GUIDELINES FOR DETERMINING YOUR PURPOSE

1 What are the requirements of my writing project?

If I am writing to fulfill an assignment, do I understand that assignment? If I am writing on my own, do I have definite expectations of what I will accomplish?

2 As I proceed in this project, what do I need to know?

Do I have a good understanding of my subject, or do I need more information? Have I considered the possible audiences who might read my writing?

3 What hypothesis can I use as my working purpose?

How many different hypotheses can I formulate about my subject? Which of them seems to direct and control my information in the most effective manner?

4 What purpose have I discovered for this writing project?

Has my purpose changed as I learned more about my subject and audience? If so, in what ways? Have I discovered, by working with a hypothesis or hypotheses, what I want to do in my writing?

5 What is my thesis?

How can I state my main idea about my subject in a thesis sentence? Does my thesis limit the scope of my writing to what I can demonstrate in the available space? Does it focus my writing on one specific assertion? Does it make an exact statement about what my writing intends to do?

GUIDELINES FOR REVISING YOUR STYLE

1 What is my general impression of my writing?

Do I find my writing clear, unambiguous, and likely to engage my readers? Have I carried out my purpose at every level; that is, am I satisfied that the *how* of my writing—its attitude, organization, and language—conveys the *what* of my ideas?

2 What tone have I established in my writing?

Is my tone informative, affective, or a blend of both? How much distance have I maintained between myself and my readers? Is my tone appropriate for my subject and audience? Is it maintained consistently?

3 How can I characterize the overall style of my writing?

Have I written this essay in a moderate style, opting for more or less colloquialism or formality as my purpose requires? Does my purpose in fact require me to be overtly colloquial or formal?

4 Are my sentences well constructed and easy on the ear?

Have I written sentences varying in length and style so that they hold my readers' interest? Have I avoided the choppiness that comes from too many basic or loosely coordinated sentences? Have I avoided the density that comes from too many complicated sentences with multiple subordinate clauses?

5 Have I used words as effectively as possible?

Do the connotations and denotations of my words support my purpose? Have I avoided unnecessary formalities and slang? Is my language specific and, when appropriate, vivid? Have I inadvertently mixed metaphors? Have I used imagery successfully to *heighten* effects, not merely to strive after them?

WRITING

with a

PURPOSE

WRITING
with a
PURPOSE
TENTH EDITION

JOSEPH F. TRIMMER

Ball State University

HOUGHTON MIFFLIN COMPANY   BOSTON   TORONTO

Dallas   Geneva, Illinois   Palo Alto   Princeton, New Jersey

Senior Sponsoring Editor: Dean Johnson
Senior Development Editor: Martha Bustin
Assistant Design Manager: Karen Rappaport
Production Coordinator: Frances Sharperson
Manufacturing Coordinator: Holly Schuster
Marketing Manager: George Kane

Photograph credits:
Fred Maroon, photo of Great Pyramids; © Fred Maroon. Reprinted with permission.

Acknowledgments

"Colloquial" and "Style" (definitions) and "Contract" (entry facsimile), Copyright ©
1981 by Houghton Mifflin Company. Reprinted by permission of *The American Heritage
Dictionary of the English Language*.

Bill Barich, "The Crazy Life," November 3, 1986. Reprinted by permission; © 1986 Bill
Barich. Originally in *The New Yorker*.

Bill Barich, "La Frontera," December, 1990. Reprinted by permission; copyright © 1990
by Bill Barich. Originally in *The New Yorker*.

Excerpt from *WOMEN'S WAYS OF KNOWING* by Mary Field Belenky et al. Copyright
© 1986 by Basic Books, Inv. Reprinted by permission of Basic Books, a division of
HarperCollins Publishers Inc.

Acknowledgments are continued on pages 593–595, which constitute an extension of
the copyright page.

Printed in the U.S.A.

Library of Congress Catalog Number: 91-71956
ISBN: 0-395-43220-0

CDEFGHIJ-VH-9876543

Brief Contents

Note: See also complete Table of Contents on page ix.

Contents

Writing Logical and Effective Sentences

Writing Grammatical Sentences

Choosing Effective Diction

Observing the Rules of Punctuation

Observing the Rules of Mechanics 549

A Glossary of Contemporary Usage 571

Preface

Writing with a Purpose has always been distinguished by its emphasis on the role of purpose in the writing process, its comprehensive coverage of the materials and problems basic to the introductory writing course, and its effective use of examples and exercises to illustrate how writers make decisions that produce successful writing. The revisions embodied in the Tenth Edition retain and reinforce these traditional features of the text, while also incorporating the best of contemporary theory and practice in the teaching of writing. The result is a blend of familiar and new material invigorated by fresh approaches and examples and enlivened by student writing composed in different contexts and progressing through various stages of the writing process.

SPECIAL FEATURES

The two most dramatic additions to the Tenth Edition are the *Readings* and the *Writing Assignments*.

▼ *Readings:* Although each chapter continues to feature examples by professional writers and case studies of student writers, each chapter now concludes with a selection of readings. These brief anthologies, arranged in a sequence of increasing length and complexity, enrich the rhetorical and thematic content of each chapter and extend opportunities to read, analyze, and evaluate exemplary models of professional and student writing.

▼ *Writing Assignments:* Again, while each chapter continues to feature exercises on all aspects of the writing process, each chapter now concludes with *ten* carefully sequenced and contextualized writing assignments. These assignments provide opportunities to *Narrate, Observe, Investigate, Collaborate, Read, Respond, Analyze, Evaluate,* or *Argue* (two assignments) about a variety of topics. They also deepen and broaden critical thinking-in-writing skills by encouraging closer analysis of the readings in the text and creative investigation of university and community resources outside the classroom. Most significantly, these assignments offer students and teachers flexibility: students can see numerous ways to write about the information in each chapter and teachers can see numerous ways to adapt these assignments to their syllabus.

ORGANIZATION OF THE TEXT

Part One: The Writing Process

Part One, "The Writing Process," covers all aspects of composing from planning through revising. Chapter 1, which provides an overview of this process, details the variety of approaches writers use to complete their tasks and discusses those three activities common to every writing situation: selecting your subject, analyzing your audience, and determining your purpose. *Purpose* receives an expanded definition that is carefully reinforced throughout the text as the principal touchstone by which writers measure their progress through the writing process.

The remainder of Part One, enriched by new examples and exercises, focuses on the three stages of the writing process—planning, drafting, and revising. Chapter 2 offers multiple planning strategies to demonstrate how students can discover and evaluate their thinking in writing. Chapter 3 presents methods to arrange and assess the material discovered in planning to guide the creation of a discovery draft and then a more successful second draft. Chapter 4 defines the revising process, demonstrates methods for revising an essay, and provides an extended case study of revising from discovery draft to final draft. All the chapters in Part One are unified by recurring student writing-in-progress that illustrates a range of projects from expressive writing about personal experience to investigative writing about academic subjects.

Part Two: The Expression of Ideas

Part Two (Chapters 5 through 10) places the discrete skills of effective writing—methods of development, argument, paragraphs, sentences, diction, tone and style—within the composing process. This is done partly through the use of quotations from personal interviews with professional writers who explain their own method for using the skill, and partly through the work of student writers who try to employ the skill in their own writing process. In particular, Chapter 5, "Common Methods of Development," and Chapter 6, "Argument," illustrate how a student writer works with the patterns of exposition and the structures of argument to plan, draft, and revise a compelling piece of writing.

The writing examples and exercises in each chapter have been selected to cluster around a different disciplinary theme to provide readers with the opportunity to discover provocative comparisons. Chapter 5 has a thematic emphasis on animal rights and environmental awareness, Chapter 6 on citizenship and contemporary social issues, Chapter 7 on families and ethnic groups, Chapter 8 on art and medicine, Chapter 9 on biology and the physical sciences, and Chapter 10 on travel and transportation.

Part Three: Special Assignments

Part Three, "Special Assignments," demonstrates how the essay exam, the critical essay, and the research paper evolve from a writing process. Student writers, guided by the advice of professional writers, work through the special stages of each assignment. Chapter 11 illustrates how to evaluate exam questions, to abstract key concepts and phrases, and to use this material to develop ideas and reach conclusions to achieve successful essay exam answers. Chapter 12 demonstrates how the use of specific reading and writing strategies enables one student to compose a critical essay that integrates his personal response to a literary work with his understanding of the basic elements of literature.

Chapters 13 and 14 provide extensive analysis and illustrations of the many steps embedded in *planning* and *writing* the research paper. Chapter 13 demonstrates how to select a subject for research: how to use all the resources of the traditional and computerized library to select, assess, and analyze sources. Chapter 14 presents the methods by which information composed by other researchers can be incorporated into and help advance the student's own research paper. Special attention is given to the purpose and procedures of quoting, documenting and listing sources. The whole range of planning and writing activities required to produce a successful research paper is illustrated by one student's progress through the process. Her paper, "The Humanities Controversy," is fully annotated so that readers can assess the decisions made during the writing process and the methods used to embody those discussions in an appropriate format.

Appendix: Writing with a Word Processor

An Appendix covers the special applications of the word processor to the writing process of student writers. In addition to suggestions for adapting the planning, drafting, and revising strategies in the text for use on the computer, "Writing with a Word Processor" supplies additional strategies uniquely suited to work on the computer as well as advice and cautions useful for those just beginning or expanding their use of this technology.

Handbook of Grammar and Usage

The Handbook of Grammar and Usage provides a coherent coding system, clear explanations and abundant exercises, making it a useful tool for classroom or individual review on a systematic basis or in response to occasional needs and questions. (The text is also available in a brief version without the handbook for instructors who do not use a handbook or who use a separate handbook.)

ANCILLARIES

Accompanying the main text are a range of print and computer materials:

Print Ancillaries

▼ *Teaching with a Purpose* by Lolly Ockerstrom, Northeastern University. This Instructor's Resource Manual offers advice for each chapter on how to use the text in three classroom settings: conventional, collaborative, and computer-assisted. It also provides chapter synopses, suggested answers for exercises, commentary about readings, additional writing assignments, sample syllabi, and special sections on how teachers and students can use the writing center to expand and enrich classroom instruction.

▼ Instructor's Support Package. This envelope of duplicating masters contains supplemental exercises for the handbook section of the long edition of the text and three forms of a new 55-item diagnostic test.

Computer Ancillaries

▼ PEER: Practical English Exercises and Review is an interactive software program for practice in sentence editing. It consists of 300 items eliciting five different kinds of responses from students.

▼ Computerized Diagnostic Tests are three forms of a 55-item diagnostic test.

Offered at Special Prices

▼ *Writing with a Purpose* and *The American Heritage Dictionary, Second College Edition*

▼ *Writing with a Purpose* and *Fine Lines: Planning, Drafting, and Revising on the Computer.*

Fine Lines by William H. Koon and Peter L. Royston. This innovative software program of seven modules is designed to help students in all stages of the writing process. The Drafting and Revising module contains an on-line handbook with MLA and APA documentation forms.

Please contact your regional sales office for additional information on these and other items.

ACKNOWLEDGMENTS

It is a pleasure to acknowledge those who have helped shape this edition of *Writing with a Purpose*.

For her help in composing the instructor's guide, *Teaching with a Purpose*, my thanks to Lolly Ockerstrom, Northeastern University.

For their extensive comments on the plans for the Tenth Edition and for their criticism of the manuscript, I would like to thank the following people: James Barcus, Baylor University (TX); Jane Bell, Texas Tech University; Joan Bischoff, University of Wisconsin—Superior; Ken Bishop, Itawamba Junior College (MS); Patricia Cearly, South Plains College (TX); Gary Ciuba, Kent State University (OH); Emma Dawson, Florida Agricultural University; Susanna Defever, St. Clair County Community College (MI); Shirley Denboske, Berkeley College of Business (NJ); Joyce Flamm, Eastern Arizona College; Ann Mace Futrell, Louisiana Tech University; Clark Germann, Front Range Community College (CO); Jeanne K. Ghent, Monroe Community College (NY); Pam Gold, Central State University (OK); Jan Gratz, Franklin University (OH); Stephen Hahn, William Paterson College (NJ); David Hopkins, Rio Hondo College (CA); Robert Johnson, Mesa State College (CO); Jane Anderson Jones, Manatee Community College (FL); Desmond Kilkeary, Glendale Community College (CA); E. B. Kirkham, Ball State University (IN); Al Krahn, Milwaukee Area Technical College; Betty Lowrance, Hill College (TX); Mark Del Maramo, Theil College (PA); Larry McDonald, Arizona Western College; Harriet McDuffie, University of South Carolina; Nancy McLelland, Mendocino College (CA); David Ostrenga, Cardinal Stritch College (WI); Robert Peterson, Middle Tennessee State University; Vickie Ricks, Grand Valley State University (MI); Michael Spain, Arizona Western College; Sharon Light Stephenson, Lamson Junior College (AZ); R. Gregory Sutcliffe, Lehigh County Community College (PA); David Tammer, Eastern Arizona College; Victor Thompson, Thomas Nelson Community College (VA); and Walter Utroske, Eastern Montana College.

For their willingness to talk at length about the craft they practice with such precision and intelligence, I would like to thank Calvin Trillin, John McPhee, Anna Quindlen, Bill Barich, Richard Selzer, Annie Dillard, and Patricia Hampl.

For their eagerness to participate in a variety of writing experiments, I would like to thank the students in my composition classes. In particular, I am indebted to the inventive, humorous, and informative observations of the student authors whose writing gives this edition its unique voice: Wallace Armstrong, Robert Scheffel, Joanne Malbone, Ray Peterson, Amy Lindsay, Susan Reidenback, Paul Singer, Ellen Haack, Rod Meyers, Jane Graham, Matt Fisher, Richard Gant, Julia Miller, and Robin Jensen.

Special thanks also go to Karen Taylor for her assistance in preparing the manuscript.

Joseph F. Trimmer

PART 1

The Writing Process

1
Toward Purposeful Writing

Some people find writing easy. They sit down and write, work until they are finished, and turn out a first draft that is so good that it is their final draft. Everyone has heard stories about students who dash off perfect term papers the night before the assignment is due. And many people know the story of how Jack Kerouac wrote his novel *On the Road*—composing it in fourteen days and typing it on a role of Teletype paper to avoid changing pages. But such ease of composition is rare. Kerouac himself had been writing and rewriting his book for years before hammering out its final version. Most people—whether they are students writing papers, teachers researching articles, journalists assembling news stories, business people composing memos, or novelists—find writing hard work.

But writing is also *opportunity*. It allows you to express something about yourself, to explore and explain ideas, and to assess the claims of other people. By formulating and organizing ideas, and finding the right words to present them, you gain power. At times the task may seem overwhelming, but the rewards make the hard work worthwhile. As you come to see writing positively, as an opportunity for communication, you will develop the confidence you need to overcome its occasional frustrations.

You can gain this confidence by writing and learning from your own work and that of others. Experienced writers are one source of lessons that you may find helpful. Consider what Ernest Hemingway says about his early writing experiences in Paris in the 1920s.

> It was wonderful to walk down the long flights of stairs knowing that I'd had good luck working. I always worked until I had something done and I always stopped when I knew what was going to happen next. That way I could be sure of going on the next day. But sometimes when I was starting a new story and I could not get it going, I would sit in front of the fire and squeeze the peel of the little oranges into the edge of the flame and watch the sputter of blue that they made. I would stand and look out over the roofs of Paris and think, "Do not worry. You have always written before and you will write now. All you have to do is write one true sentence. Write the truest sentence that you know." So finally I would write one true sentence, and then go on from there. It was easy then because there was always one true sentence that I knew or had seen or had

heard someone say. If I started to write elaborately, or like someone introducing or presenting something, I found that I could cut that scrollwork or ornament out and throw it away and start with the first true simple declarative sentence I had written. Up in that room I decided that I would write one story about each thing that I knew about. I was trying to do this all the time I was writing, and it was good and severe discipline. (Ernest Hemingway, *A Moveable Feast*)

Hemingway's account contains some helpful pointers for all writers.

1. *Develop writing habits that work for you and trust in them.* Because they have written successfully before, experienced writers believe they will write successfully again. They put this belief at risk each time they write, for each new piece of writing will inevitably contain new challenges. At times their confidence may fluctuate, but they do not lose faith. They believe the habits that have worked before—composing in a special environment, maintaining a disciplined schedule, and using familiar tools—will work again.

2. *Understand the stages of the writing process.* Identifying the predictable stages of the writing process builds confidence. Experienced writers recognize the obstacles they encounter in each stage, the strategies that help them overcome those obstacles, and the signs that prompt them to repeat one or all of the stages. As they move forward from stage to stage, or backward to repeat a stage, they are confident that they are making progress because they are identifying and solving problems.

3. *Rely on three basic elements—subject, audience, and purpose—to guide you, whatever your writing task.* Experienced writers may talk from time to time about "inspiration" or "good luck," but they do not depend on such mysterious forces. Effective writing emerges from effective decision making, and effective decisions are made when writers focus on the constants in every writing situation: their subject, audience, and purpose.

One of the primary aims of this book is to offer you experience, and thereby confidence, in writing. In the following chapters, you will learn and practice writing strategies. This chapter will discuss the writer's environment and habits, the three-stage division of the writing process, and the central elements—subject, audience, and purpose—that shape each piece of writing.

THE WRITER'S ENVIRONMENT AND HABITS

Asked to describe their writing process, students usually begin by identifying their writing habits—the conditions and tools they believe they need whenever they write. Some of these habits are formed by chance. If you completed a good paper by secluding yourself in a quiet area of the library, inscribing neatly shaped words in a spiral notebook with a Number 2 lead pencil, then you may be convinced that you need isolation, silence, and simple tools to write successfully. If you produced a good paper seated at your desk at home, your fish tank humming in the background, banging out your sentences on your new word processor, you might believe that to write effectively you require a familiar environment, reassuring noises, and modern equipment. After a time, some writers look on their writing habits as rituals, procedures to be followed faithfully each time they write. They wear the same flannel shirt, choose the same background music, or sharpen an entire box of pencils before they begin.

Although many writing habits are formed by chance and take on the nature of ritual, most come about almost unconsciously and conform to a writer's other personal habits. If, like Felix (the finicky character in Neil Simon's comedy, *The Odd Couple*), you must have a carefully organized environment to accomplish any task—from brushing your teeth to preparing dinner—then you will no doubt develop precise writing habits. You will write regularly, at approximately the same time each day, and for almost the same time, in a serene atmosphere. On the other hand, if, like Oscar (Felix's opposite), you can tolerate disorder, then your writing habits are likely to reflect your preference for flexibility. Within reason and within the confines of your deadline, you will probably write in bursts of energy, at different hours of the day and night, for varying stretches of time, and in a number of different locations.

Most people fall somewhere in between these two extremes of working styles. You will probably experiment with several approaches before finding the environment and habits that work best for you. What matters is that you develop habits that enhance your concentration rather than interfere with it. If you try to write at an uncomfortable desk and chair where the light is too dim and the temperature too high, where friends or family members are likely to interrupt, you are sabotaging your chances for success. Find a comfortable, quiet, well-lit spot where you are as free as possible from internal and external distractions.

Consider, finally, that writing is both a *solitary* and a *social* act. At times you need isolation and silence to search for words that make meaning. At other times you need community and conversation to see if your words make sense. What matters is that you find the environment and habits that work best for you.

_____*Exercise*   1. What type of physical environment do you need to write effectively? What happens to you when you are forced to write in a "hostile" environment?

2. What kind of writing tools do you prefer? What happens when you have to write with "alien" tools?

3. How do your writing habits match other aspects of your life and personality? How do they differ?

4. What experiences or people helped you form your writing habits?

5. a. What steps have you taken to eliminate external distractions (noise, music, talking, wrong light or temperature, uncomfortable furniture, lack of adequate supplies) from your writing environment?

    b. What steps have you taken to eliminate internal distractions (hunger, fatigue, boredom, anxiety, daydreaming, restlessness) from your writing environment?

    c. What other steps could you take to enhance your ability to concentrate?

THE STAGES OF THE WRITING PROCESS

Whatever your writing environment and habits, they are simply the enabling conditions that allow you to enter and complete your writing process. They are the physical and psychological setting for the central action—the mental procedures you perform as you move through the stages of composition. The writing process may be divided into three stages: *planning, drafting,* and *revising.* They will be discussed briefly in this chapter and at greater length, with examples, in Chapters 2, 3, and 4.

Planning

Planning is a systematic process of developing your ideas and giving them shape. As the first stage in the writing process, *planning is a series of strategies designed to find and formulate information in writing.* When you begin a writing project, you need to discover what is possible within the confines of the assignment—to explore a variety of subjects and invent alternative ways to think and write about each subject. To create and shape your text, you need to consider all the ideas, however mundane or unsettling, that come to you. In Chapter 2 you will learn several planning strategies for generating information you can transform into a first draft.

Drafting

Drafting is a procedure for executing a preliminary sketch. As the second stage in the writing process, *drafting is a series of strategies designed to organize and develop a sustained piece of writing.* Once planning has enabled you to identify several subjects and gather information on those subjects from different perspectives, you need to select one subject, organize your information into meaningful clusters, and then discover the links that connect those clusters. In Chapter 3 you will learn how to use drafting techniques to produce a preliminary text. Chapters 5 through 10 will give you additional techniques for composing your preliminary draft.

Revising

Revising is a procedure for improving a work in progress. As the third and final stage in the writing process, *revising is a series of strategies designed to reexamine and reevaluate the choices that have created a piece of writing.* After you have completed your preliminary draft, you need to stand back from your text and decide whether to embark on *global revision*—a complete re-creation of the world of your writing—or to begin *local revision*—a concerted effort to perfect the smaller elements in your writing. In Chapter 4, you will learn how to use global revision to rethink, reenvision, and rewrite your work. In Chapters 7 through 10, you will learn strategies for making the small rearrangements and subtle refinements that will help you achieve your most effective writing.

Working Within the Process

The division of the writing process into three stages is deceptive because it suggests that *planning, drafting,* and *revising* proceed in a linear sequence. According to this logic, you would complete all the activities in one stage and then move to the next. But writing is a complex mental activity that usually unfolds as a more flexible and "recursive" sequence of tasks. You may have to repeat the activities in one stage several times before you are ready to move on to the next, or you may have to loop back to an earlier stage before you can move forward again. For example, you may have to try a number of planning strategies until you generate enough information to work with. Or, in the middle of drafting, you may have to return to planning because you discover that the relationships you thought you saw in your material are not there after all. When you revise, you may find that your essay doesn't explain certain assumptions or illustrate important assertions, so that you must return to planning or drafting. Indeed, although planning, drafting, and revising can be seen as distinct activities, at any point in the writing process you are likely to be doing all three at once.

Experienced writers seem to perform within the process in different ways. Some spend an enormous amount of time planning every detail before they write; others prefer to dispense with planning and discover their direction in drafting or revising. The American humorist James Thurber once acknowledged that he and one of his collaborators worked quite differently when writing a play:

> Elliot Nugent . . . is a careful constructor. When we were working on
> *The Male Animal* together, he was constantly concerned with plotting the

play. He could plot the thing from back to front—what was going to happen here, what sort of situation would end the first-act curtain and so forth. I can't work that way. Nugent would say, "Well, Thurber, we've got our problem, we've got all these people in the living room. Now what are we going to do with them?" I'd say that I didn't know and couldn't tell him until I'd sat down at my typewriter and found out. I don't believe the writer should know too much where he's going. (James Thurber, *Writers at Work: The Paris Review Interviews*)

Even experienced writers with established routines for producing a particular kind of work admit that each project inevitably presents new problems. Virginia Woolf planned, drafted, and revised some of her novels with great speed, but she was bewildered by her inability to repeat the process with other novels:

> . . . blundering on at *The Waves.* I write two pages of arrant nonsense, after straining; I write variations of every sentence; compromises; bad shots; possibilities; till my writing book is like a lunatic's dream. Then I trust to inspiration on re-reading; and pencil them into some sense. Still I am not satisfied. . . . I press to my centre. I don't care if it all is scratched out . . . and then, if nothing comes of it—anyhow I have examined the possibilities. (Virginia Woolf, "Boxing Day" 1929, *A Writer's Diary*)

Writers often discover a whole set of new problems when they are asked to write in a different context. Those writers who feel comfortable telling stories about their personal experience, for example, may encounter unexpected twists and turns in their writing process when they are asked to describe the lives of other people, explain a historical event, or analyze the arguments in an intellectual controversy. Each context requires them to make adjustments in the way they typically uncover, assess, and assert information. Calvin Trillin, one of our most versatile writers, admits that he changes his writing process dramatically when he shifts from writing investigative reports to writing humorous essays or weekly columns.

> In my reporting pieces, I worry a lot about structure. Everything is there—in interviews, clippings, documents—but I don't know how to get it all in. I think that's why I do what we call around the house the vomit-out. I just start writing—to see how much I've got, how it might unfold, and what I've got to do to get through to the end. In my columns and humor pieces, I usually don't know the end or even the middle. I might start with a joke, but I don't know where it's going, so I fiddle along, polishing each paragraph, hoping something will tell me what to write next. (Personal interview)

This range of responses suggests that what appears to be a simple three-stage procedure may at times be a disorderly, contradictory procedure. But experienced writers know that disorder and contradiction may be inevitable but temporary disturbances in the composition of most pieces of writing. Confusion occurs when you know too little about your writing project; contradiction occurs when you think too little about what you know. The secret to moving through temporary impasses is to keep your eye on the constants in every writing context.

MAKING DECISIONS IN THE WRITING PROCESS

As you write, you discover that you are constantly making decisions. Some of these decisions are complex, as when you are trying to shape ideas; others are simple, as when you are trying to select words. But each decision, large or small, affects every other decision you make so that you are continuously adjusting and readjusting your writing to make sure it is consistent, coherent, and clear. You can test the effectiveness of your decisions by measuring them against this dictum: in every writing situation, a writer is trying to communicate a *subject* to an *audience* for a *purpose*.

Initially, think of these three elements as *prompters,* ways to consider what you want to write about and how you want to write about it. Later, as you move through planning to drafting and revising, think of them as *touchstones,* ways to assess what you set out to accomplish. But mainly think of them as *guidelines,* ways to control every decision you make throughout the writing process, from formulating ideas to refining sentences.

SELECTING YOUR SUBJECT

Many student writers complain that their biggest problem is finding a subject. Sometimes that problem seems less complicated because the subject is named in the writing assignment. But assignments vary in how they are worded, what they assume, and what they expect. Suppose, for example, you are asked to discuss two characters in a play. This assignment does not identify a subject; it merely identifies an area in which a subject can be found. Another version of that assignment might ask you to compare and contrast the way two characters make compromises. This assignment identifies a more restricted subject but assumes you know how to work with a specific form (the comparison and contrast essay) and expects you to produce specific information (two ways of defining and dealing with compromise). In other words, the second assignment selects your subject but requires you to select and develop the subject matter of your essay.

At the end of this chapter (and every other chapter of this book) you will find a sampler of writing assignments. As you browse through each assignment, consider how the subject is defined and how you are expected to develop it. Also consider how you might respond to or reformulate each assignment in terms of your own experience. You may decide that none of the assignments strike your fancy but that part of one assignment or parts of several assignments suggest a subject that is worth pursuing.

Whether you are responding to an assignment or creating one, you need to take certain steps to find a suitable subject. First, select a subject you know or can learn something about. The more you know about a subject, the more likely you are to make it your own, shaping it to your own perspective. If, in addition, you select a subject, such as television, that is familiar to most of your readers, you will know that you share an area of common knowledge that allows you more freedom to explore *your* observations, ideas, and values. Second, select a subject you can restrict. A subject such as television is really a broad category that contains an unlimited supply of smaller, more specific subjects. The more you can restrict your subject, the more likely you are to control your investigation, identify vivid illustrations, and maintain a unified focus. The general category *television* can be divided into all sorts of subtopics, each of which can be restricted further into specific subjects.

- ▼ situation comedies—the portrayal of women
- ▼ detective series—the methods of finding evidence
- ▼ news broadcasts—the image projected by news anchors
- ▼ sports broadcasts—the language of play-by-play commentators
- ▼ soap operas—the strategies for resolving conflict
- ▼ quiz shows—the symbolism of set designs
- ▼ music videos—the gestures of defiance

Although the subjects on the right could profit from further restriction, they illustrate why selecting a specific subject simplifies your writing task: it helps you focus on and form judgments about a concrete topic.

Finally, as you consider possible topics, ask yourself three questions: Is it significant? Is it interesting? Is it manageable? A significant subject need not be ponderous or solemn. In fact, many significant subjects grow out of ordinary observations rather than grandiose declarations. But you do need to decide whether a specific subject raises important issues (the reliability of television journalism) or appeals to the common experience of your readers (familiar methods for settling arguments). Similarly, an interesting subject need not be dazzling or spectacular, but it does need to capture your curiosity. If it bores you, it will surely bore your readers. You need to decide why a specific subject fascinates you (why you are attracted to quiz shows that give away money) and how you can make the subject more intriguing for your readers (how private detectives manipulate their friends in high places to gather evidence). A manageable subject is neither so limited that you can

"Write about dogs!"

Drawing by Booth; © 1976 The New Yorker Magazine Inc.

exhaust it in a few pages (the language of one sportscaster) nor so vast that lengthy articles or books would be required to discuss it adequately (the evolution of female stereotypes in situation comedies).

Ultimately you must develop your own methods for answering these questions each time you examine the choice of subjects available and as you consider your audience and purpose. When you compare subjects in the context of the complete writing situation, you will naturally prefer some to others. To decide which one will enable you to produce the most suitable subject, measure it against the criteria set forth in the following guidelines.

Guidelines for Selecting Your Subject _____

1. **What do I know about my subject?**
   Do I know about my subject in some depth, or do I need to learn more about it? What are the sources of my knowledge—direct experience, observation, reading? How does my knowledge give me a special or unusual perspective on my subject?

2. **What is the focus of my subject?**
   Is my subject too general? How can I restrict it to a more specific subject that I can develop in greater detail?

3. **What is significant about my subject?**
   What issues of general importance does it raise? What fresh insight can I contribute to my readers' thinking on this issue?

4. **What is interesting about my subject?**
   Why is this subject interesting to me? How can I interest my readers in it?

5. **Is my subject manageable?**
   Can I write about my subject in a particular form, within a certain number of pages? Do I feel in control of my subject or confused by it? If my subject is too complicated or too simplistic, how can I make it more manageable?

ANALYZING YOUR AUDIENCE

Most inexperienced writers assume that their audience is their writing teacher. But writing teachers, like writing assignments, often vary in what they teach, what they assume, and what they expect. Such variation has often prompted inexperienced writers to define their writing tasks as "trying to figure out what the teacher wants." This definition is naive and smart at the same time. Superficially, it suggests that the sole purpose of any writing assignment is to satisfy another person's whims. On a deeper level, it suggests that when writers analyze the knowledge, assumptions, and expectations of their readers, they develop a clearer perception of their subject and purpose. To make this analysis truly effective, though, writers must remember that they are writing for multiple audiences, not a single person.

The most immediate audience is *you*. You write not only to convey your ideas to others but also to clarify them for yourself. To think of yourself as an audience, however, you must stop thinking like a writer and begin thinking like a reader. This change in perspective offers advantages, for you are the reader you know best. You are also a fairly representative reader because you share broad concerns and interests with other people. If you feel that your writing is clear, lively, and informed, other readers will probably feel that way, too. If you sense that your text is confused or incomplete, the rest of your audience is likely to be disappointed, too.

The main drawback to considering yourself as audience is your inclination to deceive yourself. You want every sentence and paragraph to be perfect, but you know how much time and energy you invested in composing them, and that effort may blur your judgment. You may accept bad writing from yourself even though you wouldn't accept it from someone else. For that reason you need a second audience. These readers—usually your friends, classmates, and teachers—are your most attentive audience. They help you choose your subject, coach you through various stages of the writing process, and counsel you about how to improve your sentences and paragraphs. As you write, you must certainly anticipate detailed advice from these readers. But you must remember that writing teachers and even peers are essentially collaborators and thus are not your ultimate audience. They know what you have considered, cut, and corrected. The more they help you, the more eager they are to commend your writing as it approaches their standards of acceptability.

Your most significant audience consists of readers who do not know how much time and energy you invested in your writing or care about how many choices you considered and rejected. These readers want writing that tells them something interesting or important, and they are put off by writing that is tedious or trivial. It is this wider audience that you (and your collaborators) must consider as you work through the writing process.

At times this audience may seem like a nebulous creature, and you may wonder how you can direct your writing to it if you do not know any of its distinguishing features. In those cases, it may be helpful to imagine a single significant reader—an attentive, sensible, reasonably informed person who will give you a sympathetic reading as long as you do not waste his or her time. Imagine an important person whom you respect and whose respect you want. This reader, specifically imagined though often termed the "general reader," the "universal reader," or the "common reader," is essentially a fiction, but a helpful fiction. Your writing will benefit from the objectivity and sincerity with which you address this reader.

Many times, however, especially as you learn more about your subject, you discover a real-world audience for your writing. More precisely, as you consider your subject in a specific context, you may identify a number of audiences, in which case you will ultimately have to choose among them. Suppose, for example, your knowledge of contemporary music suggests that music videos might make an interesting subject, but you are finding it difficult to focus this knowledge. You decide to identify your audience, and after some deliberation you see that you have at least three possible audiences: (1) those who love music videos—MTV addicts who relish the creative nuances of each new film; (2) those who hate music videos—MTV critics who despise the commercial hype in every three-minute tape; and (3) those who are indifferent to music videos—a group whose members have never heard of MTV or have seen only an occasional clip.

Now that you have identified your audience, analyze the distinctive features of each group. What do they know? What do they think they know? What do they need to know? The more you know about each group, the more you will be able to direct your writing to their assumptions and expectations. If you know the contemporary music scene, you will have little difficulty analyzing MTV's devotees and detractors. You have heard the addicts applaud the imaginative performances, costumes, plots, and technical innovations that they believe enrich their appreciation of music. Similarly, you have heard the critics complain that the videos present contrived performances, outrageous costumes, pointless plots, and haphazard trick photography—antics, they say, that destroy their appreciation of music by reducing it to a single, often bizarre interpretation of each song.

At first you may have difficulty with the third group because those readers have no preconceptions of music videos either as a new art form or as a grotesque commercial. In some ways, readers in the third group are like the "general reader"—thoughtful, discerning people who are willing to read about music videos if you can convince them that the subject is worth their attention.

As you consider addressing each of these audiences, you should be able to anticipate their interests. As you think about the addict, for example, you might decide to describe the innovative techniques video makers have used to render one of the many recurring themes in contemporary music. As you think about the critics, you might decide to portray the plight of performers who must redirect their creative and financial resources toward producing effective videos rather than inspiring music. As you think about the neutral readers, you may decide that although they may have no interest in music videos (or even contemporary music), they may be intrigued by a demonstration of how this art form has influenced another art form, feature films.

Although this sort of audience analysis helps you visualize a group of readers, it does not help you decide which group is most suitable for your essay. If you target one group, you may fall into the trap of allowing its preferences to determine the direction of your writing. If you try to accommodate all three groups, you may waiver indecisively among them, so that your writing never finds any direction. Your decision about audience, like your decision about subject, has to be made in the context of the complete writing situation. Both decisions are ultimately related to your discovery of purpose—what you want to do in your essay. In the next several pages, you will learn how purpose guides your decisions in writing. But first, look at the following guidelines for analyzing your audience.

Guidelines for Analyzing Your Audience _____

1. **Who are the readers that will be most interested in my writing?**
   What is their probable age, sex, education, economic status, and social position? What values, assumptions, and prejudices characterize their general attitudes toward life?

2. **What do my readers know or think they know about my subject?**
   What is the probable source of their knowledge—direct experience, observation, reading, rumor? Will my readers react positively or negatively toward my subject?

3. **Why will my readers read my writing?**
   If they know a great deal about my subject, what will they expect to learn from reading my essay? If they know only a few things about my subject, what will they expect to be told about it? Will they expect to be entertained, informed, or persuaded?

4. **How can I interest my readers in my subject?**
   If they are hostile toward it, how can I convince them to give my writing a fair reading? If they are sympathetic, how can I fulfill and enhance their expectations? If they are neutral, how can I catch and hold their attention?

5. **How can I help my readers read my writing?**
   What kind of organizational pattern will help them see its purpose? What kind of guideposts and transitional markers will they need to follow this pattern? What (and how many) examples will they need to understand my general statements?

DETERMINING YOUR PURPOSE

The central idea of this book is that writers write most effectively when they are "writing with a purpose." Inexperienced writers occasionally have difficulty writing with *a* purpose, because they see many purposes: to complete the assignment, to earn a good grade, to publish their writing. These "purposes" lie outside the writing situation, but they certainly influence the way you think about your purpose. If you want a good grade, you will define your purpose in terms of your teacher's writing assignment. If you want to publish your essay, you will define your purpose in terms of a given publisher's statement about its editorial policies.

When *purpose* is considered as an element inside the writing situation, the term has a specific meaning: *purpose is the overall design that governs what writers do in their writing.* Writers who have determined their purpose know what kind of information they need, how they want to organize and develop it, and why they think it is important. In effect, purpose directs and controls all the decisions writers make. It is both the *what* and the *how* of that process—that is, the specific subject the writer selects *and* the strategies, from creating an organization to refining the style, that the writer uses to communicate the subject most effectively.

The difficulty with this definition is that finding a purpose to guide you through the writing process *is* the purpose of the writing process. Writing is both a procedure for *discovering* what you know and a procedure for *demonstrating* what you know. For that reason, you must maintain a double vision of your purpose. You must think of it as a preliminary objective that helps illuminate the decisions you have to make. You must also think of it as a final assertion that helps you implement what you intend to do in your writing.

Forming a Working Purpose: The Hypothesis

As you begin writing, you start to acquire a general sense of your purpose. You make tentative decisions about your subject and audience, and you begin to formulate ideas about what you want to accomplish in a given context. Suppose again that you choose to write about music videos. You could approach this subject in many ways, but you have to start somewhere, so you decide to focus on their intent. This preliminary decision will help you gather and sort information, but as you assess it, you may see that you do not know what you want to do with it. You do not have a purpose; you only have a general notion that suggests a number of perspectives. Any one of these perspectives might provide an interesting angle from which to investigate your subject, and you can use any one of them to form a *hypothesis*—a working purpose.

Forming a hypothesis is a major step in determining your purpose. Sometimes you come to your writing certain of your hypothesis: you know from the outset what you want to prove and what you need to prove it. More often, you need to consider various possibilities; to convey something meaningful in your writing, something that bears your own mark, you need to keep an open mind and explore your options fully. Eventually, however, you must choose one hypothesis that you think most accurately says what you want to say about your subject and how you want to say it.

How do you know which hypothesis to choose? There is no easy answer to this question. The answer ultimately emerges from your temperament, experiences, and interests, and also from the requirements of the context— whether you are writing for yourself or on an assignment. Sometimes you can make the choice intuitively as you proceed: in thinking about your subject and audience, you see at once the perspective you want to adopt and how it will direct your writing. At other times you may find it helpful to write out various hypotheses and then consider their relative effectiveness. Which will be most interesting to write about? Which best expresses your way of looking at things? With which can you make the strongest case or most compelling assertions?

For example, as you look at the information you have gathered about the intent of music videos, you might see several hypotheses:

- Videos are merely advertising gimmicks.
- Videos are an imaginative new art form.
- Videos are a simple pictorial translation of a song.
- Videos reinterpret music in complex visual images.

Any one of these or other hypotheses might guide you to the next stage of your writing. You must decide which one suits you best, and your decision must take into account the nature of your subject and intended audience.

Testing Your Hypothesis: The Discovery Draft

After you have chosen your hypothesis, you need to determine whether this preliminary statement of purpose really provides the direction and control you need to produce an effective piece of writing. You can test your hypothesis by writing a first, or *discovery,* draft. Sometimes your discovery draft demonstrates that your hypothesis works. More often, however, as you continue the writing process, you discover new information or unforeseen complications that cause you to modify your original hypothesis. In other cases, you discover that you simply cannot prove what your hypothesis suggested you might be able to prove.

Whatever you discover about your hypothesis, you must proceed in writing. If your discovery draft reveals that your hypothesis represents what you want to prove and needs only slight modification, then change your perspective somewhat or find the additional information so that you can modify it. If, on the other hand, your discovery draft demonstrates that your hypothesis lacks conviction or that you do not have (and suspect you cannot get) the information you need to make your case, then choose another hypothesis that reflects your intentions more accurately.

For example, if you choose the hypothesis that music videos are simply advertising gimmicks and start your discovery draft, you may realize that even though you have gathered information to illustrate the effect of videos on record sales, you don't find the evidence overwhelming or particularly interesting. Because much contemporary music has mixed commercial and artistic intentions, it comes as no surprise that music videos exhibit a similar mixture. You see flaws in your reasoning, holes in your draft. If you remember the conclusions of a recent opinion poll revealing that most consumers prefer to hear a record before they see the video or an interview with a film director who acknowledges that videos have influenced his work, you have uncovered evidence that makes your hypothesis less compelling. You need to modify it or, more likely, find another.

Purpose and Thesis

Whether you proceed with your original hypothesis, modify it, or choose another, you must eventually arrive at a final decision about your purpose. You make that decision during revision, when you know what you want to do and how you want to do it. Once you have established your purpose, you can make or refine other decisions—about your organization, examples, and style. One way to express your purpose is to state your thesis. A *thesis* is a sentence that usually appears in the first paragraph of your essay and states the main idea you are going to develop. Although the thesis is often called a purpose statement, thesis and purpose are not precisely the same thing. Your purpose is both contained in and is larger than your thesis: it consists of all the strategies you will use to demonstrate it in a sustained and successful piece of writing.

Your thesis makes a *restricted, unified,* and *precise* assertion about your subject—an assertion that can be developed in the amount of space you have, that treats only one idea, and that is open to only one interpretation. Devising a thesis from the information you have about your subject and stating it well are key steps in the writing process; for that reason they will be discussed in more detail in Chapter 3. For now, remember that your thesis is stated after you have determined your purpose and that it expresses your main idea about your subject. For example, if you finally determine that you want to write about the kind of music that benefits most by transformation into videos, your thesis might be stated in this way: "The most innovative videos are created from music whose lyrics do not prescribe a specific story line."

In certain writing situations you do not need to state your thesis explicitly. This does not mean that your writing will lack purpose, only that you do not need to compose a purpose statement. Narrating a story or describing an object, for example, does not usually require a stated thesis; the thesis is suggested, or implied.

In many ways the difference between a hypothesis (a working purpose) and a thesis (a final assertion) explains why you can speculate about your purpose *before* you write but can specify your purpose only *after* you have written. This connection between your writing process and your writing purpose requires you to pause frequently to consult the criteria set forth in the following guidelines.

Guidelines for Determining Your Purpose ────────────

1. ***What are the requirements of my writing project?***
   If I am writing to fulfill an assignment, do I understand that assignment? If I am writing on my own, do I have definite expectations of what I will accomplish?

2. ***As I proceed in this project, what do I need to know?***
   Do I have a good understanding of my subject, or do I need more information? Have I considered the possible audiences who might read my writing?

3. ***What hypothesis can I use as my working purpose?***
   How many different hypotheses can I formulate about my subject? Which of them seems to direct and control my information in the most effective manner?

4. ***What purpose have I discovered for this writing project?***
   Has my purpose changed as I learned more about my subject and audience? If so, in what ways? Have I discovered, by working with a hypothesis or hypotheses, what I want to do in my writing?

5. ***What is my thesis?***
   How can I state my main idea about my subject in a thesis sentence? Does my thesis limit the scope of my writing to what I can demonstrate in the available space? Does it focus my writing on one specific assertion? Does it make an exact statement about what my writing intends to do?

COORDINATING DECISIONS IN THE WRITING PROCESS

You need to understand how each of the three elements—subject, audience, and purpose—helps you measure your progress through the writing process. But you must not assume that these guidelines lock you into the fixed sequence of selecting your subject, analyzing your audience and then determining your purpose. Subject, audience, and purpose are too interconnected to allow you to follow such a simple formula. Indeed, they resemble the elements in a complex chemical formula. You can isolate the elements in the formula, but you cannot understand what they create until you combine them. And each time you alter one element, however slightly, you change the character of the other elements, setting off another chain of relationships and a new formula. To make informed and purposeful decisions about your writing, therefore, you must not only understand the separate contributions of subject, audience, and purpose, but also learn to coordinate the complex and shifting relationships among them each time you write.

_____Exercise   Describe the conceptions of subject, audience, and purpose implied in each original hypothesis, and then explain how each new decision will affect the three elements. Write a new hypothesis that reflects the changes.

1. *Original hypothesis:* Videos have had an enormous influence on contemporary cinema.
   New decision: You decide to discuss earlier films featuring music, such as *Fantasia,* that influenced videos.

2. *Original hypothesis:* Videos are shown almost exclusively on cable television.
   New decision: You decide to address your essay to someone trying to decide whether to subscribe to cable television.

3. *Original hypothesis:* Videos enrich our understanding and appreciation of a song's lyrics.
   New decision: You decide to prove that film makers (not songwriters or musicians) are in charge of creating videos.

Becoming a Writer | Gail Godwin

In this brief excerpt from her essay "Becoming a Writer," novelist Gail Godwin remembers the way she identified with her mother's work as a writer. She also remembers the importance of her grandmother's work as a reader. What does this selection suggest about how people choose role models? What makes her mother's work seem more interesting to Godwin than her grandmother's work?

On weekend mornings my mother sat at the typewriter in a sunny breakfast nook and wrote stories about women, young women like herself, who, after some difficulty necessary to the plot, got their men. In the adjoining kitchen, my grandmother washed the breakfast dishes and kept asking, "What do you two think you could eat for lunch?" My mother and I would groan in unison. Who could imagine lunch when we'd just finished breakfast? Besides, there were more important things to do than eat.   **1**

Already, at five, I had allied myself with the typewriter rather than the   **2** stove. The person at the stove usually had the thankless task of fueling. Whereas, if you were faithful to your vision at the typewriter, by lunchtime you could make two more characters happy—even if you weren't so happy yourself. What is more, if you retyped your story neatly in the afternoon and sent it off in a manila envelope to New York, you'd get a check back for $100 within two or three weeks (300 words to the page, 16–17 pages, 2¢ a word: in 1942, $100 went a long way). Meanwhile, she at the stove ran our mundane life. Still new to the outrageous vulnerability of widowhood, she was glad to play Martha to my mother's Mary. In our manless little family, she also played mother and could be counted on to cook, sew on buttons, polish the piano, and give encouragement to creative endeavors. She was my mother's first reader, while the stories were still in their morning draft; "It moves a little slowly here," she'd say, or "I didn't understand why the girl did this." And the tempo would be stepped up, the heroine's ambiguous action sharpened in the afternoon draft; for if my grandmother didn't follow tempo and motive, how would all those other women who would buy the magazines?

Brandon's Clown | Wallace Armstrong

In this essay, Wallace Armstrong describes the process he followed as he completed his first commissioned painting. In what ways does the process of painting *Brandon's Clown* resemble the three-stage process of writing?

Godwin, Gail. "A Writing Woman." *Atlantic,* October 1979: 84. Reprinted in *The Writer on Her Work.* Ed. Janet Sternburg. New York: Norton, 1980. 231–32.

How does Armstrong select the subject, analyze the audience, and determine the purpose of his painting? What is the subject, who is the audience, and what is the purpose of his essay?

Few of those words of wisdom that are passed from father to son are followed. Most are simply acknowledged and forgotten. My father's advice about my adolescent love for painting was simple and direct: "Son, you have a special talent. Be smart. Use it to make money." With his words guiding me, I took my love to the marketplace. I began accepting commissions, painting fantasies for those who didn't have the skill or desire to paint their own.   **1**

Creating artwork for a client, I soon discovered, demands much more than talent and a lust for money. A friend of mine in Art History 110 was offered $175 to paint a mural in the lobby of her home-town bank. Her only direction from the bank manager was to paint "something rural looking." Obviously, rural looking can be anything from cows lapping at a sunlit pond to combines ripping the heads from a field of golden wheat. Somewhere in that wide spectrum was the painting the manager wanted. Such flexibility forces the artist to play mind reader or simply follow his own desires and hope the client likes the result. A less common, perhaps even less desirable commission is the verbal blueprint. The client knows exactly what he wants. "I want a portrait," he says, "that makes me look like General Patton. I want two American flags in the background and a Doberman at my side." Although there is some security in knowing what the client expects, most artists aren't desperate enough to follow such instructions.   **2**

Once the actual work begins, the question that most frequently plagues the artist is "Why am I doing this?"—especially when the commission calls for an uncharacteristic shift in creative expression. I am known on campus as "the guy who paints screaming faces," a tag I am quite happy with. I am proud of the dark maelstroms of anxiety I can create on my canvas. For hours after leaving the easel, I will walk about with my shoulders stooped and head down, frowning, lost in reflections on man's inability to overcome despair.   **3**

Naturally, my first commission was for a nursery painting. A young mother expecting her first child wanted an oil painting to hang in a newly remodeled nursery. Mutual friends had informed her that I was willing, able, and cheap. My father's advice prompted me to take the job and I soon found myself discussing infant tastes with the mother-to-be, a pleasant young woman whose only exposure to art was probably the Sunday funnies.   **4**

"You know, something happy and cheery," she said between snatches of dialogue on *General Hospital*. "The usual stuff for a kid's room."   **5**

"Is there any kind of theme to your nursery?" I asked hesitantly.   **6**

"Well, it's blue," she said. "If it's a boy, we're going to call him Brandon. Something like that would be nice."   **7**

I followed her finger to a baby stroller, decorated with circus animals. "Oh," I said, as the room began to darken and spin. "I see."   **8**

For the next several weeks, I had nightmares of pink giraffes and smil-   **9** ing zebras parading across my empty canvas. I spent hours hunched over my sketchbook, filling page after page with oddly shaped animal skeletons. Before long, the book looked like a Disneyland mortuary. The entire project seemed so pointless that I was exhausted with frustration. How would I satisfy my cheerful client and remain true to my creative vision?

Resolved to compromise my pride for a buck, I began gathering my paints, brushes and canvas with all the enthusiasm of the only girl in the eighth grade not chosen for the pompom squad. I reviewed my sketches hoping to find a subject and suddenly spotted a quick drawing I had made of a clown. Eureka! The answer seemed obvious: a clown. Of course. Clowns had screaming faces, even though they concealed their real pain behind their painted masks. I would mask my true intentions by painting a clown with a slightly sorrowful expression lurking behind his grease paint. He would hold the strings of two balloons, suggesting comparisons to a man behind prison bars.   10

So I began to paint. Every morning before class, I ran to my studio to reappraise the work I had done the night before. The glistening, bright arts were so inviting. Algebra could wait. I picked out my favorite brush and dove back into the painting, detailing areas I had sketched before bedtime, making the highlights lighter and the shadows darker. Gradually, the clown's face began to emerge from the swirl of color. "Brandon's Clown" was my best work to date!   11

Feeling every bit like the proud parent myself, I carried the finished canvas home from my college studio to unveil it for my mother. As I held it up for her reaction, I was certain she would gush with glee and call the neighbors. But after a few moments of silence, she said "It's dark."   12

My defenses flew to Red Alert. "It's supposed to be dark. How can you emphasize light and shadow without making it dark?"   13

Leaving Mom to her *Reader's Digest,* I drove to my client's house in hopes of a better reception. Occasionally I glanced at the painting lying next to me on the seat. Perhaps it *was* a bit dark—for a nursery painting, that is. The expression on the clown's face suddenly seemed harsh and scolding. How could defenseless little Brandon lie in his crib and stare at this all day long?   14

"How do you like your painting, Mrs. Hobbs?" I asked meekly. For some reason, the canvas which had seemed so perfect that morning in my studio now looked totally out of place in Brandon's nursery. A beautiful, tiny wooden rocking horse swayed peacefully on the dresser top. An 8 × 10 hospital glossy of little Brandon, looking fresh and innocent, hung on the wall. And in the corner, nearly lost in the bundle of blankets, was Brandon himself, fast asleep and completely unaware of this ugly black thing that was about to disturb the harmony of his world.   15

"It's fine. Will you take a check?" his mother asked as she hung the painting right above Brandon's head.   16

As I left holding my first commission, I did not think about my father's advice or my artistic reputation. I thought only of poor Brandon. I will not be surprised if, twenty years from now, a deranged young man stops me on the street and smashes a clown painting over my head. I probably deserve worse.   17

Brandon's Clown, original painting by Wallace L. Armstrong

The Inheritance of Tools | Scott Russell Sanders

In this essay, reprinted from his collection of personal narratives, The Paradise of Bombs (1987), Scott Russell Sanders weaves together stories about his grandfather, his father, himself, and his children as he reflects on the subject of craftsmanship. What lessons did his father teach him? How does he demonstrate his mastery of those lessons? How might his discussion of carpentry apply to writing?

Sanders, Scott Russell. *The Paradise of Bombs.* Athens: U of Georgia P, 1987. 102–10.

At just about the hour when my father died, soon after dawn one Febru-   1
ary morning when ice coated the windows like cataracts, I banged my
thumb with a hammer. Naturally I swore at the hammer, the reckless thing,
and in the moment of swearing I thought of what my father would say: "If
you'd try hitting the nail it would go in a whole lot faster. Don't you know
your thumb's not as hard as that hammer?" We both were doing carpentry
that day, but far apart. He was building cupboards at my brother's place in
Oklahoma; I was at home in Indiana putting up a wall in the basement to
make a bedroom for my daughter. By the time my mother called with news
of his death—the long distance wires whittling her voice until it seemed
too thin to bear the weight of what she had to say—my thumb was swollen.
A week or so later a white scar in the shape of a crescent moon began to
show above the cuticle, and month by month it rose across the pink sky of
my thumbnail. It took the better part of a year for the scar to disappear,
and every time I noticed it I thought of my father.

    The hammer had belonged to him, and to his father before him. The   2
three of us have used it to build houses and barns and chicken coops, to
upholster chairs and crack walnuts, to make doll furniture and bookshelves
and jewelry boxes. The head is scratched and pockmarked, like an old
plowshare that has been working rocky fields, and it gives off the sort of
dull sheen you see on fast creek water in the shade. It is a finishing hammer, about the weight of a bread loaf, too light really for framing walls, too
heavy for cabinetwork, with a curved claw for pulling nails, a rounded
head for pounding, a fluted neck for looks, and a hickory handle for
strength.

    The present handle is my third one, bought from a lumberyard in   3
Tennessee down the road from where my brother and I were helping my
father build his retirement house. I broke the previous one by trying to pull
sixteen-penny nails out of floor joists—a foolish thing to do with a finishing hammer, as my father pointed out. "You ever hear of a crowbar?"
he said. No telling how many handles he and my grandfather had gone
through before me. My grandfather used to cut down hickory trees on his
farm, saw them into slabs, cure the planks in his hayloft, and carve handles
with a drawknife. The grain in hickory is crooked and knotty, and therefore tough, hard to split, like the grain in the two men who owned this
hammer before me.

    After proposing marriage to a neighbor girl, my grandfather used this   4
hammer to build a house for his bride on a stretch of river bottom in northern Mississippi. The lumber for the place, like the hickory for the handle,
was cut on his own land. By the day of the wedding he had not quite finished the house, and so right after the ceremony he took his wife home and
put her to work. My grandmother had worn her Sunday dress for the wedding, with a fringe of lace tacked on around the hem in honor of the occasion. She removed this lace and folded it away before going out to help my
grandfather nail siding on the house. "There she was in her good dress," he
told me some fifty-odd years after that wedding day, "holding up them long
pieces of clapboard while I hammered, and together we got the place covered up before dark." As the family grew to four, six, eight, and eventually
thirteen, my grandfather used this hammer to enlarge his house room by
room, like a chambered nautilus expanding his shell.

By and by the hammer was passed along to my father. One day he was   5
up on the roof of our pony barn nailing shingles with it, when I stepped
out the kitchen door to call him for supper. Before I could yell, something
about the sight of him straddling the spine of that roof and swinging the
hammer caught my eye and made me hold my tongue. I was five or six
years old, and the world's commonplaces were still news to me. He would
pull a nail from the pouch at his waist, bring the hammer down, and a moment later the *thunk* of the blow would reach my ears. And that is what
had stopped me in my tracks and stilled my tongue, that momentary gap
between seeing and hearing the blow. Instead of yelling from the kitchen
door, I ran to the barn and climbed two rungs up the ladder—as far as I
was allowed to go—and spoke quietly to my father. On our walk to the
house he explained that sound takes time to make its way through air. Suddenly the world seemed larger, the air more dense, if sound could be held
back like any ordinary traveler.

By the time I started using this hammer, at about the age when I dis-   6
covered the speed of sound, it already contained houses and mysteries for
me. The smooth handle was one my grandfather had made. In those days I
needed both hands to swing it. My father would start a nail in a scrap of
wood, and I would pound away until I bent it over.

"Looks like you got ahold of some of those rubber nails," he would tell   7
me. "Here, let me see if I can find you some stiff ones." And he would
rummage in a drawer until he came up with a fistful of more cooperative
nails. "Look at the head," he would tell me. "Don't look at your hands,
don't look at the hammer. Just look at the head of that nail and pretty soon
you'll learn to hit it square."

Pretty soon I did learn. While he worked in the garage cutting dovetail   8
joints for a drawer or skinning a deer or tuning an engine, I would hammer
nails. I made innocent blocks of wood look like porcupines. He did not talk
much in the midst of his tools, but he kept up a nearly ceaseless humming,
slipping in and out of a dozen tunes in an afternoon, often running back
over the same stretch of melody again and again, as if searching for a way
out. When the humming did cease, I knew he was faced with a task requiring great delicacy or concentration, and I took care not to distract him.

He kept scraps of wood in a cardboard box—the ends of two-by-fours,   9
slabs of shelving and plywood, odd pieces of molding—and everything in it
was fair game. I nailed scraps together to fashion what I called boats or
houses, but the results usually bore only faint resemblance to the visions I
carried in my head. I would hold up these constructions to show my father,
and he would turn them over in his hands admiringly, speculating about
what they might be. My cobbled-together guitars might have been alien
spaceships, my barns might have been models of Aztec temples, each
wooden contraption might have been anything but what I had set out
to make.

Now and again I would feel the need to have a chunk of wood shaped   10
or shortened before I riddled it with nails, and I would clamp it in a vice
and scrape at it with a handsaw. My father would let me lacerate the board
until my arm gave out, and then he would wrap his hand around mine
and help me finish the cut, showing me how to use my thumb to guide the

blade, how to pull back on the saw to keep it from binding, how to let my shoulder do the work.

"Don't force it," he would say, "just drag it easy and give the teeth a 11 chance to bite."

As the saw teeth bit down the wood released its smell, each kind with 12 its own fragrance, oak or walnut or cherry or pine—usually pine, because it was the softest and the easiest for a child to work. No matter how weathered and gray the board, no matter how warped and cracked, inside there was this smell waiting, as of something freshly baked. I gathered every smidgen of sawdust and stored it away in coffee cans, which I kept in a drawer of the workbench. When I did not feel like hammering nails I would dump my sawdust on the concrete floor of the garage and landscape it into highways and farms and towns, running miniature cars and trucks along miniature roads. Looming as huge as a colossus, my father worked over and around me, now and again bending down to inspect my work, careful not to trample my creations. It was a landscape that smelled dizzyingly of wood. Even after a bath my skin would carry the smell, and so would my father's hair, when he lifted me for a bedtime hug.

I tell these things not only from memory but also from recent observa- 13 tion, because my own son now turns blocks of wood into nailed porcupines, dumps cans full of sawdust at my feet and sculpts highways on the floor. He learns how to swing a hammer from the elbow instead of the wrist, how to lay his thumb beside the blade to guide a saw, how to tap a chisel with a wooden mallet, how to mark a hole with an awl before starting a drill bit. My daughter did the same before him, and even now, on the brink of teenage aloofness, she will occasionally drag out my box of wood scraps and carpenter something. So I have seen my apprenticeship to wood and tools reenacted in each of my children, as my father saw his own apprenticeship renewed in me.

The saw I use belonged to him, as did my level and both of my 14 squares, and all four tools had belonged to his father. The blade of the saw is the bluish color of gun barrels, and the maple handle, dark from the sweat of hands, is inscribed with curving leaf designs. The level is a shaft of walnut two feet long, edged with brass and pierced by three round windows in which air bubbles float in oil-filled tubes of glass. The middle window serves for testing whether a surface is horizontal, the others for testing whether it is plumb or vertical. My grandfather used to carry this level on the gun rack behind the seat in his pickup, and when I rode with him I would turn around to watch the bubbles dance. The larger of the two squares is called a framing square, a flat steel elbow so beat up and tarnished you can barely make out the rows of numbers that show how to figure the cuts on rafters. The smaller one is called a try square, for marking right angles, with a blued steel blade for the shank and a brass-faced block of cherry for the head.

I was taught early on that a saw is not to be used apart from a square: 15 "If you're going to cut a piece of wood," my father insisted, "you owe it to the tree to cut it straight."

Long before studying geometry, I learned there is a mystical virtue in 16 right angles. There is an unspoken morality in seeking the level and the plumb. A house will stand, a table will bear weight, the sides of a box will hold together only if the joints are square and the members upright. When the bubble is lined up between two marks etched in the glass tube of a level, you have aligned yourself with the forces that hold the universe together. When you miter the corners of a picture frame, each angle must be exactly forty-five degrees, as they are in the perfect triangles of Pythagoras, not a degree more or less. Otherwise the frame will hang crookedly, as if ashamed of itself and of its maker. No matter if the joints you are cutting do not show. Even if you are butting two pieces of wood together inside a cabinet, where no one except a wrecking crew will ever see them, you must take pains to insure that the ends are square and the studs are plumb.

I took pains over the wall I was building on the day my father died.   17
Not long after that wall was finished—paneled with tongue-and-groove boards of yellow pine, the nail holes filled with putty and the wood all stained and sealed—I came close to wrecking it one afternoon when my daughter ran howling up the stairs to announce that her gerbils had escaped from their cage and were hiding in my brand-new wall. She could hear them scratching and squeaking behind her bed. Impossible! I said. How on earth could they get inside my drum-tight wall? Through the heating vent, she answered. I went downstairs, pressed my ear to the honey-colored wood, and heard the scritch scritch of tiny feet.

"What can we do?" my daughter wailed. "They'll starve to death,   18
they'll die of thirst, they'll suffocate."

"Hold on," I soothed. "I'll think of something."   19

While I thought and she fretted, the radio on her bedside table delivered   20
ered us the headlines. Several thousand people had died in a city in India from a poisonous cloud that had leaked overnight from a chemical plant. A nuclear-powered submarine had been launched. Rioting continued in South Africa. An airplane had been hijacked in the Mediterranean. Authorities calculated that several thousand homeless people slept on the streets within sight of the Washington Monument. I felt my usual helplessness in face of all these calamities. But here was my daughter weeping because her gerbils were holed up in a wall. This calamity I could handle.

"Don't worry," I told her. "We'll set food and water by the heating   21
vent and lure them out. And if that doesn't do the trick, I'll tear the wall apart until we find them."

She stopped crying and gazed at me. "You'd really tear it apart? Just   22
for my gerbils? The *wall*?" Astonishment slowed her down only for a second, however, before she ran to the workbench and began tugging at drawers, saying, "Let's see, what'll we need? Crowbar. Hammer. Chisels. I hope we don't have to use them—but just in case."

We didn't need the wrecking tools. I never had to assault my hand-   23
some wall, because the gerbils eventually came out to nibble at a dish of popcorn. But for several hours I studied the tongue-and-groove skin I had nailed up on the day of my father's death, considering where to begin prying. There were no gaps in that wall, no crooked joints.

I had botched a great many pieces of wood before I mastered the right   24
angle with a saw, botched even more before I learned to miter a joint. The knowledge of these things resides in my hands and eyes and the webwork of muscles, not in the tools. There are machines for sale—powered miter

boxes and radial arm saws, for instance—that will enable any casual soul to cut proper angles in boards. The skill is invested in the gadget instead of the person who uses it, and this is what distinguishes a machine from a tool. If I had to earn my keep by making furniture or building houses, I suppose I would buy powered saws and pneumatic nailers; the need for speed would drive me to it. But since I carpenter only for my own pleasure or to help neighbors or to remake the house around the ears of my family, I stick with hand tools. Most of the ones I own were given to me by my father, who also taught me how to wield them. The tools in my workbench are a double inheritance, for each hammer and level and saw is wrapped in a cloud of knowing.

All of these tools are a pleasure to look at and to hold. Merchants   **25**
would never paste NEW NEW NEW! signs on them in stores. Their designs are old because they work, because they serve their purpose well. Like folksongs and aphorisms and the grainy bits of language, these tools have been pared down to essentials. I look at my claw hammer, the distillation of a hundred generations of carpenters, and consider that it holds up well beside those other classics—Greek vases, Gregorian chants, *Don Quixote,* barbed fishhooks, candles, spoons. Knowledge of hammering stretches back to the earliest humans who squatted beside fires chipping flints. Anthropologists have a lovely name for those unworked rocks that served as the earliest hammers. "Dawn stones" they are called. Their only qualification for the work, aside from hardness, is that they fit the hand. Our ancestors used them for grinding corn, tapping awls, smashing bones. From dawn stones to this claw hammer is a great leap in time, but no great distance in design or imagination.

On that iced-over February morning when I smashed my thumb with   **26**
the hammer, I was down in the basement framing the wall that my daughter's gerbils would later hide in. I was thinking of my father, as I always did whenever I built anything, thinking how he would have gone about the work, hearing in memory what he would have said about the wisdom of hitting the nail instead of my thumb. I had the studs and plates nailed together all square and trim, and was lifting the wall into place when the phone rang upstairs. My wife answered, and in a moment she came to the basement door and called down softly to me. The stillness in her voice made me drop the framed wall and hurry upstairs. She told me my father was dead. Then I heard the details over the phone from my mother. Building a set of cupboards for my brother in Oklahoma, he had knocked off work early the previous afternoon because of cramps in his stomach. Early this morning, on his way into the kitchen of my brother's trailer, maybe going for a glass of water, so early that no one else was awake, he slumped down on the linoleum and his heart quit.

For several hours I paced around inside my house, upstairs and down,   **27**
in and out of every room, looking for the right door to open and knowing there was no such door. My wife and children followed me and wrapped me in arms and backed away again, circling and staring as if I were on fire. Where was the door, the door, the door? I kept wondering. My smashed thumb turned purple and throbbed, making me furious. I wanted to cut it off and rush outside and scrape away the snow and hack a hole in the frozen earth and bury the shameful thing.

I went down into the basement, opened a drawer in my workbench, **28** and stared at the ranks of chisels and knives. Oiled and sharp, as my father would have kept them, they gleamed at me like teeth. I took up a clasp knife, pried out the longest blade, and tested the edge on the hair of my forearm. A tuft came away cleanly, and I saw my father testing the sharpness of tools on his own skin, the blades of axes and knives and gouges and hoes, saw the red hair shaved off in patches from his arms and the backs of his hands. "That will cut bear," he would say. He never cut a bear with his blades, now my blades, but he cut deer, dirt, wood. I closed the knife and put it away. Then I took up the hammer and went back to work on my daughter's wall, snugging the bottom plate against a chalkline on the floor, shimming the top plate against the joists overhead, plumbing the studs with my level, making sure before I drove the first nail that every line was square and true.

Writing Assignments

Narrate **1.** Make a list of your earliest memories of writing—e.g., learning to form your letters, drafting a letter to Santa Claus, composing your first report for school. Select the memory that had the most powerful effect on you. Then write the story, dramatizing the process and explaining what you learned.

Observe **2.** Describe the habits of someone who uses writing to conduct business. The person need not be a professional writer. For example, you might describe how a family friend drafts business letters or a former boss writes up reports. Your purpose is to describe how writing works in the world beyond school.

Investigate **3.** Using the questions about writing habits on pages 5–6, interview a classmate about his or her writing habits. After you have compiled your information, write an essay addressed to the rest of the class, explaining the rituals your partner believes he or she must perform to write successfully.

Collaborate **4.** Form a small writing group (three to four students), interview each other, focusing particularly on those problems that make writing difficult in each stage of the writing process. Then write a collaborative report for each member of the group, suggesting ways he or she might solve those problems.

Read **5.** Focus on the grandmother in Gail Godwin's "Becoming a Writer." Then construct a profile of your *first* reader. What qualities does the person possess? What do you want this reader to tell you? How do you take praise or criticism from such a reader? You may want to read the rest of Godwin's comments on "Becoming a Writer" in *The Writer on Her Work*. Ed. Janet Sternburg. New York: Norton, 1980. 231–55.

Respond **6.** Respond to Wallace Armstrong's "Brandon's Clown" by trying to remember some words of wisdom that your parents or trusted friend passed on to you as guidelines for giving your life a sense of purpose. Then describe an incident in which you tried to follow those guidelines.

Analyze **7.** Examine the details in Wallace Armstrong's painting, "Brandon's Clown." In what ways does the painting resemble its description in the essay, "Brandon's Clown"? How might this painting influence Brandon's life? Analyze how the presence of a painting (a photograph or poster) in your room has affected your life.

Evaluate **8.** Throughout his essay, "The Inheritance of Tools," Scott Russell Sanders recalls the lessons he was taught by his father during his apprenticeship. Make a list of these lessons. Then evaluate his understanding of these lessons as he builds and considers the demolition of the wall for his daughter's bedroom.

Argue **9.** Sanders argues that there is a difference between a tool and a machine. Consider various writing tasks, such as composing a thank-you note, completing an essay examination, constructing a résumé. Then persuade your readers that one of these tasks requires a specific tool or machine.

Argue   **10.**   Consider what you have learned in this chapter about the ways in which various professional writers work. Next consider the difference between the writing they do and the writing you have done as schoolwork. Then develop an argument in which you demonstrate in some detail why their advice *helps* or *hinders* the "school writer." You may want to document your argument with evidence from writing assignments you had to complete in courses other than English composition.

2
Planning

As we saw in Chapter 1, Ernest Hemingway testified that when he had trouble starting a new story he would squeeze orange peels into the fire, gaze out the window, and worry about whether he would ever write again. Although they seem to have nothing to do with writing, activities like these are not a fruitless waste of time; some may even be necessary for writers to think their way into a writing project. Random thinking may seem pointless, but it often helps writers step away from the immediate problem they face and give it a chance to "cool down" so that they can think clearly again. Random thinking *is* a waste of time, however, if it encourages writers to wait for the perfect moment to begin working. Those who wait for the perfect moment usually do a lot of waiting and very little writing. Eventually, all writers must do what Hemingway recalls he did: give themselves a strong pep talk. "Stop worrying! Start writing!"

The best way to start writing is to begin planning. Inexperienced writers mistakenly regard planning as essentially a thinking activity. First, they think, they must plan inside their heads what they want to say and then they must copy these thoughts onto a piece of paper. Unfortunately, they discover that such planning usually produces two kinds of failure: (1) They cannot think through everything they want to say before they write, and (2) they cannot simply transfer their thinking into writing. Planning, in fact, is primarily a *writing* activity, as most experienced writers can testify. Although they admit that they do some planning before they write, these writers insist that they do their most productive planning after they have begun writing. For them, planning is not so much thinking *and* writing as it is *thinking-in-writing*. Read what poet William Stafford has to say about the relationship between thinking and writing:

> When I write, I like to have an interval before me when I am not likely to be interrupted. For me, this means usually the early morning, before others are awake. I get pen and paper, take a glance out the window (often it is dark out there), and wait. It is like fishing. But I do not wait very long, for there is always a nibble—and this is where receptivity comes in. To get started I will accept anything that occurs to me. Something always occurs, of course, to any of us. We can't keep from thinking. Maybe I have

to settle for an immediate impression: it's cold, or hot, or dark, or bright, or in between! Or—well, the possibilities are endless. If I put down something, that thing will help the next thing come, and I'm off. If I let the process go on, things will occur to me that were not at all in my mind when I started. These things, odd or trivial as they may be, are somehow connected. And if I let them string out, surprising things will happen. (William Stafford, "A Way of Writing," *Writing the Australian Crawl*)

SOURCES, STRATEGIES, AND YOUR JOURNAL

As the first stage in the writing process, planning helps you uncover, explore, and evaluate a topic. Whether you are assigned a topic by your teacher or are free, like Stafford, to accept any topic that occurs to you, planning helps you locate and produce information in writing. Hemingway, you recall, found his "one true sentence" in one of three sources: (1) something he knew (*memory*); (2) something he had seen (*observation*); or (3) something he had learned (*research*).

Those three sources contain an abundance of material for writing. To tap them, however, you need to employ one of several thinking-in-writing strategies. The strategies not only identify familiar (or forgotten) information, but also create, as Stafford suggests, surprising new information. The strategies are flexible enough that you can apply them to all three sources or use them during other stages of the writing process. A strategy designed to tap your memory—such as listing—works equally well as a method for recording observations, conducting research, or solving a problem in drafting.

A good place to experiment with these strategies is in a writer's sourcebook or journal. Depending on your work habits or writing context, you can use anything from a looseleaf notebook to a computer disk for your journal. In this private, no-fault environment, you can write whatever you want. But try to avoid turning your journal into a diary that simply records the clutter of your daily schedule. Instead, use it to plan writing projects—the one due next week and the one you may want to try someday.

During planning, the writing you produce in your journal will read like "one step forward, two steps back." This movement is created by your attempt to answer two questions: (1) How much information can I *produce* about this topic in writing? (2) How much of this information can I *use* to shape an interesting piece of writing? You can answer the first question after you have worked with one or more thinking-in-writing strategies. You can answer the second by evaluating the information against the guidelines provided in Chapter 1 for selecting a subject, analyzing your audience, and determining your purpose.

USING MEMORY IN WRITING

Your own past is one of your best sources of information. Since childhood you have been accumulating memories about people, places, and things; about growing up, falling down, leaving home, staying put—the list is endless. These memories pop into your head when you least expect them. A face in the crowd reminds you of an old friend. A whiff of suntan lotion finds you playing volleyball at the beach. The sound of a word—*Schwinn*—recalls the freedom of peddling your first bike. When you begin to write, however, you cannot remember on impulse. You must remember on purpose, searching your past for information you may want to use. Select a prompt—a word, an image, or a question—to unlock your memory and focus your attention. Next, experiment in your journal with one of the following writing strategies designed to stimulate your memory: *listing* and *freewriting*.

Listing

Listing is a simple way to produce information in writing. If you are creating your own assignment, you can make a list of potential subjects. If you are responding to directions, you can list what you already know or need to know about the subject of the assignment. As you restrict your subject or identify its various subdivisions, you can make additional lists to help you recall more precise information. Begin by giving your list a title, a prompt that will evoke events, impressions, and ideas. Then, working down the page as quickly as possible, list any word or phrase that comes to mind. Don't stop to edit, organize, or evaluate the items in your list. Simply spill them down the page in whatever form they occur to you. Sometimes you will work in explosive bursts, producing ideas that instantly generate related ideas. At other times you will pause, probing for a new direction as you move from one isolated idea to another. Don't be discouraged by these occasional pauses or by the strange notions you jot down to keep the list going. The pauses may identify topics that require further consideration, and the strange notions may provoke unexpected insights into your subject.

One of the richest memory sources is probably your family. As he thought about his family, Robert focused on his relationship with his father. He selected the word *Dad* as a prompt and then produced the following list in his journal.

Dad

P.K.—preacher's kid, defensive, embarrassed, rebellious, special

friends' fathers had normal jobs—no explanations

worked at bank, factory—on weekends, slept late, played golf

Dad works at church—and at home

Saturday "Keep quiet! Dad's working on sermon"

Typing in study. No phone calls. Turn down T.V.

Skips lunch—dinner, glassy-eyed, distant

Sunday Morning—gone before breakfast—dress rehearsal

Mother checks our shoes, knots ties

Marches us to first pew—everybody looking

Organ, choir, congregation—processional

Dad in robe, carrying Bible—distinguished, important

Sunday voice—scripture, sermon (fidgety, sleepy)

Prayer—"Our Heavenly Father"—power, majesty

Heavenly father, my father—same words, same rules

Sunday afternoons—Sabbath—Keep it Holy

No football, no movies, no fun—goodie-two-shoes

Career day at school—doctor, lawyer, police chief

"What's your father do?"

"Nothing. He's a minister."

Evaluating Lists   After completing your list, examine your information carefully. What subject dominates your list? Can you identify other subjects or subjects you want to develop in greater detail? Circle and connect items that seem to go together. Pick a word or phrase and start another list. You may decide that you can use most of the information on your list, or you may discover that only a few fragments or sentences are worth pursuing. But one of those sentences may be what Hemingway called a "true sentence," a sentence that points the way to your subject, audience, and purpose.

Robert's list focuses immediately on his father's job. The initials *P.K.* evoke emotions he cannot easily explain. His friends' fathers have *normal* jobs, but his Dad's job is different. The weekend schedule clarifies that difference and suggests the possibility of a specific subject that is significant, interesting, and manageable. It also suggests at least three groups of readers (normal people, preachers' kids, and preachers) who might find the subject intriguing. But, most important, the list hints at several hypotheses about Robert's perception of his father's work that he may want to explore in greater detail, either through another list or through one of the other planning strategies described in this chapter. When he has collected enough information, he will sort through his sketchy hypotheses and select one to guide his writing during drafting.

Freewriting

Like listing, freewriting helps you write down as quickly as possible what you can remember. But freewriting differs from those strategies by encouraging you to remember in coherent blocks and to write in phrases and sentences. Freewriting is *free,* however, because you don't have to worry about writing perfect sentences. You write in your journal for a sustained period of time (usually ten to fifteen minutes) without stopping. Under these conditions, you don't have time to reflect on where you are going, where you have been, or how anything looks. You certainly don't have time to correct misspelled words, cross out awkward phrases, or reread what you have written. Once you are finished, you will have time to look it over and identify useful ideas.

You can practice freewriting as an unfocused or focused activity. In unfocused freewriting, you simply begin writing, transcribing onto the page the first ideas that pop into your head and then allowing your mind to wander to other subjects. The chief advantage of this kind of writing is that it forces you to write *immediately,* bypassing the agony of selecting the perfect topic. Its chief disadvantage is that it often forces you to write about the *immediate,* the impulses and events that have just occurred. But while you are filling up the page, you may discover a provocative idea or forgotten episode that leads to a more complex or deeply textured pattern of ideas.

Joanne, for example, completed the following unfocused freewriting in her journal during the confusion of the first day of her writing class:

Here I go again. Summer's gone. September stomach back. Worry about clothes, teachers, grades. I mean how many times did I check and double-check my schedule, and then—wrong room, wrong class. Everybody's looking at blotches on my neck. Act like you're the only one who doesn't know. If you get lucky, finding this class—surprise, write an essay. Freewriting, fat chance. First days are always a lie. I mean what do you people want? Solve the polynomial. Remember the <u>Maine</u>. Find the unknown. Never could figure out Bridgeman (Latin)—never learned to decline. My little revolt. He liked it—seemed to matter. Weird. Wonder if this matters? What are we supposed to be doing anyway? Why not "What I did on my summer vacation" or better yet "What I didn't do on my summer vacation"?

It is often difficult to evaluate unfocused freewriting because the sentences slide from subject to subject, never stopping long enough to develop. But you can underline words that seem significant or question phrases that seem suspicious. Does your writing have a common theme? Does one sentence or phrase evoke a particularly powerful memory? Answering these questions in your journal may help you select a subject for a focused freewriting exercise. Joanne, surprised that she remembered Mr. Bridgeman's Latin class, decided to reconstruct the episode suggested by the prompt "My little revolt":

My Little Revolt

"I'm a tough teacher. This is a tough class. Half of you will be gone in two weeks. The rest of you will love Latin." Tough love! Bridgeman paces behind desk like a caged panther. Knit shirts, no ties—pumps iron. Made Linda Thomas cry three days straight; then she was gone. Everybody got it. Even Tommy Hirschen, Latin ace. "Miss Reinhardt. Go to board. Decline fēmina." Stomach lurches. Don't cry in front of boys. Already sniffling—bad cold, no Kleenex. "Begin!" Nominative, genitive, dative . . . accusative? . . . Damn! Play with chalk. Read back of eraser. "Miss Reinhardt?" "I'm thinking." Thinking I need a Kleenex. Nose dripping, eyes watering. Should have stayed home. "Cease"—favorite word. Never "stop" or "that will be all". . . . "Mr. Hirschen. Finish declining fēmina." Blotches on neck. Nose running all the way to desk. Ask Mary Keller for Kleenex—too loud. "Cease." Heart pounds. "What is it now, Miss Reinhardt?" "I need a Kleenex." Long sigh—"Is there a kind soul who can give Miss Reinhardt a Kleenex?" Book bags, purses, hands—six tissues. Don't look up. Stack them slowly in pile. Reshuffle them. Make him wait. Peel off top tissue and blow. Crumple in wad. Walk slowly toward his desk. He's still waiting. Drumming pencil. Drop wad in basket. Look him in the eye—"You can continue." Turn around . . . Hirschen's mouth open. Keller's in shock. Note on my desk. "You're dead." Bell. "Miss Reinhardt. May I see you before you leave?" Class crunches out. Hirschen whispers, "Bridgeman kills." Don't cry no matter what. We're alone. He smiles . . . "Congratulations. I've been waiting a long time for somebody to do something like that." Like what? And that was it. Still can't figure it out. Never told anybody. Let 'em fight their own battles with Bridgeman. Never scared of him again. Never loved Latin. Tough luck, Bridgeman.

Evaluating Freewriting   Like Joanne, you will need to make a number of decisions about your subject, audience, and purpose, if you want to write a longer, more finished essay based on your freewriting. Reread both of Joanne's freewritings and then answer the following questions:

1. How does Joanne's decision to focus on her revolt restrict her subject? What does she find significant and interesting about this incident? What aspects has she managed effectively? What aspects need further development?

2. How might an assessment of her audience help Joanne transform her planning into a successful draft? What specific sections of her freewriting attract the sympathy of her readers? What additional information will they need to understand her revolt?

3. What is Joanne trying to prove about her subject? Is she attempting to prove more than one thing? Make a list of hypotheses she could use to clarify her intentions.

USING OBSERVATION IN WRITING

Like most people, you spend much of your life as a casual observer, acknowledging but rarely examining the blur of daily experience. You have learned to *look for* the things you must see—the date of the midterm, the light at the intersection. Occasionally, you will *look at* some person or thing that is new or unusual—a new student in the front row, a remodeled store on the corner. But for the most part, you *look through* the world the way you look through a magazine, flipping pages without any particular purpose. When you begin to write, however, you must train yourself to look for interesting subjects, significant features, and telling details. Two observation strategies that will help you compose vivid verbal pictures are *mapping* and *speculating*.

Mapping

Mapping is a strategy for studying a subject during an extended period of observation—usually twenty to thirty minutes. If you are convinced you have no artistic talent, you may hesitate to experiment with this strategy. But mapping, like freewriting, is not intended to create a perfect product; it's simply another strategy for thinking on paper. Others may be fascinated by your map, but only you can interpret its lines, figures, and legends.

You can draw three kinds of maps in your journal. Depending on your subject and purpose, you may decide to use one or combine the features of all three:

▼ *Spatial maps* resemble a traditional road map or blueprint. The map maker looks down on a static scene and then outlines the spatial relationship among its various parts.

▼ *Activity charts* use the basic outline provided by the spatial map to document the kind and amount of activity that occurs in the scene. Usually, the mapmaker uses arrows and lines to show where activities originate and concentrate.

▼ *Figure drawings* focus on your subject in two- or three-dimensional detail. Drawing this kind of map takes more time and talent, but it reveals more about your subject's unique features.

"*He's closer, but not better.*"

Drawing by Sempé: © 1984 The New Yorker Magazine, Inc.

Regardless of the format you choose, follow the same mapping procedure. First, select a subject to map. Your instructor may give you some general guidelines about the kind of subject you should observe. You may be asked, for example, to observe a local business in your community, an important gathering place on your campus, or an isolated natural environment. Or you may be free to sit in a familiar spot, wander around, or work from a list in your journal to find a specific subject that you suspect will prove worth your attention. Next, select a lookout spot. Lookout spots function like a photographer's view finder, helping you frame and center the subject you want to observe. Every subject suggests dozens of possible lookout spots, each providing a slightly different perspective. Experiment with several locations, and then select the best one for your subject and purpose.

Once you are situated, hold your hands upright in front of your eyes to form an imaginary picture frame. Expand and contract this frame to see how much you want to include within the borders of your map. Then sketch your subject in your journal, outlining and identifying the physical features, major characters, and energy centers that attract your eye. Finally, fill in the details and use annotations to correct any distortions. Study your subject like a stage designer examines a scene to create a theatrical set. Locate and list everything you would need to reconstruct this set somewhere else.

One assignment in Amy's writing class called for her to observe a major meeting place on campus and compose its profile. Armed with her journal, she prowled around her normal haunts looking for a suitable subject. She considered several possibilities—the dormitory lounge, the snack bar, the registration office—but settled on the library's reference room. Although she had been given the official library tour and had worked at the OPAC and INFOTRAC machines, she had never really observed the layout of this room where people seem to constantly come and go. She selected a lookout spot and spent almost an hour drawing the maps on pages 42 and 43.

Evaluating Maps Before leaving your lookout spot, examine your map as you would a painting. Form a general impression of the lines, figures, and shapes you have made. Next, move your eyes slowly across your subject to identify movements or to label props so you can add more precise annotations. This information will help you illuminate your subject and evoke its texture for your readers once you begin describing it. Later, look for the magnetic center—the subject that pushes itself into the foreground of your drawing. Why does it attract your attention? How does it connect to or contrast with the subjects it forces into the background? Propose several hypotheses about your map that will help you interpret your observations in writing.

Amy began by constructing a spatial map of the reference room. She selected a lookout spot across from the main desk, and in her journal she blocked out the main areas in the room (desk, OPAC monitors, reference shelves); then she added important details (change machines, card catalogue, copy machines). Occasionally, she had to leave her seat to ask one of the reference librarians to identify a prop (*Books in Print*, Library of Congress subject headings, ready reference shelf). But she returned to her lookout spot as she became more interested in observing the action in the room. Drawing an activity chart on top of her original spatial map helped her see how one librarian, Duffy, was the center of the drama. She used another page in her journal to sketch a detailed character drawing of this appealing *subject*. Her observations revealed that everyone used the reference room. Thus her *audience* could be new students (those who are intimidated by reference materials), older students (those who know how to use the major reference materials), and faculty (those who use specialized reference materials). As Amy focused on Duffy, however, she thinks less about the reference books and computer monitors and more about *him*. He is the energy center in the room, the individual who must field all the questions, however mundane or arcane. She is close to formulating a *hypothesis* to try out in a draft that reflects this growing sense of focus: "A single personality (Duffy) guides students through the impersonal resources of the library."

Speculating

Speculating will help you produce different interpretations of what you have observed. The word *speculate* suggests an imaginative, hypothetical kind of seeing: you study your subject, mull over its possible meaning, and make several conjectures about its significance. Your subject might be an observed object (the reference room), a memory (your first trip to the public library), or something you read (a character in a movie or play). As a thinking-in-writing strategy, speculating encourages you to expand your planning by seeing your subject from three different perspectives:[1]

---

[1] Based on the tagmemic theory of invention in Richard E. Young, Alton L. Becker, and Kenneth L. Pike, *Rhetoric: Discovery and Change* (New York: Harcourt, 1970).

- ▼ *Speculate about your subject as an object.*
  This perspective suggests that you see your subject at rest, as a static object or scene that at a given moment has a fixed identity.

- ▼ *Speculate about your subject as an action.*
  This perspective allows you to see your subject in motion, as a dynamic process that changes form as it progresses.

- ▼ *Speculate about your subject as a network.*
  This perspective enables you to see your subject as a series of connections, as a complex system of relationships that extend and enhance its importance.

As you think about your subject from each of these perspectives, note your speculations in your journal. If one perspective does not produce provocative information, move on to the next. Write what you see and make guesses about what you don't see. Don't try to write perfect sentences: you are still *planning.* You are looking for something interesting and significant about your subject that you can reveal to an audience for a purpose.

Speculating both generates information (if you have at least some notion of your subject) and interprets information you have already collected. Here are Amy's speculations about what she discovered from mapping the reference room.

Reference Room as an Object

The Reference Room is on the main floor of the library. The entrance is marked by the new system (OPAC—monitors/printers) and the old system (card catalog). The whole room is cluttered with books and machines. Everything is intimidating. Bibliographies, dictionaries, indexes, INFOTRAC—even the change and copy machines. At the center of the room is mission control. Three librarians manage the reference desk, waiting for questions. They stare at their monitors, answer the phone, and watch the traffic. Behind them are shelves of reference books, coded in mysterious numbers. There are signs everywhere—maps of the library, symbols for the Library of Congress classification system, instructions on how to operate data bases. This is supposed to be the "yellow pages" for the library—the place where your fingers do the walking. But it's too much. As a fixed object, it looks like a maze, a trap.

Reference Room as an Action

This must be the busiest room on campus. Students everywhere. Scowling at OPAC or INFOTRAC monitors. Acting like they know what they are doing. Hunching over the copy machine as the light flashes under their book. Then the game begins. Reference desk to OPAC, OPAC to INFOTRAC, INFOTRAC to shelves, shelves to change machine, change machine to copy machine, copy machine to reference desk. Freeze. Now, start again. Around and around. "I just need three more sources." "Anybody change a five?" Most questions go to mission control. Stand in line, like a deli. "Next." "Where's microfiche?" Librarian with beard (Duffy) seems to know everything. Occasionally he'll go hunting in the stacks. A confused student tags along, looking at watch. This wasn't supposed to take so long. Student comes back alone. Duffy still searching. Student sits with girl at study table. Search rerouted. The computer data base becomes the computer dating base.

Reference Room as a Network

The Reference Room is the key to knowledge network. Everything connects, if you know how it works. So says Duffy. He stands at mission control—silent energy, stroking his beard, waiting for action. Loves the hunt. Other librarians ask him for leads when they're stumped. Faculty call him on phone. Shows students how to think. "Got anything on toxic waste?" "What about toxic waste?" "I just need some sources." The interrogation continues—patient, personable. Looking for clues. Ways to help student get started. "Let's begin at beginning." (OED) "You need a better search word." (LOC Index) "Have you tried one of the other data bases?" (CD-ROM) Always thinking. Enthusiasm contagious. Students return carrying large books, computer printouts. Relieved. They've broken the code. Made connections. And a contact. Duffy made their day.

Evaluating Speculation   Amy's speculations have yielded a wealth of information about the reference room. Before she drafts an extended profile of this special place, she needs to reconsider her information in terms of her potential subject, audience, and purpose. Reexamine her mapping and speculation exercises, then write out your answers to the following questions. Your instructor may want you to discuss your answers in class.

1. How many specific subjects can you identify in the three speculations?
2. Which speculation produces the most interesting perspective on the reference room? How does that perspective define a significant and manageable subject?
3. What potential audience could Amy assume for her profile? What different audience does she assume in each of her speculations?
4. What hypotheses can you find in Amy's mapping and speculating exercises?
5. What purpose might Amy choose for writing an essay about the library reference room? Compose a thesis statement she could use to build an essay from.

USING RESEARCH IN WRITING

After exploring your memories and examining your observations, you may decide that you need more information about your subject to compose an effective piece of writing. Memory and observation, after all, define your subject in *your* terms—the way you remember or see it. To broaden and deepen your understanding, you must reach beyond the limits of your personal experience to determine how others have perceived your subject. Almost any subject you choose (worst flavors of ice cream, best hiking trails, most unusual junk mail) has been researched by other writers. Sometimes their research reflects and reinforces your view of the subject. More often it enlarges, confuses, or even contradicts your conclusions. You may want to reject this unsettling information and reaffirm the world as you see it. But you should resist this temptation, suspending your judgment until you have given the evidence a fair hearing. After such consideration, you will need to decide whether to dismiss this evidence entirely, accept the assertions that challenge your weakest assumptions, or integrate all its findings into your expanding interpretation of your subject.

In Chapters 13 and 14 you will learn how to follow the formal procedures for planning and writing the research paper, which is a more complex piece of writing than the simple expository writing discussed here. In this chapter you will learn how to practice two informal planning strategies designed to gather information in writing: *interviewing* and *reading.*

Interviewing

Interviewing someone is the most direct way to investigate a subject, but the process is never so simple or spontaneous as it appears on television. To use the strategy effectively, you must learn how to *prepare* for an interview, how to *manage* and *record* an interview, and how to *evaluate* the results.

How to Prepare for an Interview   Begin by compiling a list of people who may know something about your subject. The list could include *experts* (people who have studied your subject), *participants* (people who have *lived* your subject), and *information brokers* (people who may know nothing about your subject but know how to put you in touch with people who do). Contact the people on your list and ask for an interview, stating in general terms what you are trying to find out and why you think they may be able to help. Ask to talk to them for a specific amount of time—no longer than an hour—and don't overstay your welcome. As you schedule your interviews, anticipate how your subjects may respond to your questions. Are they likely to be friendly, hostile, or merely puzzled when you arrive? Sometimes you can anticipate their attitudes because you know them or because you have heard them express their opinions on your subject. At other times you can anticipate their attitudes by imagining yourself in their position. How would you feel about being interviewed on this subject? What topics would you want to be asked about? What topics would you want to avoid? What questions would you have about the interviewer's motives and methods?

Next, ask yourself what you want to learn from each subject. To feel prepared and to avoid getting sidetracked, write out a list of questions in your journal following the journalist's formula: *Who? What? Where? When?*

Why? and *How?* Although these questions will help you organize what you want to learn, most interviews are dynamic, disorganized conversations. For that reason, you must remind yourself that your questions are likely to provoke surprising answers that will inspire new questions. The best interviewers prepare to discover things they need to know and plan to uncover things they had not expected to learn.

How to Manage and Record an Interview Interviews can be formal occasions in which the interviewer acts like an attorney grilling witnesses and the interviewee acts like a jittery suspect. Or interviews can be informal occasions—pleasant and productive conversations among friends. Sometimes you cannot control the mood of an interview because the person you are talking to is suspicious before you arrive. But most of the time you can put yourself and your subject at ease by following a few basic tips:

▼ *Don't feel that you must apologize for your interview.* You may want to say something about how much you appreciate your subject's willingness to talk to you. Such remarks are part of the etiquette of interviewing. But someone who has agreed to be interviewed is probably flattered that you are there and has already made time for you on the day's schedule.

▼ *Tape recorders can supply a valuable record of your conversation, but they make some people uncomfortable.* Try your journal. Keep it out of sight as much as possible, and write in it as little as possible. When you do write, jot down words and phrases rather than complete sentences. Keep your eyes on the person you are talking to, not on your journal.

▼ *Begin your interview by talking about interesting and safe topics.* If you are conducting the interview in the subject's home or office, ask about some object or photograph you have noticed in the room. Even if you don't ask about these props, try to list them in your journal because they may help you interpret what your subject thinks is important in his or her life.

▼ *Don't tell your subject everything you want to know before your subject tells you what he or she knows.* You are trying to learn what other people think, not prove what you think. The best strategy is to encourage the interviewee to act like an expert: ask your subject to help you understand the topic at hand by answering your questions. And then LISTEN.

▼ *Use prepared questions only when the conversation drifts far away from the designated topic.* For the most part, allow the conversation to develop naturally. Before you end the interview, however, review your prepared questions as a final check.

▼ *Save two questions for the end of the interview:* (1) What should I have asked that I didn't ask? (2) Whom else do I need to interview (or what do I need to read) to understand the topic we've been discussing?

How to Evaluate an Interview   Once you have completed the interview, return to your room and immediately reconstruct the conversation. Describe the atmosphere of the room where the interview took place, the appearance of your subject, and the varying attitudes (eager, evasive, expansive) he or she displayed during the discussion. Transform your words and phrases into complete sentences. If your notes seem incomplete or if you want to be sure you are quoting your subject accurately, call the person to double-check your information. Such follow-up calls are not invitations to censor. People often want to revise what they said during an interview, but only you can decide whether their second thoughts should be yours. Your follow-up call is simply an effort to make the first version complete and accurate.

After you have reproduced the interview in writing, talk to yourself in your journal about what you learned. Did your subject provide useful answers to your prepared questions? What answers confirmed your assessment of his or her biases? What answers surprised you? What new questions did you ask? If you were to draft an essay based on this interview, could you identify a subject, anticipate an audience, and formulate a hypothesis? This last assessment suggests the degree to which even the most informal interview can propel you into further planning activities. Once you try to evaluate what other people have told you, you will discover that you are making lists of questions you should have asked, people you want to talk to next, and material you think you'd better read.

Susan decided to write about the set design in Arthur Miller's *Death of a Salesman* for a short research paper for her literature class. The university theater was scheduled to produce the play during the next semester, and she decided to interview the theater's set designer.

10/25   Decided on my research paper—"Set Design in Arthur Miller's Death of a Salesman." Theater is producing it next semester. John knows the set designer—D. C. Schwanger. Says he's easy to talk to—real creative. Got an interview Thursday at 1:30. Wonder what he'll do with Salesman? Better think up some questions so I don't look dumb.

1. Who designed the original set for Salesman?
2. What kind of problems will you have to solve in designing the set?
3. Where will you find props for the play—trophy, tape recorder, flute?
4. When will you have to start building the set to complete it on time?
5. How will you create the set for the play—follow Miller's instructions or your own intuitions?
6. Why do some playwrights provide more information than others about the significance of the set?

10/28   Notes from Interview with D. C. Schwanger

Just back from Schwanger interview. First question blew my topic. Since Jo Mielziner's prize-winning design for the original production, nobody has done much with Salesman. Schwanger says all you need is three rooms for the house and open space (apron) for other scenes— restaurant, hotel, garden. He's more interested in sets he's designing for Hedda Gabler and Waiting for Godot. Need to write down what happened.

Sign above office door: "The Miracle Worker." Room filled with props (mostly swords), drawings of sets (renderings), awards (Out- standing Creative Achievement). Next to Schwanger's desk is a drafting table stacked with blueprints (working drawings). Sign behind the table: "It's a small world, but I wouldn't want to paint it." Behind his desk Schwanger looks small, unimpressive—until he starts talking about his work. Real dynamo.

Designing set for one play, building set for another, tinkering with another in performance—complicated schedule. Set designer has to be organized. Reads play, researches how other designers staged it, then looks at history books to see what a living room should look like in a specific time (Hedda). Next collaborates with director about initial ideas—sometimes there is disagreement, but director is always in charge. Next step, makes a rendering or scale model to illustrate things like space, mood, symbolism. Then the working drawings—15–20 pages of blueprints for each play. Designer has to be architect, historian, art- ist, draftsman, engineer, carpenter, plumber, electrician, upholsterer. Turns drawings over to shop foreman for construction but may have to change everything in rehearsal. Too much furniture. Lights change color of paint. Audience can't see props.

New challenge with every play. Historical plays like Hedda you have to be accurate. Modern plays like Godot you have to be creative. Strange—less set—i.e., Godot—frees you to be more creative with what you have—tree. Each play requires you to learn something new. With Equus, weld metal masks. With Miracle Worker, get water to the pump.

Schwanger blew my paper, but fired me up about the whole process. Volunteered to work for him next semester. I could still do Salesman, but I'd rather pick another play or maybe write about several plays that present different design problems. Wonder if I could write about the job of set designer and use different plays as examples? Audience doesn't know how complicated a job it is. Just sit there and watch the actors. Never think about plumbing or electricity unless it doesn't work. Maybe I could interview some other designers. Read textbooks or something by Mielziner.

Susan's interview produced much information on the world of set design. Her original topic, "Set Design in Arthur Miller's *Death of a Salesman,*" is still feasible, but it no longer seems interesting or significant. Read through her notes, and then try to answer these questions:

1. To what extent did Susan's list of questions *prepare* her for her interview?
2. How does she *manage* Schwanger's replies to her questions?
3. Why does the interview change the focus of Susan's research paper?
4. What kind of audience does she anticipate for the new essay she is planning?
5. What hypothesis is she beginning to formulate about this new subject?

Reading

Reading what other people have written about your subject is probably the most common strategy for gathering information for writing. But merely consuming other people's words will not help you compose your own. You must be a critical consumer—*selecting, analyzing,* and *evaluating* what you read for one purpose: to help you write. In Chapters 13 and 14, you will perform these activities according to the more formal requirements of the research paper: checking bibliographies, quoting evidence, documenting sources. In this chapter, you will use reading as an informal procedure for exploring different approaches to your subject.

The easiest way to keep track of your reading is to write about it in your journal. Think of reading as another form of interviewing—a way of talking to people who have already thought and written about your subject. So, just as you did in interviewing, start by making a list of material you want to read. Be sure to look for variety in your reading material: skim magazines in a bookstore; consult with a local expert on your subject; or talk to a reference librarian. Once you start reading, each selection will refer you to others; then your problem will be deciding when you have read enough. There is no way to make that decision—you can *always* read more—but usually you know that you have read enough when the same names, ideas, and issues begin to pop up in everything you read.

On most subjects, reading material falls into three broad categories: eyewitness accounts (printed in popular magazines), expert studies (documented in technical journals or official reports), and advocates' opinions (expressed in editorial or promotional pamphlets). Although these categories suggest the kind of material you need to read, they may not help you classify a specific selection. Indeed, many selections combine the features of all three categories. An editorial, for example, may cite personal anecdotes and statistical data to advance its argument. To sort out the material on your list, you need a set of questions to help you interpret what you are reading. These questions are similar to the guidelines you follow as you write, but in this case you are deciding how another writer, writing in a specific format and context, selects a subject, analyzes an audience, and determines a purpose:

1. Who is the author? What makes the author an expert on the subject? What might have formed the author's point of view?

2. Where and when was the article or book published? You may know little about the author, but you may know something about the point of view of the magazine (*Ms., Scientific American*) and whether the date of publication makes the information current and reliable.

3. What is the author's general subject? What is the restricted subject? What does this perspective contribute to your understanding of *your* subject? Does it confirm your perception, raise new and confusing questions, or lead you into detours and dead ends?

4. To whom is the writing addressed? What attitudes does the author assume in his or her audience? What knowledge does he or she expect these readers to possess or want to obtain?

5. What is the author's purpose? Does the author state a specific thesis or imply one? How does the thesis, stated or implied, control the direction of the writing?

These questions not only help you select the most intriguing reading material from your list, they also help you analyze and evaluate it. Keep your journal with you so you can write about your reading as you *preview, read,* and *review.*

▼ *Preview:* Before you read each selection, try to anticipate the kinds of information and the point of view you will find. Annotate each entry on list, indicating what you expect to find when you read it.

▼ *Read:* As you read each selection, write a few brief notes in your journal. Comment on the major points, copy memorable sentences or important data, and write out short answers to your reading questions. You will also want to write any questions the author raises that you have not considered.

▼ *Review:* Put the material aside and write about the most vivid and thought-provoking things you remember. Thumb back through your reading notes. What did you discover that contributes to your view of the subject? Evaluate what the selection said and what it didn't say.

Paul follows this three-part procedure as he does preliminary reading for an essay on energy alternatives. He begins by reading about the most obvious alternatives—solar energy, nuclear energy, and synthetic fuels—but eventually he restricts his subject to an offbeat but plausible option: garbage. Next, he compiles a short reading list, noting his expectations for each selection.

Reading List on Garbage

Preview

1. "Where Will All the Garbage Go?" <u>Atlantic</u> (March 1985). Author is an environmentalist—wrote a book about small farms. Drawing for article shows island of Manhattan shaped like garbage scow. World Trade Towers serve as smokestacks. Probably focus on New York, but relate problems to general question in title. Who reads <u>Atlantic</u>?

2. <u>Handbook of Solid Waste Disposal</u> (1977). Long, technical book by three professors of civil engineering. One chapter on "Energy Recovery" written for experts. Charts, tables, drawings. Survey of research, case studies, bibliography, appendix on cost estimates for building a plant. Information may be dated—mostly from late 60s and early 70s.

3. "The Sweet Smell of Profits from Trash," <u>Fortune</u> (April 1985). Don't know author (Leinster), but mag. usually focuses on business. Articles grouped under "Corporate Performance," "Money and Moneymakers," etc. This article under "Looking Ahead." Written for potential investors. "Investor's Snapshot" lists sales, profit, and price per share for the two companies featured in article. Information dated? Still valid?

Finally Paul reads and reviews each selection, evaluating what the article contributes to his own planning.

Reading notes

1. "Where Will All the Garbage Go?" Focuses on Fresh Kill—(strange name)—world's largest landfill. Staten Island. 11,000 tons of garbage <u>each</u> day. Title good question. Burning garbage hot political issue. Smoke/dioxins. "Incidence of cancer." Barry Commoner against plant, then changes his mind if they promise to enforce emission standards. Right Barry! Don't you watch "60 Minutes"? Public attitude—"out of sight, out of mind." How can Fresh Kill be out of sight? Mountain peaks over 500 feet—highest on eastern seaboard south of Maine. Ends with story about a "Maintenance Artist." Builds enormous sculpture of garbage truck out of mirrored glass. Arranges "dance" for tugboats and garbage scows. Says, "If we don't blow ourselves up . . . biggest problem will be what to do with the garbage."

Review

Most striking image—mountains of garbage at Fresh Kill. Incredible name. 11,000 tons a day. How does it all get there? Who works there?

What do people who live nearby think of mountain range? How would they like a big garbage-burning plant? Smoke? Article deals with problem, not solution. No one seems to have a solution. "Garbage always wins."

Reading notes

2. <u>Handbook of Solid Waste Disposal</u>. Several plans. Combustion of <u>prepared waste</u>. What is it? Uses only residential, not industrial waste. Does that solve problem? Describes burning waste to produce a waste product that can be burned. Problem—when all this "prepared" waste burns, it produces a heavy accumulation of new waste called "bottom ash." Corrosive. Pollution not significantly higher than plants burning other fuels. Great news! Another system uses "mixed municipal waste." Problem—additional recovery system for by-products. Charts show what materials can be reclaimed and their worth. Blueprints of plants. 1,000 tons a day. Looks like something out of <u>Star Wars</u>. Six pages of charts on the chemicals that come from <u>stackgas</u>. Never say whether any of them can hurt you.

Review

<u>Waste</u>—garbage, refuse, trash, residential waste, industrial waste, mixed municipal waste. I could write my whole essay on these words. The diagrams for the plants look really complicated. Rube Goldberg cartoons. Charts are complete, but the numbers are neutral. Never say anything about environmental impact. Engineers. Talk about economic feasibility and technical problems. Should probably reread this chapter. Know one thing, 1,000 tons a day won't dent Fresh Kill.

Reading notes

3. "The Sweet Smell of Profits from Trash." Description of a groundbreaking ceremony for $80 million garbage plant in Florida. Growth industry. When <u>properly</u> run, no problem. Monaco has a plant "topped by a public tennis court with a restaurant inside, a mere 500 yards from Prince Rainier's palace." Garbage in Monaco? Prince strolls over for a "power" lunch at the plant. Spotters watch for dangerous garbage—cars, appliances, old war souvenirs (land mines and grenades). Big claws—like in penny arcades—grab garbage for fire. When it burns, you can hear the "occasional zing of aerosol cans" bouncing off furnace walls. Problems—tax reforms could prevent depreciation and investment credits. Two compounds in smoke cause cancer. Talks to Kiwanis, Chamber of Commerce, etc. Shows them a glass of cloudy water from a pond near a landfill. Says, "I'll smell the smoke if you drink this water." Projected profits for the two corporations that will dominate this "burgeoning industry." Monaco example makes plant seem harmless. Kiwanis example reduces complex problem to simple either/or. All the money talk suggests these guys are serious. Will probably battle lobbyists from

Sierra Club. Artist was right. Garbage is a big problem. Engineers are right. Should develop technology to convert garbage into energy. Business executives also right. See profit potential in all this garbage. Still, everything seems shaky.

Evaluating Reading   Paul has come a long way since he decided to restrict his paper to garbage. His view of the subject has widened so that he doubts his ability to cover it. He is astonished at how much his readers will have to know to understand the deceptively simple plan to convert garbage into energy. But as he rereads this material and searches for additional information, he discovers a working hypothesis: "Converting garbage into energy creates several kinds of problems." When he composes his discovery draft, Paul will have to refine this hypothesis into a thesis.

A FINAL WORD ABOUT PLANNING

The most important thing to learn about planning is to know when to stop. You probably know people who spend their lives making plans. If they have to study for a test, they make lists of what to study, map out a schedule for studying each item on the list, and then talk about their study plans to everyone else taking the test. Somewhere in the midst of all their planning, they lose sight of the project—the test. Planning as a part of the writing process has a specific and limited purpose: thinking-in-writing. Once you have completed this thinking, you must come to some conclusion about what you have written. You must make choices about your *subject, audience,* and *purpose.* And you must be willing to try out those choices in a fuller, more sustained piece of writing. You must begin drafting.

On Keeping a Journal

The following observations about keeping a journal were made by three important writers: Henry David Thoreau, nineteenth-century American philosopher and essayist; Virginia Woolf, twentieth-century British novelist and essayist; and Joan Didion, twentieth-century American novelist. How would you characterize the different ways these writers use their journals? Which writer's remarks seem to approximate best how you feel about keeping a journal?

Journal | Henry David Thoreau

To set down such choice experiences that my own writings may inspire me and at last I may make wholes of parts. Certainly it is a distinct profession to rescue from oblivion and to fix the sentiments and thoughts which visit all men more or less generally, that the contemplation of the unfinished picture may suggest its harmonious completion. Associate reverently and as much as you can with your loftiest thoughts. Each thought that is welcomed and recorded is a nest egg, by the side of which more will be laid. Thoughts accidentally thrown together become a frame in which more may be developed and exhibited. Perhaps this is the main value of a habit of writing, of keeping a journal—that so we remember our best hours and stimulate ourselves. My thoughts are my company. They have a certain individuality and separate existence, aye, personality. Having by chance recorded a few disconnected thoughts and then brought them into juxtaposition, they suggest a whole new field in which it was possible to labor and to think. Thought begat thought. (1852)

A Writer's Diary | Virginia Woolf

I have just re-read my year's diary and am much struck by the rapid haphazard gallop at which it swings along, sometimes indeed jerking almost intolerably over the cobbles. Still if it were not written rather faster than the fastest type-writing, if I stopped and took thought, it would never be written at all; and the advantage of the method is that it sweeps up accidentally several stray matters which I should exclude if I hesitated, but which are the diamonds of the dustheap. (January 20, 1919)

"On Keeping a Diary" | Joan Didion

So the point of my keeping a notebook has never been, nor is it now, to have an accurate factual record of what I have been doing or thinking. That would be a different impulse entirely, an instinct for reality which I sometimes envy but do not possess. At no point have I ever been able successfully to keep a diary; my approach to daily life ranges from the grossly negligent to the merely absent, and on those few occasions when I have tried dutifully to record a day's events, boredom has so overcome me that the results are mysterious at best. What is this business about "shopping, typing piece, dinner with E, depressed"? Shopping for what? Typing what piece? Who is E? Was this "E" depressed, or was I depressed? Who cares? . . .

How it felt to me: that is getting closer to the truth about a notebook. I **2** sometimes delude myself about why I keep a notebook, imagine that some thrifty virtue derives from preserving everything observed. See enough and write it down, I tell myself, and then some morning when the world seems drained of wonder, some day when I am only going through the motions of doing what I am supposed to do, which is write—on that bankrupt morning I will simply open my notebook and there it will all be, a forgotten account with accumulated interest, paid passage back to the world out there: . . . I imagine, in other words, that the notebook is about other people. But of course it is not.

The Traveling Photographer | Robert S. Winkler

In the December 1983 issue of *Travel and Leisure,* Robert S. Winkler interviews professional travel photographers about the various methods they use in selecting, framing, and interpreting their subject matter. In what ways are their *planning* strategies similar to the thinking-in-writing strategies described in this chapter?

The ways to a good travel photograph are as varied as the combinations of **1** personality and experience that can exist behind the camera. The photographers represented in this special issue recognize that; asked for their comments about their work, they agree on many matters and differ greatly on others, but the most important thing they share, aside from talent, is a willing acceptance of any photographic approach that has, as its end, a meaningful picture. It can only be encouraging for other traveling photographers to see that there is more than one way to skin a cat.

Perhaps in no area do these photographers differ more than in what **2** they do to prepare for their trips. For Pete Turner, who specializes in color and design—making his living from advertising photography but taking his pleasure from travel photographs made for himself—thorough preparation is the rule.

"I usually have a target or a plan—something in mind that I'm going **3** to photograph. For example, I might go to Kenya with the intention of photographing Mount Kilimanjaro. I'd try to make arrangements to be there at the right time of year—not in the rainy season—and I'd think about the best

Winkler, Robert S. *Travel and Leisure* Dec. 1983: 42–47.

A chance shot: A pool in Moscow. © Burt Glinn/Magnum Photos, Inc.

light to photograph in. My primary objective would be to photograph at the best time and in the best light.

"My bible is the *Pan Am World Guidebook.* You can stick it in your   4
suitcase. It covers most of the countries in the world and tells you the number of days of rain or sunshine each month, the temperature, the electric current, the places of interest. I always refer to that first because I think the two most important factors when you're photographing anywhere are temperature and rainfall. After that, I get any photographic books I can and study the images. I like to know what's been done before so that I can

A planned shot: A dramatic picture of the pyramids in Egypt. © Fred Maroon

create my own vision. If I were visiting the Sphinx and the Pyramids, I wouldn't need to do research because I've been there a number of times, but if I'd never been there, it would be useful to know that they're lit up at night. Without a plan, travel photography can be a disaster. You can't go just hoping to find something."

And yet Jay Maisel, a photographer whose work crosses several photographic disciplines and who therefore refuses to be categorized ("I'm interested in light"), believes the less preparation the better. But his approach to travel photography rests on more than just a faint hope. **5**

"You don't really know what you're looking for before you leave. Obviously, it's the juxtaposition of some kind of color and shape and light that catches you, but there's no way to say what it's going to be in advance. I try not to anticipate anything. Especially in travel photography, there's a tendency to take the pictures you've seen before you've been there. I try to avoid that by going out as clean and as stupid as I can be. I don't do a lot of research; I try not to see too much of a place before I get there. What you don't want to do is to start saying, 'I'll do that picture, but a little better.' You try to be as fresh as you can." **6**

Burt Glinn also avoids looking at other photographers' pictures of an area he will visit, "because they keep hanging up in your mind, and pretty soon you start taking pictures of other people's pictures. The only way you get things fresh is by going there and being surprised. Now, that doesn't mean you shouldn't first steep yourself in the essential character of the country. But if you're a photographer going to Russia, instead of looking at the book I did on Russia, you would do better to read Tolstoy or Chekhov to understand what the Russians are like." . . . **7**

The most important part of taking pictures—recognizing the image and 8 getting it on film—is also the most difficult. As Fred Maroon defines the problem:

"When you're hunting for images, most of the time you're saying no to 9 yourself. You always seem to see the best pictures when you're on a dead run—looking out of the corner of your eye, you see off in the distance this marvelous thing, and you're not prepared to shoot it. The worst thing a photographer can do is say, 'I'll get that later.' It's never the same. On the other hand, you can see a situation where some things are right but certain essential factors are missing—the lighting might be bad, and you're a slave to the light. But when the right circumstances develop—a big snowfall or a fog, or if you get up at four in the morning and reach that spot when there are no people or traffic or other things obstructing the view, and if the quality of light gives it some sort of magic—it can become exquisite, and then the picture is there."

Aiming always for the target he's chosen before a trip, Pete Turner at 10 the same time keeps his mind and his eyes open to "photographs of opportunity" that might occur along the way. Echoing Fred Maroon, he says that if a place you're planning to photograph is particularly attractive to tourists, the best time to photograph is dawn.

"Those places get too crowded during the day. If you want a real 11 sense of the place, a sense of experiencing something fresh for the first time, get there at first light. It's calm, it's quiet, and the light is great in the morning. Dawn is the best time to photograph, period. If it were up to me, I'd just do sunsets; I hate getting up. I never was an early person, and I have to make myself get up to do those shots, but it's worth it." . . .

John Lewis Stage takes a psychological approach. He may travel 12 around for a day or two before he starts to shoot, examining how he feels about a place.

"The photographs that grab me are the ones that transmit into visual 13 form what I feel emotionally. That could be anything from a portrait to a scenic to a still life, as long as it has the feel of the area as I see it. Even if you're an amateur, and you go to the Greek Islands, and you just love that sunbaked feeling—or anything else that gives you pleasure—then you ought to try and identify what it *really* is that gives you pleasure, and then it's surprising how automatically you start grasping those things visually if you're any kind of a photographer. Photography is no big mystery, but it's really quite individual. And thank goodness for that."

Television and Reading | Marie Winn

In this selection from *The Plug-In Drug* (1985), Marie Winn compares the process of watching television and reading books. How does her

Winn, Marie. *The Plug-In Drug*. rev. ed. New York: Viking Penguin, 1985. 57–66.

assessment of *watching* differ from the presentation of *observing* in this chapter? Similarly, how does her analysis of reading explain why it stimulates thinking-in-writing?

It is not enough to compare television watching and reading from the viewpoint of quality. Although the quality of the material available in each medium varies enormously, from junky books and shoddy programs to literary masterpieces and fine, thoughtful television shows, the *nature* of the two experiences is different and that difference significantly affects the impact of the material taken in. 1

Few people besides linguistics students and teachers of reading are aware of the complex mental manipulations involved in the reading process. Shortly after learning to read, a person assimilates the process so completely that the words in books seem to acquire an existence almost equal to the objects or acts they represent. It requires a fresh look at a printed page to recognize that those symbols that we call letters of the alphabet are completely abstract shapes bearing no inherent "meaning" of their own. Look at an "o," for instance, or a "k." The "o" is a curved figure; the "k" is an intersection of three straight lines. Yet it is hard to divorce their familiar figures from their sounds, though there is nothing "o-ish" about an "o" or "k-ish" about a "k." A reader unfamiliar with the Russian alphabet will find it easy to look at the symbol "Ш," and see it as an abstract shape; a Russian reader will find it harder to detach that symbol from its sound, *shch.* And even when trying to consider "k" as an abstract symbol, we cannot see it without the feeling of a "k" sound somewhere between the throat and the ears, a silent pronunciation of "k" that occurs the instant we see the letter. 2

That is the beginning of reading: we learn to transform abstract figures into sounds, and groups of symbols into the combined sounds that make up the words of our language. As the mind transforms the abstract symbols into sounds and the sounds into words, it "hears" the words, as it were, and thereby invests them with meanings previously learned in the spoken language. Invariably, as the skill of reading develops, the meaning of each word begins to seem to dwell within those symbols that make up the word. The word "dog," for instance, comes to bear some relationship with the real animal. Indeed, the word "dog" seems to *be* a dog in a certain sense, to possess some of the qualities of a dog. But it is only as a result of a swift and complex series of mental activities that the word "dog" is transformed from a series of meaningless squiggles into an idea of something real. This process goes on smoothly and continuously as we read, and yet it becomes no less complex. The brain must carry out all the steps of decoding and investing with meaning each time we read; but it becomes more adept at it as the skill develops, so that we lose the sense of struggling with symbols and meanings that children have when they first learn to read. 3

But not merely does the mind *hear* words in the process of reading; it is important to remember that reading involves images as well. For when the reader sees the word "dog" and understands the idea of "dog," an image representing a dog is conjured up as well. The precise nature of this "reading image" is little understood, nor is there agreement about what relation 4 it bears to visual images taken in directly by the eyes. Nevertheless images necessarily color our reading, else we would perceive no meaning, merely empty words. The great difference between these "reading images" and the images we take in when viewing television is this: we *create* our own images when reading, based upon our own life experiences and reflecting our own individual needs, while we must accept what we receive when watching television images. This aspect of reading, which might be called "creative" in the narrow sense of the word, is present during all reading experiences, regardless of *what* is being read. When we read it is almost as if we were creating our own, small, inner television program. The result is a nourishing experience for the imagination. As Bruno Bettelheim notes, "Television captures the imagination but does not liberate it. A good book at once stimulates and frees the mind."

Television images do not go through a complex symbolic transformation. The mind does not have to decode and manipulate during the television experience. Perhaps this is a reason why the visual images received directly from a television set are strong, stronger, it appears, than the images conjured up mentally while reading. But ultimately they satisfy less. A ten-year-old child reports on the effects of seeing television dramatizations of books he has previously read: "The TV people leave a stronger impression. Once you've seen a character on TV, he'll always look like that in your mind, even if you made a different picture of him in your mind before, when you read the book yourself." And yet, as the same child reports, "the thing about a book is that you have so much freedom. You can make each character look exactly the way you want him to look. You're more in control of things when you read a book than when you see something on TV."   5

It may be that television-bred children's reduced opportunities to indulge in this "inner picture-making" accounts for the curious inability of so many children today to adjust to nonvisual experiences. This is commonly reported by experienced teachers who bridge the gap between the pretelevision and the television eras.   6

"When I read them a story without showing them pictures, the children always complain—'I can't see.' Their attention flags," reports a first-grade teacher. "They'll begin to talk or wander off. I have to really work to develop their visualizing skills. I tell them that there's nothing to see, that the story is coming out of my mouth, and that they can make their own pictures in their 'mind's eye.' They get better at visualizing, with practice. But children never needed to learn how to visualize before television, it seems to me."   7

Viewing vs. Reading: Concentration

Because reading demands complex mental manipulations, a reader is required to concentrate far more than a television viewer. An audio expert notes that "with the electronic media it is openness [that counts]. Openness permits auditory and visual stimuli more direct access to the brain . . . someone who is taught to concentrate will fail to perceive many patterns of information conveyed by the electronic stimuli."   8

It may be that a predisposition toward concentration, acquired, perhaps, through one's reading experiences, makes one an inadequate television watcher. But it seems far more likely that the reverse situation obtains: 9 that a predisposition toward "openness" (which may be understood to mean the opposite of focal concentration), acquired through years and years of television viewing, has influenced adversely viewers' ability to concentrate, to read, to write clearly—in short, to demonstrate any of the verbal skills a literate society requires.

Pace

A comparison between reading and viewing may be made in respect   10
to the pace of each experience, and the relative control we have over that pace, for the pace may influence the ways we use the material received in each experience. In addition, the pace of each experience may determine how much it intrudes upon other aspects of our life.

When we read, clearly, we can control the pace. We may read as   11
slowly or as rapidly as we can or wish to read. If we do not understand something, we may stop and reread it, or go in search of elucidation before continuing. If what we read is moving, we may put down the book for a few moments and cope with our emotions without fear of losing anything.

When we view, the pace of the television program cannot be con-   12
trolled; only its beginning and end are within our control by clicking the knob on and off. We cannot slow down a delightful program or speed up a dreary one. We cannot "turn back" if a word or phrase is not understood. The program moves inexorably forward, and what is lost or misunderstood remains so.

Nor can we readily transform the material we see on television into a   13
form that might suit our particular emotional needs, as we invariably do with material we read. The images move too quickly. We cannot use our own imagination to invest the people and events portrayed on television with the personal meanings that would help us understand and resolve relationships and conflicts in our own life; we are under the power of the imagination of the show's creators. In the television experience the eyes and ears are overwhelmed with the immediacy of sights and sounds. They flash from the television set just fast enough for the eyes and ears to take them in before moving on quickly to the new pictures and sounds . . . so as *not to lose the thread.*

Not to lose the thread . . . it is this need, occasioned by the irrevers-   14
ible direction and relentless velocity of the television experience, that not only limits the workings of the viewer's imagination, but also causes television to intrude into human affairs far more than reading experiences can ever do. If someone enters the room while we're watching television—a friend, a relative, a child, someone, perhaps, we have not seen for some time—we must continue to watch or else we'll lose the thread. The greetings must wait, for the television program will not. A book, of course, can be set aside, with a pang of regret, perhaps, but with no sense of permanent loss.

A grandparent describes a situation that is, by all reports, not uncom-   15
mon:

"Sometimes when I come to visit the girls, I'll walk into their room   16
and they're watching a TV program. Well, I know they love me, but it makes me feel *bad* when I tell them hello, and they say, without even looking up, 'Wait a minute . . . we have to see the end of this program.' It hurts

me to have them care more about that machine and those little pictures than about being glad to see me. I know that they probably can't help it, but still. . . ."

Can they help it? Ultimately, when we watch television our power to release ourselves from viewing in order to attend to human demands that come up is not altogether a function of the pace of the program. After all, we might *choose* to operate according to human priorities, rather than electronic dictatorship. We might quickly decide "to hell with this program" and simply stop watching when a friend enters the room or a child needs attention.

We might . . . but the hypnotic power of television makes it difficult to shift our attention away, makes us desperate not to lose the thread of the program.

Why Is It So Hard to Stop Watching?

A number of perceptual factors unique to the television experience may play a role in making television more *fascinating* than any other vicarious experience, factors to do with the nature of the electronic images on the screen and the ways the eye takes them in.

Whereas in real life we perceive but a tiny part of the visual panorama around us with the fovea, the sharp-focusing part of the eye, taking in the rest of the world with our fuzzy peripheral vision, when we watch television we take in the entire frame of an image with our sharp foveal vision. Let us say that the image on the television screen depicts a whole room or a mountain landscape; if we were there in real life, we would be able to perceive only a very small part of the room or the landscape clearly with any single glance. On television, however, we can see the entire picture sharply. Our peripheral vision is not involved in viewing that scene; indeed, as the eye focuses upon the television screen and takes it all in sharply, the mind blots out the peripheral world entirely. Since in real life the periphery distracts and diffuses our attention, this absence of periphery must serve to abnormally heighten our attention to the television image.

Another unique feature of the television image is the remarkable activity of all contours on the television screen. While the normal contours of real-life objects and people are stationary, the electronic mechanism that creates images on a screen produces contours that are ever moving, although the viewer is hardly aware of the movement. Since the eye is drawn to fixate more strongly on moving than on stationary objects, one result of the activity of television contours is to make them more attention-binding.

Yet another consequence is to make the eye defocus slightly when fixing its attention on the television screen. The reason is this: in viewing television the steadily changing visual activity of the contour causes the eye to have difficulties in fixating properly. Now in real life when the eye does not fixate properly a signal is sent to the visual center of the brain, which then takes corrective steps. Since improper fixation is normally the result of an eye tremor or some physical dysfunction of the viewer rather than of the thing being viewed, the visual system will attempt to make corrections in the eye tremor or in some part of the viewer's visual system. However, in viewing television, it is the visual activity *at the contour of the image* that is causing the difficulties in fixation. Thus the visual system will have increasing difficulty in maintaining its normal fixation. Therefore it may be easier to give up striving for a perfect, focused fixation on a television picture, and to accommodate by a somewhat defocused fixation.

The sensory confusion that occurs as a result of the activity of television images is not unlike the state that occurs when the semicircular canals of the ears, which serve to maintain our balance and help the brain make the necessary adjustments to the body's movements, are confused by motion from external sources (as when one stands still and yet one's ear canals are moved this way and that by the motion of a car or ship or airplane). The unpleasant symptoms of seasickness or carsickness reflect this internal confusion.   23

The slight defocusing of the eyes while viewing television, while not as unpleasant as seasickness (it is barely perceptible, in fact), may nevertheless have subtle consequences that serve to make the television experience more dysfunctional for the organism than other experiences such as reading. Research shows that defocusing of the eyes normally accompanies various fantasy and daydreaming states. Thus the material perceived on television may take on an air of unreality, a dreamlike quality. Moreover, similar visual-motor conflicts are frequently described as features of many drug experiences by users. This may very well be a reason for the trancelike nature of so many viewers' television experience, and may help to explain why the television image has so strong and hypnotic a fascination. It has even been suggested that "early experiences with electronic displays are predisposing to later enjoyment of psychoactive drugs which produce similar perceptual effects."   24

All these perceptual anomalies may conspire to fascinate viewers and glue them to the television set.   25

Of course there are variations in the attention-getting and attention-sustaining powers of television images, many of which depend on such factors as the amount of movement present on the screen at any given moment and the velocity of change from image to image. It is a bit chilling to consider that the producers of the most influential program for preschool children, *Sesame Street,* employed modern technology in the form of a "distractor" machine to test each segment of their program to ensure that it would capture and hold the child's attention to the highest degree possible. With the help of the "distractor," the makers of *Sesame Street* found that fast-paced cartoons and fast-moving stories were most effective in sustaining a child's attention. This attitude toward young children and their television experiences may well be compared to that revealed by Monica Sims of the BBC who states: "We're not trying to tie children to the television screen. If they go away and play halfway through our programs, that's fine."   26

The Basic Building Blocks

There is another difference between reading and television viewing that must affect the response to each experience. This is the relative acquaintance of readers and viewers with the fundamental elements of each medium. While the reader is familiar with the basic building blocks of the reading medium, the television viewer has little acquaintance with those of the television medium.   27

As we read, we have our own writing experience to fall back upon. **28**
Our understanding of what we read, and our feelings about it, are necessarily affected, and deepened, by our possession of writing as a means of communicating. As children begin to learn reading, they begin to acquire the rudiments of writing. That these two skills are always acquired together is important and not coincidental. As children learn to read words, they need to understand that a word is something they can write themselves, though their muscle control may temporarily prevent them from writing it clearly. That they wield such power over the words they are struggling to decipher makes the reading experience a satisfying one right from the start for children.

A young child watching television enters a realm of materials completely beyond his control—and understanding. Though the images that appear on the screen may be reflections of familiar people and things, they appear as if by magic. Children cannot create similar images, nor even begin to understand how those flickering electronic shapes and forms come into being. They take on a far more powerless and ignorant role in front of the television set than in front of a book. **29**

There is no doubt that many young children have a confused relationship to the television medium. When a group of preschool children were asked, "How do kids get to be on your TV?" only 22 percent of them showed any real comprehension of the nature of the television images. When asked, "Where do the people and kids and things go when your TV is turned off?" only 20 percent of the three-year-olds showed the smallest glimmer of understanding. Although there was an increase in comprehension among the four-year-olds, the authors of the study note that "even among the older children the vast majority still did not grasp the nature of television pictures." **30**

Children's feelings of power and competence are nourished by another **31**
feature of the reading experience that does not obtain for television: the nonmechanical, easily accessible, and easily transportable nature of reading matter. Children can always count on a book for pleasure, though the television set may break down at a crucial moment. They may take a book with them wherever they go, to their room, to the park, to their friend's house, to school to read under the desk: they can *control* their use of books and reading materials. The television set is stuck in a certain place; it cannot be moved easily. It certainly cannot be casually transported from place to place by a child. Children must not only watch television wherever the set is located, but they must watch certain programs at certain times, and are powerless to change what comes out of the set and when it comes out.

In this comparison of reading and television viewing a picture begins **32**
to emerge that quite confirms the commonly held notion that reading is somehow "better" than television viewing. Reading involves a complex form of mental activity, trains the mind in concentration skills, develops the powers of imagination and inner visualization; the flexibility of its pace lends itself to a better and deeper comprehension of the material communicated. Reading engrosses, but does not hypnotize or seduce the reader from his human responsibilities. Reading is a two-way process: the reader can also write; television viewing is a one-way street: the viewer cannot create television images. And books are ever available, ever controllable. Television controls.

Writing Assignments

Narrate   **1.**   Find some photographs of a close relative in an old family album or, better yet, a letter or journal written when he or she was your age. In your journal, make a list of those features you find most familiar and most unsettling. Use this information to compose a narrative from your relative's perspective about "how it felt to be *me* at that age."

Observe   **2.**   Select a place in your neighborhood—a garden, a playground, a movie theater. Map it from memory. Revisit the place and map it again. Then in an essay addressed to your writing class, write a comparison of the same place: the way it used to be (memory) and the way it is now (observation).

Investigate   **3.**   Interview someone on your campus or community who is involved in waste management—a janitor, a garbage collector, an office manager, or the person in charge of "weeding" the library's collection of books and articles. In addition to the interview procedures discussed on page 48, ask your subject to *map* the route he or she uses to collect and deposit the waste. As your subject sketches this route, ask him or her to do some speculating about the objects, processes, and networks. You may decide to follow this route as he or she makes daily rounds. Use this information to write a "status report on garbage" for your local newspaper.

Collaborate   **4.**   Your writing group has just read about a contest called "Fantasies Unlimited." According to the rules of the contest, you (in this case your group) are to describe the distinctive features of a place you would like to visit. The contest winners will receive enough money to visit the place for two weeks. Ask each member to list possible locations. Then ask each member to freewrite about his or her nomination for *the* ideal choice. Read the freewrites, vote, and then collaborate on an essay to submit to the contest.

Read   **5.**   Expand your planning in assignment 4 by giving reading assignments about your ideal place to each member of the group—encyclopedia articles, travel essays, guidebooks. Use this additional information to revise your original essay.

Respond   **6.**   Respond to Marie Winn's essay by diagnosing your own television viewing habits. In your journal, keep a log for a week of what you watch, when you watch, and why you watch. Then write an essay for your student newspaper on "The Confessions of a Television Addict."

Analyze   **7.**   Analyze the strategies Marie Winn uses to create a special identity for her readers. In particular, notice the way she uses pronouns like "we" and "they" to distinguish between people who read and people who are addicted to television.

Evaluate   **8.**   Evaluate the two photographs on pages 57 and 58. In your journal, describe your general impression of each picture, identify its focal point and specific details, and formulate a hypothesis about the planning procedures that might have produced it. Then write an essay in which you explain why you would prefer to hang one in your room.

Argue **9.** There is an old saying that a photograph is worth a thousand words. Revise the saying so that you can argue, "A photograph *takes* a thousand words." Select photograph from one of the oversized collections in the library to demonstrate why a photograph, far from needing no explanation, actually requires extensive commentary.

Argue **10.** Winn's argument is that television is essentially a passive activity. In what ways could you make the same case for visiting an art museum, attending a musical performance, or listening to a lecture? Select one such activity, freewrite about it in your journal, and then compose an essay that demonstrates: (1) although x is usually considered an intellectual procedure, it is really a passive process, or (2) although x might seem like a passive process, it demands a great deal of intellectual activity.

3

Drafting

Through drafting, you determine whether the information you discovered in planning can be shaped into successful writing. In Chapter 2, you learned to apply thinking-in-writing strategies to explore likely topics and to assess the potential of each topic by using the guidelines for selecting a subject, analyzing an audience, and determining a purpose. Now you will learn to work the most promising of these topics into a draft.

Although drafting requires you to make specific choices about your subject, audience, and purpose, you should resist the temptation to think of these choices as final. It's tempting to assume, when you are starting out in writing, that composing the first draft is virtually the last stage in the writing process. You might believe that a little quick repair work transforms a first draft into a final draft. Experienced writers, however, know that their first draft is only a very preliminary attempt at producing a sustained piece of writing. Planning allows them to examine possible topics; drafting enables them to experiment with possible arrangements of a topic. They expect this experiment to lead to new discoveries, some of which emerge in the first draft but most of which will emerge in some subsequent draft. Experienced writers try several drafts. With each one, they come closer to what they want to say and how they want to say it.

In the following passage, May Sarton indirectly comments on the experienced writer's view of drafting when she compares the art of flower arranging to the art of writing:

> After breakfast I spend an hour or more arranging and rearranging seven or eight bunches of flowers for the house. There are flowers indoors here all the year around — in winter, bowls of narcissus, geraniums brought in from the windowboxes in the autumn, cut flowers from a local florist when all else fails. But from late May on I have a variety to play with, and the joy becomes arduous and complex. Arranging flowers is like writing in that it is an art of choice. Not everything can be used of the rich material that rushes forward demanding utterance. And just as one tries one word after another, puts a phrase together only to tear it apart, so one arranges flowers. It is engrossing work, and needs a fresh eye and a steady hand. When you think the thing is finished, it may suddenly topple

over, or look too crowded after all, or a little meager. It needs one more note of bright pink, or it needs white. White in a bunch of flowers does a little of what black does in a painting, I have found. It acts as a catalyst for all the colors. After that first hour I have used up my "seeing energy" for a while, just as, after three hours at my desk, the edge begins to go, the critical edge. (May Sarton, *Plant Dreaming Deep*)

You may be relieved to learn that drafting gives you additional opportunities to discover your subject, audience, and purpose, but you cannot lapse into inactivity. You must continue to exercise the "art of choice," evaluating your information, arranging and rearranging it, until you compose a coherent draft. The first section of this chapter presents three approaches to creating that draft: making a *scratch outline,* drafting a *hypothesis,* and composing a *discovery draft.* The second section of this chapter presents three strategies for measuring the success of that draft: constructing a *descriptive outline,* composing an *effective thesis,* and preparing a *formal outline.*

THE SCRATCH OUTLINE

To make a scratch outline you will need to study the information you created in planning. The scratch outline is not designed to impose a rigorous pattern on this material. Its main purpose is to get you started, to help you see how you might arrange the major portion (*body*) of your draft. Later, as you draft several hypotheses about this pattern, you will see how you might compose the opening section (*introduction*) that identifies your subject and explains why you are writing about it.

Begin by assembling whatever lists, maps, or reading notes you produced during planning. Then read through your material several times, looking for recurrent patterns and any unusual ideas or phrases. Use any system you like—marking key words, using numbers or circles—to identify the related information you discover. Once you have established these groups of information, connect and arrange them into a meaningful pattern, sketching the pattern onto another sheet of paper. Don't discard your planning materials: you may need to consult them again.

Sometimes you will discover that your planning has already evoked a simpler pattern, such as Joanne's narration about Mr. Bridgeman's Latin class or Amy's analysis of the activity in the reference room. More often, your information suggests several inconsistent methods of arrangement or none at all. Such confusion usually indicates that your information is too meager to work with (in which case you will have to do some more planning) or that your information is too varied to work with (in which case you will have to make some tough choices). All the cherished items you found during planning will rush forward in drafting, "demanding utterance." But if you give everything equal attention, your essay is likely to "topple over." Some information may be significant enough to form a major division in your outline; other information may be less significant, useful only as minor subdivisions or illustrative examples. Still other information—wonderful, colorful, delightful information—may have to be eliminated because it does not fit into your scheme. As you arrange and rearrange various sections of your scratch outline, you may change your mind about the status of your information: you may want to condense or eliminate significant information or expand or reshape insignificant information. All the choices you make ultimately depend on one question: "What arrangement best enables me to communicate my *subject* to an *audience* for a *purpose?*"

Ellen's assignment was to write an essay about *taste*—about how and why people decide what to eat, what to wear, what to read. During planning, she explored several ways to approach this assignment (the type of people she saw at the health food store, the problems she had selecting a necktie for a gift, and the kind of books she purchased for her personal library), but each time she tried out a thinking-in-writing strategy, she found herself thinking about her friend Barry and his habit of offering elaborate explanations for his choices. Ellen decided that Barry's behavior provided an interesting case study of "taste." Using *Barry* as her prompt, she produced the following list.

Barry

Drives me nuts

Type A—always busy, can't seem to relax

Discipline—routine, schedules, lists

Right way to do everything—always giving advice

Making granola—the right spoon, bowl

No junk food—Big Macs, doughnuts

Health nut—what's good for me

Salad bars, yogurt (?)

Sneaks ice cream—Heavenly Hash

Burns it off with exercise—but no jogging

Shin splints, tendons, new study

Rebounder—bounces to old time rock'n'roll

Says he likes opera and ballet—improves his taste

Never listens, falls asleep—the sleep of the tasteless

Books—looks at diet books, buys classics

Impress himself, never reads—dust—"I'll get around to it someday"

Movies—Siskel and Ebert vs. <u>Revenge of the Nerds</u>

Always has his reasons—getting out of the house

Naps, wine, avoiding work

Good for me

Ellen is ready to begin drafting, but she needs to find a pattern in her information. Reading through her list, she begins to circle and number certain topics. She uses arrows to suggest how something from one part of her list belongs in another and question marks and asterisks to indicate problems she needs to solve or explore in greater detail.

Barry

? Drives me nuts

1. Reasons 1. Type A—always busy, can't seem to relax 3.

1. Discipline—routine, schedules, lists

1. Right way to do everything—always giving advice *

2. Food 2. Making granola—the right spoon, bowl

2. No junk food—Big Macs, doughnuts

2. Health nut—what's good for me 1.

2. Salad bars, yogurt (?)

2. Sneaks ice cream—Heavenly Hash

3. Exercise 3. Burns it off with exercise—but no jogging

3. Shin splints, tendons, new study 1.

3. Rebounder—bounces to old time rock'n'roll 4.

4. Culture 4. Says he likes opera and ballet—improves his taste 1. *

4. Never listens, falls asleep—the sleep of the tasteless

4. Books—looks at diet books, buys classics 2.

4. Impress himself, never reads—dust—"I'll get around to it someday" 1. *

4. Movies—Siskel and Ebert vs. Revenge of the Nerds

1. Always has his reasons—getting out of the house

3. Naps, wine, avoiding work 2. 3.

* 1. Good for me

Question: In this blend of fantasy and reality, how do text and images function?

By circling and numbering, Ellen identifies and labels several information groups. Some groups evolve from the pattern of associations on the list (*food*); others form incomplete but potentially useful categories (*exercise*); still others are so cluttered that they will require additional planning to make them coherent (*culture*). Many of the items on Ellen's list could prompt the creation of new lists that relate to her assignment ("Type A," "sneaks ice cream," "sleep of the tasteless"). But Ellen decides that a phrase appearing intermittently throughout her list (*good for me*) provides the most promising topic for her first draft, one that might explain the concept of taste and pull together most of the information on her list. She continues her thinking-in-writing in a scratch outline.

Good for Me

1. Food
   you are what you eat
   health food—granola, complex carbohydrates
   junk food—Whoppers, doughnuts
   cancer—new studies—yogurt (?), salad bars (?)

2. Exercise
   keep in shape
   aerobics—jogging, swimming, rebounder (heart)
   isometrics—pumping iron, violent sports (competition, stress)
   serious injuries (shin splints), marathons—dehydration

3. Culture
   improve your mind
   novels, classics, history, philosophy
   romances, trash, junk magazines ("inquiring minds want to know")
   big tomes—fall asleep
   some reading better than none

Through her scratch outline, Ellen has discovered some new information ("you are what you eat," "pumping iron," "junk magazines") and has deleted other information that does not seem to fit into her plan ("movies," "wine," "opera"). Her outline has helped her restrict her subject to three categories of things *good for me*. Although still sketchy, they suggest an emerging pattern that is potentially significant, interesting, and manageable. Some potential audiences have also emerged: people interested in food, exercise, or culture, and people who define *taste* in terms of what is "good for me." Before she can convert this outline into an essay, however, Ellen needs to draft a preliminary hypothesis.

DRAFTING A HYPOTHESIS

A hypothesis states a possible purpose for your writing. Unlike the thesis, which formally asserts what you will prove in your essay, the hypothesis expresses a tentative purpose. You should certainly try to make your hypothesis restricted, unified, and precise, but you may discover that writing your first draft modifies rather than demonstrates your purpose. Once you have completed your first draft, in fact, you may decide to revise your purpose completely. The first draft is like a laboratory experiment: it gives you an opportunity to test one possible explanation (*hypothesis*) for the pattern you derived from your planning.

To draft a hypothesis, read through your scratch outline and then write out answers to these questions:

1. What do I want (what am I expected) to accomplish in this writing project?
2. What is my attitude toward the material I have gathered?
3. What hypotheses could I prove by writing about it?
4. Which hypothesis seems the most restricted, unified, and precise?

Your answers to the first two questions may be lengthy and provisional because you are trying to clarify your aims and analyze your assignment. You may not use this information in any direct way in your essay, but you may use it to determine your point of view toward your material and the ultimate effect you hope to achieve. Your answers to the second two questions should be simple and direct. These questions are designed to produce conditional theses, one of which you can use in your introduction to help keep your writing on track and to alert your readers to the main idea you are trying to develop.

When Ellen started to draft her hypothesis, she was confused about what she wanted to say about taste and what she wanted to prove about Barry's preoccupation with what is "good for me." Her answers to the first two questions exhibit her uncertainty, and her answers to the second two illustrate her attempt to resolve her confusion by proposing several provisional theses.

1. What do I want to accomplish with this project? I am supposed to be writing about taste. Why people prefer one thing over another. Or at least, the reasons people give for choosing one thing instead of another. Sounds pretty abstract. All I can think about is Barry. Drives me nuts with his explanations. Everything is either good or bad. I guess I wanted to show him that things aren't that simple. There are lots of Barrys in the world. Just like parents, always telling you what's good for you—body, mind, and soul. That's what I tried to do with my categories—<u>food</u>, <u>exercise</u>, and <u>culture</u>. It's not exact, but it might work. The interesting things in each group are the ones that don't fit or that change. What used to be good for you now gives you cancer. Maybe I could make something out of that.

2. I think my attitude toward this material is weird. I started out thinking about Barry. He's so compulsive he's funny. Maybe not so funny. People who think things have to be good or bad are always changing their minds or cooking up new explanations. They could be devious, dangerous. How do other people react to the Barrys of the world? Maybe they're just like me. I mean I'm always trying to figure out whether <u>he's</u> good for me. I change my mind everyday—weird.

3. Possible hypotheses:
   a. Everybody wants to know what's "good for me."

      b. Most people try to divide the world into two categories—what's good for me and what's bad for me.

      c. The most interesting things in the world cannot be classified as absolutely good or bad.

   4. I'm still not sure any of these will work, but if I had to pick one, I'd probably go with c.

As Ellen tries to draft her hypothesis, she struggles to clarify her subject, anticipate her readers, and define her purpose. She knows that this material is interesting and that she is raising significant issues that will appeal to most readers. Her scratch outline is simple enough to guide her through her first draft. As she tinkers with various ways to word her hypothesis, she feels confident enough to begin writing.

THE DISCOVERY DRAFT

Novelist Dorothy Canfield Fisher once compared writing the first draft to skiing down a slope she wasn't sure she was clever enough to manage. Although you have compiled a large body of information during planning, organized that information into a scratch outline, and drafted several hypotheses about its significance, you cannot stand at the top of the hill forever. You must push off and see if your preparation has made you clever enough to manage the long white slope of blank paper in front of you.

This first draft is called a *discovery draft* because you should expect as you write to discover something new about the subject, audience, and purpose of your essay. Some of what you discover will be disappointing. Sections of your essay that you felt certain were complete suddenly seem sketchy. Connections that you saw between sections disappear or appear in forms you had not anticipated. And individual sections may not prove useful because certain items cannot be developed in any detail, duplicate other items, or detract from your working hypothesis.

Most discoveries—even negative ones—help you learn more about what you want to say and how you want to say it. As you convert notes into sentences and group sentences into paragraphs, your writing will talk to you—telling you things you had forgotten, making unexpected connections, pointing toward things you need to find out. Sections of your scratch outline will expand and contract before your eyes; your hypothesis may reshape itself into a more subtle statement. Your discovery draft gives you something to work with—a text, a core of information that you can rearrange or refine in a subsequent draft.

Ellen's discovery draft illustrates some of these changes as she struggles to say what she means.

Good for Me

Most people divide the world into two categories: (1) things that are good for me and (2) things that are bad for me. This system works as a general rule, but the most interesting things do not fit easily into one of the two categories. 1

First, there is food. Everybody knows that raw vegetables, whole grain cereals, and fresh fruit are nutritious, and that French fries, doughnuts, and Whoppers are junk. But what about yogurt? Most advertisements claim it is a health food, but a recent study points out that one 8-ounce serving of flavored yogurt contains 9 teaspoons of sugar. And what about salad bars? They are supposed to be good for you— better than a slab of red meat or a basket of deep-fried shrimp—but recent studies charge that dangerous chemicals are sprayed on salad bar vegetables to keep them looking good. What's supposed to be good for you might give you tooth decay or cancer. 2

Next, there is exercise. Doctors are always telling you to stay fit. Exercise, particularly aerobic exercise like jogging, is supposed to be good for you because it controls your weight, lowers your cholesterol, and strengthens the efficiency of your heart muscle. But there is a trade-off. Jogging can cause serious injuries such as sprained ankles, pulled tendons, and shin splints. And there is a recent study that says severe physical exertion may actually accelerate the causes of coronary heart disease. One doctor says "jog," another says "don't," and another says "it all depends." How can people know for certain whether jogging will be "good for me"? 3

Finally, there is reading. Teachers, parents, and politicians are always saying that reading improves your mind. But what kind of reading leads to improvement? Books that are supposed to help you—diet books, or pop-psychology books—don't really improve your mind. They are stacked next to the candy near the cash register, and everybody knows they are trash. But some of the books that are supposed to be good for you—the classics—many people find too long and boring. If they can't finish the books that are supposed to be good for them, how can people improve their minds? 4

The world is really too complex for a simple good for me/bad for me system. Take ice cream, for example. On one level it is bad for me because it contains large amounts of sugar and cholesterol. On another 5 level, however, it is really good for me. After a long day of dieting, exercising, and reading, what could be better for me than a few scoops of Heavenly Hash?

THE DESCRIPTIVE OUTLINE

A descriptive outline helps you assess what you have accomplished during drafting. In it you report what you have done with the discovery draft and speculate about how to compose your next draft.

To construct a descriptive outline, place your discovery draft on one side of your desk and some blank paper on the other. Do not look at your scratch outline; your objective is to make a new outline that describes your draft. Counting the introductory paragraph as *1*, number in sequence each paragraph, and then list those numbers on your blank piece of paper. For each number, write down as briefly as possible (a) what each paragraph *says*, and (b) what each paragraph *does*.

There is a subtle but significant difference between what a paragraph *says* and what it *does*. When you identify what a paragraph *says*, you are concerned with subject matter, with the major topic discussed in the paragraph. When you identify what a paragraph *does*, you are concerned with writing strategies, with the development of each paragraph and its function within the larger design of the essay. A paragraph can do many things: it can tell a story, describe a scene, list examples, compare evidence. You will learn more about what paragraphs can do individually and collectively in Chapters 5, 6, and 7. For the moment, use your own words to describe what each paragraph in your discovery draft *says* and *does*.

After you complete the descriptive outline, read through your discovery draft again. Then record your planning and drafting material. Now return to your descriptive outline. What kind of draft does it describe? Are you delighted or disappointed by what you see? Does the outline reveal an interesting progression of carefully developed ideas? Or does it show a fairly predictable pattern of underdeveloped notions?

All this rereading should force you to assess what you have already achieved and what you still need to do. Being as honest as you can, list at the bottom of your descriptive outline your conclusions about the effectiveness of your draft's introduction, working hypothesis, body, and closing. Ellen's conclusions show that she realizes that she could do a number of things to improve her essay. After you have examined her descriptive outline, reread her discovery draft on page 76–77 and then study her conclusions here.

1. a. People divide world into two categories.
   b. Introduces hypothesis: most interesting items don't fit easily into one of two categories.

2. a. Although most people know good from bad, some items cause confusion.
    b. Identifies two examples of food whose classification has been challenged by recent studies.

3. a. Although exercise is considered good for you, it can be dangerous.
    b. Compares benefits of exercise with possible risk factors.

4. a. Reading improves your mind—if you read.
    b. Compares not reading trash with not reading classics.

5. a. The world is too complex for a simple system of good/bad.
    b. Illustrates how ice cream can be both bad and good.

Conclusions

1. Everything goes wrong in first sentence when I replace <u>Barry</u> with <u>People</u>. Sounds more scholarly, but I'm not really interested anymore. Anybody can write about people; I want to write about Barry.

2. The hypothesis is probably all right. What does <u>interesting</u> mean? It would be more interesting if it introduced Barry's explanations.

3. Three sections—food, exercise, and reading—are really predictable. This is good. This is bad. Here's a problem. If I used Barry, I could include more examples under each category—or create some new categories—and show how Barry tries to deal with the problems.

4. The conclusion is good, but it doesn't sound like me. Heavenly Hash is really Barry talking.

5. Mainly, I need to get back to Barry and develop more examples from his point of view.

Ellen's descriptive outline has helped her identify what she has done right, what she has done wrong, and what she needs to do next. Her conclusions form an *agenda* for the next stage in the writing process—*revising*. But before Ellen revises her discovery draft, she decides to transform her hypothesis into an effective thesis and construct a formal outline.

COMPOSING AN EFFECTIVE THESIS

A thesis asserts the main idea you will develop in your writing. In a sense, it summarizes your ideas about your subject and suggests your point of view toward it. You cannot make such an assertion with any confidence until you understand your purpose. You will seldom succeed if you try to compose your thesis first and then write an essay that meets its specifications. It is more efficient to work by testing various hypotheses in drafts, selecting the one that best controls your material and refining it into a thesis.

An effective thesis, then, derives from and makes a compelling statement about your writing. But once you have selected a thesis, you must word it properly if it is to be effective.

Making Your Thesis Restricted, Unified, and Precise

Restricted, unified, and *precise* theses were defined in Chapter 1. The definitions are worth amplifying here, for the more fully your thesis reflects these qualities, the better it will control your writing in your remaining drafts.

To be *restricted,* a thesis must limit the scope of an essay to what can be discussed in detail in the space available. A thesis such as "The United States has serious pollution problems" might be suitable for a long magazine article, but using it in a three-page essay would force you to make statements so broad that your readers would find them superficial and uninformative. A better thesis about pollution might be one of the following:

- ▼ The government has not been sufficiently aggressive in enforcing the regulations that control the disposal of chemical wastes.
- ▼ In Toledo, industrial expansion has created severe air and water pollution.
- ▼ Widespread use of agricultural pesticides threatens the survival of certain species of wildlife.

A good thesis is *unified* if it expresses only one idea. The thesis "The use of drugs has increased significantly in the last fifteen years; hard drugs are admittedly dangerous, but there is considerable disagreement about marijuana" commits the writer to three topics: (1) the increase in drugs, (2) the dangerous effects of hard drugs, and (3) the controversy about marijuana. Each of these topics could form the thesis of a separate essay. To try to develop all three would almost surely result in an unfocused essay consisting of three unrelated, skimpy sections.

Lack of unity most often arises when a thesis contains two or more coordinate parts. The thesis "Compared with other languages, English has a relatively simple grammar, but its spelling is confusing" could lead to separate treatments of grammar and spelling. If you wanted to relate the two topics—for example, by contrasting the ease of learning grammar with the difficulty of learning spelling—the relationship has to be implied in your thesis: "In learning English, foreigners usually have less trouble with grammar than with spelling." If your chief interest is spelling, it would be safer to ignore grammar: "Foreigners have a hard time with English spelling." Sometimes one part of a two-part thesis can be embedded in the other: "The amateur ideal of the Olympic Games is being threatened; professionalism is on the increase" can be rewritten as "Increased professionalism threatens the amateur ideal of the Olympic Games."

Finally, a thesis is *precise* when it can have only one interpretation. The thesis "My home town is one of the most unusual in the state" does not indicate the content of your essay because *unusual* is vague and can mean many things. Readers will want to know in what way the town is unusual. If they have to read the whole essay to find out, the thesis does not help them. Moreover, because the wording is vague, the thesis does not help you see what you need to develop in your essay.

Words such as *unusual, inspiring,* and *interesting* are too vague for a thesis. So are metaphors. The thesis "Where instructors are concerned, all that glitters is not gold" may seem clever, but what does it mean? That the best scholars are not always the best teachers? That the instructors who are good classroom performers do not always help students master the subject? Or does it mean something else? The precise meaning of a thesis should be immediately clear. Metaphors may be effective in the text of your essay, but they can cause trouble in your thesis.

Throughout her drafting, Ellen has had difficulty composing an effective thesis. Her first hypothesis is imprecise because it relies on the vague word *interesting:* "The most interesting things in the world cannot be classified as absolutely good or bad." A second, even more imprecise version appears in the first paragraph of her discovery draft: "The system works as a general rule, but the most interesting things do not fit easily into one of the two categories." This version also suggests two subjects—a system and things that do not fit into it—that could destroy the unity of her essay. In her conclusions to her descriptive outline, Ellen recognizes the problem word and hints that she might be able to draft a more effective thesis if she restricted it to Barry's difficulties explaining what is "good for me." This insight allows Ellen to restate her thesis. She might begin writing another draft immediately, but she decides instead to reevaluate her material and organize by constructing a formal outline.

_____*Exercise*

Some of the following statements would make acceptable theses; others, because they lack restriction, unity, or precision, would not. Explain your reasons for rejecting those that are unacceptable.

1. Foods with high fiber content are very important for your diet.
2. It's easy to see the beginning of things and harder to see the end.
3. Social historians agree that the American Dream is no more than the snows of yesteryear.
4. Although the average person thinks of gorillas as ferocious, chest-beating monsters, they are actually gentle creatures who live at peace with other animals.
5. Jane Fonda's workout tapes have enjoyed an enormous success, and they have proved that self-help videos are now a major consumer item.

PREPARING A FORMAL OUTLINE

A formal outline can serve as an additional writing tool, helping you to discover the need for more information and enabling you to organize a more precise design before you begin another draft. It breaks your topic into major units, marked by Roman numerals, and subdivides these into minor units, marked by capital letters; the next subdivision is marked by Arabic numerals; and a still smaller subdivision is marked by lower-case letters. One warning about this format: if you make any subdivision in your outline, you must have at least *two* subdivisions. You cannot divide something into only one part.

If it seems helpful, give your outline a title. Then begin to construct the formal outline by laying out the major, Roman numeral headings first; then break each Roman numeral heading into capital letter entries, and so on, completing each level of division before starting on the next lower level. This procedure keeps you in control of your outline: you will not distort your organization by developing some headings too much and others too little. As you work your way through each division, you may discover new structural patterns that will require you to revise all the headings in your outline. Such discoveries will help you prepare a consistent outline and compose a coherent draft.

When Ellen looks at her two previous outlines, she decides that she wants her formal outline to follow the same order. When she starts to work her way through each subdivision, however, she starts reclaiming information from her initial planning that applies directly to Barry. As a result, her organization—and outline—change dramatically. She drops one major division (*exercise*) and adds two new divisions (*movies* and *wine*). In the lower subdivisions, she rearranges information ("ice cream" is moved from the conclusion to the first major division) and develops new information (all the items on "movies" and "wine").

It is not always necessary to construct a formal outline to produce a new draft. Your discovery draft, descriptive outline, and reformulated thesis may give you all the direction you need. But Ellen's formal outline shows why it is such a powerful tool.

A Man with All Reasons

Thesis: Barry admits that he has difficulty explaining what's "good for me."

I. Barry has difficulty defending his eating habits
  A. He knows the foods that are nutritious
  B. He knows the foods that are junk
  C. He is attracted to foods that are both
    1. Yogurt has become a problem
    2. Ice cream presents a dilemma

II. Barry has difficulty explaining his reading habits
   A. He knows how to select good books
      1. He reads reviews
      2. He talks to friends
      3. He consults lists
   B. He resists his fascination for self-help books
   C. He buys classics
      1. He believes in the value of owning such books
      2. He never reads them

III. Barry has difficulty justifying his choice of movies
   A. He attends culturally acclaimed movies
   B. He also attends "junk" movies
   C. He contrives elaborate justifications to explain such inconsistency

IV. Barry has difficulty rationalizing his preference for wine
   A. Wine enhances his appetite
   B. Wine relaxes his activity
   C. Wine is served to French and Italian children
   D. Wine is a health risk
      1. Its high sugar content could induce diabetes
      2. Its high alcohol content could induce chemical dependency

Evaluating Outlines

Ellen can evaluate the usefulness of her formal outline as a stage in her writing process and as a completed product. For the first assessment, she compares her new outline with her previous writing on Barry's "good for me" justifications.

1. How much of the new outline derives from the original planning?
2. How many of the conclusions following the descriptive outline have been incorporated into the outline?
3. How effectively does the outline indicate possibilities for controlling *subject, audience,* and *purpose* in a final draft?

To make the *second* evaluation, Ellen considers the following criteria:

1. *Is the thesis satisfactory?* Because the thesis controls the whole outline, a faulty thesis invites trouble all along the way. A vigorous checking of the thesis is therefore the first and most important step in testing an outline.

   "Barry admits that he has difficulty explaining what's 'good for me' " is certainly more restricted, unified, and precise than Ellen's earlier hypotheses. It seems to control the whole outline, but does it say everything Ellen wants to say about her purpose? Ellen considers how she might open up her thesis to assert more about the information she is trying to present. She thinks, too, about why she feels this information is significant.

2. *Is the relationship among the parts clear and consistent?* In a good outline it should be clear how each main heading relates to the thesis and how each subdivision helps develop its main heading. If there is any doubt about the relation of any heading to the thesis, that heading is either poorly stated or indicates an inconsistency in the outline.

   Ellen's decision to focus on Barry's explanations has helped her establish a clearer connection among the four major divisions of her next draft.

3. *Does the order of the parts provide an effective progression?* Just as the sentences within each paragraph must follow a logical order, so must the parts of an outline. If any of the parts is out of order, the disorder will be magnified in the essay.

   Ellen's major divisions—*food, reading, movies,* and *wine*—suggest a progression different from the divisions of her earlier draft—*food, exercise,* and *reading.* She examines this new progression to determine if it is logical and then does the same with the material she has grouped under her capital letters and Arabic numerals.

4. *Is the outline complete?* This is not one question but two:
   a. Are all the major units of the subject represented?
   b. Is each major unit subdivided far enough to guide the development of the essay? The first question is especially important for essays that classify something or explain how something is done; all classes or steps must be included. The second question depends on the scope of the essay. For short papers, the outline may not need to go beyond the main headings. For longer papers, the outline needs to be developed in greater detail so that you can balance and control the information you group under each heading.

   Ellen's four major divisions do not represent every issue on which Barry has an opinion. She has omitted Barry's feelings about what kind of exercise is "good for me" to focus on the more interesting new subjects—movies and wine. She needs to consider whether these changes make her outline more or less complete. The other subdivisions will require the same consideration to ensure the completeness of her essay.

5. *Can each entry be developed in detail?* Each entry in the outline should be developed when the essay is written. There is no rigid rule about how much development each entry should receive. Sometimes a single entry will require two or three paragraphs; occasionally several minor entries may be dealt with in a single paragraph.

   In her discovery draft, Ellen devoted one paragraph to each of her three major divisions. She must consider whether her formal outline suggests the same coverage. The secondary divisions in Ellen's outline (those marked with capital letters) appeared singly as sentences in her discovery draft. Ellen must consider whether these, and the entries she marks with Arabic numerals, contain enough information to develop into separate paragraphs or will remain single, supporting sentences.

A FINAL WORD ABOUT DRAFTING

The most important thing to learn about drafting is to expect frustration. You certainly know people who give up on a project if their effort fails to measure up. They think that additional effort is a punishment for failing to succeed on the first try. But writing, like any other valuable work, requires effort. For that reason, think of drafting as an opportunity rather than an ordeal. Remember May Sarton's comparison of arranging flowers and drafting a piece of writing. Both processes are arduous and complex, but they are also a joy. They require a fresh eye and a steady hand and, after a while, they use up your seeing energy. In Chapter 4, you will study strategies that will help you recover that energy. Revising helps you *see* your material *again*; it helps you find a catalyst to restore your creative ingenuity and critical edge.

Comforting Thoughts | Calvin Trillin

In this essay, Calvin Trillin speculates on several research studies that are supposed to comfort him. As he considers each hypothesis, he sounds like Barry, looking for reasons to justify his behavior. Construct a descriptive outline of his essay. Then reread Trillin's comments on page 8 about how he writes his humorous columns. To what extent does your descriptive outline conform to Trillin's description of his drafting process?

February 29, 1988

First I read about a study in Meriden, Connecticut, which indicated that   **1** talking to yourself is a perfectly legitimate way of getting comfort during a difficult time. Then I saw an item about research at Yale demonstrating that stress seems to be reduced in some people by exposing them to the aromas of certain desserts. Then I started talking to myself about desserts with aromas I find soothing. Then I felt a lot better. Isn't science grand?

I didn't feel perfect. One thing that was bothering me—this is what I   **2** decided after I was asked by myself, "Well, what seems to be the trouble, guy?"—was that the ten most popular methods of comforting yourself listed in the Meriden study didn't mention sniffing desserts, even though Yale, where all the sniffing research was going on, is only about twenty miles down the road. Does this mean that some of these scientists are so busy talking to themselves that they don't talk to each other? It got me so upset that I went to the back door of a bakery in our neighborhood to sniff the aroma of chocolate chip cookies. I was talking to myself the whole time, of course.

"What the Yale people think," I said to myself, "is that a person's   **3** soothed by the smell of, say, chocolate chip cookies because it brings back pleasant memories, like the memory of his mother baking chocolate chip cookies."

"What if his mother always burned the chocolate chip cookies?" I   **4** replied.

"Are you talking about my mother?"   **5**

"Whose mother do you think I'm talking about?" I said. "We're the   **6** only one here."

"Were those cookies burnt?"   **7**

"What do you think all that black stuff was?"   **8**

"I thought that was the chocolate chips."   **9**

."No, she always forgot the chocolate chips."   **10**

I wasn't finding the conversation very comforting at all. I don't like to   **11** hear anyone making light of my mother's chocolate chip cookies, even me. I must have raised my voice, because the next thing I knew, the baker had come out to see what was going on.

Trillin, Calvin. *Enough's Enough (And Other Rules of Life)*. New York: Ticknor & Fields, 1990. 76–79.

Even though the Meriden study had shown that being with someone   **12** else was the most comforting thing of all—it finished ahead of listening to music and even watching TV—I saw right away that being with the baker wasn't going to be much more comforting than talking to myself. He said, "What are you, some kind of nut case, or what?"

I told him that I was engaging in two therapies that had been scien-   **13** tifically proven effective: sniffing chocolate chip cookies and talking to my-self. He told me that I owed him two dollars and fifty cents. "For sniffing, we charge a buck and a quarter a dozen," he explained.

"How do you know I sniffed two dozen?" I asked.   **14**

"We got ways," he said.   **15**

I told him that according to the research done at Yale, certain odors   **16** caused the brain to produce alpha waves, which are associated with relax-ation. I told him that in my case the odor of chocolate chip cookies—par-ticularly slightly burnt chocolate chip cookies—was such an odor. I told him that he ought to be proud to confirm the scientific research done at one of the great universities of the English-speaking world. That alone, I told him, ought to be payment enough for whatever small part of the aroma of his chocolate chip cookies I had used up with my sniffing.

He thought about it for a moment. Then he said, "Take a walk,   **17** buddy."

I was happy to. As it happens, going for a walk finished tenth in the   **18** Meriden study, just behind recalling pleasant memories. Naturally, I talked to myself on the way.

"Maybe I can find someplace to smell what the Yale people call 'spiced   **19** apple,'" I said to myself. "They found that the smell of spiced apple is so effective that with some people it can stop panic attacks."

"But I don't know what spiced apple smells like," I replied. "Spiced   **20** with what?"

That was bothering me enough that my walk wasn't actually very   **21** soothing. I thought about bolstering it with some of the other activities on the list, but reading or watching TV seemed impractical. Prayer was also on the list, but praying for the aroma of spiced apple seemed frivolous.

I walked faster and faster. It occurred to me that I might be getting a   **22** panic attack. Desperately I tried to recall some pleasant memories. I recalled the time before I knew about the Meriden list, when I talked to myself only in private. I recalled the time before I knew about the Yale research and didn't have to worry about finding any spiced apple. Then I felt a lot better. I didn't feel perfect, but you can't always feel perfect.

A Man with All Reasons | Ellen Haack

Ellen's final draft of her essay on "taste" focuses on Barry and his motives for choosing what he eats, reads, watches, and drinks. Compare this draft with her formal outline on page 81–82. In what ways do the divisions on her outline identify the paragraphs in her essay?

Barry's in the kitchen making granola. His long, narrow frame moves   1
deftly around the work area, pausing to scan the recipe book on the
counter or search the shelves for the ingredients—wheat germ, bran, rolled
oats, sunflower seeds, raisins, honey—he plans to mix in a large, gray earth-
enware bowl. While he works, he hums a vaguely recognizable version of
"Blue Moon," drumming on the top of the counter or the edge of the bowl
with a wooden spoon. He's happy. Making granola always has this effect
on him. He doesn't like to make granola—it's messy and time-consuming.
He doesn't like to eat granola—it's too crunchy without milk and too mushy
with it. But he likes to contemplate his reasons for eating granola—"it's
good for me."

Barry moves through the world like he moves through the kitchen,   2
carefully sorting everything into two categories: (1) things that are "good
for me" and (2) things that are "not good for me." Although he is attracted
to the simplicity of this system, he often has difficulty explaining what's
"good for me."

Since he is a health nut, Barry seems most adept at sorting food. His   3
first category includes nutritious foods such as raw vegetables, whole
grains, and fish, while his second includes junk food such as French fries,
doughnuts, and Whoppers. But not all food can be classified so easily. For
example, Barry is currently in a quandary over yogurt. For years, he ranked
it close to granola as a major "good for me." But recent reports on the
sugar content of flavored yogurt have made its position shaky. Ice cream
presents another dilemma. It contains too much sugar and cholesterol to be
"good for me," but Barry loves it. Whenever he does something that is
"good for me," he likes to reward himself with a large bowl of Heavenly
Hash—which is obviously, "not good for me."

Barry is also dedicated to improving his mind and is constantly looking   4
for books that will be "good for me." He reads reviews, talks to his more
literary friends, and consults an old mimeographed list of "150 Great Novels Every Well-Educated Person Should Read" that was given to him by his
high school English teacher. Armed with such advice, he can work his way
through a bookstore, sorting titles into his two categories. The cash register
provides the ultimate test, however. He may be attracted to *Jane Fonda's
Workout Book,* justifying his interest by saying that a strenuous exercise
program would be "good for me." But despite his attraction to Jane and his
dedication to health, he does not buy the book; exercise books are trash. Instead, he purchases *Milton Cross' Complete Stories of the Great Operas,* explaining that knowing more about opera would be "good for me." Unfortunately, the book gathers dust next to one of his other carefully chosen
purchases, H. G. Wells' *The Outline of History.* Although he has never
opened these books, he believes he will get around to them eventually because they are "good for me."

Movies present a similar difficulty. Barry believes that only critically   5
acclaimed films about significant subjects are "good for me." Following the
critics' advice, he went to see *My Dinner With Andre,* only to fall asleep
during the first course. He blinked awake during the credits, saying the nap
had been "good for me." On the other hand, he went to see *The Revenge of
the Nerds,* knowing that the critics did not think it would be "good for me."

He managed to stifle his laughter and maintain his disdain throughout the film. But walking to the car he announced that getting out of the house had been "good for me."

And finally there's wine. Barry assigns wine a high position in his ranking of things "good for me," and he has his reasons. Foremost among these is wine's appetite-enhancing properties. He is slightly underweight and views anything that encourages him to eat as "good for me." Wine is also a relaxant. Barry leans toward the Type A personality and so considers anything that helps him slow down as "good for me." And then there are the French and Italian children. He has read that French and Italian parents give even very young children wine on a regular basis. Parents couldn't possibly give their own children something that isn't good for them. He worries about wine, however, because sugar and alcohol are not "good for me."   6

Recently, as he was fretting about the onset of diabetes or alcoholism, he visited a friend in the hospital. When his friend's dinner tray arrived, he spotted a plastic glass of clear liquid between the Jello and the peas.   7

"Do they serve wine *here*?" he asked.   8

"Yeh, pretty nice, huh?" the friend replied, not realizing the cause of Barry's sudden elation.   9

"See, I told you it was good for me."   10

The Lean and Hungry Look | Suzanne Britt Jordan

Although "The Lean and Hungry Look" was originally published in *Newsweek* in 1978, the essay has been reprinted in many college anthologies because it conforms to a straightforward, logical pattern of organization. State Jordan's thesis and then construct a formal outline for her essay. What is her purpose in this essay? (Remember, purpose and thesis are not identical.)

Caesar was right. Thin people need watching. I've been watching them for most of my adult life, and I don't like what I see. When these narrow fellows spring at me, I quiver to my toes. Thin people come in all personalities, most of them menacing. You've got your "together" thin person, your mechanical thin person, your condescending thin person, your tsk-tsk thin person, your efficiency-expert thin person. All of them are dangerous.   1

In the first place, thin people aren't fun. They don't know how to goof off, at least in the best, fat sense of the word. They've always got to be ado-ing. Give them a coffee break, and they'll jog around the block. Supply them with a quiet evening at home, and they'll fix the screen door and lick S&H green stamps. They say things like "there aren't enough hours in the   2

Jordan, Suzanne Britt. "The Lean and Hungry Look." *Newsweek* 9 October 1978: 32–33.

day." Fat people never say that. Fat people think the day is too damn long already.

Thin people make me tired. They've got speedy little metabolisms that **3** cause them to bustle briskly. They're forever rubbing their bony hands together and eying new problems to "tackle." I like to surround myself with sluggish, inert, easygoing fat people, the kind who believe that if you clean it up today, it'll just get dirty again tomorrow.

Some people say the business about the jolly fat person is a myth, that **4** all of us chubbies are neurotic, sick, sad people. I disagree. Fat people may not be chortling all day long, but they're a hell of a lot *nicer* than the wizened and shriveled. Thin people turn surly, mean and hard at a young age because they never learn the value of a hot-fudge sundae for easing tension. Thin people don't like gooey soft things because they themselves are neither gooey nor soft. They are crunchy and dull, like carrots. They go straight to the heart of the matter while fat people let things stay all blurry and hazy and vague, the way things actually are. Thin people want to face the truth. Fat people know there is no truth. One of my thin friends is always staring at complex, unsolvable problems and saying, "The key thing is . . ." Fat people never say that. They know there isn't any such thing as the key thing about anything.

Thin people believe in logic. Fat people see all sides. The sides fat peo- **5** ple see are rounded blobs, usually gray, always nebulous and truly not worth worrying about. But the thin person persists. "If you consume more calories than you burn," says one of my thin friends, "you will gain weight. It's that simple." Fat people always grin when they hear statements like that. They know better.

Fat people realize that life is illogical and unfair. They know very well **6** that God is not in his heaven and all is not right with the world. If God was up there, fat people could have two doughnuts and a big orange drink anytime they wanted it.

Thin people have a long list of logical things they are always spouting **7** off to me. They hold up one finger at a time as they reel off these things, so I won't lose track. They speak slowly as if to a young child. The list is long and full of holes. It contains tidbits like "get a grip on yourself," "cigarettes kill," "cholesterol clogs," "fit as a fiddle," "ducks in a row," "organize" and "sound fiscal management." Phrases like that.

They think these 2,000-point plans lead to happiness. Fat people know **8** happiness is elusive at best and even if they could get the kind thin people talk about, they wouldn't want it. Wisely, fat people see that such programs are too dull, too hard, too off the mark. They are never better than a whole cheesecake.

Fat people know all about the mystery of life. They are the ones ac- **9** quainted with the night, with luck, with fate, with playing it by ear. One thin person I know once suggested that we arrange all the parts of a jigsaw puzzle into groups according to size, shape and color. He figured this would cut the time needed to complete the puzzle by at least 50 per cent. I said I wouldn't do it. One, I like to muddle through. Two, what good would it do to finish early? Three, the jigsaw puzzle isn't the important thing. The important thing is the fun of four people (one thin person included) sitting around a card table, working a jigsaw puzzle. My thin friend had no use for my list. Instead of joining us, he went outside and mulched the boxwoods. The three remaining fat people finished the puzzle and made chocolate, double-fudge brownies to celebrate.

The main problem with thin people is they oppress. Their good inten- 10 tions, bony torsos, tight ships, neat corners, cerebral machinations and pat solutions look like dark clouds over the loose, comfortable, spread-out, soft world of the fat. Long after fat people have removed their coats and shoes and put their feet up on the coffee table, thin people are still sitting on the edge of the sofa, looking neat as a pin, discussing rutabagas. Fat people are heavily into fits of laughter, slapping their thighs and whooping it up, while thin people are still politely waiting for the punch line.

Thin people are downers. They like math and morality and reasoned 11 evaluation of the limitations of human beings. They have their skinny little acts together. They expound, prognose, probe and prick.

Fat people are convivial. They will like you even if you're irregular 12 and have acne. They will come up with a good reason why you never wrote the great American novel. They will cry in your beer with you. They will put your name in the pot. They will let you off the hook. Fat people will gab, giggle, guffaw, gallumph, gyrate and gossip. They are generous, giving and gallant. They are gluttonous and goodly and great. What you want when you're down is soft and jiggly, not muscled and stable. Fat people know this. Fat people have plenty of room. Fat people will take you in.

Writing Assignments

Narrate   **1.**   Use the "Drives me nuts" note in the first item on Ellen's list to start a list of your own. Try to remember a certain person (your roommate or boss) or policy (your parents' or teachers' rules) that drove you nuts. Then compose a narrative that focuses on one event that reveals the maddening inconsistency in the person's behavior or rules for your behavior.

Observe   **2.**   Select a public place where people are supposed to obey certain rules of etiquette—the checkout line at the grocery store, the traffic signals at a busy street corner, the ticket booth at the local theater. Observe people's behavior for an extended period, paying particular attention to their willingness to take turns or their readiness to break the rules. Then write a column for the local paper, using your observations to comment on the status of public courtesy.

Investigate   **3.**   Interview someone who collects *unusual* artifacts—old records, baseball cards, ceramic animals. Pose some of the following questions: What prompted you to start this collection? Where did you buy your first X? How have you organized your collection? Who has the best collection? Why do you think you collect X? Use your interview material to write a profile of this person and his or her collection.

Collaborate   **4.**   Your writing group has been asked to prepare a section of a student handbook on "stress." Interview one another about what causes you to feel stress, how stress affects you, and what you do to relieve it. Then expand your research by interviewing people at the health center, counseling center, and campus ministries about their experience helping "stressed-out students." You may also read some self-help manuals or the appropriate sections in your psychology book. Pool your information and then write the section, offering new students advice about how to deal with stress.

Read   **5.**   Read several sources about *one* method of stress management—exercise, meditation, biofeedback. You may even want to test the method on yourself to see if it works. Then write a "how-to" essay in which you explain the benefits of this particular method in some detail.

Respond   **6.**   Respond to the "character" revealed in Calvin Trillin's column *or* described in Ellen Haack's essay. Imagine him as your roommate or date. Describe some of the difficulties you might have communicating with someone who "talks to himself" or is constantly explaining why something is "good for me."

Analyze   **7.**   Analyze the various outlines and drafts of Ellen's essay. Which do you like better and why? Then go back to Ellen's original assignment—to write something on the issue of *taste*. Although the assignment is vague, it probably contains certain assumptions and expectations. Write an essay to Ellen explaining why her final essay does or does not meet those assumptions and expectations.

Evaluate   **8.**   Evaluate the differences Suzanne Britt Jordan sees between thin people and fat people. In particular, assess the evidence she uses to support her generalizations. You may want to cite exceptions to Jordan's assertions or modify her argument with other sorts of evidence. A health science textbook, for example, may offer some reasons why her attitude toward fat people may require revision.

Argue   **9.**   Although Jordan makes her comparison based on two physical types, much of her analysis deals with contrasting psychological types. Construct an argument that makes the case for the "thin people" in Jordan's analysis. Try to stay away from the predictable arguments for "thin people"—physical attractiveness, for example—and focus on the value of those psychological features Jordan dislikes.

Argue   **10.**   Write your own essay on the issue of *taste*—who has it, who doesn't, and why. You may want to consider various kinds of taste—physical, aesthetic—or argue that one's taste (in food, books, or people) is a matter of education or social conditioning. Like Ellen, you may want to select a case study (or two) to illustrate your thesis.

4

Revising

Revising is the process of *seeing again,* of discovering a new vision for the writing you produced in planning and drafting. In a sense, you have been revising from the moment you began writing. As you experimented with thinking-in-writing strategies in planning, you revised your discussions about subject, audience, and purpose. As you tried to embody those decisions in drafting, you revised again when you saw a better thesis or a more effective outline. Now that you are ready to revise, you must try to gain a new perspective on writing you have already looked at several times. One thing is certain: you will not see much that is new if you think of revising as simply taking one last look.

Nothing identifies experienced writers more dramatically than the way they look at revision. For beginners, revision means *fixing* the first draft— rearrange a few phrases, substitute one word for another, correct spelling and punctuation. For experienced writers, revision means *creating* the final draft—redefining their purpose, reshaping their draft, and reworking the transitions between and the connections among their examples. They know they have overlooked minor trouble spots, but before they begin polishing and proofreading they want to be sure they are looking at a final text.

Revision is a two-stage process. During the first stage (the focus of this chapter), you use various reading strategies to help you rethink, reorder, and rewrite substantial portions of your draft. When you are satisfied with this *global revision,* you can focus your attention on the second stage, *local revision,* and begin repairing individual paragraphs, sentences, and words. (Strategies for implementing local revision are presented in Chapters 7 through 10.) Work in this second stage may propel you back to the first stage, however, as your revision of individual parts may prompt you to revise a section or even the entirety of your essay.

Revision has been made easier by the wonders of word processing. (See "The Word Processor as a Writing Tool" in the Appendix.) But revision is more than a mechanical command. It is an intellectual choice that emerges from a creative attitude toward change. In the days before *delete* and *format,* novelist Eudora Welty expresses that attitude in her comments on revision:

> My ideal way to write . . . is to write the whole first draft through in one
> sitting, then work as long as it takes on revisions, and then write the final

93

version all in one, so that in the end the whole thing amounts to one long sustained effort. . . . [Using a typewriter] helps give me the feeling of making my work objective. I can correct better if I see it in typescript. After that, I revise with scissors and pins. Pasting is too slow, and you can't undo it, but with pins you can move things from anywhere to anywhere, and that's what I really love doing—putting things in their best and proper place, revealing things at the time when they matter most. Often I shift things from the very beginning to the very end. . . .

[Writing] is so much an inward thing that reading the proofs later can be a real shock. . . . [T]here's . . . a strange moment with every book when I move from the position of writer to the position of reader, and I suddenly see my words with the eyes of the cold public. It gives me a terrible sense of exposure, as if I'd gotten sunburned. (Eudora Welty, *Writers at Work: The Paris Review Interviews*)

LOOKING TO REVISE

Once you consider revising a creative rather than a cleaning-up activity, you will look at yourself, your readers, and your text with more objectivity.

How You Look at It

Revision is always hard work, especially since you have already invested considerable effort in your writing. But try to look objectively at what you have accomplished. Rethink, don't merely glance over, every aspect of your writing from your most abstract assumptions to your most concrete assertions. Do not fall in love with your words, no matter how clever or inspiring they seem. Your real concern is effectiveness, not eloquence. Like Welty, you should look forward to making changes—to achieving coherence and clarity—by moving "things from anywhere to anywhere . . . putting things in their best and proper place, revealing things at the time when they matter most."

How Someone Else Looks at It

When you are ready to revise, you may welcome the perspective of another reader—a teacher, editor, or friend. Your readers may ask about the larger elements in your writing (its subject, audience, or purpose) or its smaller elements (sentence structure, diction, or punctuation); they may talk about their general impression (whether your writing is interesting, funny, or dull). As you revise, you must consider all reactions to your work—even if they seem threatening or trivial. You must consider what your readers saw, why they liked or disliked what they saw, and how you might use *their* observations to strengthen *your* writing. Various readers may give you confusing or contradictory advice, making it difficult for you to decide what to do next.

You will have to decide which readers you trust—and which of their recommendations you want to consider or resist. Remember, you are the *author* of your text and therefore must act as the final *authority* for deciding how it will be revised.

How It Looks

Once you start revising, your writing will often look unfamiliar. If you have neatly retyped your messy, handwritten draft, it may now look compact and complete, as if a clean page had somehow solved your writing problems. But you must look beneath this seductive surface to uncover problems that still require rethinking and rewriting.

If you have put your writing aside for a few days—or even a few hours—the mere passage of time will make your text look unfamiliar. You have been doing other things—talking, reading, thinking—while your writing has been incubating in your unconscious. Now, as you look at it again, you may see flaws that were not apparent before. Perhaps you have not restricted your subject, anticipated your audience, or defined your purpose effectively. This new perspective compels you to look for solutions that will make your writing stronger and sharper.

But mainly your writing will look unfamiliar when you revise because, like Welty, you have changed positions—from writer to reader. As a writer, your task was to create ideas; as a reader, your task is to judge the clarity of those ideas. And just as you used a set of guidelines for writing, so now you may use a set of guidelines for reading and revising what you have written.

READING TO REVISE

When you are reading to revise, you are still actively involved in the writing process. You are *not* proofreading. Proofreading presumes the existence of a completed manuscript. When you proofread, you are merely checking your writing one last time to prove that you have not mangled sentences, misplaced punctuation, or misspelled words. Reading to revise, by contrast, assumes the presence of an evolving manuscript. As you read, you are trying to identify the strengths and weaknesses of your subject. You are sharpening your perception of what your audience knows (what *is* on the page) and speculating about what your audience needs to know (what is *not* on the page). You are determining whether your purpose controls your essay and the connections among its parts.

Each of the following reading strategies suggests that you read your writing as though you were someone else—a fictitious person in a special situation who is "reading" for a particular reason. Each strategy will highlight a different facet of your work. Used jointly, they will lead to a complete revision.

Reading for Subject

Imagine you are seated in the waiting room of your dentist's office, flipping through several magazines, looking for something to read to pass the time. What subjects attract and sustain your attention? Now pick up your writing and skim through it as quickly as possible. Then put it aside and, maintaining your identity as an "impatient patient," jot down your general reactions using the following questions as a guide:

1. *Why was I attracted to this essay?* How did the title or the first few sentences—the lead—convince me that the essay was worth reading?
2. *What is the specific subject of the essay?* Did the essay focus on the subject immediately, or did I have to read a lot of preliminary material or prolonged digressions?
3. *What is significant about the subject?* Is it a subject I like reading about, one that I need to know about, or one I ought to think about?
4. *What makes the subject interesting*—the attitude of the writer, the nature of the subject, or the way the subject is presented?
5. *Does the essay seem the right length?* Is it long enough to answer all my questions yet short enough to keep my mind from wandering?

Reading for Audience

Now imagine you are seated in a large banquet hall listening to an after-dinner speech. You cannot avoid listening to the speech, so you decide to see how it's going over—how effectively the speaker has read the needs and expectations of the audience. One way to simulate this situation is to read your writing out loud to anyone who will listen—the important thing is to *hear* your writing. An excellent way to accomplish this objective is to read into a tape recorder; then, with your manuscript in hand, play back the "speech" with you as its audience. As you listen, use the following questions to identify passages that need revision. Stop the recorder each time your annotations become too detailed to keep up with the tape. Once you have copied down your comments, push *Play* and resume listening to your writing being read.

1. *What kinds of people does the speaker expect to find in the audience?* Does the speech acknowledge their values, assumptions, and prejudices?
2. *What role does the speaker invite the members of the audience to take (for example, that of dedicated, discerning people)?*
3. *What are the members of the audience likely to know about the subject of the speech?*
4. *Does the speaker ask questions that the audience would ask about the subject?* Does the speaker answer those questions when they need to be answered? Does the speaker anticipate challenging or hostile questions?

5. *Does the speaker help the audience focus on the subject and follow the development of the parts?* Where might the audience get bored, confused, or annoyed? Does the end echo and fulfill the promise of the beginning?

Reading for Purpose

Imagine you are seated in an attorney's office about to sign a contract that will have an enormous impact on your life. You must determine what the thesis of this contract promises and whether the various sections and subsections deliver on that promise. Read your writing slowly and deliberately, underlining your thesis and tracing its connection to each major topic in your essay. If there are sections that need to be rewritten, rearranged, or deleted, now is the time for renegotiation. The following guidelines will remind you of the purpose of the "contract" and call your attention to how that purpose is carried out in its various "clauses."

1. *Does the essay rest on hidden and undocumented assumptions?* How can these assumptions be introduced into the wording of the essay?

2. *What is the purpose of the essay?* Is that purpose expressed openly, or must it be inferred from the text?

3. *What is the thesis of the essay?* What specific promise does it make to its readers? Is the thesis sufficiently restricted, unified, and precise that it can be demonstrated?

4. *Does the body of the essay fulfill the promise of the thesis?* Is there a direct, logical, and dramatic connection among the various parts?

5. *Is each part of the essay sufficiently developed with evidence that is germane, reliable, and verifiable?* Does new evidence need to be introduced to clarify the thesis?

REVISION AGENDA

The detailed analysis produced by the reading-to-revise questions will help you compose a *revision agenda,* a plan for rethinking, rearranging, and rewriting the next draft of your essay.

- You may find that the subject, audience, and purpose are so intertwined that you cannot undertake three separate readings. For you, the easiest procedure may be to keep the three imaginary readers in your head simultaneously and, after one "combined" reading, to prepare a single revision agenda.

- You may prefer considering each element—subject, audience, and purpose—singly and thoroughly. If so, read through the text three times, answering the sets of questions that accompany each reading. After completing all three readings, prepare one revision agenda.

▼ A complex or difficult-to-formulate subject may invite three complete revisions. After you "read for subject," prepare a revision agenda and then a new draft. Use this text to "read for audience" and the text generated then to "read for purpose."

You will have to decide which procedure helps you produce the most effective agenda and the most polished revisions. You may discover, in fact, that each writing project you undertake requires its own procedure. If you have to write under pressure on a fairly straightforward subject, then you may be able to work with one revision agenda. If, on the other hand, you have time to allow a complex subject to evolve, then you may want to generate several revision agendas to identify and solve the problems in your writing.

Organize your revision agenda by asking yourself three questions:

1. What did I try to do in this draft?
2. What are its strengths and weaknesses?
3. What revisions do I want to make in my next draft?

Answer the third question by writing yourself prescriptions containing action verbs—for example, "Collapse section on . . . "; "Expand paragraph on . . . "; "Reword sentences in. . . ." Group the larger problems (subject, audience, purpose) at the top of the list and the smaller problems (style, mechanics, usage) at the bottom.

Remember, revision is an *intuitive* process: you may decide to relocate a paragraph or realign the parts of a sentence because a sudden impulse tells you it looks or sounds better. And revision is a *recursive* process: you are constantly stepping back from your writing to see the big picture, moving forward to touch up some detail, and stepping back again to see how the altered detail changes the composition of the whole. But revision is also a *logical* process. In any piece of writing, you will discover large problems of form and focus and smaller problems of syntax and usage. You may be tempted to fix the simple problems first and the more difficult problems later. But the logical way to proceed is to work on the difficult problems first, for in solving them you may eliminate the simple problems or at least discover an efficient method for dealing with them.

REVISING: A CASE STUDY

Early in his writing course, Rod and his classmates were asked to analyze their impressions of an American monument. Some students wrote about historical monuments in their home town. Others wrote about commercial buildings or signs that impressed them as monumental. Rod decided to write about his trip to the land of monuments—Washington, D.C. In high school, his junior class had spent almost a year preparing for the trip, traveled miles across country in a crowded bus, and then crammed a month of sightseeing into four days of frantic, nonstop touring.

Rod learned so much during this year-long experience that he had difficulty sorting out all he remembered, saw, and read before and after his trip. He decided to attack the problem slowly and systematically in several drafts—writing to discover what he remembered, reading to fill the gaps in his information, then trying a new perspective in a new draft. Most writing assignments do not require you to revise as many times as Rod does, but Rod, an architecture major, is intrigued by design problems. He wants his writing to capture the essence of his exploration of Washington's monuments. His shaping and reshaping of his material provide a case study of how one writer rethinks, revises, and rewrites his work.

Rod began by *planning.* In a listing exercise, he remembered the preparations he made for this "trip of his life." In a freewriting exercise, he tried to recapture the people, buildings, monuments, and heat of Washington in June. During *drafting,* he used a scratch outline to group his information under three chronological headings: *Preparation, Trip,* and *D.C..* He used the following hypothesis to begin his discovery draft: *Everyone cooperated through months of preparation to make our trip to Washington, D.C. a success.*

Our Trip to D.C.
(Discovery Draft)

In my junior year in high school, my class sold magazine subscrip- 1
tions to make money for a trip to Washington, D.C. Everything we did
that year seemed to focus on Washington. In first period (econ), we had
market reports and strategy sessions—we had to make our quotas or
there would be no trip. In second period (history) we learned the history of Washington. In third period (art), we learned about the architect's design for the city, the famous museums, and all the monuments.
I took really good notes in this class because I wanted to be a world-
famous architect when I graduated from college. I still have that notebook and my notes actually make sense. Art class was the high point of
my education for Washington.

By lunch, everybody had had enough—although I vaguely remem- 2
ber cutesy names on the cafeteria menu such as Lincoln Dogs and Con-
gressional Burgers. In the afternoon, we learned about how the government worked—the different branches and agencies—in civics, but I can't
remember learning anything about D.C. in math, science, and gym.

At home there was no relief. Mom and Dad were always showing 3
me articles and stuff about Washington, and my little sister pasted a

picture of the Washington Monument on my art notebook. Even Uncle Fred—the Midwest's most fanatic Bears' fan—sent me a list of the Redskins' draft choices.

The trip was a real bummer. All the junior class, plus our counselors, Mr. and Mrs. Franklin (my art teacher), and our driver Dave crammed into this bus with lousy air conditioning and headed across Indiana, Ohio, West Virginia, Pennsylvania, and Virginia to D.C. It was awful hot and kids were always asking Dave for a pit stop. When he stopped, somebody was always late getting back to the bus, so Mr. Franklin was always walking up and down the aisle counting heads before Dave could pull out.   4

We had four days in Washington to see the whole thing. We stayed in a motel in Virginia, but every morning Dave drove us into downtown D.C. On the first day we saw our congressman, the Capitol, the Supreme Court, the Library of Congress, and then we stood in line a long time to see the White House. On the second and third days, we visited the museums on the Mall. My favorite was the Air and Space Museum, especially the film about flying. After we were through at one museum, we would run to the next one just to be in an air-conditioned building.   5

Even though we drove by the monuments every day, we didn't visit them until the last day. The Jefferson and Lincoln were interesting and you could see them quickly, but you had to stand in line—a long, long line—to see the Washington Monument. But I liked that monument the best. Ever since we hit town, I kept seeing it everywhere. I'd walk around any corner and there it would be. It seemed big and yet so simple beside all those other buildings. All the postcards I sent home had pictures of the Washington Monument on them. Whenever I think of our trip, I think of that monument standing in the middle of downtown Washington like a big paperweight.   6

Revision Agenda

1. <u>What did I want to do in this draft?</u>
   Describe our junior class trip to D.C.

2. <u>What are its strengths and weaknesses?</u>
   Need more focused hypothesis. Scratch outline had three parts, but it doesn't work. Takes too long to get to D.C. Everything jammed together at the end—like the trip. I do like part about Washington Monument—paperweight.

3. <u>What revisions do I want to make in my next draft?</u>
   a. Cut material on school and trip.
   b. Focus on monument—add information—tour guides, souvenir shop, people in line.
   c. Describe view from top—impressive.
   d. Rewrite introductory paragraph, thesis?
   e. Cut out high school slang—"bummer," "lousy," "stuff."

Revising for Subject

Rod's trip to Washington seemed a specific subject, but he now realizes that it contains many small, unevenly developed subjects. He decides to focus on the Washington Monument because it represents everything he learned about and saw in Washington. He begins to think about what kind of information he can use to develop his subject in detail and how he can introduce and interpret his subject for his readers. He writes a new hypothesis—"I was impressed by my visit to the Washington Monument"—and then tries to implement his revision agenda in a second draft.

VISITING THE WASHINGTON MONUMENT
(2nd Draft)

During my junior year in high school, my class sold magazine sub- 1
scriptions to make money for a trip to Washington, D.C. Our stay was
brief, but we saw dozens of historic sites. I was certainly impressed
with the large government buildings and the elaborate architecture of
the monuments, especially the Jefferson and Lincoln Memorials, but for
simple beauty nothing could compare with the Washington Monument.

The afternoon was sunny and hot as our bus drove into the park- 2
ing lot near the Washington Monument. We jockeyed for window positions to take photographs and let out tremendous whoops to let everyone know we had arrived. Our driver parked the bus, and we squirmed
in our seats for another five minutes while Mrs. Franklin, our art
teacher, told us to take notes on what the guides said and reminded us
that young ladies and gentlemen stand quietly in line. With that said,
we stampeded off the bus and raced through the maze of cars and buses
toward the monument.

The line was over two hundred yards long and snaked along the 3
sidewalk like a Chinese dragon. It ended, oddly enough, with a middle-
aged couple from Indiana.

"Are you kids from Indiana?" the lady asked. "We seen your bus 4
pull in."

"We sure are," I answered. "We sold magazine subscriptions to get   5
here." She seemed impressed. She treated us to a detailed account of
their vacation to date, naming every battlefield, landmark, memorial,
bridge, souvenir shop, rest area, and McDonald's they had visited. She
placed special emphasis on the Jack Daniels Distillery in Tennessee.

"I wish this line would get movin'. It's hotter than blazes out   6
here," grumbled her husband. He removed his Funk Hybrids cap and
wiped the sweat off his forehead with a red handkerchief. "We got's
plenty of buildin's to see before tonight." Before his wife could tell us
about how quickly the line moved at Jack Daniels, we spotted a group
of girls in front of us. My friends and I spent the next quarter of an
hour trying to figure out how we could meet them. But the girls ignored
our leers, so we concentrated on spraying our own girls with our recently purchased "Greenie-Meanie" squirt guns.

Finally we stood at the base of the monument and craned our   7
necks to see the top. It was bigger than I ever imagined, and I thought
about the guys who had to build the thing, particularly those guys who
had to do the peak.

When we finally moved inside, we were greeted by a tour guide   8
(actually a park ranger) who told us that the Monument was 555
feet, 5-1/8 inches high, that it weighs 90,854 tons, and that it cost
$1,187,710.31 to build. While I was writing these numbers in my note-
book, he explained that we could not walk up the 898 steps to the top,
but would have to take a 13-second elevator ride. I was pleased in a
way, because it was too hot to walk, but if it were cooler it would be
fun to walk up to the top and count those steps.

Inside the elevator another park ranger told us historical facts   9
about the monument. He only had a few seconds. He called it an obelisk
and told us that it took 105 years to build because they had trouble
raising money and figuring out where to put it. The ground around the
monument used to be a swamp or something.

At the top another ranger walked us around the observation deck.   10
There was a magnificent view out of each window. To the east, you
could see down the Mall to Capitol Hill. To the west, we could see the
Lincoln Memorial. To the south, you could see the Pentagon straight
ahead and the Jefferson. To the north you could see the National Cathe-
dral on the hill and the White House below. Everybody was taking pic-

tures, pointing to places we had been, and trying to see our bus in the parking lot and our motel across the river. I asked the ranger why there were bars on the windows. He said they installed them during the Depression after three people had committed suicide by jumping out one of the windows.

After a while we came down and walked over to the souvenir 11 shop where we loaded up on pamphlets, postcards, and little models of the monument. Our heads were groggy with information and our bodies were sticky with sweat, so we walked back to the bus, spraying an occasional victim with our "Greenie-Meanies." But strangely enough, I was in no mood for horsing around. I stopped and looked back at the stark, jutting obelisk. I was impressed. The Washington Monument, like the man it honors, is a rugged individual.

Revision Agenda

1. What did I try to do in this essay?
   Describe the Washington Monument.

2. What are its strengths and weaknesses?
   Best part—when I get inside and describe what I see from the top. Also, conclusion (last few sentences)—simple, rugged design. Still sound like high school kid—"Greenie-Meanies." Funny couple from Indiana didn't know the difference between a monument and a distillery.

3. What revisions do I want to make in my next draft?
   a. Tell readers something important about monument.
   b. Cut out all the personal stuff—waiting in line, girls.
   c. Look over notes from art class, tour guides, souvenir shop.
   d. Write a straight history of monument.
   e. Fix introduction, thesis—make it more objective.
   f. Imagine I'm a historian, tour guide so that I'll talk like one—serious.
   g. Check vocabulary—no kid stuff.

Revising for Audience

Rod is beginning to recognize that he knows more about his subject than what he remembers about standing in line to observe it. He is also beginning to recognize the difference between *telling* what happened and *using* what happened to create a subject and develop a thesis. But his major reaction to his second draft is his discovery of audience. He wants to separate himself from the high school kids who don't care what they are seeing and the couple who don't understand what they are seeing. He wants to tell both groups that there is more to the monument than a place to find girls or yet another building to see. Its history is special and significant. Rod thinks that he has gathered enough information from his art teacher, the tour guides, and the souvenir shop to tell that history in some detail. This decision, made to enlighten his audience, also enlarges his subject and redefines his purpose.

THE STORY BEHIND THE WASHINGTON MONUMENT
(3rd Draft)

Since people first spoke, they have probably had a few good things 1 to say about one another. Some people receive "high fives," some just congratulations. Others live in our books, and a very few are important enough to have monuments built in their honor. When we look at those stone and steel structures, we often do not consider the time and work that went into their construction. The Washington Monument, for example, took 105 years to build and cost nearly 1.2 million dollars. Its construction was delayed repeatedly due to lack of funds and lack of interest. Once it was even stolen. The story behind the monument is in many ways as interesting as the story behind Washington himself.

The idea of building a monument to honor George Washington was 2 discussed for several decades before it was finally examined seriously. In 1783, the Continental Congress voted to erect a bronze equestrian statue depicting the father of our country. This idea was not mentioned again until 1799, when Congress proposed instead a pyramid-type mausoleum. Congress failed to provide the funds, estimated at twenty-five cents per citizen. Only faint rumblings about the monument were heard during the next thirty years.

Senator Henry Clay of Kentucky revived the notion in 1832 and   3 managed to allocate money for a twenty-ton statue of a toga-clad Washington, but this half-naked sculpture did not satisfy a group of local citizens who preferred the 150-foot shaft already erected in Washington's honor in Baltimore. The following year these people formed the Washington National Monument Society, and, during the next three years, collected $28,000 and sponsored a design competition. Robert Mills drew the winning plan, a 600-foot obelisk on a colonnade base, 250 feet in diameter, known as the National Pantheon. This temple was to contain statues of the signers of the Declaration of Independence, Revolutionary War heroes, and a colossal George Washington.

The laying of the cornerstone was scheduled for Washington's birthday in 1848, but Congress was slow in approving the site, and the ceremony was rescheduled for July 4. Fifteen thousand people, including President Polk and Congressman Lincoln, watched Benjamin B. French lay the cornerstone with the same silver trowel that Washington had used to begin construction of the Capitol in 1793. **4**

Although the cornerstone was laid, construction of the monument was delayed by a political group called the Know-Nothings. In 1855, they infiltrated the Monument Society, held a secret election, and took over the leadership of the Society, thereby "stealing" the monument. As a result, Congress promptly withdrew its pledge of $200,000 and the Society was discredited. Over the next three years, the Know-Nothings collected $285.09 and added thirteen rows of inferior marble to the monument. **5**

By 1858 the Society was back in reliable hands, but the monument remained a 176-foot stump until 1876 when the U.S. Army Corps of Engineers began removing the work of the Know-Nothings. On July 5 Congress promised $200,000, and a completion date of October 19, 1881, was announced. Meanwhile, the U.S. Minister to Italy, George P. Marsh, suggested that the monument be simplified, leaving a stark, classical obelisk. The Society agreed and on August 7, 1880, President Hayes laid the second cornerstone. Four years later the tip was set in place. On Washington's next birthday, the monument was officially dedicated; on October 9, 1888, it was opened to the public. **6**

Despite lack of funds and lack of interest, the Washington Monument finally grew to be the tallest masonry structure in the world. And despite its simple appearance, it is one of the most visited memorials in the country. It is a tribute to both the father of our country and our country itself. **7**

Revision Agenda

1. What did I try to do in this draft?
   Write a simple history of monument—how it got started, the different designs, and all the obstacles people had to overcome to build it.

2. What are its strengths and weaknesses?
   Good information on history. Could have used more statistics and stupid things people have done there (tour guide). Sound too much like tour guide—a dull one. Dan says only good part is Know-

Nothings. He's not a terrific audience—likes reruns of "Flintstones." Still, he's right. It gets dull in places. Problem may be thesis—two subjects?

3. <u>What revisions do I want to make in my next draft?</u>
   a. Cut some of the historical information. Like me, most people are probably more interested in zany stories.
   b. Revise thesis to focus on history of <u>monument</u>, not monument and man—don't know much about George.
   c. Hook reader with opening—everybody knows the facts, but here are some things you don't know.
   d. Get my experience (tourist) back into essay. Might confuse things, but may help readers see monument.
   e. Keep good paragraphs—background information makes them clear and developed—but fix them so readers see connection to thesis.
   f. Make style more upbeat—too many facts, too dull.

Revising for Purpose

By trying to write a pure information essay rather than a personal experience essay, Rod has created three problems. First, because he has allowed his information to control his essay, he sounds—to himself, at least—like a dull tour guide. Second, he has inadvertently allowed himself to write a thesis that promises a comparison between the monument and the man. Rod doesn't have the information to write the second half of this comparison— nor does he want to write it. His purpose is to discuss the history of the monument. Third, he has eliminated himself from his essay. In trying to inform his readers about the significance of the monument, he has prevented them from seeing, as he did, its impressive, simple beauty. The historical information is interesting, but Rod's attitude toward it (a mixture of admiration and amusement) does not really come through.

To tell the story behind the Washington Monument, Rod has to select and arrange his information so that it reflects *his* attitude, not that of a tour guide. By focusing on the unusual history of the monument, Rod formulates a more restricted, unified, and precise thesis, and eliminating the comparison between the man and the monument makes his subject more manageable. Rod is finally confident that his new purpose will create an interesting subject that will appeal to his readers.

REVISING THE WASHINGTON MONUMENT
(4th Draft)

The facts are simple: The Washington Monument stands 555 feet   1
5-1/8 inches. Its base is 55 feet 1-1/2 square inches. It is faced with
9,613 marble slabs, weighs 90,854 tons, can withstand a 145-mph gale,

and cost $1,187,710.31. But these statistics aren't the whole story. In the two centuries since the idea was first mentioned, the Washington Monument has been revised, moved, stolen, ignored, held hostage, and almost blown up.

It began in 1783 when the Continental Congress voted to erect a 2 bronze equestrian statue of George dressed in Roman garb, wielding a spear. Sixteen years later, Congress decided to honor George with a pyramid. Three decades later somebody thought George looked best dressed in a toga. This last idea was actually turned into a twenty-ton statue. But George looked a little cold in his toga. Not satisfied with a half-naked George, the good people of Washington formed the Washington National Monument Society in 1833 to see if they could create a fitting tribute for their hero.

In three years, the Society collected $28,000, and in 1836 they 3 held a contest to select the best design. There were a lot of crazy designs: one looked like a Gothic cathedral, another like an Egyptian sphinx. But the committee selected a drawing by Robert Mills that called for a 600-foot obelisk rising out of a colonnade base, 250 feet in diameter, to be known as the National Pantheon. This temple was to contain statues of the signers of the Declaration of Independence, Revolutionary War heroes, and a colossal statue of George. But to cut costs, the monument was stripped of all its ornamentation and shortened slightly to conform to the classical proportions of an obelisk. For years, however, artists included the National Pantheon in their drawings.

George's monument was not only modified, it was also moved. 4 Pierre Charles L'Enfant, the architect who designed the city, originally envisioned the monument in the intersection of an axis running west from the Capitol and south from the White House. This spot proved too marshy to support much weight. If they had put George there, he would have been a leaning or sinking tower. So they moved him one hundred yards south.

Finally, in 1848, Benjamin B. French, Grand Master of the capi- 5 tal's Lodge of Free and Accepted Masons, laid the cornerstone with the same silver trowel George had used to begin construction of the Capitol. Fifteen thousand people attended the ceremony, including Martha's grandson, President Polk, and Congressman Abraham Lincoln. The odd thing is that nobody remembers which stone is the cornerstone.

The Society continued to raise money for George's monument. It **6** also collected a number of carved stones from various states, Indian tribes, and foreign countries. Greece sent a block from the Parthenon; Egypt donated a stone from the Alexandrian Library; France sent a piece of Napoleon's tomb; and Italy sent a hunk of lava from Mt. Vesuvius. All these different stones (190 in all) decorate the monument—with the exception of one. On March 6, 1854, a stone sent by Pope Pius IX from the Temple of Concord was stolen. A political group called the Know-Nothings was credited with the heist, but the stone was never found.

In 1858, these Know-Nothings added another page to the crazy **7** history of the monument by infiltrating the Society, electing themselves as officers, and essentially "stealing" the monument. Congress promptly withdrew its $200,000 pledge. In their three-year reign, the Know-Nothings collected $285.09 and added thirteen rows of inferior marble to the monument.

Twenty-five years later, when serious construction finally resumed, **8** Col. Casey of the U.S. Army Corps of Engineers discovered that the rope used to lift supplies to the top of the monument had been pulled down. He solved this problem by killing a pigeon. He tied a long, thin wire to the pigeon's leg, which was attached to a rope. Then he let the bird loose inside the monument and fired a shotgun. The pigeon flew out of the monument's top carrying the wire and rope with it. But as soon as it cleared the monument, it was blown out of the sky by a sharpshooter. The wire was retrieved, and the rope pulled through.

George's memorial was opened to the public in 1888 and has been **9** involved in some bizarre stunts ever since. In 1892 "Gabby" Street caught a baseball thrown out of one of the windows at the top of the monument. In 1915, Dr. Aldredo Warsaw, a New York baritone, sang two verses of a ballad while friends dangled him from one of the windows. During the Depression, three people committed suicide by jumping out the windows. (Iron bars have since been installed.) In 1966, 76-year-old Edna Rousseau made 307 round-trip climbs on the 898 steps. In 1982, a man urging the cause of nuclear disarmament held the monument hostage and threatened to blow it up if people didn't listen to him. He was shot by a police sharpshooter, and his bomb was discovered to be a fake.

There's obviously more to George's monument than meets the eye. 10
Of course, you don't have to know the inside story to like the monument. Most people who see a picture of the monument on a calendar or
a postcard like what they see. But to truly understand and appreciate
the monument, you do need to know the inside story. When you visit
George's monument on some hot summer afternoon and have to stand
in line for over two hours for a thirteen-second elevator ride to the top,
you need to know how long it took the planners and builders to reach
the top: all those false starts, crazy designs, and engineering obstacles
that had to be overcome to produce this beautifully simple structure.
When you see people in the line who don't know why they are there or
who are just fooling around as they would at Disneyland, you need to
know that the two-hundred-year history of the monument is filled with
bewildered and misguided people. And when you have finished your
visit, you need to take time to appreciate what you have seen. Turn and
look at it one last time. There it stands—a solitary, rugged individual,
indifferent to the confusion below. It is a peaceful and impressive sight.

Revision Agenda

1. What did I try to do in this draft?
   Tell the eventful history of the Washington Monument—make the
   big paperweight more human and interesting for my reader.

2. What are its strengths and weaknesses?
   I see mainly strengths. Thesis names topics of most of my paragraphs. Other paragraphs—stones and pigeon—add to the spirit of
   thesis. Should I call Washington "Old George"?

3. What revisions do I want to make in my next draft?
   a. Not many—do I need another draft?
   b. Fix up a few sentences and find some better words—esp. verbs.
   c. Decide what to do about "the George problem."
   d. Mainly, I think I'm done. What did the guy who laid the last
      stone in the monument say when he was done?

_____*Exercises*   Consider the following questions about Rod's four revision agendas.

1. How does Rod's *subject* change from his discovery to his final draft?

2. How does Rod's concern about *audience* affect his decision making?

3. What is Rod's *purpose* for each draft? How does he try to embody that
   purpose in a thesis statement? To what extent does each thesis control
   the decisions he makes in writing?

4. How effectively does Rod follow Eudora Welty's notion of revising? For example, how does he move things around in each draft — "putting things in their best and proper place, revealing things at the time when they matter most . . . [shifting] things from the very beginning to the very end"?

5. Rod is obviously happiest with his last draft. Which draft do you like best? Explain your answer.

A FINAL WORD ABOUT REVISING

There is no final word about revising. You can revise endlessly, rearranging information, rewriting paragraphs, substituting new words. The more you look the more you will see. But at some point, revising becomes rationalizing—an excuse for idle tinkering. The test of global revision is whether it produces significant improvement. Sometimes additional revision actually destroys good writing, replacing spontaneous, original insights with self-conscious, overwrought commentary. Like Rod, you have to know when to say "I'm done." Strategies for local revision to help you polish and perfect your last draft are contained in Part Two.

Sketch 1

Sketch 3   Sketches courtesy National Archives

Photo courtesy National Park Service

Sketch 2

Question: Which of these would you have chosen to represent Washington?

Readings

Design as Revision | Henry Petroski

In this excerpt from *To Engineer Is Human: The Role of Failure in Successful Design,* Henry Petroski draws an extended comparison between the way writers and engineers view the process of revision. Petroski's thesis is that "the impulse to build and to rearrange inanimate nature is as much a part of us as our instinct to walk and dance. But just as we occasionally falter in our step, so sometimes do engineers err in their designs." Examine the specific points of Petroski's comparison. In what ways is revision different for the writer and the engineer? What is the "role of failure" in their designs?

There is a familiar image of the writer staring at a blank sheet of paper in   1
his typewriter beside a wastebasket overflowing with crumpled false starts at his story. This image is true figuratively if not literally, and it represents the frustrations of the creative process in engineering as well as in art. The archetypal writer may be thought to be trying to put together a new arrangement of words to achieve a certain end—trying to put a pineapple together, as Wallace Stevens said. The writer wants the words to take the reader from here to there in a way that is both original and familiar so that the reader may be able to picture in his own mind the scenes and the action of the story or the examples and arguments of the essay. The crumpled pages in the wastebasket and on the floor represent attempts that either did not work or worked in a way unsatisfying to the writer's artistic or commercial sense. Sometimes the discarded attempts represent single sentences, sometimes whole chapters or even whole books.

Why the writer discards this and keeps that can often be attributed to   2
his explicit or implicit judgment of what works and what does not. Judging what works is always trickier than what does not, and very often the writer fools himself into thinking this or that is brilliant because he does not subject it to objective criticism. Thus manuscripts full of flaws can be thought by their authors to be masterpieces. The obviously flawed manuscripts are usually caught by the editor and sent back to the author, often with reasons why they do not succeed. Manuscripts that come to be published are judged by critics and the general reader. Sometimes critic and reader agree in their judgment of a book; sometimes they do not. Positive judgments tend to be effusive and full of references to and comparisons with other successful books; negative judgments tend to be full of examples demonstrating why the book does not work. Critics often point out inconsistencies or infelicities of plot, unconvincing or undeveloped characters, and in general give

Petroski, Henry. *To Engineer Is Human: The Role of Failure in Successful Design.* New York: St. Martin's, 1985. 76, 78–79.

counter-examples to the thesis of author, editor, and publisher that this book works. In short, the critic points out how the book *fails*. . . .

3

The work of the engineer is not unlike that of the writer. How the original design for a new bridge comes to be may involve as great a leap of the imagination as the first draft of a novel. The designer may already have rejected many alternatives, perhaps because he could see immediately upon their conception that they would not work for this or that reason. Thus he could see immediately that his work would fail. What the engineer eventually puts down on paper may even have some obvious flaws, but none that he believes could not be worked out in time. But sometimes even in the act of sketching a design on paper the engineer will see that the approach will not work, and he crumples up the failed bridge much as the writer will crumple up his abortive character sketch.

4

Some designs survive longer than others on paper. Eventually one evolves as *the* design, and it will be checked part by part for soundness, much as the writer checks his manuscript word by word. When a part is discovered that fails to perform the function it is supposed to, it is replaced with another member from the mind's catalog, much as the writer searches the thesaurus in his own mind to locate a word that will not fail as he imagines the former choice has. Eventually the engineer, like the writer, will reach a version of his design that he believes to be as free of flaws as he thinks he can make it, and the design is submitted to other engineers who serve much as editors in assessing the success or failure of the design.

5

As few, if any, things in life are perfect, neither is the analogy between books and engineering structures. A book is much more likely to be an individual effort than is a building, bridge, or other engineering structure, though the preparation of a dictionary or an encyclopedia might be said to resemble the design of a modern nuclear power plant in that no individual knows everything about every detail of the project. Furthermore, the failure of a book may be arguable whereas the failure of a building collapsed into a heap of rubble is not. Yet the process of successive revision is as common to both writing and engineering as it is to music composition and science, and it is a fair representation of the creative process in writing and in engineering to see the evolution of a book or a design as involving the successive elimination of faults and error. It is this aspect of the analogy that is most helpful in understanding how the celebrated writers and engineers alike learn more from the errors of their predecessors and contemporaries than they do from all the successes in the world.

A George Washington Sketchbook

The following sketches describe the same person—George Washington— but "see" his character differently. As you read each sketch, consider how each writer defines his subject, audience, and purpose. Which sketch is the most interesting, the most biased, the most believable? Explain your answers.

The True Story of George Washington | Elbridge S. Brooks

Everybody likes a boy who is strong and manly, and that was what   1
George Washington was. The boy who, while in his early teens, could tame
an unbroken colt, firmly keep his seat until he had mastered the wild and
plunging thoroughbred, the boy who could "down" the best wrestlers in
the county, who could throw a stone clear across the Rappahannock, toss
bars and pitch quoits better than any man or boy about him, and sight and
fire a rifle held with one hand only; the boy who could always be trusted to
keep his promises, tell the truth, and do as he was bid without asking why,
was a boy who could be at once bold and brave, good and gentle, sturdy
and strong, wise and cautious. . . .

He would get dreadfully "mad" with other boys sometimes, and he was   2
so strong that if he had been at all bad, he might have been what is called
a bully. But, even when he was a small boy, he had learned to control his
temper; and this he always did throughout his useful life, losing it so seldom and only when there was every excuse for his getting "mad," that we
can see this splendid habit of self-control as one of the things that made
him great and noble. . . .

Even as a boy, you see, George Washington had what we call the quali-   3
ties of mind and brain, the courage, the caution and the determination to
succeed that made him, in after years, a leader of men and the chieftain
of America.

"Pater Patriae" | H. L. Mencken

If George Washington were alive today, what a shining mark he would   1
be for the whole camorra of uplifters, forward-lookers and professional pa-
triots! He was the Rockefeller of his time, the richest man in the United
States, a promoter of stock companies, a land-grabber, an exploiter of mines
and timber. He was a bitter opponent of foreign entanglements, and de-
nounced their evils in harsh, specific terms. He had a liking for forthright
and pugnacious men, and a contempt for lawyers, schoolmasters and all
other such obscurantists. He was not pious. He drank whiskey whenever
he felt chilly, and kept a jug of it handy. He knew far more profanity than
Scripture, and used and enjoyed it more. He had no belief in the infallible
wisdom of the common people, but regarded them as inflammatory dolts,
and tried to save the Republic from them. He advocated no sure cure for all
the sorrows of the world, and doubted that such a panacea existed.

Burr | Gore Vidal

When Washington became president he wanted to be styled His Might-   1
iness. The Senate was agreeable. The House of Representatives was not,
and referred the other house to the Constitution which speaks of the chief
executive as, simply, the president. In fact, the Speaker—the droll Mr.

Muhlenberg—went so far as to suggest that perhaps the General would like to be known as "His High and Mightiness." Muhlenberg's mild pleasantry was not well received by the greatest man in the world who would very much have enjoyed, I suspect, being king had he not lacked a son, a prince of Virginia, to succeed him.

Cincinnatus: George Washington and the Enlightenment | Garry Wills

Washington was asked to be heroic, but heroically restrained. Not only did he (and he alone) play a crucial role at *every* stage of the revolution—in the war, the postwar period, the passage of the Constitution, and the establishment of a working government. He had to show a complete virtue, a complementarity of competing traits, that was asked of no other. There may have been greater warriors than he—but Arnold proved venal, Gates petty, Charles Lee unstable. Others might *use* armies better; but Washington best grasped that the problem was to *create* an army, to keep it in existence, by embodying its cause. There were better philosophers of the republican ideal. But the assurance of Washington's example swayed more people than did their arguments. Jefferson and Hamilton offered brilliant analyses of events, in the first administration; but Washington steered a steadier course than either could. He did not come to describe heroism, but to enact it. . . .

Washington's disinterested service, in war and peace, in power and in retirement, was not flawless; but it was so rounded and balanced that, for people with a less classical ideal of rule, it looks *soporifically* perfect.

Two Postcards from Martha's Vineyard | Dixie D. Myers

In this personal essay, published in the Memorial Day issue of *The Vineyard Gazette*, Dixie D. Myers searches for some way to see her life differently, to "find herself and put behind forever my dark winter." Ironically, her search leads her to two memorials for the dead—one on Martha's Vineyard and one in Washington, D.C. How does her vision of these two memorials help her begin again, to revise her understanding of her life?

Last winter, something sad and awful shook my life; some sense of melancholy grabbed onto me and would not leave. It stayed for weeks on end, till

Myers, D. D. "Between a Rock and a Wall in Washington: Two Postcards from Martha's Vineyard." *The Vineyard Gazette* 25 May 1990: 15.

I lost track of time. Depression smothered me like a blanket. I felt that all my bones had gone away, that whoever I had been was no longer there. I slept a lot, and everything made me sad.

This summer, then, I came to Martha's Vineyard, to take a course, but 2 mostly I came to walk around. I hoped, somehow, that I could find myself, and put behind forever my dark winter. I'd let the Island be my healer, and in its gifts I'd find my way back into my own life again.

When I arrived at Martha's Vineyard it was storming. Rain poured 3 from buckets while the wind twisted branches off of trees and tossed boats around the harbor. Near the dock, a dinghy had broken loose and was drifting. A crowd had gathered along the beach to see if anyone cared or felt brave enough to pull the little boat back onto shore.

But no one dared. Each wave threatened to devour the boat; it spun 4 in all directions against the angry brown sea filling its little belly. It looked forlorn and helpless, alone, like some child's deserted toy. But it did not sink.

The next few days I walked around exploring different parts of the Is- 5 land. The weather had not yet cleared away the clouds; the days were gray, and so was I. I found a road that wrapped around the beach at West Chop, hidden and protected, easing gently around the edge of rocky shore. It was a narrow lane that did not welcome strangers. Do Not Enter, read the sign. But I entered anyway, past ancient trees and shaded yards where the houses, with huge, wide porches and endless windows, stood serene and strong, monuments to a different time, facing the sea. Along the road, tiger lilies the color of tangerines and roses with tangled branches seemed forgotten, growing wild wherever they found a splash of sun. The whole lane was so lovely in its stillness, asleep somehow, like a secret kept forever.

This place became my private garden. It had something to give me, I 6 could sense it; but what? It was whispering answers, I knew, to my heartache, but in the form of a puzzle to which I only held one piece.

And then, a second piece was added. One morning I walked around a 7 black-bottomed pool of water left from rain. A puddle, like an endless lake, and in its very center, a moth, caught in the water, swimming round and round, caused the water to ripple in little waves out to the very edge. The waves looked like age circles on a tree stump. The mystery of life, in a puddle: the moth, swimming in the little lake, bravely tried to fly away, but it always came back to the same place it began. I walked away, knowing that the moth would finally die. I felt a peace in that. It was not the death that mattered, but the struggle.

The next morning when I started on my familiar walk, I felt stronger. 8 All my bones were coming back; I was connected to myself again.

I don't know why I took that turn. Always, roads jut out, beckoning us 9 right, or left, tempting us off the road we're on. Some roads are chosen, but some choose us.

I turned into a road of sand cut out between two rows of pines. Wil- 10 liam T. Haggerty Drive, it said. A house or two, and then, the end, except for a large swath of grass, and in the middle, a concrete walk leading to a large rock embedded with a plaque. Beyond the rock and its little circle of landscaped shrubs, more grass, but then, a gift: a splendid view, framed in green—the ocean, blue as sky, and in the water, white butterflies, the boats; their sails like starched white handkerchiefs waving hello in the breeze.

I moved to the rock to read the plaque, "In Memory of William T. **11** Haggerty." And underneath, these words:

"Sp. 4 Medical Paratrooper in the 173rd Airbourne, 593rd Infantry. **12** First Tisbury Casualty of the Vietnam Conflict Who Fell in Action in the Battle of Dak-To, November 20, 1967."

It was not what I expected. I had intruded here, in someone else's **13** secret garden.

Then suddenly, I saw myself standing—another time, another place, **14** a different rock with names of those who'd died.

Jan. 1, 1989. It's New Year's Day, and my husband and I are up before **15** dawn. It's snowing out, and cold, 22 degrees, but we go anyway, to Washington, D.C., to run, around the monuments and the reflecting pool along the path where cherry trees bloom in spring. Damp clumps of snow are falling, and the ground has disappeared. The walks and the roads are undisturbed by traffic, and the city is without people, only us, and one miserable, frozen young guard in her brown Park Service uniform, stationed at the Lincoln Memorial.

We park the car. "I'll park here, by The Wall," Bo says. "Come back if **16** you get cold."

"The Wall?" I ask, "The Wall is here?" I look around. The world is **17** white.

"Right there," he points. **18**

I look again. I've been here many times before; I've never seen The **19** Wall.

"I don't see it." **20**

"Right there," He points again. "It's been there all along. I don't know **21** how you missed it."

We get out of the car. The snow has glazed the path with ice, and I **22** nearly fall.

"You go on and run," I say. "I'm going to see The Wall." **23**

I make my way along the slippery walk, lifting my feet carefully, cau- **24** tiously moving ahead. I wonder how I'll feel when I finally see The Wall. I did not lose one person in that war; I will not know a single name.

And then I'm there. It's risen suddenly before me—a long line of ebony **25** stone, and the world is marble white. It isn't very tall; at first, I'm not impressed. There should be more, I think.

The Wall is cold and silent in the snow. It gives nothing, just names. **26** But on the ground, a piece of paper, wrapped in plastic, lines from a poem, and a date. A Christmas wreath, with bright red bow, a birthday card that's signed, "Love, Mom." And last, a little flower box holding a dried orchid, with a letter that starts, "Dear Daddy, you never got to know me, but I wore this to graduation, and I wanted you to have it."

Row after row, the names go on forever. Not names of men who fell in **27** battle, but little boys. I pray that I may never forget this silence—the snow, The Wall, the lonely guard, and me.

And now, here I am on Martha's Vineyard. This time, a single name, **28** and a date. Nov. 20, 1967. What was it I'd been doing on the day this boy had died?

I'd started school that fall. I went to class, and made new friends, wor- **29** ried about Psych 101. That winter I slept with a boy from Rhode Island, but he was too serious, so I left him in the spring. I don't remember more than that. The next year came, my life went on. I don't think I was happy, but I can't remember. The days and nights flowed in and out. The hour-glass automatically turned when all the sand flowed through.

And then, school ended; another life began. I married, had two babies; **30** that marriage ended, and I faced my life alone. I raised my kids, and worked, and read; the years went by. I married again, and here I am.

Here I am come round again, a moth caught in the circle of days and **31** nights, winters and springs, and winter again. Every moment, something happens; every hour, I move forward, until my life comes back around to me again.

On the ground beside the plaque I found a stone, worn flat and **32** smooth. When I leave the Island, I'll carry it with me. I leave with much to do when I get home—my life goes on—but soon, I know, I'm going to see The Wall, to find a name I know, William T. Haggerty, and leave a gift: the stone, the color of sand along the beach at West Chop, and a postcard, from the Vineyard:

Dear Billy,

The world has changed a lot since you've been gone, but much has stayed **33** *the same. We still sing songs for peace. There still is war.*

Your Island is still beautiful in summer. On Sunday mornings, the boats **34** *still sail in bright blue water around West Chop, their white sails open to the wind.*

The air is clean and full of pine, and along the wooden fences by the road **35** *the tiger lilies and pink roses grow again. And little boys still ride their bikes. They're still named Tommy, or Kevin, or Chris. They stop to tie their shoes, or throw a stick, or fool around, the way boys do.*

And on West Chop Road, the light house stands; the flag flies in the sun. **36** *The fog horn is still loud and strong; it calls the boats gone out to sea, to tell them they've found home again.*

There is one more thing to add. I bought a present for myself, to keep **37** the Island with me once I've gone. A watch. I have a watch already, I do not need one more, but on this watch, in tiny miniature, the shape of the Island is traced, and underneath the words, "Martha's Vineyard." Directly in the center the hands move round and round. The second hand moves gently; it comes back to where it started and then the minute hand jumps forward, startled, then it waits to move again.

Caught in an endless circle, we too move round and round. And yet, **38** like the moth caught in the water, it is our effort that is noble, and not the end—for in a circle, there is no end that isn't a beginning, no beginning that isn't an end.

When I think of my time on Martha's Vineyard, it is not my pain that **39**

I want to recall. I know that as time moves on, the memory will fade of just what happened there.

Someday, I'll need to remember what it was to be alive on Martha's Vineyard when I was forty. So I sent myself a postcard, to find some years from now, tossed, forgotten, in a drawer. 40

Not much, just this, I write: 41

Martha's Vineyard, 1989. The summer came. I found myself. Then I went home again. 42

Writing Assignments

Narrate   **1.**   Compile a list of the natural (Grand Canyon), historic (Lincoln Memorial), or commercial (Disneyland) monuments you have visited on family vacations. Select one monument that impressed you in some significant way. Try to remember what you thought you were going to see and then what you actually saw. Then write a narrative that reveals how your experience caused you to revise your expectations.

Observe   **2.**   Visit a cemetery on a pleasant Sunday afternoon or a national holiday. Walk around the cemetery, reading headstones, examining flowers (plastic and real), and mapping the arrangement of the terrain. Find a spot where you can observe visitors as they come and go. Then write an essay in which you describe the behavior of "Sunday mourners" or speculate about the behavior of one mourner (or family of mourners) as they visit a specific plot.

Investigate   **3.**   Interview someone connected with one of your town (or university's) major monuments—the president of the local historical society, the director of the local Chamber of Commerce, or the chief groundskeeper. When and why was this monument constructed? Who was the designer? How do people react to it—do they photograph it, use it as a meeting place, or simply ignore it? Does the average visitor know what the monument commemorates? Use your interview material to write a profile of the monument, its visitors, or its keepers.

Collaborate   **4.**   Your writing group has been asked to evaluate your school's mascot (or logo) in terms of its appropriateness to the school's spirit and achievement. Members of your group may want to interview other students (or alumni) about their reaction to the mascot or read through the school's archives to discover how the mascot was selected. Then write a proposal for the student newspaper defending the current mascot or proposing a new one.

Read   **5.**   Find a magazine article that is directed toward readers interested in historic preservation. Good sources are *American Heritage, Historic Preservation,* and *Smithsonian.* Read the article carefully, and write a brief analysis of its projected audience. Then profile a completely different audience—for example, people interested in economic progress—and write down some ways in which the subject might be made appealing to them. Finally, revise the essay for presentation to this new audience.

Respond   **6.**   Respond to something you have written exclusively from the point of view of your personal experience—an extended journal entry, a letter you haven't mailed to a friend, or an essay—by transforming it into a more objective, informative piece of writing. Try to avoid the two problems Rod discovered when he tried this assignment in his third draft: (a) his information took over his writing, and (b) he lost his unique perspective on his information—his purpose in presenting it.

Analyze **7.** Using Henry Petroski's essay as a prompt, analyze how revision might work for other professionals (e.g., doctor, car mechanic, salesperson). What is the person's *text*? What causes the person to revise his or her perception of this text? What is the role of failure in creating a more successful text? How many people are involved in detecting and absorbing the cost of such failure? You may want to construct your essay in the form of a comparison (writer vs. engineer) or revise Petroski's model to focus on the role of failure in one profession.

Evaluate **8.** Using standard reference sources such as *Who's Who* or *Contemporary Authors*, study the biographies of the authors who wrote the sketches in "A George Washington Sketchbook," pages 113–115. Then write an essay in which you evaluate how the writer's life (his personal experiences, historical context, and political ideas) shaped his sketch of George Washington. An alternative version of this assignment is to research American social history during Washington's life and then, adopting the fictional point of view of a woman, slave, or Native American from that period, construct a new sketch of our first president.

Argue **9.** Analyze Dixie D. Myers' description of the two Vietnam memorials. In particular, examine the way she uses analogies (the boat, the moth, the watch) to enrich her presentation. Then argue that people can acquire a more thoughtful understanding of events such as Memorial Day through personal observation than through public ceremony. You may even wish to present your own personal observations as a way of commemorating some public rite or religious holiday.

Argue **10.** Argue for the creation of an American monument that celebrates some aspect of American culture. For example, what would a national monument commemorating America's quest for the "good life" look like? Where would it be located? Another version of this assignment is to argue that we need to revise our definition of a monument—that Disneyland or Las Vegas is America's greatest monument.

PART 2

The Expression of Ideas

5

Common Methods of Development

In Part One you learned how working through the stages of the writing process enables you to discover your subject, audience, and purpose. You also learned how these discoveries suggest various structures for shaping your writing. Once Joanne decided to write about Mr. Bridgeman, she began telling a story about her "little revolt" in his Latin class. Once Ellen decided to explain Barry's preoccupation with "what's good for me," she began to think of illustrative examples that would engage her audience. And once Rod decided to write about the Washington Monument, he reformulated his purpose to better analyze the various stages in the monument's unusual history. In each case, the method of development—the structure of the writing—emerged from material that the writer discovered in planning, drafting, and revising.

In Part Two you will learn how and when to use various structures to express your ideas more effectively. Nonfiction writer John McPhee asserts that "everything in writing is a structure within a structure within a structure down to the simple sentence, which, of course, is also a structure" (personal interview). As you work your way through particular writing assignments, you need to decide whether to impose a structure on your information or look for a structure within your information. There are occasions when you need to employ a formal structure. For example, Part Three, "Special Assignments," discusses ways of complying with very specific instructions for developing and structuring essay examinations, critical essays, and research papers. Much of your writing, however, will evolve through such a complicated process of decision making that a formal structure chosen at an early stage is likely to change later.

McPhee explains that selecting a method (or methods) of developing his writing is probably the most important decision he makes, but one he can make only after immersing himself in the writing process:

> The structure of a piece of writing arises from within the material I have collected. When I go out to gather information on a subject, I am observing, asking questions, constantly scribbling notes. Then I go to the library, read, and make more notes. I end up with this great pile of miscellaneous notes that don't reveal their important relationships. It's at this point that I go over my notes again and again, looking for a couple of things that might illuminate each other. When I find them, I think, "Well,

125

that makes sense. I could put these two things side by side." So I put them there. Once these two go together, gradually, slowly, the other segments work themselves out until I have a beginning, middle, and end. It's sort of the way the structure of some kind of mineral might get itself together. (Personal interview)

Like McPhee, you will uncover various patterns for developing your ideas throughout the writing process. In *planning,* these patterns often emerge as answers to the basic questions you might ask about any body of information: *What is it? How does it work? Why does it matter?* These questions are like the different lenses you attach to your camera: each lens gives you a different picture of your subject. If you decide to write about women artists, for example, you might formulate a series of questions such as: Why are comparatively few women ranked among the world's great artists? What historical forces may have discouraged women from becoming artists? Who is in charge of the "ranking" process and how does it work? Do the ways women look at the world differ from the ways men look at it, and if so, what implications does this difference have for women's art and its reception? As you can see, each question not only shifts your perspective on your subject, but also suggests a different method for developing your information about it.

If planning gives you the opportunity to envision your subject from a variety of perspectives, then *drafting* encourages you to develop the pattern (or patterns) that appear to you most effective for demonstrating your purpose. In some writing projects, a pattern may seem to emerge naturally from your planning. If you decide to write about your observation of a game of lacrosse, your choice seems obvious: to tell what happened. In attempting this, however, you may need to answer other questions about this unfamiliar sport: What do the field and equipment look like? How is it played? How is it similar to or different from other sports? Developing this new information may require you to develop new patterns that challenge your ability to advance your purpose without distorting your structure.

Logically, this judgment is made best during *revising.* As you look over your draft, you will need to make two decisions. First, you must decide whether individual segments or patterns of information develop or distort your original structure. The history of lacrosse—its creation by Iroquois Indians, its discovery by French explorers, and its development by Canadians—is an interesting body of information, but it may need to be reshaped, relocated, or even eliminated in revision to preserve the purpose of your original design: to tell what happened. Second, you must decide whether your original design, often mirroring the method by which you discovered the structure of your essay, is still the best method for presenting your information to your audience. Instead of using this organic structure, telling what happened, you may decide that you can best express your ideas by choosing a more formal structure, comparing lacrosse to games with which your readers are already familiar, such as soccer or hockey.

Whatever you decide, you need to understand each pattern's purpose, strategies, and effect if you are going to use it successfully to develop a paragraph, a section of your essay, or your whole essay. The remainder of this chapter presents and analyzes the most common methods of development, except for building arguments, which, because of its complexity, is given more extended explanation in Chapter 6.

WHAT HAPPENED? *Narration*

Narration tells a story to make a point. It can be used in an anecdotal, abbreviated way to introduce or illustrate a complicated subject or in an extended way to provide a detailed, personal account of "what happened." An effective narrative has a *plot*—a meaningful and dramatic sequence of action—that may or may not follow the order in which events actually occurred and usually focuses on some tension or conflict within the writer, between the writer and others, or between the writer and the environment.

A narrative depends on pace to effect its purpose. *Pace* means the speed at which events are narrated. Sometimes you need to slow the pace to describe one aspect of an event in great detail; at other times several related events can be quickly summarized in a few sentences. By making such decisions about pace, you control the development of your narrative to dramatize its purpose for your readers.

A narrative requires the selection of a *point of view,* that is, establishing the person and position of the narrator. If you tell the story as "I" or "we," you are writing in the *first person;* if you recount what "he," "she," or "they" did, you are writing in the *third person.* In addition to identity, *person* refers to the attitude and personality of the narrator. *Position* is the narrator's closeness to the action in both space and time: the narrator may be a participant or an observer and may be telling the story as it happens, shortly thereafter, or much later.

In the following passage, Francine duPlessix Gray narrates a scene that illustrates what happens when tourists invade an animal habitat.

Introduces context and intended conflict.

Driving one evening through Amboseli, at the foot of Kilimanjaro, we see twenty-one minibuses gathered near a clearing to observe three cheetahs stalking. The first cheetah curtly moves through the thicket toward a small herd of impalas, occasionally twitching her ears as a signal for her companions to move on. There is an exaggerated stylishness about these animals' features—extravagantly long, elegant forelegs, outlandishly small, heavily marked faces. These most endangered animals of East Africa— champion runners but unskilled at camouflage, their temperament as open as the plains they frequent—seem only too willing to be movie stars, and cock their heads photogenically toward the tourists.

After we have watched them for several minutes the cheetahs have approached to about a hundred and fifty yards of their prey, coming close to the distance from which they make their famous sixty-mile-per-hour dash

*Climax of narrative pro-
duces reversal of action.*

for the kill. But as they reach the critical moment minibuses start crashing about them; tourists lean on the open rooftops of their vehicles, cameras poised, and urge their drivers to get the closest possible view of the kill. Startled by the commotion, the impalas race about in circles and cough out their warning message, the baboons' terrierlike barking comes sloughing off the trees. The cheetahs must know better than we that they have lost their chance for dinner, but they go on stalking for a few minutes, as if to finish their pose. And then, amid the clicking of some fifty cameras, the head scout abruptly turns away from the impalas. The three cheetahs slink off into the plain. Their fragile rib cages seem terribly thin in the dusk, the black markings of their cheeks—like rivulets of black tears—seem to express their frustrated hunger.

*Concludes by establishing
point of narrative.*

We are going to kill these animals with sentiment. Having slain and trapped wild creatures for food, domesticated them for our amusement, and hunted them for sport, we are now decimating them by our fantasies of wilderness. How curious that photographic "shooting" is becoming deadlier to game than the ancient pastime of sport shooting. How regrettable that the tourists' most intrusive drivers tend to be Africans. The ancient code of hunting is past, a new etiquette of viewing has yet to be elaborated if the animals are to survive. I turn to Big Hunter, who, along with two other European drivers, respectfully kept his vehicle still during the cheetahs' attempted hunt. "Looking at game may become more dangerous to them than hunting," I say. "Worse that that," he remarks laconically, "it's so bloody rude to the animals." (Francine duPlessix Gray, "On Safari")

Like Gray, Jane wants to write about a journey to an animal habitat, her first whale watch. Although she was only at sea for a few hours, she was overwhelmed by events, information, and insights. She decides that one way to explore her ideas is to transcribe the sequence of events in a narrative.

1. How does Jane establish the position and attitude of the narrator?

2. What conflicts does she introduce to characterize her narrative?

3. How does the conclusion resolve conflicts and confirm the purpose of the narrative?

It was mist upon mist. The Portuguese Princess plowed out of Provincetown harbor toward Stellwagen Bank where the humpbacks had been feeding for several months. I was seated forward, so that the gasoline fumes would not combine with the rolling swell to make me sick. Nothing was going to spoil this long-anticipated adventure. My insistence chased away the mist, and we chugged along in the hot sun for about an hour. Some people tried to talk above the sound of the engine: "I've watched all the Cousteau specials." "Have you seen the skeletons at the Museum of Natural History?" Others checked their camera lenses or scanned the horizon through binoculars. "Thar she blows," yelled our tour guide. "Off the port bow. There!" I followed his finger, straining to see what he saw in the dark blue sea. Nothing. Then, suddenly, against the skyline, I saw it. A definite vertical spray. Then a pause. Then another. A whale. At last, a whale.

_____*Exercises*   1. Freewrite in your journal about an experience in which you intruded on some group's privacy. How did you disrupt its behavior? How did you feel? What alternative did you consider before you intruded?

2. List the events that contributed to your achievement of a long-anticipated goal. Then draft a narrative in which you help your readers appreciate the conflicts, large and small, you had to overcome to reach your goal.

WHAT DOES IT LOOK LIKE? *Description*

Description presents a verbal portrait of a person, place, or thing. It can be used to enrich other forms of writing or as a dominant strategy for developing a picture of a subject. A successful description does not depend solely on visual effects, however, but attempts to identify the subject's significant features by evoking all the senses. Impressions and observations are arranged in an appropriate pattern designed to capture both detail and wholeness. Specific, vivid detail makes your readers see what you see, and arranging those details in an appropriate sequence helps your readers understand why your subject is interesting and significant. Description is not merely a catalogue of facts or a collection of ornaments; like narration, it must make a point.

In the following passage from "The Courage of Turtles," Edward Hoagland describes the unique physical behavior of turtles:

Evokes senses.

Turtles cough, burp, whistle, grunt and hiss, and produce social judgments. They put their heads together amicably enough, but then one drives the other back with the suddenness of two dogs who have been conversing in tones too low for an onlooker to hear. They pee in fear when they're first caught, but exercise both pluck and optimism in trying to escape, walking for hundreds of yards within the confines of their pen, carrying the weight of that cumbersome box on legs which are cruelly positioned for walking. They don't feel that the contest is unfair; they keep plugging, rolling like sailorly souls—a bobbing, infirm gait, a brave, sea-legged momentum—stopping occasionally to study the lay of the land. For me, anyway, they manage to contain the rest of the animal world. They can stretch out their necks like a giraffe, or loom underwater like an apocryphal hippo. They browse on lettuce thrown on the water like a cow moose which is partly submerged. They have a penguin's alertness, combined with a build like a Brontosaurus when they rise up on tiptoe. They they hunch and ponderously lunge like a grizzly going forward. (Edward Hoagland, "The Courage of Turtles")

Arranges details in sequence.

Extends significance of description.

Jane saw and photographed so many whales on her voyage that she has trouble sorting out her impressions. She decides that a description of a whale will concentrate and enrich her narrative. She describes the last whale she saw—the one that saw her.

"*Fascinating, aren't they?*"

Drawing by M. Stevens; © 1991 The New Yorker Magazine, Inc.

How does Jane intro-
duce the point of her
description?

The biologist hushed us. A finback, the world's second largest whale, had been spotted swimming toward the boat. He was way off course from the usual pattern of his species. Finbacks are shy, solitary creatures and, because they are still hunted, usually stay clear of boats. The boat, its engine cut, rolled on four-foot swells. The smell of oil and gas hung in the air, making my head ache and my throat tighten as I tried to swallow. Soon, we saw him—a sea-green monolith, silhouetted several feet beneath the water. His color was uneven. The small distinguishing dorsal fin was speckled with white and gray spots. He was silent. We were silent. He swam purposefully toward the boat. Then under. More silence. I crossed to the other side in time to see his huge greenish head explode through the surface. One watery eye looked back at me before he arched his body and sounded. We did not see him again, but we knew we had seen something rare.

What senses does she
evoke?

How does she arrange
details to create a
dominant impression?

_____***Exercises***

1. Look up a description of some mythical beast—a dragon, griffin, or unicorn—in an encyclopedia. Then describe your own impressions of one of these beasts. You may want to describe the way such beasts have been portrayed in film.

2. Interview people who have extensive contacts with animals—veterinarians, zookeepers, park rangers. For them, what animal "contains the rest of the animal world"? How would they describe it?

HOW DO YOU DO IT? *Process Analysis*

A *process* is a sequence of actions or changes that bring about a result. The development of the human embryo from conception to birth is one process; the procedure by which citizens of the United States elect the president is another. To *analyze* a process effectively, you must know it thoroughly or learn as much as you can about it, and then you must divide it into steps or stages. A careful division will help you see the best way to describe the process: several small steps may be combined into one large step; certain steps may be suspended while others are completed; still other steps may require special emphasis so that they are not overlooked or reversed. After you have established an effective pattern of steps, you must explain each step, acknowledging how it connects to the next and what special knowledge or tools will be needed to complete it.

You must also make a careful assessment of your audience to determine whether you want to provide them with information about *how something works or happens* or to give them instructions on *how to do something.* In the first case, your readers may be interested in the stages and operation of a particular process even though they have no direct involvement in it. In the second case, they will want to know enough about the process so they can actually perform it.

In the following selection, humorist H. Allen Smith asks an expert, "Mr. Buttolph," to analyze the proper process for killing a wasp.

Introduces need for "campaign."

Describes "necessary" tools and strategies.

Analyzes steps—and advises additional steps.

"Don't ever think," Mr. Buttolph explained, "that you can handle a wasp the way you handle a fly. You've got to plan a campaign—figure out just exactly how you're going to proceed against him, and hope he doesn't get you while you're mapping your plans. Keep your eye on him, *but don't let him know you're looking at him.* Quietly assemble your equipment. A rubber fly swatter. Thick gloves. Put a hat on. Turn your shirt collar up and button it. Keep a ball peen hammer handy. Then go after him—but don't go directly at him. Sidle up to him. Pretend you're just walking in his direction by accident. Say something to throw him off guard, like, 'Now, I wonder what I did with those glasses.' Watch him out of the corner of your eye, and if he starts to wiggle or flap his legs ease away from him, back off, and wait a while. Give him a chance to settle down. Go outdoors and practice with the rubber swatter. Drive a tack in the wall and stand off and swat at it—develop your aim, because that's important. God help you if you ever swing at a wasp and miss him. Now, go back in and locate him again and see what sort of a mood he's in. If he's at ease, sidle up to him and when you're sure of your position, when you're certain that you've got the proper range, bust him one as hard as you can. If he falls to the floor, jump on him, stomp him—even then he may get up off the floor and stab you. Hit him with the hammer. Don't take your eye off him. No matter that he's lying there like a corpse. He may be playing possum. Get a newspaper and wrap him up in it and then set fire to it. After that it *may* be that he won't bother you again." (H. Allen Smith, "How to Kill a Wasp")

One of the real dangers Jane faced when she went on the whale watch was her susceptibility to seasickness. She had been at sea enough and sick enough to qualify as an expert on the illness. In her draft, she composes a section in which she provides instructions about how to avoid the whale watcher's curse.

1. How does Jane establish the need for an effective procedure?

2. What are the stages in the prevention process?

3. What is the effect of not following the process?

A person who suffers from motion sickness and loves whale watching has a problem. Whales do not fit under microscopes. They must be watched at sea, atop rolling four-foot swells. I have solved this problem by developing a procedure to combat the sickness that attacks me when "I go down to the sea in boats." Several hours before boarding, I eat a mild meal: toast, tea, mashed potatoes. An hour later, I take two Dramamine tablets. Then, I dress warmly, knowing that I will not be able to go below when I get cold. When I board the ship, I stay away from the engine, which spews gas and oil fumes into the air. Once underway, I stand forward, always to windward, so that I can feel the cold, salty breeze on my face. When we finally encounter some whales, I try to avoid looking too quickly from whale to whale. Finally, on the way back to port, I avoid the green tourist who has not taken these precautions. The next "Thar she blows" might be her.

_____*Exercises*

1. Map the steps in a familiar process. Divide the process into major stages and then smaller steps. Consult with an expert to see if you have overlooked some hidden steps or failed to provide the appropriate cautions.

2. Analyze a process that confuses, intimidates, or terrifies most people. Use your personal experience to demystify the process: "I did this and survived to tell the tale. So can you."

HOW IS IT SIMILAR OR DIFFERENT?
Comparison

A *comparison* systematically analyzes and evaluates the similarities of two or more things. (A *contrast* is a comparison that emphasizes differences rather than similarities.) An effective comparison demonstrates one of three general purposes: (1) two things thought to be different are shown to be quite similar; (2) two things thought to be similar are shown to be quite different; or

(3) two things, although comparable, are shown to be not equal (that is, one is shown to be better than the other). To demonstrate one of these purposes, you will need to develop your comparison according to either the divided $(A + B)$ pattern or the alternating $(A/B + A/B)$ pattern.

The Divided Pattern of Comparison: $A + B$

The *divided pattern,* the most common of the two strategies, divides the comparison into two sections, the first devoted to a discussion of A and the second to a discussion of B. Linking the examples in A to those in B—for example, by making three points about A and three similar points about B—unifies the two contrasting parts. The points should be in the same sequence and, where possible, paired points should be treated in the same amount of space. Although such exact pairings are not always necessary, in working out your purpose you should demonstrate that $A + B$ are inextricably bound.

The two main parts of an $A + B$ comparison should develop cumulatively. A simple description of two unlike houses, for example, becomes a contrast only when its thesis points out the significance of the differences. In some cases, as when one side of the contrast is so well known to readers that it need not be stated, the comparison is *implied*. If you are contrasting American football (A) with English rugby (B) for an American audience, the details of A are already in the mind of your audience and need only be mentioned in passing to explain the significant details of B.

From an interview with Richard, the marine biologist on the *Portuguese Princess,* and from her reading, Jane gathers information on two of the world's largest creatures—the diplodocus and the blue whale. Then she develops this information in a divided pattern that contrasts their enormous size with their gentle behavior.

Thesis contrasts perception with reality.

A. Diplodocus
1. Enormous size
2. Small brain
3. Gentle behavior
4. Eating habits

The creatures that seem to threaten man most with their size and power have often been quite gentle. They have banded together to care for their young, to protect one another, and to provide each other with company. Consider the big, dumb diplodocus—his huge body laboring with a slow, steady drumbeat through the prehistoric forest. Although his body was enormous, his brain was small, so small that it did not generate enough power to control his weighty tail. He needed a separate ganglion to control that end of his body. His size promised danger, but Big D spent most of his day grazing harmlessly on vegetation with his pals. When a meat-eating enemy approached, he lumbered into knee-deep water and munched on a soggy plant.

B. Blue whale
1. Enormous size
2. Large brain
3. Gentle behavior
4. Eating habits

Similarly, the blue whale, the largest creature ever to exist, is as gentle as a golden retriever. One hundred feet long, he glides soundlessly through the ocean, his enormous head concealing his fifteen-pound brain. Like Big D, Big Blue was once a pack animal, but his numbers have been so depleted by hunters that he is rarely seen alone, much less in groups. He feeds on krill and other microscopic marine life. Instead of teeth, he has baleen, long strands of tissue that hang from his upper jaw. He sifts his food through this tissue by swimming, mouth open, through tons of water. When he closes his mouth, the water strains back through the baleen, and he swallows the remaining food in gigantic gulps.

The Alternating Pattern of Comparison: A/B + A/B

The *alternating pattern* develops your material through matched pairs of *A* and *B*, expressed either in the same paragraph or in the same sentence. The divided pattern is perhaps easier to organize and control, particularly in short essays, but unless you connect the two subjects with a clear thesis, you may discover that you have written two separate essays. The alternating pattern requires you to organize your material more precisely than the divided pattern, especially in a longer essay, but the pattern is often more interesting and accessible for your reader because the point-by-point development can be written in balanced sentences that reinforce the comparison with every pair of matched details. Gretel Ehrlich uses the alternating pattern in the following passage to compare the romanticized conception (*A*) and the real character (*B*) of the American cowboy:

How does Ehrlich use the Marlboro man to introduce the two terms in her comparison?

How does she use parallel sentence structure to contrast A and B?

When I'm in New York but feeling lonely for Wyoming I look for the Marlboro ads in the subway. What I'm aching to see is horseflesh, the glint of a spur, a line of distant mountains, brimming creeks, and a reminder of the ranchers and cowboys I've ridden with for the last eight years. But the men I see in those posters with their stern, humorless looks remind me of no one I know here. In our hellbent earnestness to romanticize the cowboy we've ironically disesteemed his true character. If he's "strong and silent" it's because there's probably no one to talk to. If he "rides away into the sunset" it's because he's been on horseback since four in the morning moving cattle and he's trying, fifteen hours later, to get home to his family. If he's "a rugged individualist" he's also part of a team: ranch work is teamwork and even the glorified open-range cowboys of the 1880s rode up and down the Chisholm Trail in the company of twenty or thirty other riders. Instead of the macho, trigger-happy man our culture has perversely wanted him to be, the cowboy is more apt to be convivial, quirky, and softhearted. To be "tough" on a ranch has nothing to do with conquests and displays of power. More often than not, circumstances—like the colt he's riding or an unexpected blizzard—are overpowering him. It's not toughness but "toughing it out" that counts. In other words, this macho, cultural artifact the cowboy has become is simply a man who possesses resilience, patience, and an instinct for survival. "Cowboys are just like a pile of rocks—everything happens to them. They get climbed on, kicked, rained and snowed on, scuffed up by wind. Their job is 'just to take it,' " one old timer told me. (Gretel Ehrlich, *The Solace of Open Spaces*)

What does the comparison of cowboys with rocks contribute to her thesis?

_____ *Exercises*

1. Speculate in your journal on some of the similarities you have observed between two apparently different activities—eating and sleeping, talking and listening, reading and running. Arrange the points of your comparison in a list and then freewrite about the specific advantages and disadvantages of presenting your information according to one of the two patterns.

2. Read through several popular magazines looking for common comparisons between people and animals: the lawyer is as sly as a fox, the doctor is as busy as a beaver, the tennis player moves like a gazelle, the two political candidates are in a real dog fight, and so on. Develop an extended comparison to show how the comparison to animals may elevate or demean the true character of the two subjects.

WHAT KIND OF SUBDIVISION DOES IT CONTAIN? *Classification*

Classification organizes information into groups and categories. An effective classification begins by defining a subject and then dividing it into major categories based on a common trait. The categories are then arranged in a sequence that shows that the division is *consistent* (the same principle is used to classify each category), *complete* (no major categories are omitted), and *significant* (categories and subcategories are arranged in an order that demonstrates some purpose).

Classification, like comparison, builds on your readers' expectations for precision, balance, and order. Call your readers' attention to the principle you have used to classify each category, or clearly imply it, and devote approximately the same amount of space to each category. Finally, arrange your categories and subpoints clearly and logically so that your reader is able to follow your system.

In the following excerpts Desmond Morris employs these strategies to establish three kinds of territories people define and defend:

Establishes three kinds of territory.

A territory is a defended space. In the broadest sense, there are three kinds of human territory: tribal, family and personal. . . .

First: the Tribal Territory. We evolved as tribal animals, living in

Arranges categories in logical sequence (largest to smallest).

comparatively small groups, probably of less than a hundred, and we existed like that for millions of years. It is our basic social unit, a group in which everyone knows everyone else. Essentially, the tribal territory consisted of a home base surrounded by extended hunting grounds. Any neighbouring tribe intruding on our social space would be repelled and driven away. As these early tribes swelled into agricultural super-tribes, and eventually into industrial nations, their territorial defence systems became increasingly elaborate. The tiny, ancient home base of the hunting tribe became the great capital city, the primitive war-paint became the flags, emblems, uniforms and regalia of the specialized military, and the war-chants became national anthems, marching songs and bugle calls. Territorial boundary-lines hardened into fixed borders, often conspicuously patrolled and punctuated with defensive structures—forts and lookout posts, checkpoints and great walls, and, today, customs barriers. . . .

Second: the Family Territory. Essentially, the family is a breeding unit and the family territory is a breeding ground. At the centre of this space, there is the nest—the bedroom—where, tucked up in bed, we feel at our most territorially secure. In a typical house the bedroom is upstairs, where a safe nest should be. This puts it farther away from the entrance hall, the area where contact is made, intermittently, with the outside world. The less private reception rooms, where intruders are allowed access, are the next line of defence. Beyond them, outside the walls of the building, there is often a symbolic remnant of the ancient feeding grounds—a garden. Its symbolism often extends to the plants and animals it contains, which cease to be nutritional and become merely decorative—flowers and pets. But like a true territorial space it has a conspicuously displayed boundary-line, the garden fence, wall, or railings. . . .

Presents the same kind of information to distinguish each territory.

Third: the Personal Space. If a man enters a waiting-room and sits at one end of a long row of empty chairs, it is possible to predict where the next man to enter will seat himself. He will not sit next to the first man, nor will he sit at the far end, right away from him. He will choose a position about halfway between these two points. The next man to enter will take the largest gap left, and sit roughly in the middle of that, and so on, until eventually the latest newcomer will be forced to select a seat that places him right next to one of the already seated men. Similar patterns can be observed in cinemas, public urinals, aeroplanes, trains and buses. This is a reflection of the fact that we all carry with us, everywhere we go, a portable territory called a Personal Space. If people move inside this space, we feel threatened. If they keep too far outside it, we feel rejected. (Desmond Morris, "Territorial Behaviour," *Manwatching*)

Jane was fascinated by the many types of whales. The books she read emphasized their physical differences, and Richard, who had studied many individual whales, helped her understand their behavioral idiosyncrasies. During planning, Jane tries to combine her sources to classify whales according to their "personalities."

Although there are over one hundred kinds of whales in the world (and even more names to designate each kind), most whales can be classified

1. How does Jane attempt to establish the completeness of her classification?

2. How does she avoid the apparent contradiction in her system?

3. What is significant about the sequence in which she presents her categories?

into three major categories. The gregarious whales are outgoing, curious, and friendly toward people. This category includes extroverts, like the humpback, who have baleen and feed off microscopic marine life, and acrobats, like the porpoises, who have teeth and eat small fish. The aggressive whales are formidable, ornery, and dangerous. This category includes killer whales, who hunt in packs, stalking all sorts of marine life from penguins to baby blue whales, and sperm whales, who hunt alone, devouring such impressive prey as octopi, and who have been known to ram ships. The shy whales are solitary, enigmatic, and unpredictable. This category includes whales like the finback, who seem indifferent to other whales as well as to people, and the blue whale, who has been hunted to near-extinction by those eager to kill the world's largest creature.

_____*Exercises*

1. Interview friends or family members about their behavior in certain types of territory—tribal, family, personal. What special techniques have they discovered for claiming and defending space with "signals rather than fists"?
2. Read about an established method for classifying information, such as categories for rating films or the procedure for naming plants. Then devise a principle that will enable you to simplify and streamline the system.

HOW WOULD YOU CHARACTERIZE IT?
Definition

Definition provides a necessary explanation of a word or concept. The explanation may be a simple substitution of a familiar for an unfamiliar word, as when you substitute *cancer* for *carcinoma*. It may be the addition of a phrase, as when you follow *vintage* with "the yield of wine or grapes from a particular vineyard or district during one season." It may be a single sentence: "In the theater, a *prompter* is a person who provides cues for the actors or singers on stage." Or a definition may consist of one or more paragraphs, or even a whole essay, in which you explain your subject, such as *tradition* or *excellence,* in some depth.

Definitions may be short, stipulative, or extended. *Short* definitions, like the definition of *carcinoma, vintage,* and *prompter,* provide brief explanations similar to those in your dictionary. *Stipulative* definitions specify the exact meaning or sense of a word as you intend to use it in your writing. Some words may have favorable or unfavorable connotations, depending on the audience. In a political election, for example, a candidate, on being called *liberal,* might reply, "Yes, I am a liberal, but only in the true sense of the word. It originally meant *free,* and I believe in the freedom of individuals to think, speak, and act according to their consciences." The candidate is emphasizing one meaning and excluding others. Such definitions enable your readers to see the purpose of your words. The definition of *purpose* on page 16 is another example of a stipulative definition.

Extended definitions, usually longer pieces of writing, explain a writer's view of a subject, sometimes using short or stipulative definitions but going far beyond both. The writer adds to, modifies, and illustrates the basic definition. Any pattern of development may be used: comparison of a word's synonym, for example, an analysis of changes in its meaning. Cultural geographer Yi-Fu Tuan combines different strategies in his extended definition of *fear.*

Introduces two short definitions to answer a question that prompts an extended definition.

What is fear? It is a complex feeling of which two strains, alarm and anxiety, are clearly distinguishable. Alarm is triggered by an obtrusive event in the environment, and an animal's instinctive response is to combat it or run. Anxiety, on the other hand, is a diffuse sense of dread and presupposes an ability to anticipate. It commonly occurs when an animal is in a strange and disorienting milieu, separated from the supportive objects and figures of its home ground. Anxiety is a presentiment of danger when nothing in the immediate surroundings can be pinpointed as dangerous. The need for decisive action is checked by the lack of any specific, circumventable threat.

Explains that fear depends on emotional capacity.

Alarm and anxiety are exhibited in all higher animals. Human beings have much in common with other primates both in the causes of these sensations and in their subsequent behavioral response. Where humans differ from other species, the reason lies in their greater emotional range and superior mind.

Explains how imagination adds to the capacity to experience fear.

Emotional range is a gauge of the nervous system's complexity and hence, indirectly, of the mind. A jellyfish's repertoire of emotions is very limited compared with that of a complex animal like the rabbit, and the rabbit's range of feeling is narrow compared with that of a human being. An animal perhaps knows anger and sadness, but can it be wistful or melancholic? It shows alarm and signs of anxiety, but does it stand in dread of humiliation, of being shamed by its peers? A capacity for shame and guilt adds greatly to the scope of human fear. Can an animal living in its natural setting experience the macabre and the uncanny? Awareness of preternatural evil, unique to the human species, enables a person to see and live in phantasmagorial worlds of witches, ghosts, and monsters; these figures embody a weight of dread unknown to other animals. Fear of betrayal by a relative or friend is very different from fear of an enemy outside the familiar circle. Imagination adds immeasurably to the kinds and intensity of fear in the human world. (Yi-Fu Tuan, *Landscapes of Fear*)

During Jane's whale-watching experience, she encountered many unusual words. She heard some of them before (*breeching, spouting*) but did not appreciate their true significance until she saw the actions they identified. Others she heard for the first time on the *Portuguese Princess* (*Krill, baleen*), grasping their meaning as Richard explained them. But one term, *gam,* was used without explanation. In reviewing her notes, the word popped up again, prompting her to research and meditate on its meaning in the following definition:

1. How does the quotation from Melville add credibility to her definition?

When Herman Melville used the word <u>gam</u> in <u>Moby Dick</u>, he was certain he was the first writer to define it: "you might wear out your index finger running up and down the columns of dictionaries and never find the word." But he was equally certain that the word needed an official definition because it "has now for many years been in constant use among fifteen thousand true born Yankees" (Herman Melville, "The Gam," <u>Moby Dick</u>). Perhaps because of Melville, the word now appears in most dictionaries. <u>Gam</u>, like its equally unusual synonyms <u>pod</u> and <u>school</u>, refers to a herd of whales. By extension, <u>gam</u> refers to a meeting of two or more whaling ships at sea. Its precise origin is unknown, but some speculate that the word derives from <u>gammon</u>, a little-used word for talk or chatter. And that's what whales and whalers do when they <u>gam</u>. They socialize. Whales seem to enjoy each other's company as they feed. And whalers, once they meet at sea, stop the hunt, visit between ships, and settle down to food and conversation.

2. How does she use substitution to clarify the meaning of the word?

3. How do her closing examples extend the definition?

_____Exercise

1. Select a common word, such as *stress,* that seems to have many subtle meanings. Freewrite a few simple definitions: "Stress is . . ." Next, try a few negative definitions: "Stress is not . . ." Then look up the word in a dictionary to determine its precise meaning.

2. Select an unusual word that puzzled you when you first heard or read it. Interview several "authorities" about what the word might mean. Check the word in several dictionaries (especially a historical dictionary such as the *Oxford English Dictionary*). Then prepare your own extended definition.

WHY DID IT HAPPEN? *Causal Analysis*

Causal analysis, like process analysis, details a sequence of steps that produce a result. But rather than describing these steps, causal analysis examines them for *causes* and *effects.* Such an analysis can be developed in three ways: by describing an action or event and then demonstrating the effect; by describing an action or event and then determining its cause; or by examining two related actions or events and proving a cause and effect connection between them.

In each case, you must be careful not to exaggerate or oversimplify the cause and effect relationship. You may mistake coincidence for cause, or you may identify one cause as *the* direct cause when any number of complex causes (working independently or in combination) could have produced the same effect. In the following passage Alan Devoe analyzes the many causes of hibernation:

Suggests possible causes

1. cold
2. diminishing food supply
3. increased darkness
4. silence

The season of hibernating begins quite early for some of the creatures of outdoors. It is not alone the cold which causes it; there are a multiplicity of other factors—diminishing food supply; increased darkness as the fall days shorten; silence—frequently decisive. Any or all of these may be the signal for entrance into the Long Sleep, depending upon the habits and make-up of the particular creature. Among the skunks, it is usually the coming of the cold that sends them, torpid, to their root-lined underground burrows; but many other mammals (for instance, ground squirrels) begin to grow drowsy when the fall sun is still warm on their furry backs and the food supply is not at all diminished. This ground-squirrel kind of hibernating, independent of the weather and the food supply, may be an old race habit, an instinctual behavior pattern like the unaccountable migrations of certain birds. Weather, food, inheritance, darkness—all of these obscurely play their parts in bringing on the annual subsidence into what one biologist has called "the little death." Investigation of the causes will need a good many years before they can be understood, for in captivity, where observation is more easy than in the wild, the hibernators often do not sleep at all. (Alan Devoe, *Lives Around Us*)

Supplies another cause

5. instinctual behavior presents new effect for investigators.

Her first whale watch had a profound effect on Jane, and as she read more about whale watching she realized that many other people had had similarly significant experiences. In fact, she speculates that whale watching has produced three important effects.

1. How does Jane account for the origin of whale watching?

2. What have been the three main effects of this popularity?

Since its inception over a decade ago, whale watching has become a major industry. It began as a scientific enterprise as marine biologists, concerned about extinction, attempted to chart the feeding and migrating patterns of whales. The biologists soon became so adept at sighting whales and so enthusiastic about what they saw that they offered the experience to the public, producing three significant effects. First, whale watching has become an enormously popular recreational experience. The exhilarating voyage out to sea, the spectacular acrobatics of the whales, and the sensation of seeing something extraordinary rivals the best rides at Disneyland. Second, whale watching has increased public awareness about preservation. Once people have seen the power, grace, and agility of whales, they can never again be indifferent to their

3. Why is the third effect potentially the most important?

wholesale slaughter. Third, whale watching in America has become so profitable that entrepreneurs are trying to convince the nations that still hunt whales, such as Japan and the Soviet Union, that there is more money to be made in watching whales than in killing them.

_____Exercises

1. Analyze the possible causes for one of your common problems, such as occasional insomnia or headaches. Read a general reference work, such as *The Columbia Medical Encyclopedia,* to identify some probable causes. Then interview others who are afflicted by the same problem to see how they explain its causes.

2. Speculate on the possible effects that some dramatic change might have on your life. For example, how would one of the following events affect your life?
   a. Purchasing an expensive camera.
   b. Studying in another country (such as Kenya or New Zealand) for a semester.
   c. Acquiring a new pet.
   d. Working in a zoo.

Animals in Transit | Peter Singer

In this passage from *Animal Liberation,* animal rights activist Peter Singer explains how animals react to being transported across country in trucks. What is the dominant pattern in this passage? What other patterns does Singer use to develop his explanation? How does his explanation make you react to the last sentence in the passage?

Animals placed in a truck for the first time in their lives are likely to be frightened, especially if they have been handled hastily and roughly by the men loading the truck. The motion of the truck is also a new experience, and one which may make them ill. After one or two days in the truck without food or water they are desperately thirsty and hungry. Normally cattle eat frequently throughout the day; their special stomachs require a constant intake of food if the rumen is to function properly. If the journey is in winter, subzero winds can result in severe chill; in summer the heat and sun may add to the dehydration caused by the lack of water. It is difficult for us to imagine what this combination of fear, travel sickness, thirst, near-starvation, exhaustion, and possibly severe chill feels like to the animals. In the case of young calves who may have gone through the stress of weaning and castration only a few days earlier, the effect is still worse. Veterinary experts recommend that, simply in order to improve their prospects of surviving, young calves should be weaned, castrated, and vaccinated at least thirty days prior to being transported. This gives them a chance to recover from one stressful experience before being subjected to another. These recommendations, however, are not always followed. 1

Although the animals cannot describe their experiences, the reactions of their bodies tell us something. There are two main reactions: "shrinkage" and "shipping fever." All animals lose weight during transportation. Some of this weight loss is due to dehydration and the emptying of the intestinal tract. This loss is easily regained; but more lasting losses are also the rule. For an eight-hundred-pound steer to lose seventy pounds, or 9 percent of his weight, on a single trip is not unusual; and it may take more than three weeks for the animal to recover the loss. This "shrink," as it is known in the trade, is regarded by researchers as an indication of the stress to which the animal has been subjected. Shrink is, of course, a worry to the meat industry, since animals are sold by the pound. 2

"Shipping fever," a form of pneumonia that strikes cattle after they have been transported, is the other major indicator of stress in transportation. Shipping fever is associated with a virus that healthy cattle have no difficulty in resisting; severe stress, however, weakens their resistance. 3

Shrinkage and susceptibility to fever are indications that the animals have been subjected to extreme stress; but the animals who shrink and get shipping fever are the ones who survive. Others die before reaching their 4

Singer, Peter. *Animal Liberation. 2nd* ed. New York: Random, 1990. 148–50.

destination, or arrive with broken limbs or other injuries. In 1986, USDA inspectors condemned over 7,400 cattle, 3,100 calves, and 5,500 pigs because they were dead or seriously injured before they reached the slaughterhouse, while 570,000 cattle, 57,000 calves, and 643,000 pigs were injured severely enough for parts of their bodies to be condemned.

Animals who die in transit do not die easy deaths. They freeze to 5 death in winter and collapse from thirst and heat exhaustion in summer. They die, lying unattended in stockyards, from injuries sustained in falling off a slippery loading ramp. They suffocate when other animals pile on top of them in overcrowded, badly loaded trucks. They die from thirst or starve when careless stockmen forget to give them food or water. And they die from the sheer stress of the whole terrifying experience. The animal that you may be having for dinner tonight did not die in any of these ways; but these deaths are and always have been part of the overall process that provides people with their meat.

Watching Whales | Jane Graham

Jane's final essay incorporates much of the writing she developed during planning and drafting. Read her essay and then review her experiments with various patterns throughout the chapter. What patterns has she reshaped, relocated, or eliminated during revising? Is the dominant structure of her essay the most effective method for accomplishing her purpose? Explain your answer.

The problem with whales is that they don't fit under a microscope. As a 1 small girl, I walked around and around the large skeleton of a blue whale on the first floor of the American Museum of Natural History, trying to compare its size to the skeletons of the brontosaurus and diplodocus I had seen on the fourth floor. Like those creatures from another time, whales challenged and held my imagination. I could never see enough of them. The drawings in textbooks outlined their shape but reduced their enormous size to a few inches. The photographs in magazines suggested their magnificence but usually focused on their parts—the head rising to breech, the tail arching to dive. Last summer, hoping to see more, I booked passage on the *Portuguese Princess* out of Provincetown, Massachusetts, for my first whale watch.

A motley crowd assembled on MacMillan Pier in the early morning 2 mist. Seasoned whale watchers checked their binoculars, cameras, and lens cases. Casual tourists chased after wayward children, counted their supply of Dramamine, and looked anxiously at the *Princess* as it creaked and groaned against its moorings. Various members of the crew, dressed in T-shirts and cutoffs, peered into the engine hole or studied the sighting charts stacked on the elevated table behind the wheel house. The haunting sounds of whale songs were piped through the mist by the boat's loudspeaker system. Soon, Richard, a marine biologist, dressed like the crew but wearing a Red Sox cap, walked out of the mist and jumped aboard. He checked the charts for a few minutes and then picked up a clipboard to call the seventy names on his new manifest.

I crossed the gangplank and took a position forward, away from the engine, knowing that the combination of gasoline fumes and rolling seas could make me sick. The engine sputtered to life, drowning out the whale songs and the nervous chatter of passengers. As the *Princess* plowed out of the harbor, I looked back to watch Provincetown disappear. The streets crowded with gawking summer people blurred, and the silhouette of the old fishing village—shacks resting on huge pilings, seagulls diving behind weathered boats—lingered briefly on the horizon.

3

"We're headed for Stellwagen Bank," Richard announced from his perch behind the wheel house. "This is an area of shallow water and undersea crags that attracts microscopic marine life, plankton, and krill, the staple diet of many whales, especially the humpbacks. Humpbacks are baleen whales. They do not hunt, kill, and devour. Instead of teeth, they have baleen, long strands of tissue that hang from their upper jaws. They sift their food through this tissue by swimming, mouth open, through tons of water. When they close their mouths, the water strains back through the baleen, and they swallow the remaining food in gigantic gulps."

4

The mist had cleared, the sun burned my neck, and a cold, salty spray occasionally splashed my face as the *Princess* headed into the wind for the next half hour. The passengers talked, gestured, and looked for signs. "I've watched all the Cousteau specials," a New Hampshire bride was telling me when Richard yelled, "Thar she blows! Off the port bow! There!" We followed his finger, focusing binoculars, twisting telephoto lenses, straining to see what he had seen in the dark blue swells. Against the skyline, I saw it. A definite vertical spray. Then a pause. Then another.

5

I was actually seeing two sprays, one from each of the whale's spouts or nostrils. Whales are mammals and so, like us, cannot breathe under water. They store air in their lungs before they dive and then "blow" it out their spouts when they surface. This whale was diving and blowing steadily, heading away from Stellwagen Bank. Richard tried to identify its flukes, the large flippers at the end of its tail. The patterns and notches on a whale's flukes are like fingerprints, enabling expert whale watchers to identify individual whales. But this whale, swimming intently toward some destination, was too far away for even Richard to see its colors.

6

The *Princess* churned on for another thirty minutes. Suddenly, the captain killed the engine. "We're here." And so were they. As we drifted, several sets of feeding humpbacks swam into view. A mother, her calf beside her, dived, surfaced, and waved her flukes in a perfect vertical before diving again. Her calf, eager to imitate, tried the same maneuver over and over, but his tail and flukes flopped sideways at the last minute like a sloppy cartwheel. At our stern, an obstreperous male leaped totally out of the water and then fell sideways with an impressive clap. I could see his huge, vulnerable underbelly and the white undersides of his long flippers. When he burst out of the water, he held his flippers at a slight angle to his side. As he descended, he moved them gracefully away from his body like the arms of a ballerina finishing a pirouette.

7

After an hour of dashing around the deck, elbowing my way to the rail, and snapping pictures of everything I could see, I thought I had seen

8

enough. Other excursion boats and private craft had slowly encircled the feeding whales. Shortwave radios crackled: "Look to the west. A male is breeching." "Over to the south. Two bachelors are gamming." "In the center. The mother and calf are resting." The noise prompted thoughts of other messages delivered on distant seas: "Finback, south, southwest. Lower the boats. Aim the harpoon." Richard had apparently seen enough as well. The engine erupted, and the *Princess* began to turn. I looked forward, trying to sort it all out—the graceful, powerful gentleness of the whales; the curious, careless intrusiveness of the whale watchers. Why couldn't we simply watch? Why did people have to hunt, kill, and destroy?

The engine stopped. Richard's voice came over the loud-speaker in an   9
excited, controlled whisper. "There's a finback heading toward us. He's way off course. Finbacks are shy and solitary. They're still hunted and so usually stay clear of boats. If we're quiet, we may see something rare." Seventy watchers became still. The *Princess* rolled on four-foot swells. Soon we saw him—a sea-green monolith, his huge bulk silhouetted several feet beneath the surface. His distinguishing fin was mottled in patterns of white and gray. He was swimming purposefully toward us. We were obviously in his path, but not in his way. He was silent. We were silent. Closer, closer, and then under. More silence. I rushed to the other side. His green head exploded through the surface twenty feet away. One large, watery eye looked back at me before he arched his body into the sea. He swam in a straight line for a couple of hundred yards, blew, and then sounded.

Although we watched eagerly for him to surface again, we looked in   10
vain. Soon we began to look at one another. We smiled, but we did not talk. Neither did Richard. No explanation was necessary. We had watched a whale. A whale had watched us. Finally, the engine coughed, and the *Portuguese Princess* resumed her journey back to Provincetown.

Under the Snow | John McPhee

Before reading this essay, review John McPhee's comments on how he organizes his writing (pages 125–126). Next, as you read this, identify McPhee's predominant pattern and the way he employs other patterns to enhance his purpose. Which of these patterns seems to emerge naturally from the material? Which patterns seem imposed on the material?

When my third daughter was an infant, I could place her against my   1
shoulder and she would stick there like velvet. Only her eyes jumped from place to place. In a breeze, her bright-red hair might stir, but she would not. Even then, there was profundity in her repose.

When my fourth daughter was an infant, I wondered if her veins were   2
full of ants. Placing her against a shoulder was a risk both to her and to the shoulder. Impulsively, constantly, everything about her moved. Her head seemed about to revolve as it followed the bestirring world.

McPhee, John. *Table of Contents*. New York: Farrar, 1985. 3–12.

These memories became very much alive some months ago when—one   3
after another—I had bear cubs under my vest. Weighing three, four, 5.6
pounds, they were wild bears, and for an hour or so had been taken from
their dens in Pennsylvania. They were about two months old, with fine
short brown hair. When they were made to stand alone, to be photographed in the mouth of a den, they shivered. Instinctively, a person would
be moved to hold them. Picked up by the scruff of the neck, they splayed
their paws like kittens and screamed like baby bears. The cry of a baby
bear is muted, like a human infant's heard from her crib down the hall.
The first cub I placed on my shoulder stayed there like a piece of velvet.
The shivering stopped. Her bright-blue eyes looked about, not seeing much
of anything. My hand, cupped against her back, all but encompassed her rib
cage, which was warm and calm. I covered her to the shoulders with a flap
of down vest and zipped up my parka to hold her in place.

I was there by invitation, an indirect result of work I had been doing   4
nearby. Would I be busy on March 14th? If there had been a conflict—if,
say, I had been invited to lunch on that day with the Queen of Scotland
and the King of Spain—I would have gone to the cubs. The first den was a
rock cavity in a lichen-covered sandstone outcrop near the top of a slope, a
couple of hundred yards from a road in Hawley. It was on posted property
of the Scrub Oak Hunting Club—dry hardwood forest underlain by laurel
and patches of snow—in the northern Pocono woods. Up in the sky was
Buck Alt. Not long ago, he was a dairy farmer, and now he was working
for the Keystone State, with directional antennae on his wing struts angled
in the direction of bears. Many bears in Pennsylvania have radios around
their necks as a result of the summer trapping work of Alt's son Gary, who
is a wildlife biologist. In winter, Buck Alt flies the country listening to the
radio, crissing and crossing until the bears come on. They come on stronger
the closer to them he flies. The transmitters are not omnidirectional.
Suddenly, the sound cuts out. Buck looks down, chooses a landmark, approaches it again, on another vector. Gradually, he works his way in, until
he is flying in ever tighter circles above the bear. He marks a map. He is
accurate within two acres. The plane he flies is a Super Cub.

The den could have served as a set for a Passion play. It was a small   5
chamber, open on one side, with a rock across its entrance. Between the
freestanding rock and the back of the cave was room for one large bear,
and she was curled in a corner on a bed of leaves, her broad head plainly
visible from the outside, her cubs invisible between the rock and a soft
place, chuckling, suckling, in the wintertime tropics of their own mamma-
lian heaven. Invisible they were, yes, but by no means inaudible. What biologists call chuckling sounded like starlings in a tree.

People walking in woods sometimes come close enough to a den to   6
cause the mother to get up and run off, unmindful of her reputation as a
fearless defender of cubs. The cubs stop chuckling and begin to cry: possibly three, four cubs—a ward of mewling bears. The people hear the crying.
They find the den and see the cubs. Sometimes they pick them up and
carry them away, reporting to the state that they have saved the lives of
bear cubs abandoned by their mother. Wherever and whenever this occurs,
Gary Alt collects the cubs. After ten years of bear trapping and biological
study, Alt has equipped so many sows with radios that he has been able to

conduct a foster-mother program with an amazingly high rate of success. A mother in hibernation will readily accept a foster cub. If the need to place an orphan arises somewhat later, when mothers and their cubs are out and around, a sow will kill an alien cub as soon as she smells it. Alt has overcome this problem by stuffing sows' noses with Vicks VapoRub. One way or another, he has found new families for forty-seven orphaned cubs. Forty-six have survived. The other, which had become accustomed over three weeks to feedings and caresses by human hands, was not content in a foster den, crawled outside, and died in the snow.

With a hypodermic jab stick, Alt now drugged the mother, putting her to sleep for the duration of the visit. From deeps of shining fur, he fished out cubs. One. Two. A third. A fourth. Five! The fifth was a foster daughter brought earlier in the winter from two hundred miles away. Three of the four others were male—a ratio consistent with the heavy preponderance of males that Alt's studies have shown through the years. To various onlookers he handed the cubs for safekeeping while he and several assistants carried the mother into the open and weighed her with block and tackle. To protect her eyes, Alt had blindfolded her with a red bandanna. They carried her upside down, being extremely careful lest they scrape and damage her nipples. She weighed two hundred and nineteen pounds. Alt had carried her and weighed her some months before. In the den, she had lost ninety pounds. When she was four years old, she had had four cubs; two years later, four more cubs; and now, after two more years, four cubs. He knew all that about her, he had caught her so many times. He referred to her as Daisy. Daisy was as nothing compared with Vanessa, who was sleeping off the winter somewhere else. In ten seasons, Vanessa had given birth to twenty-three cubs and had lost none. The growth and reproductive rates of black bears are greater in Pennsylvania than anywhere else. Black bears in Pennsylvania grow more rapidly than grizzlies in Montana. Eastern black bears are generally much larger than Western ones. A seven-hundred-pound bear is unusual but not rare in Pennsylvania. Alt once caught a big boar like that who had a thirty-seven-inch neck and was a hair under seven feet long. **7**

This bear, nose to tail, measured five feet five. Alt said, "That's a nice long sow." For weighing the cubs, he had a small nylon stuff sack. He stuffed it with bear and hung it on a scale. Two months before, when the cubs were born, each would have weighed approximately half a pound—less than a newborn porcupine. Now the cubs weighed 3.4, 4.1, 4.4, 4.6, 5.6—cute little numbers with soft tan noses and erectile pyramid ears. Bears have sex in June and July, but the mother's system holds the fertilized egg away from the uterus until November, when implantation occurs. Fetal development lasts scarcely six weeks. Therefore, the creatures who live upon the hibernating mother are so small that everyone survives. **8**

The orphan, less winsome than the others, looked like a chocolate-covered possum. I kept her under my vest. She seemed content there and scarcely moved. In time, I exchanged her for 5.6—the big boy in the litter. Lifted by the scruff and held in the air, he bawled, flashed his claws, and curled his lips like a woofing boar. I stuffed him under the vest, where he shut up and nuzzled. His claws were already more than half an inch long. Alt said that the family would come out of the den in a few weeks but that **9** much of the spring would go by before the cubs gained weight. The difference would be that they were no longer malleable and ductile. They would become pugnacious and scratchy, not to say vicious, and would chew up the hand that caressed them. He said, "If you have an enemy, give him a bear cub."

Six men carried the mother back to the den, the red bandanna still tied **10** around her eyes. Alt repacked her into the rock. "We like to return her to the den as close as possible to the way we found her," he said. Someone remarked that one biologist can work a coon, while an army is needed to deal with a bear. An army seemed to be present. Twelve people had followed Alt to the den. Some days, the group around him is four times as large. Alt, who is in his thirties, was wearing a visored khaki cap with a blue-and-gold keystone on the forehead, and a khaki cardigan under a khaki jump suit. A lithe and light-bodied man with tinted glasses and a blond mustache, he looked like a lieutenant in the Ardennes Forest. Included in the retinue were two reporters and a news photographer. Alt encourages media attention, the better to soften the image of the bears. He says, "People fear bears more than they need to, and respect them not enough." Over the next twenty days, he had scheduled four hundred visitors—state senators, representatives, commissioners, television reporters, word processors, biologists, friends—to go along on his rounds of dens. Days before, he and the denned bears had been hosts to the BBC. The Brits wanted snow. God was having none of it. The BBC brought in the snow.

In the course of the day, we made a brief tour of dens that for the time **11** being stood vacant. Most were rock cavities. They had been used before, and in all likelihood would be used again. Bears in winter in the Pocono Plateau are like chocolate chips in a cookie. The bears seldom go back to the same den two years running, and they often change dens in the course of a winter. In a forty-five-hundred-acre housing development called Hemlock Farms are twenty-three dens known to be in current use and countless others awaiting new tenants. Alt showed one that was within fifteen feet of the intersection of East Spur Court and Pommel Drive. He said that when a sow with two cubs was in there he had seen deer browsing by the outcrop and ignorant dogs stopping off to lift a leg. Hemlock Farms is expensive, and full of cantilevered cypress and unencumbered glass. Houses perch on high flat rock. Now and again, there are bears in the rock—in, say, a floor-through cavity just under the porch. The owners are from New York. Alt does not always tell them that their property is zoned for bears. Once, when he did so, a "FOR SALE" sign went up within two weeks.

Not far away is Interstate 84. Flying over it one day, Buck Alt heard **12** an oddly intermittent signal. Instead of breaking off once and cleanly, it broke off many times. Crossing back over, he heard it again. Soon he was in a tight turn, now hearing something, now nothing, in a pattern that did not suggest anything he had heard before. It did, however, suggest the interstate. Where a big green sign says, "MILFORD 11, PORT JERVIS 20," Gary hunted around and found the bear. He took us now to see the den. We went down a steep slope at the side of the highway and, crouching, peered into a culvert. It was about fifty yards long. There was a disc of daylight at the opposite end. Thirty inches in diameter, it was a perfect place to stash a body, and that is what the bear thought, too. On Gary's first visit, the disc of daylight had not been visible. The bear had denned under the eastbound lanes. She had given birth to three cubs. Soon after he found her, heavy rains were predicted. He hauled the family out and off to a vacant den. The cubs weighed less than a pound. Two days later, water a foot deep was racing through the culvert.

Under High Knob, in remote undeveloped forest about six hundred **13** metres above sea level, a slope falling away in an easterly direction contained a classic excavated den: a small entrance leading into an intimate ovate cavern, with a depression in the center for a bed—in all, about twenty-four cubic feet, the size of a refrigerator-freezer. The den had not been occupied in several seasons, but Rob Buss, a district game protector who works regularly with Gary Alt, had been around to check it three days before and had shined his flashlight into a darkness stuffed with fur. Meanwhile, six inches of fresh snow had fallen on High Knob, and now Alt and his team, making preparations a short distance from the den, scooped up snow in their arms and filled a big sack. They had nets of nylon mesh. There was a fifty-fifty likelihood of yearling bears in the den. Mothers keep cubs until their second spring. When a biologist comes along and provokes the occupants to emerge, there is no way to predict how many will appear. Sometimes they keep coming and coming, like clowns from a compact car. As a bear emerges, it walks into the nylon mesh. A drawstring closes. At the same time, the den entrance is stuffed with a bag of snow. That stops the others. After the first bear has been dealt with, Alt removes the sack of snow. Out comes another bear. A yearling weighs about eighty pounds, and may move so fast that it runs over someone on the biological team and stands on top of him sniffing at his ears. Or her ears. Janice Gruttadauria, a research assistant, is a part of the team. Bear after bear, the procedure is repeated until the bag of snow is pulled away and nothing comes out. That is when Alt asks Rob Buss to go inside and see if anything is there.

Now, moving close to the entrance, Alt spread a tarp on the snow, lay **14** down on it, turned on a five-cell flashlight, and put his head inside the den. The beam played over thick black fur and came to rest on a tiny foot. The sack of snow would not be needed. After drugging the mother with a jab stick, he joined her in the den. The entrance was so narrow he had to shrug his shoulders to get in. He shoved the sleeping mother, head first, out of the darkness and into the light.

While she was away, I shrugged my own shoulders and had a look in- **15** side. The den smelled of earth but not of bear. The walls were dripping with roots. The water and protein metabolism of hibernating black bears has been explored by the Mayo Clinic as a research model for, among other things, human endurance on long flights through space and medical situations closer to home, such as the maintenance of anephric human beings who are awaiting kidney transplants.

Outside, each in turn, the cubs were put in the stuff sack—a male and **16** a female. The female weighed four pounds. Greedily, I reached for her when Alt took her out of the bag. I planted her on my shoulder while I wrote down facts about her mother: weight, a hundred and ninety-two pounds; length, fifty-eight inches; some toes missing; severe frostbite from a bygone winter evidenced along the edges of the ears.

Eventually, with all weighing and tagging complete, it was time to go. **17**

Alt went into the den. Soon he called out that he was ready for the mother. It would be a tight fit. Feet first, she was shoved in, like a safe-deposit box. Inside, Alt tugged at her in close embrace, and the two of them gradually revolved until she was at the back and their positions had reversed. He shaped her like a doughnut—her accustomed den position. The cubs go in the center. The male was handed in to him. Now he was asking for the female. For a moment, I glanced around as if looking to see who had her. The thought crossed my mind that if I bolted and ran far enough and fast enough I could flag a passing car and keep her. Then I pulled her from under the flap of my vest and handed her away.

Alt and others covered the entrance with laurel boughs, and covered   18
the boughs with snow. They camouflaged the den, but that was not the purpose. Practicing wildlife management to a fare-thee-well, Alt wanted the den to be even darker than it had been before; this would cause the family to stay longer inside and improve the cubs' chances when at last they faced the world.

In the evening, I drove down off the Pocono Plateau and over the   19
folded mountains and across the Great Valley and up the New Jersey Highlands and down into the basin and home. No amount of intervening terrain, though—and no amount of distance—could remove from my mind the picture of the covered entrance in the Pennsylvania hillside, or the thought of what was up there under the snow.

Writing Assignments

Narrate   **1.**   Freewrite in your journal about your memories of a specific animal you remember from books (*The Black Stallion*), films (*Gorillas in the Mist*), or television (*The Muppets*). Identify those features that encouraged you to identify with the animal. Then write a narrative that records your adventures with this imaginary companion.

Observe   **2.**   Keep a log in which you list the various ways people respond to your pet or to an animal you know. In particular, describe the tone of voice, body language, and emotional temperament that signals whether people are frightened or relaxed by the presence of an animal. Then write an essay in which you classify the types of responses you have observed.

Investigate   **3.**   Interview faculty and students who work with laboratory animals. You may want to contrast those who simply observe animal responses with those who dissect animals. Develop your interview notes into a profile that documents the use of laboratory animals on your campus.

Collaborate   **4.**   Most universities have a formal policy governing the use of animals in laboratory experiments. Your writing group has been asked to revise that policy. Read the policy carefully, then ask members of your group to conduct more interviews (with faculty researchers and animal rights advocates) and to read more documents (policies from other research institutions and criticism from activists like Singer). Then revise or defend your university's policy.

Read   **5.**   Read some articles and books on the history (and philosophy) of zoos (e.g., H. Hediger, *Man and Animal in the Zoo* or Virginia McKenna *et al.*, eds., *Beyond the Bars*). Visit a zoo in your area. Talk to attendants and visitors. Finally, write an analysis, based on personal experience and historical documentation, that speculates on the causes and effects of zoos in our culture.

Respond   **6.**   Respond to Singer's analysis of the "process that provides people with their meat." You may want to interview ranchers who raise cattle or doctors who recommend vegetarian diets. In either case, you are looking for information that will help you understand your attitude toward eating meat.

Analyze   **7.**   Analyze the way Jane expands, contrasts, or relocates her experiments with the common patterns of development in her essay. Jane's essay seems to be driven by a narrative question: What happened. What other questions emerge as the result of her attempt to tell what happened? How do those questions affect Jane's overall purpose? You may want to alter this assignment by using one of Jane's experiments as a prompt to write a longer essay of your own.

Evaluate   **8.**   Compare and contrast the attitudes expressed by Jane Graham and Francine duPlessix Gray toward "animal watching." What motivates each of them to watch? Why does Gray (and her guide) object to the watching? Why does Jane (and her guide) savor it? Evaluate each writer's perspective in relation to each other or write an essay suggesting a third.

Argue   **9.**   Reread Devoe's analysis of "hibernation." Then review McPhee's "Under the Snow." Identify the steps the Alts follow to intrude on the bear without interrupting its hibernation. Then construct an argument that explains why the Alts's "wildlife management" tactics are justified.

Argue   **10.**   Using the information gathered from your reading or experience, argue for or against a "wilderness ethic" that forbids people from studying, managing, and rearranging the behavior of animals.

6

Argument

Argument, in a sense, underlies all writing. In expressing your ideas, no matter what method or combination of methods you use, you are "arguing" some point about your subject. In Chapter 5, for example, each of Jane's writing ventures attempts to demonstrate a certain thesis: whales can be understood best when seen at sea; whales may seem threatening but are really gentle; whale watching has helped increase public support for whale preservation. Jane uses these informal arguments to advance her primary purpose—explaining her impressions of a whale watch.

Formal arguments, too, commonly employ expository patterns to convey information. But because their primary purpose is to convince others—to accept a proposal, to challenge a situation, to support some cause—formal arguments must be developed according to rules of evidence and logical reasoning. These demands may seem formidable, but in many ways they are simply extensions of what you have learned about those elements that govern the writing process.

You begin composing an argument by planning, by investigating a variety of sources so that you can discover a subject. Next, you organize your argument into a draft so that it most effectively and fully expresses your subject to persuade your audience. Finally, you examine your text to revise those features that obscure the clarity or weaken the credibility of your purpose.

As you move through these stages, you will expand your appreciation of other arguments (particularly those of the opposition), develop your authority to present those features of your argument that matter most, and increase your understanding of those aspects of your argument or your opponent's argument that might be negotiated or that might never be resolved.

INVESTIGATING THE ARGUMENT:
Planning

In planning an argument, you *select a subject, collect and use evidence,* and *consider the opposition.*

153

Selecting a Subject

Not every subject can be treated in a formal argument. Common sense tells you that there is no point in arguing about *facts*. You may like to argue about when the Red Sox last won the World Series or how many times Katharine Hepburn has won an Oscar, but such trivial disputes can be settled quickly by looking up the correct answer in an almanac. You may like to argue that chocolate chocolate chip is the best flavor of ice cream in the world or that all politicians are corrupt—but these assertions are merely *opinions,* based on preference (or prejudice) rather than evidence.

A formal argument must focus on a subject that can be debated. Such subjects are open to interpretation because opposing opinions can be supported with evidence and the audience is free to consider both claims and to choose sides.

As you think about possible subjects for an argument, review "Guidelines for Selecting Your Subject" in Chapter 1 (page 12). Your subject should be one you know something about, consider interesting and significant, and can restrict to a manageable size. When you develop your subject into an argument, you will need to view it as a controversy with at least two contending sides. What you know about a subject (or what you can find out about it) will lead you to take a side. But to convince your readers that yours is the right side (or at least the better side), you will need to support your position.

Exercise Matt is an older student who, after working for several years in a factory, has returned to college to study pre-law. In his business law course, he is asked to write an argument about a controversy in the work place. Read his list of potential subjects and identify those that are (a) facts, (b) opinions, or (c) open to debate. Explain your choices.

1. Unions have ruined free enterprise in America.
2. Random drug testing is an invasion of privacy.
3. Health care for alcoholics and their families are double the costs for nonalcoholics and their families.
4. Workers on the day shift are more conscientious than those on the night shift.
5. Less than 10 percent of the upper management of America's major corporations belongs to a minority group.

Collecting and Using Evidence

Once you have selected a subject, start gathering evidence. You might begin by making lists or freewriting in your journal. Such activities help you identify what you already know (or think you know) about your subject, but eventually you will need to expand and deepen your knowledge by conducting some research. Anna Quindlen, a columnist for the *New York Times*, suggests that an effective investigation requires several planning strategies:

> I begin by reading, reading, reading. I have to understand my subject before I interview people, otherwise I won't understand the terms they use or the issues they raise. Also, I have to understand where they're coming from. You need to watch out for those red flags, those people on one side of an argument who distort issues by making highly inflammatory statements. Sometimes you can catch their bias when you ask other people to comment on their remarks. So much of reporting is bouncing from one person to another, trying to get all sides of the story. You never get it all. You simply run out of time. (Personal interview)

Whatever planning strategy you use, follow Quindlen's advice and collect information from all sides of your subject, not just your side. The most common kinds of evidence are *facts, judgments,* and *testimony.*

Facts   Facts are a valuable ally in building an argument because they cannot be debated. It is a fact that the stock market crashed on October 29, 1929. It is a fact that the Dow Jones Industrial Average first exceeded 3000 on April 17, 1991. But not all facts are are so clear cut, and some statements that look like facts may not be facts. A stock analyst who announces a company's projected earnings for the next five years is making an estimate, not a statement of fact.

Judgments   Judgments are conclusions inferred from facts. Unlike opinions, judgments lend credibility to an argument because they result from careful reasoning. A doctor considering a patient's symptoms reaches a tentative diagnosis of either tuberculosis or tumor. If a laboratory test eliminates tuberculosis, then the patient probably has a tumor that is either malignant or benign, questions that can be settled by surgery. The doctor's judgment emerges from the following chain of reasoning:

1. *The patient's symptoms are caused by tuberculosis or a tumor.*
   This diagnosis is based on knowledge of the symptoms of or facts about the two conditions.
2. *The patient does not have tuberculosis.*
   This is a judgment based on the results of a laboratory test that produces certain factual information.
3. *The patient has a tumor.*
   This judgment is inferred from the facts of statements 1 and 2.
4. *The patient does not have cancer.*
   This judgment is determined after surgery, which reveals the fact that the tumor is benign.

Testimony   Testimony affirms or asserts facts. A person who has had direct experience (an *eyewitness*) or who has developed expertise in a subject (an *expert witness*) can provide testimony based on fact, judgment, or both. An eyewitness is asked to report facts, as when an observer reports seeing a man drown in strong current. An expert witness is asked to study facts and render a judgment, as when a coroner reports that an autopsy has shown that the victim did not drown but died of a heart attack.

Both kinds of testimony can constitute powerful evidence. Eyewitness testimony provides authenticity. Expert testimony provides authority. Each has its limitations, however. An eyewitness is not always trustworthy; eyewitness testimony can be distorted by faulty observation or biased opinion. An expert witness is not infallible or always unbiased; expert testimony, though often difficult for the nonexpert to challenge, can be disputed by other experts employing a different method of investigation. Each type of testimony can be abused. An eyewitness account of an event may be convincing, but it should not be used to draw parallels to unrelated events. And expert credentials in one field, whatever eminence they convey, do not automatically carry over to other (even related) fields.

Using the Evidence   Evaluate your evidence by determining whether it is *pertinent, verifiable,* and *reliable.* A stock analyst who uses the success of the polio vaccine as a reason for investing in a drug company researching a vaccine for the common cold is not presenting evidence *pertinent* to the argument. A historian who claims that Amelia Earhart's flying ability was impaired by Alzheimer's disease is using an argument that is not *verifiable.* And an attorney who builds a case on the eyewitness testimony of a person who has been arrested several times for public intoxication is not using the most *reliable* evidence (see "Evaluating Sources," Chapter 13).

As you collect your evidence, be careful to identify and record its source. Your readers will want to know where you found the information important to your argument. If you cannot identify your source, your reader may question your knowledgeability. If your information comes from dubious sources, your readers may doubt your credibility. Identify information from printed and other sources in the text of your paper (see "Documenting Sources," Chapter 14).

———— *Exercise*   Matt has decided to write about drug testing in the work place. During his last year at the factory, the subject became a hot issue in contract negotiations: management proposed random drug testing on the job; the union opposed all forms of drug testing. As he investigated the subject, Matt gathered evidence from many sources. Examine these items from his notes to determine for each: (1) whether it is a fact, a judgment, or eyewitness or expert testimony, and (2) whether it is likely to be *pertinent, verifiable,* and *reliable* evidence.

1. "According to the Research Triangle Institute, a respected North Carolina business-sponsored research organization, drug abuse cost the United States economy $60 billion in 1983, or nearly 30% more than the $47 billion estimated for 1980."

Castro, Janice. "Battling the Enemy Within." *Time* 17 March 1986: 53.

2. "Right now, if the foreman doesn't like somebody, he can ask him to take a drug test—claiming probable cause. That makes the guy look suspicious. Even though Fred's test came back clean, everybody said, 'Well, there must be something in it.' That's not fair."
Factory worker, personal interview, 10 November 1986.

3. "Employers have always had rules to govern the work place. You can't be late or absent without just cause. There are some capital offenses that are just cause for firing. You can't be intoxicated on the job. Your work is impaired, you jeopardize your co-workers, and you destroy the reliability of the company's product. Testing for drug abuse is just another way to ensure safety in the work place."
Chief counsel at local factory. Personal interview. 15 Nov. 1986.

4. The Centers for Disease Control reports that in the thirteen laboratories they studied, there was "up to 67% error rate in false positive identification of drugs."
Hansen, Hugh J. "Crisis in Drug Testing." *Journal of American Medical Association* April 1985: 2382.

5. "An estimated 45% of the Fortune 500 corporations will be involved in drug testing next year."
Chapman, Fern Schumer. "The Ruckus Over Medical Testing." *Fortune* 19 August 1985: 58.

6. "Drug abuse is hard to detect. There's no odor. People seem to act normally. Management wants to use this urine test as a cheap way to see if they have a problem. What if they do? Are they going to invest in a rehabilitation program or just fire people?"
Local union leader. Personal interview. 12 November 1986.

7. "It costs over $10,000 to hire and train even an entry level employee. For the average employee this cost exceeds $25,000. Before I terminate an employee for drug abuse I need to be confident that he or she is really a drug abuser. I can't afford to fire a productive employee on the basis of a test that isn't much better than flipping a coin."
Maltby, Lewis L. "An Employer's Perspective." *The Drug Testing Debate: Remedy or Reaction.* Washington, D.C.: American Civil Liberties Union, 1986. 4.

Considering the Opposition

If you have selected a debatable subject and collected a broad range of evidence, you have discovered that controversies are tricky. You may remain convinced that your side is the right side; you may be tempted, given your discovery of new information, to change sides; or you may feel confused as you try to balance the evidence on both sides of the debate. To complete your investigation and test your original position (or to write your way out of your current confusion), you must give serious consideration to the opposition.

Assume the identity of your opposition and draft an argument entitled "Their Side." This planning exercise will enable you to understand the important evidence that makes your opponents' position credible—evidence that you may have to concede when you present your side of the argument. The exercise will also help you uncover the weak spots in their argument—points that you will have to disguise when you write "Their Side," but points that you can dispute when you write "My Side." And finally, this exercise will encourage you to identify the points, often overlooked in the heat of argument, on which both sides agree.

If you are going to compose an effective "Their Side," you have to be *knowledgeable* and *fair*. You must present your opponents' best arguments in such a way that they will recognize it as a thorough and accurate statement of their position. If you set up a "straw man," presenting your opponents' weakest evidence in the most unfavorable light with the intention of knocking it down, the exercise will not be useful to you. Knowledge of your opponents' best argument and a sincere effort to avoid bias will help you avoid an unfair, unproductive effort. Common signs of such unfairness are *distortion, slanting,* and *quoting out of context.*

Distortion   You distort your evidence if you intentionally exaggerate your opponents' views. Councilwoman Jones supports Planned Parenthood because the agency provides valuable information on birth control. Councilman Smith distorts his opponent's position by claiming that support for Planned Parenthood is an endorsement of an extreme form of birth control such as abortion.

Slanting   If you select facts favorable to your position and suppress those unfavorable to it, you are slanting the evidence. A business executive who says there can be no real poverty in a country where the average annual income is $10,000 ignores two facts: (1) the average includes incomes of $1 million or more, and (2) a great many incomes fall far below the average.

Quoting Out of Context   If you remove words deliberately (or carelessly) from their original context and reuse them in a new context that changes their meaning, you are quoting out of context. In reviewing a play, a critic writes: "The plot is fascinating in a strange way: you keep waiting for something to happen, but nothing does. The characters never come close to greatness, and the few witty lines are out of place among the predictable dialogue." An advertisement based on this review quotes out of context if it reads: "Fascinating plot . . . characters close to greatness . . . witty lines."

_____ *Exercise*   When Matt began his investigation, he was opposed to drug testing in the work place. As a former factory worker, he resisted management's inclination to establish arbitrary rules to control employees. As a pre-law student, he was sensitive to policies that disregarded the rights of the individual. But as he collected more research on drug testing, he tried to assess the power of the opposition by composing a "Their Side" exercise. Discuss whether *those in favor of drug testing* would see Matt's presentation of their position as knowledgeable and fair: (1) What types of evidence does he present? (2) Does this evidence seem to be the best evidence—most *pertinent, verifiable, reliable*? (3) In what sections of the essay might Matt be accused of misrepresenting the opposing position?

Their Side

On January 4, 1987, an Amtrak train traveling north of Baltimore 1 collided with three Conrail engines, causing the worst accident in Amtrak's history. Sixteen passengers were killed, 170 were injured, and five locomotives from the two trains were destroyed. Investigators have since discovered that the crew operating the Conrail engines had been using marijuana.

The Amtrak disaster near Baltimore is not an isolated example. 2 Every day news stories report truck drivers in drug-related accidents, air-traffic controllers impaired on the job by drug abuse, and assembly-line workers selling and using drugs in the work place. Dr. Howard Franbrel, medical director at Rockwell, estimates that "20% to 25% of the workers at the plant responsible for the final assembly of the space shuttle were high on drugs, alcohol or both" (Castro 53). The Research Triangle Institute in North Carolina reports that "drug abuse cost the United States economy $60 billion in 1983, or nearly 30% more than the $47 billion estimated for 1980" (Castro 53).

Employers have an obligation to protect the safety of workers, the 3 efficiency of the work place, and the reliability of their products. Workers on drugs are less productive, more likely to harm themselves or their co-workers, and more likely to steal from their company. Because they are more susceptible to illness, they drive up the premiums of health insurance. And because their errors create flawed products or unreliable services, they increase the probability of lawsuits and the cost of liability insurance.

Fortunately there is a solution to this growing problem: drug test- 4
ing. Drug testing, particularly urine analysis, is now being used by a
large number of corporations to protect the safety of their employees
and the investment of their stockholders. An estimated 45% of Fortune
500 companies will be involved in drug testing by next year (Chapman
57).

There are three basic methods of drug testing currently in use: 5
pre-screening, probable cause testing, and random/massive testing. Most
employers require a physical examination for all job applicants. The additional cost of a pre-employment urine analysis is minimal and well
worth the expense since employers can thus identify drug users before
they are hired, trained, and become a problem.

The probable cause method is used when a worker's performance   6
provides sufficient reason to justify a test. Drug abuse is more difficult
to detect than alcohol abuse: there is no obvious smell, slurred speech,
or red eyes. But there are signs of possible drug abuse: excessive absenteeism, inconsistent work performance, deterioration of personal appearance, severe financial problems, and increased trips to the rest room.

In random or massive testing any part or all of the work force is   7
tested to spot abusers. This is the most costly and controversial of the
three methods. Weekly or monthly testing of an entire work force is an
enormous investment, but given the pervasiveness of drugs in our society such an investment may prevent a costly accident. There are those
who argue that without probable cause, such testing is an invasion of
workers' privacy. But if workers are drug free, then requiring such a
test is no more an invasion of privacy than requiring protective masks
or helmets. If workers are users, then they need to be placed in a rehabilitation program before they endanger themselves or their co-workers.

Employers are in business to make money. To do so, they need a   8
dependable work force. In 1982, an Illinois Central Gulf freight train
carrying hazardous chemicals derailed at Livingston, Louisiana, because
the engineer, affected by drugs, had fallen asleep. In 1984, a spectacular
rear-end collision of two trains near Newcastle, Wyoming, occurred
while six of the twelve crew members were using drugs. In July 1984,
two Amtrak trains collided in Queens, killing one and injuring 125;
traces of marijuana and cocaine were later found in the urine of the
track signal-operator. To prevent disasters like these and the one near

Baltimore, American industry must adopt a more aggressive drug-testing program.

ORGANIZING THE ARGUMENT: *Drafting*

Once you have completed your preliminary investigation, you need to develop, organize, and draft your argument, following the procedures you learned in Chapters 3, 4, and 5. Anna Quindlen points out that organizing an effective argument is terribly important and terribly difficult:

> Structure is a slippery subject. I usually like to lead with an anecdote, particularly if I can use a quote that works like a punch in the stomach. Also, up front, in what I call my *nut paragraph,* I like to spell out the issues I've discovered. "Where are we going? Where have we been? Have we gone too far?" Then I'll get into an "on the one hand, on the other hand" pattern where I present the sides in the debate. But in a true controversy, the debate is taking place on so many levels—emotional, ethical, social—that I can't choose sides. I switch back and forth and usually wind up somewhere in the middle. (Personal interview)

The final shape of an argument depends, as Quindlen suggests, on a series of interrelated decisions. To make *informed* decisions, you need to *analyze the audience, arrange the evidence,* and *monitor the appeals.*

Analyzing the Audience

In the preceding chapters you have learned that knowing your audience helps you discover and demonstrate your purpose. This is particularly true in argument because you are attempting to convince your audience to believe in your purpose. To do this, you must assess what potential audiences are likely to know about your subject, what they believe is important in the controversy, and what kind of evidence will influence their judgment.

As Quindlen points out, arguments take place in a context that contains "many levels—emotional, ethical, social." To help you clarify this context and to sort out how your readers might be affected by it, use the advice below in conjunction with "Guidelines for Analyzing Your Audience" in Chapter 1 (page 15).

Identify Specific Readers You need to identify the specific groups of readers who form the potential audience for your argument. Some may seem in the thick of things—friendly or hostile to your position. Others may seem on the edge—skeptical about any proposal or merely uncommitted. Unfortunately, the sides in controversies are rarely that clear cut, and your potential audience usually contains many people with uncertain or conflicting views. Identify these specific groups of potential readers for your argument. Then acknowledge their conflicting opinions and anticipate their various objections to your draft.

Identify With Your Readers   The "Their Side" exercise helped you see the debate from the perspective of your opponent. Now, as you identify other readers who have only partial or passing interest in the controversy, place yourself in those positions and assess the issues from those viewpoints. Who are the "friendlies"? What do they know? Who are the skeptics? What makes them resist? Who are the uncommitted? What will make them decide? Such imaginative identification helps you establish the points of conflict and areas of agreement among the various readers in your audience.

Establish Your Identity for Your Readers   In drafting your argument, you inevitably establish an identity (or a *persona*) that reveals to your readers your attitude toward your subject. You should be alert to strategies that strengthen your bond with your readers and avoid tactics that distance you from them. As the "Their Side" exercise helped demonstrate, the most effective arguments consider all sides of a controversy. In arguing, your identity should be that of a "reasonable citizen" who follows a balanced discussion with a thoughtfully rendered judgment. You must consider your readers, too, to be reasonable citizens. However indignant you are about the situation you are writing about, you cannot be indignant with your readers—not if you want their agreement. You can concede or refute certain points, but you cannot flatter or talk down to your readers, or neglect to provide logical proof of your argument—not if you want their respect. You are trying to establish a partnership of mutual inquiry. Anything that distorts your identity in that partnership will destroy your credibility.

Provide Your Readers With Appropriate Evidence   If you respect your readers, you will not ask them to accept unsupported assertions. A business executive would not ask her partners to accept her unsupported word that investing in another company will be profitable. She would provide detailed evidence for their review and would address the particular concerns (management, labor, debt, productivity, competition) of individual partners with appropriate evidence. She may believe the investment is sound, but if she wants to convince her partners, she must supply the right kind of evidence. As a writer of argument, you have an obligation to spell out in detail why you think your readers should accept your conclusion. And you must provide the specific kinds of evidence your readers will find compelling.

Draft an Argument Your Readers Can Read   You are asking your readers to agree with you, so make their job as easy as possible. Highly complex arguments, technical terminology, abstract diction, confusing statistics—all these obstructive elements make communication difficult. You want to convince your readers that you are knowledgeable, but you do not want to clutter your argument with arcane or unnecessary information that confuses and annoys them. Anticipate your readers' needs and try to fulfill them to achieve the response you seek.

_____*Exercise*   As Matt thinks about drafting his argument about drug testing in the work place, he identifies the following specific readers as potential members of his audience. Examine his list. Has he overlooked any group that has a stake in the controversy? Identify readers who might belong to more than one group. Then discuss how each group of readers might see the issue.

Employer	Health insurance claims agent
Worker (drug free)	Potential employer
Worker (abuser)	Stockholder
Drug rehabilitation counselor	Liability insurance executive
Medical laboratory analyst	American Civil Liberties Union
Union negotiator	representative
Company attorney	Consumer
Competitors (Other Employers)	

Arranging the Evidence

Because every controversy creates its own problems and possibilities, no one method of arrangement will always work best. Sometimes you may even have to combine methods to make your case. To make an informed decision, you need to consider how you might adapt your evidence to the three common methods of arrangement: *induction, deduction,* and *accommodation.*

Induction   Often called the scientific method, induction begins by presenting specific evidence and then moves to a general conclusion. This arrangement reflects the history of your investigation. You began your research with a hypothesis about what you wanted to find out and where you needed to look. You collected a cross section of examples until a pattern emerged. At this point, you made what scientists call an "inductive leap": you determined that although you had not collected every example, you had examined enough examples to risk proposing a probable conclusion.

To incorporate this arrangement into a draft, begin by posing the question that prompted your research:

Question   Why is our company losing so many valuable computer operators to other companies?

Then arrange your individual pieces of evidence in such a way that they help your readers see the pattern you discovered. You need not list all the false leads or blind alleys you encountered along the way, unless they changed your perspective or confirmed your judgment.

Evidence

1. Most computer operators are women who have preschool children. (Provide examples.)

2. A nearby day-care center used by employees has closed because it lost federal funding. (Provide examples.)

3. Other day-care centers in the area are inconvenient and under-staffed. (Provide examples.)

4. Other companies provide on-site day care for children of employees. (Provide examples.)

5. On-site day care is beneficial to the emotional well-being of both preschool children and their mothers, because of the possibility of contact during the workday.

Conclusion

Finally, present the conclusion that seems warranted by the evidence you have presented.

Therefore, our company needs to provide on-site day care to retain valuable employees.

Deduction   Usually identified with classical reasoning, deduction begins with a general statement or *major premise* that, when restricted by a *minor premise,* leads to a specific conclusion. Unlike induction, which in theory makes an assertion only in its conclusion, deduction does make initial assertions (based on evidence) from which a conclusion is derived.

To use this organization in your draft, consider the pattern of this three-step syllogism.

Major Premise

Retention of computer operators who have preschool children is promoted by on-site day care.

Minor Premise

Our company wants to retain computer operators who have preschool children.

Conclusion

Our company should establish on-site day-care centers.

To gain your audience's acceptance of your major and minor premises, you must support each assertion with specific evidence. Demonstrate that retaining computer operators who have preschool children is promoted by on-site day-care centers and that "our company" wants to retain computer operators who have preschool children. If your readers then accept your premises, they are logically committed to accept your conclusion.

Accommodation   Sometimes called "nonthreatening argument," accommodation arranges evidence so that all parties believe their position has received a fair hearing. <u>Induction reveals how a chain of evidence leads to a conclusion</u>. <u>Deduction demonstrates why certain premises demand a single conclusion</u>. Although both procedures work effectively in specific situations, they occasionally defeat your purpose. Readers may feel trapped by the relentless march of your argument; though unable to refute your logic, they are still unwilling to listen to reason. <u>Accommodation takes your audience's hesitations into account. Instead of trying to win the argument, you try to improve communication and increase understanding</u>.

To employ this strategy, begin by composing an objective description of the controversy: women computer operators who have preschool children are leaving the company. Then draft a complete and accurate statement of the contending positions, supplying the evidence that makes each position credible.

Corporation board   We need a qualified work force, but we are not in business to provide social services. (Provide evidence.)

Fellow workers (Single, male, etc.)   We understand their problem, but providing an on-site day-care center is giving expensive, preferential treatment to a small segment of the work force. (Provide evidence.)

Competitors   We need better computer operators if we are going to compete, and we will provide what is necessary to hire them. (Provide evidence.)

Next, show where and why you and the various parties agree: the corporation should not be in the day-care business; providing a center is preferential treatment; women computer operators have the right to market their skills in a competitive market. Then present your own opinion, explaining where it differs from other positions and why it deserves serious consideration: we have invested a large amount of money in training our work force; child care is an appropriate investment in view of the long-term contribution these people will provide for the corporation. Finally, present a proposal that might resolve the issue in a way that recognizes the interests of all concerned: suggest that the corporation help fund the nearby day-care center that was previously supported by government money.

Exercise   Matt decides to make a scratch outline to organize his evidence *against* drug testing. What method of arrangement does he use? What sections of his outline suggest the potential for combining several methods?

Drug Testing in the Work Place

I. Drug testing is unreliable
   Cheap screening tests

           Lab error—"sink tests" (dumping samples)
           "Black market" for urine samples
           "Chain of custody" for urine samples
           Cross reactivity—false positives from other chemicals
           Expensive confirmatory tests

II. Drug testing is counterproductive
           Decline in workers' morale
           Potential for discrimination
           Constant surveillance—time consuming
           Worker paranoia—worry about behavior, possibility of false
              positives
           Supervisors play cop—loss of rapport, cooperation with workers
           Status of productive but rehabilitated worker?
           Class bias—rehabilitate executive; fire janitor

III. Drug testing is an invasion of employees' privacy
           Presumption of guilt
           Humiliating test—objective observer
           Confidentiality of test results—liability?
           Control lifestyle outside work place
           Dangerous precedent—genetic testing for future health risks (long-
              term illness, insurance premiums)

Monitoring the Appeals

In organizing your draft, you must keep track of how you are using the three basic appeals of argument: the *emotional* appeal, the *ethical* appeal, and the *logical* appeal. These three appeals are rarely fully separate; they all weave in and out of virtually every argument. But to control their effects to your advantage, you must know when and why you are using them.

The Emotional Appeal   Readers feel as well as think, and to be thoroughly convinced they must be emotionally as well as intellectually engaged by your argument. Some people think that the emotional appeal is suspect; because it relies on the feelings, instincts, and opinions of readers, they link it to the devious manipulations of advertising or politics. The emotional appeal is often used to stampede an audience into thoughtless action, but such abuses do not negate its value. The emotional appeal should never replace more rational appeals, but it can be an effective strategy for convincing your readers that they need to pay attention to your arguments.

    The greatest strength of the emotional appeal is also its greatest weakness. Dramatic examples, presented in concrete images and connotative language, personalize a problem and produce powerful emotions. Some examples produce predictable emotions: an abandoned puppy or a lonely old woman evokes pity; a senseless accident or recurring incompetence evokes anger; a smiling family or a heroic deed evokes delight. Some examples, however, produce unpredictable results, and their dramatic presentation often works against your purpose. It would be difficult to predict, for instance, how all your readers would respond to a working mother's fears for and guilt about her preschool child in day care. Some might pity her, others might disdain her inability to solve her problems. Because controversial issues attract a range of passions, use the emotional appeal with care.

The Ethical Appeal   The character (or *ethos*) of the writer, not the writer's morality, is the basis of the ethical appeal. It suggests that the writer is someone to be trusted, a claim that emerges from a demonstration of competence as an authority on the subject under discussion. Readers trust

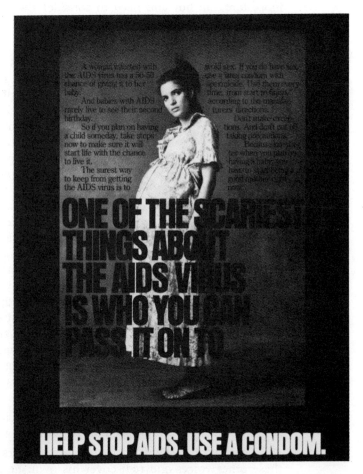

Question: How do text and image in this public service message make use of various appeals?

a writer such as Anna Quindlen and are inclined to agree with her arguments because she has established a reputation for informed, reasonable, and reliable writing about controversial subjects.

You can incorporate the ethical appeal into your argument either by citing authorities, such as Quindlen, who have conducted thorough investigations of your subject, or by following the example of authorities in your competent treatment of evidence. There are two potential dangers with the ethical appeal. First, you cannot win the trust of your readers by citing as an authority in one field someone who is an authority in another. Lee Iacocca is an established authority on building cars, but he should not be cited as an authority on nuclear disarmament. And second, you cannot convince your readers that you are knowledgeable if you present your argument exclusively in personal terms. Your own experience in trying to find reliable, convenient day-care services may make your argument for providing on-site day care more forceful, but you need to consider the experience of other people to establish your ethical appeal.

The Logical Appeal   The rational methods used to develop an argument constitute a logical appeal. Some people think that the forceful use of logic, like the precise use of facts, makes an argument absolutely true. But controversies contain many truths, no one of which can be graded simply true or false. By using the logical appeal, you acknowledge that arguments are conducted in a world of probability, not certainty; by offering a series of reasonable observations and conclusions, you establish the most reliable case.

The logical appeal is widely used and accepted in argument. Establishing the relationships that bind your evidence to your proposition engages your readers' reasoning power, and an appeal to their intelligence and common sense is likely to win their assent. But the logical appeal is not infallible. Its limit is in acknowledging limits: How much evidence is enough? There is no simple answer to this question. The amount of evidence required to convince fellow workers that your company should provide on-site day care may not be sufficient to persuade the company's board of directors. On the other hand, too much evidence, however methodically analyzed, may win the argument but lose your audience. Without emotional or ethical appeal, your "reasonable" presentation may be put aside in favor of more urgent issues. Accurate and cogent reasoning is the basis for any sound argument, but the logical appeal, like the emotional and ethical appeals, must be monitored carefully during drafting to make sure it is accomplishing your purpose.

_____*Exercise*   In his ongoing investigation of drug testing in the work place, Matt has collected a great deal of evidence, considered the position of his opponents, and analyzed the claims of his various readers. Now he wants to turn off these other voices and rediscover his own: he is ready to write "My Side" of the argument. As you read his discovery draft, identify the various appeals he has used to accomplish his purpose. Note the places that were probably strengthened by his decision to write "Their Side" first. Finally, point to the sections that would have been weaker had he written "My Side" first.

My Side

The increased public awareness of drug abuse in our society has 1 created a sense of public alarm about the potential dangers of drug abuse in the work place. Although such concern is justifiable, particularly when it affects the safety of workers and consumers, most companies are trying to solve this complex problem with a simple urine test. Whether it is used to weed out job applicants or identify suspected abusers on the job, urine testing is a misguided attempt to find a quick fix. The test is not only unreliable and counterproductive, it is a serious invasion of workers' privacy.

The biggest argument for urine testing is that it is a cheap and 2 efficient way to spot abusers. It is certainly cheap. Many test kits cost less than ten dollars. But they are hardly reliable. In order to perform an effective drug test, urine samples must be taken according to strict procedures, to guarantee the right kind of sample and to protect against sample switching from the rapidly developing "black market" for clean urine. When the test is taken at the job site, this "chain of custody" is often broken, increasing the opportunity for error and fraud.

The laboratories that analyze these samples are also suspect. 3 Many of them have been set up to make a fast buck off the high demand for drug testing. The Center for Disease Control discovered that in the thirteen laboratories they studied, there was "up to 67% error rate in false positive identification of drugs" (Hansen 2382). Some of these labs reported false negatives 100% of the time when they tested for certain drugs. Dr. Joe Boone, chief of CDC's clinical chemistry and toxicology section, reports that "if these labs would have dumped the samples down the sink and tossed a coin, they would have come up with the same reliability in their test results" (Chapman 57).

To even approach reliability, an initial urine screening needs to be 4 checked by a second, more expensive "confirmatory test." This test attempts to offset the problem of "cross-reactivity." According to David Greenblatt, chief of clinical pharmacy at Tufts New England Medical Center, "many chemicals in the body, such as caffeine, cough syrup, or antiasthmatic medication can throw off findings" (Chapman 59). Employers who do not invest in a confirmatory testing procedure will never know whether job applicants or employees who tested positive were abusing drugs or following doctor's orders.

Questions about the reliability of drug testing contribute to a decline in workers' morale. Rather than ensuring productivity, urine testing has created a climate of paranoia. Workers distrust the motives of their employers and worry about the potential for discrimination. If they become too emotional, make too many trips to the rest room, or behave in any way that is viewed as suspicious, they could be asked to take a urine test. Even if the results are negative, they are "on record" as former suspects. Supervisors, who should focus their attention on workers' productivity, are not responsible for worker surveillance. They may know little about the symptoms of drug abuse, but they are expected to look for telltale signs. By playing super-cop, they destroy their rapport with their workers.

A more serious threat to workers' morale emerges from the debate about the purpose of drug testing. Does the company want to pacify its stockholders, protect its workers, or identify abusers? More to the point, what is the fate of those who are identified as abusers? Are they replaced or rehabilitated? If the latter, who pays for the rehabilitation? Workers' morale is certainly not bolstered by rumors that executives are counseled in rehabilitation programs paid for by company insurance, whereas workers are quickly fired.

The most significant objection to urine testing, particularly random/massive testing, is that it is an invasion of workers' privacy. The test may seem simple enough, like other tests in a routine physical, but the legal and ethical consequences are hardly routine. First, the institution of the test raises serious concerns regarding an employer's right to control an employee's activities off duty. Second, the test presumes the guilt of all workers until the "results" establish their innocence. Third, these highly debatable results may ruin the career of a valuable employee who has no way to appeal a decision or reform his or her behavior. And finally, such testing sets a dangerous precedent. There is already significant corporate support for genetic testing—a test that determines an employee's predisposition toward such "costly" diseases as diabetes and cancer (Chapman 60).

There is reason for the public to be alarmed about drug abuse in   8
the work place, but the evidence on urine testing suggests that the public should be equally alarmed about the abuse of drug testing in the
work place.

ELIMINATING FALLACIES: *Revising*

Once you have organized your argument, reexamine your draft to see if it
accomplishes your purpose. Revision, as you learned in Chapter 4, can mean
global revision—the rethinking, reordering, and rewriting of your text—or
local revision often necessitated by a small problem: a faulty thesis, an undeveloped paragraph, or an unclear sentence. In argument, many local problems are the result of errors in reasoning, known as *fallacies*. Some fallacies
are unintentional, created in the haste of composition. Others are intentional, created to deceive readers. In either case, they oversimplify or distort
evidence, thus making an argument unreliable. Read the following list as a
guide to finding and eliminating fallacies from your writing during revision,
or to detecting them in the writing of others.

- *Faulty analogy* attempts to argue that because two things are alike in
  some ways they are alike in all ways. Attending school may be analogous
  to working at a factory in that both require long hours to complete
  specific tasks for a supervisor. School work and factory work are not
  the same, however. An analogy can be useful in helping your readers
  understand how something complex or unknown is similar to something
  simple and familiar, but such illustrations should not be confused with
  proof. Arguments by analogy are particularly suspect when an insignificant resemblance is proposed as evidence for a more relevant (but unsup-
  portable) comparison.

- *Hasty generalizations* are conclusions drawn from inadequate or atypical
  evidence. Suppose there are twelve women and ten men in your section
  of business law. On the final exam, the four highest scores were made
  by men and the four lowest scores by women. On the basis of this
  evidence, you conclude that women are unqualified for business law.
  There is no justification for that generalization because twelve women
  in one section are not typical of all women, and twelve is hardly an
  adequate sample to justify such a sweeping conclusion. To avoid hasty
  generalizations, make sure you provide sufficient and appropriate evidence to support your conclusions.

- *Post hoc, ergo propter hoc* (Latin for "after this, therefore because of
  this") asserts that one event caused another because it preceded it. Low-
  ering the drinking age in your state should not be claimed as the direct
  cause of the increased crime rate. The first event may have contributed
  in some way to the other, but the two events may be merely coincidental.

Because direct cause and effect relationships are difficult to establish, do not overstate your claims for events that may have many plausible explanations.

▼ *Begging the question* occurs when part of what has to be proved is assumed to be true. When a lawyer seeks to use as evidence the results of a polygraph test because such tests verify the truth, he begs this question: Are polygraph tests reliable? Sometimes begging the question can produce a *circular argument* that restates in different words what you are trying to prove: "Polygraph tests do not provide reliable evidence because their results cannot be trusted." As you revise, check each of your claims to make sure you advance your argument with evidence; do not assume a claim is credible because you have used "new and improved" language.

▼ *Either-or* states a position in such categorical terms—either *A* or *B*—that it ignores (or denies) the possibility of other alternatives. An economist who argues that "the United States must either adopt a new industrial policy or face financial ruin" does not see (or prefers not to see) that there are many possible ways to solve our economic difficulties and that financial ruin does not inevitably follow from the failure to adopt one policy. If you have conducted a thorough investigation, you know that there are more than two sides to your subject.

▼ *Ad hominem* (Latin for "to the man") distorts an argument by attacking the character of the opponent to arouse the emotions or prejudices of the audience. This strategy attempts to discredit an opponent by using labels (or stereotypes) with highly unfavorable connotations: "Senator Hoover is an avowed feminist. Her antidiscrimination bill just expresses her radical political views." As you have seen, an expert witness's trustworthiness is always on trial. If Senator Hoover's opinions are not supported by evidence, then her credibility should be discounted. But as long as she presents evidence for her case, you should resist calling her names and address her argument.

▼ *Red herring* is a smoked fish that has a reddish color and strong odor. A hunter may drag a red herring across a trail to distract the hounds and trick them into following a new scent. In argument, a *red herring* is an unrelated issue introduced to divert attention from the real issue: "As long as we are discussing whether women should receive equal pay, we should also discuss whether women still want to retain preferred treatment on social occasions, as when men open doors for them and pay for their meals. It seems to me that women want equal and preferred treatment at the same time." Such diversions confuse the issue by introducing irrelevancies. Economic equality and social courtesy are two different issues.

_____*Exercises*   1. In checking through his planning notes and preliminary drafts, Matt found several assertions that looked like fallacies. In the following list, identify the probable fallacies and then discuss how they might be revised to avoid oversimplifying or distorting the evidence.

    a. Every Monday morning he shows up at work looking tired and acting moody. He must be using drugs on the weekend.

    b. We must face the problem of drug abuse with an aggressive testing program or face the possibility of a serious industrial accident.

    c. The union leadership is against drug testing. But most of those guys dress like back-alley thugs. What else would you expect from people who look like they belong on *Miami Vice*?

    d. Requiring urine tests is no more an invasion of workers' privacy than requiring protective masks or helmets.

    e. What would happen if the executive vice president was arrested for drunk driving? Executives often have drinks when they conduct business over long lunches.

    f. Several corporations have started talking about genetic testing. In a few years, all workers in the United States will be tested to see if they have a predisposition toward "costly" diseases like diabetes or cancer.

    g. Drug testing violates workers' civil rights by invading their privacy.

2. Review Matt's two drafts, "Their Side" (pages 159–161) and "My Side" (pages 169–171), examining each for fallacies. Speculate on how Matt could eliminate those fallacies to make the same point in a more reliable and effective way.

Drug Abuse in the Work Place | Matt Fisher

When Matt finished his "My Side" draft, he knew that he had only presented one side of a complex argument. Combining "Their Side" with "My Side," he composed this final draft of his argument. Compare Matt's three drafts. Which one is the most convincing? Does everyone in your writing group agree? What "emotional, ethical, social" issues influence your choice?

In the last decade drug abuse has reached epidemic proportions in our   1
country—destroying the lives of our young people, exhausting the energies of our legal system, and eroding our fundamental values. Nowhere is the problem more alarming than in the work place, where drug abuse costs the American economy in excess of $60 billion a year. All of us—employers, workers, and consumers—want to cure this plague that threatens the health of our culture. Unfortunately, there is as much controversy about the cure as there is about the disease.

Employers, rightfully concerned about the investments of their stock-   2
holders, the safety of their workers, and the credibility of their goods and services, favor various forms of urine testing to identify drug abusers. Many employers now include a urine test as part of the routine preemployment physical. Such a test allows them to spot abusers before they are hired, trained, and become problems. Other employers use urine testing when a worker's behavior suggests that drug abuse is a reasonable explanation for impaired performance. Such testing enables employers to restore the productivity of their work force and to encourage rehabilitation of abusers. Employers whose workers' tasks directly affect the safety of fellow workers or consumers, or whose workers are engaged in sensitive security positions, may employ massive or random testing to guarantee the integrity of the work place.

Workers are concerned about protecting the integrity of the work   3
place, but they are equally concerned about protecting their own integrity. The initial urine test now being administered by most employers is highly unreliable. False results (positive and negative) can be produced by careless procedures in taking the sample or by inaccurate procedures in testing the sample. In fact, the Centers for Disease Control reported that in the thirteen laboratories they studied, there was "up to 67% error rate in false positive identification[s]" (Hansen 2382). The reliability of these tests is compromised by the problem of "cross-reactivity"—chemicals in the body such as caffeine or cough syrup that can corrupt the results.

If urine testing is judged unreliable, workers are justifiably concerned   4
about the potential for discrimination. Uninformed supervisors may misread their behavior and ask for a drug test. If the results are falsely positive, they are uncertain about their right to appeal. If the results are negative, they are uncertain about their status as "former suspects." And if the re-

sults are positive, they are uncertain of their fate. Is the employer interested in replacing or rehabilitating employees?

This question is at the heart of the controversy. Putting aside the issues of efficiency, reliability, and discrimination, and the most serious issue of invasion of workers' privacy, all of us need to be clear about the purpose of drug testing. Employers need a reliable work force; workers want a safe environment; and consumers expect dependable goods and services. But is drug testing the best way to satisfy these needs and expectations?   5

Pre-employment drug screening does not guarantee that workers have never used drugs or, once employed, will not become drug abusers. It simply provides highly questionable evidence about one sample of a worker's urine. Testing for probable cause may prevent or determine the cause of some accidents, but it does not solve the larger problem of ensuring a drug-free work place. And massive or random testing of a large work force (like the testing of "suspicious workers") may identify a few abusers, but it could also discredit innocent employees. The whole procedure, rather than increasing productivity, destroys the mutual trust between employer and workers so essential to quality performance.   6

In order to solve the complex problem of drug abuse in the work place, we need more than a simple urine test. What we need is a comprehensive drug policy developed by all those concerned. Under such a policy, drug testing might still be used, but employers would make a concerted effort to establish and monitor the credentials of urinalysis laboratories. They would also spell out in detail the purpose and procedures of all drug testing. Job applicants would be told in advance that drug screening is required and informed about the results. Workers on the job would help establish the specific criteria for impairment. If they fail to meet those criteria and then fail the test, they would have the right to ask for a series of confirmatory tests. In all cases, especially those that involved massive or random testing, the employer would protect the confidentiality of test results and provide an agreed-upon counseling procedure for those who do not pass.   7

More important than mere drug testing, however, is an enlightened employee assistance program. Such a program would have as its primary goals the well-being and long-term productivity of employees. For example, employers would be more concerned about obtaining detailed references about an applicant's qualifications and work history than in collecting a urine sample. On the job, workers and supervisors would be given extensive educational programs about the causes and consequences of drug abuse. If detailed medical examinations confirm drug abuse, workers would be given sick leave and assigned to a designated drug treatment program. For those who refuse treatment or who become multiple offenders, a predetermined administrative action is justified. But for those who enter rehabilitation, the prospects are good. Companies that provide such treatment report a 70% to 75% success record (Castro 57).   8

Lewis L. Maltby, Vice President, Drexelbrook Controls, Inc., describes the kind of consensus policy that should cure drug abuse in the work place: "We can attack drug abuse with drug testing. It's quick, it's easy, and it's cheap. It just doesn't work. It gives us inaccurate and irrelevant information and undermines the trust of good employees who resent being ordered to pee in a bottle when they've done nothing wrong. Or, we can take the   9

time to learn about our employees, watch their job performance, and help
them when it starts to slip. It's time consuming, difficult, and expensive.
But it works. Not just in preventing work place drug abuse, but in creating
a committed and productive work place" (Maltby 4).

The Penalty of Death | H. L. Mencken

One of America's most prolific journalists, H. L. Mencken was never bash-
ful about taking a stand on an issue. In fact, he published six volumes of
essays, aptly titled *Prejudices* (1919–1927). In this essay, Mencken tries to
refute the two common arguments against capital punishment. How carefully does he present "Their Side" of the argument? In what ways does
Mencken use the emotional, ethical, or logical appeals? Identify specific
places where he oversimplifies or distorts evidence.

Of the arguments against capital punishment that issue from uplifters, two   1
are commonly heard most often, to wit:

1. That hanging a man (or frying him or gassing him) is a dreadful business,
   degrading to those who have to do it and revolting to those who have to
   witness it.

2. That it is useless, for it does not deter others from the same crime.

The first of these arguments, it seems to me, is plainly too weak to   2
need serious refutation. All it says, in brief, is that the work of the hangman is unpleasant. Granted. But suppose it is? It may be quite necessary to
society for all that. There are, indeed, many other jobs that are unpleasant,
and yet no one thinks of abolishing them—that of the plumber, that of the
soldier, that of the garbage-man, that of the priest hearing confessions, that
of the sand-hog, and so on. Moreover, what evidence is there that any actual hangman complains of his work? I have heard none. On the contrary,
I have known many who delighted in their ancient art, and practised it
proudly.

In the second argument of the abolitionists there is rather more force,   3
but even here, I believe, the ground under them is shaky. Their fundamental error consists in assuming that the whole aim of punishing criminals is
to deter other (potential) criminals—that we hang or electrocute A simply
in order to so alarm B that he will not kill C. This, I believe, is an assumption which confuses a part with the whole. Deterrence, obviously, is *one* of
the aims of punishment, but it is surely not the only one. On the contrary,
there are at least half a dozen, and some are probably quite as important.
At least one of them, practically considered, is *more* important. Commonly,
it is described as revenge, but revenge is really not the word for it. I borrow
a better term from the late Aristotle: *katharsis. Katharsis,* so used, means a
salubrious discharge of emotions, a healthy letting off of steam. A school-

Mencken, H. L. *A Mencken Chrestomathy.* New York: Knopf, 1954. 118–21.

boy, disliking his teacher, deposits a tack upon the pedagogical chair; the teacher jumps and the boy laughs. This is *katharsis*. What I contend is that one of the prime objects of all judicial punishments is to afford the same grateful relief (*a*) to the immediate victims of the criminal punished, and (*b*) to the general body of moral and timorous men.

These persons, and particularly the first group, are concerned only   **4**
indirectly with deterring other criminals. The thing they crave primarily is the satisfaction of seeing the criminal actually before them suffer as he made them suffer. What they want is the peace of mind that goes with the feeling that accounts are squared. Until they get that satisfaction they are in a state of emotional tension, and hence unhappy. The instant they get it they are comfortable. I do not argue that this yearning is noble; I simply argue that it is almost universal among human beings. In the face of injuries that are unimportant and can be borne without damage it may yield to higher impulses; that is to say, it may yield to what is called Christian charity. But when the injury is serious Christianity is adjourned, and even saints reach for their sidearms. It is plainly asking too much of human nature to expect it to conquer so natural an impulse. A keeps a store and has a bookkeeper, B. B steals $700, employs it in playing at dice or bingo, and is cleaned out. What is A to do? Let B go? If he does so he will be unable to sleep at night. The sense of injury, of injustice, of frustration will haunt him like pruritus. So he turns B over to the police, and they hustle B to prison. Thereafter A can sleep. More, he has pleasant dreams. He pictures B chained to the wall of a dungeon a hundred feet underground, devoured by rats and scorpions. It is so agreeable that it makes him forget his $700. He has got his *katharsis*.

The same thing precisely takes place on a larger scale when there is a   **5**
crime which destroys a whole community's sense of security. Every law-abiding citizen feels menaced and frustrated until the criminals have been struck down—until the communal capacity to get even with them, and more than even, has been dramatically demonstrated. Here, manifestly, the business of deterring others is no more than an afterthought. The main thing is to destroy the concrete scoundrels whose act has alarmed everyone, and thus made everyone unhappy. Until they are brought to book that unhappiness continues; when the law has been executed upon them there is a sigh of relief. In other words, there is *katharsis*.

I know of no public demand for the death penalty for ordinary crimes,   **6**
even for ordinary homicides. Its infliction would shock all men of normal decency of feeling. But for crimes involving the deliberate and inexcusable taking of human life, by men openly defiant of all civilized order—for such crimes it seems, to nine men out of ten, a just and proper punishment. Any lesser penalty leaves them feeling that the criminal has got the better of society—that he is free to add insult to injury by laughing. That feeling can be dissipated only by a recourse to *katharsis*, the invention of the aforesaid Aristotle. It is more effectively and economically achieved, as human nature now is, by wafting the criminal to realms of bliss.

The real objection to capital punishment doesn't lie against the actual   **7**
extermination of the condemned, but against our brutal American habit of putting it off so long. After all, every one of us must die soon or late, and a murderer, it must be assumed, is one who makes that sad fact the

cornerstone of his metaphysic. But it is one thing to die, and quite another thing to lie for long months and even years under the shadow of death. No sane man would choose such a finish. All of us, despite the Prayer Book, long for a swift and unexpected end. Unhappily, a murderer, under the irrational American system, is tortured for what, to him, must seem a whole series of eternities. For months on end he sits in prison while his lawyers carry on their idiotic buffoonery with writs, injunctions, mandamuses, and appeals. In order to get his money (or that of his friends) they have to feed him with hope. Now and then, by the imbecility of a judge or some trick of juridic science, they actually justify it. But let us say that, his money all gone, they finally throw up their hands. Their client is now ready for the rope or the chair. But he must still wait for months before it fetches him.

That wait, I believe, is horribly cruel. I have seen more than one man   8
sitting in the death-house, and I don't want to see any more. Worse, it is wholly useless. Why should he wait at all? Why not hang him the day after the last court dissipates his last hope? Why torture him as not even cannibals would torture their victims? The common answer is that he must have time to make his peace with God. But how long does that take? It may be accomplished, I believe, in two hours quite as comfortably as in two years. There are, indeed, no temporal limitations upon God. He could forgive a whole herd of murderers in a millionth of a second. More, it has been done.

Some Thoughts about Abortion | Anna Quindlen

Reread Anna Quindlen's comments on the difficulties she encounters when she tries to organize an argument on a controversial subject (page 161). Then read her essay about the emotionally charged issue of abortion. How does she present evidence for the contending positions? How does she introduce and support her own opinions? How does her accommodation of the opposing positions make a compelling argument?

It was always the look on their faces that told me first. I was the freshman   1
dormitory counselor and they were the freshmen at a women's college where everyone was smart. One of them would come into my room, a golden girl, a valedictorian, an 800 verbal score on the S.A.T.'s, and her eyes would be empty, seeing only a busted future, the devastation of her life as she knew it. She had failed biology, messed up the math; she was pregnant.

That was when I became pro-choice.   2

It was the look in his eyes that I will always remember, too. They were   3
as black as the bottom of a well, and in them for a few minutes I thought I saw myself the way I had always wished to be—clear, simple, elemental,

Quindlen, Anna. *Thinking Out Loud.* New York: Random, 1988. 209–12.

at peace. My child looked at me and I looked back at him in the delivery room, and I realized that out of a sea of infinite possibilities it had come down to this: a specific person, born on the hottest day of the year, conceived on a Christmas Eve, made by his father and me miraculously from scratch.

Once I believed that there was a little blob of formless protoplasm in there and a gynecologist went after it with a surgical instrument, and that was that. Then I got pregnant myself—eagerly, intentionally, by the right man, at the right time—and I began to doubt. My abdomen still flat, my stomach roiling with morning sickness, I felt not that I had protoplasm inside, but, instead, a complete human being in miniature to whom I could talk, sing, make promises. Neither of these views was accurate; instead, I think, the reality is something in the middle. And that is where I find myself now, in the middle—hating the idea of abortions, hating the idea of having them outlawed.   4

For I know it is the right thing in some times and places. I remember sitting in a shabby clinic far uptown with one of those freshmen, only three months after the Supreme Court had made what we were doing possible, and watching with wonder as the lovely first love she had had with a nice boy unraveled over the space of an hour as they waited for her to be called, degenerated into sniping and silences. I remember a year or two later seeing them pass on campus and not even acknowledge each other because their conjoining had caused them so much pain, and I shuddered to think of them married, with a small psyche in their unready and unwilling hands.   5

I've met fourteen-year-olds who were pregnant and said they could not have abortions because of their religion, and I see in their eyes the shadows of twenty-two-year-olds I've talked to who lost their kids to foster care because they hit them or used drugs or simply had no money for food and shelter. I read not long ago about a teenager who said she meant to have an abortion but she spent the money on clothes instead: now she has a baby who turns out to be a lot more trouble than a toy. The people who hand out those execrable little pictures of dismembered fetuses at abortion clinics seem to forget the extraordinary pain children may endure after they are born when they are unwanted, even hated, or simply tolerated.   6

I believe that in a contest between the living and the almost living, the latter must, if necessary, give way to the will of the former. That is what the fetus is to me, the almost living. These questions began to plague me—and, I've discovered, a good many other women—after I became pregnant. But they became even more acute after I had my second child, mainly because he is so different from his brother. On two random nights eighteen months apart the same two people managed to conceive, and on one occasion the tumult within turned itself into a curly-haired brunet with merry black eyes who walked and talked late and loved the whole world, and on another it became a blond with hazel Asian eyes and a pug nose who tried to conquer the world almost as soon as he entered it.   7

If we were to have an abortion next time for some reason or another, which infinite possibility becomes, not a reality, but a nullity? The girl with the blue eyes? The improbable redhead? The natural athlete? The thinker? My husband, ever at the heart of the matter, put it another way. Knowing   8 he is finding two children somewhat more overwhelming than he expected, I asked if he would want me to have an abortion if I accidentally became pregnant again right away. "And waste a perfectly good human being?" he said.

Coming to this quandary has been difficult for me. In fact, I believe the   9 issue of abortion is difficult for all thoughtful people. I don't know anyone who has had an abortion who has been casual about it. If there is one thing I find intolerable about most of the so-called right-to-lifers, it is that they try to portray abortion rights as something that feminists thought up on a slow Saturday over a light lunch. That is nonsense. I also know that some people who support abortion rights are most comfortable with a monolithic position because it seems the strongest front against the smug and some-times violent opposition.

But I don't feel all one way about abortion anymore, and I don't think   10 it serves a just cause to pretend that many of us do. For years I believed that a woman's right to choose was absolute, but now I wonder. Do I, with a stable home and marriage and sufficient stamina and money, have the freedom to choose abortion because a pregnancy is inconvenient just now? Legally I do have the right; legally I want always to have that right. It is the morality of exercising it under those circumstances that makes me wonder.

Technology has foiled us. The second trimester has become a time of   11 resurrection; a fetus at six months can be one woman's late abortion, an-other's premature, viable child. Photographers now have film of embryos the size of a grape, oddly human, flexing their fingers, sucking their thumbs. Women have amniocentisis to find out whether they are carrying a child with birth defects that they may choose to abort. Before the proce-dure, they must have a sonogram, one of those fuzzy black-and-white pho-tos like a love song heard through static on the radio, which shows some-one is in there.

I have taped on my VCR a public television program in which some-   12 how, inexplicably, a film is shown of a fetus *in utero* scratching its face, seemingly putting up a tiny hand to shield itself from the camera's eye. It would make a potent weapon in the arsenal of the antiabortionists. I grow sentimental about it as it floats in the salt water, part fish, part human be-ing. It is almost living, but not quite. It has almost turned my heart around, but not quite turned my head.

Writing Assignments

Narrate   **1.**   Select an occasion when you (or one of your fellow workers) felt as though your civil rights were abused by an employer's policy. Write a narrative about that occasion in a way that your readers will understand why the events influenced you to select "My Side" in the controversy.

Observe   **2.**   Attend a meeting of the student association, faculty senate, or town council where a controversial issue is going to be debated. In your journal, list the way proponents on each side of the issue make their case. In particular, observe the way each person's language, body language, and tone of voice evokes the emotional, ethical, or logical appeal. Then write a review for your local paper in which you describe the drama of the debaters.

Investigate   **3.**   Interview someone who has to make arguments in public for a living—a lawyer who has to make a case to jurors, a minister who has to preach to a congregation, a college president who has to address alumni groups, a professor who has to present lectures to other scholars. Ask about the special "tricks of the trade" that he or she has discovered work in difficult situations. Then write a profile about the person entitled "Speaking My Mind and Getting My Way."

Collaborate   **4.**   Your writing group has been asked to draft a "letter to the editor" about a controversial campus regulation such as library fees, preferential parking, or birth control information. An initial poll reveals that your group is undecided or perhaps even strongly divided about the issue. Discuss ways to reach *accommodation* so that you can collaborate on a text whose purpose is to increase your audience's understanding of the issue.

Read   **5.**   Read some recent articles on the issue of drug testing. You may want to read about other testing methods (hair follicles), drugs (steroids), or civil rights issues (testing athletes but not other students). Then, like Matt, draft a "Their Side," a "My Side," and an "Our Side" argument.

Respond   **6.**   Examine your emotional response to Mencken's argument for capital punishment. How do various features of his tone and language encourage you to accept or reject his argument? What personal experiences or beliefs make you more likely to agree or disagree with his position? Present your analysis in progress; that is, trace your emotional reactions as you read through each section of Mencken's essay. How did you feel when he said X? What did you think when he said Y?

Analyze   **7.**   Analyze the types of evidence that Anna Quindlen uses in her essay on "Some Thoughts about Abortion." Identify what is *fact, judgment, eyewitness,* and *expert testimony.* Then sort out the kinds of evidence that make it difficult for Quindlen to decide where she stands on the issue. As you construct your analysis, consider the problems inherent in solving difficult issues suggested by her last sentence.

Evaluate   **8.**   Evaluate each of Matt's drafts. Then write him a letter to convince him which of the three he should place in his writing portfolio for final assessment. Reread

Quindlen's advice on pages 155 and 161. Which one of Matt's essays raises "red flags" or leads with a "punch in the stomach"? Which one will Matt's teacher prefer? Which one will Matt's fellow workers prefer? Your purpose is to convince him to submit his "best" argument. Your problem is to define which of these essays is the "best" argument.

Argue   **9.**   Select an issue that is currently provoking heated discussion on the editorial page of your community newspaper but about which you have no strong opinion. Collect editorials and letters to the editor that represent the range of disagreement on the issue. Interview the local people who are involved in the controversy or who are reporting on it for the local paper. After you have completed your investigation, compose an historical analysis in which you explain how the issue became an issue.

Argue   **10.**   Write an essay for the college alumni magazine in which you argue that a current university decision is not in the spirit of your school's stated educational mission. Do your homework so that you know why the university made its decision, why the decision is in conflict with the school's educational mission. As you think through what you want to say and how you want to say it, remember that you are appealing to the best interest of the alumni, the students, the faculty, the university administration, and the specific person who made the decision you are contesting.

7 Paragraphs: Units of Development

A paragraph is a set of related sentences that express or develop a topic. A paragraph is usually part of an extended piece of writing, although in some situations you may need only one paragraph to fulfill your purpose. In narration or description, a new paragraph usually signals a shift in time, scene, or speaker. In exposition or argument, a new paragraph adds information or announces another point supporting your thesis. This chapter discusses two kinds of paragraphs: *topical paragraphs,* those that develop a topic or idea; and *special paragraphs,* those that introduce or conclude a piece of writing or provide a transition between major parts.

Paragraphs serve several purposes for you and your readers. You can use them to divide your subject into manageable units of information: by grouping ideas into paragraphs, you show the relationship of ideas to one another and their significance to your overall purpose. You can also use paragraphs to control emphasis: by placing a paragraph in a particular position, you demonstrate the relative importance of an idea in your essay. Finally, you can use paragraphs to establish rhythm: by interrupting a series of long paragraphs with a short paragraph, or creating a series of brief paragraphs, you fix and vary cadence in your writing.

Readers use your paragraphs to grasp key points and follow your reasoning. Extended, uninterrupted passages tax their attention. They expect and need to see the regularly spaced indentations that signal a new paragraph. This visual cue tells them that they have completed one topic and are about to take up another. Because the new paragraph promises new information, they refocus their attention to see how this change alters or advances your essay.

Like so many other writing procedures, making paragraphs depends on your subject, your audience, your purpose—and your own composing process. Some writers like to plan every detail of a project before they begin, assigning each subdivision of their subject to a specific paragraph. Such a procedure usually produces a blueprint for an orderly essay, but it may box the writer into a pattern that forces connections and discourages discoveries. Other writers prefer a more open-ended procedure. They know what they want to accomplish but realize that when they start writing they will discover ideas and associations that will call for paragraphs they could not have

183

anticipated. Bill Barich, a regular contributor to *The New Yorker,* admits that he prefers this more organic approach to creating paragraphs:

> When I am planning an essay or a piece of reporting, I usually have a sense of the beginning and ending, but my paragraphs tend to arrange themselves during the writing. The process is instinctive and often surprising. I have general ideas grouped together in my notes—facts and information I want to include. But I don't know where I will put them until the piece begins to unfold. Information gathers around a center and becomes a paragraph. It's a thought unit, an energy unit. When the energy runs out, I move on, establishing a rhythm that tells me how much information I can use in the next paragraph.
>
> This sounds a little disorderly, but for me a piece becomes lifeless if I know from the beginning what goes where. I am less interested in getting the information in the right place the first time through than I am in finding the rhythm that will carry the information. I like the structure to be organic, to flow naturally. Once I have finished writing, I can check for things like sequence and fullness of statement. Maybe there is something in my notes that I can insert in a phrase or use in a new paragraph. I may push myself to shorten everything, just to see what that does to the energy of the work. I'll shift, compress, and strip away extraneous material, hoping that what remains is diamond bright. (Personal interview)

Whether you chart every paragraph before you write or form paragraphs intuitively as you compose, once you have made them you must be sure, as Barich suggests, that they meet certain criteria. The following pages discuss the four characteristics of effective topical paragraphs, the primary functions of special paragraphs, and strategies for revising paragraphs.

THE REQUIREMENTS OF TOPICAL PARAGRAPHS

An effective topical paragraph must meet four requirements. First, it must discuss one topic only—that is, its statements and illustrations must display a *unity* of subject matter, often expressed in a topic sentence. Second, it must say all that your readers need to know about the topic; it must be *complete* enough to do what it is intended to do. Third, the sentences within the paragraph must exhibit an *order* that your readers can recognize and follow. Fourth, the sentences within the paragraph must display *coherence,* allowing readers to move easily from one sentence to the next without feeling that there are gaps in the sequence of your ideas.

Unity

Paragraph unity requires the considered development of the idea in your paragraph. To achieve this, each sentence must show a clear connection to

the topic. In the following paragraph, the first sentence introduces Middletown, the topic the paragraph intends to develop.

> (1) Middletown is not an actual place but an assortment of principles—
> the democratic ideal, the golden mean, the common citizen—central to
> our sense of the American experience. (2) We have located it in a middle
> landscape, somewhere between the desolation of the wilderness and the
> debauchery of the city, and we have envisioned it as a middle-sized com-
> munity, large enough to provide everything its citizens want and small
> enough to preserve everything they need. (3) Our culture contains many
> Middletowns. (4) Although their names change—Winesburg, Main Street,
> Mayberry—their image remains the same. (5) Their courthouse squares,
> tree-lined streets, and warm-hearted people represent our desire for stabil-
> ity in a century of bewildering change.

Notice that each succeeding sentence casts light on the topic; all the sentences together focus on the distinguishing characteristics of Middletown.
This close relationship among individual sentences gives the paragraph
unity.

Any sentence that digresses or drifts away from the topic blurs the
focus of the paragraph and obscures your purpose. Consider the following
paragraph.

> (1) The legend of the Old South has a certain timeless beauty. (2) On
> the veranda of stately mansions, courtly gentlemen and charming ladies
> talked quietly of family, land, and cotton. (3) Even the slaves, who
> worked the fields, were said to be content. (4) The poor whites were
> barely visible until the vigilante movement after the Civil War. (5) They
> formed secret societies such as the Klan to terrorize the black community
> and to acquire political power. (6) Political power led to economic power,
> and by the turn of the century the poor whites were no longer poor.

The first three sentences deal with the legend of the Old South, and the
reader assumes that this "timeless beauty" will be the topic of the rest of
the paragraph. In sentence 4, however, the writer shifts to poor whites, a
topic that is "barely visible" in the legend. The remaining sentences build
on the allusion to the vigilante movement and shift the focus of the paragraph
to the Klan and its use of violence to acquire political and economic power.
Most readers can follow this digression, but as they proceed past the first
few sentences they become less sure about the main topic of the paragraph
and more certain that the paragraph lacks unity.

_____*Exercise*   Read the following paragraph, checking for unity by marking shifts in focus.
Each sentence should clearly refer to the topic of Oregon as an ideal place
to live. Suggest revisions where you think they are needed.

> (1) With its seaside beaches, snowcapped mountains, and extensive for-
> ests, Oregon is an ideal place to live. (2) Its magnificent forests alone, cov-
> ering more than 30 million acres, make it a natural paradise. (3) The

National Park Service protects 17 million acres in national forests, but the rest is used for Oregon's lumber industry. (4) Loggers "harvest" trees with chain saws and then send their "crop" to the mill on trucks. (5) Many sawmills that used to employ 100 or more people are now closed because of the decline in the lumber business. (6) But loggers are not like steelworkers. (7) They don't go on relief and wait for their factory to re-open. (8) Self-reliant, eccentric, and impatient, loggers simply move to other parts of the country to look for work.

The Topic Sentence

A *topic sentence* is a statement that presents the main idea to be developed in the paragraph. It is often a single sentence, although sometimes you will need two sentences to state the topic. By beginning a paragraph with a topic sentence, you immediately tell your readers what main idea you are going to develop. In turn, they expect that the remaining sentences in your paragraph will elaborate on that idea. The following example shows how an opening topic sentence controls a paragraph.

> There is no simple formula for describing the intricate logic of the Pawnee people's lives. One thing is clear—that no one is caught within the social code. Against the backdrop of his natural environment, each individual stands as his own person. The Old World design for the human personality does not apply to this New World Man. The Pawnee child was born into a community from the beginning, and he never acquired the notion that he was closed in "within four walls." He was literally trained to feel that the world around him was his home—*kahuraru,* the universe, meaning literally the inside land, and that his house was a small model of it. The infinite cosmos was his constant source of strength and his ultimate progenitor, and there was no reason why he should hesitate to set out alone and explore the wide world, even though years should pass before he returned. Not only was he not confined within four walls but he was not closed in with a permanent group of people. The special concern of his mother did not mean that he was so closely embedded with her emotionally that he was not able to move about. (Gene Weltfish, *The Lost Universe*)

Gene Weltfish begins his paragraph with a simple declarative sentence: "There is no simple formula for describing the intricate logic of the Pawnee people's lives." His purpose is to explain the complexity of that logic, and the remaining sentences in the paragraph advance that purpose by showing how the Pawnees imagined the universe and their place in it.

Not all topical paragraphs begin with topic sentences. If you begin composing and don't discover the main point of your paragraph until you reach the end, you must decide whether to move the topic sentence to the beginning, place it somewhere else, or leave it where you found it—at the end. In most cases, you will probably want to place it at the beginning to cue your readers about the significance of the sentences to come. On a few occasions, you may want to place it in mid-paragraph, where it serves as a commentary on the sentences that come before or after it.

In the following paragraph, Richard Rodriguez uses his first sentence to make a flat statement of fact: two nuns come to visit. He uses his second sentence to explain the reason for their visit: they suggest that the family speak English more often. But he defers his actual statement of topic until the third sentence, where he confirms the significance of the preceding sentences and points a direction for the rest of the paragraph.

> I remember when, 20 years ago, two grammar-school nuns visited my childhood home. They had come to suggest—with more tact than was necessary, because my parents accepted without question the church's authority—that we make a greater effort to speak as much English around the house as possible. The nuns realized that my brothers and I led solitary lives largely because we were barely able to comprehend English in a school where we were the only Spanish-speaking students. My mother and father complied as best they could. Heroically, they gave up speaking to us in Spanish—the language that formed so much of the family's sense of intimacy in an alien world—and began to speak a broken English. Instead of Spanish sounds, I began hearing sounds that were new, harder, less friendly. More important, I was encouraged to respond in English. (Richard Rodriguez, "On Becoming a Chicano," *Saturday Review*)

Sometimes you will want readers to follow the path that led to your discovery. On such occasions, build your paragraph toward a topic sentence that provides an appropriate conclusion. Ralph Ellison uses this technique skillfully in the following paragraph.

> To live in Harlem is to dwell in the very bowels of the city; it is to pass a labyrinthine existence among streets that explode monotonously skyward with the spires and crosses of churches and clutter under foot with garbage and decay. Harlem is a ruin—many of its ordinary aspects (its crimes, its casual violence, its crumbling buildings with littered area-ways, ill-smelling halls and vermin-invaded rooms) are indistinguishable from the distorted images that appear in dreams, and which, like muggers haunting a lonely hall, quiver in the waking mind with hidden and threatening significance. Yet this is no dream but the reality of well over four hundred thousand Americans; a reality which for many defines and colors the world. Overcrowded and exploited politically and economically, Harlem is the scene and symbol of the Negro's perpetual alienation in the land of his birth. (Ralph Ellison, "Harlem Is Nowhere," *Shadow and Act*)

Not every paragraph needs a topic sentence. Sometimes your readers will be able to infer your purpose from the way you express your thoughts. On such occasions a topic sentence would be gratuitous, out of place. In the following paragraph, for example, E. B. White, one of America's master stylists, evokes a summer place without composing a formal topic sentence.

> Summertime, oh, summertime, pattern of life indelible, the fade-proof lake, the woods unshatterable, the pasture with the sweetfern and the juniper forever and ever, summer without end; this was the background, and the life along the shore was the design, the cottages with their innocent and tranquil design, their tiny docks with the flagpole and the American flag floating against the white clouds in the blue sky, the little paths over the roots of the trees leading from camp to camp and the paths leading back to the outhouses and the can of lime for sprinkling, and at the souvenir counters at the store the miniature birch-bark canoes and the postcards that showed things looking a little better than they looked.
> This was the American family at play, escaping the city heat, wondering whether the newcomers in the camp at the head of the cove were "common" or "nice," wondering whether it was true that the people who drove up for Sunday dinner at the farmhouse were turned away because there wasn't enough chicken. (E. B. White, "Once More to the Lake," *Essays of E. B. White*)

As a rule, you should reserve paragraphs without topic sentences for special occasions. When used for effect, they can be powerful and memorable, but you risk misleading your readers and yourself if you routinely decline to write topic sentences.

Remember, your readers are most disoriented and most alert at the beginning of a paragraph. They look to your first sentences for help. They expect that you will tell them how to interpret the new group of sentences they are about to read. Although you don't have to place your topic sentence at the beginning of a paragraph, or even use a topic sentence, be aware that your readers will scrutinize your first sentence for a clue to the unity of your paragraph. If that opening sentence does not declare the topic of your paragraph, it must at least point your readers toward the sentence or group of sentences that does identify or evoke the main topic.

Completeness

Completeness, the second major requirement of an effective paragraph, is relative. The amount of explanation an idea requires depends on the amount your readers need. You must decide this based on your knowledge of your subject and of your audience. Too much information can overwhelm readers, too little can annoy them. Inexperienced writers tend to supply too little detail. Consider this example.

> American Sign Language is a language unto itself. It has its own rules that determine the meaning and significance of each gesture. Experts familiar with these rules can use their hands to communicate extremely complex thoughts.

If that is all the writer is going to say about American Sign Language, this paragraph is incomplete for most readers because the first two sentences merely state the topic. This paragraph would only "satisfy" readers who were already familiar with the intricacies of American Sign Language—but such readers would not even need this brief paragraph. For those who do need it, the writer must provide further explanation:

> American Sign Language—ASL—is a language unto itself, with its own syntax and grammar. Adjectives follow nouns, as in Romance languages. In sign, one says "house blue," establishing a picture of what is being described and then embellishing on that. Many sign language "sentences" begin with a time element and then proceed with what happened, thereby conjugating the verbs. The movement of the shoulders, the speed of the hands, the facial expression, the number of repetitions of a sign, combine with the actual signs to give meaning to the language. Signing is precise. The casual gestures hearing people make when talking have no meaning in sign language. Hearing people who do learn sign usually practice "signed English," a word-for-word coding of English into signs, but that translation sorely limits the language. In some hands, signing is an art equal to an actor's rendering of Shakespeare. It is not just swoops and swirls but an enormous variety of expression, just as a great actor's delivery is completely different from some ham's idea of haughty speeches. (Lou Ann Walker, *A Loss for Words*)

Detailed information is necessary to make the meaning of the short paragraph clear. Of course, you can begin with a short paragraph if your purpose is to state the idea and then develop the topic in greater detail in a subsequent paragraph. In that case, the second paragraph would complete the first.

Here is another example of an incomplete paragraph:

> A child understands far more than we suspect. She may not understand words too well, but she senses what they mean by how they are spoken.

If the writer stops there, the reader is left with only a topic sentence and a brief statement that barely begins to develop the main idea. The reader needs to know how a child can "sense" the meaning of words she does not understand. The complete version of the paragraph supplies the answer:

> There is also a sense in which a child understands far more than we suspect. Because a child doesn't understand words too well (and also because his nervous system is not yet deadened by years spent as a lawyer, accountant, advertising executive, or professor of philosophy), a child attends not only to what we say but to everything about us as we say it— tone of voice, gesture, facial expression, bodily tensions, and so on. A child attends to a conversation between grown-ups with the same amazing absorption. Indeed, a child listening is, I hope, like a good psychiatrist listening—or like a good semanticist listening—because she watches not only the words but also the nonverbal events to which words bear, in all too many cases, so uncertain a relationship. Therefore a child is in some matters quite difficult to fool, especially on the subject of one's true attitude toward her. For this reason many parents, without knowing it, are to a greater or lesser degree in the situation of the worried mother who

said to the psychiatrist to whom she brought her child, "I tell her a dozen times a day that I love her, but the brat still hates me. Why, doctor?"
(S. I. Hayakawa, "Words and Children," *Through the Conversation Barrier*)

The additions to the paragraph clarify the process children use to understand words: they pay attention to tone of voice, gestures, facial expressions, and so on. The final example illustrates that children see beyond the words we use and understand what we really mean.

These examples demonstrate that you need to spell out the implications of a topic sentence with facts, illustrations, explanations—whatever is needed. Unless you give your readers the necessary information, they will have difficulty grasping your purpose. You can easily flesh out incomplete paragraphs once you realize that every generalization must be developed with supporting details.

_____Exercise   The following paragraphs are incomplete. Complete them by adding several examples or a sustained illustration from your own experience.

1. You cannot and should not try to eliminate all anger from your life. If you react mildly to everything, you will often suppress your true feelings. You must learn to recognize situations where expressing anger is counterproductive.

2. Most families have a private set of signs that enable them to communicate with one another without having to say a word. Family members use these signs in public to warn each other about a potential problem.

Order

The third requirement for effective paragraphs is consistent *order*. You saw in the paragraph on the Old South (page 185) that when sentences point in various directions readers are likely to have trouble following the writer's line of reasoning.

Order in a paragraph is like organization in an essay, but because paragraphs are smaller in scope, it may be easier to consider order as *direction of movement*. Four directional patterns in expository paragraphs are from *general to particular*, from *particular to general*, from *whole to parts*, and from *question to answer* or *effect to cause*.

General to Particular   A common pattern in expository paragraphs moves from a general statement, often a topic sentence, to specific explanations or illustrations of that statement. The purpose of the paragraph is to help the reader understand the general statement. That meaning becomes increasingly clear as the paragraph progresses. You saw this kind of clarification in the paragraphs on American Sign Language and children's ability to make sense of nonverbal language. Here is another example.

It is easy to produce examples of the many ways in which Americans attempt to minimize, circumvent, or deny the interdependence upon which all human societies are based. We seek a private house, a private means of transportation, a private garden, a private laundry, self-service stores, and do-it-yourself skills of every kind. An enormous technology seems to have set itself the task of making it unnecessary for one human being ever to ask anything of another in the course of going about his daily business. Even within the family Americans are unique in their feeling that each member should have a separate room, and even a separate telephone, television, and car, when economically possible. We seek more and more privacy, and feel more and more alienated and lonely when we get it. What accidental contacts we do have, furthermore, seem more intrusive, not only because they are unsought but because they are unconnected with any familiar pattern of interdependence. (Philip Slater, *The Pursuit of Loneliness*)

Particular to General   A particular-to-general pattern reverses the preceding pattern. It begins with specific information and leads to a general conclusion, as in this example.

We look at old family photographs in which we stand next to black, boxy Fords and are wearing period costumes, and we do not gaze fascinated because there we are young again, or there we are standing, as we never will again in life, next to our mother. We stare and drift because there we are . . . historical. It is the dress, the black car that dazzle us now and draw us beyond our mother's bright arms which once caught us. We reach into the attractive impersonality of something more significant than ourselves. (Patricia Hampl, *A Romantic Education*)

Had Hampl chosen, she could have followed a general-to-particular order by beginning with her last sentence and then illustrating its significance with details about family photographs.

The direction of movement within an individual paragraph is often determined by the direction of movement within an extended passage. As Bill Barich points out, paragraphs develop a rhythm for carrying various kinds of information. In the paragraphs that precede the quoted example, Hampl uses several general-to-particular patterns to discuss the search for a family past. In the example, she reverses the order to emphasize the particulars—family photographs. She returns to the general-to-particular order in the next paragraph, when she explores the impersonality of history.

Whole to Parts   Sometimes the purpose of a paragraph is to show the parts or divisions of a topic, as in this example.

There are medium friends, and pretty good friends, and very good friends indeed, and these friendships are defined by their level of intimacy. And what we'll reveal at each of these levels of intimacy is calibrated with care. We might tell a medium friend, for example, that yesterday we had a fight with our husband. And we might tell a pretty good friend that this fight with our husband made us so mad that we slept on the couch. And we might tell a very good friend that the reason we got so mad in that fight that we slept on the couch had something to do with that girl who works in his office. But it's only to our very best friends that we're willing to tell all, to tell what's going on with that girl in his office. (Judith Viorst, "Friends, Good Friends—and Such Good Friends," *Redbook*)

This order is also called *partitive* or *enumerative*. The opening statement announces the divisions of the topic, often indicating their number; the rest of the paragraph identifies and defines each of the parts. The partitive or enumerative paragraph is often used in argument, either to introduce the issues to be considered or to summarize a discussion. In exposition, it is used to introduce the categories to be analyzed. Such paragraphs are usually less detailed than Viorst's paragraph because succeeding paragraphs supply information about the categories.

Question to Answer, Effect to Cause   A paragraph may begin with a question and give the answer or with an effect and explain the cause. Such a paragraph may have no specific topic sentence beyond the opening question or statement of the effect. This paragraph begins with a question, which it proceeds to answer.

> So what are we to do, those of us whose habit and pleasure and doom is our tendency, as a Georgia lady put it, to "fly off at every other whip-stitch"? Think in terms of movable feasts, for a start. Live here, wherever here may be, as if we were going to belong here for the rest of our lives. Learn to hallow whatever ground we happen to stand on or land on. Like medieval knights who took their tapestries along on Crusades, like modern Afghanis with their yurts, we must pack such totems and icons as we can to make short-term quarters feel like home. Pillows, small rugs, watercolors can dispel much of the chilling anonymity of a sublet apartment or motel room. When we can, we should live in rooms with stoves or fireplaces or anyway candlelight. The ancient saying still is true: Extinguished hearth, extinguished family. Round tables help, too, and as a friend of mine once put it, so do "too many comfortable chairs, with surfaces to put feet on, arranged so as to encourage a maximum of eye-contact." Such rooms inspire good talk, of which good clans can never have enough. (Jane Howard, *Families*)

The next paragraph begins with an effect and then considers some of the causes of that effect.

> There is something very wrong with an institution that so often disintegrates at the very point it is supposed to be the most useful. It is obviously absurd that we should marry, have children, get divorced, and then start the whole thing over in an even more difficult and complicated way. The "reconstituted" families of remarriage give statistical stability to the big picture. But the clue to what is wrong with the big picture lies in the "transition period to new family life," which is likely to be three or four years when a woman is caring for very small children. Nearly half the

children born today will spend a significant part of their lives in a single-parent home. Raising a child or—worse—children, alone, is the wrong way to do it. It is too hard, not on the children—if recent studies mean anything—but on the mother. Of American women divorced and separated, only 4 percent receive alimony, and only 23 percent with children receive child support. Women earn, on the average, fifty-nine cents for every dollar men earn. And of all female-headed families, 41.8 percent live below the poverty level. (Jane O'Reilly, "But Who Will Take Care of the Children?")

Summary of Main Orders of Movement Within Paragraphs

1. **General to particular**
   Opening general statement or topic sentence followed by illustration or details of explanation or proof. The paragraph may conclude with a restatement of the topic sentence.

2. **Particular to general**
   From a series of detailed statements to a conclusion drawn from them. If there is a topic sentence, it occurs at or near the end of the paragraph.

3. **Whole to parts**
   Paragraph begins with an introductory statement about the number of parts and then explains each part: often a first, second, third order.

4. **Question to answer, or effect to cause**
   Paragraph begins with question or effect, then answers the question or shows the cause.

Coherence

A paragraph is coherent when the sentences are woven together in such a way that readers move easily from one sentence to the next and read the paragraph as an integrated discussion rather than as a series of separate sentences.

If you have a sense of purpose when you begin writing, then you are not likely to have trouble with coherence. Lack of coherence often results if you think about your topic one sentence at a time: you write one sentence, stop, think a minute, write a second sentence, stop, and continue in a series of spurts and pauses. Paragraphs written in this way are likely to lack coherence because your ideas do not flow from one sentence to the next and continuity is lost.

A paragraph can exhibit unity, completeness, and order but still lack coherence. The writer of the following paragraph is composing a paper to describe the ordeals of the immigration experience. Here he tries to illustrate the processing procedure at Ellis Island in New York Harbor, the official place of entry for most European immigrants from 1892 until 1943.

The immigrants were herded off the boat onto Ellis Island. Inspectors talking in a strange language pushed them into a building where metal railings divided them into lines. They waited as the doctors examined them for diseases and defects. Some were separated from their families and sent to other parts of the building. The rest moved on to the next test. They were asked about their relatives, their politics, their work, their money. The questions were confusing, and they were never sure they gave the right answers.

Although this paragraph moves in an orderly sequence, it requires revision. Consider the following points:

▼ What is the purpose of the paragraph? You know from the description of the paper that the writer wants to describe the ordeal of immigration. The information does illustrate this experience, but its significance would be clearer if the paragraph possessed a topic sentence that bound the individual sentences together. Without such a sentence, a reader may not see the writer's purpose in describing the activity on Ellis Island.

▼ What is the relationship between this paragraph and the one that preceded it? The reader is told that the immigrants were on a boat, but there is no introductory statement that explains the transition from boat to island.

▼ Although the repetition of *they* provides some coherence, the sentence structure becomes monotonous, emphasizing the paragraph's disjointedness.

Now consider this revised version.

Although the immigrants endured many physical hardships during the crossing, they were not prepared for the psychological ordeal of Ellis Island. They had come so far, and now they realized that they could be sent back. Inspectors shouting strange words herded them into a massive building where metal railings divided them into lines. There they waited in silent humiliation as one doctor after another poked at their bodies, looking for diseases and defects. Occasional screams followed family members who were pulled out of line and led off to another part of the building. The rest moved on to the next test. Interpreters asked

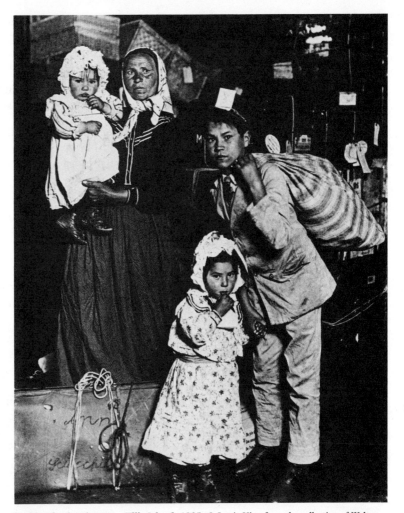

Looking for lost baggage, Ellis Island, 1905. © Louis Hine from the collection of Walter and Naomi Rosenblum.

them about their relatives, their politics, their work, their money. Every question seemed like a trap. If they told the truth, they might be turned away. If they lied, they might be caught. If they said nothing, they might be marked dumb and sent back where they came from.

The revision achieved the following improvements:

▼ The topic sentence states the purpose of the paragraph, gives significance to all the details that follow, and connects this paragraph to preceding paragraphs.

▼ The more detailed and evocative explanation of the psychological ordeal of the inspection process helps bind the sentences together more effectively than in the unsatisfactory version, where sentences were connected only by a common subject.

▼ The concluding sentences dramatize the anxiety of those waiting for clearance and sum up the content of the whole paragraph.

This contrast of the original and revised paragraphs shows how an unsatisfactory piece of writing can better express the main idea by providing the links that reveal the relationship among the sentences. Other connective devices that increase paragraph coherence are *pronouns, contrast, repetitive structure,* and *transitional markers.*

Coherence Through Pronoun Reference   Because it refers to an antecedent, a pronoun points back (or forward) to create a simple, natural connection. Notice in the following paragraph how the pronoun *they* links the whole paragraph to the antecedent *emigrants*. Pronoun repetition reinforces the purpose of this paragraph: to illustrate that emigrants "shared certain characteristics."

Most of the emigrants shared certain characteristics as a group: they were men and women who had already made one or more moves before in a restless search for better lands. They were children of parents who themselves had moved to new lands. If ever a people could be said to have been "prepared" for the adventure of the Overland Trail, it would have to be these men and women. They possessed the assortment of skills needed to make the journey and to start again. They had owned land before, had cleared land before, and were prepared to clear and own land again. And they were young. Most of the population that moved across half the continent were between sixteen and thirty-five years of age. (Lillian Schlissel, *Women's Diaries of Westward Journey*)

Coherence Through Contrasted Elements   When a topic sentence calls for a comparison or contrast, the pairing of the contrasted elements enhances coherence. In the following paragraph, the middle sentences illustrate the contrast between the lives of Grant and Lee—a contrast that is announced in the topic sentence and summarized in the concluding sentence.

So Grant and Lee were in complete contrast, representing two diametrically opposed elements in American life. Grant was the modern man emerging; beyond him, ready to come on the stage, was the great age of steel and machinery, of crowded cities and a restless, burgeoning vitality. Lee might have ridden down from the old age of chivalry, lance in hand, silken banner fluttering over his head. Each man was the perfect champion of his cause, drawing both his strengths and his weaknesses from the people he led. (Bruce Catton, "Grant and Lee: A Study in Contrasts" *The American Story*)

Coherence Through Repetitive Structure Purposeless repetition should be avoided, but deliberate repetition of key words, phrases, or sentence patterns can make sentences flow into a coherent paragraph. In the following example, every sentence after the first has the same structure and the same opening words, "There is nothing." This kind of repetition (discussed as *parallel structure* in Chapter 8) ties the sentences together in a coherent development of the topic sentence.

> America, the richest and most powerful nation in the world, can well lead the way in this revolution of values. There is nothing to prevent us from paying adequate wages to schoolteachers, social workers and other servants of the public to insure that we have the best available personnel in these positions which are charged with the responsibility of guiding our future generations. There is nothing but a lack of social vision to prevent us from paying an adequate wage to every American citizen whether he be a hospital worker, laundry worker, maid or day laborer. There is nothing except shortsightedness to prevent us from guaranteeing an annual minimum—and *livable*—income for every American family. There is nothing, except a tragic death wish, to prevent us from reordering our priorities so the pursuit of peace will take precedence over the pursuit of war. There is nothing to keep us from remolding a recalcitrant status quo with bruised hands until we have fashioned it into a brotherhood. (Martin Luther King, Jr., *Where Do We Go from Here: Chaos or Community?*)

Coherence Through Transitional Markers *Transitional markers* are words or phrases often placed at or near the beginning of a sentence or clause to signal the relationship between the new sentence or clause and the one before it. The most common markers are the conjunctions *and, or, nor, but,* and *for*. Others—sometimes called *transitional connectives*—indicate the direction a new sentence is about to take and prepare the reader for what is to follow. The most common transitional connectives are used as follows:

- ▼ *To introduce an illustration:* for example, for instance, to illustrate
- ▼ *To add another phrase of the same idea:* second, in the second place, then, furthermore, next, moreover, in addition, similarly, again, also, finally
- ▼ *To point out a contrast or qualification:* on the other hand, nevertheless, despite this fact, on the contrary, still, however, conversely, instead
- ▼ *To indicate a conclusion or result:* therefore, in conclusion, to sum up, consequently, as a result, accordingly, in other words

Coherence Through Connection Between Paragraphs Coherence is necessary not only within a paragraph but also between the paragraphs of an essay, so that your readers can see how each paragraph is related to those that precede or follow it. The following passage begins with an assertion. At the end of the first paragraph, the writer notes a change, thus providing the transitional link to the next paragraphs and giving coherence to the whole passage.

Those of us who grew up in the fifties believed in the permanence of our American-history textbooks. To us as children, those texts were the truth of things: they were American history. It was not just that we read them before we understood that not everything that is printed is the truth, or the whole truth. It was that they, much more than other books, had the demeanor and trappings of authority. They were weighty volumes. They spoke in measured cadences: imperturbable, humorless, and as distant as Chinese emperors. Our teachers treated them with respect, and we paid them abject homage by memorizing a chapter a week. But now the textbook histories have changed, some of them to such an extent that an adult would find them unrecognizable.

One current junior-high-school American history begins with a story about a Negro cowboy called George McJunkin. It appears that when McJunkin was riding down a lonely trail in New Mexico one cold spring morning in 1925 he discovered a mound containing bones and stone implements, which scientists later proved belonged to an Indian civilization ten thousand years old. The book goes on to say that scientists now believe there were people in the Americas at least twenty thousand years ago. It discusses the Aztec, Mayan, and Incan civilizations and the meaning of the word "culture" before introducing the European explorers.

Another history text—this one for the fifth grade—begins with the story of how Henry B. Gonzalez, who is a member of Congress from Texas, learned about his own nationality. When he was ten years old, his teacher told him he was an American because he was born in the United States. His grandmother, however, said, "The cat was born in the oven. Does that make him bread?" After reporting that Mr. Gonzalez eventually went to college and law school, the book explains that "the melting pot idea hasn't worked out as some thought it would," and that now "some people say that the people of the United States are more like a salad bowl than a melting pot." (Frances FitzGerald, *America Revised*)

_____*Exercise*   Read the following passage excerpted from "The Crazy Life," Bill Barich's article on youth gangs in Los Angeles. The passage is presented without its original paragraphing. Reread Barich's comments on paragraphing (page 184); review the four requirements of effective topical paragraphs; and then discuss how you would break this passage into manageable units.

The landmark work in the sociology of gangs is Frederic M. Thrasher's "The Gang," which was published in 1927. Thrasher was a founder of the Chicago school, a methodology that stressed the importance of interviews and direct observation. In pursuing his study, he observed more than a thousand Illinois gangs before arriving at his well-known theory that gangs are largely a phenomenon of immigrant communities. According to Thrasher, they represent an ethnic group in transition, waiting out its adolescence until it can be assimilated into the mainstream. The underlying assumption is that the attractions of a so-called "normal" life—a job, a family, a house in the suburbs—far outweigh the attractions of a life of crime. Over the years, Thrasher's ideas would be repeated, with variations, in many other studies, monographs, and books, and they still echo in current sociological theory, coloring the way youth-gang members are perceived, making them seem distant, opposite, always somewhat less than human. In Los Angeles County, there are Hispanic youth gangs whose histories go back almost a century, involving three and sometimes four generations of men. There are black gangs of such size, sophistication, and economic well-being that they put many small corporations to shame. There are gangs of Chinese teen-agers who run gambling emporiums as skillfully as old Vegas hands. When immigrants, legal or illegal, come to Southern California, their children form gangs—Korean, Vietnamese, Filipino, Honduran, Salvadoran, Nicaraguan, Guatemalan. There are Samoan gangs in Los Angeles County, and gangs from Tonga, and they feud with each other just as their ancestors did on the islands. Increasingly, in affluent suburban towns, there are gangs of white teen-agers, kids from decent homes, who—the saying goes—"have everything," and still take to the streets. (Bill Barich, "The Crazy Life," *The New Yorker*)

SPECIAL PARAGRAPHS

So far in this chapter you have examined topical paragraphs, the main paragraphs in an essay that develop your topic or some aspect of it. Special paragraphs are used to *introduce* or *conclude* an essay and to *mark transitions* from one unit to another.

Introductory Paragraphs

Readers want to know what you are writing about and whether they will find your subject interesting and significant. Your introductory paragraph leads into your essay, giving your readers a preview. Most introductions contain attention-getting statements that engage the readers' interest or statements that suggest the organization or indicate the scope, focus, or thesis of your essay. Notice how Bill Barich blends these in his introductory paragraph to "The Crazy Life."

The first time I met Manuel Velazquez, he greeted me awkwardly, unable to shake hands. He had cut himself on a broken bottle while crawling around in a tunnel to read a new graffito, and a doctor at a local clinic had sewed him up with seventeen stitches and then wrapped the wound in cotton, gauze, and tape. Manuel was stoical about his injury, seeing it as an unfortunate but perhaps necessary consequence of his job, which is to keep teen-age gang members in the San Fernando Valley, in California, from killing one another in wars. In Los Angeles County, of which the valley is a part, there are an estimated fifty thousand youth-gang members, and about three hundred of them are expected to be murdered this year. In the old days of youth-gang warfare, the days of "Blackboard Jungle" and "West Side Story," a boy might arm himself with a knife or a homemade zip gun, but now in times of trouble he has access to .357 magnum pistols, hunting rifles with pinpoint scopes, and Uzi semi-automatics from Israel. (Bill Barich, "The Crazy Life")

You can utilize many strategies in your introductory paragraph to suggest your intentions. The writers whose essays you have examined in previous chapters have used the following techniques:

Direct Statement   Matt uses direct statement to introduce two of his essays on drug abuse in the work place. In one version, he begins with a general statement about the effect of drug abuse, restricts this statement to drug abuse in the work place, and then offers further clarification (see Chapter 6, page 174):

> In the last decade drug abuse has reached epidemic proportions in our country—destroying the lives of our young people, exhausting the energies of our legal system, and eroding our fundamental values. Nowhere is the problem more alarming than in the work place, where drug abuse costs the American economy in excess of $60 billion a year. All of us—employers, workers, and consumers—want to cure this plague that threatens the health of our culture. Unfortunately, there is as much controversy about the cure as there is about the disease.

In his "My Side" essay Matt begins with three statements about the problem of drug abuse in the work place (see Chapter 6, p. 169). These narrow the focus of the paragraph but build toward a direct statement of his thesis—that drug testing is unreliable, counterproductive, and an invasion of workers' privacy.

> The increased public awareness of drug abuse in our society has created a sense of public alarm about the potential dangers of drug abuse in the work place. Although such concern is justifiable, particularly when it affects the safety of workers and consumers, most companies are trying to solve this complex problem with a simple urine test. Whether it is used to weed out job applicants or identify suspected abusers on the job, urine testing is a misguided attempt to find a quick fix. The test is not only unreliable and counterproductive, it is a serious invasion of worker's privacy.

Factual Information   Rod experimented with several opening paragraphs before deciding on this opening statement: "The facts are simple." He follows this with a barrage of facts about the Washington Monument that sets up the "hook" of the monument's dramatic story (see Chapter 4, pages 106–7):

> The facts are simple: The Washington Monument stands 555 feet $5^1/_8$ inches. Its base is 55 feet $1^1/_2$ square inches. It is faced with 9,613 marble slabs, weighs 90,854 tons, can withstand a 145-mph gale, and cost $1,187,710.31. But these statistics aren't the whole story. In the two centuries since the idea was first mentioned, the Washington Monument has been revised, moved, stolen, ignored, held hostage, and almost blown up.

Quotation   Wally uses his father's "words of wisdom" to set up his essay about painting "Brandon's Clown" (see Chapter 1, page 22). The quotation guides the reader through the narration and serves as an ironic commentary on Wally's subject and purpose:

> Few of those words of wisdom that are passed from father to son are followed. Most are simply acknowledged and forgotten. My father's advice about my adolescent love for painting was simple and direct: "Son, you have a special talent. Be smart. Use it to make money." With his words guiding me, I took my love to the marketplace. I began accepting commissions, painting fantasies for those who didn't have the skill or desire to paint their own.

Dramatic Episode   Ellen's description of Barry making granola dramatizes the unique features of Barry's personality (see Chapter 3, page 87). She concludes the episode with his infamous words, "it's good for me"—words with which Barry, as the reader soon discovers, justifies everything:

> Barry's in the kitchen making granola. His long, narrow frame moves deftly around the work area, pausing to scan the recipe book on the counter or search the shelves for the ingredients—wheat germ, bran, rolled oats, sunflower seeds, raisins, honey—he plans to mix in a large, gray earthenware bowl. While he works, he hums a vaguely recognizable version of "Blue Moon," drumming on the top of the counter or the edge of the bowl with a wooden spoon. He's happy. Making granola always has this effect on him. He doesn't like to make granola—it's messy and time-consuming. He doesn't like to eat granola—it's too crunchy without milk and too mushy with it. But he likes to contemplate his reasons for eating granola—"it's good for me."

Anecdote   After her attention-getting first sentence, Jane uses an anecdote about her trip to the American Museum of Natural History to introduce her reasons for her whale-watching trip (see Chapter 5, page 143). The purpose of her allusions to textbooks and magazines is to arouse the curiosity of her readers, making them want to "see more":

> The problem with whales is that they don't fit under a microscope. As a small girl, I walked around and around the large skeleton of a blue whale on the first floor of the American Museum of Natural History, trying to compare its size to the skeletons of the brontosaurus and diplodocus I had seen on the fourth floor. Like those creatures from another time, whales challenged and held my imagination. I could never see enough of them. The drawings in textbooks outlined their shape but reduced their enormous size to a few inches. The photographs in magazines suggested their magnificence but usually focused on their parts—the head rising to breech, the tail arching to dive. Last summer, hoping to see more, I booked passage on the *Portuguese Princess* out of Provincetown, Massachusetts, for my first whale watch.

Transitional Paragraphs

A transitional paragraph signals a change in content. It tells your readers that they have finished one main unit and are moving to the next, or it tells them that they are moving from a general explanation to specific examples or applications. A transitional paragraph is often as brief as one sentence:

> So much for the parents. We come now to the children.

> Let us see how this theory works in practice.

> And this brings us to the final ordeal of the crossing: Ellis Island.

> A few examples will make this explanation clear.

Sometimes you will need to supplement such signals with a concise summary of what has been covered or with a statement of what is to come, as John McPhee did in this paragraph from "Under the Snow" (see Chapter 5, page 146).

> These memories became very much alive some months ago when—one after another—I had bear cubs under my vest. Weighing three, four, 5.6 pounds, they were wild bears, and for an hour or so had been taken from their dens in Pennsylvania. They were about two months old, with fine short brown hair. When they were made to stand alone, to be photo-graphed in the mouth of a den, they shivered. Instinctively, a person would be moved to hold them. Picked up by the scruff of the neck, they splayed their paws like kittens and screamed like baby bears. The cry of a baby bear is muted, like a human infant's heard from her crib down the hall. The first cub I placed on my shoulder stayed there like a piece of velvet. The shivering stopped. Her bright-blue eyes looked about, not seeing much of anything. My hand, cupped against her back, all but en-compassed her rib cage, which was warm and calm. I covered her to the shoulders with a flap of down vest and zipped up my parka to hold her in place.

Concluding Paragraphs

Not every essay needs a concluding paragraph. If you have adequately dem-onstrated your thesis, nothing more is necessary. You do not need to add a paragraph that mechanically restates the obvious: "Thus I have shown. . . ."

A good concluding paragraph does not necessarily sum up the ideas in an essay. Bill Barich concludes "The Crazy Life" with a quotation from Manuel, the man he introduced at the beginning of the essay. This paragraph echoes the introduction, but it also opens up the essay by suggesting that Manuel will always have more work to do.

> "You can't get depressed about it," he said. "You know, with the people on my team, I tell them they have to make their job fun—even though it's a crummy job. It's got lots of negatives, but lots of positives, too. Once you start an input into somebody's life, you begin to influence them, you break the monotony. Some kids, they don't know any other kind of life.

What we do, it's like throwing a wrench inside an engine. It screws up the structure. Suddenly, you're a part of their lives. That's good to feel. Sometimes it's like I can almost control what's going on. It's like having a sixth sense. Like seeing into the future and controlling it. That's when you know you're doing your job." (Bill Barich, "The Crazy Life")

An effective concluding paragraph leaves the reader with a sense of completeness, a conviction that the point has been made, that nothing else needs to be said; it contributes something significant to the essay that could not have been accomplished by a "Thus I have shown . . ." conclusion.

The following examples, taken from essays in previous chapters, show various strategies for concluding paragraphs.

Restatement and Recommendation   Rod summarizes the main points he has made about the inside story of the Washington Monument and goes on to suggest how that information can help you appreciate this "peaceful and impressive sight" (see Chapter 4, page 109):

There's obviously more to George's monument than meets the eye. Of course, you don't have to know the inside story to like the monument. Most people who see a picture of the monument on a calendar or a postcard like what they see. But to truly understand and appreciate the monument, you do need to know the inside story. When you visit George's monument on some hot summer afternoon and have to stand in line for over two hours for a thirteen-second elevator ride to the top, you need to know how long it took the planners and builders to reach the top: all those false starts, crazy designs, and engineering obstacles that had to be overcome to produce this beautifully simple structure. When you see people in the line who don't know why they are there or who are just fooling around as they would at Disneyland, you need to know that the two-hundred-year history of the monument is filled with bewildered and misguided people. And when you have finished your visit, you need to take time to appreciate what you have seen. Turn and look at it one last time. There it stands—a solitary, rugged individual, indifferent to the confusion below. It is a peaceful and impressive sight.

Prediction   Wally begins his conclusion by drawing on the information he has discussed in other paragraphs—his father's advice, his artistic reputation. But he concludes by predicting that in twenty years Brandon may pay him back for his creation (see Chapter 1, page 23):

As I left holding my first commission, I did not think about my father's advice or my artistic reputation. I thought only of poor Brandon. I will not be surprised if, twenty years from now, a deranged young man stops me on the street and smashes a clown painting over my head. I probably deserve worse.

Resolution   Jane presents a chronological wind-up to her narrative and a final, climactic insight into her experience (see Chapter 5, page 145):

Although we watched eagerly for him to surface again, we looked in vain. Soon we began to look at one another. We smiled, but we did not talk. Neither did Richard. No explanation was necessary. We had watched a whale. A whale had watched us. Finally, the engine coughed, and the *Portuguese Princess* resumed her journey back to Provincetown.

Quotation   Sometimes a single line of dialogue makes an effective ending, especially when the words resonate like Ellen's (see Chapter 3, page 88):

> "See, I told you it was good for me."

At other times, a carefully chosen quotation from an expert can strengthen the authority of your conclusion. Matt uses this strategy to make his final points about drug testing in the work place (see Chapter 6, pages 175–6):

> Lewis L. Maltby, Vice President, Drexelbrook Controls, Inc., describes the kind of consensus policy that should cure drug abuse in the work place: "We can attack drug abuse with drug testing. It's quick, it's easy, and it's cheap. It just doesn't work. It gives us inaccurate and irrelevant information and undermines the trust of good employees who resent being ordered to pee in a bottle when they've done nothing wrong. Or, we can take the time to learn about our employees, watch their job performance, and help them when it starts to slip. It's time consuming, difficult, and expensive. But it works. Not just in preventing work-place drug abuse, but in creating a committed and productive work place" (Maltby 4).

REVISING TOPICAL PARAGRAPHS

As you learned in Chapter 4, there are two types of revision: *global revision,* employed while you are still creating your final draft, and *local revision,* in which you fine-tune your final draft. Local revision of paragraphs ensures that each paragraph in your essay not only works externally, to advance the purpose of your essay, but also works internally, to create a sensible sequence of thought. The discussion of topical paragraphs in this chapter has shown you some ways to think about local revision, especially in the case of the paragraph about Ellis Island (pages 194–5). To identify problems in your own paragraphs, you must view your paragraphs as your readers will see them. In other words, after you have refined your subject, audience, and purpose through global revision, and after you have established a reasonably firm organization, you must give your work a sentence-by-sentence reading, concentrating on the relation of sentences to each other and to the topic sentence.

One helpful technique in such close reading is creating a descriptive outline (see Chapter 3). As you recall, in a descriptive outline you describe what each paragraph in an essay says (that is, its main idea) and does (that is, how the paragraph supports the main idea). You should be able to state succinctly the main idea of every topical paragraph you write. If in reading a paragraph you find that you cannot succinctly state its main idea, you probably need to reconsider your topic sentence—or create one in the first place. If you find that you cannot determine what a paragraph does, the problem may be that it does nothing: it may fail to support the topic sentence or fail to add up to any particular meaning.

You need then to consider the paragraph's internal qualities: unity, completeness, order, and coherence. A paragraph that does not exhibit each of these qualities will not effectively advance your purpose. It will leave questions unanswered, details unsupported, transitions incomplete; and your readers will receive less from your writing than you intended. You must question both the meaning and function of each sentence in your paragraph and the overall effect of all the sentences.

In the following example a writer reports a series of impressions:

> (1) On Bourbon Street in the French Quarter of New Orleans there are a 50-cent peepshow and a theater that shows pornographic movies. (2) Pictures painted by talented artists are for sale in a shop down the street. (3) Canned music blares through doors held partly open by hustlers of strip joints. (4) There is a concert hall with no doors and no admission fee, where the crowd is entertained by jazz musicians. (5) In some places there are "dancing girls" who just walk across the stage and do "bumps" in what is supposed to be a dancer routine. (6) Sometimes there is a young woman who dances gracefully. (7) She has mastered the techniques that the better burlesques made popular in earlier years.

This paragraph does not lack detail; it is a series of details that try to capture the confusion of Bourbon Street. But the paragraph is all detail and no pattern: it has no unifying idea, no recognizable order, and no semblance of coherence.

The details in the paragraph fall into two groups: sentences 1, 3, and 5 show an unfavorable impression of Bourbon Street; sentences 2, 4, 6, and 7 suggest a more favorable impression. By classifying the details in this way, you can discern that the writer probably intends to contrast the two impressions. This purpose stated in a topic sentence is: "Bourbon Street in the French Quarter of New Orleans is a contrast of vulgarity and art." With that topic sentence as the controlling idea of the paragraph, you can revise its order in one of two ways:

- Use an *A* + *B* contrast in which all the details suggesting vulgarity (*A*) are placed in the first half of the paragraph and all those suggesting art (*B*) are placed in the second half, with a transitional marker (*but* or *on the other hand*) to mark the change.
- Use an *A/B* + *A/B* contrast in which matched details of vulgarity and art alternate within each sentence.

For this paragraph, the second arrangement is better because it is truer to the constant contrasts the writer is trying to describe. Here is a revised version:

Bourbon Street in the French Quarter of New Orleans is a contrast of vulgarity and art. Just a few doors down the street from a 50-cent peepshow and a theater that presents pornographic movies is a shop displaying for sale paintings by talented artists. At strip joints canned music blares out from doors kept ajar by hustlers seeking to entice passers-by; yet not far away is a concert hall with no admission fee, where musicians play first-rate jazz. Even the "dancing girls" offer a sharp contrast: most limit themselves to a slow walk across the stage, interrupted by exaggerated "bumps"; but a few gracefully demonstrate the techniques that once made burlesque at its best an art form.

REVISING SPECIAL PARAGRAPHS

Because introductory, transitional, and concluding paragraphs are used for special purposes, they require a somewhat different approach in revision. In judging how well they do what they are meant to do, you should focus less on method than on effect.

Be sure that your introductory paragraph clearly states the thesis you intend to develop and that the thesis is advantageously positioned within the paragraph. Or, if you have used an attention-getting device, you need to look carefully at this "hook" to see that it entices rather than confuses your readers.

Check to see that your opening paragraph fits your final draft. An introductory paragraph written before the final draft was completed may no longer be appropriate. Does your opening seem misleading, flat, or simply uninspiring? View it with an open mind, and do not hesitate to revise it completely if your other revisions make a different opening necessary.

As you revise, pay particular attention to transitional paragraphs, the structural seams of your essay. Significant revisions elsewhere may require you to revise your transitional paragraphs or to delete them and use a concluding sentence or an opening phrase in existing paragraphs. Or you may discover that changes in your essay require you to add a transitional paragraph to clarify the movement from one unit to another. Such decisions require you to reexamine the connections between your ideas to be certain that you have chosen the most effective strategy for communicating those connections to your readers.

When you revise a concluding paragraph, consider whether your essay needs a formal conclusion. You do not want to belabor the obvious. If your conclusion merely repeats what you have already said, delete it. If you decide that your essay does need a conclusion, consider the impression you want to leave in closing. You will sometimes discover that other revisions—both global and local—have weakened the effectiveness of your original conclusion. After revising the other parts of your essay, you will know what you must do to round off your work effectively, perhaps even memorably.

_____*Exercises*   Identify the problems in the following paragraphs and then revise each paragraph.

1. The front porch was once a door sill. It became a square platform large enough to hold two chairs. It lengthened and began to expand around the sides of the house. At one time, it was long and narrow, just wide enough for a row of chairs. People sat there watching and talking about their neighbors. Porches were a status symbol of economic prosperity and social prominence. Architects complained that they were too ornate. Cars created dust and fumes, so families went inside. The car also gave young lovers more privacy than the porch swing. Air conditioning made it unnecessary to go outside for air. People built backyard patios so the family could have some privacy.

2. It is unusual for one family to live in the same community for more than two generations. The average American family moves once every five years. Americans want to look for their roots. Many have complex ties to different parts of the world and are proud of their heritage. It's hard to trace the effects of immigration. Most families are scattered all over the country. Parents or grandparents who used to bring everyone together for Christmas spend December in trailer parks in Florida.

3. The Gateway Arch in St. Louis is a 630-foot stainless-steel arch. It marks the most prominent point of embarkation for those who traveled into the new territories. A Museum of Westward Expansion, near the arch, commemorates the frontier experience. Inside the steel structure is a contraption like a Ferris wheel that travels to the apex of the arch. The small windows provide a thirty-mile view in any direction. On the Mississippi River, tied to a dock near the arch, is a fast-food restaurant designed to look like a riverboat.

4. The people whose ancestors built the Great Wall of China made one of the most widely acclaimed contributions to American history. Over thirteen thousand Chinese built the western half of the transcontinental railroad. Digging tunnels through mountains and track beds across deserts, they laid 10 miles of track a day. On May 10, 1869, when a golden spike was driven at Promontory Point, Utah, no Chinese were visible. Americans resented the strength and skill of the "little yellow men." Anti-Chinese resentment was so high that Congress passed a series of Exclusion Acts that prohibited Chinese immigration. These laws were repealed in 1943, and Chinese were admitted under a strict quota system.

Family: The One
      Social Glue | Ellen Goodman

In her syndicated newspaper column, Ellen Goodman takes occasion to comment on a variety of social issues. In this column her subject is the American family, the "only place where we remember we're all related." How do you account for the difference in length between Goodman's and Barich's paragraphs? How does the size and sequence of Goodman's paragraphs contribute to her purpose?

They are going home for Thanksgiving, traveling through the clogged arteries of airports and highways, bearing bridge chairs and serving plates, Port-a-Cribs and pies. They are going home to rooms that resound with old arguments and interruptions, to piano benches filled with small cousins, to dining-room tables stretched out to the last leaf.   1

They no longer migrate over the river and through the woods straight into that Norman Rockwell poster: Freedom from Want. No, Thanksgiving isn't just a feast, but a reunion. It's no longer a celebration of food (which is plentiful in America) but of family (which is scarce).   2

Now families are so dispersed that it's easier to bring in the crops than the cousins. Now it's not so remarkable that we have a turkey to feed the family. It's more remarkable that there's enough family around to warrant a turkey.   3

For most of the year, we are a nation of individuals, all wrapped in separate cellophane packages like lamb chops in the meat department of a city supermarket. Increasingly we live with decreasing numbers. We create a new category like Single Householder, and fill it to the top of the Census Bureau reports.   4

For most of the year, we are segregated along generation lines into retirement villages and singles complexes, young married subdivisions and college dormitories, all exclusive clubs whose membership is defined by age.   5

Even when we don't live in age ghettos, we often think that way. Those who worried about a generation gap in the sixties worry about a generation war in the seventies. They see a community torn by warring rights: the Elderly Rights vs. the Middle-Aged Rights vs. the Children Rights. All competing for a piece of the pie.   6

This year, the Elderly Rights fought against mandatory retirement while the Younger Rights fought for job openings. The Children Rights worried about the money to keep their schools open, while the Elderly Rights worried about the rising cost of real estate taxes.   7

The retired generation lobbied for an increase in Social Security payments, while the working generation lobbied for a decrease in Social Security taxes. The elderly wanted health care and the children wanted day care   8

Goodman, Ellen. *Close to Home.* New York: Simon, 1979. 150–51.

and the middle-aged were tired of taking care. They wanted the right to lead their own lives.

At times it seemed as if the nation had splintered into peer pressure groups, panthers of all ages. People who cried, not "Me First" but, rather, "My Generation First." 9

But now they have come home for Thanksgiving. Even the Rights are a family who come together, not to fight for their piece of the pie this day, but to share it. 10

The family—as extended as that dining-room table—may be the one social glue strong enough to withstand the centrifuge of special interests which send us spinning away from each other. There, in the family, the Elderly Rights are also grandparents and the Children Rights are also nieces and nephews. There, the old are our parents and the young are our children. There, we care about each other's lives. There, self-interest includes concern for the future of the next generation. Because they are ours. 11

Our families are not just the people (if I may massacre Robert Frost) who, "when you have to go there, they have to let you in." They are the people who maintain an unreasonable interest in each other. They are the natural peacemakers in the generation war. 12

"Home" is the only place in society where we now connect along the ages, like discs along the spine of society. The only place where we remember that we're all related. And that's not a bad idea to go home to. 13

Black Men and Public Space | Brent Staples

In this essay, which first appeared in *Ms.* magazine, Brent Staples analyzes the effects his appearance creates in a public environment. What kind of strategies does he use in his introductory paragraph to attract his readers' attention? How does he arrange and develop the topical paragraphs in the body of his essay? How does his concluding paragraph echo his introductory paragraph while suggesting new dimensions to his purpose?

My first victim was a woman—white, well dressed, probably in her early twenties. I came upon her late one evening on a deserted street in Hyde Park, a relatively affluent neighborhood in an otherwise mean, impoverished section of Chicago. As I swung onto the avenue behind her, there seemed to be a discreet, uninflammatory distance between us. Not so. She cast back a worried glance. To her, the youngish black man—a broad six feet two inches with a beard and billowing hair, both hands shoved into the pockets of a bulky military jacket—seemed menacingly close. After a few more quick glimpses, she picked up her pace and was soon running in earnest. Within seconds she disappeared into a cross street. 1

That was more than a decade ago, I was twenty-two years old, a graduate student newly arrived at the University of Chicago. It was in the echo 2

Staples, Brent. "Black Men and Public Space." *Ms.* September 1986. 54, 88.

of that terrified woman's footfalls that I first began to know the unwieldy inheritance I'd come into—the ability to alter public space in ugly ways. It was clear that she thought herself the quarry of a mugger, a rapist or worse. Suffering a bout of insomnia, however, I was stalking sleep, not defenseless wayfarers. As a softy who is scarcely able to take a knife to a raw chicken—let alone hold one to a person's throat—I was surprised, embarrassed, and dismayed all at once. Her flight made me feel like an accomplice in tyranny. It also made it clear that I was indistinguishable from the muggers who occasionally seeped into the area from the surrounding ghetto. That first encounter, and those that followed, signified that a vast, unnerving gulf lay between nighttime pedestrians—particularly women—and me. And I soon gathered that being perceived as dangerous is a hazard in itself. I only needed to turn a corner into a dicey situation, or crowd some frightened, armed person in a foyer somewhere, or make an errant move after being pulled over by a policeman. Where fear and weapons meet—and they often do in urban America—there is always the possibility of death.

In that first year, my first away from my hometown, I was to become thoroughly familiar with the language of fear. At dark, shadowy intersections, I could cross in front of a car stopped at a traffic light and elicit the *thunk, thunk, thunk, thunk* of the driver—black, white, male, or female—hammering down the door locks. On less traveled streets after dark, I grew accustomed to but never comfortable with people crossing to the other side of the street rather than pass me. Then there were the standard unpleasantries with policemen, doormen, bouncers, cabdrivers, and others whose business it is to screen out troublesome individuals *before* there is any nastiness.   3

I moved to New York nearly two years ago and I have remained an avid night walker. In central Manhattan, the near-constant crowd cover minimizes tense one-on-one street encounters. Elsewhere—in SoHo, for example, where sidewalks are narrow and tightly spaced buildings shut out the sky—things can get very taut indeed.   4

After dark, on the warrenlike streets of Brooklyn where I live, I often see women who fear the worst from me. They seem to have set their faces on neutral, and with their purse straps strung across their chests bandolier-style, they forge ahead as though bracing themselves against being tackled. I understand, of course, that the danger they perceive is not a hallucination. Women are particularly vulnerable to street violence, and young black males are drastically overrepresented among the perpetrators of that violence. Yet these truths are no solace against the kind of alienation that comes of being ever the suspect, a fearsome entity with whom pedestrians avoid making eye contact.   5

It is not altogether clear to me how I reached the ripe old age of twenty-two without being conscious of the lethality nighttime pedestrians attributed to me. Perhaps it was because in Chester, Pennsylvania, the small, angry industrial town where I came of age in the 1960s, I was scarcely noticeable against a backdrop of gang warfare, street knifings, and murders. I grew up one of the good boys, had perhaps a half-dozen fistfights. In retrospect, my shyness of combat has clear sources.   6

As a boy, I saw countless tough guys locked away; I have since buried several, too. They were babies, really—a teenage cousin, a brother of twenty-two, a childhood friend in his mid-twenties—all gone down in episodes of bravado played out in the streets. I came to doubt the virtues of in-   7 timidation early on. I chose, perhaps unconsciously, to remain a shadow—timid, but a survivor.

The fearsomeness mistakenly attributed to me in public places often 8 has a perilous flavor. The most frightening of these confusions occurred in the late 1970s and early 1980s, when I worked as a journalist in Chicago. One day, rushing into the office of a magazine I was writing for with a deadline story in hand, I was mistaken for a burglar. The office manager called security and, with an ad hoc posse, pursued me through the labyrinthine halls, nearly to my editor's door. I had no way of proving who I was. I could only move briskly toward the company of someone who knew me.

Another time I was on assignment for a local paper and killing time 9 before an interview. I entered a jewelry store on the city's affluent Near North Side. The proprietor excused herself and returned with an enormous red Doberman pinscher straining at the end of a leash. She stood, the dog extended toward me, silent to my questions, her eyes bulging nearly out of her head. I took a cursory look around, nodded, and bade her good night.

Relatively speaking, however, I never fared as badly as another black 10 male journalist. He went to nearby Waukegan, Illinois, a couple of summers ago to work on a story about a murderer who was born there. Mistaking the reporter for the killer, police officers hauled him from his car at gunpoint and but for his press credentials would probably have tried to book him. Such episodes are not uncommon. Black men trade tales like this all the time.

Over the years, I learned to smother the rage I felt at so often being 11 taken for a criminal. Not to do so would surely have led to madness. I now take precautions to make myself less threatening. I move about with care, particularly late in the evening. I give a wide berth to nervous people on subway platforms during the wee hours, particularly when I have exchanged business clothes for jeans. If I happen to be entering a building behind some people who appear skittish, I may walk by, letting them clear the lobby before I return, so as not to seem to be following them. I have been calm and extremely congenial on those rare occasions when I've been pulled over by the police.

And on late-evening constitutionals I employ what has proved to be an 12 excellent tension-reducing measure: I whistle melodies from Beethoven and Vivaldi and the more popular classical composers. Even steely New Yorkers hunching toward nighttime destinations seem to relax, and occasionally they even join in the tune. Virtually everybody seems to sense that a mugger wouldn't be warbling bright, sunny selections from Vivaldi's *Four Seasons*. It is my equivalent of the cowbell that hikers wear when they know they are in bear country.

La Frontera | Bill Barich

In this opening section of a much longer essay, Bill Barich describes the movement across the "most heavily travelled border in the world." Reread his comments on composing paragraphs on page 184. Then examine the

Barich, Bill. "La Frontera." *New Yorker*. December 1990. 72–74.

unity, completeness, order, and *coherence* of his paragraphs. How does the size and sequence of his paragraphs contribute to his purpose?

The most heavily travelled border in the world is a strip of scrubby California desert that runs for fifteen miles between the United States and Mexico, starting at the Pacific Ocean and ending at a thriving yet isolated spot called Otay Mesa. A chain-link fence follows the border for much of its course, but it is torn in many places and trampled in many others, and in some places it has fallen down. Where the fence is still standing, you find litter on both sides of it which illegal aliens have left behind—beer and soda cans, cigarette packs, diapers, syringes, candy wrappers, and even comic-book *novelas* that feature cautionary tales about the perils of a trip to *El Norte.* These *novelas* tell of dishonest employers, horrible living conditions, and the corruptive power of American dollars. In their most dramatic stories, families come apart, brothers murder brothers, and lovers' hearts are broken beyond mending. The stories offer a liberal blend of truth and fiction, but that is an accurate reflection of the border, where nothing is ever absolute.

Between the ocean and the mesa, the only town of any size is San Ysidro, California, just across from Tijuana. About forty-three million people pass through its legal port of entry every year, in vehicles, on bicycles, and on foot, but nobody knows for certain how many undocumented migrants slip illegally over *la frontera.* An educated guess would be about five thousand every day. They come primarily from Mexico and Central America, and they carry their most precious belongings with them in knapsacks or plastic supermarket bags. The Border Patrol, in its San Diego Sector—a territory roughly as big as Connecticut—apprehends about a third of them, logging almost fifteen hundred arrests every twenty-four hours, but the others drift on to Los Angeles or San Francisco or Sacramento, or to farms in the great Central Valley, staying with relatives and friends while they look for work. If they fail to be hired anywhere, they go farther north, to Oregon and Washington, ready to pick fruit or to gut salmon in a packing-house, willing to do anything to earn their keep.

Like many border towns, San Ysidro is conducive to paranoia. Set in the midst of sagebrush and dry, brown mountains covered with chaparral, it has the harmless look of an ordinary suburb, but this is deceptive and does not hold up under close inspection. For instance, there is a blood bank on the edge of its largest mall, and all day you can watch donors come out the door with balls of cotton pressed to their forearms, bound for a shopping spree at a nearby K mart before going home to Tijuana. The sky above San Ysidro is often full of ravens and buzzards, and skulls of small animals turn up in its playgrounds. Its population is mostly Hispanic, but more and more Anglos—retired people, and people who commute to San Diego—are buying property in the tile-roofed housing tracts that are devouring the last farms and ranches, and they get very angry the first time some illegal aliens dash through their back yards, trampling the shrubbery and pausing to drink from garden hoses.

The Border Patrol is the uniformed arm of the Immigration and Naturalization Service, and it is supposed to control the flow of uninvited for-

1

2

3

4

eigners into the States. In California, as in Texas, its stations are under-staffed and underfunded, and are asked to perform a nearly impossible task. In the San Diego Sector, agents must police all of San Diego County, as well as substantial parts of Orange and Riverside Counties, scouring not only the canyons and the backwoods but also the teeming barrios in cities, where aliens frequently seek shelter. Although the sector captures more illegal aliens than any other sector in the country—more than four hundred and seventy thousand in fiscal year 1990, almost half the United States total—this record does little for the morale of the agents, since there is no real penalty imposed on those who are apprehended, unless they have some contraband or resist arrest. Mexicans are given a brief interview, then returned to Tijuana, sometimes so quickly that they get caught crossing again on the same night.

The law isn't the only obstacle that the Border Patrol faces in dispatching its duty. It used to be easy for agents to spot new arrivals because they dressed like field hands and looked dirty and frightened, but now the aliens disguise themselves in clothes fresh off the rack, relying on such items as bluejeans, Reeboks, and L.A. Dodgers caps for protective coloration. The business of providing goods and services to migrants has grown enormously, forming a closed economy worth millions, and they have an elaborate network of support, which often involves extended families and functions in the manner of an underground railroad. Then, too, illegal aliens are always testing agents by devising new tricks for sneaking into California. On a hot summer day, they like to put on bathing suits and wander up the coast, or they dive from a boat and swim to shore. They wade through raw sewage in the Tijuana River and slip into Imperial Beach, just north of San Ysidro. They jam themselves into car trunks and into boxcars, and they ride across the border spread-eagled on top of freight trains. The boldest ones merely sprint through the backed-up traffic at the port of entry, defying the Border Patrol to chase them.

Once illegal aliens get by this first line of defense, they can relax and blend into the crowd of legal Hispanics in San Ysidro. They treat the town as a sort of flea market, making connections and buying Stateside necessities, usually on the sly. If they require fake documents—anything from birth certificates to green cards—they seek out a dealer in such papers and begin negotiations. A high-quality document might cost more than a thousand dollars. Only an expert can detect that it's a forgery, while a so-called "fifty-footer" looks bad even at that distance and can be bought without much haggling. If migrants have some pesos to be laundered, they speak to the fellows hanging around the pay phones by the United States Customs gate. Those phones, supplied by half a dozen different companies, are the conduit through which, a fortune in drug profits—from the sale of cocaine, marijuana, and methamphetamines—is annually rerouted. The men who smuggle in aliens use the phones, too, arranging transportation for their customers. The smugglers are known as *coyotes,* on account of their predatory habits, and they flourish on the border, where expediency is the rule of thumb.

In San Ysidro, there are also safe houses, where, for a price, a migrant can hole up for a while. The safe houses look like the houses around them, but everybody on a given block can point them out. As it happens, secrecy tends to play a very limited role in illegal immigration. Anyone who wants to see how openly aliens cross the border, even in broad daylight, can take a drive on Dairy Mart Road, which winds from the outskirts of town through beanfields, pastures, and fallow land scattered with junked farm machinery. On any morning or afternoon, in any season, you'll have to brake to a halt as people streak by in front of your car, speeding from one hiding place to another. For the most part, they are young men in their late teens and early twenties, and they never seem the slightest bit afraid. They emerge from arroyos, from stands of bamboo and pampas grass, from copses of trees, and from vacant buildings. One morning as I cruised on Dairy Mart Road, I counted twenty-two people in a two-hour period.

The action at night is even more spectacular, and it occurs on a much   8
larger scale. At dusk, you start hearing sirens and whistles all over San Ysidro, as if several robberies were in progress, and then comes the chopping sound of helicopter blades slashing up the clouds. Step outside your motel room and you notice beams from above shining down on a Carl's, Jr., restaurant, on kids in baseball uniforms and elderly folks out for an evening stroll. Sometimes a beam illuminates a drainage ditch, and a human form scampers away, like a rabbit rousted from its burrow. It's disconcerting to find normal life going on in what appears to be a suburban war zone. If you walk to a weedy field near the blood bank, you can look toward the concrete levee of the Tijuana River, where, in the glare of I.N.S. floodlights and in full view of the Border Patrol, more than five hundred people will be congregated in little bands, waiting for an opportune moment to begin their journey to the United States.

Writing Assignments

Narrate   **1.**   Your family, like most, probably has a relative about whom you like to tell stories. Freewrite about this person without stopping to divide your information into paragraphs. Then reread your material to determine how you might group and sequence your information into paragraphs that present a coherent biographical sketch of your family's favorite hero or villain.

Observe   **2.**   Examine old pictures in a family photograph album. Select a photograph taken during a significant or a revealing occasion. Reread Patricia Hampl's comments on old family photographs on page 191, then write a letter to a member of your family describing the photograph and your interest in this historical moment.

Investigate   **3.**   Interview a student or someone in your university's office of student affairs who is concerned with the status of minority students on your campus. Inquire about the social, intellectual, and emotional difficulties specific minority students face as they acquire an education with students (and faculty) from the dominant culture. Then write a profile for your student newspaper on "A Day in the Life" of a minority student on your campus.

Collaborate   **4.**   Your writing group has been asked to compile a group-portrait that describes its ethnic diversity. Pair up with a member of your group. Interview one another. Then talk to relatives to explore your family's ethnic history. When did the first member of your family immigrate to the United States? What advantages or difficulties did members of your family face because of their ethnicity? Is your family in touch or out of touch with its ethnic heritage? Use such questions to collect information that can be transformed into topical paragraphs. Then write a collaborative portrait of your group in which you select a similar sequence of paragraphs to present the biographical profile for each member of your group.

Read   **5.**   Select a cultural group you are unfamiliar with—Amish, Lithuanian and Zuni—and then read several articles about how that group has been treated in the United States. Draft several topic sentences that advance an explanation for this treatment. Then compose an essay by developing those sentences into topical paragraphs. Experiment with each paragraph by placing the topic sentence in a different position.

Respond   **6.**   Respond to Brent Staple's essay "Black Men and Public Space" by writing an opinion column for your daily newspaper in which you describe experiences you may have had in being stereotyped as a member of a group. You may have been ignored, belittled, or mistreated because of your ethnicity, sex, age, accent or dialect, style of dress, physical characteristics or home town. Reserve some of your paragraphs, as Staples does, to reveal the strategies you have developed for dealing with this stereotyping.

Analyze **7.** Compare and contrast the paragraphs by Ellen Goodman and Bill Barich. The most obvious difference, size, can be explained by the context for their essays—a short newspaper column (Goodman) and a long magazine feature (Barich). You may want to analyze the effectiveness of these conventions. For example, are Goodman's paragraphs *complete*? Are Barich's paragraphs *unified*? You may also want to consider the appropriateness of form and purpose—short paragraphs about social fragmentation (Goodman); long paragraphs about social crowding (Barich). Write an analysis explaining these concepts, using examples from these sources.

Evaluate **8.** Reread the paragraphs on the status of the American family in this chapter (Philip Slater, page 191; Jane Howard, page 192; Jane O'Reilly, pages 192–3). Reexamine Goodman's argument about the stresses and strengths within the American family. Then argue that (a) the power of the American family was always more an ideal than a reality, (b) the American family is breaking up beneath the forces of contemporary culture, or (c) the contemporary American family, though changed in character, is as strong as it ever was.

Argue **9.** Reread the paragraphs on Ellis Island on pages 194–5. You may want to read additional material on immigration in the 1890s. (Some good sources are Oscar Handlin's *Uprooted: The Epic Story of the Great Migrations that Made the American People* and Wilson Tifft and Thomas Dunne's *Ellis Island*). Reread Barich's description of "La Frontera." You may want to read the whole essay (*New Yorker* 17 December 1990: 72–92). Then argue either that (a) there is no real difference between the way immigrant groups were treated at Ellis Island and the way they are treated along the Mexican border, or (b) specific issues—economic, social, legal—account for contemporary attitudes toward those who want to cross America's borders.

Argue **10.** Examine your university catalogue and reading lists for courses. What opportunities are available for studying the history and culture of various ethnic groups in your college curriculum? Use this information to compose an open letter to the faculty and administration, arguing either that a) such opportunities already exist, but students need better advice about why they should study such material; or that b) such opportunities do *not* exist in the current curriculum, but faculty can enrich existing courses or create new ones that would meet this need.

8

Sentences: Patterns of Expression

A s you saw in Chapter 7, the sentences in a well-written paragraph are not isolated statements; they exist in complex interrelationships with each other. Although traditionally called units of composition, sentences are units chiefly in the grammatical sense that each sentence has its own subject and predicate and is not part of another sentence. Beyond these basic attributes, however, sentences vary widely in style—and therefore in the effect they create. By varying the arrangement of words, phrases, and clauses in sentences, writers reveal emphasis, shade meaning, and create various kinds of movement in their writing.

Richard Selzer, surgeon and writer, composes sentences in two stages:

> The *first* propels me across the page with an armful of language. It's like the technique of the abstract painter. He will make a brush stroke on a bare canvas. That stroke leads to another and the combination to a third until the canvas is done and he realizes what he has made. The *second* is the fully conscious tinkering that goes on. The artist is always blacking out parts of his canvas and correcting small details until the painting is done in his mind. So one of my essays isn't finished until I cross out half of it and revise its individual parts. I try to respond to the marvellous elasticity of the language by constantly opening up or compressing my sentences. When I am done, they possess a distinctive rhythm and resonance. I can pick them out immediately on any page of prose. They're like my signature. (Personal interview)

This chapter will take a close look at how writers such as Selzer express their purpose by expanding, combining, and revising their sentences.

EXPANDING AND COMBINING SENTENCES

Like a brush stroke, a basic sentence moves across the page in a simple line. It consists of a subject and a predicate. The predicate may be a complete verb or a verb that needs something to complete it. For example, the sentence

"The doctor smiled" consists of the subject *doctor* and the complete verb *smiled.* But in the following two sentences the verb requires completion:

The doctor + *examined* + the patient. [Subject, verb, and object]

The doctor + *was* + courteous. [Subject, verb, and complement]

A *basic sentence,* then, is a main clause consisting of subject and verb and any object or complement required to complete the verb.

Any element in a basic sentence may be modified by adjectives, adverb phrases, or clauses that describe or limit the words being modified. Or the whole main clause rather than one of its elements may be modified. For example, in the sentence "If you can't do it, I'll ask Dr. Helena," the introductory *if* clause modifies the whole main clause and is called a *sentence modifier.*

In the following examples the basic sentence is underscored; the modifiers are italicized and are connected by arrows to the words they modify.

Many students *enrolled in the pre-med curriculum* find *organic* chemistry *extremely* difficult.

To prepare for a test they study *for hours* with *incredible* concentration.

Some, *recognizing their limitations in math,* hire *private* tutors *to help them prepare for each exam.*

Others study alone, *because they are driven to master the material in seclusion.*

If their study habits predict how they will behave as doctors, some will consult with colleagues, while others will insist on making their own diagnosis.

As those examples show, modifiers may be single words or phrases (*many, private, for hours*) or subordinate clauses (*because they are driven to master the material in seclusion*). The modifiers may come before, after, or within the main clause. In the last two sentences, the subordinate clauses modify the whole main clause and are therefore sentence modifiers.

———*Exercise* Distinguish between basic sentences and modifying words or phrases in the following passage from Richard Selzer's "An Absence of Windows." First underline the basic sentence; then circle the modifiers.

(1) Part of my surgical training was spent in a rural hospital in eastern Connecticut. (2) The building was situated on the slope of a modest hill. (3) Behind it, cows grazed in a pasture. (4) The operating theater occu-

pied the fourth, the ultimate floor, wherefrom high windows looked down upon the scene. (5) To glance up from our work and see lovely cattle about theirs, calmed the frenzy of the most temperamental of prima donnas. (6) Intuition tells me that our patients had fewer wound infections and made speedier recoveries than those operated upon in the airless sealed boxes where we now strive. (7) Certainly the surgeons were of gentler stripe.

Expanding Sentences by Modification

In effective writing, details communicate specific information and hold the reader's interest. Any sentence can be enriched by modification. Notice how much detail is added by the italicized modifiers in the following sentences.

My father kept his own books, *in a desk calendar that recorded in his fine Spencerian handwriting the names of the patients he had seen each day, each name followed by the amount he charged, and that number followed by the amount received.* (Lewis Thomas, "Amity Street," *The Youngest Science: Notes of a Medicine Watcher*)

I debated whether I should major in zoology *so early in the term before I knew whether my high school science courses had prepared me for the difficult challenges of the college curriculum.*

The drug companies, *usually operating through private physicians with access to the prisons,* can obtain healthy human subjects *living in conditions that are difficult, if not impossible, to duplicate elsewhere.* (Jessica Mitford, *Kind and Unusual Punishment*)

In this portion of the chart, *after all the histories are taken, after the chest has been thumped and the spleen has been fingered, after the white cells have been counted and the potassium surveyed,* the doctor can be *seen to abandon the position of recorder and assume that of* natural scientist. (Gerald Weissman, "The Chart of the Novel," *The Woods Hole Cantata: Essays on Science and Society*)

In sentences like these, the effect comes not from the main clause, which provides no details, but from the specific information provided by the modifiers. You can easily see that this is so by isolating the main clause from the modifiers:

My father kept his own books.

I debated whether I should major in zoology.

The drug companies can obtain healthy human subjects.

In this portion of the chart the doctor can be natural scientist.

Effective modifiers such as the ones shown in the full sentences here have two qualities. First, they are not tacked on as afterthoughts but are essential parts of the writers' purposes. A significant portion of Thomas's recollection of his father's books focuses on the shape of the handwriting and the pattern of the accounts; the student's debate about majoring in zoology is occasioned by her doubts about her high school preparation in science; Weissman's description of a doctor's writing process is based on the details he has to record. In each case the modifying details are necessary to express the writer's complete thought.

Second, effective modification is grounded in observation or experience. Weissman knows from experience how to keep a patient's chart. Mitford has researched her subject and knows about the doctor's cooperation and the conditions that made prisoners ideal subjects for experiments. In each example, the writer has used modification to get his or her observations into the sentences.

Suppose you were asked to expand these three sentences by modification:

> I am uncomfortable in my doctor's office.
>
> My doctor always seems impatient.
>
> Doctors study the human body.

To complete the assignment, you need to know the context in which the writer is working and his or her purpose for composing the sentences. Without that knowledge, asking you to expand them is asking you to supply a context and purpose. By drawing on your own experience, you can describe why doctors' offices make you uncomfortable, what makes your doctor appear impatient, and how doctors study the human body. You might expand the first sentence like this:

> I am uncomfortable in my doctor's office because while I sit in the posh chairs of the waiting room I imagine that my body is being secretly afflicted with all sorts of life-threatening diseases.

_____ *Exercise*   Drawing on your own experience, expand the following basic sentences to make them fuller expressions of the ideas they suggest to you.

1. My doctor always seems impatient.
2. I don't like to read reports about medical studies.
3. I always get sick on vacations.
4. Doctors study the human body.
5. I don't know if an ache is a symptom or something that will just go away.

Combining Sentences
by Coordination

Coordination is combining or joining similar elements into pairs or series. As in the following pairs of examples, sentences can be combined by using a common subject or predicate and compounding the remaining element:

Medical technology contributes to the high cost of health care. Medical liability insurance is also extremely expensive.

Compound subject/
Compound predicate

Medical technology and medical liability insurance both contribute to the high cost of health care.

Doctors must complete their charts under pressure. They also must carefully think through their comments and notations.

Compound predicate/
Compound subject

Doctors completing their charts must carefully think through their comments and notations and must write under pressure.

_____*Exercise*   By combining parts through coordination, compress the sentences in each group into a single sentence.

1. Coronary heart disease is the major cause of death in this country.
   Cancer also causes many deaths.

2. My doctor warned me about trying to lose weight too fast.
   My coach reminded me of the danger involved.
   My mother told me the same thing.

3. The first documented case of AIDS within the United States occurred in 1977.
   The AIDS crisis continues to grow.
   The number of newspaper and magazine articles on AIDS has declined in the last few years.

4. Breakfast cereals contain fiber.
   Oat bran may reduce cholesterol.
   Advertisers stress the health advantages of their products.

5. The cost of running shoes is escalating.
   Most people are very selective about the kind of running shoes they buy.

Using Parallel Structure

When two or more coordinate elements have the same form, they are said to have *parallel structure*. Such structures may be unnoticed in any sentence, but when the parallelism is conspicuous, the whole sentence may be called a *parallel sentence*. Thus, "He was without a job, without money, without opportunity, and without hope" is a parallel sentence in which the four phrases have the same form (they all start with *without*) and the same grammatical function (they all complete the verb *was*).

Consider these contrasted sentences:

I am in favor of equal economic rights for women. Women should be able to compete with men for jobs for which they are both qualified. The pay should be the same for the same jobs. There should be the same opportunities for advancement.	I am in favor of equal economic rights for women: the right to compete with men for jobs for which they are both qualified, the right to get the same pay for the same job, and the right to equal opportunities for advancement.

Both versions assert the same three rights. The version on the left advances the assertions in four sentences, each using a different subject. The version on the right states all three rights in one sentence and focuses the reader's attention by the repetition of the phrase "the right to." The parallel structure of the second version gives it the unity, coherence, and emphasis that the first version lacks.

Parallel elements may be single words, phrases, clauses, or sentences (contributing to a paragraph with parallel structure); they may act as subjects, objects, verbs, or adverbial or adjectival modifiers. But for elements in a pair or a series to be parallel, all members must have the same form and serve the same grammatical function. You cannot coordinate nouns with adjectives, verbs with infinitives, or phrases with clauses. Any attempt to do so disrupts parallelism, disappoints your readers, and produces awkwardness.

In each of the following sentences, the italicized element disrupts parallelism by switching from one grammatical form to another:

The children were laughing, squealing, and *danced*. [To restore parallelism, *danced* should be changed to *dancing*.]

My two ambitions are to become a doctor and *having* enough money to give my children a good education. [Parallelism requires that *to become* must be matched with *to have*.]

My parents taught me such things as honesty, faith, *to be fair,* and *having patience*. [Parallelism with the two nouns would be sustained by replacing the infinitive and participial phrases with the nouns *fairness* and *patience*.]

The following diagrams show the similarity in form and function of various parallel structures:

Parallel predicates

He   walked past the information desk,

                   followed the signs to obstetrics,

                   selected a seat in the waiting room, and

                   watched the other expectant fathers pace the floor.

Prepositional phrases in a series

Fat people know all about the mystery of life. They are the ones acquainted	with the night,
	with luck,
	with fate,
	with playing it by ear.
	(Suzanne Britt Jordan)

Participial phrases in a series

This was the American family at play	escaping the city heat,
	wondering whether the newcomers in the camp at the head of the cove were "common" or "nice,"
	wondering whether it was true that the people who drove up for Sunday dinner at the farmhouse were turned away because there wasn't enough chicken.
	(E. B. White)

_____ *Exercise*

1. Identify and diagram the parallel elements in the following sentences.
   a. We hold these truths to be self-evident: that all men are created equal, that they are endowed by their Creator with certain unalienable Rights. . . .
   b. Berton Roueche's narratives of "medical detection" are full of patients with unusual symptoms, of laboratory technicians with specialized knowledge, and of doctors with extraordinary diagnostic powers.

2. The notes that follow list the distinguishing characteristics of people who exhibit Type A and Type B behavior. Organize the items into parallel lists, and then write a parallel sentence coordinating the information in the two series.

Type A behavior	*Type B behavior*
Obsessed with deadlines	Evokes serenity in others
Intense need to win at all costs	Enjoys creating images and metaphors
Conversation dominated by numbers	Secure sense of self-esteem
Harshly critical of others	Rarely wears a watch

3. Create a list of notes on the brain suggested by the notes on the computer. Then compose a parallel sentence contrasting the advantages of the brain over the computer as a thinking "machine."

Computer	*Brain*
Circuits	
Blank disk	
Storage	
Program	

When parallelism is extended through a paragraph, each sentence becomes an element in a series. An example of a series of parallel sentences appears on page 196, in the paragraph by Dr. Martin Luther King in which each sentence begins with the phrase "There is nothing." Such deliberate repetition binds individual sentences into a coherent paragraph. Consider the features of conspicuous parallelism in the following paragraph.

> H. G. Wells continues to be a biographer's dream and book reviewer's waltz. His life stretches very nearly from Appomattox to Hiroshima. He was one of the world's great storytellers, the father of modern science fiction, an autobiographic novelist of scandalous proportions, a proselytizer for world peace through brain power, an unsurpassed popular historian, a journalist and inexhaustible pamphleteer, the friend and worthy adversary of great men and the lover of numerous and intelligent women. (R. Z. Sheppard, *Time*)

Combining Sentences by Subordination

Subordination reduces one sentence to a subordinate clause or to a phrase that becomes part of another sentence. Consider the following basic sentences.

> We left early. We had work to do.

The second of these sentences may be embedded in the first as a subordinate clause.

> We left early *because we had work to do.*

In the next example, a basic sentence is reduced to a phrase.

> The man was evidently in great pain. He was taken to a hospital.

> The man, *evidently in great pain,* was taken to the hospital.

As those examples show, when two sentences are combined by subordination, the information in one sentence is embedded in the other. Using subordination, a writer can pack a great deal of information into a sentence and still emphasize what is most important. This does not mean that short, basic sentences are always inappropriate. Often they are useful to create variety and achieve emphasis. But consistent use of basic sentences in a sustained piece of writing can seem repetitive and dull.

In the following example, a complex sentence is created through the subordination of four basic sentences.

1. Last weekend I saw a science fiction film.
2. Three friends went with me.
3. The film focused on the experiments of a mad doctor.
4. He altered his patients' lives by manipulating their dreams.

Last weekend three friends and I saw a science fiction film in which a mad doctor altered his patients' lives by manipulating their dreams.

The original four sentences contain 32 words. Using subordination to embed sentences 2, 3, and 4 in sentence 1 creates a denser sentence in which the same information is expressed economically, in 24 words, and the monotony of the original sentences is eliminated.

_____ *Exercise*   Practice creating denser sentences through subordination by reducing each of the following sets of sentences to a single sentence without omitting any of the information.

1. Scientists use guinea pigs in their laboratory experiments.
   They inject them with a disease.
   They observe their behavior.
   They dissect them.
   They examine the effect of the disease on their organs.

2. Michelangelo studied anatomy.
   He dissected cadavers.
   Such gruesome work helped him understand human bones and muscles.
   His sculptures celebrate the human body.

3. X-rays can penetrate the human body.
   They produce images on photographic film.
   Shadows on the picture reveal changes in body tissue.

4. The early history of medicine is filled with guesswork.
   Doctors did not know what caused disease.
   They developed cures through trial and error.
   Most of the cures did not work.
   Cures that worked were considered magical.

5. People went to spas to restore their health.
   Most spas were located in beautiful settings.
   They featured special mineral waters.
   The waters were supposed to purge the body of disease.
   These watering spots developed into vacation resorts.

Combining for a Purpose

When you combine basic sentences into denser structures through coordination and subordination, you should choose the sentence pattern that best suits your purpose. If you are writing a paper on the latest developments in frozen foods for a nutrition class, you might collect the following information.

1. Frozen food has long been part of the American way of life.
2. Frozen dinners once consisted of such dull items as lima beans, gooey potatoes, and mystery meat.
3. Currently available frozen-dinner entrées include beef bourguignon with glazed carrots, asparagus crepes with Mornay sauce, and vegetarian lasagna.
4. Some frozen-food companies have even developed gourmet dietetic dinners.
5. Americans have fast-paced, busy lifestyles these days.
6. They are also more concerned than before about eating healthful, interesting, and balanced meals.

Strung together in that order, these sentences have little meaning. They trace a sequence, to be sure, but what is significant about that sequence and what are its implications? The answer, of course, depends on your purpose. If you have a purpose, you can combine the sentences through coordination or subordination to achieve focus and establish relationships among the facts.

For example, if you want to propose a cause and effect relationship between the change in American lifestyles and the change in frozen food, you can reduce sentence 1 to a subordinate clause and embed it in sentence 2.

Frozen dinners, long part of the American way of life, once consisted of such dull items as lima beans, gooey potatoes, and mystery meat.

Through a similar process you can combine sentences 5 and 6 and 3 and 4.

To satisfy busy Americans' concern for healthy, interesting, and balanced meals, today's frozen-food companies have developed more sophisticated fare: beef bourguignon with glazed carrots, asparagus crepes with Mornay sauce, vegetarian lasagna, and even gourmet dietetic dinners.

With a coordinating conjunction you can combine the two sentences into one.

Frozen dinners, long part of the American way of life, once consisted of such dull items as lima beans, gooey potatoes, and mystery meat, but to satisfy busy Americans' concern for healthy, interesting, and balanced meals, today's food companies have developed more sophisticated fare: beef bourguignon with glazed carrots, asparagus crepes with Mornay sauce, vegetarian lasagna, and even gourmet dietetic dinners.

But if you want to demonstrate that those who once found frozen dinners unappetizing now have a reason to try them, you can combine the original sentences for this purpose.

Busy Americans once identified frozen dinners with such dull items as lima beans, gooey potatoes, and mystery meat, but today those same consumers are tempted by a new variety of healthy, interesting, and balanced frozen meals: beef bourguignon with glazed carrots, asparagus crepes with Mornay sauce, vegetarian lasagna, and even dietetic dinners.

The last version focuses on the customer rather than on the company, but the focus is still achieved by subordination and coordination.

The three devices you have been studying—modification, coordination, and subordination—allow you to combine and present information in complex sentences. Organizing ideas into an effective form is just as important in a sentence as it is in a paragraph or essay. In a series of simple sentences, each idea is stated separately; the statements lack coherence, and relationships among the ideas are not clear. Moreover, such sentences lack emphasis; all information appears to be of equal importance. By subordinating the less important to the more important, or by showing the equality of ideas through coordination, you can revise such sentences so that they exhibit variety, clarity, and emphasis.

_____*Exercise*   For each of the following clusters, combine as many of the items as you need (you may not need or want to use them all) into a sentence that fulfills each of the two purposes specified for each cluster. Combine any remaining items into a second, supporting sentence.

Cluster A

1. Clothes reveal an individual's personality and attitudes.
2. Clothes like blue jeans and T-shirts make a statement.
3. Dark blue suits and white laboratory jackets also make a statement.
4. Certain occasions, situations, or jobs require appropriate attire.
5. "Appropriate" attire is often formal: a dress, suit, tie.
6. People should be free to dress as they please.
7. In many professional situations, people judge others by their appearance.

Purpose 1   You want to assert that people should be free to dress as they please.
Purpose 2   You want to argue that people should dress appropriately in professional situations.

Cluster B

1. Hospitals are often the setting for television soap operas.
2. Characters spend more time discussing their personal problems than their professional responsibilities.
3. Doctors are seen making rounds; nurses are seen keeping charts.
4. Soap operas rarely show medical procedures.
5. Characters conveniently develop illnesses to complicate the plot.
6. Doctors use vague medical terminology to discuss cases.

Purpose 1   You want to demonstrate that soap operas show superficial treatment of illness.
Purpose 2   You want to illustrate that soap operas use hospitals as a convenient setting for dramatic conflict.

Cluster C

1. Many of today's sports injuries are treated with arthroscopic surgery.
2. Major surgery requires doctors to cut through the muscle to find the damaged area.
3. Such surgery requires many months of rehabilitation.
4. An arthroscopic surgeon punctures the muscle with a catheter carrying a microscopic television camera and another catheter carrying appropriate surgical tools.
5. He locates the injury with the camera and uses the tool to repair it.
6. Players can often return to action within several weeks.
7. Any injury requires sufficient recuperation.
8. Reinjury of damaged areas can result in disability.

Purpose 1   You want to argue that arthroscopic surgery is a major medical breakthrough.
Purpose 2   You want to suggest that the availability of arthroscopic surgery can give players a false sense of security.

TYPES OF SENTENCES AND THEIR EFFECTS

In this section you will learn to use to good effect three important sentence types: the *balanced* sentence, the *periodic* sentence, and the *cumulative* sentence.

The Balanced Sentence

In a balanced sentence, two coordinate but contrasting structures are set off against each other like the weights on a balance scale. In each of the following sentences the underlined parts balance each other:

> Many are called but few are chosen. (Matthew 22:14)
>
> I came to bury Caesar, not to praise him. (William Shakespeare, *Julius Caesar*)
>
> Where I used to suture the tissue of the body together, now I suture words together. (Richard Selzer)

When you read a balanced sentence aloud, you tend to pause between the balanced parts. That pause is often marked by a coordinating conjunction (*but, or, nor, yet, and*), sometimes by *not* (as in the second sentence), and sometimes by punctuation alone (as in the third sentence). Whatever the marker, it serves as a fulcrum, the point at which the contrasted parts balance against each other, as the following diagram illustrates:

| | but |
| When a man dies on shore, his body remains with his friends, and the "mourners go about the streets," | when a man falls overboard at sea and is lost, there is a sudden-ness in the event . . . which gives it an air of awful mystery. |

(Richard Henry Dana)

The balanced structure points up the contrast in thought. It is effective when two subjects are to be contrasted within the same sentence.

_____*Exercises*

Compose a sentence about each item in each pair. Then combine the two sentences into a balanced sentence.

jogging—swimming   pain—stress
doctors—dentists   painting—photograph
smokers—nonsmokers   mural—miniature

Periodic and Cumulative Sentences

A *periodic* sentence builds to a climactic statement in its final main clause. The writer withholds the main idea until the end of the sentence. Here is an example:

> Just before I went away to college, my father took me aside, as I had expected, and said, as I had not expected, "Now, Son, if a strange woman comes up to you on a street corner and offers to take your watch around the corner and have it engraved, don't do it." (Eric Lax)

The father's remarks lead up to the advice given in the final main clause—"don't do it"—which provides a climax, like the punch line of a joke. All the rest of the sentence has been a preparation for that statement.

Cumulative sentences, also called *loose sentences,* reverse the order of periodic sentences. Instead of withholding the main idea until the last clause, the writer states it immediately and then adds examples and details. Compare the style and effect of the cumulative and periodic sentence in these two examples.

> I fought migraine then, ignored the warnings it sent, went to school and later to work in spite of it, sat through lectures in Middle English and presentations to advertisers with involuntary tears running down the right side of my face, threw up in washrooms, stumbled home by instinct, emptied ice trays onto my bed and tried to freeze the pain in my right temple, wished only for a neurosurgeon who would do a lobotomy on house call, and cussed my imagination. (Joan Didion, "In Bed," *The White Album*)

> For doctors, who confront death when they go to work in the morning as routinely as other people deal with balance sheets and computer print outs, and for me, to whom a chest x-ray or a blood test will never again be a simple routine procedure, it is particularly important to face the fact of death squarely, to talk about it with one another. (Alice Trillin, "Of Dragons and Garden Peas: A Cancer Patient Talks to Doctors," *The New England Journal of Medicine*)

Both writers could have reversed the order of their sentences. Didion could have listed her agonies first, building to her main clause, "I fought migraine." But by announcing her struggle first and then providing the details, she exhausts the main idea and forces her reader to experience some of the exhaustion she feels. Similarly, Trillin could have begun with a clause that states her main idea—that doctors and patients talk squarely to each other about death—and then added the details to illustrate her assertion. But by suspending her assertion until she establishes the contrasting perspectives of doctors and patients, she gains the reader's sympathy and interest. In each example the style and effect of the sentence advance the writer's purpose.

_____*Exercise*   Write a periodic sentence describing the most frustrating, fulfilling, or comic day you have had recently. Use your opening clauses to build suspense and reveal your final assertion in the last clause. Then reverse this order and write a cumulative sentence. Make your assertion first and then accumulate detailed examples. Which pattern is more effective? Explain your answer.

REVISING SENTENCES

You have been examining the structure of different types of sentences and techniques for increasing the density of sentences through modification, co-ordination, and subordination. The process of shaping ideas into sentences is a learning process, and as you grope toward a satisfactory statement of your meaning you will try out different sentence structures, revising your sentences while you write them. But in this section you will be trying, through local revision, to make your sentences more effective expressions of the ideas you intend them to convey, to improve sentences that have already been written—to "tinker," as Selzer suggests, with your completed draft—by revising for *clarity, emphasis, economy,* and *variety.*

Revising for Clarity

This section is concerned only with revising confusing sentence structure, even though lack of clarity can result from faulty grammar or punctuation, misleading pronoun reference, or vague or ambiguous wording, as well. Un-clear sentence structure sometimes occurs when a writer tries to pack too much information into one sentence. The following sentence illustrates this problem:

> Last month while I was visiting the federal buildings in Washington on a guided tour, we went to the National Art Gallery, where we had been for an hour when the rest of the group was ready to move on to the Treasury Building and I told a friend with the group that I wanted to stay in the Art Gallery a while longer and I would rejoin the group about a half an hour later, but I never did, even though I moved more quickly than I wanted to from room to room, not having seen after about four more hours all that I wanted to see.

As written, this sentence of 108 words consists of three main clauses and eight subordinate clauses. This involved structure is hard going for both writer and reader. The goal of revision should be to simplify the structure by reducing the number of clauses. This can be done by (1) distributing the clauses into two or more sentences, or (2) omitting material irrelevant to the writer's purpose.

Here is a revision that follows the first strategy:

> While I was visiting the National Art Gallery with a group tour last month, I decided to stay longer when the group left after an hour, and so I told a friend that I would rejoin the group at the Treasury Building in about half an hour. I moved from room to room much more quickly than I wanted to, but after four more hours I had not seen all I wanted to see. I never did rejoin the tour group that day.

This revision distributes all the original material into three sentences and makes the passage easier to read. In addition, the revision uses 25 fewer words, a reduction of over 23 percent.

Here is a revision that follows the second strategy, cutting the original drastically by leaving out irrelevant material.

> While visiting the National Art Gallery with a tour group last month, I stayed four hours after the group left. Even then I did not see all that I wanted to.

This version reduces the original eleven clauses to four and compresses the 108-word sentence to 31 words in two sentences.

Both revisions are clearer than the original. The first revision is minor, since it makes little change in content. The second is major, since it both selects and reorganizes the content. In addition to these revisions, others are possible. Try a few variations to see which you prefer.

Notice that the revisions above reduce the amount of information in the original sentence. This may seem to contradict what was said earlier about combining sentences to increase their density. But in fact there is no contradiction. Some sentences should be combined to achieve greater density; others should be separated into several sentences to achieve greater clarity. The decision to combine or to separate, to enrich or to simplify, depends on your material and your best judgment about your audience and purpose.

_____*Exercises*   Simplify the structure of the following sentences to make them easier to read.

1. For centuries artists have known that the paint that they keep in their studios and that they allow to collect on their clothing, and that they are constantly touching and breathing, so that it penetrates their skin and gets into their blood stream, contains lead, which can poison them, causing them to have convulsive cramps, fatigue, and making them look sickly by comparison to the portraits of the healthy subjects they paint.

2. In the movies, artists are often portrayed as tormented and anguished people who live in poverty and squalor that causes them to contract all sorts of strange diseases that make them suffer so that they become more sensitive than normal people, which enables them to create beautiful art in the midst of their illness, even though they have to die for their art and only become famous once they are dead.

3. One of the conceptions not founded in fact that many people have about abstract painters is that they don't possess the skills necessary to draw a landscape or a face. In fact, most abstract painters have developed the ability to be extremely adept at drawing objects and people with photographic accuracy. Instead of painting such realistic portraits, however, they design thickly woven textures of paint that enable them to create more universal symbols that express aspects of all human experience. Some of these symbols are called "biomorphic" because they appear to resemble organic forms or fragments of human anatomy sandwiched into densely packed spatial landscapes. These symbols are often interpreted to express the abstract painter's sense of fragmentation in modern society.

Revising for Emphasis

Emphasis reflects your purpose and helps you convey that purpose to your readers. Among the numerous ways available to express any idea, the most effective are those that underscore your purpose—that best achieve the effect you have in mind. You can create purposeful emphasis by means of *emphatic word order, emphatic repetition, climactic order,* and *emphatic voice.*

Emphatic Word Order   To employ emphatic word order, you must know what you want to emphasize and which positions in a sentence provide the most emphasis. In an English sentence the positions of greatest emphasis are the beginning and the end. The most important material should be placed in those positions; less important material, in mid-sentence. Unimportant details piled up at the end of a sentence get more emphasis than they deserve and make your readers feel that the sentence is "running out of gas."

Notice the difference between the following statements.

Unemphatic order	*Emphatic order*
From 1904 to 1914, Americans built the 50-mile Panama Canal, which caused over five thousand workers to die of malaria in the jungles of Central America.	Over five thousand workers died of malaria in the jungles of Central America when Americans labored from 1904 to 1914 to build the 50-mile Panama Canal.

The most important information in this sentence is that over five thousand workers died of malaria to build a 50-mile canal—about one hundred workers per mile. The version on the left puts the number of deaths and the size of the canal in the least important position, lessening the impact. The version on the right puts this information where it will get the most emphasis, relegating the less important information to the middle of the statement.

_____*Exercises*   Revise the order of each sentence to emphasize the points you think most important.

1. It is entirely possible that longevity depends on the luck of your genes, I sometimes think.

2. A proposal that has caused much discussion about our national health policy is the one about insurance for catastrophic illness that is now before Congress.

3. Dr. Albert Schweitzer, even when he was 90, worked in his clinic all day and played his piano at night because he believed that a sense of purpose and creativity was the best medicine for any illness he might have.

4. Thomas Eakins, in his painting *Gross Clinic* (p. 234), reveals his extensive knowledge of anatomy by portraying Samuel Gross, the famous surgeon, standing next to the operating table with a scalpel in his hand, lecturing to his students as his assistant probes the patient's open wound.

5. One of America's leading authors and child psychiatrists, Robert Coles, learned about sickness when he was a medical student from the stories he heard from the patients he met as he went on rounds with poet and physician Dr. William Carlos Williams.

Emphatic Repetition   Unintentional repetition generally weakens a sentence, as the following examples show:

The disappointing results were all the more disappointing because we were sure that the experiment would be a success, and so were disappointed in the results.

Thomas Eakins (1844–1916), *The Gross Clinic,* **oil on canvas (1875).**
From the Jefferson Medical College of Thomas Jefferson University, Philadelphia.

The writer who wrote the novel that won the award for the best novel of
the year did not attend the awards ceremony.

Deliberate repetition, by contrast, can produce a desired emphasis. You have
seen how the repetition of words can help unify a paragraph and how the
use of parallel and balanced structures creates coherence. The following
examples show the effective use of deliberate repetition:

If we *write* about our scientific *observations,* our *observations* inevitably color
our *writing.* (Leigh Hafrey, "Write About What You Know: Big Bang or
Grecian Urn")

And this hell was simply, that he had never in his life owned anything—*not
his* wife, *not his* house, *not his* child—which could *not,* at any instant, be
taken from him by the power of white people. (James Baldwin)

Paul Gauguin (1848–1903), *Where Do We Come From? What Are We? Where Are We Going?*, oil on canvas (1897).
Tompkins Collection. Courtesy, Museum of Fine Arts, Boston.

Climactic Order   Climactic word order achieves emphasis by building to a major idea. The effect of a periodic sentence depends on climactic order, but climax may be used in other sentences as well. The following example contrasts anticlimactic and climactic order. Study both versions of the sentence to determine what changes were made in revision.

Anticlimactic order

Paul Gauguin, near the end of his life, painted *Where Do We Come From? What Are We? Where Are We Going?* in the hopes of glimpsing the life we live from infancy to our last years.

Climactic order

Near the end of his life, in the hopes of glimpsing the life we live from infancy to our last years, Paul Gauguin painted *Where Do We Come From? What Are We? Where Are We Going?*

Emphatic Voice   Although it is a commonplace that writers should use verbs in the active rather than in the passive voice, this sound advice is worth repeating. The active voice creates natural, vigorous sentences; the passive voice encourages awkward shifts in structure and anemic, evasive wordiness.

Weak passive

Fantasies of the self are created by modern artists.

Real people afflicted by real diseases have been helped by medical science.

More emphatic active voice

Modern artists create fantasies of the self.

Medical science helps real people afflicted by real diseases.

_____*Exercises*   Revise the following sentences by changing passive verbs to the active voice.

1. Changing the criteria for what people consider ugly has been proposed by critics as the goal of much modern art.

2. It must surely be recognized by the American Hospital Association that such costs cannot be afforded by many families.

3. The critic said that the winners in the photographic competition would be announced by her within three days.

4. Once the danger was gone, the safety precautions that had been so carefully observed by us were abandoned.

But in some cases, the passive voice may provide greater emphasis than the active voice. Passive constructions can be used to bypass a sentence's grammatical subject in order to emphasize a more important element, such as a significant action or object of an action. For example:

Active voice	*Passive voice*
A person may not smoke in the museum.	Smoking is prohibited in the museum.
The doctor performed the emergency surgery under battery-operated lights.	The emergency surgery was performed under battery-operated lights.

Choosing active or passive voice is like any other choice you make in the writing process. You must judge by results: Which form provides the emphasis you want? But to avoid the awkward or ungrammatical sentences that can result from misuse of the passive, use the active voice unless the passive advances your purpose more effectively.

Revising for Economy

Economical prose achieves an equivalence between the number of words used and the amount of meaning they convey. A sentence is not economical because it is short, or wordy because it is long. Consider these two statements:

I should like to make it entirely clear to one and all that neither I nor any of my associates or fellow workers had anything at all to do in any way, shape, or form with this illicit and legally unjustifiable act that has been committed.	I want to make it clear to everyone that neither I nor any of my associates had anything to do with this illegal act.

The version on the left takes 46 words to say what is more clearly said on the right in 24. The 22 additional words do not add significant information: they merely make reading more difficult and annoy the reader by useless repetition.

Now contrast the following statements:

His defense is not believable.

His defense is not believable: at points it is contradicted by the unanimous testimony of other witnesses, and it offers no proof that that testimony is false; it ignores significant facts about which there can be no dispute, or evades them by saying that he does not recollect them; it contains inconsistencies that he is unable to resolve, even when specifically asked to do so.

The version on the right contains over twelve times more words than the one on the left, and its greater length is justified by the greater information it provides. Both versions express the same judgment, but the second presents the reasons for that judgment. If the writer believes these reasons must be stated, it would be foolish to omit them simply to compose a shorter sentence. Decisions about economy must always be made in relation to meaning and purpose.

Wordiness—the failure to achieve economy—is a common writing problem. Essays can be wordy because of scanty planning, corrected through global revision, or a monotonous style, corrected through better use of coordination and subordination. To eliminate wordiness *within* a sentence entails local revision. The two most common methods are deleting useless words and phrases and substituting more economical expressions for wordy ones.

Cutting Out Useless Words and Phrases

~~It seems unnecessary to point out that~~ the purpose of chemistry lab is to give students ~~the kind of~~ practical experience ~~they need~~ in testing chemical formulas.

~~I would say in response to your question that~~ the task of the art teacher is to help students ~~develop the ability~~ to understand the function of shape, line, color, and light.

Picasso ~~was an artist who~~ took ~~everyday~~ common objects such as a ~~bicycle~~ seat and the handlebars of an old bicycle and ~~through the process of his imagination~~ transformed them into ~~a work of art called~~ *Bull's Head.*

Substituting an Economical Expression for a Wordy One

Contemporary researchers in
~~The forward looking thinking of those working in the area of~~ coronary

emphasize
artery disease ~~tends to place a great deal of emphasis on~~ the potential of

laser technology.

an international

The Armory Show, ~~a famous~~ exhibition of painting and sculpture ~~that~~

~~brought together the works of artists from throughout the world and dis-~~
held
~~played them~~ in the Armory of the 69th Regiment in New York City in 1913,

introduced
~~enabled~~ the American public to ~~see for the first time artistic movements~~

~~such as~~ Cubism and Expressionism.

Over   *ago*   *argued that*
~~It has been more than~~ thirty years ~~since~~ C. P. Snow ~~presented his argument~~
our
~~that the~~ world ~~we live in~~ is divided into *two cultures*—one ~~of these cultures~~
dedicated to   *to*
~~was preoccupied with~~ the humanities; the other ~~was interested only in~~ the
sciences.

_____*Exercise*   Eliminate wordiness in the following sentences.

1. As far as the average citizen is concerned, it is probable that most people are not greatly concerned with the latest critical reaction to the new fads in the world of art.

2. When we studied the parts of the human face, which we did in our art class, I discovered that I knew most of the parts that were discussed in the textbook.

3. Concerning the question of whether there are more gifted men artists than women artists, it seems to me that the answer is variable depending on how one interprets the word *gifted*.

4. When, after much careful and painstaking study of the many and various problems involved, the administrators in charge of the different phases of the operation of the hospital made the decision to build a rehabilita- tion center for patients with all sorts of disabilities, a completely new staff of doctors, nurses, and physical therapists had to be hired.

5. Many doctors, after trying many different methods of relaxing, have discovered that taking up a pleasurable pastime or hobby such as paint- ing calms them down and reduces the amount of stress in their lives.

Revising for Variety

Variety is a characteristic not of single sentences but of a succession of sentences, and it is best seen in a paragraph. But variety is achieved through modification, coordination, subordination, and changes in word order as shown in the following example:

1. Maxwell Perkins was born in 1884 and died in 1947.

2. He worked for Charles Scribner's Sons for thirty-seven years.

3. He was the head editor for Scribner's for the last twenty of those thirty-seven years.

4. He was almost certainly the most important American editor in the first half of the twentieth century.

5. He worked closely with Thomas Wolfe, Scott Fitzgerald, and Ernest Hemingway.

6. He also worked closely with a number of other well-known writers.

The sentences are of similar length (10, 9, 15, 17, 11, and 11 words, respectively) and structure (subject + predicate). Their lack of variety becomes monotonous.

Now contrast the same passage revised for variety:

Maxwell Perkins (1884–1947), head editor of Charles Scribner's Sons for the last twenty of his thirty-seven years with that company, was almost certainly the most important American editor in the first half of the twentieth century. Among the many well-known writers with whom he worked closely were Thomas Wolfe, Scott Fitzgerald, and Ernest Hemingway.

The revision combines the original into two sentences of 37 and 18 words, respectively, and results in greater economy (57 words instead of 73), greater density, and more variety. The following operations produced the revision.

▼ Sentences 1, 2, 3, and 4 of the original were combined into a new sentence by: (a) making *Maxwell Perkins* the subject of the new sentence; (b) placing his dates in parentheses; (c) reducing sentences 2 and 3 to a phrase in apposition with the subject of the new sentence; and (d) making sentence 4 the complement of the new sentence.

▼ Sentences 5 and 6 of the original were combined into a new sentence by: (a) having them share a common verb, *were;* and (b) making sentence 6 the subject of *were* and sentence 5 the complement.

Exercise   Consider the possible revisions listed after the paragraph about Nathaniel Hawthorne's story "The Birthmark." Decide which of those procedures you want to use to revise the paragraph. You do not need to use them all; use those that will give you the best paragraph.

(1) Nathaniel Hawthorne's "The Birthmark" is one of his most famous short stories. (2) It is essentially a story about the limits of science and human perfectibility. (3) Aylmer has conducted many previous experiments in the attempt to improve nature, but all of them have failed. (4) Even so, he decides to perfect his wife Georgiana's beauty by removing a tiny birthmark on her cheek. (5) At the beginning of his experiment, Aylmer is confident he will succeed. (6) He secludes Georgiana in a private chamber. (7) Then he doctors her with strange medicines concocted in his laboratory. (8) He soon discovers that the birthmark is stronger than he thought. (9) He tries to avoid another failure by giving Georgiana

an extremely powerful potion. (10) At the climax of the story, Aylmer sees his experiment succeed. (11) Unfortunately, it does so at a price. (12) Georgiana loses her birthmark. (13) She also loses her life.

Consider these revisions:

- Combine 1 and 2 by omitting everything after *is* in 1 and adding everything after *essentially* in 2. Write the revised sentence.
- Reduce most of 3 to a subordinate clause, "whose previous attempts to improve nature have failed," and insert it after *Aylmer* in 3 and before *decides* in 4. Write the revised sentence.
- Leave 5 as it is.
- Combine 6, 7, and 8 into a parallel structure using *but* to separate 7 and 8. Write the revised sentence.
- Change the pattern of 9 by beginning the sentence with an introductory phrase, "To avoid another failure," and converting "by risking" to "he decides to risk." Write the revised sentence.
- Join 10 and 11 by adding a dash after *succeed* and then inserting the phrase "at a price." Write the revised sentence.
- Combine 12 and 13 with coordinating conjunction *and.* Write the revised sentence.

Using any of those revised sentences, or any revisions of your own, rewrite the complete paragraph.

THREE PIECES OF ADVICE ON SENTENCE VARIETY

1. *Don't overdo it.* It is neither necessary nor effective to give every sentence a different structure. Within a paragraph, try to have *some* variety in the pattern of your sentences. Most of your sentences will probably be basic sentences containing about 20 words. Individual sentences will range from 10 words or fewer to 30 words or more and will include balanced, periodic, or cumulative structures.

2. *Postpone revising for variety until you have written your first draft.* As Richard Selzer suggests, the process of *tinkering,* of opening up and compressing sentences, takes place after you have a number of sentences on the page. As you rework your completed sentences, read them aloud, listening for the variations in sound and rhythm that Selzer says are essential to effective writing. You can even *see* recurring structures in sentences, just as Barich sees unvaried patterns in paragraphs, by noticing that they all occupy about the same number of lines.

3. *Be aware of the effect that sentence length has on your readers.* In general, long sentences slow down reading, and short ones speed it up. Short sentences are often effective as topic sentences because they state the general idea simply; longer sentences are often needed to develop the idea. Short sentences are excellent for communicating a series of actions, emotions, or impressions; longer sentences are more appropriate for analysis and explanation. Short sentences are closer to the rhythms of speech and are therefore suitable when you want to adopt an intimate tone and a conversational style. The more formal the tone and style, the more likely you are to use long and complex sentences.

Keep in mind that those statements are relative to the particular material and perspective you are trying to present to your readers. As in all writing, your choice should reflect your purpose.

Excerpts from a Painter's Studio Notes | Pam Smith

In these excerpts from her "studio notes," Pam Smith comments on her creative process in progress. What kind of sentences does she use to describe different stages of her process? How might her sentences be compared to brush strokes?

June 1981

When confusion visits me these days, I tell myself it is the blur of growth.   1

Suggestion is too coy for the real meaning of a painting. I struggle with whether my images are complete or incomplete, not with what they may suggest.   2

July 1981

It is color, color, color that moves me.   3
I am an ambassador for the color green, a spy for the color red, and a surgeon sent to insert the color blue.   4
In private life, I am white's lover. And gray's.   5

No painting I have ever painted has ended up being the same painting I started.   6
Some days, I feel like I'm a dictionary in reverse, cataloguing all the possible meanings, and then coming up with a word.   7

I'm concerned about showing my work. I feel this is forced on me, to "prove" my serious intentions. But when I finish a painting, I am only interested in what I am going to paint next.   8

I had a dream last night. I kept saying in this dream, "I am in love with a green painting." Then I would paint it. This happened over and over, each time the painting was different and beautiful.   9

October 1981

The point of a painting is not to say, "This way, and only this way." That's fascism. The point of a painting is, "There's something extra here because it is done this way."   10

Smith, Pam. "Powerful Red Dogs: Excerpts from a Painter's Studio Notes." *Georgia Review* 34 (Spring/Summer 1990): 184–86.

My paintings these days are renegades. Such unruly things. Each paint- 11
ing is its own world. I try to rework a problem from another painting, and
I end up getting a completely different painting. These paintings slip away
from my understanding, like baffling children, they elude me. I listen for
them to speak to me.

Some days, in my studio, I feel like a plumber who's always fixing 12
leaks. Which is to say, I don't approach a canvas with solemn ceremony,
I squint and gyrate in front of a canvas, to see what needs to be fixed.

Art is adjustment. 13

November 1982

My new paintings are pretty good. They may even be still lifes and 14
landscapes, it's possible.

Some of these new paintings are all gray, some of them have new 15
color.

They are sassy. I love that. 16

You can look in, but some of them just roar off the wall. 17

I think it's wonderful, because the painting goes from being a view of 18
something, a canvas window with a set scene, to BEING something.

When I paint, my colors are a shape and a placement. I paint their 19
boundaries. Just this much I paint. Here. And how.

Sometimes I enhance the boundaries by painting them as lines. Some- 20
times I let the boundaries be where two areas bump into each other.

The way to become an artist is to apprentice yourself and make a 21
thousand stupid mistakes from the heart.

When I paint, the world is malleable. It is up to some definition the 22
paint and I work out.

February 1983

I started a new painting today. Large, silky, sexy, lush geometry. I am 23
doing this painting from a casual sketch in an old notebook. I have lifted
the bones of the sketch intact and put it on the canvas, but painting this
painting is a battle between chaos and control.

There is such texture to this experience, the painting comes into and 24
out of focus all the time. Possibilities flash by, and each one of them dic-
tates a completely different painting. Literally every stroke affects this large
painting. I understand the original image which spawned the sketch, but I
want to do more to it. I simultaneously curse myself for not having planned
the whole painting out beforehand, and feel exhilarated by the discoveries
that are made.

I believe that a painting reveals itself. It reveals itself while it is being 25
painted.

I believe the motion of my right hand, drawing or painting, is another 26
form of thought.

Irises | Calvin Tomkins

In this excerpt from his essay on Vincent van Gogh's *Irises,* Calvin Tompkins describes the illness that placed van Gogh in a mental asylum and the discoveries the artist made about his painting as he tried to recover. In the rest of his essay, Tompkins documents the history of *Irises,* painted one year before the artist died in poverty and sold almost a hundred years later to an unknown bidder for $53.9 million. What kind of sentences does Tompkins use to describe van Gogh's illness? What kind of sentences does he use to describe van Gogh's painting?

Vincent van Gogh painted "Irises" during his first week in the mental asylum at Saint-Rémy-de-Provence, in the spring of 1889. His work had undergone a radical transformation over the preceding fourteen months. Living in Arles, seventeen miles south of Saint-Rémy, and going out every morning into the Provençal countryside, where he sometimes finished three canvases in a single day, he had come to see nature with a new eye. Instead of trying to reproduce exactly what he saw, the way Monet and Pissarro did, van Gogh had started, as he wrote to his brother Theo, "to exaggerate the essential, and, with set purpose, to leave the obvious vague." He used stronger colors than he had used before, and he used them more arbitrarily, seeking through odd combinations and violent contrasts to release the emotions that his subjects held for him. "Nature here is so *extraordinarily* beautiful!" he wrote to Theo. "Everywhere and over all the vault of the sky is a marvellous blue, and the sun sheds a radiance of pure sulphur. . . . It absorbs me so much that I let myself go without thinking of any rules." 1

Van Gogh's brushwork became looser and more visible, animating the planes of color with contrasting textures and with undulating lines that seemed to echo the movement of living forms. Having started to paint only eight years earlier, when he was twenty-seven, he now found the courage to follow his own path as an artist. But the strain on his unstable mental and physical capacities was tremendous. Paul Gauguin's arrival in Arles the previous fall, which van Gogh had looked forward to with such intensity, precipitated the most famous catastrophe in modern art—hallucinations, the mutilated ear, Gauguin's flight. A month later, van Gogh's second seizure led to his being held in the local hospital by police order, his neighbors having lodged an official protest against him as a dangerous lunatic. Calm once more, shattered in spirit but not without hope, the artist discussed his situation with Frédéric Salles, the Protestant pastor who had become his friend. Salles reported to Theo, "He is fully aware of his condition and speaks to me with touching candor and simplicity about what has happened and what, he fears, may happen again. 'I am unable,' he told me yesterday, 'to look after myself and control myself; I feel that I am quite different from what I used to be.' " The pastor suggested the private asylum of Saint-Paul-de-Mausole, at Saint-Rémy. Theo, who had been supporting his brother on 2

Tompkins, Calvin. "Irises." *New Yorker* 4 April 1988: 37–67.

his modest earnings as an art dealer in Paris, agreed to pay the asylum's charges, and van Gogh seemed content with this temporary solution to his problems—he thought it might take him a year to recover fully. He was given a private room and, since the asylum was far from fully occupied, another room to use as a studio.

A week later, he wrote to Theo's wife, Johanna, "The fear and horror **3** of madness that I used to have has already lessened a good deal. And although here you continually hear terrible cries and howls like beasts in a menagerie, in spite of that people get to know each other very well and help each other when their attacks come on." He had already started painting again. His first subjects were the flowers in the asylum's untended garden—"some violet irises and a lilac bush," he wrote his brother. The lilac-bush painting is now in the Hermitage Museum, in Leningrad. The finished "Irises," which he described to Theo as an "étude" rather than a "tableau," is unique in van Gogh's œuvre. The frieze-like composition, in which the purple flowers and their pale-green sword-shaped leaves are seen in extreme closeup, is neither a landscape nor a still-life but something in between. One white iris stops the eye at the far left, and intensifies the jewel-like richness of the purples and greens. The bold, slashing lines were undoubtedly influenced by the Japanese prints that he had admired so much in Paris—quite possibly by Hokusai's "Irises," from a woodblock series done in the late eighteen-twenties. Van Gogh treated the subject quite realistically, without arbitrary color or agitated brushwork. The style is calm, assured, and exquisitely controlled.

"Irises" was among the eleven canvases that van Gogh shipped to Theo **4** in Paris that July. Although Vincent called it a "study," meaning that it had been taken directly from nature, without imaginative restructuring, Theo liked the picture so much that he selected it, together with "The Starry Night," for submission to the Salon des Indépendants exhibition in September. "The Starry Night" was hung badly, but "the other one makes an extremely good showing," Theo wrote. "They have put it on the narrow wall of the room, and it strikes the eye from afar. It is a beautiful study full of air and life." Félix Fénéon, the most alert art critic of the time in Paris, noticed "Irises" at the Salon and made a favorable comment on it in *La Vogue*. Several artists saw it and were deeply impressed, according to Theo. There were no buyers, but Theo was hopeful nonetheless. "I think we can wait patiently for success to come," he wrote reassuringly a few months later. "You'll surely live to see it . . . and it will come of its own accord by reason of your beautiful pictures."

The Knife | Richard Selzer

In this selection, Richard Selzer uses a language of poetic intensity to describe the steps of a surgical process. Review his comments on composing sentences on page 217. In the selection here, what kind of sentences does Selzer use to create a "distinctive rhythm and resonance"? When does he

Selzer, Richard. *Mortal Lessons*. New York: Simon, 1976. 92–97.

use short sentences? When does he build long sentences? How do such sentences contribute to his purpose?

One holds the knife as one holds the bow of a cello or a tulip—by the stem. Not palmed nor gripped nor grasped, but lightly, with the tips of the fingers. The knife is not for pressing. It is for drawing across the field of skin. Like a slender fish, it waits, at the ready, then, go! It darts, followed by a fine wake of red. The flesh parts, falling away to yellow globules of fat. Even now, after so many times, I still marvel at its power—cold, gleaming, silent. More, I am still struck with a kind of dread that it is I in whose hand the blade travels, that my hand is its vehicle, that yet again this terrible steel-bellied thing and I have conspired for a most unnatural purpose, the laying open of the body of a human being.   1

A stillness settles in my heart and is carried to my hand. It is the quietude of resolve layered over fear. And it is this resolve that lowers us, my knife and me, deeper and deeper into the person beneath. It is an entry into the body that is nothing like a caress; still, it is among the gentlest of acts. Then stroke and stroke again, and we are joined by other instruments, hemostats and forceps, until the wound blooms with strange flowers whose looped handles fall to the sides in steely array.   2

There is sound, the tight click of clamps fixing teeth into severed blood vessels, the snuffle and gargle of the suction machine clearing the field of blood for the next stroke, the litany of monosyllables with which one prays his way down and in: *clamp, sponge, suture, tie, cut.* And there is color. The green of the cloth, the white of the sponges, the red and yellow of the body. Beneath the fat lies the fascia, the tough fibrous sheet encasing the muscles. It must be sliced and the red beef of the muscles separated. Now there are retractors to hold apart the wound. Hands move together, part, weave. We are fully engaged, like children absorbed in a game or the craftsmen of some place like Damascus.   3

Deeper still. The peritoneum, pink and gleaming and membranous, bulges into the wound. It is grasped with forceps, and opened. For the first time we can see into the cavity of the abdomen. Such a primitive place. One expects to find drawings of buffalo on the walls. The sense of trespassing is keener now, heightened by the world's light illuminating the organs, their secret colors revealed—maroon and salmon and yellow. The vista is sweetly vulnerable at this moment, a kind of welcoming. An arc of the liver shines high and on the right, like a dark sun. It laps over the pink sweep of the stomach, from whose lower border the gauzy omentum is draped, and through which veil one sees, sinuous, slow as just-fed snakes, the indolent coils of the intestine.   4

You turn aside to wash your gloves. It is a ritual cleansing. One enters this temple doubly washed. Here is man as microcosm, representing in all his parts the earth, perhaps the universe.   5

I must confess that the priestliness of my profession has ever been impressed on me. In the beginning there are vows, taken with all solemnity. Then there is the endless harsh novitiate of training, much fatigue, much sacrifice. At last one emerges as celebrant, standing close to the truth lying curtained in the Ark of the body. Not surplice and cassock but mask and   6 gown are your regalia. You hold no chalice, but a knife. There is no wine, no wafer. There are only the facts of blood and flesh.

And if the surgeon is like a poet, then the scars you have made on countless bodies are like verses into the fashioning of which you have poured your soul. I think that if years later I were to see the trace from an old incision of mine, I should know it at once, as one recognizes his pet expressions. **7**

But mostly you are a traveler in a dangerous country, advancing into the moist and jungly cleft your hands have made. Eyes and ears are shuttered from the land you left behind; mind empties itself of all other thought. You are the root of groping fingers. It is a fine hour for the fingers, their sense of touch so enhanced. The blind must know this feeling. Oh, there is risk everywhere. One goes lightly. The spleen. No! No! Do not touch the spleen that lurks below the left leaf of the diaphragm, a manta ray in a coral cave, its bloody tongue protruding. One poke and it might rupture, exploding with sudden hemorrhage. The filmy omentum must not be torn, the intestine scraped or denuded. The hand finds the liver, palms it, fingers running along its sharp lower edge, admiring. Here are the twin mounds of the kidneys, the apron of the omentum hanging in front of the intestinal coils. One lifts it aside and the fingers dip among the loops, searching, mapping territory, establishing boundaries. Deeper still, and the womb is touched, then held like a small muscular bottle—the womb and its earlike appendages, the ovaries. How they do nestle in the cup of a man's hand, their power all dormant. They are frailty itself. **8**

There is a hush in the room. Speech stops. The hands of the others, assistants and nurses, are still. Only the voice of the patient's respiration remains. It is the rhythm of a quiet sea, the sound of waiting. Then you speak, slowly, the terse entries of a Himalayan climber reporting back. **9**

"The stomach is okay. Greater curvature clean. No sign of ulcer. Pylorus, duodenum fine. Now comes the gallbladder. No stones. Right kidney, left, all right. Liver . . . uh-oh." **10**

Your speech lowers to a whisper, falters, stops for a long, long moment, then picks up again at the end of a sigh that comes through your mask like a last exhalation. **11**

"Three big hard ones in the left lobe, one on the right. Metastatic deposits. Bad, bad. Where's the primary? Got to be coming from somewhere." **12**

The arm shifts direction and the fingers drop lower and lower into the pelvis—the body impaled now upon the arm of the surgeon to the hilt of the elbow. **13**

"Here it is." **14**

The voice goes flat, all business now. **15**

"Tumor in the sigmoid colon, wrapped all around it, pretty tight. We'll take out a sleeve of the bowel. No colostomy. Not that, anyway. But, God, there's a lot of it down there. Here, you take a feel." **16**

You step back from the table, and lean into a sterile basin of water, resting on stiff arms, while the others locate the cancer. **17**

Writing Assignments

Narrate   **1.** Compose a freewriting exercise about your most memorable experience with illness. Follow Richard Selzer's advice and simply make one "brush stroke" after another until you have painted a fairly complete portrait of the experience. Then "doctor" your sentences—expanding and combining them to revise your freewriting into a finished essay.

Observe   **2.** Visit your local art museum or look through one of the oversized art books in your library. Select a particular painting that "speaks to you." *Study* the way the painter arranges the subject for your observation. Then write a letter to a close friend describing the painting and speculating about why it has had such a powerful impact on you.

Investigate   **3.** Visit the studio of a local artist or the studios in your university's art department. Ask for permission to observe a painter at work. Watch the way he or she uses different techniques—applying paint with fingers, brushes, spray devices, or palette knives—to "compose" the painting. Ask a few questions, but encourage the painter to talk about his or her work as it is being created. You may have to visit the studio several times to see the project through to completion. Then write a "biography of the painting" to introduce it to the students in your writing group.

Collaborate   **4.** Your writing group has been asked to draft a program for an exhibit of student paintings. Assign each member of your group to write the copy for one painter. Study previous programs to see how many and what kinds of sentences have been used to describe the painters and their work. Decide if you want to *expand* or *modify* that pattern. Then interview the student painters, study their work, design the layout for the program, and collaborate on creating the final copy.

Read   **5.** Read selections from some of Richard Selzer's other books about surgery, *Rituals of Surgery* (1974), *Confessions of a Knife* (1979), and *Letters to a Young Doctor* (1982). Compose a series of sentences on the reasons why you *would* or *would not* want to become a surgeon. After you have compared one set of reasons with the other, subordinate one group to the other to explain why "I Want . . ." [or] "I Don't Want . . . to Be a Surgeon."

Respond   **6.** Read the rest of Calvin Tompkins' essay on Vincent van Gogh's *Irises* (*The New Yorker*, 4 April 1988: 37–67). At the end of that essay, Tompkins reports that the painting was purchased by an unknown, private bidder. The painting has since reappeared in the J. Paul Getty Museum (Malibu, California). Draft letters to Tompkins (c/o *The New Yorker*) and the Director of Education (c/o the J. Paul Getty Museum) asking for specific information that will help you write "the missing chapters" in the history of the painting.

Analyze   **7.** Analyze the sentences in Pam Smith's "Excerpts from a Painter's Studio Notes." Reread Selzer's comparison of sentences and brushstrokes on page 217. Then write an essay, citing specific sentences from Smith's "studio notes," to demonstrate the appropriateness of Selzer's comparison between painting and writing.

Evaluate **8.** Richard Selzer uses many comparisons in "The Knife" to illustrate the process he is describing. Analyze each of these comparisons—the surgeon is like a priest, a poet, a traveler in a dangerous country. Then select one—for example, the artistry of the surgeon is similar to the artistry of the writer—and evaluate the points of the comparison that Selzer leaves out, the points that suggest that the two processes are radically different.

Argue **9.** You have been asked by a friend or your employer to select a painting by a local artist to be hung in a special location. Visit local galleries or art shows, looking for the *right* painting. Consider your immediate audience (the person who asked you to select the painting), your ultimate audience (the people who will see the painting), and the context (where the painting will be hung). Compose a series of sentences (or reasons) why you think a particular painting is the *right* painting. Then write a letter recommending your choice to your friend or employer. (You may want to reread Wallace Armstrong's "Brandon's Clown" in Chapter 1 to remind yourself about how such purchases affect the painter.)

Argue **10.** As an experiment in revising sentences, work with the following sentences by expanding, modifying, or combining them into an effective argument. Add other sentences to fill out your portrait and fulfill your purpose.
a. Surgeons are revered as medical priests.
b. They are cloaked and masked in green vestments.
c. They have acquired a secret knowledge.
d. They are given absolute authority over life and death.
e. They cut the human body with special tools.
f. They eliminate disease.
g. They stitch the body together.
h. They wash their hands after the ritual.
i. The people they restore to health view the process as a miracle.

9

Diction: The Choice of Words

As you think your way through a sentence, you inevitably search for the best words to convey your thoughts. Sometimes, especially when you are quite clear about what you want to say, the words come so easily that you are hardly aware of choosing them. At other times, especially when you are trying to discover what you want to say, you find yourself scratching out one choice after another as you search for the exact word to express your meaning. Such revisions are not necessarily a sign of indecision. The best writers worry constantly about diction—the selection and use of words for effective communication. Perhaps they are the best writers partly because they take pains to choose the best word.

Words are not right or wrong in themselves. What makes a particular word right is the effect it creates in the context of your sentence or paragraph. Annie Dillard, celebrated for her evocative descriptions of nature, explains how she chooses words.

> I learn words by learning worlds. Any writer does that out of simple curiosity. When I choose words, I think about their effect—of course. I like to create a rich prose surface that pommels the reader with verbs and images. I think of them as jabs. Jab, jab, jab, left. Jab, jab, jab, right. That's the vigor I want. (Personal interview)

To create vigor in your writing and to advance your purpose, you must, like Dillard, learn the words that represent the "worlds" you want to write about and learn to use words for their effect. You must learn the denotations and connotations of words.

DENOTATION AND CONNOTATION

The most familiar use of words is to name things—plants, people, oceans, stars. When words are used in this way, the things they refer to are called their *denotations*. The word *molecule* most commonly denotes small structures of atoms. The denotation of *Mars* is the fourth planet from the sun. The denotation is a word's explicit meaning.

But some words acquire connotations as well as denotations. A connotation is an *implicit* meaning, an implied or suggested attitude that is not

250

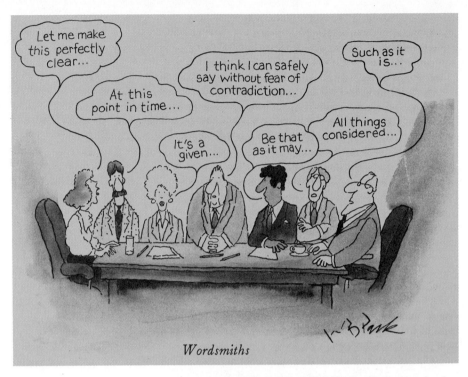

Wordsmiths

Drawing by W. B. Park; © 1988 The New Yorker Magazine, Inc.

stated outright. When you label theories about life on Mars "improbable" or "preposterous," you are not only describing them, you are also expressing, and inviting your readers to share, an attitude toward them.

In each of these sentences, the writer implies a different attitude toward similar events.

> My wife asked me why I was *slashing* the shrubbery. I told her I was merely *pruning* it.

> The difference between *childish pranks* and acts of *vandalism* depends on whose child does the mischief.

> Although most bathers thought the high surf looked *threatening,* a few thought it looked *challenging.*

> When our team of scientists traveled across the crater to *collect samples,* they encountered another team *stealing evidence.*

The contrast in each example is not between denotations and connotations but between favorable and unfavorable connotations. *Slashing* and *pruning* refer to similar actions; but the first implies destructive recklessness, and the second suggests careful cutting.

The words you choose should support your purpose. If you wish to report objectively, select words that suggest a neutral attitude: *collect samples,* not *stealing evidence.* If you wish to convey a tolerant or approving attitude, use words that invite a tolerant or approving response: *pruning, childish pranks, challenging.* If you wish to suggest disapproval, select words with unfavorable connotations: *slashing, act of vandalism, threatening.*

_____*Exercise* In the following sentences the blank may be filled with any of the words in parentheses, but each choice creates different connotations. Discuss how each choice affects the writer's intention and the reader's interpretation of the sentence.

1. The roses _____ the trellis. (climbed, adorned, strangled)
2. She was a _____ reader. (compulsive, critical, perceptive)
3. The children were _____. (sleepy, exhausted, weary)
4. The reef _____ beneath the surface. (appeared, loomed, glimmered)
5. The comet _____ across the night sky. (shot, blinked, blazed)

THREE QUALITIES OF EFFECTIVE DICTION

Choice of diction is always made with reference to a particular sentence and to the total context of your writing. For this reason no dictionary or thesaurus will give you *the* right word. A dictionary presents a word's various meanings, and a thesaurus provides a list of synonyms, words with slightly varying meanings. You must decide which word and meaning meet your needs. To make this decision, consider the qualities of effective diction: *appropriateness, specificity,* and *imagery.*

Appropriateness

Words are appropriate when they are suited to your subject, audience, and purpose. Imagine an astronomer reporting the discovery of a new star to a convention of scientists and then to the viewers of a morning television show. The subject is the same, but the audience and purpose are so different that the speaker alters the content, manner, and language of the report. Choices to accommodate audience and purpose affect not only diction, the subject of this chapter, but tone and style, the subjects of the next chapter. Diction, tone, and style are alike in requiring you to make important decisions about the degree of formality appropriate for a given context. Jeans and a T-shirt are not appropriate for a formal dance; an evening gown or tuxedo is conspicuously inappropriate for the classroom; in the same way, some words inappropriate in some situations are perfectly acceptable in others. The best way to understand this distinction is to consider four types of words: *learned, popular, colloquial,* and *slang.*

Learned and Popular Words   Most words in English, as in other languages, are common to the speech of educated and uneducated speakers alike. These words are the basic elements of everyday communication. They are called *popular words* because they belong to the whole populace.

By contrast, there are words that you read more often than you hear, write more often than you speak—words used more widely by educated than by uneducated people, and more likely to be used on formal than on informal occasions. Such words are called *learned words.*

The following list contrasts pairs of popular and learned words that have similar denotations.

Popular	*Learned*	*Popular*	*Learned*
agree	concur	help	succor
begin	commence	move easily	facilitate
clear	lucid	secret	esoteric
disagree	remonstrate	think	cogitate
end	terminate	wordy	verbose

Colloquialisms   The term *colloquial* is defined by the *American Heritage Dictionary* as "characteristic of or appropriate to the spoken language or writing that seeks its effect; informal in diction or style of expression." Colloquialisms are not "incorrect" or "bad" English. They are the kinds of words people, educated and uneducated alike, use when they are speaking together informally. Their deliberate use in writing conveys the impression of direct and intimate conversation. To achieve this effect you might use contractions (*don't, wasn't, hasn't*) or clipped words (*taxi, phone*). Other typical colloquialisms are:

awfully (*for* very)	fix (*for* predicament)	movie (*for* film)
back of (*for* behind)	it's me	over with (*for* completed)
cute	kind of (*for* somewhat)	peeve (*for* annoy)
exam	a lot of; lots of	plenty (*as an adverb*)
expect (*for* suppose)	mad (*for* angry)	sure (*for* certainly)

Slang   The *Oxford English Dictionary* defines slang as "language of a highly colloquial type." Notice that the adjective used is *colloquial,* not *vulgar* or *incorrect.* Slang is used by everyone. The appropriateness of slang, however, depends on the occasion. A college president would probably avoid slang in a public speech but might use it at an informal gathering.

Slang satisfies a desire for novelty of expression. It is often borrowed from the vocabularies of particular occupations or activities: *input* (computer technology), *on the beam* (aerial navigation), *behind the eight ball* (pool), *dunk* (basketball). Some slang words are from the "insider" languages of those who commit crimes or take drugs: *sting, torch, grass, stoned.* Much slang is borrowed from the popular vocabulary and given new meanings: *flipped, split, cool, soul, rap, high, trip, wheels, vibes, bread.* Some slang proves so imaginative and useful that it becomes part of the popular vocabulary, but most quickly becomes dated and obscure and loses its impact.

The scale below shows the four types of diction within the range of formality.

Learned	Popular	Colloquial	Slang

← *Most formal*   *Least formal* →

In most of your writing, words from the middle of this scale will be appropriate. Unfortunately, some inexperienced writers think that formality is a virtue and that big, fancy words are more impressive than short, common ones. If writers cannot maintain an appropriate level of formality, their diction becomes strained and inconsistent.

The following passage provides a humorous illustration of such inconsistency. In this scene from George Bernard Shaw's play *Pygmalion* (from which the musical *My Fair Lady* was created), Liza Doolittle, a cockney flower girl who is being taught by Professor Higgins to speak like a lady, meets her first test at a small party at the home of Mrs. Higgins, the professor's mother. Notice the contrast between Liza's first speech and her last.

> Mrs. Higgins: Will it rain, do you think?
>
> Liza: The shallow depression in the west of these islands is likely to move slowly in an easterly direction. There are no indications of any great change in the barometrical situation.
>
> Freddy: Ha! Ha! How awfully funny!
>
> Liza: What is wrong with that, young man? I bet I got it right.
>
> Freddy: Killing!
>
> Mrs. Eynsford Hill: I'm sure I hope it won't turn cold. There's so much influenza about. It runs right through our whole family regularly every spring.
>
> Liza: My aunt died of influenza: so they said. . . . But it's my belief they done the old woman in. . . . Why should *she* die of influenza? She come through diphtheria right enough the year before. I saw her with my own eyes. Fairly blue with it, she was. They all thought she was dead; but my father he kept ladling gin down her throat 'til she came to so sudden that she bit the bowl off the spoon. . . . What call would a woman with that strength in her have to die of influenza? What become of her new straw hat that should have come to me? Somebody pinched it; and what I say is, them as pinched it done her in.

The obvious switch from formal to highly colloquial speech is justified by Shaw's purpose, which is to show Liza in a transitional stage at which she cannot yet consistently maintain the pose of being a well-educated young woman. Liza does not see that her learned comment on the weather is inappropriate in this situation, and therefore she has no idea why Freddy is laughing. When the subject changes to influenza, she forgets she is supposed to be a lady and reverts to her natural speech—which is much more expressive and colorful than her phony formality. Her inconsistency is amusing, as Shaw meant it to be.

But in the compositions of inexperienced writers, most inconsistencies are not intended for humorous effect. They slip in when the writer is not in control of *how* to say *what* he or she wants to say. The writer may start off like Liza, hoping to make a good impression, but the writer's natural voice asserts itself and the result is neither formal nor informal diction but an embarrassing mixture. Try to choose words consistently appropriate to your purpose throughout the writing process, and, of course, in revision, stay alert for unintentional shifts in diction.

_____ *Exercise*   The following paragraph does not maintain a consistent level of diction. Identify the words and phrases that seem too formal or too informal. Then rewrite the paragraph, substituting more appropriate diction to make the language of the paragraph consistent.

> In my perusal of the morning paper, I often pause to take a gander at my horoscope. This stuff is supposed to be figured out on a chart of the heavens, which manifests the positions of the sun, moon, and the signs of the zodiac at the honest to goodness time and location of your birth. These configurations are then juxtaposed to the twelve hours of the celestial sphere. The signs are presumed to hold sway over certain parts of the body, and the houses are supposed to tell you what's happening in the various conditions of life. The degree of influence attributed to these houses depends on a bunch of factors. Sometimes my horoscope predicts the orb of my daily activities with confounding accuracy. But most of the time it's just hogwash.

Specificity

General and *specific* are opposite terms. Words are general when they refer not to individual things but to groups or classes: *mother, flowers, hurricane.* Words are specific when they refer to individual persons, objects, or events: *Joe's mother, the flowers in the vase near the window, Hurricane Bob.* A general term may be made more specific with a modifier that restricts the reference to a particular member of the group or class.

Specific and *general* are also relative terms: a word may seem specific in one context and general in another, as this diagram shows.

Most general	Vegetation
Less general	Grass Bush Tree Fern Weed
Still less general	Elm tree Maple tree Apple tree Oak tree Cedar tree
Specific	The crabapple tree in my yard

_____*Exercise*   For each set of terms, show the gradation from general to specific. Place the most general term at the left and the most specific at the right, as in this example:

matter, food, fruit, citrus fruit, orange

1. Labrador retriever, quadruped, bird dog, animal, dog
2. protons, molecule, electrons, atom, nucleus
3. bush, rosebush, plant, decorative bush, Tropicana rosebush
4. Jupiter, Milky Way, sun, solar system, galaxy
5. Scientist, chemist, Marie Curie, Nobel Prize winner

Your context determines whether a specific or a general word is required. Some purposes require generalities. A president's inaugural address, for example, does not deal with specifics; it states general policies and intentions. The best policy is to be as specific as the situation permits. Notice how the specific language in the examples on the right communicates meaning that is not conveyed by the general diction on the left.

A drop of water contains particles.	A drop of water contains microscopic strands of algae and multicellular aquatic organisms.
Saturn has rings.	Saturn is surrounded by a vast swarm of meteoric fragments revolving in various orbits.

The term *concrete* is used to describe some kinds of specific diction. *Concrete* is the opposite of *abstract*. Concrete words refer to particular things or qualities that can be perceived by your senses: details of appearance, sounds, smells, textures, tastes. Abstract words refer to qualities shared by many people or things: newness, width, size, shape, value, joy, anger. Abstract qualities cannot be perceived directly by observation; they are concepts that you infer from what you see.

In the following paragraph, Annie Dillard uses concrete, sensory detail to illustrate her abstract opening sentence. The image of successive flocks of red-winged blackbirds materializing from the dense, green foliage of the Osage orange tree remains in the mind in a way impossible for concepts such as *nature* or *revelation*.

For nature does reveal as well as conceal; now-you-don't-see-it, now-you-do. For a week this September migrating red-winged blackbirds were feeding heavily down by Tinker Creek at the back of the house. One day I went out to investigate the racket; I walked up to a tree, an Osage orange, and a hundred birds flew away. They simply materialized out of the tree. I saw a tree, then a whisk of color, then a tree again. I walked closer and another hundred blackbirds took flight. Not a branch, not a twig budged: the birds were apparently weightless as well as invisible. Or, it was as if the leaves of the Osage orange had been freed from a spell in the form of red-winged blackbirds; they flew from the tree, caught my eye in the sky, and vanished. When I looked again at the tree, the leaves had reassembled as if nothing had happened. Finally I walked directly to the trunk of the tree and a final hundred, the real diehards, appeared, spread, and vanished. How could so many hide in the tree without my seeing them? The Osage orange, unruffled, looked just as it had looked from the house, when three hundred red-winged blackbirds cried from its crown. I looked upstream where they flew, and they were gone. Searching, I couldn't spot one. I wandered upstream to force them to play their hand, but they'd crossed the creek and scattered. One show to a customer. These appearances catch at my throat; they are the free gifts, the bright coppers at the roots of trees. (Annie Dillard, "Sight into Insight," *Pilgrim at Tinker Creek*)

Words that refer to sensory experiences—to what you see, hear, touch, taste, and smell—call up sensory images (particularly when they are embedded in strong verbs) and create the "rich prose surface" Dillard uses to "jab" her reader. The following list gives additional examples (some words fit into more than one sensory category):

Touch   chill, clammy, cold, grainy, gritty, jarring, knobby, moist, numb, rough, smooth, sting, tingle

Taste   bland, bitter, brackish, metallic, minty, peppery, salty, sour, spicy, sweet

Smell   acrid, fetid, greasy, musky, musty, pungent, putrid, rancid, rank, reek, stench

Sound   bellow, blare, buzz, chime, clang, clatter, clink, crackle, crash, creak, gurgle, hiss, hum, murmur, pop, purr, rattle, rustle, screech, snap, squeak, whine, whisper

Sight   blaze, bleary, bloody, chalky, dappled, ebony, flame, flicker, florid, foggy, gaudy, glare, glitter, glossy, grimy, haze, inky, leaden, muddy, pallid, sallow, shadow, smudged, streak, tawny

_____*Exercise*   1. Read the following passage and note the words or phrases that seem most concrete. Then copy the passage over without those words or phrases. In what ways is the meaning of the second version diminished?

A single knoll rises out of the plain in Oklahoma, north and west of the Wichita Range. For my people, the Kiowas, it is an old landmark, and they gave it the name Rainy Mountain. The hardest weather in the world is there. Winter brings blizzards, hot tornadic winds arise in the spring, and in summer the prairie is an anvil's edge. The grass turns brittle and brown, and it cracks beneath your feet. There are green belts along the rivers and creeks, linear groves of hickory and pecan, willow and witch hazel. At a distance in July or August the steaming foliage seems almost to writhe in fire. Great green and yellow grasshoppers are everywhere in the tall grass, popping up like corn to sting the flesh, and tortoises crawl about on the red earth, going nowhere in plenty of time. Loneliness is an aspect of the land. All things in the plain are isolate; there is no confusion of objects in the eye, but *one* hill or *one* tree or *one* man. To look upon that landscape in the early morning, with the sun at your back, is to lose the sense of proportion. Your imagination comes to life, and this, you think, is where Creation was begun. (N. Scott Momaday, "The Way to Rainy Mountain")

2. The following contrasted statements deal with the same subject. From each pair, choose the statement that you think is more concrete. Explain the specific reasons for your choice.

In the past, girls in rural communities had no facilities for bathing except those offered by some neighboring stream. In such circumstances a bathing suit was not always a necessity, but if one was worn it was likely to consist of nothing more than some discarded article of clothing tailored to fit the occasion.	Forty years ago, if the farmer's daughter went swimming she swam in the crick below the pasture, and if she wore a bathing suit, which was not as customary as you may think, it was likely to be a pair of her brother's outgrown overalls trimmed with scissors as her discretion might suggest.
Suddenly I felt something on the biceps of my right arm—a queer light touch, clinging for an instant, and then the smooth glide of its body. I could feel the muscles of the snake's body slowly contract and relax. At last I saw a flat, V-shaped head, with two glistening, black, protruding buttons. A thin, pointed, sickening yellow tongue slipped out, then in, accompanied by a sound like that of escaping steam.	Suddenly I felt the snake moving over my arm. I felt the contraction of its muscles as it moved. Then I saw its ugly head and its evil-looking eyes. All the time its tongue kept moving in and out, making a kind of hissing noise.

Imagery

Imagery has two general meanings when applied to diction: the images or pictures that concrete words sometimes suggest and figures of speech such as similes and metaphors. The first meaning includes the pictorial quality of phrases such as *an anvil's edge, green belts, popping up like corn.* In this section you will learn about the second meaning—the use of figurative language.

The chief element in all figures of speech is an imaginative comparison in which dissimilar things are described as having a meaningful similarity.

The writer, by thus linking the unfamiliar with the familiar, creates a context in which the reader may more easily or clearly understand a new aspect of the subject or new information and ideas. Here is an example:

> The moon was a ghostly galleon tossed upon cloudy seas. (Alfred Noyes)

The line of poetry compares the moon to a sailing ship. Now in most ways the moon is quite unlike a ship. But as the poet watches it alternately emerging from behind the clouds and disappearing into them again, he thinks of a ship alternately emerging and disappearing from view as it rides the troughs and crests of the waves. In his imagination the moon is being tossed by the clouds as a ship is tossed by the waves.

The most commonly used figures of speech are *simile, metaphor, analogy, personification,* and *allusion.* Each figure makes a comparison, but each has its own characteristic form and use.

Simile   A simile compares two things—*A* and *B*—by asserting that one is like the other. A simile usually contains the word *like, as,* or *so* and is used to transfer to *A* the qualities or feelings associated with *B.* Thus, when Annie Dillard in "Total Eclipse" describes a solar eclipse, she imagines that the sky (*A*)—or more precisely the moon—functions like the lens cover (*B*) on a camera, covering the lens and shutting out all light:

> The sky snapped over the sun like a lens cover.

Here are some other similes:

> Insects in the first frosts of autumn all run down like little clocks. (Loren Eiseley, "How Flowers Changed the World," *The Star Thrower*)
>
> When, as you approach, [the iguanas] swish away, there is a flash of azure, green and purple over the stones, the colour seems to be standing behind them in the air, like a comet's luminous tail. (Isak Dinesen, *Out of Africa*)
>
> Floating on one's back is like riding between two skies. (Edward Hoagland, "Summer Pond")
>
> His face was as blank as a pan of uncooked dough. (William Faulkner)
>
> Laverne wasn't too bad a dancer, but the other one, old Marty . . . was like dragging the Statue of Liberty around the floor. (J. D. Salinger)

Metaphor   A metaphor compares two things by identifying one with the other. It does not say that *A* is like *B* but instead states that *A* is *B.* Lewis Thomas is using metaphor when he suggests that the sky encloses the earth just as a membrane surrounds an organ or cell.

> Aloft, floating free beneath the moist, gleaming membrane of bright blue sky, is the rising earth, the only exuberant thing in this part of the cosmos. (Lewis Thomas, "The World's Biggest Membrane," *The Lives of a Cell*)

Here are other metaphors:

> Time is but a stream I go a-fishing in. (Henry David Thoreau, *Walden*)
>
> Suddenly the whole room broke into a sea of shouting, as they saw me rise. Waves of rejoicing swept the place. (Langston Hughes, *The Big Sea*)
>
> Each rich nation is a lifeboat full of comparatively rich people. In the ocean outside each lifeboat swim the poor of the world who want to get in, or at best to share some of the wealth. (Garrett Hardin, "Lifeboat Ethics: The Case Against Helping the Poor")

Many words and phrases no longer thought of as figures of speech were originally metaphors or similes. "At bay" originally described a hunted animal cornered by pursuers and forced to turn and fight the baying hounds. "Crestfallen" first described a cock that had been humbled in a cockfight. Many other expressions can be analyzed as metaphors although you no longer think of them as figures of speech—expressions such as the "mouth" of a river, the "face" of a clock, the "brow" of a hill. Such expressions are often called, metaphorically, *dead* or *frozen metaphors.* They are so common in the language that it is hard to write a paragraph without them, but you should try to avoid those (such as "rosy red," "dirt cheap," and "face the music") that have become clichés.

Analogy   An analogy is an extended metaphor that, through several sentences or paragraphs, explains an abstract idea or seeks to persuade readers that because two things are alike, a conclusion drawn from one suggests a similar conclusion from the other. In the following passage, Robert Jastrow uses analogy to explain the shape of our galaxy:

> The Galaxy is flattened by its rotating motion into the shape of a disk whose thickness is roughly one-fifth of its diameter. Most of the stars in the Galaxy are in this disk, although some are located outside it. A relatively small, spherical cluster of stars, called the nucleus of the Galaxy, bulges out of the disk at the center. The center structure resembles a double sombrero with the gigantic nucleus as the crown and the disk as the brim. The sun is located in the brim of the sombrero about three-fifths of the way out from the center of the edge. When we look into the sky in the direction of the disk we see so many stars that they are not visible as separate points of light, but blend together into a luminous band stretching across the sky. This band is called the Milky Way. (Robert Jastrow, "The Size of Things," *Red Giants and White Dwarfs*)

Personification   Personification is a figure of speech by which inanimate objects or abstractions are given human or animal characteristics. Thus winds are said to "roar" or "bite"; flames "eat hungrily" at a burning house and many even "devour" it; a tree may "bow" before a gale or in fair weather "stretch" its branches; truth or virtue emerges "triumphant"; and justice is "blind." In these examples, the writer imagines a resemblance between the actions observed and the actions of an animal or person.

Such implied comparisons are often effective, but they should be used with restraint. If they seem exaggerated ("the waves roared their threat to the listening clouds while the palm trees nodded their approval"), your reader is likely to reject them as far fetched or as an unsuccessful attempt to be "literary."

Allusion   An allusion is a comparison between a historical, literary, or mythological event or person and the subject under discussion. When a scientific discovery is said to possess Copernican significance, it is being associated with Copernicus' theory that revolutionized the way we saw the universe (the earth rotating around the sun rather than the sun rotating around the earth). Or when a film is called another *Star Wars,* it is being likened to one of the most extraordinary films ever made about outer space.

A successful allusion provides a flash of wit or insight and gives your readers the pleasure of recognition. But you must be reasonably sure that an allusion is suited to your audience; if your readers do not recognize or understand the allusion, they will be confused and not appreciate its effect. Calling writing a research paper a "Sisyphean task" is amusing only if your audience remembers that Sisyphus was condemned forever to roll a huge stone up a steep hill in Hades, only to have it roll back down again just as it neared the top.

_____*Exercises*   1. In the following selections, underline effective examples of specificity and imagery.

When wild ducks or wild geese migrate in their season, a strange tide rises in the territories over which they sweep. As if magnetized by the great triangular flight, the barnyard fowl leap a foot or two into the air and try to fly . . . and a vestige of savagery quickens their blood. All the ducks on the farm are transformed for an instant into migrant birds, and into those hard little heads, till now filled with humble images of pools and worms and barnyards, there swims a sense of continental expanse, of the breadth of seas and the salt taste of the ocean wind. The duck totters to the right and left in its wire enclosure, gripped by a sudden passion to perform the impossible and a sudden love whose object is a mystery. (Antoine de Saint Exupéry, *Wind, Sand and Stars*)

The word is terracide. As in homicide, or genocide. Except it's terra. Land.

It is not committed with guns and knives, but with great, relentless bulldozers and thundering dump trucks, with giant shovels like mythological creatures, their girdered necks lifting massive steel mouths high above the tallest trees. And with dynamite. They cut and blast and rip apart mountains to reach the minerals inside, and when they have finished there is nothing left but naked hills, ugly monuments to waste, stripped of everything that once held them in place, cut off from the top and sides and dug out from the inside and then left, restless, to slide down on houses and wash off into rivers and streams, rendering the land unlivable and the water for miles downstream undrinkable.

Terracide. Or, if you prefer, strip-mining. (Skip Rozin, "People of the Ruined Hills," *Audubon*)

"On nights like that," Raymond Chandler once wrote about the Santa Ana, "every booze party ends in a fight. Meek little wives feel the edge of the carving knife and study their husbands' necks. Anything can happen." That was the kind of wind it was. I did not know then that there was any basis for the effect it had on all of us, but it turns out to be another of those cases in which science bears out folk wisdom. The Santa Ana, which is named for one of the canyons it rushes through, is a *foehn* wind, like the *foehn* of Austria and Switzerland and the *hamsin* of Israel. There are a number of persistent malevolent winds, perhaps the best known of which are the mistral of France and the Mediterranean sirocco, but a *foehn* wind has distinct characteristics: it occurs on the leeward slope of a mountain range and, although the air begins as a cold mass, it is warmed as it comes down the mountain and appears finally as a hot dry wind. Whenever and wherever a *foehn* blows, doctors hear about headaches and nausea and allergies, about "nervousness," about "depression." In Los Angeles some teachers do not attempt to conduct formal classes during a Santa Ana, because the children become unmanageable. In Switzerland the suicide rate goes up during the *foehn,* and in the courts of some Swiss cantons the wind is considered a mitigating circumstance for crime. Surgeons are said to watch the wind, because blood does not clot normally during a *foehn.* A few years ago an Israeli physicist discovered that not only during such winds, but for the ten or twelve hours which precede them, the air carries an unusually high ratio of positive to negative ions. No one seems to know exactly why that should be; some talk about friction and others suggest solar disturbances. In any case the positive ions are there, and what an excess of positive ions does, in the simplest terms, is make people unhappy. One cannot get much more mechanistic than that. (Joan Didion, "Los Angeles Notebook," *Slouching Towards Bethlehem*)

2. Evaluate the effectiveness of the following figures of speech from the student writing used in previous chapters. Discuss how each figure contributes to the writer's purpose.

a. Wally, "Brandon's Clown" (Chapter 1):

Before long, the book looked like a Disneyland mortuary.

b. Rod, "Our Trip to D.C." (Discovery draft, Chapter 4):

Whenever I think of our trip, I think of that monument standing in the middle of downtown Washington like a big paperweight.

c. Jane, "Watching Whales" (Chapter 5):

When he burst out of the water, he held his flippers at a slight angle to his side. As he descended, he moved them gracefully away from his body like the arms of a ballerina finishing a pirouette.

d. Matt, "Drug Abuse in the Work Place"(Chapter 6):

All of us—employers, workers, consumers—want to cure this plague that threatens the health of our culture.

REVISING DICTION

In considering the qualities of effective diction, you evaluated ways of expressing ideas, and your evaluation included a great deal of revision. In this stage of local revision, you need to change your emphasis from expressing yourself effectively to rooting out the ineffective. Work through your text slowly, looking for words that don't fully express your purpose. Four major weaknesses to watch for are *vagueness, jargon, triteness,* and *ineffective imagery.*

Eliminating Vagueness

Words are vague when, in context, they do not convey a single, specific meaning to your readers. Consider this sentence:

I could tell by the funny look on her face that she was mad.

Funny and *mad* can have quite specific meanings, but not in that sentence. What does *funny* mean here—a purposeful attempt to create laughter? What does *mad* mean—"insane," as it might in another sentence? Certainly not. "Angry," then, or "annoyed" or "irritated" or "offended"? A reader cannot be sure. The writer can remove doubt by using more specific diction.

I could tell by the *way her face stiffened* that she was *offended.*

Words like *funny* and *mad* belong to a group called *utility words.* Such words, as their name implies, are useful. In ordinary conversation, which does not usually permit or require deliberate choice and offers little chance for revision, utility words are common and often pass unnoticed. In writing, they may be adequate if the context limits them to a single, clear interpretation. But because their meaning is often left vague, they should be used with caution. The following list shows some of the most common utility words:

affair	funny	marvelous	regular
awful	gadget	matter	silly
business	glamorous	nature	situation
cute	goods	neat	stuff
fantastic	gorgeous	nice	terrible
fierce	great	outfit	terrific
fine	line	peculiar	weird
freak	lovely	pretty	wonderful

Usually the simplest way to clarify a vague utility word or phrase is to substitute a specific word or phrase, as in the following examples:

puzzling
It was a ~~peculiar~~ statement.

alarming.
The news is ~~terrible.~~

clear, sunny, and in the low 80s.
The weather will be ~~fantastic~~.

Vagueness is not limited to unclear utility words. Any word or phrase that is more general than the intended meaning should be revised. The substitutions in these sentences make the information more specific.

Annie Dillard's "Total Eclipse."
The class was discussing ~~an essay~~.

how this winter's storms eroded the sand dunes on Cape Cod.
Professor Jones is studying ~~erosion~~.

_____Exercises

1. Assume that the italicized words are not made clear by context. Substitute more specific diction to give a precise meaning.
   a. She is a scientist, but I don't know what her *line* is.
   b. Our *group* thought the *samples* were *peculiar*.
   c. One *aspect* of the *project* is its effect on prices.
   d. What a *terrific* surprise to meet so many *important* people at the same *affair*.
   e. The lab fees for this course are *something else*.

2. Circle the more specific expression in each parenthetical set.

   The whole surface of the ice was (*a chaos–full*) of movement. It looked like an enormous (*mass–jigsaw puzzle*) stretching away to infinity and being (*pushed–crunched*) together by some invisible but irresistible force. The impression of its (*titanic–great*) power was heightened by the unhurried deliberateness of the motion. Whenever two thick (*pieces–floes*) came together, their edges (*met–butted*) and (*moved–ground*) against one another for a time. Then, when neither of them showed signs of yielding, they rose (*uncertainly–quiveringly*), driven by the (*implacable–tremendous*) power behind them. Sometimes they would stop (*altogether–abruptly*) as the unseen forces affecting the ice appeared mysteriously to lose interest. More frequently, though, the two floes—often ten feet thick or more— would continue to rise (*rearing up–tenting up*) until one or both of them toppled over, creating a pressure ridge.

Eliminating Jargon

Jargon originally meant meaningless chatter. Later it meant the specialized language of a group or profession, as in *habeas corpus* (law) and *cursor* (computer technology). There is no reason not to use learned and technical terms for audiences and situations for which they are appropriate, but to use them unnecessarily when addressing a general audience is a violation of the basic rule that your style should fit your purpose and audience. Jargon in informal writing is pretentious and frustrating to your audience. The following contrast shows inappropriate jargon that results in vague, indirect writing. The version on the left comes from the King James translation of the Bible; the version on the right is George Orwell's "translation" of the same material into modern jargon.

I returned and saw under the sun, that the race is not to the swift, nor the battle to the strong, neither yet bread to the wise, nor yet riches to men of understanding, nor yet favor to men of skill; but time and chance happeneth to them all.

Objective considerations of contemporary phenomena compel the conclusion that success or failure in competitive activities exhibits no tendency to be commensurate with innate capacity, but that a considerable element of the unpredictable must invariably be taken into account.

Although the Biblical version first appeared in 1611, it makes more sense and is easier to read than the "translation," which smothers simplicity and clarity under a blanket of vague, polysyllabic words. As Orwell points out:

> The first contains forty-nine words but only sixty syllables, and all of its words are those of everyday life. The second contains thirty-eight words of ninety syllables; eighteen of its words are from Latin roots, and one from Greek. The first sentence contains six vivid images, and only one phrase ("time and chance") that could be called vague. The second contains not a single fresh, arresting phrase, and in spite of its ninety syllables it gives only a shortened version of the meaning contained in the first. ("Politics and the English Language," *Shooting an Elephant and Other Essays*)

Jargon has three chief characteristics:

▾ Highly abstract, often technical, diction that shows a fondness for learned rather than popular words: *have the capability to* for *can, maximize productivity* for *increase production,* and *utilization of mechanical equipment* for *use of machinery.*

▾ Excessive use of the passive voice. If machines break down, they "are found to be functionally impaired." If a plan does not work, "its objectives were not realized." If management failed to consider the effects of certain changes on the workers, the error is reported like this: "With respect to employee reactions, management seems to have been inadequately advised."

▾ Conspicuous wordiness, as illustrated in the previous examples.

Jargon combines inappropriateness, vagueness, and wordiness into one consistently unintelligible style. Writers who lapse into jargon do so because they believe that ordinary language is not good enough. Like Liza Doolittle, they are trying to make a good impression. But the best way to make a good impression with your writing is to have something to say and to say it clearly.

The only way to revise jargon is to get rid of it. Leaving it in your writing forces your readers to do mentally the rewriting that you should have done, with the difficulty that they may not be sure what you meant.

Notice how the following passage creates ambiguity for the reader.

(1) Rigorous comprehension and innermost instincts are the features of collaborative inquiry that spelunkers must engage when they delve into

the unexplored terrain of a new cave. (2) They must scrutinize the formation of the rocks and the current of the river, establish their directional
movement with the assistance of a compass, and maintain a precise topo-
graphical record so that they can renegotiate their expedition to its inception. (3) But since they have no established record, they must still commit
their full confidence to their instincts when they reach an intersection. At
that juncture they must contemplate whether traversing one passageway
will bring them into contact with a chamber enlarged by a high ceiling or
with a corridor that narrows into a cul-de-sac.

The writer probably consulted a thesaurus to dress up the language of that
needlessly "learned" paragraph. If you rewrite the paragraph, reducing each
sentence to a summary of what the writer was trying to say, you get this:

1. Spelunkers use knowledge and instincts to explore a new cave.

2. They study rock formations and river currents; they use a compass;
and they need to find their way out.

3. Since they have no maps, at intersections they must rely on their
instincts.

4. They may turn into big chambers or dead ends.

If you join the revised sentences, you get a paragraph that says all the original
was trying to say, but says it more clearly and in fewer words—51 words
instead of 119. You might get a still better revision by tinkering with the
sentence structure, adding or subtracting words where appropriate:

When they explore a new cave, spelunkers rely on educated guesswork.
They study the rock formation and river current, chart their movement
with a compass, and mark their trail so that they can find their way out.
But since they have no map, they must trust their instincts at each intersection. They may select a passage that turns into a vaulted chamber or a
dead end.

The revised paragraph says nothing that was not said in the revised sentences. But it sharpens the focus by beginning with a clear topic sentence
and then explaining that sentence. The pomposities of the original version
have been eliminated, and the meaning is conveyed in half the space.

_____*Exercise*   Using the procedure just shown, revise this paragraph.

Last month as I was perambulating through the stacks, I happened to encounter a book filled with photographs of volcanoes. Not yet having realized my latent interest in such geological formations, I was surprised at
the manner in which this book enthralled my attention. The color displays of the spectacular discharge of Washington's St. Helens and the
florid lava flows of Hawaii's Kilauea I found to be particularly disquiet-
ing. It was these photographs which led me to the decision to espouse volcanoes as the subject of my research paper.

Eliminating Triteness

The terms *trite, hackneyed,* and *cliché* are used to describe expressions, once colorful and apt, that have been used so often that they have lost their freshness and force. Like outdated slang, trite expressions once evoked images and conveyed a sense of discovery through language. Striking when new, such phrases become meaningless when they are overused. Note these examples:

apple of her eye	hook, line, and sinker
birds of a feather	lock, stock, and barrel
black sheep	mountains out of molehills
blind as a bat	sober as a judge
budding genius	teeth like pearls
diamond in the rough	thick as thieves
fly in the ointment	water over the dam

Trite diction blocks thought. Writers who use ready-made phrases instead of creating their own soon find it difficult to think beyond stereotyped expressions: any change in personnel becomes a "shakeup"; all hopes become "fond," "foolish," or "forlorn"; defeats are "crushing"; changes in the existing system are "noble experiments" or "dangerous departures"; unexpected occurrences are "bolts from the blue"; and people who "sow wild oats" always have to "pay the piper" even though they are "as poor as church mice."

When you spot triteness in your writing, you should remove it. The way to learn to detect and avoid triteness in your writing is to learn to recognize triteness in the speech and writing of others. Notice the italicized clichés in this paragraph.

> *Money doesn't grow on trees,* and how well I've learned that. What a *rude awakening* when I realized that the odd change I used to ask for at home was not available at school. I had thought my allowance was enormous but, before I knew it, it had *trickled through my fingers.* College has taught me that *"A penny saved is a penny earned."* I have learned to live within my allowance and even to *save something for a rainy day.* What I have learned in college is *not all in the books.* I have learned to *shoulder my responsibilities.*

How many of those phrases do you recognize as prefabricated units that can be inserted into any sentence? If you can identify triteness in another writer's work, you can identify it in your own.

_____*Exercises*

1. Politics, television, popular music, and sports seem to encourage the use of trite expressions. Although some writers interpret these subjects with originality and insight, most seem to type their texts on a cliché machine. Examine the following paragraph to determine whether it provides any insights into football or simply repeats clichés.

Wherever the gridiron game is played in the United States—on a sandlot, a high school field, or in a college or professional stadium—the players learn through the school of hard knocks the invaluable lesson that only by the men's blending together like birds of a feather can the team win. It is a lesson they do not forget on the gridiron. Off the field, they duly remember it. In society, the former player does not look upon himself as a lone wolf on the prowl who has the right to do his own thing—that is, to observe only his individual social laws. He knows he is a part of the big picture and must conduct himself as such. He realizes that only by playing as a team man can he do his share in making society what it should be—the protector and benefactor of all. The man who has been willing to make the sacrifice to play football knows that teamwork is essential in this modern day and age and that every citizen must pull his weight in the boat if the nation is to prosper. So he has little difficulty in adjusting to his roles in family life and in the world of business and to his duties as a citizen in the total scheme of things. In short, his football training helps make him a better citizen and person, better able to play the big game of life.

2. Rewrite that paragraph to eliminate the major objections made about it during class discussion.

3. Choose as a general subject a current issue in the world of politics, television, or popular music. Restrict that general subject to a topic that you think is important to students, and write a letter to the campus newspaper expressing your opinion. Then reread your letter to catch any trite language you may have used.

Eliminating Ineffective Imagery

An effective figure of speech can make your writing concrete; a figure that is trite, far fetched, obscure, or confused mars your writing and distracts your readers. *Mixed metaphors*—metaphors that combine two or more incompatible images in a single figure—are especially ineffective. Consider the following:

> The scientist decided to gauge the political water by throwing his hat into the ring as a trial balloon.

This sentence mixes three overused, equally unimaginative images. "Testing the water" has a literal meaning in cooking and bathing. "Throwing one's hat into the ring" was a conventional way of issuing a challenge in the days of bareknuckle prize fights. Trial balloons were once used to determine wind direction and velocity. Each of these images can be used in a political context, but fitting all three into one consistent figure of speech is impossible. And because the subject of the sentence is "the scientist," these figures distract the reader by suggesting that the sentence is about science rather than politics. The writer of the sentence should abandon metaphor and simply say,

"The scientist tried to evaluate his chances of being nominated by announcing his intention to seek the position."

A poor figure of speech is worse than none at all. Imagery is ruined if the picture it conveys is preposterous or dull. If the figure you intended to strengthen your writing weakens it, delete or revise it. Test every figure of speech by *seeing* the picture it represents. If you visualize what your words are saying, then you will see and eliminate ineffective or mixed images during revision.

_____*Exercise* These sentences try unsuccessfully to combine discordant elements in the same figure of speech. Visualize the images they suggest, and then revise each sentence by creating an acceptable figure or restating the idea without a figure.

1. A host of music fans flocked into the arena like an avalanche.

2. The president's ill-advised action has thrown the ship of state into low gear, and unless the members of Congress wipe out party lines and carry the ball as a team, it may take months to get the country back on the track.

3. When I try to focus my microscope, I do something that throws a monkey wrench into the ointment.

4. NASA expressed confidence that the hearing would allow the real facts of the case to come out in the wash.

5. Although the members of our writing group have difficulty forgetting where the hatchet is buried, we decided that was water behind the dam.

The Microscope | James Thurber

In this episode from his classic essay "University Days," humorist James Thurber explains his frustration in trying to see through a microscope. How would you characterize the *appropriateness* of Thurber's diction? On the scale of most formal to least formal, where would you place Thurber's choice of words? Select specific examples to demonstrate your choice.

I passed all the other courses that I took at my university, but I could 1 never pass botany. This was because all botany students had to spend several hours a week in a laboratory looking through a microscope at plant cells, and I could never see through a microscope. I never once saw a cell through a microscope. This used to enrage my instructor. He would wander around the laboratory pleased with the progress all the students were making in drawing the involved and, so I am told, interesting structure of flower cells, until he came to me. I would just be standing there. "I can't see anything," I would say. He would begin patiently enough, explaining how anybody can see through a microscope, but he would always end up in a fury, claiming that I could *too* see through the microscope but just pretended that I couldn't. "It takes away from the beauty of flowers anyway," I used to tell him. "We are not concerned with beauty in this course," he would say. "We are concerned solely with what I may call the *mechanics* of flars." "Well," I'd say, "I can't see anything." "Try it just once again," he'd say, and I would put my eye to the microscope and see nothing at all, except now and again a nebulous milky substance—a phenomenon of maladjustment. You were supposed to see a vivid, restless clockwork of sharply defined plant cells. "I see what looks like a lot of milk," I would tell him. This, he claimed, was the result of my not having adjusted the microscope properly, so he would readjust it for me, or rather, for himself. And I would look again and see milk.

I finally took a deferred pass, as they called it, and waited a year and 2 tried again. (You had to pass one of the biological sciences or you couldn't graduate.) The professor had come back from vacation brown as a berry, bright-eyed, and eager to explain cell-structure again to his classes. "Well," he said to me, cheerily, when we met in the first laboratory hour of the semester, "we're going to see cells this time, aren't we?" "Yes, sir," I said. Students to right of me and to left of me and in front of me were seeing cells; what's more, they were quietly drawing pictures of them in their notebooks. Of course, I didn't see anything.

"We'll try it," the professor said to me, grimly, "with every adjustment 3 of the microscope known to man. As God as my witness, I'll arrange this glass so that you see cells through it or I'll give up teaching. In twenty-two years of botany, I—" He cut off abruptly for he was beginning to quiver all over, like Lionel Barrymore, and he genuinely wished to hold onto his temper; his scenes with me had taken a great deal out of him.

Thurber, James. "University Days." *My Life and Hard Times.* New York: Harper, 1961. 88–90.

So we tried it with every adjustment of the microscope known to man. **4**
With only one of them did I see anything but blackness or the familiar lac-
teal opacity, and that time I saw, to my pleasure and amazement, a varie-
gated constellation of flecks, specks, and dots. These I hastily drew. The instructor, noting my activity, came back from an adjoining desk, a smile on
his lips and his eyebrows high in hope. He looked at my cell drawing.
"What's that?" he demanded, with a hint of a squeal in his voice. "That's
what I saw," I said. "You didn't, you didn't, you *didn't*!" he screamed, losing control of his temper instantly, and he bent over and squinted into the
microscope. His head snapped up. "That's your eye!" he shouted. "You've
fixed the lens so that it reflects! You've drawn your eye!"

Knothole Cavern | Edwin Way Teale

In this selection naturalist Edwin Way Teale describes a nighttime discovery in his garden. In what ways does Teale use *imagery* to describe the
events he observes in the "knothole cavern"? What specific figures of
speech does he use to describe the "larvae of a Syrphid fly, *Eristalis tenax*"?

The drooping branches of the tree, with their thick thatching of green **1**
leaves, descend almost to the ground. Supported by the central column of
the tree trunk, they form an arboreal hut that protects me from the rain.
Here the drumming of the downpour seems more remote.

For a moment I listen in the darkness before I switch on my light. The **2**
beam glides upward along the gray tree trunk. Five feet from the ground, it
encounters the black, unblinking eye of a knothole. A dozen times a day, in
full sunlight, I have passed this opening without a second glance. But now,
surrounded by the vast blackness of the night, the three-inch opening assumes a new interest.

Rain from previous showers has collected in the hollow within. In the **3**
beam of my flashlight the scene resembles some unexplored cave or subter-
ranean lake in miniature. The weathered wood, sloping downward along
the roof of this teacup-sized cavern, has the appearance of shelving rock.
Half a dozen sow bugs, like trilobites from a remote geological past, glide
away on the flowing action of a succession of slender legs, to crowd into
the darker corners of the cave. Two black ants are bending down at the
edge of the water as though drinking on the shore of a lake.

On the surface of this knothole pool floats the body of a dead cranefly. **4**
While looking at it, I catch a glimpse of one of the sow bugs hurrying from
one dark corner to another with a baby sow bug clinging firmly to its back.

Under the lip of the opening, where I had missed them before, I see a **5**
dozen grayish water midgets, hardly more than an eighth of an inch long.
Hanging by the tips of their tails from the surface film of the water, they
swing back and forth in steady, leisurely arcs. They suggest acrobats on
gymnasium rings. Two, side by side, are swinging in unison, first this way,
then that. What are they? What are they doing? The best guess I can make

Teale, Edwin Way. *Adventures in Nature.* New York: Dodd, 1959. 37–40.

is that they are some sort of immature gnats living out the underwater stage of their existence.

All around them, and all through this knothole lake, move the lighter, more active forms of the mosquito wigglers. Like slender, whitish tadpoles, these larvae swim about with lashing tails. They start, stop, dart forward again, whip-tails in action. They are the most numerous of the midget swimmers that dwell in this Lilliputian lake.

From the debris at the bottom of the flooded cavern rise a score or more slender white stalks, apparently sprouts from seeds scattered singly and in little clusters. Among these pale vertical columns ascending through the brown water, the tiny wigglers keep up their incessant and seemingly aimless darting and pausing.

As the beam of my flashlight shoots low over the water, I observe a curious thing. The surface is not smooth but has a dozen dimples that suggest the "knots" in an imperfect pane of glass. Under each dimple there are from one to seven of the sprouts. Where there are more than one, the thin stalks come together like the poles of a tepee. Some attraction seems to pull them to a common center. Using a straw, I push one of these clusters apart. With a slow, stately motion, the component stalks swing back and assume their former position.

The dimples above such clusters are larger than where a single sprout reaches the surface. And here is another surprising thing: Not one sprout has pushed above the water. All reach exactly to the surface and no farther. I am puzzling over this when an amazing thing takes place before my eyes.

One of the sprouts, as I watch it, telescopes slowly downward like a moving picture running in reverse. It steadily becomes shorter until it reaches the debris below. The other stalks remain as before. The whitish wigglers keep up their endless darting and halting. And the little acrobats of the surface film continue swinging back and forth in rhythmic oscillations.

But something has happened at the spot where the descending sprout has reached the debris. Half an inch of white is moving among the black decayed wood of the pond-bottom. In a flash, I know. These are no sprouts. These slender stalklike columns are the air-hoses of the world's first diving suits. At the bottom of my knothole cavern are not seeds but some of the strangest, most incredible creatures of the insect world.

These larvae of a Syrphid fly, *Eristalis tenax,* feed upon decaying matter underwater. Their tubelike, telescoping tails reach to the surface and carry air to the creatures below. Aeons before man first appeared on earth, Nature thus invented the prototype of the diving gear. Réaumur, the great natural scientist of eighteenth century France, studied and named this larva. He called it "the rat-tailed maggot" and the name has stuck.

The larvae themselves are at most only two-thirds of an inch long. But their remarkable tails, formed of two tubes, one sliding within the other and both capable of tremendous elongation and contraction, can be extended as much as eight times the length of the larva's body. In his pioneer researches Réaumur added water, little by little, to a vessel in which several of these creatures were feeding. He saw the breathing tubes extend to each new level until the water reached a height of almost six inches. The tails, now no thicker than horsehairs, had stretched to their limit. When more water was added, the larvae either crept up the side of the vessel or floated up to a height from which their breathing tubes could reach the air supply.

Total Eclipse | Annie Dillard

Compare Annie Dillard's comments (page 250) on choosing and using words with her diction in this excerpt from "Total Eclipse." Select specific examples where her word choice exhibits the three qualities of effective diction—appropriateness, specificity, and imagery. How does each example advance her purpose?

The hill was five hundred feet high. Long winter-killed grass covered it, as 1 high as our knees. We climbed and rested, sweating in the cold; we passed clumps of bundled people on the hillside who were setting up telescopes and fiddling with cameras. The top of the hill stuck up in the middle of the sky. We tightened our scarves and looked around.

East of us rose another hill like ours. Between the hills, far below, was 2 the highway which threaded south into the valley. This was the Yakima valley; I had never seen it before. It is justly famous for its beauty, like every planted valley. It extended south into the horizon, a distant dream of a valley, a Shangri-la. All its hundreds of low, golden slopes bore orchards. Among the orchards were towns, and roads, and plowed and fallow fields. Through the valley wandered a thin, shining river; from the river extended fine, frozen irrigation ditches. Distance blurred and blued the sight, so that the whole valley looked like a thickness or sediment at the bottom of the sky. Directly behind us was more sky, and empty lowlands blued by distance, and Mount Adams. Mount Adams was an enormous, snow-covered volcanic cone rising flat, like so much scenery.

Now the sun was up. We could not see it; but the sky behind the band 3 of clouds was yellow, and, far down the valley, some hillside orchards had lighted up. More people were parking near the highway and climbing the hills. It was the West. All of us rugged individualists were wearing knit caps and blue nylon parkas. People were climbing the nearby hills and setting up shop in clumps among the dead grasses. It looked as though we had all gathered on hilltops to pray for the world on its last day. It looked as though we had all crawled out of spaceships and were preparing to assault the valley below. It looked as though we were scattered on hilltops at dawn to sacrifice virgins, make rain, set stone stelae in a ring. There was no place out of the wind. The straw grasses banged our legs.

Up in the sky where we stood the air was lusterless yellow. To the 4 west the sky was blue. Now the sun cleared the clouds. We cast rough shadows on the blowing grass; freezing, we waved our arms. Near the sun, the sky was bright and colorless. There was nothing to see.

It began with no ado. It was odd that such a well-advertised public event 5 should have no starting gun, no overture, no introductory speaker. I should

Dillard, Annie. *Teaching a Stone to Talk*. New York: Harper, 1982. 88–93.

have known right then that I was out of my depth. Without pause or pre-amble, silent as orbits, a piece of the sun went away. We looked at it through welders' goggles. A piece of the sun was missing; in its place we saw empty sky.

I had seen a partial eclipse in 1970. A partial eclipse is very interesting. **6** It bears almost no relation to a total eclipse. Seeing a partial eclipse bears the same relation to seeing a total eclipse as kissing a man does to marrying him, or as flying in an airplane does to falling out of an airplane. Although the one experience precedes the other, it in no way prepares you for it. During a partial eclipse the sky does not darken—not even when 94 percent of the sun is hidden. Nor does the sun, seen colorless through protective devices, seem terribly strange. We have all seen a sliver of light in the sky; we have all seen the crescent moon by day. However, during a partial eclipse the air does indeed get cold, precisely as if someone were standing between you and the fire. And blackbirds do fly back to their roosts. I had seen a partial eclipse before, and here was another.

What you see in an eclipse is entirely different from what you know. **7** It is especially different for those of us whose grasp of astronomy is so frail that, given a flashlight, a grapefruit, two oranges, and fifteen years, we still could not figure out which way to set the clocks for Daylight Saving Time. Usually it is a bit of a trick to keep your knowledge from blinding you. But during an eclipse it is easy. What you see is much more convincing than any wild-eyed theory you may know.

You may read that the moon has something to do with eclipses. I have **8** never seen the moon yet. You do not see the moon. So near the sun, it is as completely invisible as the stars are by day. What you see before your eyes is the sun going through phases. It gets narrower and narrower, as the waning moon does, and, like the ordinary moon, it travels alone in the simple sky. The sky is of course background. It does not appear to eat the sun; it is far behind the sun. The sun simply shaves away; gradually, you see less sun and more sky.

The sky's blue was deepening, but there was no darkness. The sun was a **9** wide crescent, like a segment of tangerine. The wind freshened and blew steadily over the hill. The eastern hill across the highway grew dusky and sharp. The towns and orchards in the valley to the south were dissolving into the blue light. Only the thin river held a trickle of sun.

Now the sky to the west deepened to indigo, a color never seen. A **10** dark sky usually loses color. This was a saturated, deep indigo, up in the air. Stuck up into that unworldly sky was the cone of Mount Adams, and the alpenglow was upon it. The alpenglow is that red light of sunset which holds out on snowy mountaintops long after the valleys and tablelands are dimmed. "Look at Mount Adams," I said, and that was the last sane moment I remember.

I turned back to the sun. It was going. The sun was going, and the world **11** was wrong. The grasses were wrong; they were platinum. Their every detail of stem, head, and blade shone lightless and artificially distinct as an art photographer's platinum print. This color has never been seen on earth. The hues were metallic; their finish was matte. The hillside was a nineteenth-century tinted photograph from which the tints had faded. All the people you see in the photograph, distinct and detailed as their faces look, are now dead. The sky was navy blue. My hands were silver. All the distant hills' grasses were finespun metal which the wind laid down. I was watching a faded color print of a movie filmed in the Middle Ages; I was standing in it, by some mistake. I was standing in a movie of hillside grasses filmed in the Middle Ages. I missed my own century, the people I knew, and the real light of day.

I looked at Gary. He was in the film. Everything was lost. He was a platinum print, a dead artist's version of life. I saw on his skull the darkness of night mixed with the colors of day. My mind was going out; my eyes were receding the way galaxies recede to the rim of space. Gary was light-years away, gesturing inside a circle of darkness, down the wrong end of a telescope. He smiled as if he saw me; the stringy crinkles around his eyes moved. The sight of him, familiar and wrong, was something I was remembering from centuries hence, from the other side of death: yes, *that* is the way he used to look, when we were living. When it was our generation's turn to be alive. I could not hear him; the wind was too loud. Behind him the sun was going. We had all started down a chute of time. At first it was pleasant; now there was no stopping it. Gary was chuting away across space, moving and talking and catching my eye, chuting down the long corridor of separation. The skin on his face moved like thin bronze plating that would peel. 12

The grass at our feet was wild barley. It was the wild einkorn wheat which grew on the hilly flanks of the Zagros Mountains, above the Euphrates valley, above the valley of the river we called *River*. We harvested the grass with stone sickles, I remember. We found the grasses on the hillsides; we built our shelter beside them and cut them down. That is how he used to look then, that one, moving and living and catching my eye, with the sky so dark behind him, and the wind blowing. God save our life. 13

From all the hills came screams. A piece of sky beside the crescent sun was detaching. It was a loosened circle of evening sky, suddenly lighted from the back. It was an abrupt black body out of nowhere; it was a flat disk; it was almost over the sun. That is when there were screams. At once this disk of sky slid over the sun like a lid. The sky snapped over the sun like a lens cover. The hatch in the brain slammed. Abruptly it was dark night, on the land and in the sky. In the night sky was a tiny ring of light. The hole where the sun belongs is very small. A thin ring of light marked its place. There was no sound. The eyes dried, the arteries drained, the lungs hushed. There was no world. We were the world's dead people rotating and orbiting around and around, embedded in the planet's crust, while the earth rolled down. Our minds were light-years distant, forgetful of almost everything. Only an extraordinary act of will could recall to us our former, living selves and our contexts in matter and time. We had, it seems, loved the planet and loved our lives, but could no longer remember the way of them. We got the light wrong. In the sky was something that should not be there. In the black sky was a ring of light. It was a thin ring, an old, thin silver wedding band, an old, worn ring. It was an old wedding band in the sky, or a morsel of bone. There were stars. It was all over. 14

Writing Assignments

Narrate **1.** Mark Twain once said, "The difference between the right word and the nearly right word is the difference between lightning and a lightning bug." Compose a narrative essay about the consequences of your inability to select the right word(s) to explain your behavior on an important occasion.

Observe **2.** Select several students and observe their use of certain words in conversation. Make a list of the words they use most often to describe certain social events on campus. Pay particular attention to their use of *slang.* Then compile a "dictionary of slang" for next year's freshman class. Ask your friends to help compose definitions.

Investigate **3.** Interview an expert on your campus (botany professor) or in your community (car mechanic) about some aspect of his or her job. As you conduct the interview, make a list of all the words you don't understand. Ask your expert to help you with your list. Which words would he or she classify as *popular, learned,* or *jargon*? Ask your expert to define the words on the jargon list. Then write an essay for uninformed readers explaining some of the jargon they need to know to understand this area of expertise.

Collaborate **4.** Each month *The Atlantic* concludes with a page called "Word Watch." The four or five words presented each month are being tracked by the editors of the *American Heritage Dictionary* to see if they exhibit sustained use over time and therefore merit inclusion in a future edition of the dictionary. In the August 1987 issue, for example, one of the words presented is *dink,* an acronym for "double income, no kids" couples. Your writing group has been asked to conduct a "Word Watch," using a word in *The Atlantic* or a word you have heard on campus. Consider its origin, definition, synonyms. Compile your evidence. Then collaborate on a letter to the editors of the *American Heritage Dictionary* arguing for the inclusion of your word in the next edition of the dictionary.

Read **5.** Select a troublesome word you have encountered in your reading about science—such as *entropy, refraction,* or *void.* Examine the history of the word in the *Oxford English Dictionary.* See if the word is given an expanded definition in a general or specialized encyclopedia such as *Encyclopedia Britannica* or the *McGraw-Hill Encyclopedia of Science and Technology.* Look up some of its synonyms in *Roget's Thesaurus.* Then compose an extended definition of the word, pointing out its denotative and connotative meanings.

Respond **6.** Respond to Thurber's essay by describing your own experiences seeing what you are supposed to see. You may want to describe your difficulties seeing a microscopic world (a cell) or a cosmic world (a constellation). You may want to expand this assignment to include the "lab report"—that is, to describe the difficulty you had describing *in writing* what you saw to a professor who knows already exactly what you were supposed to see.

Analyze **7.** Analyze Edwin Way Teale's use of imagery in "Knothole Cavern." Identify those places in the text where Teale uses *similes, metaphors, analogy, personifi-*

cation, and *allusion.* Pay particular attention to the way Teale uses verbs to create mental pictures. Then write an essay explaining how Teale's use of imagery contributes to his purpose.

Evaluate   **8.**   Evaluate Annie Dillard's diction in the selection from "Total Eclipse." Begin by finding words that document the range of her word choice (from *popular* to *learned*). Next, assess her use of imagery (see in particular her comparison of a partial eclipse to a total eclipse). Then evaluate how Dillard's diction deepens and extends her description of the event.

Argue   **9.**   In an essay designed for a popular nature magazine (or the Life Style section of your Sunday newspaper), argue that physical events create certain psychological reactions. You may want to select an extraordinary event, such as a solar eclipse, tornado, or flood, and speculate on why it produces extreme reactions. Or you may want to select a more common event, such as sunshine, rain, or humidity, and set up correlations between external and internal weather.

Argue   **10.**   When the emperor asked Confucius what could be done to restore harmony to his troubled land, the wise man replied, "Purify the language." Select an example of language that needs purifying from, for example, a political speech or a product warranty. Identify those places in the text that need revision. Then write a letter to the appropriate authority using your revisions to demonstrate how effective diction can create social harmony.

10
Tone and Style

In Chapters 8 and 9, you examined sentence structure and diction separately, but you must also consider their joint impact on the tone and style of a piece of writing. You are generally familiar with the words *tone* and *style*, of course. When someone says, "Don't speak to me in that tone," or, "The style of that book is difficult," you know what is meant. In this chapter, however, *tone* and *style* are technical concepts that you need to understand and control to improve your writing.

As you work your way through the stages of the writing process, you try to sort out what you think about your material and how you want your readers to think about it. For example, Ellen's initial planning (in Chapter 3) captured much of Barry's quirkiness, but her scratch outline reduced his behavior to abstractions (*food, exercise,* and *culture*). This led her to eliminate Barry as a subject and adopt an academic tone for her working hypothesis and discovery draft. She discovered this problem through her descriptive outline and concluded that her draft sounded scholarly but wasn't very interesting. By returning to Barry in her new outline and subsequent draft, she achieved a more entertaining tone and engaging style and revealed Barry's quirkiness to her readers.

TONE

Essayist Patricia Hampl, like Ellen, finds that the right tone is essential for an effective writing style.

> The issue of tone is central to me because I want my readers to know that another human being is speaking to them. I've never had much interest in the objective tone of the godlike narrator. It's supposed to give your writing a kind of neutral authority, but I don't think it exists. Even God has a personality. There's the God of light. The God of mercy. The philosophical issue at stake here is how to maintain the middle position, the position of a human being who possesses both authority and reliability. I try to create that balance by mixing a formal tone with a more conversational tone. You can deal with only so much operatic truth. Then you have to acknowledge the popcorn stand and the peanut gallery. (Personal interview)

"When I say 'Please pass the butter,' why do
you say 'Hey, no problem'?"

Drawing by Saxon; © 1987 The New Yorker Magazine, Inc.

Range of Tone: Informative
to Affective

As Hampl suggests, writers can adopt an objective or a subjective tone. You adopt the first when your purpose is to give your readers authoritative information. You adopt the second when your purpose is to affect or influence your readers in some way. The following two excerpts demonstrate these two extremes of tone.

> The United States was the first nation in history so many of whose citizens could go so far simply in quest of fun and culture. The size of this phenomenon made international travel, for the first time, a major element in world trade, a new problem for the American economy and for

American balance of payments, and a new opportunity for the destination countries. In 1970 the Department of Commerce estimated that the expenditures of American travelers overseas had reached $2 billion each year. In the United States, economists began to count foreign travel as a major import, and other countries began to plan for tourism by Americans as a principal export. (Daniel Boorstin, *The Americans: The Democratic Experience*)

Notice the following characteristics of this passage:

▼ Boorstin is principally concerned with giving readers information about his subject. He assumes that they will be interested in the historic and economic significance of travel.

▼ Boorstin's writing is informative and objective—he does not show his personal feelings. He supports his judgment about America's preoccupation with travel by citing experts: the Department of Commerce and economists.

▼ As a result of Boorstin's purpose and strategies, his tone is informative, factual, and impersonal.

Contrast Boorstin's passage with this one:

I don't know where we got the idea we have to go away for a vacation. I suppose the travel industry sold it to us. The travel business is the second largest industry in the United States. It's always trying to get us to go someplace *else* to spend our money when most of us don't have any trouble spending it right here where we are. The industry tries to make us feel cheap if we don't go on an expensive trip.

Well, I've got my plans all made for my vacation. I'm not going *anywhere*. How do you like that, travel industry? Show me all the luxurious accommodations you want, tempt me with pictures of bikini-clad girls with windswept hair on pearl-white beaches—I'm not going. I'm staying put is what I'm doing. We've been tourists, and none of us likes being a tourist, so this summer I'll be somewhere I've never been on vacation— right where I live. (Andy Rooney, *A Few Minutes with Andy Rooney*)

This sample is quite different from Boorstin's.

▼ Rooney's purpose is to offer his opinion, not to give information. He does tell his readers that the travel industry is the second largest in the United States, but he tells them little more about it—except how it makes him feel.

▼ Rooney's writing is affective and *subjective*. Rooney writes almost exclusively about how *he* feels about the subject of vacations: "I've got my plans," "I'm not going *anywhere*," "I'm staying put." His language reveals his defiant attitude: "How do you like that, travel industry?"

▼ As a result of Rooney's purpose and strategies, his tone is affective, opinionated, and personal.

These two passages represent the extremes of tone on a scale ranging from informative to affective.

Boorstin passage   Rooney passage

←———→

Informative   *Affective*

Between the extremes, you could place other samples that show varying degrees of objectivity and subjectivity; those in the middle would be equally balanced between the two.

Each time you write, you will have to decide how informative or affective your writing should be. Certain assignments—laboratory reports, summaries of books or events, essay examinations—usually require an informative tone. Persuasive essays, intended to convince a reader to believe or do something, are usually affective. But, as Hampl indicates, a balance of informative and affective elements produces the most flexible and natural tone. The balance in your essays will depend on your subject and purpose. Rod's final essay on the Washington Monument (in Chapter 4) is informative because it provides facts about the monument's history, but it is also affective because Rod tries to show his readers why he feels that there is "more to George's monument than meets the eye."

Inexperienced writers sometimes believe that the way to be objective is to avoid writing in the first person. When you are writing about your own experience, ideas, and feelings, however, you need to use the pronoun *I*. Moreover, a third-person account is not necessarily an objective treatment of the subject. The statement "I saw the car run through a red light" is more objective than "The crazy fool drove through a red light," even though the first sentence contains *I* and the second does not.

_____*Exercise*   Where on the informative/affective scale would you place the following passages? Examine each passage closely so that you can support your judgment by reference to specific details.

Passage 1   Why is it almost impossible to gaze directly at the Grand Canyon under these circumstances and see it for what it is—as one picks up a strange object from one's back yard and gazes directly at it? It is almost impossible because the Grand Canyon, the thing as it is, has been appropriated by the symbolic complex which has already been formed in the sightseer's mind. Seeing the canyon under approved circumstances is seeing the symbolic complex head on. The thing is no longer the thing as it confronted the Spaniard; it is rather that which has already been formulated—by picture postcard, geography book, tourist folders, and the words *Grand Canyon*. As a result of this preformulation, the source of the sightseer's pleasure undergoes a shift. Where the wonder and delight of the Spaniard arose from his penetration of the thing itself, from a progressive discovery of depths, patterns, colors, shadows, etc., now the sightseer measures his satisfaction *by the degree to which the canyon conforms to the preformed complex.* If it does so, if it looks just like the postcard, he is pleased; he might even say, "Why it is every bit as beautiful as a picture postcard!" He feels he has not been cheated. But if it does not conform, if the colors are somber, he will not be able to see it directly; he will only be conscious of the disparity between what it is and what it is supposed to be. He will say later that he was unlucky in not being there at the right time. The highest point, the term of the sightseer's satisfaction, is not the sovereign discovery of the thing before him; it is rather the measuring up of the thing to the criterion of the preformed symbolic complex. (Walker Percy, "The Loss of the Creature," *The Message in the Bottle*)

Passage 2

Everything comes onto the island: nothing much goes off, even by evaporation. Once it was a gateway to a New World, now it is a portal chiefly to itself. Manhattan long ago abandoned its melting-pot function. Nobody even tries to Americanize the Lebanese or the Lithuanians now, and indeed the ethnic enclaves of the island seem to me to become more potently ethnic each time I visit the place. Nothing could be much more Italian than the Festival of St. Anthony of Padua down on Mulberry Street, when the families of Little Italy stroll here and there through their estate, pausing often to greet volatile contemporaries and sometimes munching the soft-shelled crabs which, spread-eagled on slices of bread like zoological specimens, are offered loudly for sale by street vendors. Harlem has become almost a private city in itself, no longer to be slummed through by whities after dinner, while Manhattan's Chinatown is as good a place as anywhere in the world to test your skill at that universal challenge, trying to make a Chinese waiter smile. (Jan Morris, "Manhattan: The Islanders," *Destinations: Essays from Rolling Stone*)

Passage 3

The next day when I was already in full flight—aboard a northward bound train—I could not have accounted, if it had been demanded of me, for all the varied forces that were making me reject the culture that had molded and shaped me. I was leaving without a qualm, without a single backward glance. The face of the South that I had known was hostile and forbidding, and yet out of all the conflicts and the curses, the blows and the anger, the tension and the terror, I had somehow gotten the idea that life could be different, could be lived in a fuller and richer manner. As had happened when I had fled the orphan home, I was now running more away from something than toward something. But that did not matter to me. My mood was: I've got to get away; I can't stay here. (Richard Wright, *Black Boy*)

Distance

Another element of tone is the impression of distance between writer and reader.

Consider a professor lecturing to a large class. She is separated from her listeners by her position on a platform; she cannot speak to each student in the audience individually. The situation requires her to speak more slowly, more loudly, and more formally than if she were conferring with a student in her office. The lecture room produces both physical and stylistic distance. Consider the distance in a statement in a printed syllabus that "Students are expected to hand in assignments on the date stipulated" and an instructor's after-class remark, "Joe, you've got to get your papers in on time." In the first statement the writer is impersonal and remote; in the second the speaker is personal and close.

The following selections illustrate the difference between writing that tries to get close to the reader and writing that addresses the reader from a distance.

Example 1

Did you ever wonder, looking at a map or whirling a globe, how the intricate shape of continents, shorelines, rivers and mountains came to be mapped, and who designed the system of parallels and meridians? Or how people found out, in the first place, that the earth is shaped like a globe? If we had not been told so I am not ever sure that you or I would have found it out for ourselves. (Erwin Raisz, *Mapping the World*)

Here the distance between writer and reader is very slight. By using the second person, Raisz gives the impression of speaking personally to each reader. His conversational and questioning tone and his diction suggest that he identifies with his readers.

Example 2

The map predates the book (even a fairly ordinary map may contain several books' worth of information). It is the oldest means of information storage, and can present the most subtle facts with great clarity. It is a masterly form of compression, a way of miniaturizing a country or society. Most hill-climbers and perhaps all mountaineers know the thrill at a certain altitude of looking down and recognizing the landscape that is indistinguishable from a map. The only pleasure I take in flying in a jet plane is the experience of matching a coastline or the contour of a river to the corresponding map in my memory. A map can do many things, but I think its chief use is in lessening our fear of foreign parts and helping us anticipate the problems of dislocation. Maps give the world coherence. It seems to me one of man's supreme achievements that he knew the precise shape of every continent and practically every river-vein on earth long before he was able to gaze at them whole from the window of a rocketship. (Paul Theroux, "Mapping the World," *Sunrise with Seamonsters*)

This paragraph is addressed not to any particular reader but to all readers. Theroux does not address his readers as "you" or try to appeal to their special interests. He is more interested in what he has to say than in his audience. His tone establishes greater distance between writer and reader than existed in the passage by Raisz.

The impression of distance comes chiefly from sentence structure and diction, the linguistic bases of tone, discussed below under "Style." Remember that the tone of your writing depends in part on decisions you make about the distance, or degree of separation, you want to maintain between yourself and your readers. The decision is not arbitrary; it is related to decisions about your attitude toward your subject, and it should be consistent with your purpose.

STYLE

The *American Heritage Dictionary* defines style as "the way in which something is said or done, as distinguished from its substance." In writing, *style* refers to "how something is said"—the way a writer arranges sentences and words; *substance* means "what is said"—the ideas or message that the writer wishes to convey. The difficulty with the dictionary definition is that it assumes that what is said can somehow be examined apart from how it is said. In writing, however, the *what* and the *how* are virtually indistinguishable. The most subtle changes in sentences or diction can change the ideas or message. A simple, though more accurate definition, then, would be, "Style is the way something is written."

How do you describe the way something is written? Consider the following passage from *The Adventures of Huckleberry Finn,* by Mark Twain. Huck, staying with the Grangerfords after his raft has been wrecked, has been reading a "poem" written by the youngest daughter, now dead. The poem, intended to be a sad poem about a young man who fell into a well and drowned, is so maudlin and so badly written that it is funny. Huck thinks it is very good. After reading it, he says:

> If Emmeline Grangerford could make poetry like that before she was fourteen, there ain't no telling what she could a done by-and-by. Buck [her younger brother] said she could rattle off poetry like nothing. She didn't ever have to stop and think. He said she would slap down a line, and if she couldn't find anything to rhyme with it she would just scratch it out and slap down another one, and go ahead. She warn't particular; she could write about anything you choose to give her to write about just so it was sadful. Every time a man died, or a woman died, or a child died, she would be on hand with her "tribute" before he was cold. She called them tributes. The neighbors said it was the doctor first, then Emmeline, then the undertaker—the undertaker never got in ahead of Emmeline but once, and then she hung fire on a rhyme for the dead person's name, which was Whistler. She warn't ever the same, after that; she never complained, but she kinder pined away and did not live long.

Notice the following things about this passage:

▼ Mark Twain is having fun with the subject. He knows the poem is sentimental to the point of being ridiculous, and he expects the reader to see that too.

▼ Huck himself is serious. Huck, the narrator, says what a boy like him, but not a man like Twain, would say. Even though Twain is the writer, the *voice* you hear is that of Huck Finn. Twain creates an ironical situation in which everything Huck says about Emmeline's poetry confirms a different judgment in his readers.

▼ The diction is appropriate to the speaker. The humorous effect would be lost if Huck were made to speak like a sophisticated adult. He must speak in his own voice.

▼ All these elements are so interrelated that a change in any one of them would spoil the total effect.

Even this brief sample suggests that when you write something you must consider your attitude toward your subject, your relationship with your readers, and the language you use to express your ideas. The tone of your writing reveals the decisions you have made about the first two. The third is expressed in the choices you make as you develop your purpose. As you have seen throughout this text, a clear sense of purpose guides you through all the choices you make from planning through revision. If these choices are consistent, your writing will exhibit a distinctive *style* that will express your attitude toward and embody your understanding of your purpose.

Range of Style: Sentence Structure, Diction, and Tone

Style, of course, rests finally on language. Look closely at the sentence structure, diction, and tone of the following passages to see what generalizations you can make about them.

Example 1

Airplanes are invariably scheduled to depart at such times as 7:54, 9:21 or 11:37. This extreme specificity has the effect on the novice of instilling in him the twin beliefs that he will be *arriving* at 10:08, 1:43 or 4:22, and that he should get to the airport on time. These beliefs are not only erroneous but actually unhealthy, and could easily be dispelled by an attempt on the part of the airlines toward greater realism. Understandably, they may be reluctant to make such a radical change all at once. In an effort to make the transition easier I offer the following graduated alternatives to "Flight 477 to Minneapolis will depart at 8:03 P.M.":
a. Flight 477 to Minneapolis will depart oh, let's say, eightish.
b. Flight 477 to Minneapolis will depart around eight, eight-thirty.
c. Flight 477 to Minneapolis will depart while it's still dark.
d. Flight 477 to Minneapolis will depart before the paperback is out.
(Fran Leibowitz, "Fran Leibowitz's Travel Hints," *Social Studies*)

Analysis of Example 1: Sentence Structure

The nine sentences in this passage average only 17 words in length, and almost half of them are set apart in a list of brief announcements. Most of the sentences consist of one or two independent clauses. Only the second sentence has a slightly inverted construction. The rest of the sentences follow a subject-verb-object order.

Diction

In the whole passage there are proportionately few words more than two syllables long. *Invariably, specificity* and *graduated* are the most notable. Except for *novice* and *erroneous* there are no learned words. There are a few contractions (*let's, it's*) and one example of slang (*eightish*).

Tone

Leibowitz's attitude toward her subject is humorous and ironic.

Supposedly informative—after all, she is offering advice—her attitude is really affective because she wants to exploit her readers' exasperation over airline schedules. The distance between writer and reader is slight. Leibowitz writes as a fellow sufferer commenting on a common frustration. You hear the voice of a world-weary crank, slightly angry about a situation over which she has no control.

Summary

With simple sentences and diction, Leibowitz establishes her tone and creates a style that achieves ease and clarity. The diction and the pace of her sentences are those of informal conversation, creating an impression of talking in print. In Chapter 9 the word *colloquial* was used to describe diction of this sort. That term can apply to a style as well. A colloquial style is not common in college writing, but it is by no means inappropriate when it is used—as it is here—to fulfill the writer's purpose.

Now contrast the next example with Leibowitz's writing. Read the following passage aloud, slowly, to hear how it sounds.

Example 2

What a fierce weird pleasure to lie in my berth at night in the luxurious palace-car, drawn by the mighty Baldwin—embodying, and filling me, too, full of the swiftest motion, and most resistless strength! It is late, perhaps midnight or after—distances join'd like magic—as we speed through Harrisburg, Columbus, Indianapolis. The element of danger adds zest to it all. On we go, rumbling and flashing, with our loud whinnies thrown out from time to time, or trumpet-blasts, into the darkness. Passing the homes of men, the farms, barns, cattle—the silent villages. And the car itself, the sleeper, with curtains drawn and lights turn'd down—in the berths the slumberers, many of them women and children—as on, on, on, we fly like lightning through the night—how strangely sound and sweet they sleep! (They say the French Voltaire in his time designated the grand opera and a ship of war the most signal illustrations of the growth of humanity's and art's advance beyond primitive barbarism. Perhaps if the witty philosopher were here these days, and went in the same car with perfect bedding and feed from New York to San Francisco, he would shift his type and sample to one of our American sleepers.) (Walt Whitman, *Specimen Days*)

Analysis of Example 2: Sentence Structure

The paragraph has only eight sentences. Although there are two short sentences (one a fragment), most of the sentences are long. The average sentence length is 26 words, against 17 in the Leibowitz passage; the last three sentences are 42, 32, and 39 words long. The sentences are not simple. Subjects and verbs are often separated—sometimes widely—by modifiers. Several of the sentences exhibit extremely complicated punctuation. Throughout the paragraph, parallel and periodic structures are used for rhythmic and other effects.

Diction

About 27 percent of the words in the passage are more than two syllables long, and it contains a smaller proportion of monosyllables than the Leibowitz example. Whitman's diction is sprinkled with learned words—*resistless, slumberers, barbarism.* Several phrases have a lofty, poetic ring—"embodying, and filling me, too, full of the swiftest motion, and most resistless strength!"

Tone   Whitman is celebrating the mythic adventure of train travel, and his attitude toward his subject is clearly subjective. The distance between writer and reader is great; the emphasis is on the subject, not on the reader. The affective tone is impersonal, dignified, eloquent.

Summary   As in the Leibowitz example, all the components blend into a consistent style. But what a different style! Whitman aims at eloquence, not ease or familiarity. You would not use this style to give directions, explain a process, answer an examination, or report a story in a newspaper. Whitman's style shares many of the characteristics of nineteenth-century prose, characteristics still found in prose seeking similar effects. It could be called a *grand* style, but the usual name for it is *formal*.

Example 3   In those days differences in vegetation between a main highway and a side road were even greater than now. There weren't many state highways but the best of them stretched straight ahead with mathematical perfection, even though just of gravel. These rights-of-way were usually wide and from the road edge to the boundary fences were mowed pretty much as now, though road building had not been preceded by earth moving. As a result, there were more native plants in among the grass and fewer of those cosmopolitan tramps which take so readily to disturbed habitats. But the side roads, those fascinating side roads, they are mostly gone and there is nothing in the modern road system to compare with them. The wheel track wound here and there, depending upon the slope and the vegetation and the character of the land. Sometimes it was straight for a little way; frequently it wobbled. There was often grass in the roadway outside the actual wheel tracks; shrubs like sumac and elderberry pressed so close to the road that you could smell them as you drove by and children snatched at the flowers. Accommodating drivers of the local stage-line learned to snip off small twigs with a snap of the buggy whip and present them to lady passengers. (Edgar Anderson, "Horse-and-Buggy Countryside," *Landscape*)

Analysis of Example 3:
Sentence Structure   This paragraph has nine sentences, all following the standard pattern: subject-verb-object with modifiers and subordinate clauses appearing in predictable places. There are no conspicuous periodic sentences. Sentences do vary in length, from 11 to 38 words, but most fall between 19 and 26, averaging 21 (between the 17-word Leibowitz average and the 26-word Whitman average).

Diction   In this 214-word passage, only 15 words (or about 7 percent) are more than two syllables long. There are a few learned words such as *cosmopolitan* and *habitat,* but they are counterbalanced by popular words such as *snip* and *snap.*

Tone   Anderson's attitude toward his subject is both informative and affective. He wants to inform his readers about country roads, and he wants to describe how it must have looked and felt to ride down one of these roads in a horse-and-buggy. His choice of details—children snatching flowers, stage drivers snipping off flowers with their buggy whips—helps establish his

Summary

informal, familiar tone. The distance between writer and reader is greater than in the first example but less than the second example.

Anderson's style is neither so simple as Leibowitz's nor so involved as Whitman's. It has none of Leibowitz's chattiness and none of the poetry or exaltation that pervades Whitman's writing. Its balance of sentence length, diction, and tone produces a *moderate* style.

Whitman passage	Anderson passage	Leibowitz passage
Formal	*Moderate*	*Colloquial*

The diagram suggests three things.

▽ *The scale indicates degree of formality, from most to least.* It does not measure degree of excellence; no one style is better than another. All three are standard styles, and each is appropriate in some situations—although the moderate style is appropriate for most writing situations.

▽ *Each classification embodies a range.* A particular sample may be more or less formal than others. For example, a legal contract is more formal than Whitman's paragraph.

▽ *There is no clear division between styles.* The overlapping in the diagram is intended to suggest that the moderate style has such a broad range that it may include some formal and colloquial elements. Such inclusions, however, must be consistent with the writer's purpose. Edgar Anderson's use of *habitat,* for example, was justified because his purpose was to identify the characteristics of a particular landscape.

Summary of the Formal, Moderate, and Colloquial Styles

	Formal	*Moderate*	*Colloquial*
Sentences	Relatively long and involved; likely to make considerable use of parallel, balanced, and periodic structures; fragments rare.	Of medium length, averaging between 15 and 25 words; mostly standard structure but with some use of parallelism and balanced and periodic sentences; fragments occasional.	Short, simple structures; mainly subject-verb-object order; almost no use of balanced or periodic sentences; fragments common.
Diction	Extensive vocabulary, some use of learned and abstract words; no slang; almost no contractions or clipped words.	Ranges from learned to colloquial but mostly popular words; both abstract and concrete diction; occasional contractions and clipped words; may contain some inconspicuous slang.	Diction limited to popular and colloquial words, frequent contractions, and clipped words; frequent use of utility words; more slang than in moderate style.

Tone	Always a serious attitude toward an important subject; may be either subjective or objective and informative or affective; no attempt to establish closeness with reader, who is almost never addressed as "you"; personality of the writer often inconspicuous; whole tone usually dignified and impersonal.	Attitude toward subject may be serious or light, objective or subjective, informative or affective; relationship with reader close but seldom intimate; writer often refers to himself or herself as "I" and to reader as "you"; but the range of moderate style is so broad that it can vary from semiformal to semicolloquial.	Attitude toward subject may be serious or light but is usually subjective; close, usually intimate, relation with reader, who is nearly always addressed as "you"; whole tone is that of informal conversation.
Uses	A restricted style used chiefly for scholarly or technical writing for experts, or for essays and speeches that aim at eloquence or inspiration; a distinguished style, but not one for everyday use or practical affairs.	The broadest and most usable style for expository and argumentative writing and for all but the most formal of public speeches; the prevailing style in nontechnical books and magazines, in newspaper reports and editorials, in college lectures and discussions, in all student writing except some fiction.	Light, chatty writing as in letters to close friends; a restricted style that is inappropriate to most college writing except fiction.

_____Exercise   Analyze the sentence structure, diction, and tone of each of the following passages, using supporting details. Then rate each passage on the scale provided.

Most Formal				*Most Colloquial*

Competitors in conquest have overlooked the vital soul of Africa herself, from which emanates the true resistance to conquest. The soul is not dead, but silent, the wisdom not lacking, but of such simplicity as to be counted non-existent in the tinker's mind of modern civilization. Africa is of an ancient age and the blood of many of her peoples is as venerable and as chaste as truth. What upstart race, sprung from some recent, callow century to arm itself with steel and boastfulness, can match in purity the blood of a single Masai Murani whose heritage may have stemmed not far from Eden? It is not the weed that is corrupt; roots of the weed sucked first life from the genesis of earth and hold the essence of it still. Always the weed returns; the cultured plant retreats before it. Racial purity, true aristocracy, devolve not from edict, nor from rote, but from the preservation of kinship with the elemental forces and purposes of life

whose understanding is not farther beyond the mind of a Native shepherd than beyond the cultured fumblings of a mortar-board intelligence.
(Beryl Markham, *West with the Night*)

We were sitting in a restaurant called Orchid Garden, in the Wanchai
district, beginning our first meal in Hong Kong, and I had just sampled
something called fish-brain soup. I was about to comment. Alice was
looking a bit anxious. She was concerned, I think, that over the years I
might have created a vision of Hong Kong in my mind that could not be
matched by the reality—like some harried businessman who finally arrives
in what he has pictured as the remote, other-worldly peace of a Tahiti
beach only to be hustled by a couple of hip beach-umbrella salesmen
wearing "Souvenir of Fort Lauderdale" T-shirts. Even before we had a

Question: How does the tone and style of the text
compare and contrast with that of the image?

meal, she must have noticed my surprise at discovering that most of the other visitors in Hong Kong seemed to be there for purposes other than eating. That's the sort of thing that can put a visionary off his stride. How would the obsessed mountain climber feel if he arrived in Nepal after years of fantasizing about a clamber up the Himalayas, and found that most of the other tourists had come to observe the jute harvest? It appeared that just about everyone else had come to Hong Kong to shop. Hong Kong has dozens of vast shopping malls—floor after floor of shops run by cheerfully competitive merchants who knock off 10 percent at the hint of a frown and have never heard of sales tax. There are restaurants in some of the shopping malls, but most of the visitors seemed too busy shopping to eat. It was obvious that they would have come to Hong Kong even if it had been one of those British colonies where the natives have been taught to observe the queen's birthday by boiling brussels sprouts for an extra month. That very morning, in the lobby of a hotel, we had noticed a couple in late middle age suddenly drawing close to share some whispered intimacy in what Alice, the romantic, took to be a scene of enduring affection until one of the softly spoken phrases reached her ears— "customs declaration." (Calvin Trillin, "Hong Kong Dream," *Third Helpings*)

If you want to get something done, here is a professional secret: don't try to rush it by laying down the law that it *must be done* within a given time, but come back, each day if need be, and ask again, and do it with a smile. While evidences of irritation are fatal, persistence is never resented if it is clothed in good manners and good temper. When you can't wait any longer, the thing to do is to take an unfair advantage of your Brazilian friend—appeal to him to arrange matters for you because, first, you are in trouble with your principals; second, you are embarrassed by your own failure; third, you are obliged to leave by a given boat and will be humiliated if matters have not been arranged—anything to put it on a personal basis. When you do this your Brazilian is lost. He feels that you have been reasonable and patient and that he cannot throw you to the wolves. And in arranging matters for you he probably has to make a series of appeals more or less similar to yours. (Hugh Gibson, *Rio*)

Some Practical Advice about Style

You have examined the elements of style in passages by other writers. Now you are ready to apply what you have learned to your own writing. As you revise your writing, keep these stylistic considerations in mind.

1. *Let your purpose be your guide.* A clear sense of purpose controls all the choices you make at every stage in writing. Style results from that control.

2. *Generally, choose a moderate style.* There is nothing wrong with a formal or a colloquial style when it is appropriate. Unnecessary formality, however, often leads to pretentiousness and wordiness. The writer tries too

hard to be impressive or literary when it would be enough to clearly express his purpose. The colloquial style, if used for serious treatment of a serious subject, can undermine the writer's purpose. The best policy, as Hampl suggests, is to maintain the middle position, "the position of a human being who possesses both authority and reliability." You can then mix objective and subjective—informative and affective—as your purpose demands.

3. *Keep your style consistent.* Probably the worst stylistic defect is inconsistency. An inconsistent style is not the same as a moderate style in which formal and colloquial elements are balanced for a purpose. Writing that is totally inconsistent has no discoverable purpose and therefore no discoverable style. The inconsistencies in tone and diction that often occur in individual paragraphs, sentences, or words can be removed in revision.

   a. *Inconsistency in tone.* Conspicuous inconsistency in tone is likely to jar a reader. It is most obvious when colloquial elements appear in a formal style or formal elements in a colloquial style. Because a moderate style can range from semiformal to semicolloquial, it can tolerate usages that would be conspicuous in the extreme styles.

   b. *Inconsistency in diction.* As you begin planning and drafting your essay, you gradually commit yourself to a recognizable approach to both your subject and your reader. Your choice of words will either contribute to stylistic consistency or obscure the pattern in your writing. You are most likely to confuse readers by choosing words that are close but not close enough to your meaning. Do you want to say that your traveling companions are *insensitive, naive,* or *undiscriminating?* Your purpose determines the "best" choice of words.

4. *Try to see your writing as your readers will see it.* This advice may be the hardest to follow. People assume that what is clear to them will be clear to others, but common experience demonstrates that this assumption is not always true. In everyday conversation, a frequently asked question is "What do you mean by that?" Because your readers will not have the opportunity to ask you that question, try to anticipate their need for clarity and completeness.

5. *Be as specific as you can.* Writing is a difficult medium because it is abstract. The word *apple* is more abstract than any apple you ever ate, because it leaves out your actual experience with apples—their shape, size, color, texture, and taste. The problem all writers face is how to make abstractions concrete. The two common solutions are to (a) illustrate the meaning of general statements with examples, and (b) choose words that are specific.

6. *Revise for style.* You revise for style when you undertake global revision. Your style is dependent on your purpose, so if you revise your purpose, you must revise your style. Likewise, if you revise your subject or audience, you must make new decisions about sentence structure, diction,

and tone. For example, when Rod changed the focus of his essay on the Washington Monument and directed it toward a wider audience, he modified his style to avoid colloquial terms and breezy references.

Local revision—arranging your sentences, selecting your words, and adjusting your tone—involves the nuts and bolts of style. In fact, the changes you make in local revision will probably make the most improvement in your style. Follow your local revision with one last reading—just for style. Read the text aloud or, better yet, listen to it read aloud, and concentrate on its overall effect. Imagine yourself listening to a band or a singer performing a piece of music. As you listen to your own writing, concentrate on the style of the piece and keep alert for any false notes.

The following guidelines provide some basic questions to ask yourself when you revise for style.

Guidelines for Revising Your Style

1. **What is my general impression of my writing?**
   Do I find my writing clear, unambiguous, and likely to engage my readers? Have I carried out my purpose at every level; that is, am I satisfied that the *how* of my writing—its attitude, organization, and language—conveys the *what* of my ideas?

2. **What tone have I established in my writing?**
   Is my tone informative, affective, or a blend of both? How much distance have I maintained between myself and my readers? Is my tone appropriate for my subject and audience? Is it maintained consistently?

3. **How can I characterize the overall style of my writing?**
   Have I written this essay in a moderate style, opting for more or less colloquialism or formality as my purpose requires? Does my purpose in fact require me to be overtly colloquial or formal?

4. **Are my sentences well constructed and easy on the ear?**
   Have I written sentences varying in length and style so that they hold my readers' interest? Have I avoided the choppiness that comes from too many basic or loosely coordinated sentences? Have I avoided the density that comes from too many complicated sentences with multiple subordinate clauses?

5. **Have I used words as effectively as possible?**
   Do the connotations and denotations of my words support my purpose? Have I avoided unnecessary formalities and slang? Is my language specific and, when appropriate, vivid? Have I inadvertently mixed metaphors? Have I used imagery successfully to *heighten* effects, not merely to strive after them?

Once you have completed all your revisions and have typed your final draft, you should proofread your writing very carefully. Proofreading is a close reading of the final version to catch errors in grammar, spelling, and punctuation, as well as typographical errors, that survived your revisions or crept into the final copy. Proofreading should be done slowly, preferably aloud. If possible, you should allow some time to elapse between your final typing and your proofreading. In that way you are more likely to read with a fresh eye.

Third World Driving
   Hints and Tips | P. J. O'Rourke

In this selection from *Holidays in Hell,* P. J. O'Rourke demonstrates the particular style that he has exhibited as an editor for *The National Lampoon* and International Affairs Desk Chief at *Rolling Stone.* The title of the essay suggests that its purpose is to inform. At what point in the essay do you realize that O'Rourke's purpose is to entertain? How does purpose affect his tone?

During the past couple of years I've had to do my share of driving in the   1
Third World—in Mexico, Lebanon, the Philippines, Cyprus, El Salvador, Africa and Italy. (Italy is not technically part of the Third World, but no one has told the Italians.) I don't pretend to be an expert, but I have been making notes. Maybe these notes will be useful to readers who are planning to do something really stupid with their Hertz #1 Club cards.

Road Hazards

What would be a road hazard anywhere else, in the Third World is   2
probably the road. There are two techniques for coping with this. One is to drive very fast so your wheels "get on top" of the ruts and your car sails over the ditches and gullies. Predictably, this will result in disaster. The other technique is to drive very slowly. This will also result in disaster. No matter how slowly you drive into a ten-foot hole, you're still going to get hurt. You'll find the locals themselves can't make up their minds. Either they drive at 2 m.p.h.—which they do every time there's absolutely no way to get around them. Or else they drive at 100 m.p.h.—which they do coming right at you when you finally get a chance to pass the guy going 2 m.p.h.

Basic Information

It's important to have your facts straight before you begin piloting a   3
car around an underdeveloped country. For instance, which side of the road do they drive on? This is easy. They drive on your side. That is, you can depend on it, any oncoming traffic will be on your side of the road. Also, how do you translate kilometres into miles? Most people don't know this, but one kilometre = ten miles, exactly. True, a kilometre is only 62 per cent of a mile, but if something is one hundred kilometres away, read that as one thousand miles because the roads are 620 per cent worse than anything you've ever seen. And when you see a 50-k.p.h. speed limit, you might as well figure that means 500 *m.p.h.* because nobody cares. The Third World does not have Broderick Crawford and the Highway Patrol. Outside the cities, it doesn't have many police at all. Law enforcement is in the hands of the army. And soldiers, if they feel like it, will shoot you no matter what speed you're going.

O'Rourke, P. J. *Holidays in Hell.* New York: Atlantic Monthly Press, 1988. 78–82.

Traffic Signs and Signals

Most developing nations use international traffic symbols. Americans 4
may find themselves perplexed by road signs that look like Boy Scout merit
badges and by such things as an iguana silhouette with a red diagonal bar
across it. Don't worry, the natives don't know what they mean, either. The
natives do, however, have an elaborate set of signals used to convey information to the traffic around them. For example, if you're trying to pass
someone and he blinks his left turn signal, it means go ahead. Either that
or it means a large truck is coming around the bend, and you'll get killed if
you try. You'll find out in a moment.

Signalling is further complicated by festive decorations found on many 5
vehicles. It can be hard to tell a hazard flasher from a string of Christmas-
tree lights wrapped around the bumper, and brake lights can easily be confused with the dozen red Jesus statuettes and the ten stuffed animals with
blinking eyes on the package shelf.

Dangerous Curves

Dangerous curves are marked, at least in Christian lands, by white 6
wooden crosses positioned to make the curves even more dangerous. These
crosses are memorials to people who've died in traffic accidents, and they
give a rough statistical indication of how much trouble you're likely to have
at that spot in the road. Thus, when you come through a curve in a full-
power slide and are suddenly confronted with a veritable forest of cruci-
fixes, you know you're dead.

Learning to Drive Like a Native

It's important to understand that in the Third World most driving is 7
done with the horn, or "Egyptian Brake Pedal," as it is known. There is a
precise and complicated etiquette of horn use. Honk your horn only under
the following circumstances:

1. When anything blocks the road.
2. When anything doesn't.
3. When anything might.
4. At red lights.
5. At green lights.
6. At all other times.

Road-Blocks

One thing you can count on in Third World countries is trouble. 8
There's always some uprising, coup or Marxist insurrection going on, and
this means military road-blocks. There are two kinds of military road-block,
the kind where you slow down so they can look you over, and the kind
where you come to a full stop so they can steal your luggage. The important thing is that you must *never* stop at the slow-down kind of road-block.
If you stop, they'll think you're a terrorist about to attack them, and they'll
shoot you. And you must *always* stop at the full-stop kind of road-block. If
you just slow down, they'll think you're a terrorist about to attack them,
and they'll shoot you. How do you tell the difference between the two
kinds of road-block? Here's the fun part: you can't!

(The terrorists, of course, have road-blocks of their own. They always 9
make you stop. Sometimes with land mines.)

Animals in the Right of Way

As a rule of thumb, you should slow down for donkeys, speed up for 10
goats and stop for cows. Donkeys will get out of your way eventually, and
so will pedestrians. But never actually stop for either of them or they'll take
advantage, especially the pedestrians. If you stop in the middle of a crowd
of Third World pedestrians, you'll be there buying Chiclets and bogus an-
tiquities for days.

Drive like hell through the goats. It's almost impossible to hit a goat. 11
On the other hand, it's almost impossible *not* to hit a cow. Cows are im-
mune to horn-honking, shouting, swats with sticks and taps on the hind
quarters with the bumper. The only thing you can do to make a cow move
is swerve to avoid it, which will make the cow move in front of you with
lightning speed.

Actually, the most dangerous animals are the chickens. In the United 12
States, when you see a ball roll into the street, you hit your brakes because
you know the next thing you'll see is a kid chasing it. In the Third World,
it's not balls the kids are chasing, but chickens. Are they practising punt
returns with a leghorn? Dribbling it? Playing stick-hen? I don't know. But
Third Worlders are remarkably fond of their chickens and, also, their children (population problems not withstanding). If you hit one or both, they
may survive. But you will not.

Accidents

Never look where you're going—you'll only scare yourself. Nonethe- 13
less, try to avoid collisions. There are bound to be more people in that bus,
truck or even on that moped than there are in your car. At best you'll be
screamed deaf. And if the police do happen to be around, standard procedure is to throw everyone in jail regardless of fault. This is done to forestall
blood feuds, which are a popular hobby in many of these places. Remember
the American consul is very busy fretting about that Marxist insurrection,
and it may be months before he comes to visit.

If you do have an accident, the only thing to do is go on the offensive. 14
Throw big wads of American money at everyone, and hope for the best.

Safety Tips

One nice thing about the Third World, you don't have to fasten your 15
safety belt. (Or stop smoking. Or cut down on saturated fats.) It takes a lot
off your mind when average life expectancy is forty-five minutes.

The Ugly Tourist | Jamaica Kincaid

Although she now lives in New York and is a staff writer for *The New
Yorker,* Jamaica Kincaid has a special perspective on the issues of travel
and tourism. Born in St. John's, Antigua, in the West Indies, she has seen

Kincaid, Jamaica. *A Small Place.* New York: Farrar, 1988. 14–9.

and (as she suggests in this excerpt from *A Small Place*) been an "ugly tourist." How would you characterize Kincaid's style—formal, moderate, colloquial? What distinctive features of her style—sentence structure, diction, tone—influence your assessment?

The thing you have always suspected about yourself the minute you become a tourist is true: a tourist is an ugly human being. You are not an ugly person all the time; you are not an ugly person ordinarily; you are not an ugly person day to day. From day to day, you are a nice person. From day to day, all the people who are supposed to love you on the whole do. From day to day as you walk down a busy street in the large and modern and prosperous city in which you work and live, dismayed, puzzled (a cliché, but only a cliché can explain you) at how alone you feel in this crowd, how awful it is to go unnoticed, how awful it is to go unloved, even as you are surrounded by more people than you could possibly get to know in a lifetime that lasted for millennia, and then out of the corner of your eye you see someone looking at you and absolute pleasure is written all over that person's face, and then you realize that you are not as revolting a presence as you think you are (for that look just told you so). And so, ordinarily, you are a nice person, an attractive person, a person capable of drawing to yourself the affection of other people (people just like you), a person at home in your own skin (sort of; I mean, in a way; I mean, your dismay and puzzlement are natural to you, because people like you just seem to be like that, and so many of the things people like you find admirable about yourselves—the things you think about, the things you think really define you—seem rooted in these feelings): a person at home in your own house (and all its nice house things), with its nice back yard (and its nice back-yard things), at home on your street, your church, in community activities, your job, at home with your family, your relatives, your friends—you are a whole person. But one day, when you are sitting somewhere, alone in that crowd, and that awful feeling of displacedness comes over you, and really, as an ordinary person you are not well equipped to look too far inward and set yourself aright, because being ordinary is already so taxing, and being ordinary takes all you have out of you, and though the words "I must get away" do not actually pass across your lips, you make a leap from being that nice blob just sitting like a boob in your amniotic sac of the modern experience to being a person visiting heaps of death and ruin and feeling alive and inspired at the sight of it; to being a person lying on some faraway beach, your stilled body stinking and glistening in the sand, looking like something first forgotten, then remembered, then not important enough to go back for; to being a person marvelling at the harmony (ordinarily, what you would say is the backwardness) and the union these other people (and they are other people) have with nature. And you look at the things they can do with a piece of ordinary cloth, the things they fashion out of cheap, vulgarly coloured (to you) twine, the way they squat down over a hole they have made in the ground, the hole itself is something to marvel at, and since you are being an ugly person this ugly but joyful thought will swell inside you: their ancestors were not clever in the way yours were and not ruthless in the way yours were, for then would it not be you who would be in harmony with nature and backwards

1

in that charming way? An ugly thing, that is what you are when you become a tourist, an ugly, empty thing, a stupid thing, a piece of rubbish pausing here and there to gaze at this and taste that, and it will never occur to you that the people who inhabit the place in which you have just paused cannot stand you, that behind their closed doors they laugh at your strangeness (you do not look the way they look); the physical sight of you does not please them; you have bad manners (it is their custom to eat their food with their hands; you try eating their way, you look silly; you try eating the way you always eat, you look silly); but they do not like the way you speak (you have an accent); they collapse helpless from laughter, mimicking the way they imagine you must look as you carry out some everyday bodily function. They do not like you. *They do not like me!* That thought never actually occurs to you. Still, you feel a little uneasy. Still, you feel a little foolish. Still, you feel a little out of place. But the banality of your own life is very real to you; it drove you to this extreme, spending your days and your nights in the company of people who despise you, people you do not like really, people you would not want to have as your actual neighbour. And so you must devote yourself to puzzling out how much of what you are told is really, really true (Is ground-up bottle glass in peanut sauce really a delicacy around here, or will it do just what you think ground-up bottle glass will do? Is this rare, multicoloured, snout-mouthed fish really an aphrodisiac, or will it cause you to fall asleep permanently?). Oh, the hard work all of this is, and is it any wonder, then, that on your return home you feel the need of a long rest, so that you can recover from your life as a tourist?

That the native does not like the tourist is not hard to explain. For every native of every place is a potential tourist, and every tourist is a native of somewhere. Every native everywhere lives a life of overwhelming and crushing banality and boredom and desperation and depression, and every deed, good and bad, is an attempt to forget this. Every native would like to find a way out, every native would like a rest, every native would like a tour. But some natives—most natives in the world—cannot go anywhere. They are too poor. They are too poor to escape the reality of their lives; and they are too poor to live properly in the place where they live, which is the very place you, the tourist, want to go—so when the natives see you, the tourist, they envy you, they envy your ability to leave your own banality and boredom, they envy your ability to turn their own banality and boredom into a source of pleasure for yourself. 2

Prague | Patricia Hampl

In this excerpt from her memoirs *A Romantic Education,* Patricia Hampl tries to explain why she revised her intention to visit her grandparents' birthplace. Reread Hampl's comments on tone and style at the beginning of this chapter. Identify the specific passages in Hampl's essay where you sense that "another human being is speaking to" you. Where does Hampl use a formal tone? Where does she use a more conversational tone? How

Hampl, Patricia. *A Romantic Education.* Boston: Houghton, 1981. 145–48; 149–52.

does this mixture help her readers understand the conclusions she makes in the last paragraph?

In May 1975, during the spring music festival that opens every year with a performance of Smetana's "Ma Vlast" ("My Homeland"), I went to Prague for the first time. The lilacs were in bloom everywhere: the various lavenders of the French and Persian lilac, and the more unusual—except in Prague—double white lilac. Huge flat red banners with yellow lettering were hoisted everywhere too, draped across homely suburban factories and from the subtle rose and mustard baroque buildings of Staré Město (the Old City).

The banners were in honor of the thirtieth anniversary of the liberation of Prague by the Soviet Army in May 1945. 30 *Let,* "30 years," it said everywhere, even on the visa stamp in my passport. Many offices and stores had photographs in their windows, blowups from 1945 showing Russian soldiers accepting spring bouquets from shy little girls, Russian soldiers waving from tanks to happy crowds. For the first time, I was in a city where the end of the Second World War was really celebrated, where history was close at hand. Prague was the first Continental European city I had seen (I had come from London) and it was almost weirdly intact, not modern. On the plane from America to London I had reminded myself that London would be modern; *my* England was so much a product of the nineteenth-century novels and poetry I'd been reading all my life that I knew I would be shocked to see automobiles. And in fact, nothing could prepare me for the slump I felt in London: I wanted the city of Becky Sharpe, of Daniel Deronda, even of Clarissa Dalloway, not the London of Frommer's guidebooks and the thrill of finding lunch for 5 pence.

Prague stopped my tourism flat. The weight of its history and the beauty of its architecture came to me first as an awareness of dirt, a sort of ancient grime I had never seen before. It bewitched me, that dirt, caught in the corners of baroque moldings and decorative cornices, and especially I loved the dusty filth of the long, grave windows at sunset when the light flared against the tall oblongs and caused them to look gilded.

I had arrived in a river city, just as I had left one in St. Paul. But the difference . . . On the right bank of the Vltava (in German, the Moldau) the buildings were old—to me. Some of them were truly old, churches and wine cellars and squares dating from the Middle Ages. But the real look, especially of the residential and shopping areas of Nové Město (New City—new since the fourteenth century when Charles IV founded it), was art nouveau, highly decorative, the Bohemian version of the Victorian. Across the river, in Malá Strana (Small Side—Prague's Left Bank), the city became most intensely itself, however; it rose baroquely up, villa by villa, palace crushed to palace, gardens crumbling and climbing, to the castle that ran like a great crown above it on a bluff.

The city silenced me. It was just as well I didn't know the language and was traveling alone. There was nothing for me to say. I was here to look.

My original intention in going to Prague was simple: to see the place my grandparents had come from, to hear the language they had spoken. I knew Prague was Kafka's city, I knew Rilke had been born here, and I had read his *Letters to a Young Poet* many times. I was a young poet myself. But my visit wasn't for them. Mine was the return of a third generation American, the sort of journey that is so inexplicable to the second generation: "What are you going to *do* there?" my father asked me before I left Minnesota.

That spring, the lines at the Prague Čedok office (the government agency that runs tourism in Czechoslovakia) were dotted here and there with young Americans looking for family villages. The young couple in front of me in the line had come from Cleveland. The man was asking a young travel agent, who was dressed in a jeans skirt and wore nail polish the color of an eggplant, how he and his wife could get to a village whose name he couldn't manage to pronounce.   7

"There does not seem to be such a place," she told him. She couldn't find a name on the map with a spelling that corresponded to the one the young man had brought from Cleveland on the piece of paper he was holding out to his wife. ("It's *his* family," she said to me. "I'm Irish.")   8

They decided to set out, anyway, for a village in Moravia that had a similar spelling. "I guess that's the place," the young man said, without much conviction.   9

I asked my father's question: "What are you going to *do* there?"   10

"Look around," he said. "Maybe somebody"—he meant a relative— "will be there."   11

My own slip of paper, which I'd brought from St. Paul, had the name of my grandmother's village ("spelling approximate," my cousin had written next to the name when he gave it to me) which was supposed to be near Třeboň, a small town in southern Bohemia. On the map, Třeboň was set among lakes (like Minneapolis, I had thought); here, the guidebook said, "the famous carp" were caught.   12

Suddenly, just then, as my turn came up, I had no heart for the approximate name of the village, for the famous carp, the kind of journey the Cleveland couple had set for themselves. ("We're going to do the same thing in Ireland," the wife said.) I stepped out of the line, crumpled up my piece of paper, and left it in an ashtray. The absurdity of trying to get to Třeboň, and from there to wherever this village with the approximate spelling was supposed to be, lay on me like a plank. I felt like a student who drops out of medical school a semester before graduation; I was almost there and, suddenly, it didn't matter, I didn't want what I'd been seeking. Apparently I wanted something else.   13

"Do you want to get something to eat?" I asked the couple from Cleveland.   14

But they didn't have time. "We have to split," she said.   15

"Yeah," said her husband. "It's a long way. . . ."   16

I put Třeboň out of my mind and spent the rest of the week walking aimlessly around Prague. If I had answered my father's question—what was I *doing*—I would have said I was sitting in coffeehouses, in between long, aimless walks. A long trip for a cup of coffee, but I was listless, suddenly lacking curiosity and I felt, as I sat in the Slavia next to the big windows that provide one of the best views of the Hradčany in the city, that simply by staring out the window I was doing my bit: there it was, the castle, and   17

I was looking at it. I had fallen on the breast of the Middle European coffeehouse and I was content among the putty- and dove-colored clothes, the pensioners stirring away the hours, the tables of university students studying and writing their papers, the luscious waste of time, the gossip whose ardor I sensed in the bent heads, lifted eyebrows—because of course I couldn't understand a word.

In Vienna the coffeehouses—not all of them, thank God—lose their 18
leases to McDonald's and fast-food chains. But in Prague the colors just fade and become more, rather than less, what they were. The coffeehouse is deeply attached to the idea of conversation, the exchange of ideas, and therefore, to a political society. In *The Agony of Czechoslovakia '38/'68,* Kurt Weisskopf remembers the Prague coffeehouses before the Second World War.

> You were expected to patronize the coffeehouse of your group, your 19
> profession, your political party. Crooks frequented the Golden Goose,
> or the Black Rose in the centre of Prague. Snobs went to the Savarin,
> whores and their prospective clients to the Lind or Julis; commercial
> travelers occupied the front part of Cafe Boulevard, while the rear was
> the traditional meeting place of Stalinists and Trotskyites, glaring at
> each other as they sat around separate marble tables. The rich went to
> the Urban, "progressive" intellectuals to the Metro. Abstract painters
> met at the Union, and surrealists at the Manes where they argued with
> impressionists. You were still served by the black-coated waiters if you
> did not belong, but so contemptuously that you realized how unwel-
> come your presence was. The papers in their bamboo frames and the
> magazines in their folders, an essential part of the Central European
> coffeehouse service, were regrettably not available to intruders. If you
> went to the wrong coffeehouse you were just frozen out.
>
> But if you fitted in, socially, politically, philosophically, artistically 20
> or professionally, well, then the headwaiter and the manager treated
> you almost as a relative and you were even deemed worthy of credit.
>
> "Rudolf, switch on the light over the Communists, they can't read 21
> their papers properly," old Loebl, manager of the Edison, used to in-
> struct the headwaiter. "And see that the Anarchists get more iced wa-
> ter." Once you had ordered your coffee you were entitled to free
> glasses of iced water brought regularly by the trayload; this was called
> a "swimming pool."

The water was still brought, as I sat at the marble table of the Slavia, 22
though not by the trayload. Perhaps there were political conversations, even arguments: I couldn't tell. But the newspapers were the official ones of the Communist Party, including, in English, the *Daily Worker.* When I asked someone I'd struck up a conversation with, who was quoted as a source on American news, I was told, "Gus Hall," the president of the American Communist Party. "As a typical American?" I asked incredulously. "As the voice of the people," I was told. It struck me as funny, not sinister, although later I realized I was annoyed.

I walked around Prague, hardly caring if I hit the right tourist spots, 23
missing baroque gems, I suppose, getting lost, leaving the hotel without a map as if I had no destination. I just walked, stopping at coffeehouses,

smoking unfiltered cigarettes and looking out from the blue wreath around me to other deep-drawing smokers. Everyone seemed to have time to sit, to smoke as if smoking were breathing, to stare into the vacancy of private thought, if their thoughts were private. I was in the thirties, I'd finally arrived in my parents' decade, the men's soft caps, the dove colors of Depression pictures, the acquiescence to circumstance, the ruined quality. For the first time I recognized the truth of beauty: that it is brokenness, it is on its knees. I sat and watched it and smoked (I don't smoke but I found myself buying cigarettes), smoked a blue relation between those coffeehouses and me. For this sadness turned out to be, to me, beautiful. Or rather, the missing quality of beauty, whatever makes it approachable, became apparent in Prague. I could sit, merely breathing, and be part of it. I was beautiful—at last. And I didn't care—at last. I stumbled through the ancient streets, stopped in the smoke-grimed coffeehouses and added my signature of ash, anonymous and yet entirely satisfied. I had ceased even to be a reverse immigrant—I sought no one, no sign of my family or any ethnic heritage that might be mine. I was, simply, in the most beautiful place I had ever seen, and it was grimy and sad and broken. I was relieved of some weight, the odd burden of happiness and unblemished joy of the adored child—or perhaps I was free of beauty itself as an abstract concept. I didn't think about it and didn't bother to wonder. I sat and smoked; I walked and got lost and didn't care because I couldn't get lost. I hardly understood that I was happy: my happiness consisted of encountering sadness. I simply felt *accurate*.

Writing Assignments

Narrate   **1.** Write a brief guidebook to a place you remember well and with great affection. Provide a map, a brief (informative) history, and the kind of information your readers will want—how to get there, where to stay, what to see, how much things cost. Reserve a section to explain why this place has special, personal significance for you.

Observe   **2.** Select a place you have visited on several occasions and compare how two means of travel—driving a car, or flying in a plane—affected what you saw on your way and altered your attitude toward your destination. Consider why you prefer one style of travel to the other. Then draft an essay, "The Best Way to Get There," describing your observations and the reasons for your choice.

Investigate   **3.** In "Girl Talk–Boy Talk," *Science 85* (January/February 1985), John Pfeiffer reports that researcher "Sally McConnell-Ginet of Cornell finds that women's voices are more colorful—they vary their pitch and change pitch more frequently than do men's voices. In one experiment, women immediately assumed a monotone style when asked to imitate men's speech. McConnell-Ginet regards speaking tunefully as an effective strategy for getting and holding attention, a strategy used more often by women than men." Use McConnell-Ginet's research as a starting point for developing your own investigation of the way gender, class, profession, or place may affect the tone of speech of the people you talk with during your daily travels.

Collaborate   **4.** Your writing group has been asked to write and produce a series of language/culture tapes for a group of exchange students visiting your campus for a semester. Make a list of the kind of information you think they should have about America, your region, and campus. Interview other exchange students from that country already on your campus to see what specific difficulties they have encountered. Ask these students to evaluate the sentence structure, diction, and tone in your scripts. Then audition members of your group and select those people with the most engaging *voices* to read the scripts on tape.

Read   **5.** Select a place people commonly visit for vacations—the Caribbean, Europe, California, Florida. Collect a range of guidebooks that provide information on the same place—comprehensive (*Baedeker's Great Britain*), discount (*Great Britain on $50 a Day*), and quaint (*England's Wonderful Little Hotels and Inns*). Compare and contrast the tone and style of these books in a review for the "Travel and Leisure" section of your newspaper. Focus on one specific spot—such as Stratford-on-Avon—so that you restrict the terms of your comparison.

Respond   **6.** Write a response to P. J. O'Rourke's "Third World Driving Hints and Tips." Your experience driving in other countries or particular sections of our country, for example, may encourage you to imitate O'Rourke's essay, detailing the many comic aspects of driving in a strange land. On the other hand, you may wish to take issue with O'Rourke's attitude toward the people of the *third* world. In that case, you may want to use specific driving experiences to demonstrate why good guests should learn and respect the customs of their hosts.

Analyze **7.** Study the *you* Jamaica Kincaid addresses in "The Ugly Tourist"—the various contexts *you* inhabits, the reactions *you* elicits, the adjectives *you* ordinarily uses to describe *yourself,* and the changes *you* experiences when encountering people from another country. Then write an analysis explaining how Kincaid uses this strategy to personalize the conflict between tourists and natives.

Evaluate **8.** Evaluate Hampl's style (sentence structure, diction, tone) in those sections where she is talking about the history of Prague and those sections where she is talking about herself. Use the information to explain how Prague "silenced" Hampl, "stopped my tourism flat." Then write an essay illustrating how her decision to stop touring and get lost helped her understand this alien culture, helped her "feel accurate."

Argue **9.** Reread Robert Winkler's essay "The Traveling Photographer" at the end of Chapter 2 (pages 56–9) and Walker Percy's description of the Grand Canyon in this chapter (pages 281–2). Then, using a specific experience to illustrate your case, write an opinion column arguing that tourists adopt a particular style. For example, some tourists see what they expect to see, some something less than what they were led to believe they would see, and some see something no one else has ever seen.

Argue **10.** Using your own experience, your knowledge of American history, and the readings in this chapter, write a speech for the "travel lecture series" at your local public library about America's fascination with travel. You could argue, for example, that such fascination is a deficiency: Americans are continually traveling because we are unable to find happiness in any place. Or you could argue that such fascination is a virtue: Americans are flexible, capable of change, and tolerant of other lifestyles.

PART 3

Special Assignments

11

The Essay Examination

The essay examination is one of the most practical of all academic writing assignments. By asking you to compose an answer to a specific question, with a limited amount of time for organizing your thoughts, it calls on most of the skills you have developed as a writer. As historian T. H. White points out in his book *In Search of History,* "One must grasp the question quickly; answer hard, with minimum verbiage; and do it all against a speeding clock."

Instructors frequently complain that students produce their worst writing on essay examinations. Of course, the "speeding clock" makes it impossible for you to work slowly and carefully through the stages of planning, drafting, and revising your responses. And certainly, the pressure of taking an examination does not encourage stylistic polish. But in spite of these limitations, you can still plan what you want to say, develop your purpose into an adequate essay, and reserve some time to review and proofread your answer. If you simply begin writing without using those strategies, you are likely to produce an essay that is irrelevant, inadequate, unclear, and even self-contradictory.

If you practice the major principles of purposeful writing discussed in Parts One and Two of this book, you will be able to improve the quality of your essay answers. Of course, you will not learn the subject matter of your examinations in this chapter. But many weak responses to essay examination questions are caused not by ignorance of the subject matter but by carelessness, haste, or panic. The recommendations in this chapter will help you avoid such pitfalls.

READ THE QUESTION CAREFULLY

Before you begin to answer any part of an examination, read the question carefully to see what it asks you to write about and how it asks you to write about it. If you misinterpret the question, your answer may be inadequate, even if it shows detailed knowledge of the subject and is otherwise well written. Essay questions are generally carefully written to identify a specific subject and indicate a specific approach. So before you begin to write, ask yourself, "What subject does this question require me to write about and how does it require me to

309

UPI/Bettmann Newsphotos

write about it?" Look for key words—such as *evaluate, trace,* or *contrast*—that indicate the appropriate organization for your information. If you are asked to *analyze* a passage, a summary or a paraphrase will not satisfy the requirement. If you are asked to *compare* two characters in a play, a description of each character may not develop the comparison. *Never begin to write until you have a clear idea of the form and content of the answer required.*

Study the following question and the two answers to it to see the difference in answers derived from a careful and from a careless reading of the question.

Examination Question

FDR and JFK had different conceptions of the presidential press conference. Using these two photographs as evidence, describe and contrast their conceptions.

Answer 1

FDR and JFK had different conceptions of the presidential press conference. FDR saw it as a private discussion with a small group of friendly reporters; JFK saw it as a public performance in front of a large audience that included reporters and the American people. In the two photographs, these contrasting views can be seen in each president's choice of setting, characters, and activity.

Photo courtesy The John F. Kennedy Library, Boston, Photo No. AR 6703B.

FDR chose the Oval Office for his intimate press conferences. The informality of this setting is illustrated by the small group of reporters standing close to the president, the bouquet of flowers on his desk, and the good will evident in the president's smile. By contrast, JFK chose the auditorium at the State Department for his more imposing press conferences. The formality of this setting is illustrated by the way reporters are separated from the president by theater seating, by the elevated stage and rostrum, and by the microphones on the lectern. Instead of the casual bouquet of flowers, the flags and official seals of the president suggest that this press conference is a ceremonial occasion.

FDR invited thirty or so reporters to his weekly press conferences. He thought of them as "family" and was eager to talk with them about various issues of public policy. Because all of them were print journalists, he provided them with information that they could use to write their stories. JFK held open news conferences, and usually the four-hundred-seat auditorium was filled to overflowing. He thought of reporters as "friendly adversaries" and enjoyed making news by sparring with them on live television. In the first photo, FDR seems prepared to answer questions by himself. In the second, JFK is flanked by a group of advisors who can help him if he is asked a complicated question.

The drama captured in the FDR photo suggests the activity of a family council. FDR allowed each reporter to ask questions, but he conducted his conferences like after-dinner discussions, lecturing leisurely to reporters about the state of the economy or foreign policy and dictating when they could or could not quote him directly. JFK called on reporters, but since he staged his press conferences as thirty-minute television shows, he had to be selective about which questions he acknowledged and which answers he developed in detail. In the first photo, FDR seems like a beneficent father who has stopped discussion to pose for a family photograph. In the second, JFK seems like a matinee idol performing not just for the reporters in the room but for the millions of people watching on television.

This is an excellent response to the examiner's question. The first paragraph asserts a basic contrast in the two presidents' conception of the press conference that is based on supporting evidence from the photographs. The three paragraphs that follow use the alternating pattern to contrast FDR's and JFK's choice of, respectively, setting, characters, and dramatic activity. Each detail develops the contrast announced in the opening paragraph. There are no digressions. And each paragraph concludes with a brief summary that reaffirms the basic contrast. The writer knows what the question requires. That determines her purpose and controls what she has to say.

Answer 2

The photograph of FDR's press conference is very crowded. About twenty people, not all of them smiling, are trying to squeeze themselves into the shot. It is not clear from the photograph that all these people are reporters—only one seems to be writing. All seem aware of the photographer, who has apparently asked them to stop their discussion and pose. The president's desk is covered, but not cluttered, with paper. Other objects on his desk are an inkstand, a telephone, and a large bouquet of flowers. The president is seated in a large, comfortable chair. Because FDR was crippled by polio, photographers agreed to maintain the illusion of his good health by taking his picture only when he was seated. His smile suggests that the press conference has been productive.

The photograph of JFK's press conference is also crowded, but most of the reporters are seated in (or standing around the rim of) an auditorium, while the president stands on a platform behind a large lectern. Some of his advisors appear to be seated on his left. Near the double doors to his right are two television cameras. Behind the windows on the second floor is the control center. Barely visible behind the glass are the technicians who control the light and sound for the president's performance and broadcast it to the American public. The president seems to be making a thoughtful reply to an important question. Most of the reporters in the room are either listening to his response or writing significant quotes in their notebooks.

Even though it shows good observation of details, answer 2 is unsatisfactory, chiefly because it does not respond directly to the question. The purpose imposed by the directions was to use the two photographs to *describe and contrast* the different conceptions FDR and JFK had of the presidential press conference. Answer 2 describes each photograph separately but pays almost no attention to the contrast the descriptions were to demonstrate. The writer digresses by mentioning FDR's polio, which is irrelevant to the description of the press conference. This answer lacks a thesis; it tells readers what each press conference looks like but says nothing about the two presidents' differing conceptions of them.

THINK OUT YOUR ANSWER BEFORE WRITING

Plan your answer before you begin to write it. Because in an essay examination you will have almost no chance for composing a discovery draft or for extensive revising, your answer must be drafted correctly the first time. Most examination questions attempt to restrict your subject, specify a method of development and organization, and suggest a thesis. Thinking about the implications of the information given in the question itself will bring to mind explanatory or illustrative details that you can use in your answer. For many questions, it is wise to start, as you learned in Chapter 3, by making a scratch outline to organize the information you want to use and then formulating a thesis statement or, in the case of brief answers, a topic sentence.

Answer 1 below shows a carefully planned response to this question:

Explain how the Arctic region supports various forms of plant and animal life.

The student thinks over the question and frames a topic sentence:

The seasonal changes in the permafrost enable the Arctic region to support various forms of plant and animal life.

The topic sentence (or thesis) shows that the writer understands that the question is asking him to discuss *how* a specific characteristic of the Arctic region—the seasonal changes in the permafrost—supports various forms of plant and animal life. His topic sentence will require him to define *permafrost,* to explain how seasonal changes affect it, and to demonstrate how these changes support plant and animal life. Notice how his answer satisfies the requirements of both the question and his own topic sentence.

Answer 1

The seasonal changes in the permafrost enable the Arctic region to support various forms of plant and animal life. During most of the year the ground is covered with snow, and permafrost freezes the sublayers of the soil to depths ranging from 50 to 4,800 feet. But during the spring months the snow melts and the top layer of the permafrost thaws into a swampy marsh. This layer is not deep enough to support trees, whose roots need from 4 to 8 feet of unfrozen soil to grow, but it does support a wide variety of stunted vegetation, composed mostly of mosses, lichens, and grasses. These plant communities, some featuring brightly colored flowers, support the life of insects, migrating birds, and grazing mammals such as reindeer.

This answer is an excellent example of purposeful writing in a paragraph: topic sentence, followed by supporting detail, followed by a concluding sentence that expands the reference to "plant and animal life." Because the writer planned his whole answer from beginning to end, he controls his paragraph and demonstrates his understanding of the content behind the question.

Answer 2 does not show the same careful thought about the requirements of the question or the use of an appropriate topic sentence to control the answer. Instead the student plunges into a summary of the facts without considering how they relate to the question she is supposed to be answering.

Answer 2

The Arctic region is able to support a wide range of plant and animal life. Although most of the area is virtually treeless, it does support specialized vegetation such as grasses and sedges. These plants have brightly colored flowers but thrive in swampy soil that makes walking extremely difficult. They provide habitation for many insects, including flies and mosquitoes that make what appears to be a beautiful meadow unbearable for most travelers. The most common mammals in this region are lemming, reindeer, Arctic fox, and wolf. Birds, mainly hawks, also migrate to the Arctic region during the summer months.

This paragraph does not answer the question. It catalogues the variety of plant and animal life in the Arctic region but fails to analyze the factor (the spring thaw of the top layer of the permafrost) that enables this life to thrive. The answer also digresses by its allusion to the difficulties encountered by travelers.

Failure to read the question carefully enough to see what it asks and failure to plan your answer are related faults. If you know the subject, careful reading of the question will suggest an answer, and planning the answer will give you a check against the wording in the question. If you miss the first step, you will probably miss the second also.

WRITE A COMPLETE ANSWER

Unless the directions specify a short answer, do not write a one- or two-sentence response in an essay examination. Be sure to distinguish between a short-answer test and an essay examination. A short-answer test tests your ability to recall facts, and each question can usually be answered in one or two minutes. Usually there are from twenty to thirty such questions in a fifty-minute quiz. An essay examination, by contrast, tests your ability to interpret facts—to select and organize information that supports a thesis. Because such an answer requires more extended writing, the examiner assumes that you may need as much as fifty minutes to compose each answer. Sometimes the directions specify how much time to allow for each answer, but if they do not, the number of questions in the test indicates approximately how much time you should devote to each answer.

A complete answer is one that deals with the subject as fully as possible within the time limits. An answer that is complete for a short-answer test will be inadequate for an essay examination. For example, with a few additions, the second sentence of answer 1 contrasting FDR's and JFK's conceptions of press conferences would be a complete answer for a short-answer test.

FDR saw [the presidential press conference] as a private discussion with a small group of friendly reporters; JFK saw it as a public performance in front of a large audience that included reporters and the American people.

But this would be an inadequate answer for an essay examination because it lacks the detailed analysis of the two photographs required by the question.

The answers to the following essay examination question further illustrate the difference between a complete and an incomplete answer.

What lessons did American military strategists learn from the French experience in Vietnam?

Answer 1

American military strategists learned little from the French experience in Vietnam because, like the French, they failed to understand the culture of the country and the dedication of the enemy. For example, the Americans ignored the lesson of the French "agroville" experiment when they adopted the Strategic Hamlet program. Both programs violated ancient Vietnamese traditions by removing peasants from their sacred villages and herding them into secure but alien fortresses. In each case, many peasants sneaked back to their homes, and those who remained nursed a growing hostility toward those who were trying to save them.

Similarly, the U.S. did not understand the lesson of Dien Bien Phu. The French assumed that a massive increase in highly trained forces could overpower a poorly armed enemy. At Dien Bien Phu, however, the Vietminh used superhuman effort to haul their small supply of large guns through dense jungles to trap and capture the superior French forces. Like the French, American military and political leaders failed to learn that increases in personnel and weapons were insufficient to dispose of a dedicated army fighting for its homeland.

Answer 2

The United States never made the error of Dien Bien Phu, where the French troops were trapped in a valley by enemy artillery. But, by and large, the United States repeated the central French mistake of failing to understand the country it was trying to save from communism.

Answer 2 is incomplete for two reasons: first, it does not mention the real lesson of Dien Bien Phu (that a small, dedicated army can outmaneuver large forces), and second, it fails to illustrate how the Americans repeated the central French mistake of ignoring the culture of the country it was trying to help. Although the second answer may be adequate for a short-answer examination, it is not developed in enough detail for an essay examination.

Completeness in an essay examination resembles completeness in paragraphs (discussed in Chapter 7). The topic sentence of a paragraph or the thesis of an essay is necessarily a general statement. To make that statement clear and convincing, you must develop it with specific details. This is especially true when an examination question, such as the one on Vietnam, calls for a judgment. Your judgment is only an assertion until you support it with evidence. If the writer of answer 1 on Vietnam had stopped with the assertion in his first sentence, he would have written an incomplete answer. His explanatory details provide the evidence that makes his answer complete.

DO NOT PAD YOUR ANSWER

Padding an answer with needless repetition or irrelevant detail is more likely to hurt than to help. A padded answer suggests that you are trying to conceal a lack of knowledge. Graders are not easily persuaded that an answer is good just because it is long. They are more likely to be annoyed at having to sort through all the padding to find the information that might be relevant to the question. It is your responsibility to select, present, and develop the essential information called for in the question.

The answer below is a padded response to the question of what lessons American strategists learned from the French experience in Vietnam. The grader's comments identify the two major weaknesses of the answer—failure to explain the lesson learned and the useless repetition of the content of the first paragraph in the second. The thesis statement reveals that the writer was not prepared to answer the question. She said all she had to say in the first paragraph, but she seemed to feel that saying it over again, from a slightly different perspective, would somehow make her answer acceptable. Through the use of marginal comments and editorial suggestions, the grader calls attention to these deficiencies.

vague

What specific lesson did the United States learn from the French defeat at Dien Bien Phu?

The Americans learned a <u>great deal</u> from the French war with the revolutionary army called the Vietminh, headed by the communist leader Ho Chi Minh. Throughout their war with these guerrillas, the French continuously increased their troop commitments ~~to higher and higher numbers~~ because they believed that more soldiers and more guns could bring about a speedy victory against a small and poorly armed enemy. At Dien Bien Phu, the French parachuted over 6,000 crack troops into a valley to begin an all-out assault on the Vietminh. But they did not realize that the enemy had worked its way through the jungles to occupy the high ridges above the valley where it had a superior military position.

This paragraph merely restates the ideas in paragraph 1 and further delays your response to the question about what Americans may have learned from this battle.

~~The capture of the French troops at Dien Bien Phu is an example of how important military mistakes are often made by miscalculation of the enemy's strategy. The French assumed that they could confront the enemy in a traditional ground war. But because the Vietminh was a guerrilla army, it never allowed the French the opportunity to engage in this kind of military action. Instead, it hauled its guns to the top of a high ridge and surprised the French.~~

Your problem seems to begin with your vague thesis sentence. You seem uncertain about what the United States learned from the French, so you simply present (rather than interpret) the facts of Dien Bien Phu.

PROOFREAD YOUR ANSWER

Reserve some time at the end of the examination to reread and correct your answer. You will not have time to write a second draft, but you may have enough time for a quick review and revision. First, reread the question. Then, as you read your answer, determine whether you supplied all the required information. Sometimes a subtle change in diction or sentence structure will clarify your answer. At other times you may need to add a sentence or paragraph to develop or redirect your answer. Use a caret (∧) to indicate where such insertions belong, then place the additional information in a numbered box in the margin or at the end of your paper. Help your instructor follow these revisions by writing a brief note near the insertion. If the writer of the essay here had reserved time for such revisions, she might have sharpened her thesis, added a few sentences about what the United States learned from Dien Bien Phu, and deleted the repetitious second paragraph.

_____ *Review*
    Exercise   Examine each of the following paired answers to questions on literature, psychology, and cultural geography. Decide which is the better answer, and be prepared to explain the reasons for your choice. Even if you are unfamiliar with the subjects, you should be able to decide which answer satisfies the requirements of the question.

Question 1

Just before he dies, Laertes says to Hamlet, "Mine and my father's death come not on thee, nor thine on me." In view of the facts of the play, how do you interpret this statement?

Answer 1

Laertes' statement fits some of the facts but not all of them and is best understood as a request to let bygones be bygones. True, Hamlet is not responsible for Laertes' death, because Hamlet thought he was engaging in a friendly bout with blunted swords. When he picked up Laertes' sword in the mix-up, he did not know it was poisoned. Since Laertes deliberately put the poison there, he was responsible for both Hamlet's death and his own. Hamlet killed Polonius by mistake, thinking that the person behind the curtain was the king. To that extent it was an accidental killing, but a killing nevertheless. I think Laertes' statement is intended not as a literal description of the facts but as a reconciliation speech. I interpret the statement to mean: "We have both been the victims of the king's treachery. Forgive me for your death, as I forgive you for mine and my father's."

Answer 2

Laertes returns from France and learns that his father has been killed by Hamlet. He is almost mad with grief and rage, and in a stormy scene with the king he demands revenge. He and the king conspire to arrange a duel between Laertes and Hamlet in which Laertes will use a poisoned sword. The duel takes place after Ophelia's funeral, and Laertes cuts Hamlet with the poisoned sword. Then, in a scuffle, their swords are knocked from their hands, and Hamlet picks up Laertes' poisoned sword and wounds him. Meanwhile the king has put poison in a goblet of wine he intends for Hamlet, but the queen drinks the wine by mistake. When Hamlet sees that she is dying, he kills the king; then both Hamlet and Laertes die.

Question 2

Explain the chief differences between neurosis and psychosis.

Answer 1

The chief differences between neurosis and psychosis are the extent to which a person is alienated from reality and his or her chances of making a workable adjustment to normal living. The boundary between the two cannot be precisely drawn; therefore the differences are best illustrated at their extremes.

A person suffering from neurosis may feel serious anxieties but still be able to handle the ordinary activities of daily living. For example, a woman may have a phobia about being left alone with a red-headed man because a male with red hair once assaulted her. But as long as she avoids that particular situation, she is able to fulfill her domestic and business responsibilities. Through psychiatric counseling she may learn to understand the cause of her phobia and either get rid of it or control it. Fears of heights and of crowds are examples of other neuroses. They are not central to the way one organizes one's life and can be alleviated either by counseling or by avoidance of situations in which the neurotic response is likely to occur.

A psychotic person is so divorced from reality that in severe cases, like paranoid schizophrenia, he or she lives in a private world that has little relation to the real one. A man who thinks he is Moses and feels a divinely granted right to punish those who break any of the Ten Commandments has reorganized experience around a delusion that makes life bearable for him. His delusion is necessary to his continued existence. In a sense he has found a therapy that works for him. He will resist psychiatric help because he thinks he no longer has any problem: it is the sinners who have problems. Such a person may be helped to some degree by specialized, institutional care, but the chances of a complete recovery are slim.

Between these extremes are conditions classifiable as either neurosis or psychosis. In such cases psychiatrists may disagree in their diagnoses.

Answer 2

Because there is some neurosis in all of us, we all utilize defense mechanisms against our frustrations. For that matter, a psychotic person may also use such defenses, but is less likely to be aware of what he or she is doing. We may repress our frustrations—simply refuse to think about them. Or we may defend by consciously developing characteristics that are the opposite of those we disapprove of. For example, a person who is troubled by a tendency toward greediness may force himself or herself to generously give away prized possessions. We can also escape frustration and low self-esteem by projection of our faults, blaming them on other people. Or we can use rationalization by devising excuses to justify our behavior. Finally, we may save our pride by fantasizing. That is, a young man may imagine that the girl who has declined to date him is cheering wildly in a basketball gymnasium when he sets a new scoring record and that she will be waiting for him with bated breath at the locker-room door.

Neurotic people may need the help that defense mechanisms can give them, but excessive use of such devices can make a problem worse. And if a neurotic condition becomes so serious that the person is out of touch with the real world and locked into his or her private world, that person is psychotic. As I think back over my answer, it seems to me that a psychotic person would be more likely to use some of these mechanisms than others.

Question 3

Contrast the different concepts of *border* that are illustrated by these two maps of North America.

Answer 1

These two maps provide a dramatic contrast between the geopolitical and theoretical concepts of border. The first map designates the official borders of the United States, which have been formed by three methods. First, there are natural borders. Rivers such as the Ohio and Mississippi, lakes such as Michigan and Erie, and mountains such as the Smokies and Sierra Nevada provide natural ways to separate various regions of the country from one another. Second, the map documents historical borders that were negotiated as the result of specific military conflicts—for example, the border separating Canada and Maine was negotiated to end the Aroostook War (1842), and the border separating Mexico and Texas was negotiated to end the Mexican War (1848). And third, this map illustrates political borders that were formed by the process of achieving statehood. After the formation of the thirteen original colonies, large blocks of land, particularly west of the Mississippi, were shaped by local politicians and federal agencies into territories that eventually became states. The borders of these structures—for example, Colorado and Oklahoma—were often drawn without reference to the contours of the land or the interests of the inhabitants.

By contrast, the second map illustrates Joel Garreau's theory that the United States can be understood only by reshaping its borders into "the nine nations of North America." By ignoring the principles used to establish the borders of the first map, Garreau is able to speculate about how people's attitudes toward issues such as economics and ecology give

Map by Graf-Tech, Inc.

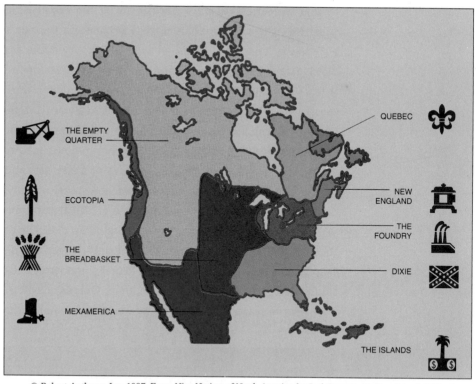

© Robert Anthony, Inc. 1987. From *Nine Nations of North America,* by Joel Garreau, © Houghton Mifflin Co.

rise to more natural alliances—and hence more meaningful borders—than those on the geopolitical map. For example, Garreau says that the neatly boxed borders of Colorado make no sense. The wheat farmers in the eastern part of the state feel a more natural alliance with farmers in "The Breadbasket" than with the industrialists in Denver who want to mine the resources of "The Empty Quarter." Similarly, the thin strip along the Pacific coast contains not three states, but two nations. What separates them, Garreau argues, is their attitude toward water. "Ecotopia" is the only place in the West with enough water, whereas "MexAmerica" must suck water from other places to support its dry, sunny climate.

Answer 2

The first map illustrates the international borders separating the United States from Canada and Mexico, and the national borders separating the states. Some of these borders are irregular because they are formed by the shoreline of the ocean or the banks of a river. Other borders are extremely regular because they were drawn by surveyors who were marking out plots of land for the United States government. For example, the borders of the western states look like rectangular blocks, whereas the borders of the eastern states look like oddly shaped pieces of a puzzle.

The second map does not acknowledge the borders that separate the United States from Canada and Mexico, or the borders that separate the various states from one another. It illustrates Joel Garreau's nine "nations" of North America. Each nation has an identifying name, symbol, and border. Some of these nations are vaguely recognizable as traditional regions in the United States. For example, the borders of "The Foundry" enclose most of the industrial Northeast, whereas the borders of "Dixie" enclose most of the Old South. But most of the map rearranges the traditional borders of North America. For example, "The Empty Quarter" includes most of the underdeveloped land of the United States and Canada, and "MexAmerica" joins southern California, the Southwest, and Mexico.

The Value of C | Jean Shepherd   **Readings**

In this excerpt, humorist Jean Shepherd remembers the one time he could not avoid a question in algebra and the extraordinary luck he had in formulating an answer. In what ways does Shepherd avoid *reading the question carefully* and *thinking out his answer*? What kind of guerrilla tactics does he employ as alternative strategies?

Wednesday, two days before the end, arrived like any other spring day.   1
A faint breeze drifted from the south, bringing with it hints of long summer afternoons to come, of swung bats, of nights in the lilac bushes. But not for such as me. I stumped into algebra class feeling distinctly like the last soul aboard the *Titanic* as she was about to plunge to the bottom. The smart-asses were already in their seats, laughing merrily, the goddamn A's and B's and C's and even the M's. I took my seat in the back, among the rest of the condemned. Schwartz sat down sullenly and began his usual moan. Helen Weathers squatted toadlike, drenched in sweat. The class began, Pittinger's chalk squeaked, hands waved. The sun filtered in through the venetian blinds. A tennis ball pocked back and forth over a net somewhere. Faintly, the high clear voices of the girls' glee club sang, "Can you bake a cherry pie, charming Billy?" Birds twittered.

My knot of fear, by now an old friend, sputtered in my gut. In the past   2
week, it had grown to roughly the size of a two-dollar watermelon. True, I had avoided being called on even once the entire year, but it was a hollow victory and I knew it. Minute after minute inched slowly by as I ducked and dodged, Pittinger firing question after question at the class. Glancing at my Pluto watch, which I had been given for Christmas, I noted with deep relief that less than two minutes remained before the bell.

It was then that I made my fatal mistake, the mistake that all guerrilla   3
fighters eventually make—I lost my concentration. For years, every fiber of my being, every instant in every class, had been directed solely at survival. On this fateful Wednesday, lulled by the sun, by the gentle sound of the tennis ball, by the steady drone of Pittinger's voice, by the fact that there were just two minutes to go, my mind slowly drifted off into a golden haze. A tiny mote of dust floated down through a slanting ray of sunshine. I watched it in its slow, undulating flight, like some microscopic silver bird.

"You're the apple of my eye, darling Billy . . . I can bake a cherry   4
pie . . ."

A rich maple syrup warmth filled my being. Out of the faint distance,   5
I heard a deadly rasp, the faint honking of disaster.

For a stunned split second, I thought I'd been jabbed with an electric   6
cattle prod. Pittinger's voice, loud and commanding, was pronouncing my name. He was calling on ME! Oh, my God! With a goddamn minute to go, he had nailed me. I heard Schwartz bleat a high, quavering cry, a primal

Shepherd, Jean. *A Fistful of Fig Newtons.* New York: Doubleday, 1981. 192–95.

scream. I knew what it meant: If they got him, the greatest master of them all, there's no hope for ANY of us!

As I stood slowly at my seat, frantically bidding for time, I saw a great **7** puddle forming around Helen Weathers. It wasn't all sweat. Chester had sunk to the floor beneath his desk, and behind me Zynzmeister's beads were clattering so loudly I could hardly hear his Hail Marys.

"Come to the board, please. Give us the value of C in this equation." **8**

In a stupor of wrenching fear, I felt my legs clumping up the aisle. On **9** all sides the blank faces stared. At the board—totally unfamiliar territory to me—I stared at the first equation I had ever seen up close. It was well over a yard and a half long, lacerated by mysterious crooked lines and fractions in parentheses, with miniature twos and threes hovering above the whole thing like tiny barnacles. Xs and Ys were jumbled in crazy abandon. At the very end of this unholy mess was a tiny equal sign. And on the other side of the equal sign was a zero. Zero! All this crap adds up to nothing! Jesus Christ! My mind reeled at the very sight of this barbed-wire entanglement of mysterious symbols.

Pittinger stood to one side, arms folded, wearing an expression that **10** said, At last I've nailed the little bastard! He had been playing with me all the time. He knew!

I glanced back at the class. It was one of the truly educational mo- **11** ments of my life. The entire mob, including Schwartz, Chester, and even Zynzmeister, were grinning happily, licking their chops with joyous expectation of my imminent crucifixion. I learned then that when true disaster strikes, we have no friends. And there's nothing a phony loves more in this world than to see another phony get what's coming to him.

"The value of C, please," rapped Pittinger. **12**

The equation blurred before my eyes. The value of C. Where the hell **13** was it? What did a C look like, anyway? Or an A or a B, for that matter. I had forgotten the alphabet.

"C, please." **14**

I spotted a single letter C buried deep in the writhing melange of Ys **15** and Xs and umlauts and plus signs, brackets, and God knows what all. One tiny C. A torrent of sweat raged down my spinal column. My jockey shorts were soaked and sodden with the sweat and stink of execution. Being a true guerrilla from years of the alphabetical ghetto, I showed no outward sign of panic, my face stony; unyielding. You live by the gun, you die by the gun.

"C, please." Pittinger moodily scratched at his granite chin with **16** thumb and forefinger, his blue beard rasping nastily.

"Oh my darling Billy boy, you're the apple of my eye . . ." **17**

Somewhere birds twittered on, tennis racquet met tennis ball. My **18** moment had finally arrived.

Now, I have to explain that for years I had been the leader of the **19** atheistic free-thinkers of Warren G. Harding School, scoffers all at the Sunday School miracles taught at the Presbyterian church; unbelievers.

That miracle stuff is for old ladies, all that walking on water and **20** birds flying around with loaves of bread in their beaks. Who can believe that crap?

Now, I am not so sure. Ever since that day in Pittinger's algebra class **21**

I have had an uneasy suspicion that maybe something mysterious is going on somewhere.

As I stood and stonily gazed at the enigmatic Egyptian hieroglyphics of that fateful equation, from somewhere, someplace beyond the blue horizon, it came to me, out of the mist. I heard my voice say clearly, firmly, with decision: 22

"C . . . is equal to three."   23

Pittinger staggered back; his glasses jolted down to the tip of his nose.   24

"How the hell did you know?!" he bellowed hoarsely, his snap-on bow tie popping loose in the excitement.   25

The class was in an uproar. I caught a glimpse of Schwartz, his face pale with shock. I had caught one on the fat part of the bat. It was a true miracle. I had walked on water.   26

Instantly, the old instincts took over. In a cool, level voice I answered Pittinger's rhetorical question.   27

"Sir, I used empirical means."   28

He paled visibly and clung to the chalk trough for support. On cue, the bell rang out. The class was over. With a swiftness born of long experience, I was out of the room even before the echo of the bell had ceased. The guerrilla's code is always hit and run. A legend had been born.   29

What Does a Woman Need to Know? | Mary Field Belenky
Blythe McVicker Clinchy
Nancy Rule Goldberger
Jill Mattuck Tarule

This selection from *Women's Ways of Knowing* compares two stories about the "limitations of firsthand experience as a source of knowledge." What important differences can you identify between the teachers and students in the two stories? How do the authors use this information to support the main point in their concluding paragraph?

We begin with the reminiscences of two ordinary women, each recalling an hour during her first year at college. One of them, now middle aged, remembered the first meeting of an introductory science course. The professor marched into the lecture hall, placed upon his desk a large jar filled with dried beans, and invited the students to guess how many beans the jar contained. After listening to an enthusiastic chorus of wildly inaccurate estimates the professor smiled a thin, dry smile, revealed the correct answer, and announced, "You have just learned an important lesson about science. Never trust the evidence of your own senses."   1

Thirty years later, the woman could guess what the professor had in mind. He saw himself, perhaps, as inviting his students to embark upon an   2

Belenky, Mary Field, et al. *Women's Ways of Knowing: The Development of Self, Voice and Mind.* New York: Basic, 1986. 191–93.

exciting voyage into a mysterious underworld invisible to the naked eye, accessible only through scientific method and scientific instruments. But the seventeen-year-old girl could not accept or even hear the invitation. Her sense of herself as a knower was shaky, and it was based on the belief that she could use her own firsthand experience as a source of truth. This man was saying that this belief was fallacious. He was taking away her only tool for knowing and providing her with no substitute. "I remember feeling small and scared," the woman says, "and I did the only thing I could do. I dropped the course that afternoon, and I haven't gone near science since."

The second woman, in her first year at college, told a superficially simi- 3 lar but profoundly different story about a philosophy class she had attended just a month or two before the interview. The teacher came into class carrying a large cardboard cube. She placed it on the desk in front of her and asked the class what it was. They said it was a cube. She asked what a cube was, and they said a cube contained six equal square sides. She asked how they knew that this object contained six equal square sides. By looking at it, they said. "But how do you know?" the teacher asked again. She pointed to the side facing her and, therefore, invisible to the students; then she lifted the cube and pointed to the side that had been face down on the desk, and, therefore, also invisible. "We can't look at all six sides of a cube at once, can we? So we can't exactly *see* a cube. And yet, you're right. You know it's a cube. But you know it not just because you have eyes but because you have intelligence. You invent the sides you cannot see. You use your intelligence to create the 'truth' about cubes."

The student said to the interviewer, 4

It blew my mind. You'll think I'm nuts, but I ran back to the dorm and 5 I called my boyfriend and I said, "Listen, this is just incredible," and I told him all about it. I'm not sure he could see why I was so excited. I'm not sure I understand it myself. But I really felt, for the first time, like I was really in college, like I was—I don't know—sort of *grown up*.

Both stories are about the limitations of firsthand experience as a 6 source of knowledge—we cannot simply see the truth about either the jar of beans or the cube—but there is a difference. We can know the truth about cubes. Indeed, the students did know it. As the science professor pointed out, the students were wrong about the beans; their senses had deceived them. But, as the philosophy teacher pointed out, the students were right about the cube; their minds had served them well.

The science professor was the only person in the room who knew 7 how many beans were in that jar. Theoretically, the knowledge was available to the students; they could have counted the beans. But faced with that tedious prospect, most would doubtless take the professor's word for it. He is authority. They had to rely upon his knowledge rather than their own. On the other hand, every member of the philosophy class knew that the cube had six sides. They were all colleagues.

The science professor exercised his authority in a benign fashion, 8 promising the students that he would provide them with the tools they needed to excavate invisible truths. Similarly, the philosophy teacher planned to teach her students the skills of philosophical analysis, but she was at pains to assure them that they already possessed the tools to construct some powerful truths. They had built cubes on their own, using only their own powers of inference, without the aid of elaborate procedures or fancy apparatus or even a teacher. Although a teacher might have told them once that a cube contained six equal square sides, they did not have to take the teacher's word for it; they could have easily verified it for themselves.

9   The lesson the science professor wanted to teach is that experience is a source of error. Taught in isolation, this lesson diminished the student, rendering her dumb and dependent. The philosophy teacher's lesson was that although raw experience is insufficient, by reflecting upon it the student could arrive at truth. It was a lesson that made the student feel more powerful ("sort of grown up").

10   No doubt it is true that, as the professor in May Sarton's novel *The Small Room* says, the "art" of being a student requires humility. But the woman we interviewed did not find the science lesson humbling; she found it humiliating. Arrogance was not then and is not now her natural habitat. Like most of the women in our sample she lacked confidence in herself as a thinker; and the kind of learning the science teacher demanded was not only painful but crippling.

11   In thinking about the education of women, Adrienne Rich writes, "Suppose we were to ask ourselves, simply: What does a woman need to know?" A woman, like any other human being, does need to know that the mind makes mistakes; but our interviews have convinced us that every woman, regardless of age, social class, ethnicity, and academic achievement, needs to know that she is capable of intelligent thought, and she needs to know it right away. Perhaps men learn this lesson before going to college, or perhaps they can wait until they have proved themselves to hear it; we do not know. We do know that many of the women we interviewed had not yet learned it.

In Laboratory with Agassiz | Samuel H. Scudder

In this memoir, scientist Samuel H. Scudder (1837–1911) recalls how his teacher, Louis Agassiz (1807–1873), required him to examine a fish in scrupulous detail, reflect on what he had seen, and speculate on what he had not expected to see. What does Scudder learn by following Agassiz's injunction to "look, look, look"? What would Agassiz consider a *complete* answer to his examination?

1   **I**t was more than fifteen years ago that I entered the laboratory of Professor Agassiz, and told him I had enrolled my name in the Scientific School as a student of natural history. He asked me a few questions about my object in coming, my antecedents generally, the mode in which I afterwards proposed to use the knowledge I might acquire, and, finally, whether I wished to study any special branch. To the latter I replied that, while I wished to

Scudder, Samuel H. *Every Saturday*. 4 April 1874. 369–70.

be well grounded in all departments of zoology, I purposed to devote myself specially to insects.

"When do you wish to begin?" he asked. 2

"Now," I replied. 3

This seemed to please him, and with an energetic "Very well!" he reached from a shelf a huge jar of specimens in yellow alcohol. "Take this fish," he said, "and look at it; we call it a haemulon; by and by I will ask what you have seen." 4

With that he left me, but in a moment returned with explicit instructions as to the care of the object entrusted to me. 5

"No man is fit to be a naturalist," said he, "who does not know how to take care of specimens." 6

I was to keep the fish before me in a tin tray, and occasionally moisten the surface with alcohol from the jar, always taking care to replace the stopper tightly. Those were not the days of ground-glass stoppers and elegantly shaped exhibition jars; all the old students will recall the huge necklace glass bottles with their leaky, wax-besmeared corks, half eaten by insects, and begrimed with cellar dust. Entomology was a cleaner science than ichthyology, but the example of the Professor, who had unhesitatingly plunged to the bottom of the jar to produce the fish, was infectious; and though this alcohol had a "very ancient and fishlike smell," I really dared not show any aversion within these sacred precincts, and treated the alcohol as though it were pure water. Still I was conscious of a passing feeling of disappointment, for gazing at a fish did not commend itself to an ardent entomologist. My friends at home, too, were annoyed when they discovered that no amount of eau-de-Cologne would drown the perfume which haunted me like a shadow. 7

In ten minutes I had seen all that could be seen in that fish, and started in search of the Professor—who had, however, left the Museum; and when I returned, after lingering over some of the odd animals stored in the upper apartment, my specimen was dry all over. I dashed the fluid over the fish as if to resuscitate the beast from a fainting fit, and looked with anxiety for a return of the normal sloppy appearance. This little excitement over, nothing was to be done but to return to a steadfast gaze at my mute companion. Half an hour passed—an hour—another hour; the fish began to look loathsome. I turned it over and around; looked it in the face—ghastly; from behind, beneath, above, sideways, at a three-quarters' view—just as ghastly. I was in despair; at an early hour I concluded that lunch was necessary; so, with infinite relief, the fish was carefully replaced in the jar, and for an hour I was free. 8

On my return, I learned that Professor Agassiz had been at the Museum, but had gone, and would not return for several hours. My fellow-students were too busy to be disturbed by continued conversation. Slowly I drew forth that hideous fish, and with a feeling of desperation again looked at it. I might not use a magnifying-glass; instruments of all kinds were interdicted. My two hands, my two eyes, and the fish: it seemed a most limited field. I pushed my finger down its throat to feel how sharp the teeth were. I began to count the scales in the different rows, until I was convinced that was nonsense. At last a happy thought struck me—I would draw the fish; and now with surprise I began to discover new features in the creature. Just then the Professor returned. 9

"That is right," said he; "a pencil is one of the best of eyes. I am glad 　**10**
to notice, too, that you keep your specimen wet, and your bottle corked."

With these encouraging words, he added: 　**11**

"Well, what is it like?" 　**12**

He listened attentively to my brief rehearsal of the structure of parts 　**13**
whose names were still unknown to me: the fringed gill-arches and mov-
able operculum; the pores of the head, fleshy lips and lidless eyes; the lat-
eral line, the spinous fins and forked tail; the compressed and arched body.
When I finished, he waited as if expecting more, and then, with an air of
disappointment:

"You have not looked very carefully; why," he continued more ear- 　**14**
nestly, "you haven't even seen one of the most conspicuous features of the
animal, which is plainly before your eyes as the fish itself; look again, look
again!" and he left me to my misery.

I was piqued; I was mortified. Still more of that wretched fish! But 　**15**
now I set myself to my task with a will, and discovered one new thing after
another, until I saw how just the Professor's criticism had been. The afternoon passed quickly; and when, towards its close, the Professor inquired:

"Do you see it yet?" 　**16**

"No," I replied, "I am certain I do not, but I see how little I saw 　**17**
before."

"That is next best," said he, earnestly, "but I won't hear you now; 　**18**
put away your fish and go home; perhaps you will be ready with a better
answer in the morning. I will examine you before you look at the fish."

This was disconcerting. Not only must I think of my fish all night, 　**19**
studying, without the object before me, what this unknown but most visible
feature might be; but also, without reviewing my discoveries, I must give an
exact account of them the next day. I had a bad memory; so I walked home
by Charles River in a distracted state, with my two perplexities.

The cordial greeting from the Professor the next morning was reassur- 　**20**
ing; here was a man who seemed to be quite as anxious as I that I should
see for myself what he saw.

"Do you perhaps mean," I asked, "that the fish has symmetrical sides 　**21**
with paired organs?"

His thoroughly pleased "Of course! Of course!" repaid the wakeful 　**22**
hours of the previous night. After he had discoursed most happily and
enthusiastically—as he always did—upon the importance of this point,
I ventured to ask what I should do next.

"Oh, look at your fish!" he said, and left me again to my own devices. 　**23**
In a little more than an hour he returned, heard my new catalogue.

"That is good, that is good!" he repeated; "but that is not all; go on"; 　**24**
and so for three long days he placed that fish before my eyes, forbidding me
to look at anything else, or to use any artificial aid. "Look, look, look," was
his repeated injunction.

This was the best entomological lesson I ever had—a lesson whose in- 　**25**
fluence has extended to the details of every subsequent study; a legacy the
Professor had left to me, as he has left it to so many others, of inestimable
value, which we could not buy, with which we cannot part.

A year afterward, some of us were amusing ourselves with chalking 　**26**
outlandish beasts on the Museum blackboard. We drew prancing starfishes;

frogs in mortal combat; hydra-headed worms; stately crawfishes; standing on their tails, bearing aloft umbrellas; and grotesque fishes with gaping mouths and staring eyes. The Professor came in shortly after, and was as amused as any at our experiments. He looked at the fishes.

"Haemulons, every one of them," he said; "Mr. _____ drew them."   27

True; and to this day, if I attempt a fish, I can draw nothing but haemulons.   28

The fourth day, a second fish of the same group was placed beside the first, and I was bidden to point out the resemblances and differences between the two; another and another followed, until the entire family lay before me, and a whole legion of jars covered the table and surrounding shelves; the odor had become a pleasant perfume; and even now, the sight of an old, six-inch, worm-eaten cork brings fragrant memories.   29

The whole group of haemulons was thus brought in review; and, whether engaged upon the dissection of the internal organs, the preparation and examination of the bony framework, or the description of the various parts, Agassiz's training method of observing facts and their orderly arrangement was ever accompanied by the urgent exhortation not to be content with them.   30

"Facts are stupid things," he would say, "until brought into connection with some general law."   31

At the end of eight months, it was almost with reluctance that I left these friends and turned to insects; but what I had gained by this outside experience has been of greater value than years of later investigation in my favorite groups.   32

Writing Assignments

Narrate **1.** List the memorable examinations you have faced in your academic career—those where you studied the wrong thing, misread the question, or earned a high grade. Select one that taught you a lesson you were not expecting to learn about yourself. Then write a narrative of that experience addressed to a specific audience (e.g., a group of high school students).

Observe **2.** Take your journal to the library (or some other place where students are studying for examinations). Select a group of students. Log the amount of time each one seems to devote to certain activities—reading, writing, staring, talking to others, and so on. Then write a column (perhaps a humorous one) for your student paper in which you classify the behavior of students on "The Night Before the Big One."

Investigate **3.** Interview one of your favorite teachers about his or her philosophy of examinations. Begin by asking about his or her own experience as a student taking exams. Then ask about the assumptions and expectations that are buried in a recent examination (perhaps one you have taken). How would the teacher have prepared for the exam? What specific thinking and writing strategies did the exam require? What specific problems did the teacher encounter in evaluating the answers? Finally, write an essay in which you use the information from your interview to compose a profile on "How to Succeed in Professor X's Class."

Collaborate **4.** Your writing group has been asked to compose a "Study Guide" for one of the General Studies courses that requires essay examinations—History 101, Anthropology 151, Philosophy 100, or a comparable course. Determine which members of your group (or students you know) have performed successfully or unsuccessfully in the class. Establish the reasons for their performance. Visit several sections of the class, take notes on the lectures, read the text. Study an old examination question and some exemplary answers. What writing strategies do successful students seem to use? Do students know these strategies in advance or do teachers coach them? What seems to be the main cause of student failure? Collect your data and, with the help of teachers or tutors, write a guide that anticipates ways to overcome the problems you have discovered.

Read **5.** Visit the study skills center on your campus. Talk to teachers and tutors about the research they use to counsel students. Read one research study that has developed a successful method for helping students prepare for written examinations. You may want to test the findings of the study by using its methodology on your next examination. Then write an essay on "What They Never Told Me about Writing Essay Examinations."

Respond **6.** Respond to Jean Shepherd's "The Value of C" by recalling an experience (or a dream) in which you had to take an examination on a subject about which you knew nothing (or next to nothing). How did you feel—about yourself, your teacher, the subject, education? How did you react to your feelings?

Then write an essay that tries to show your readers what it feels like to be "unprepared."

Analyze **7.** Examine the gender stereotypes illustrated in the two examples in "What Does a Woman Need to Know?" How are men (particularly the male professor) characterized in the selection? What gender stereotypes are represented by the women students? Using this hypothesis, and your own observations about the way men and women use and abuse authority in education, analyze the concluding paragraph of this selection.

Evaluate **8.** Study the teaching-learning process as it is exemplified in Samuel H. Scudder's "In Laboratory with Agassiz." This essay was written about education in the nineteenth century at Harvard University. How have things changed? For example, how would you and your friends define a good teacher? How would you assess Agassiz's ability as a teacher? How would you assess Scudder's abilities as a student? How would students you know respond to Agassiz's assignment? Use your answers to these questions to draft a speech that evaluates the motivation of contemporary teachers and students for a specific audience (the local PTA, teachers' union, or state legislature).

Argue **9.** In a letter to the chair of your department major or some other administrator, argue that most teachers do not prepare students to take their examinations. Describe the kind of teachers whose philosophy of testing or inattentiveness to student confusion provide little or no advance coaching on how to do well on a written examination. By contrast, describe the kind of teachers who employ specific strategies to help students prepare for and perform better on written examinations.

Argue **10.** In a letter to the Dean of Undergraduate Programs, argue that teachers who understand the writing process—particularly, the need for planning, drafting, and revising—should not give impromptu or timed written examinations. Acknowledge teacher arguments: (1) students need to learn to write under pressure, (2) teachers need to verify that student work is original. But provide examples and alternatives that demonstrate how teachers can design writing assignments to help students learn more effectively.

12 The Critical Essay

The critical essay helps readers understand a subject. The word *critical* in this context does not mean to find fault. Its Greek root means "to separate, discern, or choose." Thus, the critical essay attempts to enhance the reader's understanding of a subject by analyzing its parts and interpreting its meaning. It may deal with any subject worthy of serious study—a painting, a film, a social movement. In most writing classes, however, the critical essay assignment focuses on literature. Although procedures for composing a critical essay resemble procedures followed in writing other essays, the success of the critical essay depends on another process—the informed reading of imaginative literature.

BASIC ELEMENTS OF LITERATURE

Reading literature is different from reading a newspaper or magazine. In reading those texts, you may be a "speed reader," grasping the main point early, skimming through the middle, and glancing at the end to see how it turns out. Such habits can cause trouble when you read a poem or a play. As novelist William Gass points out, reading a work of literature is a "slow, old-fashioned . . . complicated, profound, silent, still, very private, very solitary yet civilizing activity" ("Of Speed-Readers and Lip-Movers"). To engage in that sort of reading, you need to distinguish among three literary genres—*fiction, poetry,* and *drama,* each with its own history, conventions, and subcategories—and recognize five elements common to nearly every literary work—*plot, characterization, setting, point of view,* and *theme.*

These elements may be combined with such subtlety that you may not see them as separate concepts, or one or two of them may be given special attention. Some works may require you to consider additional elements. In much poetry, for example, you will need to consider rhyme, sound patterns, meter, and form. In considering dramatic productions, you will need to evaluate actors, costumes, lighting, and sets. But in most cases, your ability to recognize the interaction of the five basic elements will enable you to complete the informed reading essential for writing a critical essay.

Plot

The plot is a coherent, unified, and meaningful sequence of events that forms the beginning, middle, and end of a work of literature. The author must begin by revealing where and when the events take place, who the characters are, and what situation has brought them together. This introductory material is termed the *exposition*. In some cases, as in a brief poem, the exposition may be short because the author expects the readers to understand immediately the circumstances and setting. In other cases, such as in a complex drama, the playwright may need to provide a lengthy exposition to help the audience understand the events that are about to occur.

The middle section of the plot begins when a new set of complications develops to disrupt the existing order. These complications are almost always the result of *conflict*—conflicts among characters, conflicts between characters and their environment, conflicts in the thoughts, desires, or choices of a single character. In some works, all three types of conflict occur together. As conflict intensifies, a moment of crisis, called the *climax,* is reached. The climax usually marks the end of the major action of the plot. All that remains is the revelation of the consequences of whatever occurred during the climax. This final clarification or unraveling of the plot is called the *dénouement,* from a French word that means to untangle knots.

All plots have a beginning, middle, and end, but they do not always follow a chronological or predictable sequence. Some begin in the middle of the action or near the end. In such instances, the author may use a *flashback* to take the reader back in time to witness a scene that explains the current action. Early in a work, an author may use *foreshadowing* to suggest how the action might be resolved. Occasionally such hints turn out to be false clues, and the plot resolves itself in an unexpected way. This reversal of expectations is called *situational irony.*

Characterization

The method by which an author creates, reveals, and develops characters is called *characterization.* An author may describe characters directly, telling the reader what people look like, how they behave, and what they think; or an author may reveal characters indirectly, suggesting their appearance, personality, and values through their words and deeds or through the words and deeds of others.

A literary work usually focuses on a single character. In a poem, this character is often the speaker, who reveals thoughts or describes events. In fiction or drama, this character, the *protagonist,* is often opposed by another character or characters, the *antagonist.* The antagonist need not be a person; it might be the environment, society, or some aspect of the protagonist's personality.

Central characters who change in some significant way as a result of the conflicts they must resolve are often called *dynamic.* Characters who remain unchanged by the experiences they encounter are called *static.* Another way to distinguish between characters is to use the terms *round* and *flat.* A round character, usually the central character, is a fully developed, complex, often contradictory personality. A flat character, usually a minor character, possesses no depth or complexity but is so predictable in words and deeds that he or she is often called a stock character, or *stereotype.*

In thinking about literary characters, your main concern is to interpret their behavior. When a character makes choices or fails to make choices, you need to explain his or her *motivation.* In some cases, motivation can be explained by acknowledging that the character is responding to external factors such as social expectations. In other cases, motivation can be explained only by assessing internal factors such as psychological perception. A mixture of social and psychological factors motivates the most complex characters. When characters reveal their inability to understand their own motivation, making choices that the reader knows are uninformed or incorrect, they create a situation known as *dramatic irony.*

Setting

In simple terms, setting is the place, time, and social context established by a work of literature. Sometimes an author's choice of a physical place—a living room in a play, for example—seems relatively insignificant. More often, an author chooses a specific physical location—a farm in the rural South, a ghetto in the urban North—because it embodies the conflict in the plot and the choices available to the characters. Similarly, some authors seem to be indifferent to the constraints of time. A poet may evoke a mood in a kind of timeless present; a novelist may establish a story in a particular historical period. To interpret a literary work effectively, you need to determine the author's purpose in ignoring or exploiting restrictions of place and time.

The combination of place and time creates the *social context* for a literary work. Certain stories, poems, and plays evolve from the assumptions, rituals, and shared beliefs that shape the characters and their world. Understanding this context may help you explain an author's *tone,* or attitude toward the world he or she is describing, or an author's use of *symbols,* the evocation of artifacts, images, and ideas that illuminate the meaning of the work.

Point of View

Literally, point of view is the position one occupies in viewing an object. Applied to literature, the phrase refers to both *position* (the narrator's or speaker's proximity to the action in time and space) and *person* (the narrator's or speaker's personality and attitude). The term *narrator* is usually reserved for novels and short stories; the term *speaker* is used for poems. Neither term suits drama, because in a play the action unfolds as each character speaks.

In determining how to reveal the action and ideas in a literary work, an author may choose from four basic points of view.

- ▼ *Third-person omniscient*   The narrator, usually assumed to be the author, tells the story. He or she can move at will through time, across space, and into the minds of each character to tell the reader anything that is necessary to understand the story.

- ▼ *Third-person limited omniscient*   Although the author is still the narrator, he or she gives up total omniscience and limits the point of view to the experience and perception of one character in the story. Instead of knowing everything, the reader knows only what this one character knows or is able to learn.

- ▼ *First person*   The author selects one character to tell the story or express an idea. The character may be involved in the action or reflect on it from afar. This character may tell about events as they are happening or recall events many years after they have taken place.

- ▼ *Dramatic*   The author presents the external action of the story directly, as if it were being acted on stage or filmed by a movie camera. The author does not attempt to comment on or interpret the character's actions, thoughts, or feelings. All the reader knows about the action is inferred from the character's public words and deeds.

Through your ability to identify a point of view, you can understand other literary elements, such as *tone and style*. In Chapter 10, you learned how to use tone and style to enhance the purpose of your writing. In a work of imaginative literature, the tone and style of the narrator or speaker also further the author's purpose. The tone may be straightforward or ironic, bitter or enthusiastic. The style may be colloquial or formal, simple or complex. In each case the author makes choices that shape the meaning of the work. Your ability to assess the significance of these choices will help you interpret a work more effectively.

Theme

In addition to showing characters in conflict, a work of literature expresses several ideas about human experience. Different readers, working from different perspectives, may respond to the same work in dramatically different ways. Their disagreement prompts further discussion and analysis, encouraging additional reading of a work to find support for a particular interpretation.

To discover and state the theme that seems to integrate your perceptions and responses to a literary work, look for general statements about human experience. These statements are sometimes presented by the omniscient narrator and sometimes by individual characters. In the case of statements by a character, you need to examine the statement in light of your understanding of events. A character who makes a generalization that seems directly opposite to the author's intended meaning may be using *verbal irony*.

If you cannot find any direct statement of theme, ask yourself what the central characters have learned from their experience, or ask yourself what you have learned, from reading of this experience, that the characters have somehow failed to perceive.

You may also gain insight into theme by looking at how authors express their meaning through literary devices such as symbol and allusion. A *symbol* is a person, act, or thing that has both literal significance and metaphorical meaning. A symbol often pulls together several complex, interrelated ideas. An author may use one symbol or a series of related symbols to suggest a theme. An *allusion* suggests a thematic connection between some aspect of the story and something similar in literature, history, or myth. Such references suggest significant comparisons or ironic contrasts that illuminate the theme.

Guidelines for Reading Literature

Now that you have some knowledge of the basic elements that interact within any work of literature, you need to approach the reading of a specific work by following some practical reading strategies. Some of these strategies resemble those discussed in Chapter 2 (pages 50–1). Others are especially suited to reading literature.

Preview

It is often possible to learn a few important things about a literary work before you read it.

▼ Begin with a careful consideration of the title, which, as the first clue to the world you are about to enter, may reveal significant information about what you are about to discover. After you have finished reading, you should reconsider the title to see if your first impression was accurate. In most instances, you will discover that the title anticipated what you found and provides a focus for your interpretation.

▼ Next, consider what you know about the author. If you have read other works by the same author, you may be familiar with her or his themes or techniques. Read whatever introduction or headnote is provided; it may contain important biographical information. If such information is not provided, you may want to use a standard reference guide such as *Who's Who* to find out something about the author's life and work.

▼ Finally, consider the genre of the literary work. Recalling the basic differences between genres may give you some initial insight into the text you are about to read.

Read

As you read a literary text, do not be a passive observer, simply absorbing words and turning pages. Be an active reader, analyzing characters and speculating about their behavior.

▼ As you read, annotate the work. Use any convenient method. Underline words or sentences that seem important, mark transitions, or star statements that may help you once you begin to compose your interpretation.

▼ Ask yourself questions about what you are reading. If you are confused about a character's motives, reactions, or observations, take time to write out your questions in the margin of the work. Even though further reading may answer your questions, the act of writing them down encourages you to analyze what seems to be happening and why.

▼ As you read, and particularly when you reread a work, mark the places in the text where the five basic elements are most apparent—for example, divisions within the plot, clues to character motivation, shifts in point of view.

Review

Once you have finished reading a work, you will want to reread it, both to analyze how it achieves its effect and to contemplate the ways it might be interpreted. A poem with a difficult meter or one that remains opaque after a first reading, or a story whose ending surprised you, may send you back to the text for an immediate rereading, causing you to postpone using the following planning strategies. Often, however, using these strategies immediately after a first reading produces unexpected insights and interesting questions to guide your second reading.

▼ Make a list of the ideas and images that come to mind as you think about the work. You need not organize this information according to any particular pattern. Consult your memory to determine what aspects of the story made the strongest impression.

▼ Using the freewriting techniques you learned in Chapter 2, compose a more extended response to the story, using statements or questions or both. Your purpose is to write out your immediate reaction to the work. Did you like it or not? More important, what confused you about the characters and the way they attempted to resolve their problems?

▼ Compose (or consult) a series of questions about the five basic elements in the work. Some anthologies (or instructors) provide such questions. These questions, like yours, are composed by active readers who are attempting to achieve an informed reading of the work. You may discover that you have already answered some of them in your first reading. Other questions, however, may send you back to the work to look more closely at specific elements of plot, characterization, setting, point of view, or theme.

Now use these guidelines to read and draft your initial responses to the following short story. A headnote introduces the author, and study questions are provided in the exercise on pages 348–9.

Everyday Use | Alice Walker

Alice Walker was born in 1944 in Eatonton, Georgia. After graduating from Sarah Lawrence College, she became active in the civil rights movement, helping to register voters in Georgia, teaching in the Head Start program in Mississippi, and working on the staff of the New York City welfare department. In subsequent years she developed her own writing career while working as writer-in-residence at several universities. She has written a biography for children, *Langston Hughes, American Poet* (1973), edited an important literary anthology, *I Love Myself When I'm Laughing . . . and Then Again When I'm Looking Mean and Impressive: A Zora Neale Hurston Reader* (1979), and compiled two collections of her essays, *In Search of Our Mothers' Gardens* (1983) and *Living By the Word* (1988). These works reveal her interest in the themes of sexism and racism, themes embodied in her four widely acclaimed novels: *The Third Life of Grange Copeland* (1970), *Meridian* (1976), *The Color Purple* (1982), and *The Temple of My Familiar* (1989). Her stories, collected in *In Love and Trouble: Stories of Black Women* (1973) and *You Can't Keep a Good Woman Down* (1981), also examine the complex experiences of black women.

for your grandmamma

1   I will wait for her in the yard that Maggie and I made so clean and wavy yesterday afternoon. A yard like this is more comfortable than most people know. It is not just a yard. It is like an extended living room. When the hard clay is swept clean as a floor and the fine sand around the edges lined with tiny, irregular grooves anyone can come and sit and look up into the elm tree and wait for the breezes that never come inside the house.

2   Maggie will be nervous until after her sister goes: she will stand hopelessly in corners homely and ashamed of the burn scars down her arms and legs, eyeing her sister with a mixture of envy and awe. She thinks her sister has held life always in the palm of one hand, that "no" is a word the world never learned to say to her.

3   You've no doubt seen those TV shows where the child who has "made it" is confronted, as a surprise, by her own mother and father, tottering in weakly from backstage. (A pleasant surprise, of course: What would they do if parent and child came on the show only to curse out and insult each other?) On TV mother and child embrace and smile into each other's faces. Sometimes the mother and father weep, the child wraps them in her arms and leans across the table to tell how she would not have made it without their help. I have seen these programs.

4   Sometimes I dream a dream in which Dee and I are suddenly brought together on a TV program of this sort. Out of a dark and soft-seated limousine I am ushered into a bright room filled with many people. There I meet a smiling, gray, sporty man like Johnny

Walker, Alice. *In Love & Trouble*. New York: Harcourt, 1973. 47–59.

Carson who shakes my hand and tells me what a fine girl I have. Then we are on the stage and Dee is embracing me with tears in her eyes. She pins on my dress a large orchid, even though she has told me once that she thinks orchids are tacky flowers.

In real life I am a large, big-boned woman with rough, man-working hands. In the winter I wear flannel nightgowns to bed and overalls during the day. I can kill and clean a hog as mercilessly as a man. My fat keeps me hot in zero weather. I can work all day, breaking ice to get water for washing. I can eat pork liver cooked over the open fire minutes after it comes steaming from the hog. One winter I knocked a bull calf straight in the brain between the eyes with a sledge hammer and had the meat hung up to chill before nightfall. But of course all this does not show on television. I am the way my daughter would want me to be: a hundred pounds lighter, my skin like an uncooked barley pancake. My hair glistens in the hot bright lights. Johnny Carson has much to do to keep up with my quick and witty tongue. 5

But that is a mistake. I know even before I wake up. Who ever knew a Johnson with a quick tongue? Who can even imagine me looking a strange white man in the eye? It seems to me I have talked to them always with one foot raised in flight, with my head turned in whichever way is farthest from them. Dee, though. She would always look anyone in the eye. Hesitation was no part of her nature. 6

"How do I look, Mama?" Maggie says, showing just enough of her thin body enveloped in pink skirt and red blouse for me to know she's there, almost hidden by the door. 7

"Come out into the yard," I say. 8

Have you ever seen a lame animal, perhaps a dog run over by some careless person rich enough to own a car, sidle up to someone who is ignorant enough to be kind to him? That is the way my Maggie walks. She has been like this, chin on chest, eyes on ground, feet in shuffle, ever since the fire that burned the other house to the ground. 9

Dee is lighter than Maggie, with nicer hair and a fuller figure. She's a woman now, though sometimes I forget. How long ago was it that the other house burned? Ten, twelve years? Sometimes I can still hear the flames and feel Maggie's arm sticking to me, her hair smoking and her dress falling off her in little black papery flakes. Her eyes seemed stretched open, blazed open by the flames reflected in them. And Dee. I see her standing off under the sweet gum tree she used to dig gum out of; a look of concentration on her face as she watched the last dingy gray board of the house fall in toward the red-hot brick chimney. Why don't you do a dance around the ashes? I'd wanted to ask her. She had hated the house that much. 10

I used to think she hated Maggie, too. But that was before we raised the money, the church and me, to send her to Augusta to school. She used to read to us without pity; forcing words, lies, other folks' habits, whole lives upon us two, sitting trapped and ignorant underneath her voice. She washed us in a river of make-believe, 11 burned us with a lot of knowledge we didn't necessarily need to know. Pressed us to her with the serious way she read, to shove us away at just the moment, like dimwits, we seemed about to understand.

Dee wanted nice things. A yellow organdy dress to wear to her graduation from high school; black pumps to match a green suit she'd made from an old suit somebody gave me. She was determined to stare down any disaster in her efforts. Her eyelids would not flicker for minutes at a time. Often I fought off the temptation to shake her. At sixteen she had a style of her own: and knew what style was.   12

I never had an education myself. After second grade the school was closed down. Don't ask me why: in 1927 colored asked fewer questions than they do now. Sometimes Maggie reads to me. She stumbles along good-naturedly but can't see well. She knows she is not bright. Like good looks and money, quickness passed her by. She will marry John Thomas (who has mossy teeth in an earnest face) and then I'll be free to sit here and I guess just sing church songs to myself. Although I never was a good singer. Never could carry a tune. I was always better at a man's job. I used to love to milk till I was hoofed in the side in '49. Cows are soothing and slow and don't bother you, unless you try to milk them the wrong way.   13

I have deliberately turned my back on the house. It is three rooms, just like the one that burned, except the roof is tin; they don't make shingle roofs any more. There are no real windows, just some holes cut in the sides, like the portholes in a ship, but not round and not square, with rawhide holding the shutters up on the outside. This house is in a pasture, too, like the other one. No doubt when Dee sees it she will want to tear it down. She wrote me once that no matter where we "choose" to live, she will manage to come see us. But she will never bring her friends. Maggie and I thought about this and Maggie asked me, "Mama, when did Dee ever *have* any friends?"   14

She had a few. Furtive boys in pink shirts hanging about on washday after school. Nervous girls who never laughed. Impressed with her they worshiped the well-turned phrase, the cute shape, the scalding humor that erupted like bubbles in lye. She read to them.   15

When she was courting Jimmy T she didn't have much time to pay to us, but turned all her faultfinding power on him. He *flew* to marry a cheap gal from a family of ignorant flashy people. She hardly had time to recompose herself.   16

When she comes I will meet—but there they are!   17

Maggie attempts to make a dash for the house, in her shuffling way, but I stay her with my hand, "Come back here," I say. And she stops and tries to dig a well in the sand with her toe.   18

It is hard to see them clearly through the strong sun. But even the first glimpse of leg out of the car tells me it is Dee. Her feet were always neat-looking, as if God himself had shaped them with a certain style. From the other side of the car comes a short, stocky man. Hair   19 is all over his head a foot long and hanging from his chin like a kinky mule tail. I hear Maggie suck in her breath. "Uhnnnh," is what it sounds like. Like when you see the wriggling end of a snake just in front of your foot on the road. "Uhnnnh."

Dee next. A dress down to the ground, in this hot weather. A dress so loud it hurts my eyes. There are yellows and oranges enough to throw back the light of the sun. I feel my whole face warming from the heat waves it throws out. Earrings, too, gold and hanging down to her shoulders. Bracelets dangling and making noises when she moves her arm up to shake the folds of the dress out of her armpits. The dress is loose and flows, and as she walks closer, I like it. I hear Maggie go "Uhnnnh" again. It is her sister's hair. It stands straight up like the wool on a sheep. It is black as night and around the edges are two long pigtails that rope about like small lizards disappearing behind her ears. **20**

"Wa-su-zo-Tean-o!" she says, coming on in that gliding way the dress makes her move. The short stocky fellow with the hair to his navel is all grinning and he follows up with "Asalamalakim, my mother and sister!" He moves to hug Maggie but she falls back, right up against the back of my chair. I feel her trembling there and when I look up I see the perspiration falling off her chin. **21**

"Don't get up," says Dee. Since I am stout it takes something of a push. You can see me trying to move a second or two before I make it. She turns, showing white heels through her sandals, and goes back to the car. Out she peeks next with a Polaroid. She stoops down quickly and lines up picture after picture of me sitting there in front of the house with Maggie cowering behind me. She never takes a shot without making sure the house is included. When a cow comes nibbling around the edge of the yard she snaps it and me and Maggie *and* the house. Then she puts the Polaroid in the back seat of the car, and comes up and kisses me on the forehead. **22**

Meanwhile Asalamalakim is going through the motions with Maggie's hand. Maggie's hand is as limp as a fish, and probably as cold, despite the sweat, and she keeps trying to pull it back. It looks like Asalamalakim wants to shake hands but wants to do it fancy. Or maybe he don't know how people shake hands. Anyhow, he soon gives up on Maggie. **23**

"Well," I say. "Dee." **24**

"No, Mama," she says. "Not 'Dee,' Wangero Leewanika Kemanjo!" **25**

"What happened to 'Dee'?" I wanted to know. **26**

"She's dead," Wangero said. "I couldn't bear it any longer being named after the people who oppress me." **27**

"You know as well as me you was named after your aunt Dicie," I said. Dicie is my sister. She named Dee. We called her "Big Dee" after Dee was born. **28**

"But who was *she* named after?" asked Wangero. **29**

"I guess after Grandma Dee," I said. **30**

"And who was she named after?" asked Wangero. **31**

"Her mother," I said, and saw Wangero was getting tired. "That's **32** about as far back as I can trace it," I said. Though, in fact, I probably could have carried it back beyond the Civil War through the branches.

"Well," said Asalamalakim, "there you are."   33

"Uhnnnh," I heard Maggie say.   34

"There I was not," I said, "before 'Dicie' cropped up in our family, so why should I try to trace it that far back?"   35

He just stood there grinning, looking down on me like somebody inspecting a Model A car. Every once in a while he and Wangero sent eye signals over my head.   36

"How do you pronounce this name?" I asked.   37

"You don't have to call me by it if you don't want to," said Wangero.   38

"Why shouldn't I?" I asked. "If that's what you want us to call you, we'll call you."   39

"I know it might sound awkward at first," said Wangero.   40

"I'll get used to it," I said. "Ream it out again."   41

Well, soon we got the name out of the way. Asalamalakim had a name twice as long and three times as hard. After I tripped over it two or three times he told me to just call him Hakim-a-barber. I wanted to ask him was he a barber, but I didn't really think he was, so I didn't ask.   42

"You must belong to those beef-cattle peoples down the road," I said. They said "Asalamalakim" when they met you, too, but they didn't shake hands. Always too busy: feeding the cattle, fixing the fences, putting up salt-lick shelters, throwing down hay. When the white folks poisoned some of the herd the men stayed up all night with rifles in their hands. I walked a mile and a half just to see the sight.   43

Hakim-a-barber said, "I accept some of their doctrines, but farming and raising cattle is not my style." (They didn't tell me, and I didn't ask, whether Wangero [Dee] had really gone and married him.)   44

We sat down to eat and right away he said he didn't eat collards and pork was unclean. Wangero, though, went on through the chitlins and corn bread, the greens and everything else. She talked a blue streak over the sweet potatoes. Everything delighted her. Even the fact that we still used the benches her daddy made for the table when we couldn't afford to buy chairs.   45

"Oh, Mama!" she cried. Then turned to Hakim-a-barber. "I never knew how lovely these benches are. You can feel the rump prints," she said, running her hands underneath her and along the bench. Then she gave a sigh and her hand closed over Grandma Dee's butter dish. "That's it!" she said. "I knew there was something I wanted to ask you if I could have." She jumped up from the table and went over in the corner where the churn stood, the milk in its clabber by now. She looked at the churn and looked at it.   46

"This churn top is what I need," she said. "Didn't Uncle Buddy whittle it out of a tree you all used to have?"   47

"Yes," I said.   48

"Uh huh," she said happily. "And I want the dasher, too."   49

"Uncle Buddy whittle that, too?" asked the barber.   50

Dee (Wangero) looked at me.   51

"Aunt Dee's first husband whittled the dash," said Maggie so low   52
you almost couldn't hear her. "His name was Henry, but they called
him Stash."

"Maggie's brain is like an elephant's," Wangero said, laughing. "I   53
can use the churn top as a centerpiece for the alcove table," she said,
sliding a plate over the churn, "and I'll think of something artistic to
do with the dasher."

When she finished wrapping the dasher the handle stuck out. I   54
took it for a moment in my hands. You didn't even have to look close
to see where hands pushing the dasher up and down to make butter
had left a kind of sink in the wood. In fact, there were a lot of small
sinks; you could see where thumbs and fingers had sunk into the
wood. It was beautiful light yellow wood, from a tree that grew in
the yard where Big Dee and Stash had lived.

After dinner Dee (Wangero) went to the trunk at the foot of my   55
bed and started rifling through it. Maggie hung back in the kitchen
over the dishpan. Out came Wangero with two quilts. They had been
pieced by Grandma Dee and then Big Dee and me had hung them on
the quilt frames on the front porch and quilted them. One was in the
Lone Star pattern. The other was Walk Around the Mountain. In
both of them were scraps of dresses Grandma Dee had worn fifty and
more years ago. Bits and pieces of Grandpa Jarrell's Paisley shirts.
And one teeny faded blue piece, about the size of a penny matchbox,
that was from Great Grandpa Ezra's uniform that he wore in the
Civil War.

"Mama," Wangero said sweet as a bird. "Can I have these old   56
quilts?"

I heard something fall in the kitchen, and a minute later the   57
kitchen door slammed.

"Why don't you take one or two of the others?" I asked. "These   58
old things was just done by me and Big Dee from some tops your
grandma pieced before she died."

"No," said Wangero, "I don't want those. They are stitched   59
around the borders by machine."

"That'll make them last better," I said.   60

"That's not the point," said Wangero. "These are all pieces of   61
dresses Grandma used to wear. She did all this stitching by hand.
Imagine!" She held the quilts securely in her arms, stroking them.

"Some of the pieces, like those lavender ones, come from old   62
clothes her mother handed down to her," I said, moving up to touch
the quilts. Dee (Wangero) moved back just enough so that I couldn't
reach the quilts. They already belonged to her.

"Imagine!" she breathed again, clutching them closely to her   63
bosom.

"The truth is," I said, "I promised to give them quilts to Maggie,   64
for when she marries John Thomas."

She gasped like a bee had stung her.   65

"Maggie can't appreciate these quilts!" she said. "She'd probably   66
be backward enough to put them to everyday use."

"I reckon she would," I said. "God knows I been saving 'em for long enough with nobody using 'em. I hope she will!" I didn't want to bring up how I had offered Dee (Wangero) a quilt when she went away to college. Then she had told me they were old-fashioned, out of style.   67

"But they're *priceless!*" she was saying now, furiously; for she has a temper. "Maggie would put them on the bed and in five years they'd be in rags. Less than that!"   68

"She can always make some more," I said. "Maggie knows how to quilt."   69

Dee (Wangero) looked at me with hatred. "You just will not understand. The point is these quilts, *these* quilts!"   70

"Well," I said, stumped. "What would *you* do with them?"   71

"Hang them," she said. As if that was the only thing you *could* do with quilts.   72

Maggie by now was standing in the door. I could almost hear the sound her feet made as they scraped over each other.   73

"She can have them, Mama," she said, like somebody used to never winning anything, or having anything reserved for her. "I can 'member Grandma Dee without the quilts."   74

I looked at her hard. She had filled her bottom lip with checker-berry snuff and it gave her face a kind of dopey, hangdog look. It was Grandma Dee and Big Dee who taught her how to quilt herself. She stood there with her scarred hands hidden in the folds of her skirt. She looked at her sister with something like fear but she wasn't mad at her. This was Maggie's portion. This was the way she knew God to work.   75

When I looked at her like that something hit me in the top of my head and ran down to the soles of my feet. Just like when I'm in church and the spirit of God touches me and I get happy and shout. I did something I never had done before: hugged Maggie to me, then dragged her on into the room, snatched the quilts out of Miss Wangero's hands and dumped them into Maggie's lap. Maggie just sat there on my bed with her mouth open.   76

"Take one or two of the others," I said to Dee.   77

But she turned without a word and went out to Hakim-a-barber.   78

"You just don't understand," she said, as Maggie and I came out to the car.   79

"What don't I understand?" I wanted to know.   80

"Your heritage," she said. And then she turned to Maggie, kissed her, and said, "You ought to try to make something of yourself, too, Maggie. It's really a new day for us. But from the way you and Mama still live you'd never know it."   81

She put on some sunglasses that hid everything above the tip of her nose and her chin.   82

Maggie smiled; maybe at the sunglasses. But a real smile, not scared. After we watched the car dust settle I asked Maggie to bring me a dip of snuff. And then the two of us sat there just enjoying, until it was time to go in the house and go to bed.   83

PLANNING THE CRITICAL ESSAY

An informed reading of a literary work is the most important stage in planning the critical essay. But to transform your reading into writing, you need to try out some of the thinking-in-writing strategies suggested as "review" activities (page 339). For example, after Richard read "Everyday Use," he made a list of the characters, scenes, and images that he remembered most vividly.

Mama—fat, proud, smart—sledgehammer

Johnny Carson reunion vs. real reunion

Maggie—fire, ugly, afraid of Dee, knows how to make a quilt

Dee—educated, ashamed of family (Wangero), Hakim-a-barber

Butter dish, churn

Quilts—bits and pieces, suddenly fashionable

Hang on the wall

Mama's choice

After looking over this list, Richard decided to focus his attention on Dee's attempt to take the quilts. In a freewriting exercise, he explored his reaction to this event:

I was really furious with Dee, or Wangero, or whatever her name is. She didn't want those quilts when she was in college. Out of style. Now that they're "in," she wants to hang one in her apartment. Probably put spotlights on them with a brass plaque explaining how priceless they are. Good thing Mama saw through her. Maggie would have given them to her. She can always make others. But that's not the point. It's the principle. They're Maggie's quilts. Shouldn't have to give them up.

Not everybody reacts to a particular literary work in the same way. For example, Julia's freewriting exercise expresses a slightly different interpretation of Dee's behavior.

Dee is not completely at fault for the way she acts. She's what her family wanted her to become—educated. Mama and Maggie think she's famous. Johnny Carson. Every family has somebody that outgrows it. Dee lives in a different world. Different values. Car, dress, bracelets, boyfriend. Wangero. Trying to discover roots. Knows what style is. People should respect heritage. Try to make something out of themselves.

By contrast to Richard's emotional reaction to the story, Julia's response seems thoughtful and objective. Her analysis may explain Dee's behavior, but it does not account for Mama's decision to give the quilts to Maggie. Richard, on the other hand, may need to think through the reasons for his anger, but his assessment provides a more complete picture of the story's events. Obviously, Julia and Richard have a great deal to discuss with each other about "Everyday Use." Each response adds some insight to the other, prompting both writers to rethink their views and perhaps return to the story to look for evidence that supports their positions.

To test their reactions to the story, they need to consider the five basic elements contributing to the story's effect. One way is to compose and answer questions about these elements or attempt to answer questions provided by their instructor.

_____Exercise   Answer the following questions about how the five basic elements interact in "Everyday Use." Respond to each question in three or four sentences. For some questions, you may need to reread sections of the story before you compose your answer.

Questions About Plot

1. How does Mama's dream about a family reunion on television introduce the conflicts in the story?

2. How does Mama's decision to give the quilts to Maggie mark the climax of the story?

3. How do Wangero's comments about heritage and self-development bring the story to an ironic conclusion?

Questions About Characterization

1. How does Mama's description of her working ability establish her character?

2. How do Maggie's scars explain her lack of self-esteem?

3. How do Dee's attire, boyfriend, and new name justify Mama's comment that Dee "knew what style was"?

Questions About Setting

1. How do Mama's opening and closing comments about the yard evoke the physical and social setting of the story?

2. Why does Mama suspect that Dee will want to "tear down" the house?

3. Why does Wangero photograph the house and pay so much attention to the benches, churn, and quilts?

Questions About Point of View

1. Why is it appropriate for Mama to tell this story? For example, how might the story change if it were told by Maggie or Dee?

2. What is Mama's attitude toward Maggie's accident and Dee's education?

3. What attitude toward her story does Walker suggest by her dedication, "*for your grandmamma*"?

Questions About Theme

1. How does the conflict about the quilts symbolize the themes of tradition and progress?

2. How do you interpret Wangero's comment that her sister should "make something" of herself?

3. How do you interpret Mama's observation that "Maggie knows how to quilt"?

DRAFTING THE CRITICAL ESSAY

After you have worked your way through several thinking-in-writing strategies, you should have learned enough about a particular literary work to draft your essay.

Selecting Your Subject

Sort through the subject ideas you uncovered during planning. Even a subject assigned by your instructor and restricted to a specific aspect of a story, poem, or play should enable you to integrate your planning material into a unified essay. If your instructor asks you to select your own subject, be sure to restrict it to a specific aspect of the work. You cannot discuss everything you know about "Everyday Use," for example, but you can focus your attention on an aspect of the story that will enable you to compose a thoughtful and thorough analysis.

Analyzing Your Audience

You must assume that your audience for a critical essay is a group of informed readers. This means that your readers have read the story you are about to interpret and have probably formed their own opinions about its meaning and significance. For that reason, you do not need to summarize the plot. But you do need to analyze relevant aspects of the plot (and even quote certain passages) so that your readers can see how you arrived at your interpretation.

Determining Your Purpose

Restricting your subject will help determine your purpose, but remember that you need to prove something about your subject. In a critical essay on a literary work, this means proving that your particular interpretation is supported by a careful examination of the text. To put your purpose into operation, compose a thesis that embodies the interpretation you are trying to prove.

As Richard began drafting his essay on "Everyday Use," he decided that he wanted to restrict his subject to the conflicting attitudes toward the word *heritage* that he discovered in the story. He began by making a scratch outline grouping words and details that reveal how Mama and Dee might use the word.

1. Mama
   House-yard-homestead
   Hard work, hog killing
   Family—children, all the Dees (Civil War)
   Church songs
   Skills—whittling, quilts
   Saving for "everyday use"
   Can always make another

2. Dee
   School—discovers other habits (heritages)
   Wanted nice things—style (vs. heritage)
   Rediscovers heritage: Afro, pigtails, jewelry
   New name (oppression vs. tradition)
   Photographs—artifacts, something artistic
   Skills—admired, appreciated, priceless
   New Day

Making this simple division lets Richard see the significance of some aspects of the story that were not on his original list or in his freewriting exercise and lets him draft a preliminary hypothesis about this information.

In "Everyday Use," Alice Walker presents two attitudes toward heritage: Mama's and Maggie's is something used everyday, and Wangero's is a matter of what is in style.

As he thinks about this hypothesis, Richard decides to use his knowledge of the basic elements of literature to provide a more critical perspective on his material. He revises his thesis to focus on *how* Alice Walker develops this *theme* through *characterization*.

In "Everyday Use," Alice Walker presents contrasting attitudes toward heritage through her characters' appearance, actions, and appreciation of family possessions.

The advantage of this thesis is that it sets up a structure for Richard's essay. He can contrast the two attitudes toward heritage as he contrasts the characters in three separate sections: (a) *appearance,* (b) *actions,* and (c) *appreciation of family possessions.* His use of the various stages of the reading and writing process enables him to compose the following draft.

The Meaning of Heritage in "Everyday Use"
Richard Gant

Alice Walker's short story "Everyday Use" is about the conflict   1 between a mother and a daughter over their heritage. Heritage for Mama and her daughter Maggie is a matter of everyday living, or "everyday use" as the title of the story suggests. Mama and Maggie are not conscious of their heritage because it is so much a part of their lives. For Mama's daughter Dee, however, heritage is a matter of style, a fashionable obsession with one's roots. Walker develops these contrasting attitudes through her characters' appearance, actions, and appreciation of family possessions.

The description of the characters in the story introduces the   2 conflicting attitudes toward heritage. Mama admits that she is fat and manly. Her hands are calloused and rough from a lifetime of hard work. Maggie is described as homely, wearing a pink skirt and red blouse, and bearing scars from a fire that burned down the family home. Dee, however, is beautiful and stylish, wearing a striking, brightly colored African dress, earrings, bracelets, sunglasses, and hair in the full-bodied African style that, according to Mama, "stands straight up like the wool on a sheep." Even Dee's feet are pretty, "as if God himself had shaped them with a certain style."

The characters' actions further develop the theme of heritage.   3 By telling us that she can butcher hogs "as mercilessly as a man" or break ice "to get water for washing," Mama suggests that she possesses necessary survival skills. She is at home in her world, sweeping the front yard as though it were "an extended living room." And she prepares and eats chitlins, corn bread, and collards because they are inexpensive and readily available. Although she is less assertive, Maggie displays similar domestic skills, particularly her ability to make quilts. Both women live their heritage. Dee, however, thinks of herself as outside this world. When she was a girl, she used to read things to her family that they "didn't necessarily need to know," washing them "in a river of make-believe."

She wanted to dress nicely and impress others with a "well-turned phrase." Now that she has become educated and fascinated by African culture, she changes her name to Wangero Leewanika Kemanjo. She does not want to bear the name of the "people who oppress me," even though, ironically, her name has a long history in the family. Unaware of this inconsistency, Wangero returns home with her Muslim boyfriend, Hakim-a-barber, to take pictures of her mother and sister with the house and cow, probably to show her friends the "down home" aura of the homestead.

The characters' appreciation of certain family possessions intensifies the difference between the two notions of heritage. Dee-Wangero rediscovers Mama's wooden benches: "I never knew how lovely these benches are. You can feel the rump prints." She also views the churn top and the dasher as quaint because they were created by a primitive skill, whittling, and because she can use them to create something else, such as an artistic centerpiece for her alcove table. And finally, she is captivated by the quilts that Grandma Dee and Big Dee stitched together out of bits and pieces of family clothing from as far back as the Civil War. She wants to hang them on a wall as she would priceless paintings. To Mama and Maggie, however, these objects are indispensable to their everyday living. The churn top, dasher, benches, and quilts are for "everyday use," not for stylish decoration.

At the climax of the story, Maggie is tempted to give her quilts to Dee-Wangero. Mama has been saving them for Maggie to use when she starts her own home, but Maggie says that she can remember "Grandma Dee without the quilts." Mama acknowledges that Maggie "can always make some more," and then suddenly she feels "something hit me in the top of my head and ran down to the soles of my feet." She hugged Maggie, "snatched the quilts out of Miss Wangero's hands and dumped them into Maggie's lap." This decision leaves Maggie speechless and Dee-Wangero momentarily annoyed. But clearly Mama and Maggie understand their heritage better than Dee-Wangero thinks they do. The final scene of the story reveals the difference between an artificial and a real heritage. Dee-Wangero puts on her sunglasses and rides away in the dust, while Mama and Maggie finish the day by sitting there "just enjoying."

4

5

Conclusion

REVISING THE CRITICAL ESSAY

To assess what you have accomplished in your draft, use the strategies for global and local revision that you have already learned to clarify the internal focus and development of your text. To complete this revision process, however, reread the literary work, using your draft as a guide. If your draft helps you understand the interaction of the basic elements in the work, then you have probably composed a fairly complete essay. But if, as you reread the work, you discover important features of plot, characterization, setting, point of view, or theme that you have overlooked or underestimated, then you may need to revise your essay. Sometimes such discoveries will require you to rethink the wording of your thesis or the transitions between the major divisions of your paper. At other times, they will remind you that by adding a detail, modifying an assertion, or quoting a particular passage, you can make a more compelling case for your interpretation.

Poem/Student Essay

Examine Edwin Arlington Robinson's poem "Mr. Flood's Party" by using the reading strategies described in the Guidelines for Reading Literature (pages 338–9). Then read Julia Miller's essay, "Old Eben and Mr. Flood." In what ways does your response differ from the student's response? What aspects of the poem did you overlook in your reading? What aspects did she overlook in her writing?

Mr. Flood's Party | Edwin Arlington Robinson

Old Eben Flood, climbing alone one night
Over the hill between the town below
And the foresaken upland hermitage
That held as much as he should ever know
On earth again of home, paused warily.   5
The road was his with not a native near;
And Eben, having leisure, said aloud,
For no man else in Tilbury Town to hear:

"Well, Mr. Flood, we have the harvest moon
Again, and we may not have many more;   10
The bird is on the wing, the poet says,
And you and I have said it here before.
Drink to the bird." He raised up to the light
The jug that he had gone so far to fill,
And answered huskily: "Well, Mr. Flood,   15
Since you propose it, I believe I will."

Alone, as if enduring to the end
A valiant armor of scarred hopes outworn,
He stood there in the middle of the road
Like Roland's ghost winding a silent horn.   20
Below him, in the town among the trees,
Where friends of other days had honored him,
A phantom salutation of the dead
Rang thinly till old Eben's eyes were dim.

Then, as a mother lays her sleeping child   25
Down tenderly, fearing it may awake,
He set the jug down slowly at his feet
With trembling care, knowing that most things break;
And only when assured that on firm earth
It stood, as the uncertain lives of men   30
Assuredly did not, he paced away,
And with his hand extended paused again:

"Well, Mr. Flood, we have not met like this
In a long time; and many a change has come

Collected Poems of Edwin Arlington Robinson. New York: Macmillan, 1921. 573–5.

To both of us, I fear, since last it was 35
We had a drop together. Welcome home!"
Convivially returning with himself,
Again he raised the jug up to the light;
And with an acquiescent quaver said:
"Well, Mr. Flood, if you insist, I might. 40

"Only a very little, Mr. Flood—
For auld lang syne. No more, sir; that will do."
So, for the time, apparently it did,
And Eben evidently thought so too;
For soon amid the silver loneliness 45
Of night he lifted up his voice and sang,
Secure, with only two moons listening,
Until the whole harmonious landscape rang—

"For auld lang syne." The weary throat gave out,
The last word wavered, and the song was done. 50
He raised again the jug regretfully
And shook his head, and was again alone.
There was not much that was ahead of him,
And there was nothing in the town below—
Where strangers would have shut the many doors 55
That many friends had opened long ago.

Old Eben and Mr. Flood | Julia Miller

"**M**r. Flood's Party" embraces two separate worlds. The first world is one 1
of reality, consisting of Eben's consciousness of his present state, in which
he is lonely and desolate; the other world is one of illusion, made up of Mr.
Flood's dreams of his fellowship with friends of bygone days. The distinction between the poem's two worlds is emphasized by the figure of the
"two moons." One moon is real, but the other moon is just a part of Mr.
Flood's illusion.

Robinson begins the poem by placing Eben in the world of reality. In 2
the first words of the first line, "Old Eben Flood, climbing alone," the
reader gets a hint of Eben's age and solitude. In the next line, the phrase
"Over the hill" continues to express the concept of age. Eben's position
"between the town below/And the forsaken upland hermitage" strengthens
the idea of loneliness. Here, he is caught in the middle. In the words of the
last stanza, "there was nothing in the town below," and yet "There was
not much that was ahead of him." The world of reality continues for Eben
in the second stanza. In addressing himself, Eben recognizes his age in the
passage: "we have the harvest moon/Again, and we may not have many
more." He also acknowledges the movement of time in the statement, "The
bird is on the wing." On this note old Eben takes a drink, and his world of
reality begins to fade.

In the third stanza, Eben is still aware of his state of solitude, but this 3
awareness has taken on a heroic quality. He is described as "enduring to
the end/A valiant armor of scarred hopes outworn." This is a very noble
image of Mr. Flood, who has merely outlasted his expectations and outlived
his time. "Like Roland's ghost winding a silent horn," so Mr. Flood calls
for the help of his comrades by raising the jug to his mouth. In the world

of illusion, Flood's friends answer the call. At the end of the third stanza, these "friends of other days" who "had honored him" greet Mr. Flood in a "phantom salutation of the dead." Old Eben's desolation is forgotten in this illusion. He is living in a dream of the past through his imagined reunion with his deceased friends. Feeling secure in the company of his party, Mr. Flood sings "For auld lang syne."

Robinson then informs the reader that "The weary throat gave out,/   4
The last word wavered, and the song was done." Likewise, Mr. Flood's world of illusion fades, and the party is over.

As the party ends, the world of reality returns. Eben, as if he were   5
waking from a dream, "shook his head, and was again alone." In the line that states, "There was not much that was ahead of him," Eben recognizes that there is neither much left of his life, nor much left in his life. The words of the last three lines sum up Eben's situation: "there was nothing in the town below—/Where strangers would have shut the many doors/ That many friends had opened long ago." In the realm of reality, Eben knows that the world has changed. He also knows that all of his contemporaries are gone. As the poem ends, Eben returns to being a lonely old man with time passing rapidly by him.

In conclusion, the name Eben Flood is most appropriate for the main   6
character in this poem. The name can be broken down into "ebb and flood." The flood describes the high tide of Eben's life. This is the period in which Eben had friends and hopes. At that time, life held much in store for him. The image of the flood also describes the flood of memories from his past, which pour in the flood from the jug. All of Mr. Flood's dreams of a bygone era comprise the world of illusion. The ebb describes the decline of Eben's life and the low level of his present existence. The ebb also represents the world of reality, in which Mr. Flood must face up to loneliness, desolation, and age. Eben may always want to live in the flood of illusion, but he must always return to the ebb of reality. After all, time and tide wait for no man.

Family Feud | Mark Crispin Miller

In his analysis of the popular television game show *Family Feud*, Mark Crispin Miller points out important features of plot, characterization, setting, point of view, and theme as he tries to answer several questions: "What is this all about? Why is the show so popular, why so engrossing?" In what ways does Miller use the show's title to answer these questions? How does Miller use his analysis to raise larger questions about the relationship of the family to television culture?

Family Feud" may well be the cleverest game show on TV. It's certainly   1
the most absorbing. "Family Feud" has been on the air since 1975, it comes on (in most cities) twice a day, and yet it hasn't lost its fascination, and probably never will, as long as millions stare at millions of TV sets. When

Miller, Mark Crispin. *Boxed In: The Culture of TV.* Evanston, IL: Northwestern University Press, 1988. 51–55.

Mark Goodson and his associates first cooked this trifle up, they created one of TV's few abiding things, a spectacle as durable and bright as Johnny Carson, or a no-wax floor.

If you aren't a regular viewer of "Family Feud," you might enjoy a leisurely description. Of course, trying to describe a game show is a bit like trying to describe the kind of dreams you have when half-asleep with fever. Even the weirdest of fantasies, however, has its own implicit structure, and so does "Family Feud," whose generic craziness conceals a form as rigid and significant as the plan of any other public ritual.

The show starts with the usual sudden uproar. "It's time for—'*Family Feud*'!!" someone yells, backed by a screechy din that sounds like bluegrass music played by speed freaks. We see the title, its dark red letters rendered in mock needlepoint across a yellow oval, like an enormous sampler, and then the title turns into some surname—PFISTER, say—also lettered in mock needlepoint. The studio audience goes nuts, the music yelps and twangs, as the oval zips leftward like a sliding door, revealing a sort of mock-Victorian parlor, where the five immobile Pfisters pose in wacky imitation of some old-fashioned family portrait. After the announcer shouts their names, the Pfisters break out of this *tableau vivant* and line up, five abreast, applauding back at the applauding crowd. This rapid process then repeats itself, showing us the Pfisters' rival house—say, GRUBB—and then both little clans come bounding out onto the stage, a hectic edifice of lurid hues and tiny winking lights, and face off gaily, five abreast, each standing in a happy row behind a sort of elongated podium.

Now the music turns to brass, hiccuping and blaring in the Vegas mode, and everybody's clapping. Then, ". . . the *star* of 'Family Feud,' " whoops the announcer, "—*Richard Dawson*!!" The place goes crazier, and out strolls this aging, deeply suntanned figure, resplendent in a roomy three-piece suit of glossy brown or gray, a huge carnation shining on his left lapel. He meanders downstage between the cheering Grubbs and Pfisters, as a much-loved drunk might join a raucous party thrown in his honor, and halts to do a spot of mellow shtick. We see at once that Dawson is no typical M.C., not an unctuous, chortling "host," beaming like a salesman, but rather comes on with the boozy self-possession of a weathered libertine. He seems pure show biz, a veteran of unnumbered poolside hangovers. As he glistens on the screen, his asides a little slurred, his shirt cuffs vast and blinding, you start to feel a little groggy, and your Sony starts to smell of aftershave. And yet, while Dawson thus evinces the authority of smooth decay, he also wears, incongruously, the uniform of high-paid middle management—the ample suit, the boutonniere, a glittering watch chain. He is, in short, an ingenious combination of intimidating traits. With his gray Neronian bangs, his puffy, umbered face, and his obtrusive vest, he looks like some old Roman debauchee now working as a district manager for Burger King.

The families on "Family Feud" clearly regard this wry and shiny boss, not just with something like affection, but with deep respect. At first, this seems a little strange, given the glaring contrast between him and them. For, whether the Grubbs and Pfisters claim to hail from L.A., the Bronx, or Salt Lake City, they really represent our fabled heartland. Invariably bright-eyed, cheery, vigorous, and neat, these folks all look as stolid and clean-cut as Dawson seems unwholesome. Although he's clearly not their type, however, Dawson counteracts his daunting aura with intense displays of flattering concern. He falls all over them from start to finish, with an oleaginous noblesse oblige perhaps unrivaled on TV.

After his moment downstage, he turns to do some quick preliminary schmoozing with each team's captain, usually the Dad or elder brother. Leaning forward chummily, with a familiar drawl, Dawson orders Mr. Pfister to identify the family, and the eager patriarch booms back at him, with strained heartiness: "Well, Richard," Pfister thunders, "this is my beautiful wife Adele—my lovely daughter Gina—my good lookin' son Todd," and so on, as the camera pans across this taut ménage, each Pfister greeting "Richard" with a bellow or a chirp, according to gender. There's some talk about how Pfister earns his livelihood, and then, at the chat's conclusion, the team formally presents the star of "Family Feud" with some homely offering, usually handmade, such as a bag of cookies, a necklace made of chestnuts, or an inscribed hat.

After a similar brief visit with the Grubbs, Dawson shouts, "Let's play the feud!" and swaggers over to his central place behind a smaller podium, beneath a big bright board comprised of numbered slats. A Pfister and a Grubb stand ready at his left and right, as Dawson reads a question, which he always introduces with the same revealing formula: "One hundred people surveyed, top six answers on The Board, here's the question: Name an appliance that's always plugged in." Grubb and Pfister each lunge forward, and the first to smack a massive button on Dawson's podium gets to answer first: "A vacuum cleaner!" hollers Grubb, who is not, perhaps, as quick as his right hand. Chuckling, Dawson looks up at The Board: "*Vacuum cleaner?*" he calls out, but The Board is still, and there flashes over it a coarse red "X," emphasized by a derisive honk. Dawson turns to Pfister, who, knowing her appliances, shrieks out, "A *toaster*!" Dawson addresses The Board with this wiser answer, whereupon one of the slats turns over with a ping, revealing the word "toaster" and a certain number, representing points.

The Pfisters exult, because they've won the chance to play this question out. Dawson proceeds down the line along their podium, asking each of them to name another ever-plugged-in thing. Until the schedule starts to tighten, Dawson will conduct each brief interrogation with an efficient stream of cagey banter; and he always greets each female panelist with a loud kiss on the lips, as the menfolk stand there, grinning tightly. (The kiss is Dawson's trademark.) The Pfisters keep it up until they win or lose the round. That is, they either guess every answer on The Board, thereby winning all the points available, or they come up with three "wrong" answers, whereupon the Grubbs jump in and try to guess one answer yet unchosen, stealing the round if they succeed.

The game goes on through several rounds, each devoted to another mundane question—one that refers either to the world of goods ("Name something you have two of in your bathroom"), the teachings of TV ("Name the wealthiest man in show business"), or the routines of daily life ("Name the first thing you do when you wake up in the morning"). Finally, whichever family earns three hundred points gets to play the "Lightning Round." After a show of deft commiseration with the losing Grubbs, who, no less upbeat, promptly disappear, Dawson moves down front and center, as one quivering Pfister comes to stand beside him and another prances off stage left. All is quiet; the Pfister's head, inclined, eyes closed, as if in prayer, appears in closeup and then Dawson reads off five quick questions, the Pfister blurting out an answer to each one, as fifteen seconds tick away. When time's up, both turn around to hot applause, and face a sort of scoreboard at the rear of the stage. With one familiar arm around the Pfister's neck, Dawson repeats each question and reply, pausing as each answer shows up on the scoreboard with some number next to it. Once we get the grand subtotal, Pfister No. 2 sprints back to undergo the same ordeal. The suspense is captivating, as we wait to find out if the Pfisters have racked up two hundred points, which will win them $10,000.

If the family succeeds, the crowd once again goes berserk, and the winning Pfisters grab each other, bouncing up and down as if attempting a collective levitation. As Dawson wanders offstage, many further Pfisters, hitherto unknown, come bolting down the aisles to join their kin. We cut to a commercial. When the show comes back, the much-augmented house of Pfister stands spread out, euphorically, across the stage, and Dawson hands one of them (usually a tot or oldster) a big sheet of white cardboard, with the amount they've won inscribed in Magic Marker, in a childish scrawl. Sometimes, if there are any kids onstage, he hands out lollipops. Finally, we see the credits, and, under them, the Pfisters frolicking and clapping to the rhythm of the grating theme. 10

What is this all about? Why is this show so popular, why so engrossing? Unlike other game shows, "Family Feud" is never heatedly competitive, nor does the cash prize ultimately matter. Dawson tends to discourage the grim desire to score, turning faintly chilly when confronted with impatient avarice. Usually, however, he doesn't need to convey such scorn, since the players are nearly always buoyant, either good winners or good losers. In fact, both families have more or less cleaned up before the game begins, since the show pays for their trips west, puts them up in a hotel for two nights, and provides them with a car and a comfortable per diem. 11

If the point of "Family Feud" is not the prize, then maybe it's the emphasis on kinship. "Family Feud" would seem the most straightforward *family* show on television. Its "stars" appear to be just plain folks, exemplars of the old domestic virtues. For one thing, each household sticks together with amazing loyalty. No matter how stupid someone's answer, even if Dawson gets the giggles, the others show maniacal support, clapping hard and roaring out, "Good answer! Good answer!" Such clannishness seems out of place on television, whose impulse is to shatter families, not unite them, ceaselessly exhorting each and every "individual" to go his/her "own way," i.e., to live a "life" of nonstop buying. "Family Feud" appears a broad exception to the TV rule, from its opening title, with "family" proclaimed in scarlet letters, through its closing video portrait of the Pfisters/Grubbs/O'Rourkes/Barzinis/Goldbergs/Jeffersons/Wongs/Romeros, each group rewarded, seemingly, for its intense togetherness. 12

And yet, in fact, it isn't the familial bond that wins the prize on "Family Feud," but the family's successful self-erasure. Each of Dawson's questions is a test of sameness, its answers based on tallies of "one hundred people surveyed," well ahead of time, by the show's producers. A "correct" 13 reply is therefore not the smartest, but the *least* inventive answer, matching an alleged "consensus" expertly defined and validated by the show itself. Thus the irresistible appeal of "Family Feud" is also the attraction of TV, which tells us endlessly what "we" believe, thereby using our supposed group sentiments to reconfirm its own authority. "Family Feud" is basically a festive variant of those other forms of modern tabulation, the marketing survey and the opinion poll. And so it is precisely like TV itself — a pseudopopulist diversion based on crude statistics.

For all its seeming family pride, then, each group that plays on "Fam-   **14** ily Feud" does not come on to manifest its own discrete identity, but rather struggles to get rid of it. Victory demands the absolute suppression of any wayward thought or preference, any eccentricity that might define the family apart from TV's bland reconstruction of ourselves. If they want to win, the players must respond with ready minds of total emptiness, letting the mythic mass speak through them. Thus "Family Feud" is actually a high-speed ritual of absorption, which has its consummation only when five beings demonstrate their own ecstatic averageness. In visual terms, the real reward is not the money, which we never glimpse, nor even Dawson's cardboard token, but the climactic moment when those nameless others pour from the audience onto the stage, creating the illusion of an oceanic merger, as the separated clan now happily dissolves into the gathering flood of erstwhile watchers.

Once we recall its proper meaning, the title too suggests this terminal   **15** absorption. A "family feud" is not, in fact, a dispute between two separate houses, but one that divides a *single* family into warring factions. The show's real purpose is to celebrate, not specific households, but the encroaching, all-inclusive tribe of viewers, that unseen mass into which those households long to be reintegrated, nervously competing for acceptance like extruded siblings. In other words, all the families on "Family Feud" appear to be related to each other, seeming fundamentally alike, however various their surnames, hue, or points of origin.

In Search of Our Mothers' Gardens | Alice Walker

In this essay, Alice Walker searches for and honors the legacy left by generations of anonymous black women. How does she evaluate the contributions of the black slave poet Phillis Wheatley? How does she use the quilt at the Smithsonian Institution and her mother's garden to demonstrate that "we have constantly looked high, when we should have looked high—and low" for evidence of the black creative spirit? How does Walker's quotations from Virginia Woolf's *A Room of One's Own* broaden (and narrow) the subject of her essay?

Walker, Alice. *In Search of Our Mothers' Gardens*. San Diego: Harcourt, New York, 1983. 231–243.

I described her own nature and temperament. Told how they needed a larger life for their expression. . . . I pointed out that in lieu of proper channels, her emotions had overflowed into paths that dissipated them. I talked, beautifully I thought, about an art that would be born, an art that would open the way for women the likes of her. I asked her to hope, and build up an inner life against the coming of that day. . . . I sang, with a strange quiver in my voice, a promise song.

                                                                Jean Toomer ("Avey," *Cane*)

The poet speaking to a prostitute who falls asleep while he's talking—

When the poet Jean Toomer walked through the South in the early twen- 1
ties, he discovered a curious thing: black women whose spirituality was so intense, so deep, so *unconscious,* that they were themselves unaware of the richness they held. They stumbled blindly through their lives, creatures so abused and mutilated in body, so dimmed and confused by pain, that they considered themselves unworthy even of hope. In the selfless abstractions their bodies became to the men who used them, they became more than "sexual objects," more even than mere women: they became "Saints." In- stead of being perceived as whole persons, their bodies became shrines: what was thought to be their minds became temples suitable for worship. These crazy Saints stared out at the world, wildly, like lunatics—or quietly, like suicides; and the "God" that was in their gaze was as mute as a great stone.

Who were these Saints? These crazy, loony, pitiful women? 2

Some of them, without a doubt, were our mothers and grandmothers. 3

In the still heat of the post-Reconstruction South, this is how they 4
seemed to Jean Toomer: exquisite butterflies trapped in an evil honey, toil- ing away their lives in an era, a century, that did not acknowledge them, except as "the *mule* of the world." They dreamed dreams that no one knew—not even themselves, in any coherent fashion—and saw visions no one could understand. They wandered or sat about the countryside croon- ing lullabies to ghosts, and drawing the mother of Christ in charcoal on courthouse walls.

They forced their minds to desert their bodies and their striving spirits 5
sought to rise, like frail whirlwinds from the hard red clay. And when those frail whirlwinds fell, in scattered particles, upon the ground, no one mourned. Instead, men lit candles to celebrate the emptiness that remained, as people do who enter a beautiful but vacant space to resurrect a God.

Our mothers and grandmothers, some of them: moving to music not 6
yet written. And they waited.

They waited for a day when the unknown thing that was in them 7
would be made known; but guessed, somehow in their darkness, that on the day of their revelation they would be long dead. Therefore to Toomer they walked, and even ran, in slow motion. For they were going nowhere immediate, and the future was not yet within their grasp. And men took our mothers and grandmothers, "but got no pleasure from it." So complex was their passion and their calm.

To Toomer, they lay vacant and fallow as autumn fields, with harvest 8
time never in sight: and he saw them enter loveless marriages, without joy;

and become prostitutes, without resistance; and become mothers of children, without fulfillment.

For these grandmothers and mothers of ours were not Saints, but Artists; driven to a numb and bleeding madness by the springs of creativity in them for which there was no release. They were Creators, who lived lives of spiritual waste, because they were so rich in spirituality—which is the basis of Art—that the strain of enduring their unused and unwanted talent drove them insane. Throwing away this spirituality was their pathetic attempt to lighten the soul to a weight their work-worn, sexually abused bodies could bear.   9

What did it mean for a black woman to be an artist in our grandmothers' time? In our great-grandmothers' day? It is a question with an answer cruel enough to stop the blood.   10

Did you have a genius of a great-great-grandmother who died under some ignorant and depraved white overseer's lash? Or was she required to bake biscuits for a lazy backwater tramp, when she cried out in her soul to paint watercolors of sunsets, or the rain falling on the green and peaceful pasturelands? Or was her body broken and forced to bear children (who were more often than not sold away from her)—eight, ten, fifteen, twenty children—when her one joy was the thought of modeling heroic figures of rebellion, in stone or clay?   11

How was the creativity of the black woman kept alive, year after year and century after century, when for most of the years black people have been in America, it was a punishable crime for a black person to read or write? And the freedom to paint, to sculpt, to expand the mind with action did not exist. Consider, if you can bear to imagine it, what might have been the result if singing, too, had been forbidden by law. Listen to the voices of Bessie Smith, Billie Holiday, Nina Simone, Roberta Flack, and Aretha Franklin, among others, and imagine those voices muzzled for life. Then you may begin to comprehend the lives of our "crazy," "Sainted" mothers and grandmothers. The agony of the lives of women who might have been Poets, Novelists, Essayists, and Short-Story Writers (over a period of centuries), who died with their real gifts stifled within them.   12

And, if this were the end of the story, we would have cause to cry out in my paraphrase of Okot p'Bitek's great poem: 13

O, my clanswomen
Let us all cry together!
Come,
Let us mourn the death of our mother,
The death of a Queen
The ash that was produced
By a great fire!
O, this homestead is utterly dead
Close the gates
With *lacari* thorns,
For our mother
The creator of the Stool is lost!
And all the young women
Have perished in the wilderness!

But this is not the end of the story, for all the young women—our **14** mothers and grandmothers, *ourselves*—have not perished in the wilderness. And if we ask ourselves why, and search for and find the answer, we will know beyond all efforts to erase it from our minds, just exactly who, and of what, we black American women are.

One example, perhaps the most pathetic, most misunderstood one, can **15** provide a backdrop for our mothers' work: Phillis Wheatley, a slave in the 1700s.

Virginia Woolf, in her book *A Room of One's Own,* wrote that in order **16** for a woman to write fiction she must have two things, certainly: a room of her own (with key and lock) and enough money to support herself.

What then are we to make of Phillis Wheatley, a slave, who owned **17** not even herself? This sickly, frail black girl who required a servant of her own at times—her health was so precarious—and who, had she been white, would have been easily considered the intellectual superior of all the women and most of the men in the society of her day.

Virginia Woolf wrote further, speaking of course not of our Phillis, **18** that "any woman born with a great gift in the sixteenth century [insert "eighteenth century," insert "black woman," insert "born or made a slave"] would certainly have gone crazed, shot herself, or ended her days in some lonely cottage outside the village, half witch, half wizard [insert "Saint"], feared and mocked at. For it needs little skill and psychology to be sure that a highly gifted girl who had tried to use her gift for poetry would have been so thwarted and hindered by contrary instincts [add "chains, guns, the lash, the ownership of one's body by someone else, submission to an alien religion"], that she must have lost her health and sanity to a certainty."

The key words, as they relate to Phillis, are "contrary instincts." For **19** when we read the poetry of Phillis Wheatley—as when we read the novels of Nella Larsen or the oddly false-sounding autobiography of that freest of all black women writers, Zora Hurston—evidence of "contrary instincts" is everywhere. Her loyalties were completely divided, as was, without question, her mind.

But how could this be otherwise? Captured at seven, a slave of **20** wealthy, doting whites who instilled in her the "savagery" of the Africa they "rescued" her from . . . one wonders if she was even able to remember her homeland as she had known it, or as it really was.

Yet, because she did try to use her gift for poetry in a world that **21** made her a slave, she was "so thwarted and hindered by . . . contrary instincts, that she . . . lost her health. . . ." In the last years of her brief life, burdened not only with the need to express her gift but also with a penniless, friendless "freedom" and several small children for whom she was forced to do strenuous work to feed, she lost her health, certainly. Suffering from malnutrition and neglect and who knows what mental agonies, Phillis Wheatley died.

So torn by "contrary instincts" was black, kidnapped, enslaved Phillis **22** that her description of "the Goddess"—as she poetically called the Liberty she did not have—is ironically, cruelly humorous. And, in fact, has held Phillis up to ridicule for more than a century. It is usually read prior to hanging Phillis's memory as that of a fool. She wrote:

> The Goddess comes, she moves divinely fair,
> Olive and laurel binds her *golden* hair.
> Wherever shines this native of the skies,
> Unnumber'd charms and recent graces rise. [My italics]

It is obvious that Phillis, the slave, combed the "Goddess's" hair every 23 morning; prior, perhaps, to bringing in the milk, or fixing her mistress's lunch. She took her imagery from the one thing she saw elevated above all others.

With the benefit of hindsight we ask, "How could she?" 24

But at last, Phillis, we understand. No more snickering when your 25 stiff, struggling, ambivalent lines are forced on us. We know now that you were not an idiot or a traitor; only a sickly little black girl, snatched from your home and country and made a slave; a woman who still struggled to sing the song that was your gift, although in a land of barbarians who praised you for your bewildered tongue. It is not so much what you sang, as that you kept alive, in so many of our ancestors, *the notion of song.*

Black women are called, in the folklore that so aptly identifies one's 26 status in society, "the *mule* of the world," because we have been handed the burdens that everyone else—*everyone* else—refused to carry. We have also been called "Matriarchs," "Superwomen," and "Mean and Evil Bitches." Not to mention "Castraters" and "Sapphire's Mama." When we have pleaded for understanding, our character has been distorted; when we have asked for simple caring, we have been handed empty inspirational appellations, then stuck in the farthest corner. When we have asked for love, we have been given children. In short, even our plainer gifts, our labors of fidelity and love, have been knocked down our throats. To be an artist and a black woman, even today, lowers our status in many respects, rather than raises it: and yet, artists we will be.

Therefore we must fearlessly pull out of ourselves and look at and 27 identify with our lives the living creativity some of our great-grandmothers were not allowed to know. I stress *some* of them because it is well known that the majority of our great-grandmothers knew, even without "knowing" it, the reality of their spirituality, even if they didn't recognize it beyond what happened in the singing at church—and they never had any intention of giving it up.

How they did it—those millions of black women who were not Phillis 28 Wheatley, or Lucy Terry or Frances Harper or Zora Hurston or Nella Larsen or Bessie Smith; or Elizabeth Catlett, or Katherine Dunham, either—brings me to the title of this essay, "In Search of Our Mothers' Gardens," which is a personal account that is yet shared, in its theme and its meaning, by all of us. I found, while thinking about the far-reaching world of the creative black woman, that often the truest answer to a question that really matters can be found very close.

In the late 1920s my mother ran away from home to marry my father. 29 Marriage, if not running away, was expected of seventeen-year-old girls. By the time she was twenty, she had two children and was pregnant with a third. Five children later, I was born. And this is how I came to know my mother: she seemed a large, soft, loving-eyed woman who was rarely impatient in our home. Her quick, violent temper was on view only a few times a year, when she battled with the white landlord who had the misfortune to suggest to her that her children did not need to go to school.

She made all the clothes we wore, even my brothers' overalls. She   **30**
made all the towels and sheets we used. She spent the summers canning vegetables and fruits. She spent the winter evenings making quilts enough to cover all our beds.

During the "working" day, she labored beside—not behind—my father   **31**
in the fields. Her day began before sunup, and did not end until late at night. There was never a moment for her to sit down, undisturbed, to unravel her own private thoughts; never a time free from interruption—by work or the noisy inquiries of her many children. And yet, it is to my mother—and all our mothers who were not famous—that I went in search of the secret of what has fed that muzzled and often mutilated, but vibrant, creative spirit that the black woman has inherited, and that pops out in wild and unlikely places to this day.

But when, you will ask, did my overworked mother have time to   **32**
know or care about feeding the creative spirit?

The answer is so simple that many of us have spent years discover-   **33**
ing it. We have constantly looked high, when we should have looked high—and low.

For example: in the Smithsonian Institution in Washington, D.C.,   **34**
there hangs a quilt unlike any other in the world. In fanciful, inspired, and yet simple and identifiable figures, it portrays the story of the Crucifixion. It is considered rare, beyond price. Though it follows no known pattern of quilt-making, and though it is made of bits and pieces of worthless rags, it is obviously the work of a person of powerful imagination and deep spiritual feeling. Below this quilt I saw a note that says it was made by "an anonymous Black Woman in Alabama, a hundred years ago."

If we could locate this "anonymous" black woman from Alabama, she   **35**
would turn out to be one of our grandmothers—an artist who left her mark in the only materials she could afford, and in the only medium her position in society allowed her to use.

As Virginia Woolf wrote further, in *A Room of One's Own*:   **36**

> Yet genius of a sort must have existed among women as it must have existed among the working class. [Change this to "slaves" and "the wives and daughters of sharecroppers."] Now and again an Emily Brontë or a Robert Burns [change this to "a Zora Hurston or a Richard Wright"] blazes out and proves its presence. But certainly it never got itself on to paper. When, however, one reads of a witch being ducked, of a woman possessed by devils [or "Sainthood"], of a wise woman selling herbs [our root workers], or even a very remarkable man who had a mother, then I think we are on the track of a lost novelist, a suppressed poet, of some mute and inglorious Jane Austen. . . . Indeed, I would venture to guess that Anon, who wrote so many poems without signing them, was often a woman. . . .

And so our mothers and grandmothers have, more often than not   **37** anonymously, handed on the creative spark, the seed of the flower they themselves never hoped to see: or licked a sealed letter they could not plainly read.

And so it is, certainly, with my own mother. Unlike "Ma" Rainey's **38** songs, which retained their creator's name even while blasting forth from Bessie Smith's mouth, no song or poem will bear my mother's name. Yet so many of the stories that I write, that we all write, are my mother's stories. Only recently did I fully realize this: that through years of listening to my mother's stories of her life, I have absorbed not only the stories themselves, but something of the manner in which she spoke, something of the urgency that involves the knowledge that her stories—like her life—must be recorded. It is probably for this reason that so much of what I have written is about characters whose counterparts in real life are so much older than I am.

But the telling of these stories, which came from my mother's lips as **39** naturally as breathing, was not the only way my mother showed herself as an artist. For stories, too, were subject to being distracted, to dying without conclusion. Dinners must be started, and cotton must be gathered before the big rains. The artist that was and is my mother showed itself to me only after many years. This is what I finally noticed:

Like Mem, a character in *The Third Life of Grange Copeland,* my **40** mother adorned with flowers whatever shabby house we were forced to live in. And not just your typical straggly country stand of zinnias, either. She planted ambitious gardens—and still does—with over fifty different varieties of plants that bloom profusely from early March until late November. Before she left home for the fields, she watered her flowers, chopped up the grass, and laid out new beds. When she returned from the fields she might divide clumps of bulbs, dig a cold pit, uproot and replant roses, or prune branches from her taller bushes or trees—until night came and it was too dark to see.

Whatever she planted grew as if by magic, and her fame as a grower **41** of flowers spread over three counties. Because of her creativity with her flowers, even my memories of poverty are seen through a screen of blooms—sunflowers, petunias, roses, dahlias, forsythia, spirea, delphiniums, verbena . . . and on and on.

And I remember people coming to my mother's yard to be given cut- **42** tings from her flowers; I hear again the praise showered on her because whatever rocky soil she landed on, she turned into a garden. A garden so brilliant with colors, so original in its design, so magnificent with life and creativity, that to this day people drive by our house in Georgia—perfect strangers and imperfect strangers—and ask to stand or walk among my mother's art.

I notice that it is only when my mother is working in her flowers that **43** she is radiant, almost to the point of being invisible—except as Creator: hand and eye. She is involved in work her soul must have. Ordering the universe in the image of her personal conception of Beauty.

Her face, as she prepares the Art that is her gift, is a legacy of respect **44** she leaves to me, for all that illuminates and cherishes life. She has handed down respect for the possibilities—and the will to grasp them.

For her, so hindered and intruded upon in so many ways, being an   45
artist has still been a daily part of her life. This ability to hold on, even in
very simple ways, is work black women have done for a very long time.

This poem is not enough, but it is something, for the woman who   46
literally covered the holes in our walls with sunflowers:

> They were women then
> My mama's generation
> Husky of voice—Stout of
> Step
> With fists as well as
> Hands
> How they battered down
> Doors
> And ironed
> Starched white
> Shirts
> How they led
> Armies
> Headragged Generals
> Across mined
> Fields
> Booby-trapped
> Kitchens
> To discover books
> Desks
> A place for us
> How they knew what we
> *Must* know
> Without knowing a page
> Of it
> Themselves.

Guided by my heritage of a love of beauty and a respect for strength—   47
in search of my mother's garden, I found my own.

And perhaps in Africa over two hundred years ago, there was just   48
such a mother; perhaps she painted vivid and daring decorations in oranges
and yellows and greens on the walls of her hut; perhaps she sang—in a
voice like Roberta Flack's—*sweetly* over the compounds of her village; perhaps she wove the most stunning mats or told the most ingenious stories of
all the village storytellers. Perhaps she was herself a poet—though only her
daughter's name is signed to the poems that we know.

Perhaps Phillis Wheatley's mother was also an artist.   49

Perhaps in more than Phillis Wheatley's biological life is her mother's   50
signature made clear.

Writing Assignments

Narrate   **1.**   List three or four of your favorite stories, such as the ones that were read to you as a child, the first one you read on your own, and those that gave you particular pleasure or difficulty in school. Select one from the list and, making use of the basic elements of literature (*plot, characterization, setting, point of view,* and *theme*), tell a story about your experience with that story.

Observe   **2.**   Select a member of your family or a teacher who is a gifted storyteller. Document those techniques of storytelling that make your storyteller effective. Another version of this assignment would be to document the skills of your favorite show business storyteller (e.g., Bill Cosby, Whoopi Goldberg, Garrison Keillor, Hal Holbrook as Mark Twain). Or you may want to document the flaws of someone you know who *thinks* he or she is a good storyteller but who usually bores an audience to distraction. After you have collected your information, identify the most telling talents of a good storyteller.

Investigate   **3.**   Interview someone on your campus or in your community who writes stories for a living—a creative writer on your faculty, a columnist on your local newspaper, a local "master of ceremonies" who is famous for his or her "good stories." Select a specific text (or performance) as evidence and then question its creator about how he or she created it. What came first—the plot, the characters, the point of view? What difficulties did the creator have in fashioning and presenting the text? What point does the creator hope his or her readers will see in the story? Then write a profile for the entertainment section of your newspaper that gives your readers the "inside story" on how the story was made.

Collaborate   **4.**   Your writing group has been asked to perform a dramatic version of "Everyday Use." Conduct a "story conference" to map the "set," select the props, pick those parts of the story (especially dialogue) that can be dramatized effectively, cast the members of your group for different parts, and discuss how your audience might interpret (or misinterpret) your version of the story. Do not depend on "winging it." Write down your adaptation as you would a playscript. Perform it. Then wait for the reviews.

Read   **5.**   Following the Guidelines for Reading Literature (pages 338–9), examine the two poems printed here. Then compose a critical essay on this topic: Compare the tension between romantic love and everyday reality in Richard Wilbur's "A Late Aubade" and Adrienne Rich's "Living in Sin."

A Late Aubade | Richard Wilbur

You could be sitting now in a carrel
Turning some liver-spotted page,
Or rising in an elevator-cage
Toward Ladies' Apparel.

You could be planting a raucous bed   5
Of salvia, in rubber gloves,
Or lunching through a screed of someone's loves
With pitying head,

Or making some unhappy setter
Heel, or listening to a bleak   10
Lecture on Schoenberg's serial technique.
Isn't this better?

Think of all the time you are not
Wasting, and would not care to waste,
Such things, thank God, not being to your taste.   15
Think what a lot

Of time, by woman's reckoning,
You've saved, and so may spend on this,
You who had rather lie in bed and kiss
Than anything.   20

It's almost noon, you say? If so,
Time flies, and I need not rehearse
The rosebuds-theme of centuries of verse.
If you *must* go,

Wait for a while, then slip downstairs   25
And bring us up some chilled white wine,
And some blue cheese, and crackers, and
     some fine
Ruddy-skinned pears.

Living in Sin | Adrienne Rich

She had thought the studio would keep itself;
no dust upon the furniture of love.
Half heresy, to wish the taps less vocal,
the panes relieved of grime. A plate of pears,
a piano with a Persian shawl, a cat   5
stalking the picturesque amusing mouse
had risen at his urging.
Not that at five each separate stair would writhe
under the milkman's tramp; that morning light
so coldly would delineate the scraps   10
of last night's cheese and three sepulchral bottles;
that on the kitchen shelf among the saucers
a pair of beetle-eyes would fix her own—
envoy from some village in the moldings . . .
Meanwhile, he, with a yawn,   15
sounded a dozen notes upon the keyboard,
declared it out of tune, shrugged at the mirror,
rubbed at his beard, went out for cigarettes;
while she, jeered by the minor demons,

> pulled back the sheets and made the bed and found   20
> a towel to dust the table-top,
> and let the coffee-pot boil over on the stove.
> By evening she was back in love again,
> though not so wholly but throughout the night
> she woke sometimes to feel the daylight coming   25
> like a relentless milkman up the stairs.

Respond   **6.**   Compare Alice Walker's characterization of Mama in "Everyday Use" with her portrait of her mother in "In Search of Our Mothers' Gardens." Then write a response to Walker's poem, "Women," printed near the end of the essay. You may want to consider this poem from Dee's point of view. That is, compare how Dee's and Walker's education has prevented or enabled them to understand the true value of their heritage.

Analyze   **7.**   Analyze Miller's analysis of *Family Feud*. How does Miller "set up" his readers with the following comment: "If you aren't a regular viewer of 'Family Feud,' you might enjoy a leisurely description." How does Miller interpret the features of plot, character, setting, point of view, and theme in this "leisurely description"? What is Miller's attitude toward game shows and the kind of culture it represents? Miller's analysis was originally published in *The New Republic.* Think of your analysis as a letter that might be published in the "Readers' Reply" section of that magazine. Then organize your analysis to confirm or challenge Miller's conclusions.

Evaluate   **8.**   Evaluate the effectiveness of Julia Miller's essay on Edwin Arlington Robinson's "Mr. Flood's Party." To supplement your own response, you may wish to read some other critical commentaries on the poem. See, for example, Hoyt Franchere, *Edwin Arlington Robinson* (New York: Twayne, 1968); or Francis Murphy, *Edwin Arlington Robinson: A Collection of Critical Essays* (Englewood Cliffs, N.J.: Prentice, 1970). Then write an extended commentary to Julia explaining those aspects of the poem you and other commentators have noticed that might enrich this student's interpretation of the poem should she decide to revise her essay.

Argue   **9.**   Read some biographical and critical analyses of one of the black women writers Walker mentions in her essay—e.g., Phillis Wheatley, Nella Larsen, Zora Neale Hurston. Select one poem or story by that writer that seems to support Walker's thesis about "contrary instincts." Then write a critical essay in which you demonstrate how the poem or story reveals the specific causes of those "contrary instincts."

Argue   **10.**   Compile a brief anthology of poems that focus on a theme—childhood, education, nature, war. Select and organize the poems so that they develop engaging perspectives on the theme. Then write an introduction presenting the specific thesis your readers will discover by reading your anthology.

13

Planning the Research Paper

You will probably write a number of research papers (also called library or term papers) during your formal education, papers that will figure prominently in your course grades but also provide you with an opportunity to discover new ways of thinking and writing. Noted historian Barbara Tuchman remembers researching her undergraduate honors thesis as "the single most formative experience of my career. . . . It was not a tutor or a teacher or a fellow student or a great brook or the shining example of some famous lecturer. . . . It was the stacks at Widener [library]. They were *my* Archimedes' bathtub, my burning bush, my dish of mold where I found my personal penicillin" (Barbara Tuchman, "In Search of History," *Practicing History*).

The assignment to write a research paper is similar to other writing assignments in that you must discover information to fulfill a specific purpose. But it differs from other writing assignments in that your major source of information is not memory, observation or informal reading (as in most personal essays), your textbook or lecture notes (as in the essay examination), or one or more literary texts (as in the critical essay) but—as Tuchman suggests—the books, articles, and documents housed in your university library. To locate the information you need and then to use it in your paper require skills in thinking, reading, and writing that you do not draw on in other assignments.

Chapter 13 introduces the stages you must work through in *planning* a research paper:

▼ Understanding the assignment
▼ Making a schedule
▼ Selecting a subject
▼ Finding sources
▼ Evaluating sources
▼ Taking notes
▼ Filling gaps

Chapter 14 takes up the stages involved in *writing* the paper. In these chapters you will follow Robin Jensen, a student writer, as she plans, drafts, and

371

revises her paper on the controversy over the required humanities course. Robin's final paper, along with readings on each side of the controversy, appears fully annotated at the end of Chapter 14 so that you can see how she made important decisions about her sources and used those sources to clarify her own position in the controversy.

UNDERSTANDING THE ASSIGNMENT

Before you begin working, you need to determine the kind of paper you are to write. There are two basic kinds of research papers. In one you are expected to compile a *survey;* in the other you are expected to conduct an *argument.*

The Survey

The survey is a factual review of what other researchers have written about a subject. When you select a subject for a survey, focus on an issue or problem that has provoked extensive commentary or controversy, such as the causes of acid rain, the effects of gun control, the merits of educational reform. Imagine that your readers are curious about your subject but uncommitted to any particular position. They expect you to examine all sides of the subject objectively and to document your sources accurately so that they can read more about the subject. Your purpose is not to present your own argument about the subject but to identify and summarize the major arguments of others.

The Argument

The argument presents your analysis of a subject that has been researched by others; you interpret the information you uncovered in your research. You work from the perspective you have chosen, and you devise your own method of organizing and analyzing sources. Imagine that your readers are curious and uncommitted but ready to be convinced by a compelling argument. They expect you to acknowledge opinions that do not support your own, but they also expect you to present a forceful analysis, citing the proper authorities to support your viewpoint. Your purpose is not to compile a neutral summary of what others have written but to make your own contribution to a growing body of knowledge. (See Chapter 6, Argument.)

MAKING A SCHEDULE

Your instructor will specify when your paper is due and may require you to submit your work in stages so that both of you can track your progress. If your instructor does not provide a timetable, make one yourself. Start with the deadline and then work backward through the process, assigning a specific amount of time to each stage. Be cautious; allow yourself plenty of time to complete each activity. Be conscientious; work in the library for a certain number of hours each week. And be pragmatic; produce some kind of written material (journal entries, note cards, drafts) at the end of each stage. Post your schedule in a prominent place and consult it often. A schedule for a research paper might look like this:

Time	*Activity*	*Written Product*
Week 1	Study assignment. Make out schedule. Use journal to assess subject, audience, and purpose. Pick general subject. Read background material.	Schedule; journal entries; general subject; notes on background reading
Week 2	Select a specific subject. Formulate several hypotheses. Begin compiling bibliography of possible sources.	Specific subject; several hypotheses; source cards
Week 3	Locate and evaluate possible sources. Begin reading and taking notes.	Note cards
Week 4	Restrict subject. Analyze most valuable sources. Identify gaps in research.	Restricted-subject note cards; new source cards
Week 5	Locate and read additional sources. Take notes.	New note cards
Week 6	Select hypothesis. Develop outline.	Hypothesis; outline
Week 7	Write first draft. Prepare revision agenda for next draft. New outline.	First draft; revision agenda; new outline
Week 8	Write final draft. Check quotations. Complete documentation. Compile "works cited" list. Type and proofread final manuscript.	Completed assignment

Even if you start planning your paper the day you receive your assignment and follow a schedule like this one, inevitably you will have to adjust your timetable as your work proceeds. A good rule of thumb is to add two weeks to your schedule for unexpected difficulties. You may need this time for situations like these:

➤ *Some things take more time than you planned.* Because the article you must read by Friday has to be ordered through interlibrary loan, you have to wait two weeks to complete your background reading.

▼ *Some stages prove more difficult than you expected.* Because your search strategy turns up only a few sources that deal directly with your subject, you have to find new sources or a new angle on your subject.

▼ *Deadlines on your schedule have to be adjusted, making it more difficult to meet subsequent deadlines.* Difficulties composing the final draft cut into time set aside for typing and proofreading.

Writers who start promptly, map out a reasonable timetable, make allowances for setbacks, and work efficiently can produce a research paper on time. Those who leave everything to the last minute will discover too late that they cannot throw together a satisfactory paper overnight. You need to live with your project for several weeks, reading and assimilating sources. A realistic schedule is a written reminder of your goal and encourages you to work at a steady pace, committing your discoveries and ideas to writing as soon as possible.

SELECTING A SUBJECT

Selecting a subject for a research paper is like staking a prospector's claim. You *hope* the claim will produce gold, but you won't *know* until you begin digging. Some instructors, therefore, ask students to select a subject from a pretested list. If your instructor instead asks you to select your own subject, assess potential subjects according to the following criteria of successful research subjects. (Review the Guidelines for Selecting a Subject discussed in Chapter 1 on page 12.)

1. *Select a subject you can research.* This may seem an obvious requirement, but many subjects cannot be researched.
   a. *Some subjects are too autobiographical.* A paper that draws primarily on your own experience—"Growing Up in Oklahoma City"—does not require you to search for information in other sources.
   b. *Some subjects are too subjective.* No amount of research will resolve a question of personal taste, such as "Which is the better poet—Yeats or Eliot?"
   c. *Some subjects are too restricted.* A mechanical process—"How to Operate a VCR"—that can be explained by only one source does not require significant research.
   d. *Some subjects are too current.* Events that produce today's headlines—"Scandal at the State House"—have not been studied in sufficient depth for you to find enough information about them.
   e. *Some subjects are too specialized.* A subject such as "Reactions of German-American Pacifists to the Great Sioux Massacre of 1864" cannot be researched if your library does not own or have access to the required special documents.

2. *Select a subject you can restrict.* Before you begin your research, you may worry that you will not be able to find enough information. Once

you begin, however, you are likely to find that nearly every source reveals new aspects of your subject. Instead of feeling overwhelmed, take control of your subject and reduce it to a manageable size. Two factors will help you:

   a. *The time you scheduled for planning your paper.* Whether you select a subject that you already know something about or one that is new to you, be realistic about how much you can learn in the time available. A subject such as heart disease, for example, will lead to more sources than you will have time to read, analyze, and understand. Restrict your subject to a specific aspect of heart disease, such as one of its suspected causes. Restricting your subject even further, to one method used to control a cause of heart disease, might lead to an even better focus for your paper.

   b. *The space available to develop your paper.* If your assignment restricts the length of your paper, be realistic about how much you can cover in the specified number of pages. A subject such as word processors, for example, will reveal more sources than can be listed in ten pages, let alone usefully developed into an argument. Restricting your subject to changes in American business correspondence or even changes in *one* American business's correspondence with its customers will be more manageable.

3. *Select a subject you can live with.* Writing a research paper requires you to work with one subject for a long time. If this subject does not fascinate you, if you do not care about the questions it poses or the answers you can provide, you will become bored; your planning will be careless and your writing uninspired. Be sure to select a subject that holds your interest.

4. *Select a subject that will appeal to other readers.* Although the immediate audience for your research paper is your instructor, imagine at least two other audiences. One is the authors you have come to know while doing your research. In a sense, you are carrying on an extended conversation with these writers about a new direction in an area familiar to them. The other audience is the intelligent "general reader," who is always interested in new information or new approaches. You are asking this reader to consider your thesis. As you select your subject, strike a balance between the expectations of these two audiences. Previous researchers should consider your work substantive, not trendy; the general reader should find it innovative, not shopworn.

5. *Select a subject you can prove something about.* If you are writing an *argument*, not a *survey*, the purpose of your paper is to use sources to support a thesis. You must be sure to select a subject that will yield a thesis, not a summary of other researchers' arguments. Your subject must be focused, so that you can control your evidence to support your argument, and complex, so that you can develop and sustain your argument throughout your paper.

_____*Exercise*   One way to discover a subject is to explore, in your journal, what you already know about certain subjects. Robin, an education major, tries this approach as she thinks about possible subjects for a research paper in her English class. Read her journal entry and then discuss how she has applied the above criteria for selecting a subject.

2/16 Got research paper assignment. Johnson says write about some issue in our major, but I don't know enough. Only taken two courses—History and Philosophy of Education, Reading in the Secondary Schools. Not even sure I want to be a teacher. I like Lloyd's course in humanities. Great reading. "What can you do with that?" Dad's question. "Well, you can always teach." Mom's answer. So here I am—an education major.

Actually, the hottest education issue is my humanities course. What Lloyd is teaching—or more exactly, what she's *not* teaching. She says it's all political. Part of a national debate. Kilpatrick's column today, "We're Poisoning the Groves of Academe." Am I being poisoned? What's wrong with reading multicultural stuff? Good place to begin. Ask Lloyd about this debate. Maybe she can help me restrict subject. Identify sources. Johnson will ask what I'm trying to prove. Trying to prove I can find a subject. What else?

FINDING SOURCES

Once you have selected your general subject, begin the formal process of researching it in the library. Most libraries, like most cities, try to help visitors by providing tours, publishing maps and directories, and hiring guides (librarians) to work at specific locations throughout the building. Because no two libraries are organized exactly alike, even the most experienced researchers depend on this kind of assistance to help them work in an unfamiliar library.

One reason you will need this advice is because in the last five years libraries, like most other institutions in our culture, have gone through a technological revolution. They still provide traditional resources, but more and more libraries are providing computerized versions of nearly every reference tool mentioned in this chapter. The card catalogue is available on an On-line Public Access Catalogue (OPAC), and most periodical indexes are available on Compact Disk–Read Only Memory (CD–ROM). In addition, most libraries now provide a battery of terminals and printers at convenient locations throughout the building and computer ports in other buildings (including faculty offices and student dormitory rooms) all over campus.

Clearly such technological devices change the way researchers track and compile their sources. But not every library has the same technological capacity. And every technological wonder has built-in limitations that can often frustrate rather than facilitate your research. You will save yourself much needless confusion at the outset if you realize that your best allies are librarians. No matter how difficult or ridiculous your question seems, the librarians have probably heard it or one like it before. And if they cannot give you an answer, they can show you where and how to look for one. Indeed, they can direct you to many more sources than are mentioned in this chapter. You have already considered how to select a subject. Librarians will help you formulate a *search strategy*—a systematic procedure for finding information on your subject. The Search Strategy diagram shows you the sequence of steps in a search strategy.

Background Information

Read several overviews of your general subject so that you can learn about its history, major themes, and principal figures. Such background information can be found in general and specialized encyclopedias located in the reference collection of the library.

General Encyclopedias   These reference works, written for a general audience, cover a wide variety of subjects. The entries, generally arranged in alphabetical order, are not technical or scholarly, but they often contain a brief list of sources that do treat the subject in depth. You can find the main entry about your general subject by looking in the appropriate volume. To locate every reference to your subject in the encyclopedia, you can consult the index, which is usually the last volume. The latter method enables you to see how your subject is subdivided and cross-referenced, and reading the additional entries may give you a perspective that will help you restrict or

Search strategy

revise your subject. Standard encyclopedias include

Collier's Encyclopedia

New Columbia Encyclopedia

Encyclopedia Americana

New Encyclopaedia Britannica

World Book

Specialized Encyclopedias   These books are usually devoted to one or two disciplines or to specific subject areas. They provide a narrow, detailed coverage of particular topics. The entries tend to be more technical than those in a general encyclopedia, with longer lists of sources. Because specialized encyclopedias are available on a wide range of academic and general interest subjects, you will need to use OPAC or the card catalogue to locate them. Look up your general subject and then look for the subheading "Dictionaries." The *Encyclopedia of Philosophy,* for example, is listed under the subject heading "Philosophy—Dictionaries." The following brief list of specialized encyclopedias shows the variety of material available.

International Encyclopedia of Higher Education

McGraw-Hill Encyclopedia of Science and Technology

Rock On: The Illustrated Encyclopedia of Rock 'n' Roll

Biographical Sources   These works give brief accounts of notable figures, listing such information as family history, educational background, major accomplishments, and significant publications. A short list of additional sources is often included. If your background reading points to one or two people significant in the development of your general subject, you should research these figures in a biographical source. Some examples are

Biography Index

Dictionary of American Biography

International Who's Who

Exercise   Robin uses her journal to make notes on the information she discovered in encyclopedias about the humanities. Read her notes and consider how her background reading helps her shape her subject. Note what information enriches, confuses, or expands her original subject.

___

2/18 Only one citation on <u>humanities</u> in <u>Americana</u> index. Entry identifies it as branches of learning that deal with human thought and culture, excluding [?] the sciences" (555). What about Darwin, Freud? Says term originally identified with Greece and Rome, but now covers all [?] languages and literatures, the arts, history, and philosophy. Two cross-references: Humanism and a long list of subjects from Architecture to Theology—probably subclassified by country or culture (i.e., Greek Architecture, Catholic Theology). Humanism. Long entry on preceding pages (553–554) written by Leona C. Gobel, editor of "The Commentaries of Pius II." Strict interpretation (surprise, surprise) of term to refer to New Learning of the Renaissance—revival of Greek and Roman studies. Last few paragraphs devoted to its importance for modern education—"man's [?] single and most important enterprise" (554). No women? Give me a break, Leona! No listing in Americana for multiculturism or cross-cultural studies. Citation for culture all anthropology—subtopics Archeology, Folk Music, Superstition. Maybe I'm using the wrong word. Everything with humanities refers to what Lloyd calls DWEMs (Dead White European Males).

International Encyclopedia of Higher Education by Joseph Satin much better. Based on UNESCO's International Standard Classification of Education (Paris, 1976). First paragraph mentions Renaissance artist Luce Signorelli (woman) and Persian poet Firdausi. Lists all the ways humanities study the human experience. Discussion of literature—comparative literature. Examples also multicultural. Philosophy—I Ching (the ancient Chinese Book of Changes). Art—Japanese and African influence on 20th-century painting. Ancient traditions and new outreaching directions. Contemporary core curriculum features humanities broadening internationalism. Sounds more like Lloyd. But maybe UNESCO line is just as slanted as Leona's. New search words core curriculum, comparative literature, internationalism. Lists good annotated bibliography. Rogers, A. R., The Humanities: A Selective Guide to Information Services (1974)—"best available guide. . . . Essays on fields of study" 1974—dated?

Subject Headings

When you have done some background reading, you will discover that there are many ways to classify, subdivide, and cross-reference your topic. This cluster of categories should tell you three things:

1. You must restrict your general subject (in Robin's case, humanities) to the specific subject you want to write about (the contemporary controversy over what should be taught in humanities courses).

2. You may find your specific subject listed under several headings (core curriculum, comparative literature, internationalism).

3. You may have to read material that does not deal directly with your subject in order to discover a perspective that will organize your information (cultural literacy, feminist criticism, racism, history of publishing, theories of pedagogy).

The best way to discover subject headings related to your subject is to consult the reference book entitled *Library of Congress Subject Headings.* This guide, usually located near the card catalogue and the main OPAC terminals, shows you how your subject is classified and cross-referenced in the card catalogue. Sometimes you will have to use some ingenuity to determine how your subject might be listed. For example, Robin found fairly traditional subject headings under *humanities* and only one subject heading under *multi-culturism.* But a cross-reference to *Pluralism* produced headings such as *cultural pluralism, ethnicity,* and *biculturalism* that might have sources on her subject.

Throughout your research you will revise your subject headings. Some will be eliminated because they fail to turn up sources that focus on your subject. Others will be added because they lead you to sources that will give you valuable insights. In fact, one of the most powerful features of the computerized systems is the "keyword," a feature that encourages you to strike out in a new direction, using a word or combination of words to find a new angle on your subject. If the keyword is listed in the book's title, subject headings, description, or abstract, it will appear in a list of possible sources on your computer screen.

For example, Robin added to her initial headings, *humanities* and *multi-culturalism,* the following: *cultural pluralism, cultural literacy, intercultural education, literacy canon.* She considered but discarded *humanism* and *bilingualism.* Although her subject may seem to be getting out of control, Robin is actually developing several hypotheses about the controversy that focuses on what books she ought to read in her humanities course. Her hypothesis will help shape her draft.

Bibliographies

When you have compiled a preliminary list of subject headings, you are ready to begin building your bibliography. You begin with a *working bibliography,* a list of books and articles you intend to consult as you plan your paper. (When you finish writing your research paper, you will have a *final bibliography,* a typewritten list of "works cited".) Consult a reference guide to reference books, such as the American Library Association's *Guide to Reference Books* (10th ed., 1986), compiled by Eugene P. Sheehy. This guide will reveal whether someone has already published a specialized bibliography on your subject. Specialized bibliographies not only save you time but also ensure that you consult the most significant sources. Such bibliographies are often

```
LB        Hirsch, E. D. (Eric Donald), 1928-
45            Cultural literacy : what every American needs to know/
.H57      E.D. Hirsch, Jr. ; with an appendix, What literate
1987      Americans know [by] E.D. Hirsch, Jr., Joseph Kett,
          James Trefil. — Boston : Houghton Mifflin, 1987.
             xvii, 251 p. : ill. ; 22 cm.
Bibliography note ──────────▶Bibliography: p. 216-238.
          Includes index.
          BSU HAS: 2 copies.
          (KZclt)
          ISBN 0-395-43095-X
          1. Educational anthropology—United States. 2. Culture.
          3. Intercultural education—United States.  4. Literacy
          —United States.  I. Kett, Joseph
             F.  II. Trefil, James S., 1938-   III. Title
InMuB     15 SEPT 89    14411877     IBSUme    86-21352r88
```

annotated, providing a brief description (and perhaps evaluation) of each book and article listed. Specialized bibliographies, however, may not cover recent works. A bibliography published in 1950, for example, leaves you to track down elsewhere the research done in the last four decades.

Three other ways to locate specialized bibliographies are to

- ▼ Check the *Bibliography Index,* a reference work that lists articles, parts of books, and pamphlets devoted in whole or in part to bibliographies.

- ▼ Check the card catalogue or OPAC under your subject headings for the subheading "Bibliography": for example, Ethnicity—Bibliography; Humanities—Bibliography; Intercultural Education—Bibliography.

- ▼ Check the catalogue card under your subject heading or the source listed on your computer screen to see if it contains a notation indicating that a source contains a bibliography, as in the following example:

Card Catalogue/OPAC

After locating a specialized bibliography or determining that none is available, begin constructing your bibliography with the two major research tools in the library—the *card catalogue/OPAC* and the *periodical indexes/CD–ROMs.* The card catalogue, arranged alphabetically by subject, author, and title, lists books and other material in the library. OPAC lists material in the same format but also enables you to find sources through the "keyword" feature discussed above.

Author Card/A = If you know the author of a book on your subject or suspect that a certain author might have written about the subject, look in card catalogue for the *author (or main) card.* If you are working with OPAC, strike A = and type the author's name (last name first). The screen will

Author Card

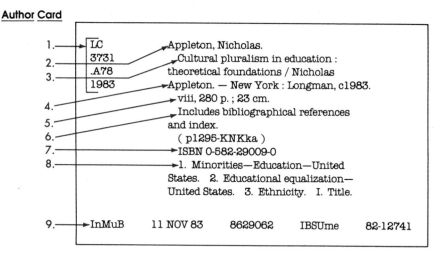

1. ──▸ LC
2. ──── 3731
3. ──── .A78
        1983
4. ────
5. ────
6. ────
7. ────────
8. ────────

9. ──▸ InMuB   11 NOV 83   8629062   IBSUme   82-12741

Appleton, Nicholas.
  Cultural pluralism in education :
theoretical foundations / Nicholas
Appleton. — New York : Longman, c1983.
  viii, 280 p. ; 23 cm.
  Includes bibliographical references
and index.
    (p1295-KNKka)
  ISBN 0-582-29009-0
  1. Minorities—Education—United
States. 2. Educational equalization—
United States. 3. Ethnicity. I. Title.

display all the books the author has written. Type the number of the entry you want and the author card will appear on the screen. It will give you all sorts of useful information:

Author Card

1. *Call number and location symbol (if applicable).* The letters and numbers, in the exact order in which they appear on the card, constitute the call number, which indicates the book's location on the library's shelves.

2. *Author's name.* The last name appears first, followed by additional data, such as birth and death dates.

3. *Title.* The title is given as it appears on the title page of the book.

4. *Imprint.* The imprint information includes the place of publication, the publisher and the year of publication.

5. *Number of pages; size of book; and maps, charts, or illustrations.* Numbers in small Roman numerals (xii) are sometimes used to indicate the number of pages of front matter.

6. *Special features.* These may include the bibliography, appendixes, or index.

7. *ISBN number.* This is the International Standard Book Number assigned by booksellers to identify the book for those who wish to purchase it.

8. *Tracings.* These list the subject headings under which the book is catalogued. Tracings are most useful for locating other subject areas that might pertain to your subject.

9. *Codes.* Codes provide librarians with computer cataloguing information; this information is *not* pertinent to your research or for locating the book.

Title
Card

Title

Cultural pluralism in education

LC
3731
.A78
1983

Appleton, Nicholas.
    Cultural pluralism in education :
theoretical foundations / Nicholas
Appleton. — New York : Longman, c1983.
    viii, 280 p. ; 23 cm.
    Includes bibliographical references
and index.
    (p1295–KNKka)
    ISBN 0–582–29009–0

Title Card/T =   If you know the title of the book but have forgotten the author, or if you suspect one of your subject headings might be included in a book title, look for a *title card* in the catalogue or strike T = and type the title on your OPAC terminal.

Subject Card/S =   If you know only your subject or several related subject areas, look for subject cards. If you are working with OPAC, your screen will tell you how many books the library owns on that subject and will list the books according to date of publication (most recent first). Once you have selected the book you want, your screen will display the subject card.

After you have located a book in the card catalogue or your computer terminal, write down the call number (or print out your data on the com-

Subject
Card

General
subject
heading

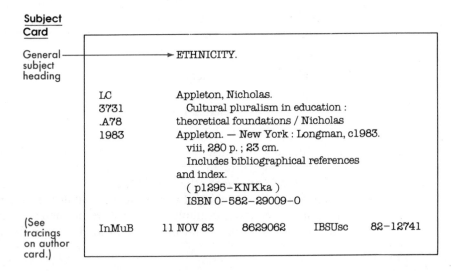

ETHNICITY.

LC
3731
.A78
1983

Appleton, Nicholas.
    Cultural pluralism in education :
theoretical foundations / Nicholas
Appleton. — New York : Longman, c1983.
    viii, 280 p. ; 23 cm.
    Includes bibliographical references
and index.
    (p1295–KNKka)
    ISBN 0–582–29009–0

(See
tracings
on author
card.)

InMuB   11 NOV 83   8629062   IBSUsc   82–12741

puter next to your terminal) and then locate it on the shelf. Most libraries now arrange books according to the *Library of Congress system,* although some libraries retain the *Dewey decimal system* or are in the process of converting to the Library of Congress system and so have part of their collection classified by one system and part by the other.

Library of Congress

A	General works		**M**	Music
B	Philosophy, Psychology, Religion		**N**	Fine Arts
			P	Language and Literature
C–D	History and Topography (except America)		**Q**	Science
			R	Medicine
E–F	America		**S**	Agriculture, Forestry
G	Geography, Anthropology, Sports and Games		**T**	Engineering and Technology
H	Social Sciences		**U**	Military Science
J	Political Science		**V**	Naval Science
K	Law		**Z**	Bibliography and Library Science
L	Education			

Dewey decimal system

In the Dewey decimal system, materials are arranged by numbers that represent subject areas.

000–099	General works		**700–799**	The arts. Fine and decorative arts
100–199	Philosophy and related disciplines		**800–899**	Literature (belles-lettres)
200–299	Religion		**900–999**	General geography and history and their auxiliaries
300–399	Social sciences			
400–499	Language			
500–599	Pure sciences			
600–699	Technology (applied sciences)			

Knowing which classification system your library uses will help you find a specific book. Because books in both systems are shelved by subject, however, browsing through the shelves where you found one book you were looking for may reveal other intriguing, relevant titles you failed to notice when you were thumbing through the card catalogue or scrolling down your computer screen. For example, browsing on the shelf where she found Nicholas Appleton's *Cultural Pluralism in Education,* Robin found other books on multicultural education. Similarly, by browsing in the general area designated "Education (L)," she found books on a wide range of issues related to theories of education.

Periodical Indexes/CD–ROMs Periodicals (magazines and journals) exist on almost every conceivable subject. Their value in research is their currency and specificity, and back issues can show the ways your subject has been treated in the past. Indexes to periodicals are of two types, general and specific, and are available in two formats—printed volumes and computer disks (CD–ROMs).

General indexes list articles from hundreds of nontechnical and scholarly magazines. Individual articles are classified by author and by subject, and most broad topics are subdivided. The most useful general indexes are *Reader's Guide to Periodical Literature* and *INFOTRAC*.

Subject indexes list articles on specific subjects. The articles tend to be more detailed and scholarly than those listed in the general indexes. Here is a brief sampling of the subject indexes available both in print and on computerized disk:

Art Index	Humanities Index
Business Periodicals Index	Music Index
Education Index	Social Science Index

Note: InfoTrac begins by telling the reader how many articles it has record of—in the case above there were 25. The reader then scans and selects which articles are worth reading: 3, 4, 8.

INFOTRAC (CD–ROM)

3.   The humanities in the school—source of enrichment and wisdom. (National Endowment for the Humanities chairman Lynne V. Cheney) (interview) by Tom Koerner il v73 NASSP Bulletin Dec '89 p51(10)
     LIBRARY SUBSCRIBES TO JOURNAL

4.   The liberal arts must be reformed to serve democratic ends. (column) by Henry A. Giroux and Harvey J. Kaye il v35 The Chronicle of Higher Education March 29 '89 pA44(1)
     LIBRARY SUBSCRIBES TO JOURNAL

8.   Thoughts on the humanities. (Three Decades of Daedalus Issue) by Roger W. Shattuck v117 Daedalus Summ '88 p143(7) 45F1962
     LIBRARY SUBSCRIBES TO JOURNAL

Education Information Resources Center/ERIC (CD–ROM)

: AN: EJ361248
: CHN: HE523042
: AU: Smith,-Richard-J.
: TI: China and the West: Some Comparative Possibilities.
: PY: 1987
: JN: Liberal-Education; v73 n4 p6-11 Sep-Oct 1987
: AV: UMI
: DT: Journal Articles (080); Reports - Evaluative (142); Opinion Papers (120)
: LA: English
: DE: Higher-Education; Humanistic-Education
: DE: *Chinese-Culture; *Comparative-Analysis; *Cultural-Differences; *Liberal-Arts; *Multicultural-Education; *Western-Civilization
: IS: CIJFEB88
: AB: Humanist educators must attempt bold cross-cultural comparisons both to test general theories of language, thought, or behavior and to refine concepts central to the humanities, such as aesthetics and ethics. China's ancient cultural tradition is a fertile area for cross-cultural comparisons with Western civilization in the search for enlightenment. (MSE)

Humanities Index (Print)	Readers' Guide to Periodical Literature

Education, Humanistic
    See also
        Humanism
Academic excellence: cliché or humanizing vision? M. Westphal. bibl <u>Thought</u> 63:348-57 D '88
Allan Bloom's battle for man's soul: metaphor as revelation [review article] B. H. Gelfant. <u>N Engl Rev Bread Loaf Q</u> 12:93-7 Aut '89
Is teaching "western culture" racist or sexist? letter from Stanford. S. Hook. <u>Encounter</u> 73:14-16+ S/O '89
Johann Sturm's method for humanistic pedagogy. B. S. Tinsley. <u>Sixteenth Cent J</u> 20:23-40 Spr '89
Liberal education and democracy. S. L. Schweizer. bibl <u>Midwest Q</u> 31:70-92 Aut '89
Making thought possible. D. Bromwich. <u>Times Lit Suppl</u> no4483:220 Mr 3-9 '89
Presidential address 1988; limelight: reflections on a public year. B. H. Smith. <u>PMLA</u> 104:285-93 My '89
A rally for the academic left. J. F. Peterman and D. E. Richardson. <u>Sewanee Rev</u> 97:622-7 Fall '89
What can we do to make and keep peace? L. Kumley. <u>Humanist</u> 48:37 S/O '88
	HUMANISTIC EDUCATION See Liberal Education
	HUMANITIES
	    See also
	      Medicine and the humanities
	      National Endowment for the Humanities
	      Science and the humanities
	          Study and teaching
	    See also
	      American Association for the Advancement of the Humanities
	Blossom time for the humanities. <u>America</u>. 160:283-4. Ap 1 '89
	Civilization and its malcontents [cover story] S. Hook. il <u>National Review</u> 41:30-3 O 13 '89
	The core of the humanities: can the center hold? T. Todorov. <u>Current</u> (Washington, D.C.) 318:12-17 D '89
	Crimes against humanities [cover story] T. Todorov. <u>The New Republic</u> 201:26-30 Jl 3 '89

Most periodical indexes are located in the reference area of your library (see the map on page 42 in Chapter 2). When you have selected the best indexes for your subject, look under your subject headings to find major listings and then check any subheadings or cross-references for additional information. When you look at a specific entry, you will see that it contains (1) the title of the article, (2) the name of the author, (3) the abbreviated title of the periodical, (4) the volume number of the periodical, (5) page references, and (6) date of publication (see the Humanities Index example). In some of the computer indexes, this information is arranged in a different format (see the ERIC example). These indexes provide a guide to the abbreviations that will help you identify the information you need. Also, most computer indexes indicate how many articles your search words has allowed it to find on your subject heading and whether your library subscribes to the journals where those articles are published (see the INFOTRAC example).

In the case of print indexes, you will need to copy this information on a source card (see "Taking Notes," pages 391–6). In the case of computer indexes, you will need to read through the sources available and type *print* for the individual entries you want printed on computer paper (see "Taking Notes," pages 391–6).

Robin checked INFOTRAC, the Humanities Index, and ERIC for periodical sources. She discovered that in INFOTRAC the best search words were *EDUCATION, HUMANITIES*. Indeed, most computerized indexes enable you to expand your search by adding or restricting words. For example, Robin tried *EDUCATION, HUMANITIES, CURRICULUM* and then discovered that INFOTRAC listed all sorts of subheadings. She selected *AIMS AND OBJECTIVES* and found 24 entries. As she scrolled through those entries, she decided to print three that seemed to focus on her subject. Using the same search words for the Humanities Index, Robin uncovered articles on the debate over Allan Bloom's book *The Closing of the American Mind* and the controversy over the humanities curriculum at Stanford University. Her ERIC search was less successful, but she did find one article in a journal she did not know, *Liberal Education,* on the value of cross-cultural comparisons for the humanities curriculum.

Newspapers, Documents, Microforms, and Computer Searches

In addition to the card catalogue/OPAC and periodical indexes/CD–ROMs, four other tools will help you find information on your subject.

Newspapers   Many major newspapers, such as the *New York Times, The Times* (London), and the *Washington Post,* publish their own indexes in both print and computer disk. Newspapers give day-to-day accounts of events and provide details often omitted in later, more general discussions. Consulting them will help you identify important factual information about your subject and enable you to trace its historical development.

Government Documents and Publications   The U.S. government publishes an enormous amount of information on a wide variety of subjects. These publications are housed in a separate area of the library and catalogued according to a separate classification system. There are print and computer disk indexes to this information, such as *American Statistics Index* and the *Monthly Catalogue of United States Government Publications,* but to use the collection effectively you will need help from someone familiar with government documents. A documents librarian or a member of your library's reference staff will be able to provide this guidance.

Microforms   Most libraries do not have space for all the documents they wish to keep. Thus many periodicals and other materials are photographically reduced in size and stored on *microfilm* (reels of film), *microfiche* (transparent sheets of film), or *microcard* (opaque prints). With the aid of mechanical viewers you can enlarge and read these documents easily or make photocopies of the enlarged images. Librarians can tell you which books and periodicals are stored in microform and show you how to operate the microreaders.

Computer Search   With the increasing use of computers throughout the library, the specialized computer search is no longer an essential tool for most researchers. But not all libraries own every computerized index and some disks do not pick up specialized sources.

If your library offers computer searchers, consult with the librarian about your subject and subject headings to determine if a computer search is appropriate. If so, the librarian will use your subject headings to search data bases for books, articles, and other documents. Computer searches may cost as little as $10; some cost a good deal more. Your librarian can advise you whether, given your subject, you should invest in the service.

EVALUATING SOURCES

To compile a working bibliography of books and articles that might pertain to your subject, you must decide which items are likely to prove most useful. The best way to make this decision is through careful reading, but you will *never* have time to read every possible source. The additional flexibility of the computer can also be a significant frustration simply because it produces so many sources. If Robin attempts to read everything she find on humanities and cultural pluralism, she will never finish reading, much less begin writing. If she decides to read, in addition, all the books and articles she can find on education and multicultural studies, she will spend her life trying to keep up with an ever-growing reading list.

All researchers need guidelines and short cuts to help them make intelligent guesses about the potential value of the sources they uncover. Following such guidelines will help you eliminate some sources immediately, discard others after determining that they do not focus on your subject, and concentrate on the sources or parts of sources that will make the most significant contribution to your research.

Guidelines for Evaluating Sources

1. ***The source should be relevant.***
   Whether a particular source is relevant is not always apparent. When you first begin your research, your lack of perspective on your subject may make every source seem potentially relevant. Sometimes the titles of articles and books may be misleading or vague, leading you to examine a work unrelated to your subject or to assume that a work is too general or theoretical when actually it focuses on an essential aspect of your subject. Finally, your reading will occasionally change the status of some sources. What seemed irrelevant to yesterday's perspective on your subject may suddenly seem crucial to today's more informed definition of your purpose. The key to assessing the relevance of a source is to restrict your subject. The sooner you limit your subject, the sooner you can determine the relevance of a particular book or article.

2. ***The source should be current.***
   You want to be sure that the information in your sources is reliable and up to date. A paper on the latest cures for cancer should not rely on an article published in 1945. On the other hand, if you are

analyzing the public's attitude toward cancer at different times, the 1945 article might be relevant. Not all old works are dated, however. Experts in many subjects acknowledge standard or "classic" books or articles that have advanced major interpretations. You should read those that pertain to your subject.

3. ***The source should be comprehensive.***
   Some sources will focus on an extremely narrow aspect of your subject; others will cover its every feature and many related topics as well. Always begin your reading with the most comprehensive source, because it will probably provide the essential information contained in the more specialized sources, and you may not have to read the second source.

4. ***The source should direct you to other sources.***
   Catalogue cards will show whether a book contains a bibliography. Skimming will reveal whether an article contains extensive notes. The most helpful notes include annotations about the sources cited. Books and articles that describe and evaluate other sources help you decide whether you want to read sources you have already found and point you toward sources you have overlooked.

Short Cuts for Evaluating Sources

Locate Annotated Bibliographies   If you are lucky enough to find an annotated bibliography on your subject or if the notes in an article contain extensive annotations, you can determine quickly whether the sources they describe are worth reading.

Read Book Reviews   If you want to determine whether a particular book is reliable, see how it was reviewed when it was first published. Reference guides, such as the *Book Review Digest* and the *New York Times Index,* contain either summaries or references to book reviews that should help you evaluate the book's content and critical reception.

Obtain the Advice of Experts   Many people on your campus or in your community are experts on certain subjects. A quick phone call or visit to these people can help you identify the "must-reads" or classic treatments of your subject. They can also direct you to annotated bibliographies and special indexes. And, finally, they can refer you to unusual sources that you would not find by following a normal search strategy. Such books and articles, often dealing with other subjects, may introduce you to new ideas or new methods of interpretation.

Review the Table of Contents   To determine the way a book develops its major ideas, study the table of contents. The chapter titles and subheadings work like an outline, giving you a general sense of the author's understanding and organization of the subject.

Read the Introduction   To discover the particular focus of a source, read its introduction—the preface and often the first chapter of a book, the first few paragraphs of an article. A few pages is usually enough to detect the author's thesis and decide whether it is relevant and the source valuable.

Browse Through the Index   An index works like a miniature card catalogue, helping you see whether a source has information on your subject, how it classifies and cross-references your subject, how much information it devotes to each of your subject's features, and precisely where that information is located.

_____*Exercise*   The following titles come from Robin's working bibliography on the controversy about the books that should be taught in a college humanities course. (Robin is using the Modern Language Association's citation form, given in Chapter 14 on pages 423–30.) Using the Guidelines for Evaluating Sources (pages 388–9), what guesses would you make about the usefulness of these sources to Robin's project?

Berbusse, Edward J. "The Foreign Student on the American Catholic
     Campus," Liberal Education 45 (October 1959): 428–37.

Bobbitt, John F. The Curriculum. Boston: Houghton, 1918.

Gates, Henry Louis, Jr. "The Master's Pieces: On Canon Formation and
     the African-American Tradition," South Atlantic Quarterly 89 (Winter 1990): 89–112.

Hall, James W., and Barbara L. Keivles, eds. In Opposition to Core Curriculum: Alternative Models for Undergraduate Curriculum. Westport: Greenwood, 1982.

Joyce, William W., and James A. Banks. Teaching Language Arts to Culturally Different Children. Reading: Addison, 1971.

Klassen, Frank H., and Donna M. Gollnick, eds. Pluralism and the American Teacher: Issues and Case Studies. Washington: Ethnic Heritage Center for Teacher Education, 1977.

Leavis, F. R. Education and the University: A Sketch for an "English School." New York: Stewart, 1948.

Ravitch, Diane. "Multiculturalism: E Pluribus Plures." American Scholar 59 (Summer 1990): 337–54.

Seabury, Paul, ed. Universities in the Western World. New York: Free, 1975.

Wright, Louis B. <u>The Cultural Life in the American Colonies.</u> New York:

Harper's, 1924.

TAKING NOTES

As you find your sources and select those that you suspect will prove most useful, start making source cards (or printing the sources on your computer screen) and begin taking notes.

Source Cards/Print Screen

The traditional procedure for keeping track of your sources is to fill out a $3'' \times 5''$ source card for every item you intend to read. The card will help you keep track of each source from the beginning of your research (when you locate the source in the card catalogue or periodical index) to the point at which you type up the results of your research (when you enter the source in your list of "works cited").

The more recent procedure is to take advantage of the availability of computer terminals and printers and simply *print* the source that appears on your computer *screen.* Each procedure has advantages and disadvantages. The source card takes time to fill out but is easier to code and sort as you work on your paper. The computer printout provides a quicker (and more accurate) record, but the computer paper is difficult to sort and is easily damaged or misplaced. Here is a sample source card and computer printout for the same source.

Source Card

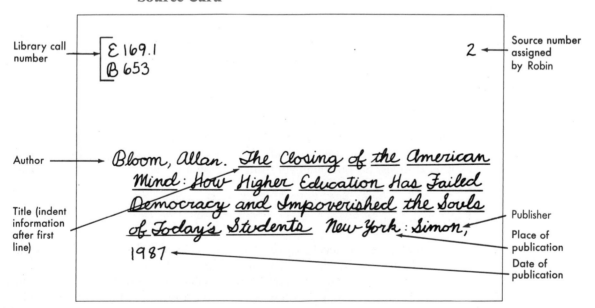

Library call number → E 169.1 B 653

2 ← Source number assigned by Robin

Author → Bloom, Allan. <u>The Closing of the American Mind: How Higher Education Has Failed Democracy and Impoverished the Souls of Today's Students</u> New York: Simon, 1987

Title (indent information after first line)

Publisher

Place of publication

Date of publication

Print Screen (Computer Printout)

```
Bloom, Allan David, 1930-
  The closing of the American mind : how higher education
has failed democracy and impoverished the souls of
today's students / Allan Bloom. - New York : Simon and
Schuster, c1987.
  392 p. ; 25 cm.
  Includes index.
SUBJECT HEADINGS (Library of Congress; use s= ):
    United States-Intellectual life-20th century.
    Education, Higher-United States-Philosophy.

LOCATION: General Collection
CALL NUMBER: E169.1 .B653 1987
```

*Source number
assigned by Robin*

Two pieces of information on the source card/print screen will help you during your research. The *call number* (at the left on the source card and at the bottom of the computer printout) enables you to locate the book in the library. The *source number* (on right) enables you to code your sources so that you can identify the source without recopying the bibliographic information. Note that Robin has copied the bibliographic information on Bloom's book onto her source card in the format she will use when she types her list of "Works Cited" (see Listing Sources, pages 423–30). In contrast, she will have to rearrange the information on the computer printout so that it will conform to the appropriate format. If you use source cards, remember to copy the information accurately, even though you are not yet sure which sources will surface in your paper. If you rely on computer printouts, remember to arrange the bibliographic information in the correct format if you decide to cite it in your paper.

After you make your source cards or print the sources you find on your screen, use the Evaluation Guidelines on pages 388–9 to establish some priorities for your reading. What sources seem most crucial? What sources will take the most time to read? What sources are likely to help you find other sources? Sort through your information and plan your reading to make the best use of your time.

Note Cards

Note taking is the most critical stage in the research process because it demands that you read, select, interpret, and evaluate the information that will form the substance of your paper. When you return the books and articles to the library, your notes will be your only record of your research.

If you have taken notes carelessly, you will be in trouble when you begin writing. Many students inadvertently plagiarize because they work from inaccurate note cards. The wise procedure is to take your notes precisely from the beginning.

Most researchers prefer to use large cards (4″ × 6″ or 5″ × 7″) for note cards and small cards (3″ × 5″) for source cards. The two sizes make it easy to distinguish between the types of cards, and the large cards provide more space for information. Just as your source cards may become part of your "Works Cited" list, so each of your note cards may produce one of the ideas you will present in the final text of your paper.

Make a separate card for every piece of important information you discover in each source. Identify the note card with the source-card number, the author, and the pages where you found the information. By using separate cards for each note, you can shuffle your cards as you begin to look for ways to organize your material. As you become familiar with your subject, you may wish to write a subheading on the top of each card.

Before you actually write down a note, read quickly through your source to determine if it contains any worthwhile information. If it does, then during a second, more careful reading, use one of the three methods to take notes: *quoting, summarizing, paraphrasing.* No matter which method you use, leave room at the bottom of each card for your own comment. In this space, consider how you might use the note or how it might connect to other note cards you have written.

To understand how to read, react, and write during the notetaking process, consider the following passage from Allan Bloom's *The Closing of the American Mind: How Higher Education Has Failed Democracy and Impoverished the Souls of Today's Studies* and Robin's note cards on it, appearing on pages 394–6.

One of the techniques of opening young people up is to require a college course in a non-Western culture. Although many of the persons teaching such courses are real scholars and lovers of the areas they study, in every case I have seen this requirement—when there are so many other things that can and should be learned but are not required, when philosophy and religion are no longer required—has a demagogic intention. The point is to force students to recognize that there are other ways of thinking and that Western ways are not better. It is again not the content that counts but the lesson to be drawn. Such requirements are part of the effort to establish a world community and train its member—the person devoid of prejudice. But if the students were really to learn something of the minds of any of these non-Western cultures—which they do not—they would find that each and every one of these cultures is ethnocentric. All of them think their way is the best way, and all others are inferior. Herodotus tells us that the Persians thought that they were the best, that those nations bordering on them were next best, that those nations bordering on the nations bordering on them were third best, and so on, their worth declining as the concentric circles were farther from the Persian center. This is the very definition of ethnocentrism. Something like this is as ubiquitous as the prohibition against incest between mother and son.

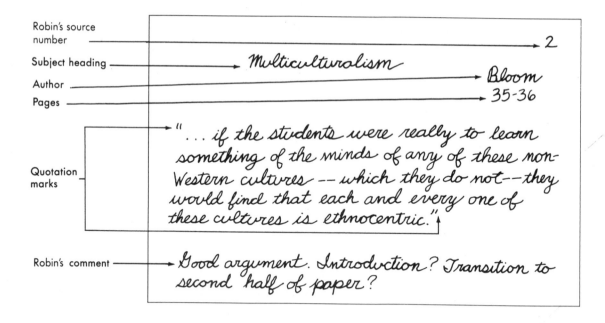

Robin's source number ——→ 2

Subject heading ——→ *Multiculturalism*

Author ——→ *Bloom*

Pages ——→ 35-36

Quotation marks

" ... *if the students were really to learn something of the minds of any of these non-Western cultures -- which they do not--they would find that each and every one of these cultures is ethnocentric.*"

Robin's comment ——→ *Good argument. Introduction? Transition to second half of paper?*

Quoting Sources

Quoting an author's text word for word is the easiest way to record information, but you should use this method selectively. Quote only the passages that deal directly with your subject in particularly memorable language. When you write a quotation on your note card, place quotation marks at the beginning and end of the passage to indicate you are quoting. If you decide to leave out part of the text, use *three* ellipsis points (. . .) to indicate that you have omitted words from the beginning or middle of the sentence and *four* ellipsis points (. . . .) to indicate that you have omitted one or more sentences. (See the discussion of ellipsis points in Section 28 of the Handbook of Grammar and Usage.) Finally, proofread your quotation against the original to confirm that every word and mark of punctuation is in its proper place.

Summarizing Sources

Summarizing an author's views is an effective way to record the essence of a text. Use this method when the author states a thesis or analyzes evidence in a way that either anticipates or contradicts your emerging perception of your argument. Use key words or two or three phrases to briefly restate the principal points in the argument.

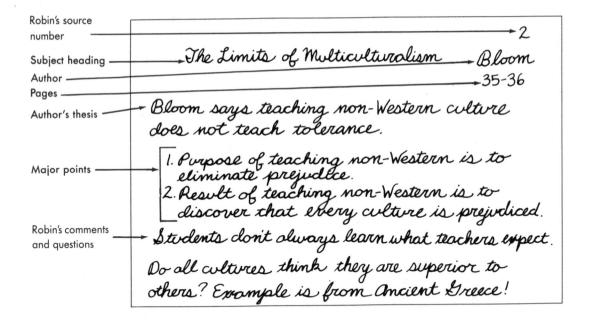

Robin's source number → 2

Subject heading → *The Limits of Multiculturalism* → *Bloom*

Author

Pages → 35-36

Author's thesis → *Bloom says teaching non-Western culture does not teach tolerance.*

Major points →
1. *Purpose of teaching non-Western is to eliminate prejudice.*
2. *Result of teaching non-Western is to discover that every culture is prejudiced.*

Robin's comments and questions → *Students don't always learn what teachers expect.*

Do all cultures think they are superior to others? Example is from Ancient Greece!

Paraphrasing Sources

Paraphrasing an author's views is both the most useful and the most misused method of note taking. It is *not* simply a casual way for you to reproduce the author's views nearly word for word without using quotation marks. Rather, paraphrasing requires you to think through what the author has said and

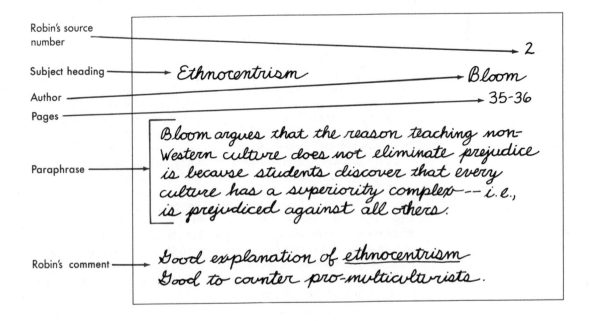

Robin's source number → 2

Subject heading → *Ethnocentrism* → *Bloom*

Author → 35-36

Pages

Paraphrase → *Bloom argues that the reason teaching non-Western culture does not eliminate prejudice is because students discover that every culture has a superiority complex --- i.e., is prejudiced against all others.*

Robin's comment → *Good explanation of ethnocentrism*
Good to counter pro-multiculturists.

then restate the information *in your own words.* To accomplish this objective you must understand what the author has said and then reformulate her or his opinion without adding or deleting significant information and without distorting the intent of the original passage. The paraphrase combines the advantages of quoting and summarizing because it allows you to reproduce the essence of the author's argument and adapt it to the flow of your own argument.

Exercise

Read carefully the following passage by Gerald Graff and then, following the procedures discussed, make out three note cards. On the first, quote a few important sentences. On the second, summarize the major points of the passage. On the third, paraphrase Graff's thesis. At the bottom of each card, state the significance of the note and how you might use it in the paper.

To teach or not to teach the great books? High culture or popular culture? Classics or commercials? Western lit or Westerns as lit? Open canons or closed American minds? *King Lear* or *King Kong*? Rimbaud or *Rambo*? Plato or Puzo? These are just a few of the conflicts that divide the educational world today.

In recent writings, I have been proposing a solution to these conflicts that I think is both practical and democratic: *teach* them. My argument is that the most educationally effective way to deal with present conflicts over education and culture is to teach the conflicts themselves. And not just teach the conflicts in separate classrooms, but structure them into the curriculum, using them to give the curriculum the coherence that it badly lacks.

Not that we should spurn consensus when it proves possible to get it. But when it does not, we should recognize that such conflicts are here to stay and start looking for ways to make them educationally productive. We should use the "dissensus" (in Sacvan Bercovitch's useful term) to make education more coherent and interesting to students than it is now.

The mistake of traditional educational thinking has been to assume that schools and colleges have to *resolve* disagreements in order to teach effectively, that without a consensus on what to teach and why, the curriculum will be chaotic, confused, and without direction. This reasoning is seductive to those outside the university and to many inside. It has inspired a great revival of a philosophy of education I call "educational fundamentalism," which urges the reorganization of the curriculum around a "common culture" based on unitary truths and values.

Unfortunately, the educational fundamentalists fail to confront the question of whose common culture it is to be. Educational fundamentalists look back fondly to a past when there was still enough consensus over the content of higher education that this question did not have to arise. They conveniently ignore the fact that that past consensus was made possible only by the narrow and exclusive social base from which educators and educated then were drawn. It is not too hard to get a consensus if you start by excluding most Jews, blacks, immigrants, women, and others who figure to make trouble. (Gerald Graff, "Teach the Conflicts," *South Atlantic Quarterly*)

Photocopying

Photocopying has had as great an impact on research as have microtexts and computer databases. When you discover a particularly valuable source, copying all of it (if it is an article) or major portions of it (if it is a book) may seem to be the most efficient thing to do. You can cut out appropriate passages and paste them onto individual note cards, thus ensuring that you have precise quotations. You can even review the pertinent information in the original when you begin to write.

But if you decide to photocopy every source you uncover, you will waste a lot of time, paper, and money. The purpose of reading and note taking is to extract the essence of an article or book, to identify the information most pertinent to your argument. Photocopying is not an alternative to evaluating your sources. Compiling a large stack of paper only postpones your examination, reading, and assessment of the material.

Filling Gaps

Planning the research paper is like planning any other paper. As you evaluate your information, you discover that you need more or different kinds of material. As you conduct your research, you constantly refine and restrict your subject. By the time you finish taking notes on the sources you first discovered and the sources you have uncovered along the way, you know where the holes in your research are, what gaps you have to fill if you are to present a thorough and coherent argument.

The research process, like the writing process, is recursive. You must loop back to the beginning to devise additional subject headings and check specialized bibliographies and other references to find the sources to fill the gaps in your information. When you begin writing your paper, you may have to make yet another loop to discover information that forges missing connections. Because you have worked through the process once and know what you are looking for, however, these further efforts should be quick and to the point.

The Homewood Library | Annie Dillard   **Readings**

In this selection from her memoir, *An American Childhood,* Annie Dillard remembers her fascination with libraries, books, and the people who use them. What attracts Dillard to *The Field Book of Ponds and Streams*? What prompts her to speculate about the book's other users? Why does she revisit the book?

The Homewood Library had graven across its enormous stone facade: FREE **1** TO THE PEOPLE. In the evenings, neighborhood people—the men and women of Homewood—browsed in the library, and brought their children. By day, the two vaulted rooms, the adults' and children's sections, were almost empty. The kind Homewood librarians, after a trial period, had given me a card to the adult section. This was an enormous silent room with marble floors. Nonfiction was on the left.

Beside the farthest wall, and under leaded windows set ten feet from **2** the floor, so that no human being could ever see anything from them—next to the wall, and at the farthest remove from the idle librarians at their curved wooden counter, and from the oak bench where my mother waited in her camel's-hair coat chatting with the librarians or reading—stood the last and darkest and most obscure of the tall nonfiction stacks: NEGRO HISTORY and NATURAL HISTORY. It was in Natural History, in the cool darkness of a bottom shelf, that I found *The Field Book of Ponds and Streams.*

The Field Book of Ponds and Streams was a small, blue-bound book **3** printed in fine type on thin paper, like *The Book of Common Prayer.* Its third chapter explained how to make sweep nets, plankton nets, glass-bottomed buckets, and killing jars. It specified how to mount slides, how to label insects on their pins, and how to set up a freshwater aquarium.

One was to go into "the field" wearing hip boots and perhaps a head **4** net for mosquitoes. One carried in a "rucksack" half a dozen corked test tubes, a smattering of screwtop baby-food jars, a white enamel tray, assorted pipettes and eyedroppers, an artillery of cheesecloth nets, a notebook, a hand lens, perhaps a map, and *The Field Book of Ponds and Streams.* This field—unlike the fields I had seen, such as the field where Walter Milligan played football—was evidently very well watered, for there one could find, and distinguish among, daphniae, planaria, water pennies, stonefly larvae, dragonfly nymphs, salamander larvae, tadpoles, snakes, and turtles, all of which one could carry home.

That anyone had lived the fine life described in Chapter 3 astonished **5** me. Although the title page indicated quite plainly that one Ann Haven Morgan had written *The Field Book of Ponds and Streams,* I nevertheless imagined, perhaps from the authority and freedom of it, that its author was a man. It would be good to write him and assure him that someone had found his book, in the dark near the marble floor at the Homewood Li-

Dillard, Annie. *An American Childhood.* New York: Harper, 1987. 81–83.

brary. I would, in the same letter or in a subsequent one, ask him a question outside the scope of his book, which was where I personally might find a pond, or a stream. But I did not know how to address such a letter, of course, or how to learn if he was still alive.

I was afraid, too, that my letter would disappoint him by betraying my   6
ignorance, which was just beginning to attract my own notice. What, for example, was this noisome-sounding substance called cheesecloth, and what do scientists do with it? What, when you really got down to it, was enamel? If candy could, notoriously, "eat through enamel," why would anyone make trays out of it? Where—short of robbing a museum—might a fifth-grade student at the Ellis School on Fifth Avenue obtain such a legendary item as a wooden bucket?

The Field Book of Ponds and Streams was a shocker from beginning to   7
end. The greatest shock came at the end.

When you checked out a book from the Homewood Library, the librar-   8
ian wrote your number on the book's card and stamped the due date on a sheet glued to the book's last page. When I checked out *The Field Book of Ponds and Streams* for the second time, I noticed the book's card. It was almost full. There were numbers on both sides. My hearty author and I were not alone in the world, after all. With us, and sharing our enthusiasm for dragonfly larvae and single-celled plants, were, apparently, many Negro adults.

Who were these people? Had they, in Pittsburgh's Homewood section,   9
found ponds? Had they found streams? At home, I read the book again; I studied the drawings; I reread Chapter 3; then I settled in to study the due-date slip. People read this book in every season. Seven or eight people were reading this book every year, even during the war.

Every year, I read again *The Field Book of Ponds and Streams*. Often,   10
when I was in the library, I simply visited it. I sat on the marble floor and studied the book's card. There we all were. There was my number. There was the number of someone else who had checked it out more than once. Might I contact this person and cheer him up? For I assumed that, like me, he had found pickings pretty slim in Pittsburgh.

The people of Homewood, some of whom lived in visible poverty, on   11
crowded streets among burned-out houses—they dreamed of ponds and streams. They were saving to buy microscopes. In their bedrooms they fashioned plankton nets. But their hopes were even more vain than mine, for I was a child, and anything might happen; they were adults, living in Homewood. There was neither pond nor stream on the streetcar routes. The Homewood residents whom I knew had little money and little free time. The marble floor was beginning to chill me. It was not fair.

The Craft | Barbara W. Tuchman

In this excerpt from her essay "In Search of History," Barbara W. Tuchman talks about the "craft" of research: looking for sources and knowing

Barbara W. Tuchman. *Practicing History: Selected Essays.* New York: Knopf, 1981. 18–21.

when to stop. What is her attitude toward secondary sources, the kind of sources you normally use to support the argument in your research paper? How does she compare the processes of *research* and *writing*?

Selection is what determines the ultimate product, and that is why I use   1
material from primary sources only. My feeling about secondary sources is that they are helpful but pernicious. I use them as guides at the start of a project to find out the general scheme of what happened, but I do not take notes from them because I do not want to end up simply rewriting someone else's book. Furthermore, the facts in a secondary source have already been pre-selected, so that in using them one misses the opportunity of selecting one's own.

I plunge as soon as I can into the primary sources: the memoirs and   2
the letters, the generals' own accounts of their campaigns, however tendentious, not to say mendacious, they may be. Even an untrustworthy source is valuable for what it reveals about the personality of the author, especially if he is an actor in the events, as in the case of Sir John French, for example. Bias in a primary source is to be expected. One allows for it and corrects it by reading another version. I try always to read two or more for every episode. Even if an event is not controversial, it will have been seen and remembered from different angles of view by different observers. If the event *is* in dispute, one has extra obligation to examine both sides. As the lion in Aesop said to the Man, "There are many statues of men slaying lions, but if only the lions were sculptors there might be quite a different set of statues."

The most primary source of all is unpublished material: private letters   3
and diaries or the reports, orders, and messages in government archives. There is an immediacy and intimacy about them that reveals character and makes circumstances come alive. I remember Secretary of State Robert Lansing's desk diary, which I used when I was working on *The Zimmermann Telegram.* The man himself seemed to step right out from his tiny neat handwriting and his precise notations of every visitor and each subject discussed. Each day's record opened and closed with the Secretary's time of arrival and departure from the office. He even entered the time of his lunch hour, which invariably lasted sixty minutes: "Left at 1:10; returned at 2:10." Once, when he was forced to record his morning arrival at 10:15, he added, with a worried eye on posterity, "Car broke down."

Inside the National Archives even the memory of Widener paled. Noth-   4
ing can compare with the fascination of examining material in the very paper and ink of its original issue. A report from a field agent with marginal comments by the Secretary of War, his routing directions to State and Commerce, and the scribbled initials of subsequent readers can be a little history in itself. In the Archives I found the original decode of the Zimmermann Telegram, which I was able to have declassified and photostated for the cover of my book.

Even more immediate is research on the spot. Before writing *The Guns*   5
I rented a little Renault and in another August drove over the battle areas of August 1914, following the track of the German invasion through Luxembourg, Belgium, and northern France. Besides obtaining a feeling of the geography, distances, and terrain involved in military movements, I saw the

fields ripe with grain which the cavalry would have trampled, measured the great width of the Meuse at Liège, and saw how the lost territory of Alsace looked to the French soldiers who gazed down upon it from the heights of the Vosges. I learned the discomfort of the Belgian *pavé* and discovered, in the course of losing my way almost permanently in a tangle of country roads in a hunt for the house that had been British Headquarters, why a British motorcycle dispatch rider in 1914 had taken three hours to cover twenty-five miles. Clearly, owing to the British officers' preference for country houses, he had not been able to find Headquarters either. French army commanders, I noticed, located themselves in *towns,* with railroad stations and telegraph offices.

As to the mechanics of research, I take notes on four-by-six index **6** cards, reminding myself about once an hour of a rule I read long ago in a research manual, "Never write on the back of anything." Since copying is a chore and a bore, use of the cards, the smaller the better, forces one to extract the strictly relevant, to distill from the very beginning, to pass the material through the grinder of one's own mind, so to speak. Eventually, as the cards fall into groups according to subject or person or chronological sequence, the pattern of my story will emerge. Besides, they are convenient, as they can be filed in a shoebox and carried around in a pocketbook. When ready to write I need only take along a packet of them, representing a chapter, and I am equipped to work anywhere; whereas if one writes surrounded by a pile of books, one is tied to a single place, and furthermore likely to be too much influenced by other authors.

The most important thing about research is to know when to stop. **7** How does one recognize the moment? When I was eighteen or thereabouts, my mother told me that when out with a young man I should always leave a half-hour before I wanted to. Although I was not sure how this might be accomplished, I recognized the advice as sound, and exactly the same rule applies to research. One must stop *before* one has finished; otherwise, one will never stop and never finish. I had an object lesson in this once in Washington at the Archives. I was looking for documents in the case of Perdicaris, an American—or supposed American—who was captured by Moroccan brigands in 1904. The Archives people introduced me to a lady professor who had been doing research in United States relations with Morocco all her life. She had written her Ph.D. thesis on the subject back in, I think, 1936, and was still coming for six months each year to work in the Archives. She was in her seventies and, they told me, had recently suffered a heart attack. When I asked her what year was her cut-off point, she looked at me in surprise and said she kept a file of newspaper clippings right up to the moment. I am sure she knew more about United States–Moroccan relations than anyone alive, but would she ever leave off her research in time to write that definitive history and tell the world what she knew? I feared the answer. Yet I know how she felt. I too feel compelled to follow every lead and learn everything about a subject, but fortunately I have an even more overwhelming compulsion to see my work in print. That is the only thing that saves me.

Research is endlessly seductive; writing is hard work. One has to sit **8** down on that chair and think and transform thought into readable, conservative, interesting sentences that both make sense and make the reader turn the page. It is laborious, slow, often painful, sometimes agony. It means rearrangement, revision, adding, cutting, rewriting. But it brings a sense of excitement, almost of rapture; a moment on Olympus. In short, it is an act of creation.

Marita | Mike Rose

Mike Rose is a thoughtful teacher who knows that there are many assumptions and expectations buried in academic assignments. In this passage from *Lives on the Boundary,* he speculates on the assignment that almost caused Marita to trip the "legal switches of the university." What kind of research papers had Marita probably written before she came to college? What conventions of academic research did she fail to understand when she wrote her paper on Bronowski?

The counselor's office was always dusky, the sun blocked by thick trees   1
outside the windows. There was an oversize easy chair by his desk. In it sat Marita, thin, head down, hands in her lap, her shiny hair covering her face. The counselor spoke her name, and she looked up, her eyes red in the half-light. The counselor explained that the graduate student who taught her English had accused Marita of plagiarism and had turned her paper over to the director of Freshman English. He asked her to continue, to tell me the story herself.

Marita had been at UCLA for about three weeks. This was her first   2
writing assignment. The class had read a discussion of creativity by Jacob Bronowski and were supposed to write papers agreeing or disagreeing with his discussion. What, Marita wondered, would she say? "What is the insight with which the scientist tries to see into nature?" asked Bronowski. Marita wasn't a scientist, and she didn't consider herself to be a particularly creative person, like an artist or an actress. Her father had always been absolute about the expression of opinion, especially with his daughters: "Don't talk unless you know." "All science is the search for unity in hidden likenesses," asserted Bronowski. "The world is full of fools who speak in ignorance," Marita's father would say, and Marita grew up cautious and reticent. Her thoughts on creativity seemed obvious or, worse yet, silly next to this man Bronowski. What did it mean anyway when he said: "We remake nature by the act of discovery, in the poem or in the theorem"? She wanted to do well on the assignment, so she went to the little library by her house and looked in the encyclopedia. She found an entry on creativity and used some selections from it that had to do with mathematicians and scientists. On the bottom of the last page of her paper, she listed the encyclopedia and her English composition textbook as her references. What had she done wrong? "They're saying I cheated. I didn't cheat." She paused and thought. "You're supposed to use other people, and I did, and I put the name of the book I used on the back of my paper."

Rose, Mike. *Lives on the Boundary: The Struggles and Achievements of America's Underprepared.* New York: Free, 1989. 179–181.

The counselor handed me the paper. It was clear by the third sentence   3
that the writing was not all hers. She had incorporated stretches of old encyclopedia prose into her paper and had quoted only some of it. I couldn't
know if she had lifted directly or paraphrased the rest, but it was formal
and dated and sprinkled with high-cultural references, just not what you'd
find in freshman writing. I imagined that it had pleased her previous teachers that she cared enough about her work to go find sources, to rely on experts. Marita had come from a tough school in Compton—an area to the
southeast of where I'd grown up—and her conscientiousness and diligence,
her commitment to the academic way, must have been a great joy to those
who taught her. She shifted, hoisting herself back up from the recesses of
the counselor's chair. "Are they going to dismiss me? Are they going to kick
me out of school?"

Marita was adrift in a set of conventions she didn't fully understand;   4
she offended without knowing why. Virtually all the writing academics do
is built on the writing of others. Every argument proceeds from the texts of
others. Marita was only partially initiated to how this works: She was still
unsure as to how to weave quotations in with her own prose, how to mark
the difference, how to cite whom she used, how to strike the proper balance between her writing and someone else's—how, in short, to position
herself in an academic discussion.

I told Marita that I would talk with her teacher and that I was sure we   5
could work something out, maybe another chance to write the paper. I excused myself and walked slowly back to my office, half lost in thought,
reading here and there in the Bronowski excerpt. It was typical fare for
Freshman English anthologies, the sort of essay you'd originally find in
places like *The New Yorker*. Bronowski, the eminent scientist, looking back
on his career, weaving poetry in with cybernetics, quoting *Faust* in German, allusive, learned, reflective.

The people who put together those freshman anthologies are drawn to   6
this sort of thing: It's in the tradition of the English essay and reflects rich
learning and polished style. But it's easy to forget how difficult these essays
can be and how developed a taste they require. When I was at Loyola,
someone recommended I buy Jacques Barzun's *The Energies of Art,* a collection of "fifteen striking essays on art and culture." I remember starting one
essay and stopping, adrift, two or three pages later. Then another, but no
go. The words arose from a depth of knowledge and a developed perception
and a wealth of received ways to talk about art and a seemingly endless reserve of allusions. I felt like a janitor at a gallery opening, silent, intimidated, little flecks of knowledge—Bagehot, Stendhal, baroque ideology—
sticking to the fiber of my broom.

Marita's assignment assumed a number of things: an ability to slip into   7
Bronowski's discussion, a reserve of personal experiences that the writer
herself would perceive as creative, a knowledge of and facility with—
confidence with, really—the kinds of stylistic moves you'd find in those *New
Yorker* essays. And it did *not* assume that someone, by family culture, by
gender, would be reluctant to engage the reading on its own terms. Marita
was being asked to write in a cognitive and social vacuum. I'm sure the
other students in her class had a rough time of it as well. Many competent
adult writers would too. But the solution Marita used marked her as an
outsider and almost tripped the legal switches of the university.

Writing Assignments

Narrate   **1.** Freewrite in your journal about some special childhood experiences you had in your school or public library. Make a list of the sights and smells you remember, the books you read, the people you met. Then compose a narrative about how the library introduced you to new worlds.

Observe   **2.** Review the mapping example in Chapter 2 (page 42). Map the activity of the people in the reference room of your own library. Observe how various students and faculty consult the reference tools and reference librarians in the room. Then write an essay (perhaps a comic one) for your student newspaper on the various *styles* of research you observed.

Investigate   **3.** Interview the head reference librarian at your university library. Ask him or her to discuss how computer technology has changed library research in the last five years. Ask him or her to speculate on what new technologies will become available in the next five years. Then write a profile of the reference librarian for your university's alumni magazine, explaining to former graduates how things have changed since they thumbed their way through the card catalogue and the *Reader's Guide.*

Collaborate   **4.** Your writing group has been asked to update your university library's "Guide." Assign each member of the group to a specific area—circulation, reference, periodicals, special collections, and so on. Ask librarians how the area is supposed to work. Ask students about problems they encounter when they work in that area. Ask librarians and students what improvements they would like to see implemented. Collect your evidence and then revise the "Guide."

Read   **5.** Read selected passages from a book such as Robert D. Altick's *The Scholar Adventurers* (New York: Macmillan, 1965). Then write an essay in which you comment on one of these adventurers or in which you discuss your own adventures tracking down and reading some piece of evidence. Consider your audience as students about to begin their first research paper and your purpose as convincing them that research is *adventurous.*

Respond   **6.** Respond to Annie Dillard's "The Homewood Library" by speculating on the other people who have borrowed and read your favorite library book. You could draft your essay in several ways—speculating about the people who sped through your favorite mystery novel (nostalgic), who skimmed through familiar sections of the the *Encyclopaedia Britannica* (comic), or who studied the theories of some specialized researcher (academic). Address your essay to the community of readers who have also checked out the book.

Analyze   **7.** Analyze the various types of evidence Tuchman discusses in her commentary on sources. What does she learn from each type? What are the advantages and limitations of each type? Then write a letter to your writing teacher explaining in specific detail how you could enrich your "library" research paper assignment by using versions of the kinds of evidence Tuchman finds valuable.

Evaluate   **8.**   Evaluate Mike Rose's assessment of Marita's problem with plagiarism. What are the conventions she did not understand? Which of these conventions "go without saying"? Then read the statements on plagiarism in your university's catalogue or student manual. Finally, evaluate the degree to which these statements provide a clear and cogent explanation of the conventions Marita did not understand.

Argue   **9.**   Argue that your library needs to provide more systematic instruction on how to use its new computer technology. Acknowledge that such explanations seem abstract unless the researcher has a specific problem to solve. For that reason, argue that instruction in the library's computer technology should be linked in some official way with instruction in the basic writing course, where students are writing their first college research paper. Address your argument to the directors of the library and the freshman writing program.

Argue   **10.**   In a letter addressed to the chair of the English Department, argue that students should be required to complete two kinds of research assignments: (1) the library research paper (based on secondary sources), and (2) the field research paper (based on observations, interviews, questionnaires, and other kinds of primary sources). To support your argument, you may want to use both secondary sources (e.g., Robin W. Winks, ed., *The Historian as Detective: Essays on Evidence* [New York: Harper, 1968]) and primary sources (e.g., interviews with students, faculty, and future employers).

14

Writing the Research Paper

For the research paper as for any writing project, eventually you must stop planning and start writing. The large stack of note cards or computer printout you have prepared points to two accomplishments: (1) you have learned a systematic procedure for gathering information (a procedure you can apply to other subjects), and (2) you have learned a great deal about the research that has already been published on your subject. But, as Barbara Tuchman suggests, most people are "overimpressed by research. People are always saying to me in awed tones, 'Think of all the *research* you must have done!' as if this were the hard part. It is not; writing, being a creative process, is much harder and takes twice as long" (Barbara Tuchman, "Problems in Writing the Biography of General Stilwell," *Practicing History*).

Your sources will guide you through the hard part of research—writing your paper. But they can also present two problems: (1) you have probably gathered more information than you can use in one paper, and (2) you have become so immersed in what other researchers have written about your subject that you may no longer know what *you* want to write about it. The most effective way to overcome these difficulties is to settle down and write a first draft.

This chapter will discuss the basic steps in writing that first draft. It will also show you some of Robin's initial difficulties getting started on her first draft. And further, it will give you detailed advice about how to quote and document sources in the final draft. Read Robin's final draft and accompanying annotations in the readings at the end of the chapter to see how she resolved her difficulties and integrated her research into her writing.

The major topics discussed in this chapter are

▼ Organizing a preliminary outline
▼ Developing a thesis
▼ Writing the first draft
▼ Creating the introduction
▼ Quoting sources
▼ Documenting sources

▼   Listing sources

▼   Typing the final draft

ORGANIZING A PRELIMINARY OUTLINE

To organize a preliminary outline, read through your note cards, matching up those that deal with specific subdivisions of your subject. If you have composed subheadings and written them at the top of each card, your large stack of cards will organize itself quickly into a series of smaller stacks. Each stack could become a major section or minor subdivision on your outline. If you discover that several stacks focus on similar aspects of your subject, contain too few cards to develop a significant subdivision, or deal with subheadings no longer appropriate to the emerging design of your paper, eliminate the irrelevant note cards or relabel them so that they fit under a more appropriate subheading (see Robin's formal outline on page 433).

Before drafting your paper, try out several *preliminary* outlines to determine the most effective pattern for your information. After you have completed your first draft, use a *descriptive* outline (or a revision agenda) to evaluate what you have written. Once you are ready to write the final draft of your research paper, prepare a *formal* outline to guide your composing process. (You may want to review the types, formats, and uses of each of these outlines in Chapter 3.) Your instructor may require you to submit your formal outline with your paper as a kind of "table of contents."

Once you have established your categories, arrange them into various patterns to find the one that seems most effective. (You may wish to review the patterns in Chapter 5, "Common Methods of Development.") Some of your subject headings may suggest a simple pattern (a *definition* of humanities); others may point to a more complicated pattern (a *causal analysis* of why universities stopped making the humanities the central feature of the curriculum). Robin's research, for example, led her to study the arguments for keeping the traditional humanities curriculum, for introducing the multicultural curriculum, and for restructuring the teaching-learning process. Because she saw the obvious conflict between the first two subjects, she considered writing a *comparison and contrast.* But she was perplexed about how to arrange her material. Which side should she analyze first, the traditional or the multiculturalist? What was her purpose in comparing the two positions? She sorted her cards again and discovered that she needed to be more precise about her purpose.

PRELIMINARY OUTLINE: THE BATTLE OF THE BOOKS

1. Traditional Humanities Curriculum
      core curriculum
      common culture

```
        teach our culture first
        teach what teachers know
        only so much time
        minority students need to learn about majority culture
  2. Multicultural Humanities Curriculum
        diverse curriculum
        multicultural world
        teach appreciation of other cultures
        teachers need to learn
        make room for excluded
        minority students need to learn about their own heritage
  3. Education Solution
        why do we have to choose?
        why do we have to cover everything?
        how do you construct a curriculum?
        what is culture?
```

A preliminary outline reveals at a glance the kind of paper your sources will allow you to write. As Robin looks at her outline, she sees that her planning has led to several interesting discussions. Her reading about the debate over the humanities curriculum has helped her match up the points of controversy in the first two sections. The sources she read on each side were convincing. Does she have to choose one or the other? That question prompts her to create a third section filled with a series of other questions. Robin suspects that if she reviews her research, she may discover some insights that will help her revise her preliminary outline so that it demonstrates a thesis.

DEVELOPING A THESIS

Developing a thesis is the most difficult task in composing the research paper. Your note cards, even when they are sorted and arranged into stacks, represent the voices of authority. It is easy to be intimidated by your own research, easy to let your sources speak for you. But remember, your aim is to advance your own argument—to discuss and analyze a topic from your own point of view. Like all other writing assignments, the research paper requires you to write with a purpose.

To find that purpose, review the comments you wrote at the bottom of your note cards. If you consistently commented on or posed questions about the ideas in your notes, then you have already established a degree of independence from your resources. As you reread your comments, look for common denominators in your thinking. What fascinated you about your subject? What connections did you see among the various sources you read?

Once you have identified some common themes, convert each into a hypothesis and try to match it to your preliminary outline. Some of your hypotheses may match up easily, leading to assertions that explain each of your subdivisions and pointing toward a thesis. Others may require you to revise the subdivisions or expand the range of categories you need to consider. Still others may suggest that you reorganize your outline completely. The particular thesis you try to advance in your first draft depends on a number of factors—your personal preference, your understanding of the information you have gathered, and your confidence in your ability to demonstrate what you propose to prove.

As Robin looked back through her comments, she discovered that two ideas expressed by other writers clarified what she wanted to prove in her own research. Although she did not always agree with Allan Bloom's analysis of what college students know, she did agree with his suggestion that they don't always learn what teachers expect them to. She was also intrigued by Gerald Graff's suggestion that instead of resolving the conflicts between the two sides, teachers should *teach them*.

Robin began to speculate that the questions she posed in the third section of her preliminary outline might place the humanities controversy in a different context. She formulated three hypotheses that might help her escape the curriculum gridlock she discovered in the first two sections of her preliminary outline.

1. Studying the great books of Western civilization will reveal that they were not written by or about many of the people in Western civilization.

2. The great books of Western civilization need to be compared with the great books of non-Western civilizations.

3. The debate about what books should be taught in the humanities course needs to be changed to focus on how books should be taught.

Exercise   Discuss how each of Robin's hypotheses matches up with her preliminary outline (page 407–8). In what ways will each hypothesis require her to change the major headings and subdivisions of her outline? What information will she have to add, eliminate, or relabel?

WRITING THE FIRST DRAFT

Writing the first draft of your research paper is like writing the first draft of any other paper—it is a discovery exercise. You have to discover whether your planning will enable you to communicate a subject to an audience for a purpose. Some of your discoveries will seem familiar because they are common in every writing situation: the information that seemed so complete in your notes now seems sketchy; and the overall purpose of your paper, so clear in your mind when you began, now strikes you as confused or inconsistent. Other discoveries may prove unsettling because they seem unique to the research paper: your first draft may follow your preliminary outline and support your thesis; but it may seem stiff, mechanical, and dull.

For most inexperienced writers, first-draft dullness derives from the inability to compose a simple, straightforward introduction that asserts a thesis and the inability to weave quoted material gracefully and naturally into the body of the paper. The following sections will illustrate and discuss some methods for solving these problems.

CREATING THE INTRODUCTION

Do not be surprised if you have to struggle with the introduction to your research paper. You have learned a great deal about your subject and are eager to display that learning in the body of your paper. But in order to "get there," you have to write an introduction that establishes the focus of your subject, attracts the attention of your readers, and asserts the purpose of your paper. Some writers cannot write such an introduction until they have discovered precisely what they are going to say in the body of the paper. For that reason, they prefer to write the introduction after they have drafted the rest of the paper—when they know exactly what they want to introduce. Other writers cannot develop the body of the paper until they have defined its exact direction. For that reason, they draft several versions of the introduction, hoping to learn what they want to introduce. Either method will require you to make a series of adjustments—some large, some small—to the introduction and to the body when you revise the final draft.

Robin is intrigued by her first hypothesis but suspects that it may prove too limited. She decides to use it in some form to develop the multiculturalism section of her paper. Her attempts to work out the implications of her other two hypotheses and to find a purpose for her paper produced two different introductions. Her revision agendas reveal her dissatisfaction with them because each failed to establish her subject and clarify her thesis. Here are both introductions and the revision agendas:

FIRST DRAFT: INTRODUCTION

According to the editorials in many of today's newspapers, the most controversial issue currently facing American education is the collapse of the core curriculum, especially that part of the curriculum called Western Civilization. Bestselling authors, government leaders, and columnists report that today's college students know little or nothing about the great ideas contained in the great books that have shaped our cultural heritage. The problem with this argument is that it assumes that Americans have only one cultural heritage. But as Catharine R. Stimpson points out, "Our records of Western culture show not a central tradition, but a multiplicity of traditions carrying on together—sometimes harmoniously, sometimes not" (28).

REVISION AGENDA

1. What did I try to do in this draft?
   I tried to establish the controversy about the collapse of Western Civ. courses and then expand the debate by suggesting that Western Civ. contains more than one great tradition.

2. What are its strengths and weaknesses?
   I focus on the controversy, although the reference to bestselling authors, government leaders, and columnists is vague. I criticize this popular side of the controversy by stating that the great tradition actually contains many traditions. Actually Stimpson states this. Need to write my own thesis. Haven't really said anything about non-Western civilization.

3. What revisions do I want to make in my next draft?
   1. Present both sides in the controversy.
   2. Explain why our culture contains many cultures.
   3. Establish the purpose of studying non-Western cultures.
   4. Compose my own thesis about controversy—something about how to avoid being forced to choose between one side or the other.

SECOND DRAFT: INTRODUCTION

One of the most controversial issues in American higher education is what American college students should be taught in the basic humanities course. On one side are the traditionalists, who argue that students should be given a strong dose of "back-to-the-basics" of Western civilization. On the other side are the multiculturalists who argue that American students need to study other cultures, including the minority cultures within our own culture. The problem with this controversy is that it poses a false dilemma. Students shouldn't have to choose between one side or the other. They need to be taught both curriculums.

REVISION AGENDA

What did I try to do in this draft?
Establish the two sides of the controversy but suggest that rather than choosing one or the other students need both.
What are its strengths and weaknesses?
I set up the two sides of the controversy. Suggest that it's a false di-

lemma. Argue that students need to be taught both Western Civ. and non-Western cultures. Solution seems fair but I'm not sure how to do it. Will students take all the courses? Will teachers know how to cover all the material. Thesis is better. Not sure it's what I want to say about controversy.

What revisions do I want to make in my next draft?
1. Clarify the arguments on both sides—add a few details.
2. Make point that controversy is a controversy because both sides make good arguments.
3. Suggest that controversy about what books should be taught overlooks problem of how they should be taught.

When she completed her second revision agenda, Robin was confident that her third hypothesis had led to a thesis and a purpose for her paper. She reworked the introduction and drafted the body of her paper, encountering a number of tricky problems. She had to decide, for example, how to weave her source material into her text and how to prepare her list of works cited. You will see how Robin handled these problems when you read her paper and the annotations that accompany it.

_____*Exercise*   Compare Robin's two draft introductions (pages 410–1) with the introduction that she uses in her final paper (page 434). How do her revision agendas help her expand her introduction to sharpen her thesis? What specific decisions seem to produce the biggest changes in her final draft?

_____

QUOTING SOURCES

The most persistent challenge posed by the research paper is deciding *when* and *where* to cite your sources to support your argument. For every division on your outline, you have a stack of cards that contains the words and ideas of other writers. If you use this material, you must acknowledge the source of your information (see Documenting Sources, pages 418–23, and Listing Sources, pages 423–30). It's a common beginner's error, however, not just to use sources but to let the sources write the paper for you. Excessive quoting distorts the balance between your writing and the writing of others and makes your paper seem to be a scrapbook of other people's opinions. And it can disrupt the flow of your argument by introducing ideas and images that may not deal directly with your thesis.

To avoid these problems, you should be selective when you quote. Because each quotation creates a special effect, ask yourself these questions when you are deciding whether to quote a passage.

1. *Will the substance of the passage make a significant contribution to my subject?* Sometimes a passage may seem significant because it provides

extensive evidence for its conclusions. But you may be able to make the same point more effectively by summarizing or paraphrasing rather than quoting the passage.

2. *Will the phrasing of the passage seem memorable to my readers?* You do not want to blur the effect of a quotation by quoting too much material. Nor do you want to waste the effect of a quotation by quoting uninspired or unintelligible writing. You should quote only key sentences or phrases—those that convey the author's meaning in especially vivid language.

3. *Will the reputation of the author give credibility to my argument?* The mere mention of certain "experts" produces controversy or distorts your argument. If the authority of your sources is suspect, there is no point in quoting them.

When you determine that you want to use a particular quotation, you have to decide how to incorporate it into your own writing. There are several methods for quoting material; the one you choose depends on why you are quoting the passage and how much you intend to quote.

Introducing Quotations

All quotations must be placed within quotation marks or set off from your text. They must be documented with a parenthetical reference that includes the exact page numbers from which the quotation was taken and, if necessary, the author's name or another word or phrase that identifies the source. A lead-in phrase or sentence identifying the person you are quoting and the reason he or she is being quoted helps your readers follow your reasoning and prepares them for the special effect conveyed by a quotation. There are at least three ways to introduce a quotation. Here is the most common method:

Rick Simonson and Scott Walker, the editors of Multi-Cultural Literacy: Opening the American Mind, argue that "Americans need to broaden their awareness and understanding of the cultures of the rest of the world" (xiii).

The people to be quoted (Rick Simonson and Scott Walker), their expertise (editors), and the source of the quotation (*Multi-Cultural Literacy: Opening the American Mind*) are all identified. But the purpose for which Simonson and Walker are being quoted is not explained; presumably, this passage would appear in a paragraph in which the context or reason for the quotation has been established. Introductory phrases such as the one here help your readers see how your argument is advanced by an authority.

In the second form of introducing a quotation, the people being quoted and the reason they are being quoted are both identified in a sentence that concludes with a colon; the quotation follows, as in this example:

The editors of <u>Multi-Cultural Literacy: Opening the American Mind</u>, Rick Simonson and Scott Walker, argue for a more complex view of the humanities: "Americans need to broaden their awareness and understanding of the cultures of the rest of the world" (xiii).

The third method of identifying a quotation relies on the assumption that you have already introduced the writers' full names and credentials earlier in the paper.

"Americans," as Simonson and Walker point out, "need to broaden their awareness and understanding of the cultures of the rest of the world" (xiii).

Compare Robin's treatment of the Simonson and Walker passage in her paper on pages 436–47.

Length of Quotations

The length (and look) of your quotation will determine its effect. A brief, pointed quotation, generally worked into the syntax of your sentence, is often the best way to advance your argument. But on rare occasions (perhaps no more than two or three times in a ten-page research paper), you may want to quote a long passage that expresses the main ideas you are trying to present.

Long quotations (four or more lines of prose; three or more lines of poetry) are usually introduced by a colon or comma, set off from your text by triple-spacing above and below, and indented ten spaces from the left margin. This special placement identifies the passage as a quotation, so do not enclose it in quotation marks. In such block quotations, the final period goes *before* rather than *after* the parenthetical reference. Here is an example.

> Afro-American scholar Henry Louis Gates, Jr. explains why some people want to challenge the traditionalists' view of the humanities:
>
> . . . the teaching of an aesthetic and political order in which no women or people of color were even able to discover the reflection or representation of their images, or hear the resonances of their cultural voices. . . . represents the return of an order in which my people were the subjugated: the voiceless, the invisible, the unrepresented and the unrepresentable. (105)

Short quotations (less than four lines of prose, less than three lines of poetry) are usually run in with your text, unless they deserve special emphasis. You can introduce a short quotation by one of the three methods described earlier. Or, as in the example below, you can work brief phrases from your source into the syntax of your sentence, using quotation marks and identifying the source with a parenthetical reference. See how Robin uses this passage in her paper on pages 437–8:

In his article "The Master's Pieces: On Canon Formation and the Afro-American Tradition," Henry Louis Gates, Jr., argues that the traditionalists' view of the humanities "represents the return of an order in which my people were the subjugated: the voiceless, the invisible, the unrepresented and the unrepresentable" (105).

Integrating Quotations

Sometimes, to make a quoted passage fit smoothly into the flow of your sentences, you will have to use *ellipsis* and *brackets.* Use ellipsis points when you want to omit part of the quoted passage to make it conform to your sentence. Use three points (. . .) to indicate omission of material within the sentence. Use four points (. . . .) to indicate the omission of a whole sentence or more. Use brackets when you need to add your own words to a quotation to make the passage complete or grammatically correct or, on occasion, when you need to make an editorial comment. (See Sections 27 and 28, on brackets and ellipsis, respectively, in the Handbook of Grammar and Usage.)

For example, Robin wants to integrate phrases from the following quotation from *Cultural Literacy: What Every American Needs to Know,* by E. D. Hirsch, Jr., into her own sentence:

> To this very day, China is a polyglot nation of mutually unintelligible dialects. And in the early years of the twentieth century China presented a cautionary picture of what can happen in the modern world to a populous nation that lacks language unification and standardization. In the absence of a standard tongue China was not able to function successfully as a modern industrial and economic unit.

Notice how Robin uses ellipsis and brackets to incorporate Hirsch's phrasing into her own:

When nations do not preserve and perpetuate a common culture, Hirsch argues, they become like China, "a polyglot nation of mutually unintelligible dialects. . . . [un]able to function successfully as a modern industrial and economic unit" (76).

See page 435 to see how Robin uses this passage to advance the argument of her paper.

Using Summary and Paraphrase

Often the most efficient way to work your sources into your own writing is to summarize or paraphrase them. As you remember from Chapter 13, a summary states the thesis or outlines the principal points of an author's argument; a paraphrase is a restatement of the author's ideas in *your own words* (see pages 394–5). Because the words of a summary or paraphrase are yours, they do not have to be enclosed by quotation marks. But because the ideas come from someone else, you do need to cite the source in your text and document the passage with a parenthetical reference.

The following passage is from one of this chapter's readings, Mary Louise Pratt's "Humanities for the Future: Reflections on the Western Culture Debate at Stanford":

> Current struggles over Western culture curricula—both challenges to them and reactionary attempts to reassert them—also emerge from urgently felt national imperatives. Among these is an imperative to reimagine cultural and civic identity in the United States in the wake of vast changes produced by the decline of its global hegemony, the rapid internationalization of capital and industry, the immigrant implosion of the "Third World" onto the "First," and the democratization of American institutions and political processes that occurred in the two decades prior to 1980.

Robin summarizes this passage in a paraphrase. See how she works this material into her paper on page 437:

The obvious reason for studying other cultures is, as Mary Louise Pratt points out, that our cultural identity is being reformed by the economic, political, and social changes throughout the globe (8).

Plagiarism

Plagiarism is the use of someone else's writing without giving proper credit—or perhaps without giving any credit at all—to the writer of the original. Whether plagiarism is intentional or unintentional, it is a serious offense that can be easily avoided by adhering scrupulously to the following advice. You should document your sources whenever you

- Use a direct quotation.
- Copy a table, chart, or other diagram.
- Construct a table from data provided by others.
- Summarize or paraphrase a passage in your own words.
- Present specific examples, figures, or factual information that are taken from a specific source and used to explain or support your judgments.

The following excerpt from William J. Bennett's *To Reclaim a Legacy: A Report on the Humanities in Higher Education* and the examples of a student's use of it illustrate the problem.

Original Version   A student can obtain a bachelor's degree from 75 percent of all American colleges and universities without having studied European history, from 72 percent without having studied American literature or history, and from 86 percent without having studied the civilizations of classical Greece and Rome.

Version A   Students can now obtain a bachelor's degree from 75 percent of all American colleges and universities without having studied European history, from 72 percent without having studied American literature or history, and from 86 percent without having studied the civilizations of classical Greece and Rome.

That is plagiarism in its worst form. Because the writer of Version A does not indicate in the text or in a parenthetical reference that the words and ideas belong to Bennett, her readers will believe the words are hers. She has stolen the words and ideas and attempted to cover the theft by changing or omitting an occasional word.

Version B   William J. Bennett points out that a student can obtain a bachelor's degree from 75 percent of all American colleges and universities without having studied European history, from 72 percent without having studied American literature or history, and from 86 percent without having studied the civilizations of classical Greece and Rome (1–2).

Version B is also plagiarism, even though the writer acknowledges his source and documents the passage with a parenthetical reference. Obviously the writer has copied the original word for word, yet he has supplied no quotation marks to indicate the extent of the borrowing. As written and documented, the passage masquerades as a paraphrase, when in fact it is a direct quotation.

Version C   In his To Reclaim a Legacy: A Report on the Humanities in Higher Education, Bennett cites the following figures: "A student can obtain a bachelor's degree from 75 percent of all American colleges and universities without having studied European history, from 72 percent without having studied American literature or history, and from 86 percent without having studied the civilizations of classical Greece and Rome" (1–2).

Robin's version (Version C) represents one, although not the only, satisfactory way of handling this source material. Robin has identified her source at the beginning of the sentence, letting her readers know who is being quoted. She then uses an introductory phrase and a colon to characterize and set up the material she plans to quote. She marks the original passage in quotation marks. Finally, she provides a parenthetical reference. By following this procedure, Robin has made perfectly clear which words are hers and which belong to Bennett. See how she uses this sentence in her paper on page 435. You may also want to reread Mike Rose's "Marita" at the end of Chapter 13 (pages 402–3) to remind yourself why it is important for students to learn the correct conventions of citation.

DOCUMENTING SOURCES

The purpose of documenting each source with a parenthetical reference is twofold: (1) to avoid the appearance of representing somebody else's work as your own and (2) to refer your readers to your list of "works cited," where they will find a complete citation on your source. Although there is general agreement about the purpose of documentation, different fields of knowledge, periodicals, and publishers prefer different styles.

The two most commonly used styles are those recommended by the Modern Language Association in its *MLA Handbook for Writers of Research Papers, Third Edition,* and by the American Psychological Association in its *Publication Manual of the American Psychological Association, Third Edition.* The two styles differ:

MLA Style	*APA Style*
Sources are documented by parenthetical reference to author's last name and to page number. No punctuation separates these elements, and no abbreviation for *page* or *pages* is used.	Sources are documented by parenthetical reference to author's last name, publication date, and page number. Commas separate these elements, and the abbreviations *p.* and *pp.* are used.

Here is the same source documented according to each style:

MLA Style

        Studying the humanities should engage students in a conversation, a "cultural conversation they have a stake in" (Graff 65).

WORKS CITED

Graff, Gerald. "Teach the Conflicts." <u>South Atlantic Quarterly</u> 89 (Winter 1990): 51–67.

APA Style

        Studying the humanities should engage students in a conversation, a "cultural conversation they have a stake in" (Graff, 1990, p. 65).

WORKS CITED

Graff, Gerald (1990). Teach the conflicts. <u>South Atlantic Quarterly</u>, 89, 51–67.

Different departments in your college or university may require a particular style; your instructors will tell you which documentation style they require. If you are writing a research paper in the social sciences, your instructor is likely to require APA style. If you are writing a research paper in the humanities, your instructor is likely to require MLA style. Because this chapter is designed to help you write a research paper in a composition class, its examples, including Robin's research paper, follow MLA style.

Sample Citations

Frequently you will need to cite sources that are not so straightforward as the Graff example, such as a book written by more than one author or several works by the same author. In these cases, follow the specific styles given here. Each example of a citation is followed by the entry that would appear in the "Works Cited" list.

Citing One Work by an Author of Two or More Works   If you are citing two or more titles by the same author, place a comma after the author's last name, add a shortened version of the title of the work, and then supply the relevant page numbers. Another solution is to cite the author's last name and title in your sentence and then add the page numbers in a parenthetical reference.

Once society reaches a certain stage of industrial growth, it will shift its energies to the production of services (Toffler, Future 221).

Toffler argues in The Third Wave that society has gone through two eras (agricultural and industrial) and is now entering another—the information age (26).

WORKS CITED

Toffler, Alvin. Future Shock. New York: Random, 1970.

---. The Third Wave. New York: Morrow, 1980.

Citing One Work by an Author Who Has the Same Last Name as Another Author in Your List of Cited Works   When you are citing two or more authors with the same last name, avoid confusion by supplying each author's first name in the parenthetical reference or in your sentence. In the list of cited works, the two authors should be alphabetized by their first names.

Critics have often debated the usefulness of the psychological approach to literary interpretation (Frederick Hoffman 317).

Daniel Hoffman argues that folklore and myth provide valuable insights for the literary critic (9–15).

WORKS CITED

Hoffman, Daniel G. <u>Form and Fable in American Fiction</u>. New York: Oxford, 1961.

Hoffman, Frederick J. <u>Freudianism and the Literary Mind</u>. Baton Rouge: Louisiana State UP, 1945.

Citing a Work by More Than One Author   If you are citing a book by two authors, you have the option of naming them in your sentence or of putting their names in a parenthetical reference. If you are citing a book by three or more authors, you should probably place their names in a parenthetical reference to sustain the readability of your sentence. The authorship of a work by three or more authors can be given in a shortened form by using the first author's last name and "et al." (an abbreviation for the Latin phrase *et alia,* meaning "and others").

Boller and Story interpret the Declaration of Independence as Thomas Jefferson's attempt to list America's grievances against England (58).

Other historians view the Declaration of Independence as Jefferson's attempt to formulate the principles of America's political philosophy (Norton et al. 124).

WORKS CITED

Boller, Paul, and Ronald Story. <u>A More Perfect Union: Documents in U.S. History</u>. Boston: Houghton, 1984.

Norton, Mary Beth, et al. <u>A People and a Nation: A History of the United States</u>. Boston: Houghton, 1984.

Citing a Multivolume Work   If you are citing one volume from a multivolume work, indicate in your parenthetical reference the specific volume you used.

William Faulkner's initial reluctance to travel to Stockholm to receive the Nobel Prize produced considerable consternation in the American embassy (Blotner 2: 1347).

WORKS CITED

Blotner, Joseph. <u>Faulkner: A Biography</u>. 2 vols. New York: Random, 1974.

Citing a Work by Title   If you are citing a source for which no author is named, use a shortened version of the title—or the title itself, if it is short—in either the text citation or a parenthetical reference. If you shorten the title, be sure to begin with the word by which the source is alphabetized in the list of cited works.

> The recent exhibit of nineteenth-century patent models at the Cooper-Hewitt Museum featured plans for such inventions as the Rotating Blast-Producing Chair, and Improved, Creeping Doll, and the Life Preserving Coffin: In Doubtful Cases of Actual Death ("Notes").

Notice that page numbers are omitted from the parenthetical reference when a one-page article is cited.

WORKS CITED

"Notes and Comments: The Talk of the Town." New Yorker. 16 July
        1984: 23.

Citing an Illustration   Place the illustrative material as close as possible to the part of the text it illustrates. The illustration—a photograph, advertisement, map, drawing, or graph—should be labeled "Figure" (often abbreviated "Fig."), assigned an Arabic number, and, if appropriate, given a caption and complete citation. In your text, use a parenthetical reference to guide the reader to the illustration: "(see Fig. 1)." Place all necessary information below the illustration:

Fig. 1. "Your Gateway to Tomorrow." Advertisement. Money Mar. 1983:
        1–2.

Citing Literary Works   Because some literary works—novels, plays, poems—are available in several editions, MLA recommends that you give more information than just a page number so that readers who are not using the same edition as you are can locate in their books the passage you are citing. After the page number, add a semicolon and other appropriate information, using lower-case abbreviations such as *pt., sec.,* and *ch.* (for *part, section,* and *chapter*).

> Although Flaubert sees Madame Bovary for what she is—a silly, romantic woman—he insists that "none of us can ever express the exact measure of his needs or his thoughts or his sorrows" and that all of us "long to make music that will melt the stars" (216; pt. 2, ch. 12).

WORKS CITED

Flaubert, Gustave. <u>Madame Bovary: Patterns of Provincial Life</u>. Trans.

     Francis Steegmuller. New York: Random-Modern Library, 1957.

When you cite classic verse plays and poems, omit all page numbers and document by division(s) and line(s), using periods to separate the various numbers. You can also use appropriate abbreviations to designate certain well-known works. For example, "*Od.* 8.326" refers to book 8, line 326, of Homer's *Odyssey.* Do not use the abbreviations "l" or "ll" to designate lines because they can be confused with numbers. Once you have established in your text which numbers indicate lines, you may omit the words *line* and *lines* and simply use the numbers.

Also, as shown in the *Odyssey* citation just given, use Arabic numbers rather than Roman numerals for division and page numbers. Some teachers prefer Roman numerals for designating acts and scenes in plays (for example, "*Macbeth* III.iv"), but if your instructor does not insist on them, use Arabic numbers with appropriate abbreviations to cite famous plays: "*Mac.* 3.4."

Citing More than One Work in a Single Parenthetical Reference   If you need to mention two or more works in a single parenthetical reference, document each reference according to the normal pattern, but use semicolons to separate the citations.

(Oleson 59; Trimble 85; Hylton 63)

WORKS CITED

Hylton, Marion Willard. "On the Trail of Pollen: Momaday's <u>House Made</u>

     <u>of Dawn</u>." <u>Critique</u> 14.2 (1972): 60–69.

Oleson, Carole. "The Remembered Earth: Momaday's <u>House Made of</u>

     <u>Dawn</u>." <u>South Dakota Review</u> 2 (1973): 59–78.

Trimble, Martha Scott. <u>N. Scott Momaday</u>. Western Writers Series.

     Boise, ID: Boise State College, 1973.

Although the MLA style provides this procedure for documenting multiple citations within parenthetical references, that kind of documentation is often the result of "scholarly" padding and may be disruptive for readers. If multiple citations are absolutely necessary, MLA recommends that they be placed in a bibliographical endnote or footnote.

Using Notes with Parenthetical References

A *superscript numeral* (a number raised above the line) placed at an appropriate place in the text—usually at the end of a sentence—signals a note. The note itself, identified by a matching number, may appear at the end of the text (as an endnote) or at the bottom of the page on which its superscript appears (as a footnote).

In MLA style, notes (preferably endnotes) are reserved for two specific purposes.

Notes Containing Additional Commentary

Thurber's reputation continued to grow until the 1950s, when he was forced to give up drawing because of his blindness.[1]

[1]Thurber's older brother accidentally shot him in the eye with an arrow when they were children, causing the immediate loss of that eye. He gradually lost the sight of the other eye because of complications from the accident and a cataract.

Notes Listing or Evaluating Sources or Referring to Additional Sources

The argument that American policy in Vietnam was on the whole morally justified has come under attack from many quarters.[2]

[2]For a useful sampling of opinion, see Buckley 20; Draper 32; Nardin and Slater 437.

Notice that the sources cited in note 2 are documented like parenthetical references. Complete citations would be given in the "Works Cited" list.

WORKS CITED

Buckley, Kevin. "Vietnam: The Defense Case." New York Times 7 Dec. 1978: 19–24.

Draper, Theodore. "Ghosts of Vietnam." Dissent 26 (1979): 30–41.

Nardin, Terry, and Jerome Slater. "Vietnam Revisited." World Politics 33 (1981): 436–48.

LISTING SOURCES: SAMPLE ENTRIES

In the MLA documentation style readers can locate complete information about your sources only in a list of cited works. The list goes at the end of your paper and, as its title "Works Cited" suggests, contains only the sources you have *cited* in your paper. Occasionally, your instructor may require a list of the works you *consulted*. Such a list would include not only the sources you cited in your paper but also the sources you consulted while conducting your research. (If you have questions about the kind of list you are to pre-pare, ask your instructor.)

Even though the list of cited works appears at the end of your paper, it must be compiled *before* you begin writing. The bibliographic information on your source cards will eventually constitute your "works cited" list. In order to create the list, you must alphabetize your source cards, being careful that each entry is complete according to the appropriate format. As you write, you may need to add or delete source cards. Be sure to identify your sources clearly and accurately in your text and to provide complete biblio-graphic information about each one in your list of cited works.

When you type your final list, follow the instructions given below. For an illustration of this format, see Robin's "Works Cited" list on pages 442–3.

1. Paginate the "Works Cited" list as a continuation of your text. If the conclusion of your paper appears on page 9, begin your list on page 10, unless there is an intervening page of endnotes.

2. List all entries in alphabetical order according to the last name of the author.

3. Double-space between successive lines of an entry and between entries.

4. After the first line of an entry, indent successive lines five spaces.

5. If you are listing more than one work by the same author, alphabetize the works according to title (excluding any initial articles—*a, an, the*). Instead of repeating the author's name with each citation, for the second and additional works, type three hyphens and a period, skip two spaces, and then give the title:

> Lanham, Richard A. <u>Literacy and the Survival of Humanism</u>. New
>   Haven: Yale, 1983.
> ---. <u>Style: An Anti-Textbook</u>. New Haven: Yale, 1974.

The form of each entry in your "Works Cited" list will vary according to the type of source you are citing. The major variations are illustrated below. If you need additional information, consult *MLA Handbook for Writers of Research Papers, Third Edition* (1988).

Books

Citations for books have three main parts—author, title, and facts of publica-tion. Separate each part with a period followed by two spaces. (The first sample entry is described completely; significant variations in subsequent entries are noted in marginal annotations.)

A Book by a Single Author or Agency

> Tuchman, Barbara W. <u>A Distant Mirror: The Calamitous 14th
>   Century</u>. New York: Knopf, 1978.

▼ The author's last name comes before the given name or initial to facilitate alphabetizing. Use the name exactly as it appears on the title page of the sources.

▼ If the book is the work of an agency (committee, organization, or department) instead of an individual, the name of the agency takes the place of the author's name.

▼ If no author or agency is given, the citation begins with and is alphabetized by the title of the source.

▼ The title and subtitle of the book are underlined.

▼ The place of publication, the publisher, and the date of publication are named in that order and are punctuated and spaced as in the preceding Tuchman citation. A colon separates the place of publication from the name of the publishing company, and a comma separates the publisher's name from the date.

▼ If more than one place of publication is given on the title page, mention only the first.

▼ If the place of publication might be unfamiliar or unclear to your readers, add an abbreviation identifying the appropriate state or country: Cambridge, MA.

▼ Shorten the publisher's name, as long as the shortened form is easily identifiable: *Houghton Mifflin* can be *Houghton; Harvard University Press* can be *Harvard UP*.

▼ When you cannot locate one or more pieces of information concerning the facts of publication, use these abbreviations in the appropriate positions.

No place: n.p.
No publisher: n.p.
No date: n.d.

A Book by Two or Three Authors

Ashby, Eric, and Mary Anderson. <u>The Rise of the Student Estate in Britain</u>. Cambridge, MA: Harvard UP, 1970.

Lee, Lawrence, George Seddon, and Frances Stephens. <u>Stained Glass</u>. New York: Crown, 1976.

A Book by Three or More Authors

Sheridan, Marion C., et al. <u>The Motion Picture and the Teaching of English</u>. New York: Appleton, 1965.

A Book with an Editor

Kuhn, Thomas, ed. <u>The Essential Tension: Selected Studies in Scientific Tradition and Change</u>. Chicago: U of Chicago P, 1977.

A Book with an Author and an Editor

Emphasis on author   Ginsberg, Allen. Journals: Early Fifties, Early Sixties. Ed. Gordon Ball. New York: Grove, 1977.

Emphasis on editor   Ball, Gordon, ed. Journals: Early Fifties, Early Sixties. By Allen Ginsberg. New York: Grove, 1977.

Works in an Anthology

Citation of one work only   Tyler, Anne. "Still Just Writing." The Writer on Her Work. Ed. Janet Sternberg. New York: Norton, 1980, 3–16.

Basis for multiple citations   Sternberg, Janet, ed. The Writer on Her Work. New York: Norton, 1980.

Multiple citations   Walker, Alice. "One Child of One's Own: A Meaningful Digression Within the Works." Sternberg 121–40.

Walker, Margaret. "On Being Female, Black, and Free." Sternberg 95–106.

An Article in an Alphabetically Arranged Reference Book

"Graham, Martha." Who's Who of American Women. 13th ed. 1983–1984.

Frequently revised work   Hayward, Jane. "Stained Glass." Encyclopedia Americana 1983 ed.

A Multivolume Work

Citing all volumes   Blotner, Joseph. Faulkner: A Biography. 2 vols. New York: Random, 1974.

Citing one volume   Blotner, Joseph. Faulkner: A Biography. New York: Random, 1974. Vol. 2.

An Edition Other than the First

Bailey, Sydney. British Parliamentary Research. 3rd ed. Boston: Houghton, 1971.

An Introduction, Preface, Foreword, or Afterword

Bernstein, Carl. Afterword. Poison Penmanship: The Gentle Art of Muckraking. By Jessica Mitford. New York: Random, 1979. 275–77.

A Book in a Series

Longley, John L., Jr. Robert Penn Warren. Southern Writers Series 2. Austin, TX: Steck, 1969.

A Republished Book

Malamud, Bernard. The Natural. 1952. New York: Avon, 1980.

Published Proceedings of a Conference

Shusterman, Alan J., ed. Capitalizing on Ideas: New Alliances for Business. Proceedings from a Conference of Indiana Business Leaders. 10–11 April 1983. Indianapolis: Indiana Committee for the Humanities, 1983.

A Translation

Mâle, Émile. Chartres. Trans. Sara Wilson. New York: Harper, 1983.

A Book with a Title Usually Italicized in Its Title

Miller, James E., Jr. A Critical Guide to Leaves of Grass. Chicago: U of Chicago P, 1957.

Articles

Citations for articles in periodicals, like citations for books, contain three parts: author, title, and facts of publication. But articles include more complicated facts of publication such as the periodical title, the volume number, year of publication, and inclusive page numbers. You can usually find this information on the first page of the article and on the cover or title page of the periodical. The first entry is discussed completely; significant variations in subsequent entries are noted in marginal annotations.

Fulwiler, Toby. "How Well Does Writing Across the Curriculum Work?" College English 46 (1984): 112–25.

▼ Cite author (last name first).
▼ Place title of article within quotation marks.
▼ Underline title of periodical.
▼ Place volume number after title of periodical.
▼ Enclose year of publication within parentheses.
▼ Use colon to separate date of periodical from inclusive page numbers of article.
▼ If a periodical pages its issues continuously through an annual volume, as does *College English,* give only the volume number, not the issue number.

An Article in a Journal that Pages Each Issue Separately or Uses Only Issue Numbers

Bird, Harry. "Some Aspects of Prejudice in the Roman World." University of Windsor Review 10.1 (1975): 64–75.

An Article from a Monthly or Bimonthly Periodical

Jacobs, Jane. "The Dynamic of Decline." Atlantic April 1984: 98–114.

An Article from a Weekly or Biweekly Periodical

Arlen, Michael J. "Onward and Upward With the Arts: Thirty Seconds." The New Yorker 15 Oct. 1979: 55–146.

Article from a Daily Newspaper

Article with byline

Whited, Charles. "The Priceless Treasure of the Marquesas." Miami Herald 15 July 1973: 1.

Separately paginated sections

"Culture Shock: Williamsburg and Disney World, Back to Back." New York Times 21 Sept. 1975: sec. 10:1.

Newspaper title that does not include city name

"Oliver North Faces Congress." Union Star [Schenectady, NY] 7 July 1987: 1.

Editorial, Letter to Editor, Review

"From Good News to Bad." Editorial. Washington Post 16 July 1984: 10.

Coldwater, Charles F., MD. Letter. The Muncie Star 17 June 1987: 4.

DeCurtis, Anthony. "Bob Dylan's Blue Highways." Rev. of The Bootleg Series, Volumes 1–3 (Rare and Unreleased), 1961–1991, by Bob Dylan. Rolling Stone 4 April 1991: 53–55.

Griswold, Charles L., Jr. "Soul Food." Rev. of Statecraft as Soulcraft: What Government Does, by George F. Will. American Scholar 53 (1984): 401–06.

An Article Whose Title Contains a Quotation or a Title Within Quotation Marks

Carpenter, Lynette. "The Daring Gift in Ellen Glasgow's 'Dare's Gift.'" Studies in Short Fiction 21 (1984): 95–102.

An Abstract from Dissertation Abstracts (DA) or Dissertation Abstracts International (DAI)

Creek, Mardena Bridges. "Myth, Wound, Accommodation: American Literary Response to the War in Vietnam." DAI 43 (1982): 3593A. Ball State U.

Other Sources

You may sometimes have to list sources other than books and articles. In fact, MLA changed the name of its concluding list of sources from "Bibliography" (literally "description of books") to "Works Cited" because of the variety of nonbook sources that may be cited. The particular treatment of "other sources" depends on what information is available and what information needs to be included to enable readers to locate the same material themselves. Here are some sample entries with brief annotations.

Government Document

United States. Cong. House Committee on the Judiciary. Immigration
 and Nationality Act with Amendments and Notes on Related Laws.
 7th ed. Washington: GPO, 1980.

Computer Software

Nota Bene. Computer software. Dragonfly Software, 1988. IBM, 512k,
 PC-DOS 2.0, disk.

Films; Radio and Television Programs

The Last Emperor. Dir. Bernardo Bertolucci. With John Lone and Peter
 O'Toole. Columbia, 1987.

"If God Ever Listened: A Portrait of Alice Walker." Horizons. Prod. Jane
 Rosenthal. NPR. WBST, Muncie. 3 Mar. 1984.

"The Hero's Adventure." Moyers: Joseph Campbell and the Power of
 Myth. Prod. Catherine Tatge. PBS. WNET, New York. 23 May 1988.

Performances

A Walk in the Woods. By Lee Blessing. Dir. Des McAnuff. With Sam Wa-
 terston and Robert Prosky. Booth Theatre, New York. 17 May
 1988.

Ozawa, Seiji, cond. Boston Symphony Orch. Concert. Symphony Hall,
 Boston. 30 Sept. 1988.

Recordings

Mozart, Wolfgang A. Cosi Fan Tutte. With Kiri Te Kanawa, Frederica
 von Stade, David Rendall, and Philippe Huttenlocher. Cond. Alain
 Lombard. Strasbourg Philharmonic Orch. RCA, SRL3-2629, 1978.

Simon, Paul. "Under African Skies." Graceland. Warner's, 7599-25447-1,
 1986.

Works of Art

Botticelli, Sandro. Giuliano de' Medici. Samuel H. Kress Collection.
    National Gallery of Art, Washington.

Rodin, Auguste. The Gate of Hell. Rodin Museum, Paris.

Maps and Charts

Sonoma and Napa Counties. Map. San Francisco: California State Auto-
    mobile Assn., 1984.

Published and Unpublished Letters

Fitzgerald, F. Scott. "To Ernest Hemingway." 1 June 1934. The Letters
    of F. Scott Fitzgerald. Ed. Andrew Turnbull. New York: Scribner's,
    1963. 308–10.

Stowe, Harriet Beecher. Letter to George Eliot. 25 May 1869. Berg Col-
    lection. New York Public Library.

Published and Unpublished Interviews

Ellison, Ralph. "Indivisible Man." Interview. With James Alan McPher-
    son. Atlantic Dec. 1970: 45–60.

McPhee, John. Personal interview. 4 November 1986.

TYPING THE FINAL DRAFT

When you type the final draft of your research paper, follow these general
specifications.

1. Use white, 20-pound bond, 8½" × 11" paper.
2. Use a pica typewriter or high quality printer.
3. Double-space the text throughout—*including* quotations, notes, and
   "works cited" list.
4. Maintain margins of 1 inch at the top and the bottom and on both sides
   of each page.
5. Indent 5 spaces at the beginning of each paragraph.
6. Leave 2 spaces after periods and other terminal marks of punctuation.
7. Leave 1 space after commas and other internal marks of punctuation.
8. Do not supply a title page. Instead, type your name, your instructor's
   name, the course title, and the date on separate lines (double-spacing
   between lines) at the upper left margin.

9. A formal outline, if required, should be attached to the front of the paper. Use topics or full sentences, and follow the outline formats discussed in Chapter 3. Type the title of your paper at the top of the first page of the outline; then type your thesis, triple-spaced below the title. Do not list your introduction or conclusion in your outline.

10. Type your title at the top of the first page of your paper. Triple space to the first sentence of your paper.

11. Number the pages of your manuscript consecutively, type your last name and the page number in the upper-right corner.

12. Label any illustrations. Position the caption 2 line-spaces below the figure, and align the caption with the left side of the figure. Mount each illustration on bond paper using rubber cement or dry-mount tissue.

When you have finished typing, proofread every page carefully— including the title page, the formal outline, captions, endnotes, and "Works Cited" list. Make a photocopy of your paper. If your instructor has asked you to hand in your note cards with your paper, arrange them in a logical order, put a rubber band around them, and place them in an envelope.

The Humanities Controversy
    [Research Paper: Student Model] | Robin Jensen

Reading the final draft of Robin's research paper will demonstrate several valuable lessons. You will see that an informed writer can make any subject, however unfamiliar, significant and interesting. You will see how a carefully crafted essay evolves from the complex and often confusing attempts to discover a subject, audience, and purpose. And you will see how Robin uses the specific techniques of analyzing, paraphrasing, quoting, and documenting sources to advance her purpose.

Consider, too, as you read, how Robin has positioned her own argument in relation to the two sides in the controversy. Then examine examples of contending positions in the two readings that follow: William J. Bennett (traditionalist) and Mary Louise Pratt (multiculturalist).

Jensen 1

Robin Jensen

Mr. Johnson

English 104, Section 32

2 May 1991

The Humanities Controversy

<u>Thesis</u>: The battle over what students should be taught in the humanities course has overlooked the question of how they learn.

   I. The traditionalists argue that students should be taught the culture of Western Civilization.

       A. The university no longer teaches the traditional humanities curriculum.

       B. Students need to become culturally literate about the great tradition of Western Civilization.

  II. The multiculturalists argue that students should be taught other cultures.

       A. The university should teach the cultures that are reforming our cultural identity.

       B. Students need to understand cultures that challenge the basic assumptions of Western Civilization.

 III. Possible ways to resolve controversy

       A. Teach separate versions of the curriculum.

       B. Combine the two curriculums.

  IV. The controversy has overlooked how students learn.

       A. Both sides see the student as passive.

       B. Teachers should invite students to participate.

       C. Students who participate in the controversy claim their legacy in the humanities.

Jensen 1

Robin Jensen

Mr. Johnson

English 104, Section 32

1 May 1991

Title: *Robin uses title to identify her subject.*

Indent five spaces

The Humanities Controversy

    For the last ten years, American education has been engaged
in a complex and contentious debate about what books ought to be
taught in the university's basic humanities course. On the one
side, the traditionalists argue that students should be taught the
great books of Western Civilization. On the other side, the
multiculturalists argue that students should be taught the great
books of other civilizations, including the neglected works of
minority writers within our culture. Like all controversies, each
side presents compelling evidence to support its position. But
their categorical assertions often prevent them from seeing what
is really at stake in the controversy. In this case, the battle
over what students should be taught has overlooked the question of
how they learn.

1

Introduction: *Robin established context for her thesis.*

    According to the traditionalists, the problem began in the
sixties when American educators exhibited what William J. Bennett
has characterized as a "loss of nerve" (<u>To Reclaim</u> 1). Confronted
by the emergence of ethnic studies and the challenges of the civil
rights movement, American educators ceased to argue for a unified
humanities curriculum that celebrated the achievements of Western
Civilization. Instead, they opened up the university curriculum
to a bewildering array of specialized courses, producing what
Allan Bloom has called "educational anarchy" (337).

2

Documentation: *Robin includes shortened title to identify which of Bennett's texts she is citing.*

Jensen 2

3

The result, according to Bloom, is that "the university now offers no distinctive visage . . . no vision . . . of what an educated human being is" (337). Graduates now are distinguished by what they do not know. In his <u>To Reclaim a Legacy: A Report on the Humanities in Higher Education</u>, Bennett cites the following figures: "A student can obtain a bachelor's degree from 75 percent of all American colleges and universities without having studied European history, from 72 percent without having studied American literature or history, and from 86 percent without having studied the civilizations of classical Greece and Rome" (1-2). Several years later, in her <u>Humanities in America: A Report to the President, the Congress and the American People</u>, Lynne V. Cheney continues to tabulate the crisis: "it is possible to graduate now, as it was five years ago, from almost 80 percent of the nation's four-year colleges and universities without taking a course in the history of Western Civilization" (5).

Such statistics explain E. D. Hirsch, Jr.'s call for "cultural literacy." He argues that "at the heart of modern nationhood is the teaching of literacy and a common culture through a national system of education" (73). When nations do not preserve and perpetuate a common culture, Hirsch argues, they become like China, "a polyglot nation of mutually unintelligible dialects. . . . [un]able to function successfully as a modern industrial and economic unit" (76). To avoid such disasters, Hirsch offers a list of terms, "What Literate Americans Know" and encourages teachers to begin teaching it (146-215).[1]

4

Introduction of Quotation: Robin names author and source to introduce quotation.

Documenting Quotation: Robin identifies author she intends to quote throughout paragraph.

Endnote: Robin uses superscript numerals to give additional information on Hirsch's "cultural literacy" project.

Jensen 3

Hirsch's argument assumes that the great tradition of Western Civilization can be represented by a basic list and that although there is <u>other</u> information citizens could learn, learning <u>this</u> information is crucial to "our national survival, as well as our national identity" (Stimpson 29). We should study Western Civilization because it is ours (Bennett "Why the West?" 39), and because it "forms the basis of our society's laws and instructions" (Cheney 12).

5

Although traditionalists such as Hirsch make a persuasive argument, Rick Simonson and Scott Walker, the editors of <u>Multi-Cultural Literacy: Opening the American Mind</u>, remain unconvinced, finding their opponents' position "overridingly static" and "shallow" (x). The traditionalists, they argue, "seem to think that most of what constitutes contemporary American and world culture was immaculately conceived by a few men in Greece around 900 B.C., came to its full expression in Europe a few centuries later, and began to decline around the middle of the nineteenth century" (x).

6

The multiculturalist side in the humanities controversy focuses on the "out-dated" notion of the traditionalists' definition of culture (Simonson and Walker x). What the traditionalists see as the fragmentation of Western Civilization, the multiculturalists see as the fulfillment of "a more democratic society in which there will be greater equality in all spheres of life" (Appleton 6). Instead of celebrating the superiority of <u>our</u> culture, the multiculturalists argue that

7

Documentation: Robin cites specific sources to document ideas paraphrased and quoted in independent clauses.

Quotation: Because Robin has established the source at beginning of paragraph, she assumes her readers know the source for this citation.

Jensen 4

"Americans need to broaden their awareness and understanding of the cultures of the rest of the world" (Simonson and Walker xiii).

Paraphrase: *Robin paraphrases Pratt's description of multicultural world.*

The obvious reason for studying other cultures is, as Mary Louise Pratt points out, that our cultural identity is being reformed by the economic, political, and social changes throughout the world (8). The goods Americans buy, the treaties they sign, and many of the students who enroll in their universities are no longer the products of a uniform Western culture. "To see . . . an entire cultural tradition as if it were a self-contained whole is," as one of Pratt's colleagues comments, "like listening to only one side of a phone conversation" (13).

8

Paraphrase: *Source identified in parentheses.*

Another reason for studying other cultures is to see how they challenge the basic assumptions of our culture (Graff 62). Sometimes those challenges come from cultures across the globe; sometimes they come from cultures that have been suppressed in our own back yard. As Gerald Graff points out, it is easy to celebrate the glories of Western Civilization if we exclude those who are likely to "make trouble" (62). Afro-American scholar Henry Louis Gates, Jr. explains why those who "make trouble" want to challenge the traditionalists' view of the humanities:

9

Longer Quotations: *Quotation of more than four typed lines is set off from text, double-spaced, and* not *included within quotations.*

> the teaching of an aesthetic and political order in which
> no women or people of color were even able to discover
> the reflection or representation of their images, or hear
> the resonances of their cultural voices. . . . represents
> the return of an order in which my people were the
> subjugated: the voiceless, the invisible, the

unrepresented and the unrepresentable. (105)
Or as Diane Ravitch points out, human history is the story of "the
clash of different cultures, races, ethnic groups and religions"
(390). If we want to live together, then we must learn to
understand the differences that divide us.

> As in all controversies, both sides in the traditionalist-
> multiculturalist debate make valid arguments. Students should be
> taught the culture that formed their heritage; they should also be
> taught that culture is not a static product, like a statue in a
> museum, but a dynamic process in which different voices challenge
> and complement each other (Stimpson 30). Students should be
> taught cultures other than their own; they should also be taught
> that these other cultures suffer from the same superiority complex
> that has made Western Civilization ethnocentric (Bloom 36).

> The simplest way to resolve this controversy is to
> acknowledge the claims of both sides: Teach students courses in
> Western Civilization <u>and</u> courses in non-Western civilization. But
> this solution only perpetuates what Graff calls the "add-on"
> principle of curricular change:

> > by this principle, whenever a new and challenging idea or
> > method arises, it is assimilated into the university by
> > the device of <u>adding</u> another unit to the existing
> > aggregate. The result is that established departments
> > and factions do not have to confront the challenge of the
> > new idea or even notice its existence. (57)

Paraphrase: Robin paraphrases Stimpson's and Bloom's arguments.

Longer Quotation: Robin cites source and term, then uses longer quotation to define term.

10

11

Thus, universities could teach both versions of the humanities in
separate courses, creating a curriculum that everybody needs and
nobody wants.

Another way to resolve the controversy would be to combine   **12**
the two courses. But even if teachers would be willing to
entertain such a compromise, they could not produce it. As

Brief Quotation: Robin cites source, then uses quotation to advance her own argument.

Catharine Stimpson points out, "no curriculum . . . can do all of
earthly time, all of earthly space" (31). And combining
curriculums often forces teachers to look for common ground and to
erase the differences that created the opposing cultures in the
first place (Graff 56).

In their constant fussing about books, both sides seem   **13**
preoccupied by what students need to be taught rather than how

Paraphrase: Robin paraphrases Emig's and Trimbur's major arguments about education.

students can learn (Emig 88). To learn effectively, students need
to participate in their own education (Emig 93). But both sides
see students as passive and powerless--children who need to be
given lots of information (Trimbur 118). The official curriculum
may focus on the classic debates in ancient Greece or the
contemporary debates between "Third World" and "First World"
cultures, but the "unofficial" curriculum tells students to keep
quiet and take notes.

Studying the humanities should engage students in a   **14**
conversation, a "cultural conversation they have a stake in"
(Graff 65). To create this conversation, teachers will need to
give students time to talk. Instead of telling them what to think
about "the Norton Anthology of World Masterpieces, we might ask
them to think about what is implied by the word 'World' in the

Jensen 7

title of a volume that collects works exclusively from the Western

tradition" (Trimbur 117-8). Instead of trying to cover centuries

of cultural achievement, in all parts of the world, teachers might

invite students to examine one historical period to see "what was

happening simultaneously in many places, and how each place

thought of the others, if indeed they did" (Stimpson 31).

Such invitations will help students see that culture is not

something that has "washed up on the beach of history"(Gates 104).

Culture is created by constant arguments about what voices to

include and what voices to exclude. Indeed, the argument about

what books should be taught in the humanities course is part of

that process. Rather than waiting for one side to win or for both

sides to resolve their disagreements (Graff 52), students should

be encouraged to examine the causes and effects of the conflict.

The real crisis in the humanities controversy is that for the most

part students have not been consulted. To "claim" their legacy

they need to participate in the complex and contentious

controversy. They need to do more than take humanities; they need

to take part in creating humanities.

Brief Quotation: Robin uses brief quotations from Trimbur and Stimpson to illustrate her thesis.

15

Paraphrase: Robin places parenthetical documentation next to her paraphrase of Graff.

Jensen 8

Notes

Note: *Robin uses note to refer readers to additional sources.*

1)   Hirsch has expanded his "preliminary list" into <u>The Dictionary of Cultural Literacy</u> (Boston: Houghton, 1988).

Jensen 9

Works Cited

Appleton, Nicholas. <u>Cultural Pluralism in Education: Theoretical Foundations</u>. New York: Longman, 1983.

Bennett, William J. <u>To Reclaim a Legacy: A Report on the Humanities in Higher Education</u>. Washington, D.C.: National Endowment for the Humanities, 1984.

---. "Why the West?" <u>National Review</u> 27 May 1988: 37-39.

Bloom, Allan. <u>The Closing of the American Mind: How Higher Education Has Failed Democracy and Impoverished the Souls of Today's Students</u>. New York: Simon, 1987.

Cheney, Lynn V. <u>Humanities in America: A Report to the President, the Congress and the American People</u>. Washington, D.C.: National Endowment for the Humanities, 1988.

Emig, Janet. "Our Missing Theory." <u>Conversations: Contemporary Critical Theory and the Teaching of Literature</u>. Eds. Charles Moran and Elizabeth Penfield. Urbana: NCTE, 1990: 87-96.

Gates, Henry Louis, Jr. "The Master's Pieces: On Canon Formation and the African-American Tradition." <u>South Atlantic Quarterly</u> 89 (Winter 1990): 89-112.

Graff, Gerald. "Teach the Conflicts." <u>South Atlantic Quarterly</u> 89 (Winter 1990): 51-67.

Hirsch, E. D. <u>Cultural Literacy: What Every American Needs to Know</u>. Boston: Houghton, 1987.

---. <u>The Dictionary of Cultural Literacy</u>. Boston: Houghton, 1988.

Works Cited: *Works cited in text (and notes) and alphabetized by the author's last name, double-spaced.*

Entry: *Two books by same author are alphabetized by title. Author's name designated by three dashes.*

Entry: *Chapter in book compiled by two editors*

Entry: *Article by single author*

Entry: *Book by single author*

Jensen 10

Pratt, Mary Louise. "Humanities for the Future: Reflections on
the Western Culture Debate at Stanford." <u>South Atlantic
Quarterly</u> 89 (Winter 1990): 7–25.

Ravitch, Diane. "Multiculturalism: <u>E Pluribus Plures</u>." <u>American
Scholar</u> 59 (Summer 1990): 337–54.

Simonson, Rick and Scott Walker, eds. <u>Multi-Cultural Literacy</u>:
<u>Opening the American Mind</u>. St. Paul, MN: Graywolf, 1988.

Stimpson, Catharine R. "Is There a Core in the Curriculum? And
Is It Really Necessary?" <u>Change</u> 20 (Mar.–Apr. 1988): 26–31.

Trimbur, John. "<u>To Reclaim a Legacy</u>, Cultural Literacy and the
Discourse of Crisis." <u>Liberal Education</u> 72 (Summer 1986):
109–19.

*Entry: Book compiled
by two editors*

Why the West? | William J. Bennett

In this excerpt from his speech, "Why the West?" originally presented at Stanford University, former Secretary of Education William J. Bennett presents his four major reasons for studying Western civilization. Which of the four reasons seem most compelling? Which ones seem most flawed? In what ways does he attempt to accommodate the multiculturalist position?

Why must we study, nurture, and defend the West? I'll give you four rea-   1
sons. First, because it is ours. It is the culture in which we live and in which most of us will continue to live, whether our grandparents are African or Asian, Hungarian or Mexican, Muslim or Shinto. Our institutions and ideals—our schools and universities and their great, still honored traditions, our churches and synagogues, our government and laws, even our notions of friendship and family—have all acquired their shape and significance through the course of Western history, largely though not exclusively through the European experience. To be sure, China, India, Africa, and other societies and cultures have made contributions to our institutions and ideals. Where contributions have been made, they must be acknowledged. Where new contributions emerge, they must be included. Historically, this has in fact been the standard Western practice: Western civilization is strong in part because it is open—it studies and learns from others.

The second reason we must study the West is that it is good. It is not   2
all good. There are certainly great blots on its record. Nevertheless, the West has produced the world's most just and effective system of government: the system of representative democracy. It has set the moral, political, economic, and social standards for the rest of the world. To quote Allan Bloom, "Our story is the majestic and triumphant march of two principles: freedom and equality." And those principles now define no less than a universal standard of legitimacy.

This leads me to the third reason—the reason that Western civiliza-   3
tion's critics seem to have entirely missed: the West is a source of incomparable intellectual complexity and diversity and depth. Western civilization is emphatically *not* an endorsement of a particular "party line." On the contrary, the West's long history of self-critical dialogue is one of its greatest strengths. Since the time of Socrates, what has distinguished the West is its insistence, in principle, on the questioning of accepted ways and beliefs—its openness to the appeal to nature, to use Socratic terms, as opposed to mere convention. It is true that the West has often failed, beginning with the death of Socrates, fully to live up to this principle but the principle has always animated the Western experience.

The point of contemporary higher education is this: the classics of   4
Western philosophy and literature amount to a great debate on the perennial questions. To deprive students of this debate is to condemn them to

Bennett, William. "Why the West?" *National Review* 27 May 1988: 37–39.

improvise their ways of living in ignorance of their real opinions and the best arguments for each. In the tradition of Peter Abelard, our civilization offers a great *sic et non* on the human condition. Consider the point/counterpoint of Western thought. On the ends of government, whom do we follow—Madison or Marx? On the merits of the religious life—Aquinas or Voltaire? On the nobility of the warrior—Homer or Erasmus? On the worth of reason—Hegel or Kierkegaard? On the role of women—Wollstonecraft or Schopenhauer? The study of Western civilizations is not, then, a case for ideology; it is a case for philosophy and for thoughtfulness. It considers not only the one hand, but the one hand *and* the other—and, just as often, the third and fourth hands as well. Those who take the study of the West seriously end up living a variety of different lives and arriving at a diversity of opinions and positions. And for this there is unparalleled tolerance and encouragement.

Indeed, some of the West's greatest teachers and statesmen are those who have participated most vigorously in this continual process of dissent, discussion, and redirection. In our time, this tradition is well exemplified by the Reverend Martin Luther King, Jr. Reverend King immersed himself in the writings of the great philosophers: "from Plato to Aristotle," as he wrote, "down to Rousseau, Hobbes, Bentham, Mill, and Locke." These great thinkers—these *Western* thinkers—helped teach and inspire Reverend King to tear down the ugly injustices of Jim Crow. 5

It is true that Reverend King was also inspired by the example of a non-Western—Gandhi. We should give credit where credit is due, and we should study Gandhi's thought and deeds, as we should study the thought and deeds of others from outside the West. But I would add that in this case, when we study Gandhi, we shall see that Gandhi was himself very much indebted to such Western philosophers as Henry David Thoreau, and to such Anglo-American traditions as the rule of law. So even in studying Gandhi's East, one cannot escape the West. Now, of course, nothing stops Stanford from requiring a course in non-Western traditions of thought; indeed much commends such an idea. But such an idea in no way diminishes the importance, the necessity, of studying the West. 6

Each year since becoming education secretary, I've been invited to the Martin Luther King Center to deliver an address marking Reverend King's birthday. And each year I speak of how Reverend King drew strength and purpose from his education, an education in the Western intellectual tradition. Last year, at Stanford, Reverend King's birthday was marked by Jesse Jackson leading a group of students in the now famous cry: "Hey, hey, ho, ho, Western Culture's got to go." Just a week earlier, I had been at the King Center talking about Reverend King's self-proclaimed debt to Western thought. Either Reverend King was right, or Reverend Jackson is right. I'll stand with King. 7

This brings me to my final reason for studying and protecting the West and its unique tradition of open discourse and philosophic inquiry: we must do so because the West is under attack. Oftentimes the assault comes from outside the West, but sometimes, sadly, it comes from within. Those who attack Western values and accomplishments do not see an America that—despite its imperfections, its weaknesses, its sins—has served 8 and continues to serve as a beacon to the world. Instead, theirs is an America hopelessly tainted—tainted by racism, imperialism, sexism, capitalism, ethnocentrism, elitism, and a host of other "isms." Such rhetoric has been used over and over again as a justification for the abolition of the Western Culture program here at Stanford. As one member of the Stanford community has said: "The Western Culture program gives intellectual justification to sexism, racism, and national chauvinism." So, the assertion goes, by diminishing the study of the West in our colleges and universities, we can make an important step toward ridding the world of these unholy "isms."

I would remind those critics that it is Western civilization that has taught much of the world about the evils of "sexism, racism, and national chauvinism." Indeed, it is the West that has given us the very language used to attack the West here at Stanford. After all, where do the concepts of rights, equality, and, yes, diversity come from? It is in the West, it is from the West, that we have learned—over time, through struggle, after bloodshed—to stand squarely behind liberty and equality for all people. An honest study of the West will provide the reasons for its protection. But how are we to protect the West if we set about systematically robbing ourselves of opportunities to know and study it?

9

Humanities for the Future: Reflections on the Western Culture Debate at Stanford | Mary Louise Pratt

In this selection, Stanford professor Mary Louis Pratt presents the multiculturalist side of the debate. Bennett's and Pratt's arguments were prompted by the controversy created in 1988 by Stanford University's decision to scrap its first-year course in Western Culture to provide a more multicultural curriculum for its students. How does Pratt regard Bennett's argument? Why does she think multiculturalism is so important? What do her opening and closing examples contribute to her argument?

SWM, 38, 5'10", N/S, Stanford scientist, average-looking, a bit eccentric, blindingly brilliant, phenomenally funny, amazingly humble, likes jogging, bicycling, all things done with racquet-like instruments, movies, literature and most aspects of western civilization, but most interested in a reasonably attractive and intelligent 25–45 PA female capable of being interested in me. Send photo & brief description of your life, liberty and pursuits of happiness. Box 65C.

This singles ad appeared late last summer in the personals column of a local weekly serving the communities of Palo Alto, California, and neigh-

1

Pratt, Mary Louise. "Humanities for the Future: Reflections on the Western Culture Debate at Stanford," *South Atlantic Quarterly* 89 (Winter 1990): 7–11, 19–25.

boring Stanford University. Apart from its intriguing characterization of the "Stanford scientist," I quote it here to suggest the extent to which Stanford's long and intense debate over its Western culture curriculum last year permeated local life. In the semiotics of representation and identity, "Western civilization" remains a constant and intensely meaningful point of reference.

The debate which took place at Stanford during the winter of 1988   2
and the resulting reform of the Western culture requirement received a great deal of national attention, largely due to the involvement of then Secretary of Education William Bennett, who chose to use the Stanford case as a platform to advocate his views, quite literally making a federal case out of it. Perhaps because of Bennett's own partisanship, the account of the Stanford debate in the national press had a shape somewhat different from the local experience. As other institutions face similar struggles, fuller accounts of the workings of change at Stanford may be helpful. At the same time, there is an urgent need to formulate the concerns that so unexpectedly made freshman book lists an object of wide public concern. What nerves had been touched?

Histories of Western culture curricula in the United States point to   3
the Western civilization course instituted at Columbia University in 1919 as a main antecedent for such courses all over the country. One recent account, however, notes that the Columbia course had a direct antecedent of its own, a War Issues course instituted in 1918 at various universities, including Columbia. Its aim was "to educate recently conscripted American soldiers about to fight in France . . . to introduce [them] to the European heritage in whose defense they were soon to risk their lives."[1] A new tie to Europe was constituted in relation to a national imperative.

Current struggles over Western culture curricula—both challenges to   4
them and reactionary attempts to reassert them—also emerge from urgently felt national imperatives. Among these is an imperative to reimagine cultural and civic identity in the United States in the wake of vast changes produced by the decline of its global hegemony, the rapid internationalization of capital and industry, the immigrant implosion of the "Third World" onto the "First," and the democratization of American institutions and political processes that occurred in the two decades prior to 1980. The question can be posed in Pierre Bourdieu's sometimes helpful language: what is to count as "cultural capital" in a culturally plural nation and a globalized human world? How will that capital be constructed and deployed, how will people be asked to identify with it? How might the United States project itself into the future as a cultural and political entity? In the words (a few of which I've emphasized) of one speaker in the Stanford debate:

> The character of U.S. society is changing. More and more North Americans insist on affirming the specificity of their class, ethnicity, gender, region, race, or sexual orientation, rather than melting into the homogeniz-

---

[1]See Gilbert Allardyce, "The Rise and Fall of the Western Civilization Course," *American Historical Review* 87 (1982): 695–743, cited by Herbert Lindenberger in his admirable essay, "On the Sacrality of Reading Lists: The Western Culture Debate at Stanford University," to appear in the British journal *Comparative Criticism*, Fall 1989. [Au.]

ing pot. They see such affirmations as *intrinsic to their citizenship.* Culture, literature, and the academy have been important sites for the affirmations: it will be neither productive nor comfortable to commit ourselves only to resisting these developments, rather than engaging with them.

Having acquiesced to change, by what visions will United Statesians be guided into a future where they and their society will be different from what they are now? What is the United States trying to become? What are the options?

The world is full of multicultural, multiethnic, multilingual nations, so there are plenty of models around. Indeed, Bloom, Bennett, Bellow, and the rest (known by now in some quarters as the Killer B's) are advocating one of them: to create a narrowly specific cultural capital that will be the normative *referent* for everyone, but will remain the *property* of a small and powerful caste that is linguistically and ethnically unified. It is this caste that is referred to by the "we" in Saul Bellow's astoundingly racist remark that "when the Zulus have a Tolstoy, *we* will read him." Few doubt that behind the Bennett-Bloom program is a desire to close not the American mind, but the American university, to all but a narrow and highly uniform elite with no commitment to either multiculturalism or educational democracy. Thus while the Killer B's (plus a C—Lynne Cheney, the Bennett mouthpiece now heading the National Endowment for the Humanities) depict themselves as returning to the orthodoxies of yesteryear, their project must not be reduced to nostalgia or conservatism. Neither of these explain the blanket contempt they express for the country's universities. They are fueled not by reverence for the past, but by an aggressive desire to lay hold of the present and future. The B's act as they do not because they are unaware of the cultural and demographic diversification under way in the country; they are utterly aware. That is what they are trying to shape; that is why they are seeking, and using, national offices and founding national foundations.

Many citizens are attracted to Bloom's and Bennett's pronouncements, on the other hand, out of fairly unreflected attachments to the past (including their own college experience), and simply have trouble seeing how good books could possibly do any harm. Many people are perfectly ready for change but remain deeply anxious about where it is all supposed to be heading. Other visions of the cultural and educational future in the United States, then, are likely to generate as much interest as the Killer B's, if they can be effectively introduced into the national discussion. The attention drawn by Bloom's intellectually deplorable *Closing of the American Mind* and Bennett's intellectually more deplorable "To Reclaim a Legacy" most directly reflects not levels of enthusiasm for their programs (though much enthusiasm does exist), but levels of anxiety that have developed around the issue of national cultural identity. Even among the many people ready for change, one seems to hear voices asking, "If I give up white supremacy, who am I? Am I still American? Am I still white? If I give up homophobia, who am I? Am I the same as gay? If I give up misogyny, am I still a man? a woman? an American? If I learn Spanish, does it make me Mexican? What ties me to these gays, these feminists, these Salvadorans, these Vietnamese, these Navaho, these white people?" And perhaps more acutely, "What ties them to me?" The sooner answers to these questions are attempted, the better. What, indeed, would it mean to adopt the "nonhierarchical, intercultural perspective on the study of culture and the West" called for by one Stanford humanist (a classicist, at that)? What can cultural citizenship and identity be in a radically plural society enmeshed in relentlessly globalizing relations? Can there be transnational national culture? Can it be good?

Alongside the understandable apprehensions such questions generate (especially late in a century), it should be possible to create some excitement and curiosity. After all, this could become, perhaps has become, a fabulously energetic and revealing cultural experiment. It has tremendous imaginative appeal. Does the United States not badly need to revitalize its image and understanding of itself? Is there not much to be learned about the fluid global cultureways that bring the music of Soweto into living rooms across the United States, and make *The Cosby Show* the most popular TV program in South Africa? Is there not much to be learned about the past by rereading it in the light of contemporary intercultural understanding? **7**

Perhaps the biggest surprise for naive observers like myself as we listened and read [about the curriculum debate at Stanford University] was what some of us came to call the "willful ignorance" factor. It was saddening to hear academics saying please don't make me read anything new. I refuse to agree there are things I am ignorant of that are important and worthwhile. "Does that make me a racist?" one old friend and colleague asked. What would Aretha Franklin reply, I wondered. At the same time, especially given the rantings of the official right, it is important to affirm the thoughtfulness and intellectual quality of the discussion that took place at Stanford, and to give you some examples. It was, for example, George Will and not an academic colleague who, amazingly, called for courses that "affirm this fact: America is predominantly a product of the Western tradition and is predominantly good because that tradition is good." It was William F. Buckley, and not a Stanford professor, who displayed his ignorance by declaring that "from Homer to the nineteenth century no great book has emerged from any non-European source." Below I offer some excerpts from what Stanford faculty and students did say, for and against the reform (the quotations are taken from statements published in the campus newspaper):   **8**

Con: Education is an exercise of modesty, a process whereby we give up some of ourselves to gain an understanding of that which is *not* ourselves, an understanding of things still shaping us. It's a kind of surrender; we learn that some things are superior in consequence to us, even to our particular gender, to our particular ethnic heritage, to all the parochialism to which we are subject. Then the apparent foreignness of the past, its record of people seemingly *unlike* ourselves, becomes much less foreign and those people much less strange and irrelevant.   **9**

Pro: The famous texts of the past cannot continue to live for us if we simply place them on a pedestal and teach our students to worship them. Only if we see them as engaged with the stuff of history, both of the times in which they were written and of those later times, can we give a continuing life to these texts and to our cultural tradition as a whole. Only if we understand how the idea of a Western culture took shape in differing ways over the centuries and how it defined itself in relation to other forms of culture, can we justify giving it the prime consideration . . . to our students.   **10**

Con: As a historian of the United States, I would be the last person to   **11** deny the ethnic, racial, and cultural complexity of American society. But, from the same perspective, I find it puzzling, if not troubling, to learn that some of the dominant and influential ideas in modern America are to be seen [in the new legislation] as originating outside the West. Few historians of the United States believe that the culture of this country has been seriously influenced by ideas from Africa, China, Japan, or indigenous North America. . . . There is no direct connection between the dominant ideas and institutions in American culture and the cultures of Africa or Eastern Asia. [The roots of American culture], if one is talking about ideas and institutions, are derived overwhelmingly from Europe. To contend otherwise, I think would cause American historians to scratch their heads in amazement.

Pro: A "liberal education" for our time should expand beyond the culture-bound, basically colonialist, horizon that relies, albeit subtly, on the myth of the cultural superiority of the "West" (an ill-defined entity, in any event, whose borders are ludicrously artificial). . . . Does the new, integrated vision of Area One entail our teaching the Greek Hermes and Prometheus alongside the North American Indian Coyote or the West African Anansi and Legba as paradigms of trickster heroes, or Japanese Noh alongside Greek drama or Indian philosophy alongside Plato? If the answer is yes, so much the better.   **12**

Pro: I was never taught in Western Culture the fact that the Khemetic or "Egyptian" Book of the Dead contained many of the dialectic principles attributed to Greece, but was written three thousand years earlier, or the fact that Socrates, Herodotus, Pythagoras, and Solon studied in Egypt and acknowledged that much of their knowledge of astronomy, geometry, medicine, and building came from the African civilizations in and around Egypt. . . . I was never told that algebra came from Moslem Arabs, or numbers from India. I was never informed when it was found that the "very dark and wooly haired" Moors in Spain preserved, expanded, and reintroduced the classical knowledge that the Greeks had collected, which led to the "renaissance." . . . I read the Bible without knowing St. Augustine looked black like me, that the ten commandments were almost direct copies from the 147 negative confessions of Egyptian initiates, or that many of the words of Solomon came from the black pharaoh Amen-En-Eope. I didn't learn that Toussaint L'Ouverture's defeat of Napoleon in Haiti directly influenced the French Revolution or that the Iroquois Indians in America had a representative democracy which served as a model for the American system. . . . I'm damned if my children have to go to a school that preaches diversity, then refuses to practice its own values because it was scared.   **13**

In the end, the reform legislation was passed, with some substantial amendments. One, for instance, required courses to "include treatment of ancient and medieval cultures"; another required faculty teaching in the program to agree each spring on a set of "common elements" which all tracks would share the following year. The latter amendment, which finally broke the deadlock, is a very big loophole. It leaves open the unlikely possibility of faculty agreeing to restore the entire core list, or of the whole battle being fought over in miniature every spring. At the moment, it seems more likely that the parties will learn to understand each other better through this compulsory conversation. The actual consequences of the re-   **14** form remain uncertain, however. With only minor alterations, the standard Great Books course *can* continue to exist at Stanford, and nobody is being required to reeducate him or herself. You can certainly talk about gender without challenging sexism, or race without challenging racism, or class without challenging classism. On the other hand, a space has been made for much greater change by those who desire it. Tracks constructed around other understandings of culture and broader perspectives on the West are now possible. Their existence and survival depends, however, on the presence of sufficient faculty to teach them, and the hiring and tenuring of such faculty is not possible without the acquiescence of those who opposed the reform. It is no accident that the final amendment passed by the senate deleted a phrase calling for the recruitment of minority faculty to teach in the new program. In the larger national picture, it seems fair to say that the new program puts Stanford in the vanguard of the rear guard, for other schools have long since left our modest reform behind. (Write, for example, for the catalog of Oglala College in Pine Ridge, South Dakota.)

Three faculty have jointly prepared a course according to the new 15 guidelines. It is a course called Europe and the Americas which studies the European, African, and native American strands of American cultures, and the history of their interaction in the Americas. Canonical European texts retain a place in the course, but rather than forming its center of gravity, they simply coexist with American, Caribbean, Spanish-American, native-American, and Anglo-American materials. "The complex interactions of colonialism, slavery, migration and immigration," says the course's preamble, "have produced on this side of the Atlantic societies that are highly diverse in origin, and in many cases multicultural and syncretic. European traditions play a prominent and indeed decisive role in these societies, *though by no means the same roles they play in Europe.*" At times the course adopts a comparative perspective—Haitian Vodun and Greek Dionysus are brought together, for instance, in a section on religious syncretism and ecstatic cults; a section on representations of the self juxtaposes the extroverted, historicized self-representation of a Navaho oral history with the confessional modes of St. Augustine and Freud. Historical dialogues are pursued—the legacy of Shakespeare's *The Tempest* in Aimé Césaire's *A Tempest,* José Enrique Rodó's *Ariel,* and Roberto Fernández Retamar's *Calibán* are examined; the give-and-take between European enlightenment discourse on human rights, American independence movements, abolitionism, and slave rebellions is considered; indigenous traditions are traced, from the ancient Mayan *Popul Vuh,* for instance, to the contemporary *testimonio* by Guatemalan indigenous activist Rigoberta Menchu, or from the pre-Columbian Inca state to the Spanish conquest (through Andean eyes) to the great Andean rebellions of the 1780's to the contemporary Quechua poetry of José María Arguedas. Terms like creolization, transculturation, and syncretism are used to develop an approach to culture that is relational and at the same time recognizes the internal fullness and integrity of particular moments and formations.

Approaches to culture and to United States culture such as those this 16 course adopts are widespread in higher education, but are scarcely to be found in official discourse on education, nor in the national media's depictions of the curricular controversy. Partisans of reform have so far had little success at getting across in the public discourse the modes of understanding against which the monumentalist approach seems narrow and impoverished. Few people reading Bloom or Bennett, even those critical of them, can bring to bear a picture of what nonhierarchical, relational approaches to culture are or what people stand to gain from learning them. Stanford's scientists, in being asked to vote for reform, had little idea of what they were voting *for*. How could they not fall back on the common sense of the man in the personals ad I quoted at the beginning who simply likes most aspects of Western civilization? (As the West Texan is supposed to have said against daylight saving time, "If central time was good enough for Jesus Christ, it's good enough for me!") When then Secretary Bennett and Stanford President Donald Kennedy debated the issue on the *MacNeil/ Lehrer Report,* neither party possessed a clear picture of alternative visions of culture, the West, or the United States. Bennett knew only vaguely what he was opposing, and Kennedy what he was defending. Lehrer also seemed to be groping for an unknown. And yet, one goes on to wonder, why should the discussion remain in the hands of those three people, a remarkably uniform group? Where are the voices of those who have the most fundamental, bodily stakes in efforts for change? For the moment, those voices are not authorized to speak for "us" all, the way Bennett, Kennedy, and Lehrer can. When they are, change will have occurred.

The final amendments-to-the-amendments on the Stanford reform **17** were resolved in the last week of May 1988. In the days that followed, a series of local events suggested with unexpected clarity the need for the experiment Stanford had embarked on. A student was expelled from his dormitory after a year of disruptive activity directed especially toward a gay resident assistant, culminating in an assault on the resident and the vandalizing of the dormitory lounge. The following evening, ten fraternity brothers, in defense of the expelled student's freedom of speech, staged a silent vigil at midnight outside the dormitory lounge wearing masks and carrying candles, a gesture that seemed to deliberately invoke the customs of the Ku Klux Klan. The reactions of black students who assembled at the site ranged from terror to outrage, and the action was treated by the university as a serious racial and homophobic incident. The ten demonstrators, however, claimed complete ignorance of the associations their vigil invoked. They did not know, they said, that masks and candles at midnight had any connotations—it is just what they thought a vigil was. The following day a group of sorority women, as part of a rush ritual, performed a mock "Indian dance" around a fountain which happened to stand in the doorway of the native American student center. Asked to stop, they refused, later saying they did not intend to offend, or see the dance as offensive. It was just a tradition.

Many people did not believe these students' pleas of ignorance. But **18** either way, the call for educational change was reinforced. If it is possible for young adults to leave the American educational system ignorant of the history of race relations in the United States (not part of standard Western culture curricula), then something needs to change. And if a person who knows the history of race relations and their symbolizations feels free to re-enact racist rituals of mockery or intimidation, something needs to change.

At the same time, blame must be placed where it belongs. In pleading ignorance, the students were following the example of many of the country's
own leaders, for whom ignorance had become an acceptable standard of
public life. Throughout their high school and college years these students
had looked to a president who consistently showed himself to be both ignorant and utterly comfortable with his ignorance. (The Stanford incidents
coincide with Reagan's extraordinary remarks in Moscow about the "cod-
dling" of native Americans.) For many of us exhausted by conflict that
spring, these discouraging incidents reminded us of what we were fighting for.

A week later a less weighty event drew local attention, when two   **19**
California students turned up as the two finalists in the National Spelling
Bee. Their names were Rageshree Ramachandran, an Indian-born American
from Fair Oaks (who won), and Victor C. Wang, a Chinese American from
Camarillo (who came in second). Nothing could have suggested more
clearly the multicultural, multiethnic future taking shape on the West
Coast. The final words in the spelling bee, the report noted, were these:
buddleia (from an Englishman's surname), araucaria (from South American
indigenous language), mhometer (from a German electrician's surname,
spelled backwards), ovoviviparous (from Latin), caoutchouc (from another
South American indigenous language, via French), stertorous (from Latin),
and elegiacal (from Greek). "Who makes up these words?" asked Victor
Wang as he went down to defeat on "stertorous." Good question, Victor.
And as you head on up the educational ladder, I hope you find a system
that will give you an honest and imaginative answer.

Writing Assignments

Narrate   **1.**   Select *one* core subject—such as history, literature, science or math—that you have taken several times during your educational career. In what ways did the material seem different each time you studied it? What was the source of that difference—teacher, students, textbook, assignments? Focus on one experience that forced you to confront that difference. Then compose a narrative essay to dramatize the factors that made you see the subject differently.

Observe   **2.**   Attend a faculty committee meeting where professors are contemplating changing the requirements for general education or your major. As the various professors conduct their meeting, sort out what is at stake in their deliberations. Who's on what side? How many sides are there? What factors (large and small) make it difficult for the committee to reach a decision? Then write a column for your student newspaper describing how faculty make decisions about what students should learn.

Investigate   **3.**   Interview two faculty members who represent opposing sides in a curriculum controversy. Ask them where and how they were taught the course that is the focus of the dispute or how they developed their own philosophy (and syllabus) for the course. Identify areas of agreement and then compose an essay in which you propose a possible compromise between the "dueling professors."

Collaborate   **4.**   For most of the semester, you have had to work through conflicts, find compromises, and acknowledge differences in order to function as a writing group. Read John Trimbur's essay, "Consensus and Difference in Collaborative Learning," *College English* 51 (October 1989): 602–16. Then write an essay on what your group has discovered about the possibilities and limitations of working together.

Read   **5.**   Read Gerald Graff's "Teach the Conflicts," *South Atlantic Quarterly* 89 (Winter 1990): 51–67. Examine his analysis of the way universities avoid conflicts and his suggestions for using conflicts to create a more coherent curriculum. Then write a proposal for the professors who are teaching the courses you are taking this semester suggesting how they might implement one of Graff's suggestions.

Respond   **6.**   Respond to Robin Jensen's argument that students need to be engaged in creating their college curriculum. What are the advantages and disadvantages of her argument? How would students in your writing class respond to the invitation to create their own curriculum? Draft a proposal for your writing teacher, suggesting ways for students to take responsibility for creating their course and see how many sign on.

Analyze   **7.**   Analyze William J. Bennett's four reasons for teaching Western civilization. Why does he arrange them in this sequence? What kind of evidence does he use to support each reason? Why does he think "the West" is under attack? Why are such attacks a problem if "the West" encourages critical inquiry? You may want to expand your analysis by considering some of the arguments—pro and con—appearing in the editorial columns of national or local newspapers.

Evaluate **8.** Evaluate Mary Louise Pratt's argument for multiculturalism. How does she assess the proponents, the teachers, and the graduates of the traditional Western Civilization course? Why does she think the multiculturalist approach is so important? Review the section on "appeals" in Chapter 6 on pages 166–8. Then evaluate how Pratt uses various appeals to make her case.

Argue **9.** Draft a letter to the Minority or Ethnic Studies departments on your campus arguing that all minority students should be required to take a traditional version of the course in Western Civilization. Find and use sources to support one of the following arguments: (1) all students—regardless of gender, race, and class—are entitled to know the version of the humanities that has been taught by the dominant culture; or (2) minority students should learn how to challenge the assumptions and assertions contained in the "universal" language of the traditional humanities course.

Argue **10.** Conduct some research on the cultural backgrounds of the students and faculty on your campus. How many students and faculty come from minority or other cultures? How many citizens in your state or region come from the same culture? How many opportunities does your university offer to faculty and students to study the cultural history of these groups? Once you have completed your research, write a letter to your state legislature's Education Committee presenting your research and suggesting reasons why they should fund more students and faculty from culturally diverse backgrounds.

Appendix Writing with a Word Processor

Writing with a word processor expands opportunities for fully exploring the writing process and thus the possibility of more fully expressing your purpose. When personal computers first gained popularity in the late 1970s, they were most commonly used for computer games. Recently, however, word processing has become the primary use of personal computers. Like a growing number of people, you can use word processors for all kinds of personal, academic, and professional writing. Your use of a word processor during your school years serves both short-term and long-term purposes: The word processor is a writing tool that can improve your academic writing by making planning, drafting, and revising easier; and the ability to use a word processor develops technical skills that will be helpful in any profession you enter.

THE WORD PROCESSOR AS A WRITING TOOL

You may have friends who talk about writing with a word processor with the enthusiasm of the newly converted, giving glowing testimonials about what this new tool has done for their writing. Although such testimonials can be boring to the uninitiated, your friends' enthusiasm is well based. The microcomputer can increase your efficiency and effectiveness, as well as your enjoyment of writing. Make no mistake: the word processor does not miraculously transform writing into a quick and simple task. After all, it cannot do for you the hard thinking that good writing requires. It can, however, encourage experimental planning and drafting and extensive revision through its capacity to save and change texts easily.

Because writing is such a personal activity, how you choose to utilize this tool is an individual matter. Some of you, especially those who have been composing on a typewriter, may very quickly begin to do all your writing on the computer—planning, drafting, and revising. Others may continue to plan and produce the first draft by hand and turn to the word processor only for second drafts and subsequent revisions. Still others may initially use the word processor like a typewriter, entering and editing only the final draft. Just as there is no one right way to write, so too there is no one right way to use the computer for writing. Over time, however, you will probably find yourself taking increasing advantage of the computer's capabilities.

As you contemplate using a word processor for the first time, you may share a common fear of many writers new to the word processor: that you will lose your work because of a mistaken command, a damaged disk, or a computer "crash." Three precautions can reduce the risk of such misfortunes:

▼ Use the "Save" command frequently to preserve the writing you are working on.

▼ After every day's work, make back-up copies of your disk.

▼ Print "hard" copies of your work regularly (that is, print out your work on paper).

USING THE WORD PROCESSOR FOR PLANNING

Some people argue that the word processor is useful for planning because typing on an electronic keyboard more closely matches the pace of thought than does writing with a pen or pencil or typing on a manual or even electric typewriter. Others suggest that writing on a word processor is like talking to onself or thinking aloud. In any case, for many, the word processor seems to encourage the "play" and experimentation with ideas and language that are the heart of planning.

Nearly all the thinking-in-writing strategies mentioned in Chapter 2 adapt readily to planning with a word processor. *Listing,* for example, can be done as easily on screen as by hand. Simply type your prompt at the top of your screen and begin listing all the ideas, associations, and images that it brings to mind. To evaluate your list, review it and highlight promising items with an asterisk, underlining, or boldface. As suggested in Chapter 2, you might then pick one of these promising ideas and begin another list or do some freewriting, using the new idea as your prompt. After that activity, you may wish to return to your original list and insert some of the new ideas that emerged. To do this you will need to save your initial lists and other plans; you can do this by keeping them at the beginning of the file for your upcoming assignment, in a separate file, or in print. Since these steps are easy to do, you should get into the habit of saving your planning so that you do not prematurely delete plans to which you later find you need to refer.

Freewriting can be done easily with the word processor. In fact, the exploratory nature of freewriting makes it an ideal strategy for generating ideas and at the same time practicing computer-assisted writing. You just begin "fishing," as poet William Stafford puts it, for whatever happens along. You should try to write without stopping for ten to fifteen minutes to get the most out of this activity. To push your freewriting a bit further, try this strategy. After ten to fifteen minutes of freewriting, stop, reread what you've written, and look for a focus. This might be a surprising phrase, a problem, an intriguing idea, or a remembered incident. Move down on the screen a few lines and type this focus as a prompt for another ten to fifteen minutes of focused freewriting.

Another computer-assisted freewriting strategy is what the composition researchers Sheridan Blau and Stephen Marcus call "invisible writing." Simply turn down the brightness control on the monitor, so that your screen appears blank. You then begin typing whatever comes to mind or, if you are using a prompt, whatever it triggers. You may find this technique liberating because you will not be distracted by what you've just written; such forced concentration on what you wish to say next can produce creative results. After you've done this for ten or fifteen minutes, turn the brightness control back up, read, save, and print what you've written. As recommended in Chapter 2, it is wise to conclude a freewriting session by reviewing and evaluating your work for interesting ideas and passages. These passages can be identified for later use by asterisks placed at the beginning and end of the passage, underlining, boldface, or brackets, or they may be transferred to a file reserved for them. You can also annotate promising passages by hand on your hard copy.

Keeping an electronic journal, an alternative to keeping a journal in a notebook, is a planning activity particularly suited to the word processor. Although an electronic journal cannot be carried around like a notebook, it offers several other advantages: it is easier to store; it is less likely to get lost (especially if you work on your word processor at home or in your dorm room and don't have to carry your disks with you); it allows you to transfer chunks of your journal writing directly into a draft; and since it is typed, it is easier to read. There are, however, several guidelines you should follow. First, be sure that an electronic journal is acceptable to your teacher. Next, use a separate disk for your journal entries. And finally, create a file on your journal disk to serve as a table of contents. Call this file "Contents"; and before or after you have written an entry, record in your contents file the date and a phrase indicating the focus of the entry. You can also keep track of your entries by making a separate file for each. Or, if you are keeping different kinds of entries—assigned freewriting entries, reading notes, self-selected freewriting entries—you may wish to create separate "contents" files for each type. If your teacher wants you to submit selected entries or the whole journal, you will need to print the required material.

If you are using your journal to evoke and store potential essay topics, you may wish to reread and evaluate your journal entries from time to time, abstracting promising entries and transferring them to another file kept for such theme-starters. If you wish to move blocks of your journal directly into the text of a paper, check your computer manual for instructions on "block moves."

The two observation strategies mentioned in Chapter 2 are not equally adaptable to the word processor. *Mapping* is adaptable only to computers that have graphics capabilities. *Speculating* is adaptable to any computer. Mapping requires you to translate your sketches or notes about your subject's relationships, activity patterns, and figures into computer maps and sketches. If you have graphics or "painting" software and know how to use it, this translation process can promote further insights into and new perspectives on your subject.

Speculating is a particularly rich planning strategy since it allows you to explore your subject from several perspectives. You can speculate on a word processor by doing a series of three focused freewritings or by using a grid. Some computer programs will create multi-celled grids. In other cases, you yourself might create the grid, using computer graphics.

Interviewing and *reading,* the two research activities mentioned in Chapter 2, will yield information that can be stored in computer files. Translating your interview notes or transcribing your interview tape into computer files works best if you do it soon after the interview. Thus, the translation process becomes an opportunity to interpret and speculate about the data you have just collected. After recording your interview notes in the actual sequence in which you took them, you may want to copy this file. You can then preserve the file containing the original version of the interview while using the duplicate file to experiment with your subjects' comments, moving them around and arranging them to best reveal the patterns and themes that emerged during the interview.

Whether you are keeping informal reading notes or working on a research paper, the word processor is a useful tool. If you type the bibliographic information about each of your sources at the beginning of your notes for that source, you will be able to keep track of that information and transfer it, if necessary, into your bibliography or "works cited" list. Some word-processing programs can take your bibliographic information and format and alphabetize it, saving you a lot of time.

Below the bibliographic information, enter a summary of the reading, paraphrases of key ideas, direct quotations, and your own comments and questions. This method of keeping notes has many advantages. You can insert additional comments when you review your notes; you can move paraphrases, quotations, or comments directly into the text of your paper; and you can merge related readings into a single file that represents a subtopic or theme. A further benefit is that such notes are less likely to be lost than those done on note cards.

In addition to transferring and expanding traditional planning techniques with the word processor, you may wish to use or your teacher may encourage you to use various invention (or planning) programs. These programs prompt you to explore your topic by asking you various questions—speculating questions similar to those found in Chapter 2; the reporter's six questions (*who? what? when? where? why?* and *how?*), mentioned in Chapter 2; and questions that ask for definition, comparison, and so on, similar to the questions on structure in Chapter 5. Some new software, called idea processors or thought processors, offers outlining programs as a planning device. These programs can be useful and can make the planning process more gamelike; most, however, are programmed versions of the planning strategies presented in Chapter 2 (which can be used on word-processing software), and so are not essential to productive planning.

As noted at the end of Chapter 2, at some point you must stop planning and begin drafting. Because of the ease of electronic word processing, you may be more tempted than usual to continue freewriting and note taking, putting off the more difficult and threatening business of drafting. The following suggestions may help you overcome this tendency. Set specific time limits on your planning, and ease into drafting by viewing it as an extension of your freewriting. Even if you think you have more planning to do—and you always will think so, for most writers end up planning and replanning throughout the writing process—begin drafting. Focused freewriting might aid in this transition. After your listing or freewriting, summarize the gist of an interesting train of thought, or form a hypothesis and begin drafting with the same sense of freedom you felt during freewriting. After all, you have nothing to lose. Computer-produced drafts can be endlessly reshaped without complete retyping.

USING THE WORD PROCESSOR FOR DRAFTING

The fluid nature of screen text counteracts a first-draft block for some writers. However, if you find yourself reluctant to begin drafting, even on a word processor, you might try one of these strategies:

▼ You may wish to try *invisible writing,* described earlier, to produce your first draft. This technique, by preventing you from becoming preoccupied with exact wording and correctness, frees you to concentrate on developing your ideas.

▼ Another strategy for overcoming a first-draft block, the *discovery draft,* is similar to freewriting. Write nonstop for a certain period of time, say thirty minutes, with the aim of producing a complete representation of your ideas. Such a draft, discussed in Chapter 3, is deliberately tentative.

▼ Try drafting a *scratch outline* and then compose your draft in chunks. Your first goal, for example, might be to draft one of the topical paragraphs. This strategy breaks the job of drafting into small segments and allows you to compose your draft in any sequence you wish. If the introductory paragraph has you stumped, begin with the first or second topical paragraph. A word processor allows you to easily reorder the chunks later.

The word processor can help you get started with your draft, and it can also help you keep going. When you get stuck, shift to freewriting or listing. This procedure can get you over the various blocks and on to other sections where your ideas are more forthcoming. If you use brackets or asterisks to mark the places at which you feel blocked, you can easily locate those places with the "Find" function on your computer when you return to drafting. Another way to get through a problem section is to make a bracketed note to yourself to work on it later and then to go on. Still another idea is to draft several versions of the problem section and decide later which works best.

If your word-processing software includes a thesaurus, you will want to use it if you are having trouble finding the right word. All you have to do is type a word that comes close to the one you want but can't quite think of. The thesaurus will suggest several alternatives. Often the discovery of the right word is exactly what you need to spur you on to further composing.

A final way in which the word processor can be useful is by helping you to evaluate your drafts. After completing your first draft, triple-space your text, print it out, read through it (or have a friend read it), and make notes for later revision. Some word processors have a "split screen" or a "window" function that allows you to annotate your screen text. In each case, a second screen is superimposed on some portion of the screen holding your text. The "split screen" function divides the screen into two sections; the "window" function opens a "window" in one corner of your screen. In both cases, you can control the portion of the screen devoted to your original text and the portion devoted to revision. You might use these functions to make on-screen comments or to compose a descriptive outline (explained in Chapter 3) of your draft. Since these functions work by merging two files, the draft and comments or descriptive outline will print out separately.

In addition to using on-screen evaluation strategies, you should always evaluate a hard copy of your draft. On a screen you can see only a very small portion of your text (usually 24 lines) at a time, so it can be difficult to keep in mind the content of preceding and following pages. Reading screen text does not offer the same complete perspective as reading the easily turned pages of a printed copy. Some writers find it helpful to move back and forth from printed text to screen text, reading and annotating the former, then making the desired changes on the latter.

Some word-processing programs will provide a word count, a useful drafting aid that will help you avoid length problems in drafts for assignments that impose a specific number of words. Programs may also offer an abbreviation feature. If your subject involves a name, title, or word that you use repeatedly—such as *photosynthesis* or *Feodor Dostoevski*—you can avoid typing and retyping all those letters (and the risk of misspellings) by pressing a special key followed by a *P*, a *D*, an asterisk, or whatever symbol you choose: the word or words will appear automatically.

USING THE WORD PROCESSOR FOR REVISING

Probably the most touted benefit of computer-assisted writing is its encouragement of revision. But to some novice computer writers, the easy revision of screen texts leads to preoccupation with word changes and mechanical corrections. Substantial revision, unlike editing and proofreading, involves reseeing and reshaping the ideas in a draft. In Chapter 4 this process is called *global revision*. In the past, you may have avoided or minimized this kind of revision because it meant changing, recopying, or retyping large portions of the draft you had worked so hard to produce. But with the computer, you can make substantial changes—adding paragraphs and sentences, deleting sentences and paragraphs, shifting and reordering paragraphs and larger sections—without recopying or retyping the entire paper. The revision process becomes physically easier and far less tedious.

On-screen revision, which should be coupled with the evaluation of printed drafts, can be divided into three categories: (1) writer-initiated activities, (2) responses to peer or teacher feedback, (3) software-generated activities.

Some writer-initiated strategies have already been mentioned—using the "split screen" function to annotate a draft, marking blocks of text for later revision, and composing several versions of a particular section. Since such on-screen revisions involve reorganizing, reworking, and experimenting with the draft, you may wish to copy the original draft so that you can retrieve portions of it if you decide you prefer them to any of your subsequent revisions.

The easiest kind of revision is addition or deletion of text. Perhaps in evaluating your draft you decide that a certain term needs a definition, a generalization needs support, or an example needs elaboration. All you need to do is position the cursor at the point where you want to insert material and begin typing. (Some programs require that you use an "Insert" function to do this; if you don't, as you type you will cover and eliminate material that you may wish to keep.) If you decide to eliminate any portion of your draft, delete the material word by word or mark the entire block of text and delete it all at once.

Manipulation of blocks of text is a revision strategy especially suited to the word processor. Easy to accomplish, block and cut-and-paste moves allow you to reorder sentences, paragraphs, or larger sections to see what effect these shifts have on the overall effectiveness and meaning of your text. Sometimes, for example, you may want to try your conclusion as an introduction or to reorder your topical paragraphs. You may decide that an example you used in one paragraph would be more effective in another. Word processors enable you to reorganize your draft with ease and yet to return readily to your earlier version if you saved your original draft.

As suggested in Chapter 4, another important guide to global revision is the feedback you receive from others. For computer-produced drafts this feedback can be offered by computer as well as on a hard copy. A peer editor, friend, or teacher who reads your draft on screen and wishes to offer comments may do so in several ways. The reader may insert his or her comments right into the text in bracketed caps, like this: [CAN YOU ILLUS-TRATE HOW THIS WOULD WORK?] Or, if your draft is triple spaced, the reader's comments may be inserted between the lines. If you find such inserted comments intrusive, the reader may place his or her comments at the end of your draft (you can read, print, and then erase them) or in a separate file kept for comments; comments from different sources can be kept in the same file or in separate files. Some teachers arrange for class members to respond to one another's drafts through electronic mail or electronic bulletin boards. If your reader will be responding to a hard copy, be sure that you triple-space or leave wide right or left margins for comments.

There are computer programs especially designed for aiding revision. You may find that the software you received with your computer includes a text-feedback program. Sometimes these programs are available in computer-assisted classrooms or campus writing labs. Although some of them are designed strictly for editing and proofreading, others (such as revision prompters, revision demonstrators, and speech synthesizers) are intended to help with global revision. Revision prompters can represent your text to you in various ways; for example, the program may show you a paragraph from your draft and ask you whether it has a clear focus. Revision demonstrators show you examples of an expert writer revising a text with a word processor. Speech synthesizers read your draft aloud to you, allowing you the different perspective of being a listener rather than a reader. Because the voice is flat and robotic, this oral reading can give you an objective view of your paper's coherence and meaning, though at times the mechanical voice can be difficult to understand.

Some of the strategies useful for global revision—annotating drafts, manipulating sentences and paragraphs, employing text feedback programs—are also useful for local revision. As discussed in Chapters 7 through 10, local revision involves fine-tuning individual paragraphs, sentences, phrases, and words. You may, for example, wish to experiment by reordering the sentences in your topical paragraphs or by drafting several versions of your introductory paragraph to vary tone or emphasis. Or ask a peer reader to mark your draft, using one of the methods discussed earlier, to show needed transitions or problems with paragraph unity, completeness, order, or coherence.

Similarly, you may experiment with sentence structure and diction, drafting several versions of a sentence or listing several possible word choices, or you may wish to ask a peer reader to annotate your draft for awkward or ineffective sentences or diction. Style-checking programs summarize the sentence types in your draft (the number or percentage of simple, compound, or compound-complex sentences), sometimes suggesting the need to vary sentence structure. Also, some style checkers calculate the number of words per sentence and flag wordy constructions. Such feedback on sentence types, constructions, and length may be helpful, but it must be evaluated in terms of your subject, audience, and purpose. As mentioned elsewhere, the computer thesaurus aids in word choice, although here, too, you will want to evaluate the computer's advice or suggestions in light of your subject or purpose.

Reading computer drafts aloud should be part of your local revision process. The computer's encouragement of constant tinkering can cause you to overlook wordiness and overly long sentences. Your ear is the best guide for catching such infelicities and for determining whether your tone and style are consonant with your purpose.

It is important to print each successive draft for evaluation and revision. The on-screen methods for revision complement but do not replace reading and annotating the hard copy. There are several reasons why this is true. First, it is hard to evaluate the overall organization and coherence of a paper by reading on screen. The slow process of scrolling from page to page to read screen text makes it difficult to remember what you have written. When you read a printed copy, you can refresh your memory by quickly referring to earlier pages. Second, as you compose or enter your paper on the computer, you inevitably make many changes. Since you are not forced to recopy or retype the entire paper to incorporate these changes, it can be difficult to see how they affect the paper as a whole. So, even though you may be impressed with the professional look of your computer-produced paper and hesitant to read it for revision and mark it up, resist the temptation to forgo this step. Another copy that is just as professional looking can easily be produced later, and this one will have the benefit of careful, thorough review and revision.

USING THE WORD PROCESSOR FOR EDITING AND PROOFREADING

The last stage of work on any assignment is editing and proofreading. Some software programs offer editing aids, but you should develop your own strategies for editing and proofreading with a word processor.

First, here is some general advice. When you read screen text for editing purposes, it is easy to miss mechanical and grammatical errors. Because the text looks so neat and you already know what's on the page, your eyes may skip over words and fail to catch errors. Computer-type errors such as double letters and undeleted words—the computer's counterpart to typos—are also easy to miss. Sometimes, as you make quick changes, you may forget to delete a word or phrase, and a sentence like this results: "The following essays *explore examine* causes and effects." At other times, you may fail to add an intended word. In any case, you need to read through your screen text carefully. First read each page line by line; then move the cursor through the page word by word. When you find errors, delete the incorrect form and add the correct one. Double-check by proofreading a hard copy.

The "Find/Replace" function is a specific word processor editing and proofreading tool that can be used in several ways to check and correct your text. If you discover that you have misspelled a word throughout your paper, you can use the "Find/Replace" function to correct all the misspellings of that word. You can also use the "Find/Replace" feature if you wish to replace one word with another throughout your paper. You might start writing about a personal experience using a pseudonym (for example, Sarah) instead of your real name (Jane). If you later decide to use your real name, you can change all the Sarahs to Janes in seconds by employing the "Find/Replace" feature.

When you are drafting or revising, you may wish to mark with asterisks all words or sentences about which you have questions of diction, style, or grammatical correctness. Instead of interrupting your writing to check your handbook or dictionary, you can use the "Find/Replace" function to return to each marked spot for later editing. You can also use this feature to find all the periods in your text if you wish to check for sentence completeness, all the commas if you wish to check for correct usage, or all instances of *is* and *are* if you wish to see whether you can replace them with stronger verbs or make passive constructions active.

Peer editors can also offer proofreading and editing advice by marking your text in certain ways—placing asterisks on either side of a misspelled word [*receive*], a *P* at the beginning of each sentence with a punctuation error, and so on. Using the "Find/Replace" function, you can locate the errors flagged by your peer editor.

You may be familiar with some programmed editing and proofreading aids—for example, spell and style checkers, thesauruses, and error detectors. Although these text-feedback programs are helpful, they must be used with caution and should accompany, not replace, self-editing and proofreading strategies.

▼ *Spell checkers* check the correctness of the spelling of each word in your text by comparing it to the contents of an online dictionary. The computer, however, does not recognize the *contexts* of the words you use and so will not pick up errors like these: *compute* for *computer* or *there* for *their*.

▼ *Style checkers* vary from program to program. Generally, they locate potential problem areas, such as passive constructions, wordy phrases, and clichés, and may suggest changes. Some style checkers give you a statistical analysis of the number of words in your essay, average word length, readability level, number and types of sentences. The advice provided by all style programs is generic and should not be followed blindly. They are meant as guides to editing, not as instructions for editing. Since computers cannot understand the context in which a certain word or phrase appears, they cannot determine the most appropriate word or phrase. Only you, perhaps with the advice of a teacher or a peer editor, can do that.

▼ A programmed *thesaurus* can suggest various alternative word choices, but you must decide which word expresses the meaning you intend.

▼ *Error detectors* are very new and relatively untried. If you use one, remember only you can determine whether the sentence fragment detected by the program is an intentional fragment that you wish to keep for stylistic effect or whether it is an error that should be corrected.

Remember, no matter how neat your printed copy may look, it still needs a careful proofreading.

In addition to the uses of the word processor mentioned here, there are other electronic aids for special writing tasks. If you are taking a business or technical writing course, you can set up certain formats (for example, tables, graphs, spreadsheets) for frequent or repeated use. A number of aids are available for writers of research papers: computer data searches, programs to translate your bibliographic entries and notes into various formats (including MLA and APA); programs to index items in a long paper.

The computer is a powerful writing tool and one that promises to continue to grow in usefulness and capacity. Exciting new advances are under development. In the not-too-distant future, for example, voice-reproduction word processors will work like dictating machines, entering the text as you speak your thoughts aloud. Already, writers working on joint projects in different cities use telephone connections to send their drafts to one another in seconds.

Powerful though they are, however, computers are not the writer's most valuable tool. Even with advances in artificial intelligence, the computer's simulation of human thought is crude and rigid. An example of an advanced computer's translation from one language to another illustrates the computer's limitations. The English saying "The spirit is willing, but the flesh is weak," when translated by computer into Russian and back into English, becomes "The vodka is good, but the meat is rotten." The complexity and resourcefulness of the human mind, the richness of human language, and the boundlessness of the human imagination are, and will remain, the writer's most powerful tools.

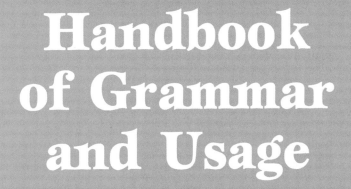

Handbook of Grammar and Usage

The Evolution of English

Understanding Sentence Elements

Writing Logical and Effective Sentences

Writing Grammatical Sentences

Choosing Effective Diction

Observing the Rules of Punctuation

Observing the Rules of Mechanics

A Glossary of Contemporary Usage

The Evolution of English

The language that Americans speak and write is descended from the language spoken by the English, Scottish, and Irish immigrants who founded the British colonies in America. Their language, in turn, was descended from the languages of Germanic tribes who, during the fifth and sixth centuries, invaded Britain and settled there. One of these tribes, the Angles, later became known as the Englisc (English) and gave their name to a country and a language, both of which they shared with other peoples—the Saxons, the Jutes, and later, the Danes and the Normans.

The language that has come down to us from that Anglo-Saxon beginning has undergone great changes. Modern college students find Chaucer's fourteenth-century English something of a puzzle. And before Chaucer—well, judge for yourself. Here is the opening of the Lord's Prayer as it was written in the ninth, fourteenth, and seventeenth centuries, respectively:

Old English	Middle English	Modern English
Fæder ūre þū þe eart on heofonum, sī þīn nama gehālgod. Tōbecume þīn rīce, Gewurþe ðīn willa on eorðan swā swā on heofonum.	Oure fadir that art in heuenes, halwid be thi name; thi kyngdom cumme to; be thi wille don as in heuen and in erthe.	Our Father which art in heaven, Hallowed be thy name. Thy kingdom come. Thy will be done on earth as it is in heaven.

A contrast of these three versions offers a brief but revealing impression of the changes that occurred in the language during eight hundred years, and these differences would seem even greater if we could reproduce also the changes in sound that took place. For example, Old English $\bar{u}$ and $\bar{\imath}$ were pronounced like the *oo* in *boot* and the *e* in *me,* respectively, so that *ūre* was pronounced "oo′ruh" and *sī,* "see."

In grammar the major change has been the simplification of grammatical forms. Old English (700–1100) was a highly *inflected* language, one that made grammatical distinctions by changes in the form of a word. For example, nouns were declined in five cases (nominative, genitive, dative, accusative, and instrumental) as well as in singular and plural numbers. Adjectives and the definite article were declined to agree with the nouns they modified. Here is the declension, in the singular only, of "the good man" with the approximate pronunciation enclosed in quotation marks at the right:

Case	Declension	Pronunciation
N. (*man* as subject)	sē gōda mann	"say goada man"
G. ("of the good man" or "the good man's")	ðaes gōdan mannes	"thas goadan mannes"
D. ("to the good man")	ðǣm gōdan menn	"tham goadan men"
A. (*man* as object)	ðone gōdan mann	"thonna goadan man"
I. ("by the good man")	ðȳ gōdan menn	"thee goadan men"

In Modern English the article and the adjective are not declined at all. The noun retains the genitive case and has singular and plural forms. We distinguish between subject and object by word order, and we have replaced the dative and instrumental endings by the prepositions *to* and *by.* As a result, the whole declensional system has been greatly simplified. Verbs still show considerable inflection, though much less than in Old English.

Along with this simplification of grammatical forms went a great increase in vocabulary as new words were introduced through association with foreign cultures. During the eighth and ninth centuries, Scandinavian raiders settled along the coast of England and brought into the language some fourteen hundred place names and about one thousand common words. In 1066 the Normans conquered England, and for three hundred years their French language dominated the court and the affairs in which the nobility was most involved—government, army, law, church, art, architecture, fashions, and recreation. Between 1100 and 1500, over ten thousand French words were absorbed into the language. During the fourteenth, fifteenth, and sixteenth centuries, English writers borrowed heavily from Latin. Language historians estimate that more than half of the present English vocabulary came from Latin, either directly or through one of the Romance languages, especially French. And as the English-speaking countries grew in political, economic, and cultural importance, their language borrowed from all over the world the words it needed to name the things and ideas that Anglo-Americans were acquiring. Today the vocabulary of the English language is international in origin, as the following list illustrates:

algebra (Arabic)
amen (Hebrew)
bantam (Javanese)
boor (Dutch)
caravan (Persian)
cashew (Portuguese)
chorus (Greek)
coffee (Turkish)
dollar (German)

flannel (Welsh)
garage (French)
garbage (Italian)
inertia (Latin)
kimono (Japanese)
leprechaun
  (Old Irish)
polka (Polish)
polo (Tibetan)

silk (Chinese)
shampoo (Hindi)
ski (Norwegian)
tag (Swedish)
toboggan
  (American Indian)
vodka (Russian)
whiskey (Gaelic)

Understanding Sentence Elements

The ability to *compose* effective sentences does not depend on an ability to describe sentences grammatically or linguistically. Rather, most proficient writers use intuitive language skills, developed over a number of years, when they compose sentences. Yet when writers understand sentence elements and structure, they are better able to *revise* sentences to achieve a clear form and purpose. To help you in effective sentence revision, the following sections offer a brief overview of basic sentence elements.

1 RECOGNIZE THE BASIC ELEMENTS OF SENTENCES

Although many sentences are complicated word structures, all sentences, even the most complicated, are built from a few basic elements: **subjects** (S), **verbs** (V), **objects** (O), and **complements** (C). These elements work together to express a central idea that may be further developed or refined by other elements: **modifiers** (M) and **conjunctions** (Conj).

The verb with its objects, complements, and modifiers is known as the **predicate** of the sentence. The predicate describes the action performed by the subject or the state of being of the subject. Subject and predicate are the two main parts of a simple sentence.

        S   V
The lawyer wrote. [Subject + Verb.]

        S   V   O
The lawyer wrote the brief. [Subject + Verb + Object.]

The trial lawyer hurriedly wrote the Hernandez brief but then carefully

V   O

revised it.

[Subject + Verb + Object + Conjunction + Verb + Object. Modifiers used throughout.]

These examples show that a sentence composed of the basic elements can be made more specific and informative through expansion.

1a   *Subjects* **identify the people, places, things, ideas, qualities, or conditions that act, are acted upon, or are described in a sentence.**

Nouns and pronouns are the most common subjects, but phrases (groups of words without verbs) or clauses (groups of words with subjects and verbs) may also be subjects.

┌─S─┐ V   C

To win is her objective. [Subject (*phrase*) + Verb + Complement.]

┌────────── S ──────────┐ V   C

What President Aquino wants most is political stability.

[Subject (*clause*) + Verb + Complement.]

1b   *Verbs* **express action (***select, walk***) or a state of being (***seem, is***). Verbs consist of single words (***develop***) or groups of words (***might have developed***).**

A verb that requires an object to complete its meaning is a *transitive verb*. A verb that does not require an object to complete its meaning is an *intransitive verb*. Notice that some verbs can be either transitive or intransitive.

┌──── S ────┐ Trans V   O

President Roosevelt **ordered** the evacuation.

Intrans V

After two years, Senator Harris **resigned**.

Trans V   O

The building inspector **examined** the wiring.

Intrans V

Pandas **eat** voraciously.

A verb connecting a complement to a subject is a *linking verb*.

The child **seemed** frightened.

After years of study, Fred **became** an aerospace engineer.

1c   *Objects* **are nouns or pronouns that complete the ideas expressed by subjects and transitive verbs.**

Direct objects answer the questions *what?* or *whom?* *Indirect objects* answer the questions *to whom?* or *for whom?*

```
             ┌── S ──┐     V        D.O.
With great care, Dr. Rodriguez completed the report.
```
[*Report* tells *what* Dr. Rodriguez completed.]

```
     ┌── S ──┐ V      I.O.        D.O.
Dr. Rodriguez sent the immunologist the report.
```
[*Report* tells *what* Dr. Rodriguez sent; *immunologist* explains to *whom* he sent it.]

1d

Complements are adjectives or nouns that complete the ideas in a sentence by modifying the subject (*predicate adjective*) or by renaming the subject (*predicate noun*).

Complements are joined to the subjects of sentences by linking verbs, such as *am, are, is, was, were, become, get, feel, look,* and *seem.*

```
                              S       V       C
Throughout the competition, Warren remained optimistic.
```
[Predicate adjective modifies the subject *Warren.*]

```
          S    V        C
In the end, Warren was first runner-up.
```
[Predicate noun renames the subject *Warren.*]

1e

Modifiers (typically adjectives, adverbs, and prepositional phrases) describe or limit subjects, verbs, objects, complements, or other modifiers.

Modifiers alter the meanings of other words by answering one of these questions: *what kind? which one? how many? whose? how? when? where? how often?* or *to what extent?*

Long speeches are unacceptable. [What kind of speeches?]

Those four-wheelers are dangerous. [Which four-wheelers?]

We received **sixty-seven** applications. [How many applications?]

The subcommittee shared **its** findings. [Whose findings?]

The immigrant **slowly** completed the form. [How did he complete it?]

After the tennis match, we celebrated. [When did we celebrate?]

Leave the carton **in the mailroom.** [Where should it be left?]

Michael called his doctor **frequently.** [How often did he call?]

The glassblower **very** skillfully formed the stem.

[What degree of skill did the glassblower use?]

Conjunctions join and relate two or more words, phrases, or clauses in a sentence.

Coordinating conjunctions (*and, but, for, nor, or, so,* and *yet*) link equivalent sentence elements.

John Kander **and** Fred Ebb collaborated on several major musicals. [Conjunction links two subjects.]

The burglars gained access to the vault **yet** left its contents intact. [Conjunction links two verbs.]

He fought unenthusiastically **but** skillfully. [Conjunction links two modifiers.]

I will not do it, **nor** will I recommend anyone else who might. [Conjunction links two clauses.]

Correlative conjunctions, such as *both . . . and, either . . . or, neither . . . nor,* and *not only . . . but also,* work in pairs and also link equivalent sentence elements.

Both Senator Robins **and** Representative Hershell received contributions from the tobacco industry. [Conjunction links two subjects.]

Marion will go **either** to Butler University to study pharmacology **or** to Indiana University to study dentistry. [Conjunction links two modifiers.]

Subordinating conjunctions, such as *after, although, because, even if, so that, until,* and *when,* join clauses but subordinate one clause to another. The subordinate clause, introduced by the subordinating conjunction, can be positioned at the beginning, in the middle, or at the end of a sentence.

Because she was outspoken on the subject of women writers, Virginia Woolf has become a central figure in feminist criticism. [Subordinate clause first.]

Virginia Woolf has become a central figure in feminist criticism **because she was outspoken on the subject of women writers.** [Subordinate clause last.]

Virginia Woolf, **because she was outspoken on the subject of women writers,** has become a central figure in feminist criticism. [Subordinate clause embedded.]

Exercise

Identify each of the underlined words or phrases as a subject (S), verb (V), object (O), complement (C), modifier (M), or conjunction (Conj). (Consider proper names as single elements but consider all other words separately.)

1. <u>Although</u> the <u>1981 baseball strike</u> lasted seven <u>weeks</u>, the 1985 baseball strike <u>lasted only three</u> days.

2. <u>Cadets</u> at West Point <u>are considered members</u> of the <u>regular</u> Army.

3. Jason <u>sent me</u> an <u>application</u> for Duke University, in hopes that <u>I</u> too <u>would apply</u> for admission.

4. In 1967, a fire <u>aboard Apollo 1</u> killed <u>Virgil Grissom</u>, <u>Edward White</u>, <u>and</u> <u>Roger Chaffee</u>.

5. <u>General Washington commissioned seven ships</u> to fight against the <u>British</u> navy.

6. <u>Universal Studios and</u> 20th Century-Fox <u>produced</u> the <u>five</u> motion pictures with the highest revenues.

7. <u>The Iliad and the Odyssey</u>, composed by the <u>Greek</u> poet Homer, are <u>mainstays</u> of <u>most humanities</u> curricula.

8. <u>Thomas à Becket was</u> the <u>archbishop of Canterbury</u> during the reign of Henry II.

9. <u>In spite of</u> recent declines in sales, <u>General Motor, Ford, and Chrysler</u> are still among the fifteen largest corporations in the United States.

10. <u>U.S. Grant was</u> an effective <u>general but</u> an <u>ineffectual president</u>.

2   RECOGNIZE BASIC SENTENCE PATTERNS

There are four basic sentence patterns: simple, compound, complex, and compound-complex.

2a

A *simple sentence* contains one independent clause, that is, a subject and verb that can stand alone as a grammatically complete sentence.

The subject and verb of a simple sentence may appear in compound form. A simple sentence need not be simplistic, but it does present a single idea. In fact, simple sentences, because they present ideas clearly, are useful for creating emphasis.

S   V   C

Hurricanes are frightening.

S   S V

Hurricanes and other tropical storms are both frightening and dangerous.

[Though more complicated than the preceding example, this is a simple sentence because it has one (compound) subject, and one predicate; the sentence also includes one compound complement.]

2b   **A *compound sentence* contains two or more independent clauses joined by a comma and a coordinating conjunction (*and, but, for, nor, or, so,* and *yet*) or by a semicolon alone.**

A compound sentence presents a balanced relationship between the clauses that are joined, thus emphasizing that the ideas in the sentence are of equal importance.

We moved to the Gulf coast to escape the cold Ohio winters, but then we were terrified by tropical storms. [Two independent clauses joined by a conjunction.]

We moved to Florida in 1978; we stayed only five years, however, and then returned to Ohio. [Two independent clauses joined by a semicolon and a conjunctive adverb.]

2c   **A *complex sentence* contains at least two clauses: one independent and one or more subordinate clauses.**

Subordinating conjunctions, such as *although, because, since, when,* and *while,* and relative pronouns, such as *that, what, which,* and *who,* join the clauses in a complex sentence. One clause, and thus the interrelationship of the ideas in the sentence, is emphasized over the others.

S V   S   V   C

Although it rains in the midmornings, the afternoons are generally sunny.

[Subordinate clause, then independent clause.]

S   V   O   S   V   O

We enjoyed our stay in Florida, even though we knew that we could not

remain. [Independent clause, then subordinate clause.]

2d   **A *compound-complex* sentence contains three or more clauses—at least two independent clauses and one subordinate clause.**

A compound-complex sentence establishes a complicated relationship among a series of ideas.

S   V   S   V   O

While we lived in Florida, we survived four minor hurricanes without

S   V   O

injuries or property damage, but we never developed the nonchalance of native Floridians. [Subordinate clause, then independent clause, then another independent clause.]

_____*Exercise*

Identify the following sentences as simple, compound, complex, or compound-complex.

1. Lightning is a discharge of electricity between two clouds or between a cloud and the earth.

2. Because of deaths during the war with the Soviet Union and because of massive emigration to Iran and Pakistan, Afghanistan's population has shrunk by one-third in the last decade.

3. According to some statistics, Northern Ireland has the highest unemployment rate in Europe.

4. The original purpose of the Crusades was to take Christianity to the non-Christian "infidels," but the holy wars also served to enrich trade and the arts in Europe.

5. Although the 1986 Tax Reform Act is supposed to be revenue neutral, it provides too many loopholes for selected businesses.

6. Mongolia is located in eastern Asia, between Siberia and China, and is slightly larger than Alaska.

7. After his notorious raid on Harpers Ferry in 1859, John Brown was captured and hanged; in the years that followed, his name became a symbol of ineffectual militant protest.

8. Although *bona fide* means "in good faith" in Latin, it is commonly used today to mean "genuine."

9. Because the costs of American materials and labor are high, sales of American-made shoes have plummeted, and sales of imports from Brazil and South Korea have risen.

10. Most Americans assume that the U.S. Navy is our oldest maritime service, yet the U.S. Coast Guard was established in 1790, eight years before the Navy.

3

EXPAND AND VARY SENTENCE PATTERNS

As writers move from drafting sentences to revising them, they make decisions about diction, about the placement of phrases and clauses, and about the structural patterns of sentences. The larger issue — sentence patterns — is important because sentence construction (and reconstruction) often determines how effectively writing communicates with readers.

3a

Use Coordination

When isolated, successive sentences present ideas that together establish an important, parallel relationship, those sentences can be effectively combined by coordination. *Coordination* is the joining of simple sentences to form compound sentences, and it is also the meshing or combining of related sentence elements through pairing or seriation.

President Reagan initially denied that the United States had traded arms

for hostages, ~~T~~*but t*he Tower Commission subsequently revealed otherwise.
[Two sentences effectively joined by a coordinating conjunction.]

Oliver North's *and John Poindexter's* activities were largely unsupervised. ~~John Poindexter's activities were also unsupervised.~~
[Combining the sentences — by using a compound subject — improves the emphasis.]

3b

Use Subordination

When isolated, successive sentences present related ideas. The sentences can be combined through subordination. *Subordination* is the joining of simple sentences to form complex or compound-complex sentences, but it is also the embedding of words, phrases, or clauses in the structure of the most important sentence.

Mark Chagall, ~~was~~ a native of Russia, ~~He~~ emigrated to France, ~~While in~~ *where* ~~France,~~ he produced vibrant and dreamlike paintings.
[Three independent clauses compressed into one complex sentence.]

Because

∧Chagall's images are often childlike, *u*ndiscerning observers sometimes
                                        and o
find his work simplistic. *O*bservant critics see an ingenious use of childhood

perception in his work.

[Three independent clauses reworked into a compound-complex sentence
that reveals a cause-and-effect relationship among the ideas.]

Subordination is a useful means of indicating emphasis and bringing
variety to sentences. Consider subordination the groundwork of a mature
and effective sentence style and work to use it to achieve your purpose.

_____*Exercise*

Use coordination and subordination to combine the following pairs of
sentences.

1. Four men from the United States have won the Olympic figure-skating
   title. Only one, Dick Button, won the title twice.

2. *Amadeus* popularized the works of Mozart. The plot of the play and film
   is historically inaccurate.

3. Ten percent of home-study lawyers pass the California Bar Exam. Sixty
   percent of law school–trained lawyers pass.

4. Alfred Smith was the first Catholic to run for president. He lost by a
   wide margin to Herbert Hoover in 1928.

5. Trademarks are usually specialized symbols, products, or company
   names. They can also be individual words and letters.

_____*Exercise*

The following paragraph contains simple sentences only. Use coordination
and subordination to combine sentences and produce an effective and varied
paragraph.

The Beatles were the most successful pop group of all time. They began
playing in Liverpool, England. The group had four members. They were
John Lennon, Paul McCartney, George Harrison, and Ringo Starr. Their
early music was characterized by a simple rhythm-and-blues style. It also

had simple harmonies and lyrics. The Beatles' early hits included "She Loves You," "Please Please Me," and "I Want to Hold Your Hand." These simple songs attracted worldwide interest. John Lennon and Paul McCartney later wrote complicated songs. The lyrics became imaginative and philosophical. The music itself became varied. It was also complex. They experimented with new instruments and recording equipment. Their later work included the albums *Rubber Soul, The White Album,* and *Abbey Road.* The Beatles' most sophisticated work was the album *Sergeant Pepper's Lonely Hearts Club Band.* It contained some of the group's most memorable songs. Each member of the band developed separate interests. The group disbanded in 1980.

Understanding Sentence Elements: Review Exercises

In the following paragraph, label each of the underlined elements as a subject (S), Verb (V), Object (O), complement (C), modifier (M), or conjunction (Conj).

Our Sun is a sphere of superheated gas. Hydrogen atoms at its core fuse, creating the atomic reactions that produce both light and energy. Scientists estimate that the temperature of the Sun's core is twenty million degrees centigrade, while the surface temperature is approximately six thousand degrees centigrade. The diameter of the Sun is roughly 850,000 miles. These figures suggest that our Sun is neither a hot nor a large star when compared with others in our solar system.

The following paragraph contains simple sentences only. Use coordination and subordination to combine sentences to make this paragraph effective. Then label your sentences by type: simple (S), compound (C), Complex (CX), and compound-complex (CCX).

The Black Death devastated Europe between 1348 and 1666. The disease was brought to Europe through Italy. Traders carried it from the Black Sea area. The epidemic of 1348 killed one-fourth of the population of Europe. The disease was carried by fleas. This was unknown in the fourteenth and seventeenth centuries. The fleas lived on rats. The disease raged, subsided, and reemerged for three hundred years. The worst epidemic in England occurred in 1665. Entire towns and villages were wiped out. London's population decreased by one-tenth. The population was approximately 450,000. People were terrified. They tried all kinds of cures. They didn't understand the nature of the disease. The cures failed. Samuel Pepys wrote about the Black Death in his *Diary*. Daniel Defoe wrote a fictional account titled *Journal of the Plague Year*.

stationary, stationery *Stationary* means "fixed" or "unchanging": "The battle front is now stationary." *Stationery* means "writing paper": "a box of stationery." Associate the *e* in *stationery* with the *e*'s in *letter*.

suit, suite The common word is *suit*: "A suit of clothes"; "Follow suit, play a diamond"; "Suit yourself." *Suite*, pronounced "sweet," means "retinue" ("The President and his suite have arrived") or "set" or "collection" ("a suite of rooms," "a suite of furniture"). When *suite* refers to furniture, an alternative pronunciation is "suit."

sure = certainly Using *sure* in the sense of "certainly" ("I am sure annoyed"; "Sure, I will go with you") is colloquial. Unless the style justifies colloquial usage, use *certainly* or *surely*.

terrific Used at a formal level to mean "terrifying" ("a terrific epidemic") and at a colloquial level as an intensive ("a terrific party," "a terrific pain"). Overuse of the word at the colloquial level has made it almost meaningless.

than, then *Than* is a conjunction used in comparison; *then* is an adverb indicating time. Do not confuse the two: "I would rather write in the morning than in the afternoon. My thinking seems to be clearer then."

that, which, who *That* refers to persons or things, *which* refers to things, and *who* refers to persons. *That* introduces a restrictive clause; *which* usually introduces a nonrestrictive clause: "John argued that he was not prepared to take the exam. The exam, which had been scheduled for some time, could not be changed." "Anyone who was not ready would have to take the test anyway."

there, their, they're Although these words are pronounced alike, they have different meanings. *There* indicates place: "Look at that dog over there." *Their* indicates possession: "I am sure it is their dog." *They're* is a contraction of "they are": "They're probably not home."

thusly Not an acceptable variant of *thus*.

tough The use of *tough* to mean "difficult" ("a tough assignment," "a tough decision") and "hard fought" ("a tough game") is accepted without qualification by reputable dictionaries. But its use to mean "unfortunate," "bad" ("The fifteen-yard penalty was a tough break for the team"; "That's tough") is colloquial and should be used only in a paper written in a colloquial style.

troop, troupe Both words come from the same root and share the original meaning, "herd." In modern usage *troop* can refer to soldiers and *troupe* to actors: "a troop of cavalry," "a troop of scouts," "a troupe of circus performers," "a troupe of entertainers."

try and *Try to* is the preferred idiom. Use "I will try to do it" in preference to "I will try and do it."

type = type of *Type* is not acceptable as a variant form of *type of*. In "That type engine isn't being manufactured anymore," add *of* after *type*.

uninterested, disinterested See **disinterested**.

unique The formal meaning of *unique* is "sole" or "only" or "being the only one of its kind": "Adam was unique in being the only man who never had a mother." The use of *unique* to mean "rare" or "unusual" ("Americans watched their television sets anxiously as astronauts in the early moon landings had the unique experience of walking on the moon") has long been popular, but some people still object to this usage. The use of *unique* to mean merely "uncommon" ("a unique sweater") is generally frowned upon. *Unique* should not be modified by adverbs that express degree: *very, more, most, rather.*

up The adverb *up* is idiomatically used in many verb-adverb combinations that act as verbs—*break up, clean up, fill up, get up, tear up.* Avoid the unnecessary or awkward separation of *up* from the verb with which it is combined, since such a separation makes *up* look at first like an adverb modifying the verb rather than an adverb combining with the verb in an idiomatic expression. For example, "They held the cashier up" and "She made her face up" are awkward. Say "They held up the cashier," "She made up her face."

use to The *d* in *used to* is often not pronounced; it is elided before the *t* in *to.* The resulting pronunciation leads to the written expression *use to.* But the acceptable written phrase is *used to:* "I am used to the noise"; "He used to do all the grocery shopping."

very A common intensive, but avoid its overuse.

wait on *Wait on* means "serve": "A clerk will be here in a moment to wait on you." The use of *wait on* to mean "wait for" ("I'll wait on you if you won't be long") is a colloquialism to which there is some objection. Use *wait for:* "I'll wait for you if you won't be long."

want in, out, off The use of *want* followed by *in, out,* or *off* ("The dog wants in"; "I want out of here"; "I want off now") is colloquial. In college writing supply an infinitive after the verb: "The dog wants to come in."

want to = ought to, should Using *want to* as a synonym for *should* ("They want to be careful or they will be in trouble") is colloquial. *Ought to* or *should* is preferred in college writing.

where . . . at, to The use of *at* or *to* after *where* ("Where was he at?" "Where are you going to?") is redundant. Simply write "Where was he?" and "Where are you going?"

whose, who's *Whose* is the possessive of *who; who's* is a contraction of *who is.* "In the play, John is the character whose son leaves town. Who's going to try out for that part?"

will, shall See **shall, will.**

-wise Avoid adding the suffix *-wise,* meaning "concerning," to nouns to form such combinations as *budgetwise, jobwise, tastewise.* Some combined forms with *-wise* are thoroughly established (*clockwise, otherwise, sidewise, weatherwise*), but the fad of coining new compounds with this suffix is generally best avoided.

Writing Logical and Effective Sentences

4

SENTENCE SENSE (SS)

Creating a uniform impression in your writing is important, especially at the sentence level, because readers need consistency to understand fully your ideas. Unnecessary shifts in point of view, tense, mood, and voice are distracting and may be confusing.

4a

Use a consistent point of view.

Point of view is the standpoint from which you present information. If you select the *first-person* point of view, then your subject (*I, we*) is the speaker. If you select the *second person,* then your subject (*you*) is being spoken to. If you select the *third person,* then your subject (*he, she, it, they*) is being spoken about. Selecting the appropriate point of view and maintaining it are important for clarity.

Swimming instructors must be patient if they work with children. ~~You~~ *They* must acknowledge that some children have never swum before, and ~~you~~ *they* must acclimate children to the water. Instructors must be willing to work slowly and teach skills gradually.

[Elimination of shift from third person (*swimming instructors*) to second person (*you*).]

4b

Use verb tenses consistently.

Verb tenses signal chronological relationships among ideas. Unnecessary shifts in tense will confuse your readers.

485

After filling out a tentative class schedule, the student goes to see his or her advisor for approval. The advisor examined *s* the schedule to see that requirements ~~were~~ *are* met, and the student submits the signed computer form.

[The shifts from present tense (*goes*) to the past tense (*examined*) to the present tense (*submits*) make these sentences confusing. It is unclear whether they describe a typically repeated sequence, for which present tense would be appropriate, or a completed sequence, for which past tense would be suitable.]

4c   **Use a consistent mood.**

Three moods indicate how you view the actions or conditions you are describing in your sentences. The ***indicative mood*** is used to make statements of fact or opinion and ask questions. The ***imperative mood*** is used to express commands. The ***subjunctive mood*** is used to indicate doubt, conditional situations, statements contrary to fact, and wishes. In most writing, mood should remain consistent.

Betting on a horse race, Mr. McMillan explained, can be risky. *He suggested that people* ~~Bet~~ only money that ~~you~~ *they* can afford to lose.

[Elimination of confusing shift from the indicative to the imperative. The first sentence *described;* the second *advised.*]

4d   **Use a consistent voice.**

Active voice and passive voice create different kinds of emphasis in sentences. They should not be mixed in successive sentences that describe the same subject. (See Section 5, "Active and Passive Sentences.")

The research assistants carefully compile the results of the questionnaire. First, they record the sex, age, race, and religion of each respondent. Then, *they record* profession, income, and education ~~were recorded.~~ Next, the assistants note responses to individual interpretive questions. [Elimination of shift into the passive voice.]

Exercise

Revise each set of sentences so that it constitutes a paragraph that is consistent in mood, point of view, voice, and tense.

1. Department of Energy spokespersons have suggested that Americans save energy in small but important ways. They suggest walking rather than driving, coordinating short trips, and driving at slower speeds. Turn off lights when you are not in a room. Wash only full loads. Lower your thermostats.

2. The U.S. Fish and Wildlife Service now restricts bird hunting in most areas. Hunters can no longer use lead shot, since it poisons birds that are wounded but not killed. You must also restrict hunting to specified seasons, and hunters must limit the number of birds they kill. Penalties are also severe if you are caught violating these protective laws.

3. The National Forest Service has made timberlands available to private logging companies. New logging roads are built, destroying the forest floor. Trees are removed, and fish and wildlife are threatened. Irreparable damage is being done.

4. In the last few years, industrial pollution of water has declined. The Clean Water Act has given government agencies the right to assign stiff fines to plants and foundries in violation of existing pollution standards. These companies then had to correct the problem or risk further fines. Most industries adapted to these procedures.

5. Spokespeople for these agencies and services address important issues at arranged press conferences. Facts are given, and violators are identified. The American people are given information by these spokespeople to help them understand these national concerns.

5   ACTIVE AND PASSIVE SENTENCES (ACT & PAS)

Active sentences emphasize the people or things responsible for actions and conditions. Passive sentences focus on people or things that are acted upon. What would be the object in an active sentence is used as the subject in a passive sentence, and a form of the verb *to be* is used with the main verb. As a result, passive sentences are always slightly longer than active sentences. Although most readers and writers prefer active sentences, you should select the sentence pattern that most effectively matches your purpose.

Active: Congress approved a multi-billion-dollar highway improvement bill. [Congress is emphasized.]

Passive: The multi-billion-dollar highway improvement bill was approved by Congress. [The highway improvement bill is emphasized.]

5a   Use Active Sentences Most of the Time

Use active sentences to indicate who takes responsibility for actions and events.

Dr. Taylor misdiagnosed and mistreated Jeremy's respiratory problem.

Use active sentences to create emphasis.

A tornado in Texas destroyed property worth over $50 million.

Use active sentences for economy of expression.

Active: Lionel Richie sang the national anthem at the opening game of the season. [13 words]

Passive: The national anthem was sung by Lionel Richie at the opening game of the season. [15 words]

5b   Use Passive Sentences Selectively

Use passive sentences when the people who are responsible for actions are not known.

The superintendent's window was broken sometime over the weekend.

Use passive sentences to emphasize the receiver of the action instead of those responsible.

Van Gogh's *Sunflowers* was sold for $39.9 million.

Use passive sentences to emphasize actions that are more important than specific people who might be responsible.

Lasers are currently being used to treat medical problems as diverse as cancer, cataracts, and varicose veins.

Exercise

The following sentences are written in the passive voice. Rewrite those that would be more effective in the active voice.

1. Twenty people were killed when a car bomb exploded in Teheran.

2. Over $800 million had been deposited in personal Swiss bank accounts by Ferdinand Marcos, the ousted president of the Philippines.

3. Favorable trade conditions with China were supported by President Bush, despite controversy over the action.

4. Details of the nuclear accident at Chernobyl were withheld by Soviet officials for several days.

5. Franklin D. Roosevelt was elected to four terms as president.

6 MAINTAIN PARALLELISM AMONG SENTENCE ELEMENTS

Parallelism in a sentence requires that similar ideas be presented in similar form and that elements that are similar in function appear in similar grammatical form. Parallelism is an important principle of both grammar and style.

Grammatically, sentence elements linked by coordinating or correlative conjunctions should be similar in form: a clause should be followed by a clause, a phrase by a phrase, a noun by a noun, a verb by a verb of the same tense, and so on. (See Consistent Verb Tenses, Section 4b.)

Stylistically, parallelism creates balance and emphasis. It can, therefore, be used to create desired effects.

6a **Maintain parallelism with coordinating conjunctions.**

The evangelist ended the service with a hymn and ~~calling on~~ *with a call for* sinners to repent.
[Two prepositional phrases separated by a coordinating conjunction.]

6b **Maintain parallelism with correlative conjunctions.**

The owners of VCRs can either tape films from network broadcasts or

can rent films from video clubs.
[Correlative conjunctions followed by two verbs without auxiliaries.]

6c **Repeat key words to clarify a parallel construction.**

The commission has the power to investigate, *to* conciliate, *to* hold hearings, *to* subpoena witnesses, *to* issue cease-and-desist commands, *to* order reinstatements, and *to* direct hiring. [Parallelism emphasized by repeating *to*.]

Exercise

Revise the following sentences to eliminate faulty parallelism.

1. The narrator of *Invisible Man* was idealistic, intelligent, and tried to advance the cause of black people.

2. Holden Caufield, the main character of *Catcher in the Rye,* rejected hypocrisy in other people but was ignoring his own hypocrisy.

3. Thornton Wilder won Pulitzer prizes not only for his plays *Our Town* and *The Skin of Our Teeth* but also he won for his novel *The Bridge of San Luis Rey.*

4. The stories of Flannery O'Connor allow readers to examine unusual characters, to explore psychological motivations, and consider macabre situations.

5. Willy Loman could neither understand his own problems nor could he accept the help of friends.

7   WORD ORDER (WD OR)

7a   Inversions

The common order of words in sentences can be briefly summarized:

- Subjects precede verbs.
- Verbs precede objects or complements.
- Indirect objects precede direct objects.
- Adjectives precede the words they modify.
- Adverbs usually follow verbs they modify, but they precede adjectives or other adverbs.
- Prepositional phrases follow the words they modify.
- Independent clauses often precede subordinate clauses, although three variations are common: (1) clauses used as adjectives follow the words they modify, (2) clauses used as adverbs often precede the independent clause, and (3) clauses used as nouns occupy the subject or object positions.
- Closely related material is best kept as close together as possible.

Although these principles usually govern word order in sentences, any element of a sentence may be moved to create emphasis or interest. Variations of common word order, however, should produce neither awkward nor unidiomatic writing.

Common Order	*Inverted Order*
The chancellor **quickly and superficially** responded to the interviewer's questions.	**Quickly and superficially,** the chancellor responded to the interviewer's questions.
The team doesn't stand a chance **without Terry.**	**Without Terry,** the team doesn't stand a chance.
The computer terminals were installed **at last.**	**At last,** the computer terminals were installed.
The company will pay relocation expenses **if employees are transferred.**	**If employees are transferred,** the company will pay relocation expenses.
Jessica said, "I can only attend the Art Institute if I receive a scholarship."	"I can only attend the Art Institute," **Jessica said,** "if I receive a scholarship."

7b   Emphatic Order

To achieve a desired effect in a sentence, writers can vary the location of key information. In a typical sentence, information placed near the beginning or end will be emphasized. Placing important information in an independent clause, instead of in a subordinate clause or phrase, strengthens emphasis.

Place important information first or last; do not bury it in the middle.

Unemphatic: On April 14, 1865, **Abraham Lincoln was shot** at Ford's Theatre.
Emphatic: **Abraham Lincoln was shot** at Ford's Theatre on April 14, 1865.
Emphatic: At Ford's Theatre on April 14, 1865, **Abraham Lincoln was shot.**
Unemphatic: That novel, **as far as I know,** was my biggest commercial failure.
Emphatic: **As far as I know,** that novel was my biggest commercial failure.
Unemphatic: She is innocent, **in my opinion.**
Emphatic: **In my opinion,** she is innocent.

Place key information in independent clauses, not in subordinate clauses or phrases.

Unemphatic: He fell from the roof, **thus breaking his neck.**
Emphatic: He fell from the roof and **broke his neck.**

Exercise

Revise the following sentences to improve awkward or unemphatic word order.

1. The Supreme Court refused to consider the appeal, according to the late news last night.

2. The major evidence had been acquired during a search without a proper warrant, thus resulting in a dismissal of the case.

3. The evidence shows, the prosecuting attorney suggested, that Marshall Tireman is guilty of stealing industrial secrets.

4. The judge agreed to admit the videotape as evidence after the defense attorney made a special appeal.

5. The lawyers, even, had not expected such a large settlement in the case.

8

POSITION MODIFIERS CAREFULLY (MOD)

A modifier must clearly relate to a word in a sentence and explain, describe, define, or limit the word to which it relates. When a modifier is not positioned properly, the modification can be both awkward and confusing.

8a

Long modifiers should not separate a subject and verb or a verb and its complement.

Although modifiers may be placed between a subject and verb or between a verb and its complement, such positioning often makes a sentence difficult to read and interpret. Reposition the modifiers so that they do not break the flow of the sentence.

The renovation, because of fund-raising activities and because of competitive bidding by major contracting firms, was delayed.

The final bid was, even though it was thousands lower than the initial bids, still too high.

8b

Avoid dangling modifiers.

Opening modifiers that do not modify the subject of a sentence are said to dangle—hence, the name **dangling modifier.** To correct such an error, either revise the independent clause so that the introductory phrase can logically modify the subject, or revise the introductory phrase to make it a subordinate clause.

To qualify for the award, ~~the committee requires that~~ candidates *must* have sixty class hours and a 3.50 GPA.

I was
While _∧waiting for my date in the lobby, two men in tuxedos got into a violent argument.

8c   Avoid squinting modifiers.

A *squinting modifier* seems to modify the word before it *and* the word after it. Reposition the modifier to clarify the meaning, or use *that* to eliminate confusion.

that

The reporter said ∧ before noon she would finish the article.

The reporter said before noon she would finish the article.

8d   Avoid split infinitives.

A *split infinitive* occurs when a modifier falls between *to* and the primary verb. Writers and readers disagree about whether split infinitives are grammatically or stylistically acceptable. To be on the safe side, reposition the modifier.

Darren began to furiously pack his luggage to try to make the nine o'clock flight.

Exercise

Eliminate ambiguities in the following sentences by changing the position of misleading modifiers.

1. At one time his parents said he had been an engineering student.

2. The stage set, based on original paintings and engravings from the eighteenth century, was breathtaking.

3. The car was in the garage that he wrecked.

4. Marc promised on his way home to pick me up.

5. They talked about going on a second honeymoon but never did.

6. My brother hung the painting in the hallway that I gave him for his birthday.

7. The short story was, because of its convoluted sentences and obscure imagery, almost incomprehensible.

8. There is a panel discussion tonight about drug addiction in the student lounge.

9. I thought of writing often but never did.

10. Reading the personal letters of famous people is a way to usefully and completely understand their reactions to public situations.

9 COMPARISONS (CP)

When you include comparisons in your sentences, consider your diction carefully to ensure that the ideas are clear and complete.

9a **Include all the words needed to make a comparison clear and complete.**

Flying to Chicago is more convenient than *taking* a train.

Levi's are more popular than any *other* jeans.

9b **Do not write an implied comparison.**

An implied comparison presents only part of the necessary context. The words *better, less, more,* and *worse* and words formed with the suffix *-er* signal the need for fully stated comparisons; use *than* and explain the comparison completely.

The house on Elm Street is better suited to our needs *than the others we've seen*.

The orchestra's performance of Beethoven's Ninth Symphony was much worse *than expected*.

─────────── *Exercise*

Revise the following sentences to make their comparisons logical and complete.

1. Once Carla began taking her medication regularly, she felt much better.

2. Having had a two-hour practice session, the students were no longer as confused.

3. Taking a taxi or riding the subway is certainly more convenient than a car.

4. Reeboks are more popular than any tennis shoe.

5. Revising a paper is much easier using a word processor.

10   CONCISENESS (CON)

Writing that is concise expresses ideas in as few words as possible; it is free of needless repetition and useless words. To make your writing concise, eliminate words, phrases, and clauses that do not further your purpose.

10a   **Do not repeat words needlessly.**

~~The car~~ *W*e were looking for ~~was~~ a car for highway travel.
[12 words reduced to 9.]

10b   **Do not repeat ideas that are already understood.**

~~The~~ frown ~~on~~ Todd's ~~face~~ suggested that he was ~~depressingly~~ saddened by his interview. [14 words reduced to 10.]

10c   **Eliminate expletive constructions whenever possible.**

Expletives, such as *it is, there is, there are, here is, here are,* and so on, add words to sentences without clarifying meaning.

~~There were~~ *J* three cars *were* involved in the accident. [8 words reduced to 7.]

10d   **Write active sentences whenever possible. (See Active and Passive Sentences, Section 5.)**

My aunt Ruth made The prize-winning quilt ~~was made by my Aunt Ruth.~~
[9 words reduced to 7.]

10e   **Replace wordy phrases with brief expressions.**

I ~~am of the opinion~~ *think* that we should resubmit the insurance claim.
[12 words reduced to 9.]

10f   **Replace forms of the verb *to be* with stronger verbs.**

Counselors ~~are responsible for~~ *must* complet~~ing~~e the transcript portion of the applications.
[11 words reduced to 9.]

10g   **When possible, replace nonrestrictive clauses with appositives.**

Nonrestrictive clauses, clauses that provide useful or interesting but nonessential information, can often be replaced with *appositives*, simple words or phrases that provide definitions for other words or phrases in a

495

sentence. (See also Section 20h.) To save words and tighten and clarify your writing, consider using appositives in place of nonrestrictive clauses.

Sandra Day O'Connor, ~~who was~~ the first woman appointed to the Supreme Court, assumed her duties in August 1981.
[19 words reduced to 17 through substitution of an appositive for a nonrestrictive clause.]

_____Exercise

Make the following wordy sentences concise. Note the number of words saved through revision.

1. There should be two waiters to serve every ten people at the banquet, or there will be unnecessary delays occurring. [20 words reduced to _____.]

2. After the violent eruption of Nevada de Ruiz, relief agencies joined together in their efforts to help the unfortunate victims. [20 words reduced to _____.]

3. Wynton Marsalis, who plays both classical and jazz trumpet, scorns pop music. [12 words reduced to _____.]

4. At this point in time, we should prepare for spring floods, in the event that the Wabash River will crest as it did last year. [25 words reduced to _____.]

5. Finalists in the oratory competition will be evaluated by seven judges. [11 words reduced to _____.]

6. The original prototype for the Ford Mustang is on display at the Ford Museum in Detroit, Michigan. [17 words reduced to _____.]

7. A house made of brick is more costly but more maintenance free than a house made of wood. [18 words reduced to _____.]

8. Secret Service agents are responsible for protecting the current president, past presidents, and their families. [16 words reduced to _____.]

9. In the humble opinion of this writer, Academy Awards present indications of popularity rather than quality. [16 words reduced to _____.]

10. The real truth is that there is no money available to support and maintain the scholarship. [16 words reduced to _____.]

_____*Exercise*

Revise the following paragraph to make it concise. Try a number of strategies and notice how much the paragraph improves when you eliminate unnecessary words and bloated phrases.

Prior to beginning the search for gainful employment, gather together necessary and essential information and materials. Assemble a list of your experiences in educational institutions and in the work place and be sure to include the months or years involved in each situation. Prepare a résumé that includes facts and information about yourself, personally, and about yourself, academically and professionally. Make sure that there are clear sections in the résumé to cover each of these important and crucial topics. Proofread the final copy of the résumé in order to be aware of and correct any errors or mistakes. Then photocopy the résumé so that you still have at your disposal a copy of the résumé for future reference.

_____*Writing Logical and Effective Sentences: Review Exercises*

Revise the following sets of sentences to create logical and effective sentences. Identify the kinds of problems that required correction.

1. Human figures were elongated and were rendered in sallow yellows and greens by the Spanish artist El Greco.

2. Cubism is, with its emphasis on presenting the surfaces of all objects—both living and inanimate—in abstract geometric forms, alien to many people's artistic sensibilities.

3. Although his work was not popular during his lifetime, van Gogh paints

with bold colors and exaggerated forms. Modern collectors have valued his work since his death.

4. It is clear that there are only a few major pop art paintings of lasting aesthetic value. There are many others that are simply cultural curiosities.

5. When one sees the work of Rembrandt in a well-lighted gallery, you will be impressed by the rich texture of his work and the subtle variations in his gold and brown tones.

6. Neoclassical artists of the eighteenth century objected to the visual excesses of Baroque and Rococo art and imitate the symmetry and simple forms of Greek and Roman art.

7. Picasso's versatility as a sculptor is evident in his ability to skillfully and ingeniously use "junk" in his welded works.

8. Da Vinci, Raphael, David, Rembrandt, van Gogh, Monet, and Picasso would surely be included if one was to make a list of major European painters.

9. New York's Chrysler Building—with its use of zigzag forms, angular metal ornamentation, and strong vertical lines—is an exemplary model of Art Deco architecture.

10. Up until the middle of our current century, most prominent and important painters and sculptors from the United States of America trained and went to school in the countries of Europe.

11. Once, painters worked almost exclusively on wood panels or plaster walls. Then stretched canvas was used. Today, wood is being used again by many artists.

12. The Louvre in Paris houses more major works of art than any museum.

13. Prior to viewing a major exhibition, I would offer encouragement to inexperienced and untrained viewers to peruse or skim the catalogue prepared to accompany the exhibition.

14. To create what he described as an unconscious interpretation of reality, paint was splattered on canvas by Jackson Pollock.

15. Stressing the dreamlike, the unusual, and the bizarre, we found Surrealistic art unsettling.

Writing Grammatical Sentences

11 ELIMINATE SENTENCE FRAGMENTS (FRAG)

A *sentence fragment* is a group of words presented as if it were a complete sentence—with a capital letter at the beginning and a period at the end. A sentence fragment, however, lacks a subject or a verb or both and does not express a complete thought. Eliminate sentence fragments in one of four ways, depending on the type of fragment.

11a **Add a subject when necessary, or join the fragment to another sentence.**

Charlie Chaplin was a multitalented man. Wrote, directed, and starred in

his own films.

Charlie Chaplin was a multitalented man. Wrote, directed, and starred in

his own films.

11b **Add a verb when necessary, or join the fragment to another sentence.**

Grigori Rasputin, a Russian monk in Czar Nicholas's court. He was assassi-

nated in 1916.

11c **Omit the subordinating conjunction, or connect the fragment to an in-dependent clause.**

Mother Teresa

~~Because she~~ tirelessly helped the poor in Calcutta. ~~Mother Teresa~~ *She* was awarded the Nobel Peace Prize in 1979.

11d   Attach a phrase to a related sentence.

Leonard Bernstein received wide acclaim on Broadway, ~~N~~otably for the score of *West Side Story*.

Exercise

Eliminate each fragment by making it into a sentence or by combining it with a sentence.

1. The *Robert E. Lee,* a renovated river boat that now operates as a restaurant. It is an excellent place to eat.

2. We made our way up the mountain trail with much difficulty. Slipping on rocks and snagging our clothes in the underbrush.

3. Chad has only one ambition. To play the violin in a major symphony.

4. Many people dread one part of medical exams more than any other. Having a blood sample taken.

5. In a political speech, candidates should appeal to the entire audience. Not just to those who believe as they do.

6. Even though the cost of automobile insurance is high. Repairs on damaged cars are even more exorbitant.

7. Having come this far. We must see the matter through.

8. Whatever challenge the office presents. I believe our new member of Congress will meet it successfully.

9. When the chairperson stated, "I will not compromise on any issue on which I have taken a stand." I began to question her judgment.

10. Rita Moreno has won all major performance awards. An Oscar, an Emmy, a Grammy, and a Tony.

12   ELIMINATE FUSED SENTENCES (FS) AND COMMA SPLICES (CS)

A *fused sentence* (also called a *run-on sentence*) results when no punctuation or coordinating conjunction separates two or more independent clauses. A *comma splice* results when two or more independent clauses are joined with only a comma. Eliminate these sentence errors in one of four ways.

12a   **Use a period to separate independent clauses, forming two sentences.**

> Lorraine Hansberry was the first black female playwright of importance. She wrote *A Raisin in the Sun.*

12b   **Use a semicolon to separate independent clauses and form a compound sentence.**

> Through flying, Charles Lindbergh gained his notoriety; Amelia Earhart lost her life.

12c   **Insert a coordinating conjunction between independent clauses to form a compound sentence.**

> Helen Keller was both blind and deaf, but she was a skillful author and lecturer.

12d   **Use a subordinating conjunction to put the less important idea in a subordinate clause and form a complex sentence.**

> Although Paul Revere is known to most people as a Revolutionary War patriot; he is known to collectors as a silversmith and engraver.

Be especially sensitive to the use of conjunctive adverbs, such as *consequently, however, moreover, nevertheless,* and *therefore.* They do not link clauses grammatically. Misinterpreting their function in sentences is a common cause of comma splices.

> Oscar Wilde fancied himself a poet and critic; however, he is most remembered as a playwright and wit.

_____*Exercise*

Correct the following fused sentences and comma splices.

1. The comma splice can confuse readers, it is usually less troublesome, however, than the fused sentence.

2. Members of the Drama Guild have rehearsed carefully for tonight's show, the director feels certain it will be a success.

3. The war is over the fighting is not.

4. The air traffic controller made the best decision he could at the time, looking back, he saw what he should have done differently.

5. It is too late to sign up for the proficiency exam this term, however, students can sign up for next term's exam.

6. Pay attention to the instructions you must follow them exactly.

7. Much has been done the Civil Liberties Union believes that much more needs to be done.

8. Stockholders don't have to liquidate their assets this week, all they need to do is sign papers of intent.

9. Clean-up is scheduled for Monday, Tuesday, and Wednesday the plant closes on Friday.

10. No conclusive evidence has been uncovered, the commissioners will meet again tomorrow.

13   AGREEMENT (AGR)

Agreement in grammar refers to the correspondence of key sentence elements in number, person, and gender. Two kinds of agreement are grammatically important in most sentences: subject-verb agreement and pronoun-antecedent agreement.

13a   Subject-Verb Agreement

In simplest terms, a singular subject requires a singular verb, and a plural subject requires a plural verb. A number of troublesome constructions can cause confusion, however, and require consideration.

When subjects are joined by *and,* use a plural verb.

Although each of the subjects may be singular, the compounding makes a plural verb necessary.

O'Connor and Rehnquist **speak** articulately for the dissenters.
[Plural verb with compound subject.]

A fool and his money **are** soon parted.

When subjects are joined by *or, nor, but, either . . . or, neither . . . nor,* or *not only . . . but also,* use a verb that agrees with the subject that is nearer to the verb.

Either Weixlmann or Stein **is** my choice for president.
[Singular verb with two singular subjects.]

The coach or the co-captains **supervise** the practices each day.
[Plural verb agrees with *co-captains,* the nearer subject.]

Neither Lewis, his two partners, nor their lawyers **were** at the press

conference.
[Plural verb agrees with *lawyers,* the nearer subject.]

Either Jean or you **are** to accept the award for the entire cast.
[Verb agrees with *you,* the nearer subject.]

When this rule produces an awkward though correct sentence, consider revising the sentence.

You ~~or he is~~ *two are* the leading contender**s**.

When a subject is followed by a phrase containing a noun that differs in number or person from the subject, use a verb that agrees with the subject, not with the noun in the phrase.

The attitude of these men **is** decidedly hostile.
[Singular verb agrees with *attitude,* the singular subject.]

The ballots with her name **have** been recalled.
[Plural verb agrees with *ballots,* the plural subject.]

When an indefinite pronoun, such as *anybody, anyone, each, either, everybody, neither, nobody,* and *someone,* is used as a subject, use a singular verb.

Ultimately, someone **has** to accept responsibility.

Anybody who wants to **has** the right to attend the hearing.

Everyone **has** the same chance.

When a collective noun is used as a subject, use a singular verb *or* a plural verb to clarify the meaning.

When a collective noun emphasizes the unity of a group, use a singular verb. When a collective noun emphasizes group members as individuals, use a plural verb.

> The clergy **is** grossly underpaid.
> [Singular verb because whole group is meant.]
> The clergy **are** using their pulpits to speak out against oppression.
> [Plural verb because individual members are meant.]

When an expletive construction, such as *here is, here are, there is,* and *there are,* is used as both subject and verb, match the verb to the noun that follows.

> Here **is** your receipt. [Singular verb with singular noun *receipt.*]
>
> Here **are** the copies you requested. [Plural verb with plural noun *copies.*]
>
> There **is** no excuse for such behavior. [Singular verb with singular noun *excuse.*]
>
> There **are** several solutions to the city's problems.
> [Plural verb with plural noun *solutions.*]

The verb in a relative clause introduced by *who, which,* or *that* agrees in number with the pronoun's antecedent.

> Jessica is one performer who **acts** with restraint.
> [Singular verb with singular antecedent *performer.*]
> Philip Roth writes books that **illustrate** the absurdities of modern life.
> [Plural verb with plural antecedent *books.*]

When a compound subject is preceded by *each* or *every,* use a singular verb.

Each and *every* indicate that persons or things are being considered individually.

> Each boy and girl **takes** shop and home economics.
> Every basket of peaches and flat of strawberries **was** sold.

When a subject is followed by a predicate noun that differs in number from the subject, the verb agrees with the subject, not with the complement.

Although predicate nouns restate the subject of the sentence, their word forms do not always agree in number; that is, the predicate noun and the subject may not be both singular or both plural. Use the subject, not the predicate noun, to determine the appropriate subject-verb agreement.

> Her chief source of enjoyment **is** books.
> [Singular verb with singular subject *source.*]
> Books **are** her chief source of enjoyment.
> [Plural verb with plural subject *books.*]

When a plural noun has a singular meaning, use a singular verb.

Some subjects may initially appear to be plural, although they are singular. *Electronics, mathematics, semantics,* and *geriatrics* appear to be in plural form but are names of individual fields of study. Expressions such as *gin and tonic* and *ham and eggs* are also singular, because they name a single drink and a single dish.

No news **is** good news.

Scotch and soda **is** not as popular as it once was.

When fractions, measurements, money, time, weight, and volume are considered as single units, use singular verbs.

Three days **is** too long to wait.

Jerrid feels that 165 pounds **is** his ideal weight.

Twenty-two percent **is** the accepted rate for credit-card financing.

With titles of individual works, even those containing plural words, use a singular verb.

All the King's Men **is** an enlightening political novel.

Dorothy Parker's "Good Souls" **is** about congenial, often exploited people.

Words used as words take a singular verb.

Amateur athletes is used to describe participants as varied as Little League pitchers and endorsement-rich track-and-field stars.

13b   Pronoun-Antecedent Agreement

Pronouns must agree with their antecedents (the nouns or pronouns to which they refer) in number and person. A singular pronoun must be used with a singular antecedent; a plural pronoun must be used with a plural antecedent. (See also Case, Section 14.)

The workers received **their** wages.
[Plural third-person pronoun with plural third-person antecedent *workers.*]
The DC 10 changed **its** course and landed at Cincinnati.
[Singular third-person pronoun with singular third-person antecedent *DC 10.*]

Singular pronouns must also agree in gender with their antecedents. A masculine pronoun must be used with a masculine antecedent; a feminine pronoun must be used with a feminine antecedent; and a neuter pronoun must be used with a neuter antecedent. (See also Case, Section 14.)

Masculine:	he	him	his	himself
Feminine:	she	her	hers	herself
Neuter:	it	it	its	itself

The generic use of masculine pronouns is no longer universally acceptable. Use both musculine and feminine pronouns when an antecedent could be either male or female (*he or she, his or hers*). Alternatively, use plural, genderless antecedents and pronouns whenever possible.

Each teacher must submit **his or her** annual report by March 15.
[Singular masculine and feminine pronouns with male or female antecedent *teacher.*]

Teachers must submit **their** annual reports by March 15.
[Plural pronoun with plural antecedent *teachers.*]

These principles of pronoun-antecedent agreement apply consistently to all situations, but a number of troublesome constructions require special consideration.

When the antecedents *each, either, neither,* and *none* are followed by a phrase that contains a plural noun, use a singular pronoun.

Although the noun in the phrase may be plural, *each, either, neither* and *none* refer to elements individually. Consequently, the pronoun must be singular.

Neither of the boys would accept the responsibility for **his** actions.
[Singular pronoun with *neither* as antecedent.]

Either of these women may lose **her** position.
[Singular pronoun with *either* as antecedent.]

When *everybody, each, either, everyone, neither, nobody,* and *a person* are antecedents, use a singular pronoun.

Although in context these words may imply plurality, the word forms are singular and therefore singular pronouns are required. Do not use masculine pronouns generically to refer to these genderless singular antecedents. Use both masculine and feminine forms, or alternatively, substitute plural antecedents and pronouns for the singular forms.

Nobody had **his or her** work completed on time.
[Singular pronouns with singular antecedent *nobody.*]

The committee members had not completed **their** work on time.
[A plural pronoun with plural antecedent *members.*]

Collective nouns used as antecedents take singular or plural pronouns depending on the meaning of the sentence.

A collective noun that identifies the group as a single unit takes a singular pronoun. A collective noun that identifies the individual members of a group takes a plural pronoun.

The judge reprimanded the jury for **its** disregard of the evidence.
[Singular pronoun because reference is to group as a whole.]

At the request of the defense attorney, the jury were polled and **their** individual verdicts recorded.
[Plural pronoun because reference is to group members individually.]

When an antecedent is a person, use *who, whom,* or *that* to introduce qualifying phrases or clauses.

This is the architect **who** planned the civic center.

The interior designer **whom** we selected was unavailable.

The landscaper **that** worked on our property has moved.

When an antecedent is an object or concept, use *which* or *that* to introduce qualifying phrases or clauses.

Here is the package **that** she left behind.

The package, **which** she left behind, could not later be found.

When an antecedent is an animal, use *that* to introduce qualifying phrases or clauses.

Secretariat is the horse **that** you're speaking of.

Exercise

Circle the correct form in parentheses.

1. Neither she nor her sons (was, were) present at the reading of the will.

2. The jury (is, are) expected to reach a verdict before midnight.

3. Each of the children is expected to bring (his, her, his or her, their) own art supplies.

4. The horse (that, who) won the Kentucky Derby went on to win the Preakness and the Belmont.

5. The team lost (its, their) first game of the season, but (it, they) won the next five games.

6. Every one of the actors who auditioned (was, were) exceptionally talented.

7. There (is, are) both food and firewood in the cabin.

8. Students (which, who) maintain grade-point averages of 3.50 or better are eligible for alumni scholarships.

9. None of the applicants presented (himself, herself, himself or herself, themselves) well in the interview.

10. Thirty hours a week (is, are) a heavy work schedule, especially if you are taking two classes.

14   CASE (CA)

Case is the form or position of a noun or pronoun that indicates its relation to other words in a sentence. English has three cases: *subjective, objective,* and *possessive.* In general, a noun or pronoun is in the subjective case when it acts as a subject, in the objective case when it acts as an object, and in the possessive case when it modifies a noun as in *"his* bicycle," "the *boy's* dog," *"their* future."

English nouns, pronouns, and adjectives once all showed case by changing their forms. In modern English, word order and idiomatic constructions have largely replaced case endings. Only pronouns—and chiefly the personal pronouns—still make any considerable use of case forms.

Personal pronouns change form dramatically to indicate case.

		Subjective	Objective	Possessive
Singular	*1st person*	I	me	my, mine
	2nd person	you	you	your, yours
	3rd person	he, she, it	him, her, it	his, hers, its
Plural	*1st person*	we	us	our, ours
	2nd person	you	you	your, yours
	3rd person	they	them	their, theirs

The indefinite or relative pronoun *who* also changes form to indicate case.

Subjective	Objective	Possessive
who	whom	whose
whoever	whomever	

The case of a pronoun is determined by the pronoun's function in its own clause. Pronouns used as subjects or predicate nouns, that is, nouns that follow linking verbs and restate the subject, are in the subjective case. Pronouns used as direct objects, as indirect objects, or as objects of prepositions are in the objective case. Pronouns that modify a noun or pronoun or that precede and modify a gerund are in the objective case. Use the following guidelines to select the appropriate case.

14a   Uses of the Subjective Case of Personal Pronouns

▪ As the subject of a verb:

I think that **we** missed the flight.

▪ As the complement of the verb *to be:*

I'm sure it was **she.**

▪ As the appositive (restatement) of a subject or predicate noun:

The surveyors, Mr. James and **he,** plotted the acreage.

14b   Uses of the Objective Case of Personal Pronouns

▪ As the direct object or indirect object of a verb:

Mother likes **her** best.
Todd gave **us** the concert tickets.

▪ As the object of a preposition:

Sara directed the salesman to **him** and **me.**

▪ As the appositive (restatement) of a direct or indirect object:

My sister and I gave them, Mrs. Lester and **her,** nothing but trouble.

▪ As the subject of an infinitive:

I want **them** to take my place.

▪ As the object of an infinitive:

Don't expect to see **her** or **me** at a classical concert.

14c   Uses of the Possessive Case of Personal Pronouns

▪ As a modifier of a noun or pronoun:

These are **my** four children, and those are **his** three.

▪ As a modifier of a gerund:

Her skiing improved rapidly.
What's wrong with **my** buying new equipment?

14d   Distinguishing Between "We" and "Us" Used with a Noun in Apposition

The subjective case form is *we;* the objective case form is *us.* Select the pronoun that would be correct if the noun were omitted.

We tenants must file formal complaints against the management firm.
[Subjective case for subject of the sentence.]

Their inattentiveness has given **us** tenants little recourse.
[Objective case for indirect object.]

14e

Personal Pronouns with "Than" or "As"

The case of a pronoun following *than* or *as* in a comparison often causes difficulty. In an elliptical (incompletely expressed) construction, use the case that would be appropriate if all the words were expressed.

He is at least as capable as **she.**
[Subjective case because *she* is the subject of the unexpressed verb *is.*]
The crowd liked Navratilova better than **them.**
[Objective case because *them* would be the object of the verb if the comparison were expressed completely; *better than it liked them.*]

14f

Uses of the Subjective Case of the Relative Pronoun "Who"

- As the subject of a clause:

Ralph Nader is a consumer advocate **who** gets media attention easily.

- As the subject of a clause stated as a question:

Who donated the carpets?

14g

Uses of "Whom"—The Objective Case of the Relative Pronoun "Who"

- As the object of a verb:

Professor Frayne is a man **whom** we admire.

- As the object of a verb in a question:

Whom should we notify?

14h

Distinguishing Between "Whoever" and "Whomever"

The subjective case form is *whoever;* the objective case form is *whomever.* Be aware that even when a subordinate clause functions as an *object,* a pronoun that functions as the *subject* of the clause belongs in the subjective case.

Invite **whoever** will come.
[Subjective case because *whoever* is the subject of *will come.*]
The committee will approve the appointment of **whomever** we select.
[Objective case because *whomever* is the object of the preposition *of.*]

Revise the following sentences to correct any errors in the use of case. Some of the sentences need no correction.

1. The police suspected Boris Kraykov's associates, but he is more likely to be responsible than them.

2. Jim, not me, must make the recommendation.

3. Us gun collectors must be aware of people's objecting to firearms.

4. Reverend Wehrenberg is the person to whom we will go for advice.

5. They gave the finalists, Sandi and he, an enthusiastic round of applause.

6. Whoever we appoint to the council must be willing to present our case with conviction.

7. There is really no excuse for him refusing to comment.

8. The comments were directed to we two, you and I.

9. Carol is at least three years older than him.

10. Sonia will have to train whoever accepts the job.

15   VERB TENSES (T)

Verb tenses indicate the time of the action or state of being expressed. Most verbs in English have four principal parts and change in a predictable way to form the six basic tenses and the six progressive tenses.

> _Present-tense form:_ walk
> _Present participle:_ walking
> _Past-tense form:_ walked
> _Past participle:_ walked

> _Present tense:_ walk, walks
> _Past tense:_ walked
> _Future tense:_ will walk, shall walk
> _Present perfect tense:_ have walked, has walked
> _Past perfect tense:_ had walked
> _Future perfect tense:_ will have walked, shall have walked

Present progressive tense: am walking, are walking, is walking
Past progressive tense: was walking, were walking
Future progressive tense: will be walking, shall be walking
Present perfect progressive tense: have been walking, has been walking
Past perfect progressive tense: had been walking
Future perfect progressive tense: will have been walking, shall have been walking

Irregular verbs form their past tenses and their past participles through changes in spelling or word form that must be memorized. The following list contains the principal parts of the most common or troublesome verbs.

Present tense	Present participle	Past tense	Past participle
am, is, are	being	was, were	been
bear	bearing	bore	borne
beat	beating	beat	beaten
begin	beginning	began	begun
bite	biting	bit	bitten
blow	blowing	blew	blown
break	breaking	broke	broken
bring	bringing	brought	brought
burst	bursting	burst	burst
cast	casting	cast	cast
choose	choosing	chose	chosen
come	coming	came	came
deal	dealing	dealt	dealt
do	doing	did	done
draw	drawing	drew	drawn
drink	drinking	drank	drunk
eat	eating	ate	eaten
fall	falling	fell	fallen
fly	flying	flew	flown
forbid	forbidding	forbade	forbidden
forsake	forsaking	forsook	forsaken
freeze	freezing	froze	frozen
give	giving	gave	given
go	going	went	gone
grow	growing	grew	grown
hang*	hanging	hung	hung
have	having	had	had
know	knowing	knew	known
lay	laying	laid	laid
lie	lying	lay	lain
ride	riding	rode	ridden

---

*The verb *to hang,* used in the sense of "to execute," is regular: *hang, hanged, hanged.*

ring	ringing	rang	rung
rise	rising	rose	risen
run	running	ran	run
see	seeing	saw	seen
shake	shaking	shook	shaken
shoe	shoeing	shod	shod
shrink	shrinking	shrank (shrunk)	shrunk
sing	singing	sang (sung)	sung
sink	sinking	sank (sunk)	sunk
sit	sitting	sat	sat
slay	slaying	slew	slain
slink	slinking	slunk	slunk
speak	speaking	spoke	spoken
spin	spinning	spun	spun
spring	springing	sprang (sprung)	sprung
steal	stealing	stole	stolen
strive	striving	strove	striven
swear	swearing	swore	sworn
swim	swimming	swam	swum
take	taking	took	taken
teach	teaching	taught	taught
tear	tearing	tore	torn
throw	throwing	threw	thrown
wear	wearing	wore	worn
weave	weaving	wove	woven
win	winning	won	won
write	writing	wrote	written

15a   Use the present tense to describe habitual action or actions that occur or conditions that exist in the present.

Pamela **listens** to classical music when she writes papers.

They **are** exhausted.

15b   Use the present tense to express general truths and scientific principles.

The earth **tilts** slightly on its axis.

15c   Use the present tense to describe or discuss artistic works, paintings, sculpture, etc., and literary works, novels, plays, poems, etc.

Polonius **offers** Laertes platitudes, not advice.

Picasso's use of black and white in his large-scale painting *Guernica* establishes a stark visual equivalent for the starkness of the artist's message.

15d   **Use the past tense to describe the completed actions or conditions that existed in the past.**

Abolitionists openly **opposed** slavery, often at personal risk.

They **were** exhausted.

15e   **Use the future tense to describe actions that will occur or conditions that will exist in the future.**

The Congress **will reconvene** after a brief recess.

15f   **Use the present perfect tense to describe actions that started or conditions that existed at an unspecified time in the past and continue in the present.**

For years, Mary Tyler Moore **has been** a spokesperson for the American Diabetes Association.

15g   **Use the past perfect tense to describe actions that started or conditions that existed before a specific time in the past.**

In large part, Czar Nicholas **had ignored** the turmoil that preceded the Russian Revolution.

15h   **Use the future perfect tense to describe actions that will be completed or conditions that will exist before a specific time in the future.**

Natalie **will have submitted** her dissertation before the school year ends.

15i   **Use the progressive tenses to express ongoing actions that occur in the present, past, or future.**

I **am learning** to ski.

Sasha **had been planning** to attend the theater opening.

Rebecca **will be working** as a receptionist this summer.

15j   **Use present participles to express action that coincides with the action described by the main verb.**

Sensing that media coverage of the takeover would be negative, Albertson decided to cancel the press conference.

15k   **Use past participles and perfect participles to express actions that occurred, or to describe conditions that existed, before the action or condition described by the main verb.**

Shocked by the disparaging comments, Senator Robertson left the hearing.

Having completed her work, Sybil sat down to read.

15l   **Generally, use the past tense or past perfect tense in a subordinate clause when the verb in the independent clause is in the past or past perfect tense.**

This combination of past tenses is used to place one past action in a temporal or other relation with another past action.

Virginia Woolf **worked** in isolation because she **needed** quiet to concentrate well.

After he **had purchased** tickets for the World Series, Karl **was** unable to use them.

15m

When the verb in the independent clause is in the present, future, present perfect, or future perfect tense, use any tense in the subordinate clause that will make the meaning of the sentence clear.

In *Camelot,* Lancelot **thinks** that he **will succeed** at every venture.

Because twenty-four-carat gold **is** soft, detailed design work **will wear** away over time.

Exercise

Select the appropriate verb tenses in the following sentences. Be ready to explain your choices.

1. Rain (is, was) water that (condenses, condensed) around dust particles and (falls, fell) to earth.

2. Normally the incidence of heart-worm disease (increases, increased) each year, but last year it (decreases, decreased).

3. On a bi-monthly basis, the Citizens' Action Coalition (sends, sent) a newsletter to its supporters.

4. Next fall, tuition at American universities (rises, will rise) to keep pace with inflation.

5. Becky Sharp (is, was) the main character of William Thackeray's *Vanity Fair,* an episodic novel published in 1847.

6. Isaac Singer (has written, had written) all of his stories in Yiddish, but they (are, were) immediately translated into English.

7. By the end of this season, we (will play, will have played) in thirty games and two tournaments.

8. (Serving, Having served) on the magazine's Board of Economic Advisors, the woman (is, was) a likely figure to head the Federal Reserve Board.

9. Because Da Vinci (experiments, experimented) with a variety of interesting pigments, many of his works (are, were) deteriorating.

10. (Opening, Having opened) the bomb casing with great care, the explosives expert (disconnects, disconnected) the timing mechanism.

16   ADJECTIVES AND ADVERBS (ADJ & ADV)

Adjectives and adverbs are both modifiers, but they serve separate purposes in sentences. Adjectives modify nouns and pronouns. Adverbs modify verbs, adjectives, and other adverbs; they may also modify phrases and clauses.

The -*ly* ending identifies many words as adverbs. It is not foolproof, however. Some adjectives end in -*ly* (*heavenly, lovely, leisurely*), and many common adverbs (*very, then, always, here, now*) do not end in -*ly*. To avoid faulty modification, be certain to use adjectives only with nouns and pronouns and adverbs with verbs, adjectives, other adverbs, or whole phrases and clauses.

16a   **Use adjectives to modify nouns and pronouns.**

                     N
His **thoughtful** assessments are always **welcome.**

PRON
They are **dependable.**

16b   **Use adverbs to modify verbs, adjectives, and other adverbs.**

               V
She **carefully** selected the flowers.

                 ADJ
She was **especially** careful when she chose the roses.

            ADV
She **very** carefully examined the buds and leaves on each stem.

16c   **Recognize the distinct uses of troublesome adjective and adverb pairs.**

The following two adjective/adverb pairs, and others you may have had trouble with in your writing, should be carefully used.

Bad/Badly: Use *bad,* the adjective form, to modify nouns and pronouns, even in conjunction with sensory verbs such as appear, look, taste, and so on. Use *badly,* the adverb form, only to modify a verb.

                   ADJ
Lendl made a series of **bad** volleys during the third match.

ADJ

His prospects may seem **bad,** but they really aren't.

Although Jimmy Stewart sang several great Cole Porter songs in films, he

ADV

acknowledged that he sang them **badly.**

Good/Well: The word *good,* an adjective, always modifies a noun or a pronoun. The word *well* can function as either an adverb or an adjective. As an adverb meaning "satisfactorily," *well* could modify a verb, an adjective, or another adverb. As an adjective meaning "healthy," *well* could only modify a noun or pronoun.

N

The lasagna smells *good.* [Adjective.]

V

Your point is *well* taken. [Adverb.]

PRON

Mrs. Biagi says that she feels *well* today. [Adjective.]

Exercise

Revise the following sentences to correct faulty modification.

1. If you move quiet and slow, you can sometimes see small wildlife in this area.

2. Miss Haversham, eccentric and oppressive, treated Pip bad.

3. Competitive cyclists must react calm and quick when they need to make repairs during tournaments.

4. Make sure that the knots are tied tight and secure, or the rocking of the waves may break the boat loose from the wharf.

5. When receiving chemotherapy treatments, most patients don't feel good.

Writing Grammatical Sentences: Review Exercise

Revise the following sentences to make them grammatical. Identify the problem in each sentence that made revision necessary.

1. Beginning in 1901, Nobel Prizes have been awarded to people who have made major contributions in the areas of peace, literature, physics, chemistry, and physiology or medicine, contributions in economics have been recognized since 1969.

2. A committee representing Yale University and the Bollingen Foundation presents their $5,000 award for poetry every two years.

3. The 1985 World Hunger Media Award was given to Bob Geldof, the rock musician who most people recognize as the organizer of the Live Aid concerts.

4. *Gödel, Escher, Bach: An Eternal Golden Braid,* Douglas R. Hofstadter's Pulitzer Prize–winning book, established philosophical and theoretical links between physics, art, and music.

5. Kennedy Center Honors have recognized the innovative work of a number of choreographers. George Balanchine, Martha Graham, Agnes de Mille, and Jerome Robbins, among others.

6. Although the musical *The Mystery of Edwin Drood* won five major Tony Awards in 1986, it has fared bad on overall ticket sales.

7. George W. Beadie and Edward L. Tatum, both of the United States, received Nobel Prizes in Physiology for their discovery that genes transmitted hereditary characteristics.

8. Each year, the Randolph Caldecott Medal, awarded by the American Library Association, recognizes whomever has produced the best illustrated book for children.

9. "We Are the World," the title cut from the album of the same name. Won Grammy Awards in 1985 for record of the year, song of the year, pop group of the year, and video–short form.

10. Henry Kissinger was Secretary of State from 1973 to 1977, under Nixon and Ford, he has received the Nobel Peace Prize (1973), the Presidential Medal of Freedom (1977), and the Medal of Liberty (n.d.).

11. Emory Holloway, Walter Jackson Bate, Justin Kaplan, Lawrence Thomp-

son, Louis Sheaffer, and Richard W. B. Lewis have all won Pulitzer Prizes for biographies of major writers. In spite of the awards, however, their books are more recognized by name than them.

12. MacArthur Foundation Fellowships boast awards of $164,000 to $300,000, spread over five years, these fellowships free recipients to pursue their interests.

13. The Enrico Fermi Award is given to scientists who demonstrated an "exceptional and altogether outstanding" body of work in the field of atomic energy.

14. Milos Forman has won Academy Awards for directing two highly distinct films, *One Flew Over the Cuckoo's Nest,* a black comedy about a mental ward, and *Amadeus,* a selectively retold biography of Mozart, also won Oscars as best film of the year.

15. The Columbia University Graduate School of Journalism won a George Foster Peabody Award for Broadcasting in 1985. Their collection *Seminars on Media and Society* were particularly acknowledged.

Choosing Effective Diction

Effective diction is the choice of words that best communicate your purpose to your audience. Your diction must be tailored to fit the specific context of your sentences and paragraphs and of your paper as a whole. Your choices of effective diction depend on your *subject, audience,* and *purpose.*

17

USING A DICTIONARY (DICT)

No writer should work without a dictionary. Unabridged dictionaries, like the *Oxford English Dictionary,* usually found in the reference rooms of libraries, contain vast numbers of words and lengthy, thorough definitions. They are useful when you need to find highly detailed information like full word histories or when you need to find the definition of an arcane word. Most of your needs, however, will be met by a standard desk-sized, collegiate dictionary such as

- *American Heritage Dictionary of the English Language*
- *Random House Dictionary of the English Language: College Edition*
- *Webster's New Collegiate Dictionary*
- *Webster's New World Dictionary of the American Language: College Edition*

Those dictionaries, and most other standard-sized collegiate dictionaries, provide a wide variety of general and useful information:

- A brief history of lexicography (the preparation and study of dictionaries)
- A brief history of the language

521

- An explanatory diagram of a sample word entry, with a key to the abbreviations that are used in the definitions
- Explanations and definitions of and guidance on matters of grammar and usage
- The dictionary of words (the main portion of the reference book)
- Lists of standard abbreviations
- Biographical entries (providing brief notes on important people)
- Geographical entries (providing brief notes on important places)
- Lists of foreign words and phrases
- Comparative tables of alphabets, calendars, and currencies
- Tables of measurements (both American and metric)
- Lists of signs and symbols in common use
- Maps and illustrations
- Pronunciation guides
- General guides to writing (business letter forms, forms of address, manuscript preparation guidelines, and so on)

Dictionaries provide much more than definitions; they offer useful information about many subjects related to writing. Most often, however, you will turn to a dictionary to find information about specific words. To make your use of a dictionary efficient and productive, familiarize yourself with its general pattern of presenting information about words.

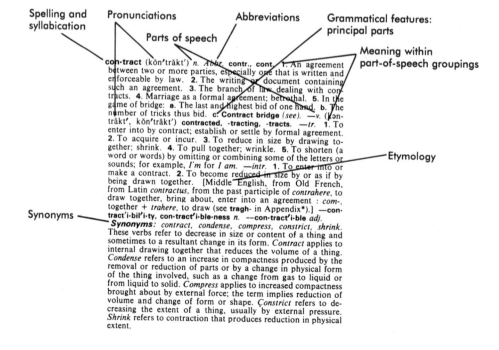

Spelling and syllabication · Pronunciations · Parts of speech · Abbreviations · Grammatical features: principal parts · Meaning within part-of-speech groupings · Etymology · Synonyms

con·tract (kŏn′trăkt′) n. Abbr. contr., cont. 1. An agreement between two or more parties, especially one that is written and enforceable by law. 2. The writing or document containing such an agreement. 3. The branch of law dealing with contracts. 4. Marriage as a formal agreement; betrothal. 5. In the game of bridge: a. The last and highest bid of one hand. b. The number of tricks thus bid. c. Contract bridge (see). —v. (kŏn-trăkt′, kŏn′trăkt′) contracted, -tracting, -tracts. —tr. 1. To enter into by contract; establish or settle by formal agreement. 2. To acquire or incur. 3. To reduce in size by drawing together; shrink. 4. To pull together; wrinkle. 5. To shorten (a word or words) by omitting or combining some of the letters or sounds; for example, I'm for I am. —intr. 1. To enter into or make a contract. 2. To become reduced in size by or as if by being drawn together. [Middle English, from Old French, from Latin contractus, from the past participle of contrahere, to draw together, bring about, enter into an agreement : com-, together + trahere, to draw (see tragh- in Appendix*).] —con·tract′i·bil′i·ty, con·tract′i·ble·ness n. —con·tract′i·ble adj.

Synonyms: contract, condense, compress, constrict, shrink. These verbs refer to decrease in size or content of a thing and sometimes to a resultant change in its form. Contract applies to internal drawing together that reduces the volume of a thing. Condense refers to an increase in compactness produced by the removal or reduction of parts or by a change in physical form of the thing involved, such as a change from gas to liquid or from liquid to solid. Compress applies to increased compactness brought about by external force; the term implies reduction of volume and change of form or shape. Constrict refers to decreasing the extent of a thing, usually by external pressure. Shrink refers to contraction that produces reduction in physical extent.

Spelling and Syllabication   Entries begin with the word spelled out and divided into syllables, usually marked with dots: **con•tract.** When a word has several acceptable spellings, each of them will be listed, but the most common spelling will be listed first. If alternative spellings are listed as *Am* (American) and *Brit* (British), use the American spelling in your writing.

Pronunciation   The pronunciation (usually enclosed in parentheses) follows, presented in a simplified phonetic transcription. The markings are matched to a pronunciation guide, which is usually printed at the bottom of each page. When words have more than one syllable, accent marks ('') indicate which syllables receive primary or secondary stress.

Part of Speech   Abbreviations such as *n.*, *v.*, and *adj.* indicate how a word can be used in a sentence. When a word can be used in various ways, the definitions are divided by parts of speech with, for instance, all meanings of the noun grouped together, followed by all meanings of the verb.

Abbreviations   If a word is commonly abbreviated, some dictionaries include the abbreviation in the entry; other dictionaries list abbreviations in a special section.

Grammatical Features   Distinctive grammatical features are noted in the entry. The principal parts of a verb are included, information that is especially helpful with irregular verbs—for example, *go, went, gone, going, goes*. Plural forms are provided for nouns that form plurals irregularly — for example, *mouse, mice*. When comparative and superlative degrees of adjectives and adverbs are formed by adding *-er* or *-est*, for example, *good, better, best* or *many, more, most,* dictionaries generally list them.

Meanings   Within part-of-speech groups, meanings are most commonly presented in order of their frequency of use. Some dictionaries, however, present definitions in historical order (from oldest to newest) or hierarchical order (from primary to secondary). Read the front matter of the dictionary you are using to see what pattern it follows.

Etymology   When word origins are known, they are provided, sometimes in abbreviated form (*Gk.* for Greek, *ME* for Middle English, and so on). Thus *contract* is one of a large class of words that came into English from Latin by way of Old French. It is made up of the prefix *con-* (from the Latin *com-*, meaning "together") and the root word *tract* (from the Latin *trahere,* meaning "to draw").

Labels   Labels are used to identify words according to a number of specific criteria: general level of usage (Nonstandard, Informal, Slang, Dial., and so on), regional usage (Brit., Southern), and usage within an area of specialization (Law, Med., Computer Sci.).

Synonyms and Antonyms Many dictionaries include brief lists of synonyms for defined words (often introduced by the abbreviation *syns.*), to illustrate comparable word choices. Some dictionaries include antonyms as well (introduced by the abbreviation *ant.*). Check the front matter of your dictionary to see whether these aids are used and where they are placed in the entries.

───────────────── *Exercise*

Use the following questions to familiarize yourself with your own collegiate dictionary. You will have to use all parts of the dictionary to find your answers—the front matter, entries, and appended materials. Keep in mind that your responses may vary slightly from those of people using other dictionaries.

1. If you have to hyphenate *maleficence* at the end of a line, where could you appropriately place a hyphen before finishing the word on the next line?

2. How are the following words pronounced: *acclimate, banal, data, impotent, Wagnerian?*

3. Which is the preferred spelling, *aesthetics* or *esthetics?* Is the word listed under both spellings or only under one?

4. What synonyms does your dictionary list for *ghastly, lure, puzzle, single,* and *yield?*

5. What is the British meaning of the word *torch?* When *torch* is used as slang, what does it mean? What idiomatic expression uses the word *torch?*

6. What is a *schlemiel?* What is the origin of the word?

7. How many meanings are recorded for the word *vulgar?* By what pattern are the definitions arranged?

8. As what parts of speech can the word *square* be used? In what order do the parts of speech appear in the entry?

9. What are the plural forms of *alumna, fungus, graffito, hippopotamus,* and *medium*?

10. What do the abbreviations *AAUW, EST, FNMA, MCAT,* and *VISTA* stand for?

11. In what years were *Marian Anderson, D. W. Griffith, Marie Antoinette, Alfred Nobel, George H. Ruth,* and *Mary Cassatt* born?

12. In what countries are *Addis Ababa, Caracas, Kuala Lumpur, Mecca,* and *Sarajevo* located?

18   CONSIDER ISSUES OF DICTION

Standard English is the language of educated speakers and writers of English. American schools, government, businesses, and the media have long used Standard English as the criterion by which speech and expository writing are judged; yet judgments about acceptable usage are sometimes hard to make because of the fluid nature of language and the effect of different writing situations. In a larger sense, word choices must be made in the context of a given piece of writing, depending on your subject, audience, and purpose. As a result, a word choice that is appropriate in one context may be inappropriate in another.

18a   Changes and Variations in Language

Language is constantly evolving, and as a result standards of usage are also constantly changing. New words are introduced, old words assume new meanings, and some words are discarded. As a writer, you must be aware of such changes and keep your diction current. A newly coined word such as *houseperson* may at the present time be questionable usage, but another fairly recent word such as *chairperson* may generally be acceptable. You need to remain sensitive to such subtleties and make your word choices on the basis of what seems to be currently acceptable. A dictionary and your instructor can provide useful guidance.

Be aware as well that language varies from one region of the country to another. *Tag* may easily be understood in some areas, but in other regions the term *license plate* may be necessary to make your meaning clear. It is therefore important to familiarize yourself with regional word choices and to use or avoid using them, depending on your writing context.

The Writing Situation—Formal or Informal

Writers vary their diction and sentence structure to suit the writing context. A letter to the editor of the local newspaper in support of its position on a local issue, for example, AIDS education in the schools, would differ at many points from a letter to a friend on the same subject. The difference is one of level of formality within Standard English. Formal usage—which typically uses an extensive vocabulary including learned words, no slang, few contractions and long, often complex sentences—may be appropriate for some topics and in some circumstances. Informal usage—generally characterized by the use of popular and colloquial words and some slang and contractions and short, simple sentences, often including fragments—may be appropriate for other topics and other circumstances. Whether a writer chooses a formal or informal style, or something in-between, depends not on "correctness," for a broad range of styles are acceptable; rather, it depends on what is *appropriate* to the specific writing situation.

The following discussions address some key issues of diction, both formal and informal, and will help you choose your words selectively. (See Chapter 9, "Diction: The Choice of Words," for a fuller discussion.)

Considering Denotation and Connotation

When you choose words, consider their **denotations** (the meaning in the dictionary) and their **connotations** (meaning derived from context). Look at these two sentences:

> Nell Gwynn, a **famous** actress during the English Restoration, became the mistress of King Charles II.
>
> Nell Gwynn, a **notorious** actress during the English Restoration, became the mistress of King Charles II.

Both of the words in bold type indicate that Nell Gwynn was well known; their denotations are similar. *Famous* and *notorious* have different connotations, however. *Famous* implies "celebrated," "renowned"; *notorious* implies "infamous," "widely but unfavorably known."

Distinguishing Between Often-Confused Words

Some words are easily mistaken for each other because of similarities in spelling or pronunciation. When such confusion occurs, ideas become jumbled or unclear. Look at these two sentences:

> In her closing remarks, the district attorney stated that the defendant had been **persecuted** because the evidence proved him guilty.
>
> Darren received a summons for **wreckless** driving.

In the first, the verb *persecute* has been mistaken for *prosecute;* in the second, *wreckless* for *reckless.*

Commonly confused words include *advice* and *advise, cite, sight,* and *site, council* and *counsel, farther* and *further, loose* and *lose,* and *principal* and *principle.* Others are listed in the "Glossary of Usage" (page 571).

18e Avoiding Trite Language

Trite language is diction that is commonplace and unimaginative and consequently ineffective. Once-original expressions like *white as snow, in the final analysis,* and *rough and ready* have been used so often, in so many contexts, that they no longer offer new insight. Avoid using clichés and instead strive to communicate your meaning in your own, specific language.

~~In an ideal world,~~ *Ideally,* boxers ~~who are over the hill~~ *aging* would retire before they ~~were past their prime.~~ *lost their strength and agility.*

18f Avoiding Jargon

Jargon, the specialized or technical language of a particular group, is sometimes appropriate when you are writing only to members of the group, but it is inappropriate when you are writing for a general audience. Keep your audience clearly in mind and use specific but common words instead.

By improving the quality and clarity of ~~horizontal transmittal correspondence,~~ *interdepartmental memos,* companies can ~~become more cost efficient.~~ *save money.*

18g Using Figurative Language

Figurative language makes imaginative comparisons, comparisons that link dissimilar things to present a significant insight. Figurative language can add interest to your writing, but you should be aware of some potential problems in its use.

■ **Mixed metaphors** bring together images that clash because they establish incompatible impressions.

Shannon dove into her studies to reach the top of the class standings. [*Dove,* denoting downward movement, clashes with *reach the top,* connoting upward movement.]

■ **Exaggerated personifications** result when inanimate objects or abstractions are given human or animal characteristics, thus creating images that are so far-fetched that readers find them strained—even laughable—rather than effective.

The craggy peak, covered with a few scraggly pines, brooded over the valley like a disapproving parent.

■ **_Unrecognizable allusions_** are references to obscure historical or literary events or people. An allusion should illuminate a discussion, so use references that are likely to be recognized by a general audience.

Jeremy's letter to the editor, a condensed **_Areopagitica,_** railed against censorship.
[The allusion to John Milton's tract on freedom of the press might be lost on many audiences.]

_____*Exercise*

Revise the following sentences to eliminate problems with diction. Consult your dictionary, if necessary.

1. The sight for the new city counsel building has already been chosen.

2. We racked our brains for solutions to our financial problems, but solutions seemed few and far between.

3. The berserk parents shouted at the school's principle and refused to believe that Danny, their pride and joy, could have done anything wrong.

4. Purchasing a residence in a noncity environment was the Smiths' fondest wish.

5. Like a ship without a sail, Scott wandered threw the office building, looking for the lawyer's office.

6. The intelligence operative arranged for telephone surveillance of Dr. Russell's office.

7. For reasons too numerous to mention, Bradley Jennerman resigned.

8. One should always masticate one's food completely.

9. Like a scared monkey, the small child clung to his mother.

10. Researchers suggest that excessive involvement in the television-viewing process can effect the way a young person preforms in an educational institution.

Revise the following paragraphs to eliminate problems with diction.

In these troubled financial times, one is likely to find adults returning to their family domiciles to cohabitant with their parents. After attaining degrees from institutions of higher learning, many offspring return to their home areas to find gainful employment and save money by sharing the family dwelling. The money they save they often invest in automobiles, stereos, and haberdashery. Some save money to allow them to later invest in living quarters of their own or save money for a rainy day.

The psychological affects of adults returning to live with parents can be unfortunate. Offspring sometimes feel that they are not establishing their independence from Mom and Pop. Parents sometimes feel that their children, now grown, are imposing on their independence, and returning children create storm and strife when they return to the nest. But at this point in time, adults living with their parents is becoming more commonplace, and many people will have to learn to live with the situation.

_____*Choosing Effective Diction: Review Exercise*

Revise the following sentences to improve their diction.

1. An effective piece of transcribed discourse must be easily decipherable.

2. Like a sponge absorbs water, the dancer listened to and analyzed the comments of her choreographer.

3. In the final analysis, the institution of higher learning's operation was not cost effective.

4. The NSC's clandestine operations in Central America and the Middle East were less than effective.

5. The aggressive salesperson amassed a sizable commission.

6. It goes without saying that in this day and age oral communication is crucial for getting ahead in this dog-eat-dog world.

7. Sometime or other everyone will have difficulties with interpersonal relations.

8. The principal's principal objection was not to the principal the students presented but to their method of implementing it.

9. The Herculean task of planning the reunion fell on the shoulders of the two organizers.

10. The microscopic listening devices implanted in the concrete structural members of the U.S. Embassy in Moscow would make surreptitious monitoring of conversations possible.

Observing the Rules of Punctuation

Marks of punctuation serve specific purposes in sentences. They show where thoughts end, where ideas are separated, and where pauses occur. Punctuate sentences according to the principles noted here. Remember that using punctuation unnecessarily is as confusing as omitting it when it is required.

19 PERIODS, QUESTION MARKS, AND EXCLAMATION POINTS (./?/!)

Three marks of punctuation end sentences: the **period (.)**, the **question mark (?)**, and the **exclamation point (!)**. Primarily indicators of completely stated thoughts, they serve, especially the period, a few additional purposes as well.

19a Accurate Use of Periods

Use a period to end a sentence that makes a statement.

Solar power is not yet a widely used energy source.

Use a period at the end of a question that is a courteously stated request or a command.

Will you please hand in your papers now.

Give your forms to the secretary when you've finished.

Use a period to end a sentence that contains an indirect question.

The landlord asked if we understood the terms of the lease.
[The sentence reports that a question was asked; it does not directly pose the question.]

Use a period with most abbreviations.

Although a period in an abbreviation indicates that letters have been omitted, some standard abbreviations do not require periods. Consult a dictionary for guidance. (See also Section 35, "Abbreviations.")

With periods	Without periods
Mr.	FCC (government agency)
M.D.	IL (state)
Trans.	PBS (television network)

Use a period before a decimal point and with dollars and cents.

Production standards vary by only .14 millimeter.
Pi equals 3.14159.
The price was reduced to $39.95.

Accurate Use of Question Marks

Use a question mark after a direct question.

The need for a question mark is usually indicated by inverted word order: part or all of the verb in the independent clause precedes the subject of the clause. In some instances, however, intent transforms a statement into a question.

Can we assume that the order has been shipped?
[*Can,* part of the verb, precedes the subject *we.*]

You mean he's ill?
[Intent, not word order, indicates that the sentence is a question; the question mark, though optional, confirms the writer's intent.]

Use a question mark in parentheses to indicate uncertainty about the accuracy of dates or numbers or other facts.

Modern scholars question whether Homer, a Greek poet of the ninth century (?) B.C., was the sole author of the famous epics attributed to him, the *Iliad* and the *Odyssey.*

It is not good usage to indicate possibly inaccurate words or to indicate irony by using a question mark in parentheses; changes in diction or sentence structure are more effective means of achieving these ends.

Use an exclamation point only to express strong emotion or to indicate unusual emphasis.

Be quiet!
Don't just stand there. Do something!

In most writing, exclamation points are not necessary or appropriate. Use them selectively.

20   **COMMAS (,)**

The comma is used to make the internal structure of a sentence clear. It does so in three general ways: (1) by separating elements that might otherwise be confused, (2) by setting off interrupting constructions, and (3) by marking words that are out of normal order.

20a   **Use commas to separate three or more coordinate items in a series.**

Using a comma before the conjunction (the word that joins the items in the series) is always correct and will avoid possible confusion.

Her favorite novelists were Melville, Lawrence, and Faulkner.
[Commas separating nouns.]

We considered displaying the statue in three places: in the lobby, in the president's office, and in the reception room. [Commas separating phrases.]

Jack designed the set, Ira did the flat painting, and Margo did the detailed painting.
[Commas separating independent clauses.]

20b   **Use commas between coordinate adjectives or adverbs that are not joined by a conjunction but that modify the same word individually.**

When each of several adjectives modifies a noun individually, or when each of several adverbs modifies a verb, adjective, or adverb individually, commas should separate the modifiers. No comma separates the last modifier from the word it modifies. (See also Section 21d.)

It was a dark, drizzly, depressing day. [Each adjective individually modifies *day*.]

Rick slowly, methodically rechecked his documentation.
[Each adverb individually modifies *rechecked*.]

20c   **In a compound sentence, use a comma before the coordinating conjunction that links the independent clauses.**

This usage prevents the subject of the second clause from being misread as an additional object in the first clause. When there is no danger of a confused reading, the comma may be omitted.

> Because of financial difficulties, the farmer sold his tractor and his plows, and his land remained uncultivated in the spring.
> [Without the comma, *land* could be misread as another direct object in a series with *tractor* and *plows*.]
> T. S. Eliot's poetry is highly regarded but his drama is not.
> [No comma necessary because no confusion is likely.]

20d **Use one comma or a pair of commas to set off a conjunctive adverb.**

Conjunctive adverbs, such as *however, moreover, therefore, consequently,* and *nevertheless,* establish logical connections between sentences. Usually they provide a transition between two statements, and they come near or at the beginning of the second statement. If no confusion will result, the comma or commas may be omitted, but using commas in these cases will always be correct.

> The warehouse was severely damaged by fire. Subsequently, the property was sold at a loss.
> Recent advances in medical research have brought hope to victims of AIDS. Some medical experts, however, feel the optimism is premature.
> Streamlining corporate management helps companies operate more smoothly; moreover, it can save on operating costs.

20e **Use a comma after an introductory subordinate clause in a complex or compound-complex sentence.**

> Because OPEC's prices were high in the 1970s, American drivers began to conserve gasoline, showing that for once they were responsive to government recommendations.
> Although Middle English is somewhat difficult to read, the rewards of reading Chaucer make learning his language worth the effort.

Use a comma after an introductory infinitive or participial phrase.

> To prepare for her language proficiency exam, Pam skimmed five study guides.
> Moving cautiously through the rubble, the insurance agent made notes for the damage report.

20f **Use a comma after introductory elements that function as adjectives or adverbs, unless the phrase is short and the meaning of the sentence is clear without the comma.**

A prepositional phrase at the beginning of a sentence that answers the questions *when, where,* or *under what conditions* is functioning like an adverb. Since such phrases modify the entire sentences of which they are a part, they should be followed by commas.

After four weeks of intensive work, Jason finished the first draft of his master's thesis.

After classes the five of us met to play basketball.
[Short phrase does not require a comma.]

Use a comma to set off an introductory adverb that modifies an entire sentence.

Finally, attending conferences and workshops is an important way to meet other professionals.

20g

Use one comma or a pair of commas to set off a nonrestrictive clause or phrase.

A *nonrestrictive clause* or *phrase* does not limit a class to a particular group or individual but modifies the whole class. It supplies additional information but can be omitted from a sentence without substantially altering the sentence's meaning.

A *restrictive clause* or *phrase* specifies a particular member or members of a group. It supplies information that is necessary to the meaning of the sentence. Restrictive clauses or phrases are not set off by commas.

The audio designer, **who creates sound effects for a play,** is an important member of a theater staff.
[*Nonrestrictive clause* could be omitted without altering sentence meaning.]

New recruits, **who may join after finishing high school,** must make numerous adjustments before they are acclimated to military life.
[*Nonrestrictive clause* could be omitted without altering sentence meaning.]

The audio designer **who worked on *Equus*** should be fired.
[*Restrictive clause* identifies a specific audio designer.]

All soldiers **who complete basic training** will be assigned to duty within three weeks. [*Restrictive clause* identifies a specific group of soldiers.]

20h

Use one comma or a pair of commas to set off nonrestrictive appositives.

An *appositive*—a word, phrase, or clause that renames a word or group of words in a sentence—can be nonrestrictive or restrictive. Nonrestrictive appositives provide nonessential information and are set off by commas. Restrictive appositives provide essential information and are not set off by commas. Appositives are grammatically equivalent to the noun or pronoun they rename.

PBS, **a nonprofit broadcasting network,** relies on corporate donations to cover most of its operating expenses.
[*Nonrestrictive appositive* could be omitted without altering sentence meaning.]

The superstation **TBS** broadcast the first colorized versions of many American film classics.
[*Restrictive appositive (TBS)* identifies a specific station.]

535

20i   **Use one or a pair of commas to set off contrasted elements.**

Young children react best to positive comments, not negative ones.

South Korea, not Japan, has the highest literacy rate in Asia.

20j   **Use commas to set off the words *yes* and *no*, mild interjections (*well, okay,* and so on) that begin sentences, and words in direct address.**

Yes, James Joyce's *Ulysses* is a difficult novel to read.

I suspect, my fellow Americans, that we are the victims of a hoax.

Sarah, would you please share your interpretation of the poem?

20k   **Use commas to separate directly quoted material from explanatory expressions.**

Expressions that signal direct quotations, such as "he said," "she replied," and so on, vary widely in form and position (they may be positioned at the beginning, in the middle, or at the end of a quotation). Wherever such expressions occur, they must be separated from the quotation, most often by using commas.

Reverend Tobias said, "State lotteries are nothing but state-sanctioned gambling."

"Lotteries, however, provide revenues that can be used to support education," **Representative Fulwiller noted.**

"If we ignore the lottery as a way of increasing revenues," **he added,** "our state's finances will continue to suffer."

20l   **Use commas with numbers containing four or more digits, dates, addresses, place names, and titles and academic degrees, according to the conventions shown below.**

- *Numbers:* Place a comma after every three digits, moving from right to left.

  1,399   2,776,100

- *Dates:* In month-day-year order, a comma separates the day and year. If a date including month, day, and year appears in the middle of a sentence, a comma also follows the year.

  No commas are required in the day-month-year order or when only the month and year are used.

  George Washington was born on February 22, 1732.

  On October 30, 1905, Tsar Nicholas issued the October Manifesto, guaranteeing individual liberties.

  Sixty percent of Hiroshima was destroyed by the atomic bomb dropped on 6 August 1945.

  Hitler annexed Austria in March 1938.

■ *Addresses:* When an address is written in a sentence, separate each element with a comma. If the address appears in the middle of a sentence, a comma must follow the last element.

> She moved to **719 Maple Avenue, Cleveland, Ohio,** shortly after the Thanksgiving holidays.
> The Convention Center in **Landover, Maryland,** was the site of the "Welcome Home" concert honoring Vietnam veterans.
> The Olympics in **Munich, West Germany,** were plagued by terrorism.

■ *Titles and academic degrees:* Use commas to set off these nonrestrictive elements.

> At Honors Convocation, Rebecca Kingsley, **professor emerita,** presented the scholarship that bears her name.
> William Leeds, **M.D.,** serves on the Marion County Health Board.

Exercise

Supply periods, question marks, exclamation points, and commas in the following sentences. Make sure that a rule guides your placement of punctuation.

1. CBS NBC and ABC America's largest networks are now advertising programs regularly on small independent cable networks

2. The novel originally priced at $2595 did not sell well but sales increased when the price was reduced to $1795

3. Address women as Ms unless you are certain that they prefer Mrs or Miss

4. Should we send our order to the Chicago Illinois distribution center or to the Atlanta Georgia center

5. Angered that her glares did not quiet the jabbering child the old woman finally shouted "Shut up"

6. The tour guide concerned that he adapt himself to the visitors' preferences asked if they wanted to spend more time in the chapel

7. The San Francisco earthquake of April 18 1906 measured 8.3 on the Richter scale but the March 2 1933 earthquake in Japan measured 8.9

8. Much to my surprise the word *calf* is used to describe young cattle elephants antelopes rhinoceroses hippopotamuses and whales

9. Even though he was working without State Department authorization Rev Jesse Jackson secured the release of Robert Goodman Jr from Syria

10. Did you know that the West Indian island Jamaica is smaller (4244 square miles) than Connecticut

11. Because she was aware of prejudice against women Amadine Aurore Dupin published her novels under the name George Sand

12. After four months of work the restorers gave up their attempts to salvage the Venetian fresco

13. Peonies irises roses and day lilies are among Americans' favorite perennial not annual flowers

14. To be competitive in a declining market American auto manufacturers slashed interest rates and offered special rebates

15. The Tyrannosaurus Rex with teeth that measured six inches long was the fiercest of the meat-eating dinosaurs

16. Passengers who need special assistance are always asked to board airplanes before other travelers

17. Ironically taking out a mortgage is considered more stressful than having a foreclosure on a mortgage

18. Many taxpayers choose to use the "short form"; however taxpayers who wish to itemize deductions must use the "long form"

19. The mineral calcium is needed to develop and maintain bones and teeth but it is lacking in many diets

20. The film *Gandhi* begins with the leader's assassination on January 30 1948 and then recounts his life in a long flashback

UNNECESSARY COMMAS ⦿

Too many commas in sentences can be as confusing as too few. To avoid excessive use of commas, observe the following rules.

21a

Do not use a comma before a coordinating conjunction that joins only two words, phrases, or dependent clauses.

Isak Dinesen married a Danish baron and subsequently moved to Africa.
[No comma with compound verb *married and moved.*]
I asked for advice first from my classmates and then from Professor Bakerman.
[No comma between two prepositional phrases joined by *and.*]

21b

Do not use a comma between subjects, verbs, and complements unless specific rules require that commas be used.

In the simplest sentences, no commas should break the subject-verb-complement pattern. When other information is added—appositives, nonrestrictive clauses, coordinate modifiers—commas may be necessary, but only as required by specific comma rules.

The angry soprano walked out of the rehearsal.
[No comma with subject-verb pattern.]
The angry soprano, **unhappy with the conductor,** walked out of the rehearsal.
[Nonrestrictive appositive set off by commas.]
Our university's pole vaulter was a strong contender for the title.
[No comma with verb-complement pattern.]
Our university's pole vaulter was, **by general agreement,** a strong contender for the title.
[Parenthetical comments, in this case a nonrestrictive prepositional phrase, require commas; see Section 20g.]

21c

Do not use a comma before the first or after the last item in a series.

Carla began attending exercise classes to build her stamina, to lose weight, and to tone her muscles.
[Comma would interrupt verb-complement pattern.]
Time, U.S. News and World Report, and *Newsweek* are the most popular weekly magazines in America.
[Comma would interrupt subject-verb pattern.]

21d

Do not use commas to separate adjectives or adverbs that cumulatively modify the same word.

When adjectives or adverbs work together to create meaning, they should *not* be separated by commas.

Four small red candles burned on the mantelpiece.
[No commas because *red* modifies *candles, small* modifies *red candles,* and *four* modifies *small red candles.*]

Do not use a comma between an adjective or an adverb and the word it modifies.

An especially͵talented͵pianist opened the recital.
[No commas because the adverb *especially* modifies the adjective *talented,* which modifies the noun *pianist.*]

Do not use commas to set off restrictive elements in sentences.

Barbra Streisand's song͵"Evergreen͵" won an Oscar in 1977.
[No commas because song title is necessary for sentence clarity. (Streisand had another Oscar-winning song in a different year.)]

Do not use a comma before an expression in parentheses.

When a comma is necessary with a parenthetical expression, it should follow the closing parenthesis.

In hopes of graduating early, Brian took six English classes͵(English 307, 320, 337, 339, 412, and 445)͵but he could not manage the reading.

Do not use a comma before either an indirect or a direct quotation introduced by *that.*

Marcos said͵that he will someday return to the Philippines.
But: Marcos said, "I will someday return to the Philippines."
Wasn't it Winston Churchill who said that "An iron curtain has descended across the Continent"?

Do not place a comma after either a question mark or an exclamation point in a direct quotation.

Question marks and exclamation points replace the commas that are frequently required with direct quotations.

"Will we never recover from the wounds created by the Vietnam War?͵" asked Representative Martin.

Exercise

Remove unnecessary commas from the following sentences. Be ready to explain why each comma you delete is not needed.

1. Sandy Koufax was named Most Valuable Player of the World Series in 1963, and in 1965.

2. Two American cities, (Chicago, and New York City) each employ more than ten thousand police officers.

3. Four, very, small cars can park in the spaces normally allotted to three full-sized cars.

4. The geriatrician said, the symptoms suggest that Uncle Rupert probably has Alzheimer's disease.

5. Chicago's O'Hare International Airport, is the busiest airport in the United States.

6. The aging movie theater, which was once the small city's pride, needed extensive, expensive, renovation.

7. The playwright, Sophocles, is known for perfecting the form, of classical Greek tragedy.

8. Since early 1982, the copper penny has been gradually replaced, by a copper-plated zinc coin.

9. "How can we expect students, who have never taken calculus, to perform well on this portion of the exam?," Professor Carino asked.

10. California, Pennsylvania, Illinois, Michigan, and Ohio, each distributes over $1.5 million annually in unemployment benefits.

22 SEMICOLONS (;)

The semicolon most often functions like a period, separating independent clauses. Though it can in some specialized instances replace a comma, the semicolon should not be used routinely as a substitute for a comma.

22a

Use a semicolon to join closely related independent clauses that are not connected by a coordinating conjunction.

In this usage, the semicolon most clearly functions like a period. As a result, make certain that each clause is, in fact, independent.

Take care of the children; let the adults take care of themselves.

22b

Use a semicolon to join independent clauses that are linked by a conjunctive adverb, or separate the clauses with a period.

The defense attorney's closing statements were brilliantly presented; however, the facts of the case favored the prosecution.

22c

Use a semicolon to separate three or more items in a series when one or more of the items contain internal commas.

In their essays, students commented on *The Fire Next Time,* an essay-novel by James Baldwin; *Soul on Ice,* a polemic by Eldridge Cleaver; and *Anger and Beyond,* a collection of critical essays edited by Herbert Hill.

22d

Do not use a semicolon in place of a comma with a subordinate clause.

Although revisions of the tax code will eliminate many deductions⟋ most Americans will benefit from a reduction in their overall tax rate.

22e

Do not introduce a list or a clarifying phrase with a semicolon.

The colon (:) and the dash (−) are traditionally used to introduce a list or a clarification. The semicolon is not interchangeable with these marks of punctuation.

A number of long-distance services vied for consumers' business⟋ AT&T, MCI, and Sprint.

23

COLONS (:)

The colon is a formal way to introduce a list or a clarification. The colon means "Note what follows." Use colons selectively to add clarity to your writing.

23a

Use a colon to introduce a list.

The items in the series should never be direct objects, predicate nouns, predicate adjectives, or objects of prepositions. An independent clause must precede the colon.

As noted in Section 22e, a dash may be used in place of the colon.

American theater and film have produced a number of notable acting families: Barrymore, Bridges, Fairbanks, Fonda, and Sheen.

23b

Selectively use a colon between two independent clauses when the second explains the first.

The second clause may start with either a lower-case letter (as shown here) or with a capital letter.

Except for differences in subject matter, the rules of grammar are like the laws of chemistry: they are generalizations describing accepted principles of operation.

23c

Use a colon to emphasize an appositive that comes at the end of a sentence.

Marlowe and Shakespeare introduced the dramatic use of blank verse: unrhymed iambic pentameter.

23d   **Use a colon in place of a comma to introduce or emphasize a long quotation.**

Churchill concluded an eloquent speech with this visionary statement: "Out of the depths of sorrow and sacrifice will be born again the glory of mankind."

23e   **Use a colon between numerals designating hours and minutes, after formal salutations in formal or official correspondence, between titles and subtitles, between chapter and verse in biblical citations, and between city and publisher in works-cited entries.**

(See "Documenting Sources" in Chapter 14.)

The speaker was scheduled to arrive on a 9:40 A.M. flight from Los Angeles.
Dear Mr. Harper: Dear Professor Smithson:
Some Sort of Epic Grandeur: The Life of F. Scott Fitzgerald
Isaiah 12:2–4
Cambridge: Harvard UP
Boston: Houghton Mifflin

23f   **Do not use a colon between a verb and its complement or between a preposition and its object.**

Jerrid's favorite restaurants are⟨ Richard's Townhouse, The Broken Blossom, and Fernucchi's.

Exercise

Revise these sentences, using semicolons or colons.

1. Two lizards found in southwestern United States and northern Mexico are venomous. They are the Gila monster and the Mexican bearded lizard.

2. The Democratic party considered five cities for its national convention. Those cities were Dallas, Texas, Chicago, Illinois, Atlanta, Georgia, Washington, D.C., and Los Angeles, California.

3. Mark Spitz was an outstanding Olympic competitor. However, he was only an adequate Olympic commentator.

4. Infertility counselor Roselle Shubin made this epigrammatic comment on parenthood, "There is more to being a mother than giving birth, and more to being a father than impregnating a woman."

5. Morocco, Algeria, Libya, Tunisia, and Egypt border the Mediterranean Sea. These are the only African countries that do.

24 DASHES (—)

A dash (made in typing with two hyphens with no space between or before or after them), serves a number of purposes in punctuating sentences. But it should be used with restraint because if overused the dash can become distracting and will lose its impact.

24a Use dashes to set off appositives in midsentence that contain commas.

Five states—Indiana, Iowa, Kentucky, Missouri, and Wisconsin—share borders with Illinois.

24b Use a dash to set off a series that introduces or ends a sentence.

Beaumont, Fletcher, Jonson, Kyd, Marlowe, and Webster—these dramatists were respected contemporaries of Shakespeare.

24c Use dashes, singly or in pairs, to set off interpretations, evaluations, or interruptions.

This answer—if we can call it an answer—is completely meaningless.
This answer is completely meaningless—if we can call it an answer.

25 PARENTHESES (( ))

Parentheses, used in pairs to set off secondary information in sentences, can foster clarity. Use them selectively, however, because they break the flow of sentences and if overused make your writing seem choppy and fragmented.

25a Use parentheses to enclose an explanation, qualification, or example that is not essential to the meaning of the sentence.

Phnom Penh is the capital of Kampuchea (known to most Americans as Cambodia).

25b

Use parentheses around numbers or letters that identify a sequence within a sentence.

> Withdrawing money from an automatic-teller machine requires seven simple steps: (1) insert your validated bank card; (2) type in your personal access code; (3) identify the account you want to take the money from; (4) indicate the amount of money you desire; (5) open the drawer and remove the money; (6) indicate that the transaction is complete; and (7) remove your bank card and the withdrawal slip.

Exercise

Using dashes and parentheses, revise these sentences.

1. In 1755, roughly 4,000 Acadians settlers in Nova Scotia, Canada, were forcibly relocated to Louisiana.

2. Sagamore Hill, Theodore Roosevelt's home at Oyster Bay, New York, became a national memorial in 1962.

3. Mali, Niger, and Nigeria these are the countries through which the river Niger flows.

4. Changing a tire requires five relatively simple steps: 1. turn off the car's engine and engage the emergency brake, 2. jack up the car on the appropriate side, 3. remove the damaged tire, 4. put on the spare, and 5. lower the car and remove the jack.

5. Margaret Higgins Sanger 1883–1966 led the birth-control movement in America during the early years of the twentieth century.

26

QUOTATION MARKS ("/")

Quotation marks are most commonly used to enclose direct quotations (but see also "Quoting Sources" in Chapter 14). The most important issues with quotation marks are accuracy in recording other people's comments and accuracy in the placement of other punctuation marks.

26a

Place commas and periods *before* quotation marks.

> My favorite story, "The Fall of the House of Usher," is by Poe.

26b Place colons and semicolons *after* quotation marks.

> Shelley creates a vivid image of a decayed civilization in his poem "Ozymandias": "Round the decay / Of that colossal wreck, boundless and bare / The lone and level sands stretch far away."

> For the university newspaper, Rachel wrote "The Dilemma of Drug Testing"; the article won the school's journalism award in the spring.

26c If a quotation is a question or an exclamation, place the question mark or exclamation point *before* the quotation marks.

If the whole sentence in which a quotation (or an exclamation) appears is a question (or an exclamation) but the quotation is not, place the question mark (or exclamation point) after the quotation marks.

> I can't remember who wrote the ballad "What'll I Do?"

> Were we supposed to read "What It Takes to Be a Leader"?

26d Use single quotation marks ('/') around material that would be enclosed by full quotation marks if it were not already within a quotation.

> Jeremy said, "Although 'Dover Beach' is one of Matthew Arnold's greatest poems, it is not one of my favorites."

27 BRACKETS ([/])

Brackets are used to enclose an editorial or a clarifying explanation or comment inserted into a direct quotation.

> Richardson commented, "Using both systems [the U.S. Customary System and the International Metric System] has caused considerable confusion for American consumers and has put U.S. industries at a trade disadvantage."

28 ELLIPSIS (. . .)

Ellipsis, three spaced periods, is used to indicate the omission of one or more words from a quotation. The three periods, or points, that form the ellipsis are considered a unit. When the omission comes at the end of a sentence, a fourth point must be added as end punctuation. When a comma is required, it follows the ellipsis.

28a Use ellipsis points to show where words have been omitted from a direct quotation.

Omit extraneous material—like parenthetical expressions or unnecessary clarifications—but do not leave out material if the omission changes the meaning of the original text.

Original Quotation	**Elliptical Quotation**
Lincoln's anti-slavery views, clarified in the Republican party platform of 1860, served to alienate not only the residents of southern states but also southern sympathizers in the North.	According to Walter Holtmire, "Lincoln's anti-slavery views . . . served to alienate not only the residents of southern states but also southern sympathizers in the North."

28b **Use ellipsis points very selectively to indicate hesitation, a trailing off of thought, or an incomplete statement.**

The deathbed scene in James Brooks's *Terms of Endearment* is . . . manipulative.

Observing the Rules of Punctuation: Review Exercise

Correct the punctuation errors in the following sentences. Be ready to identify the rules that guided your work.

1. The Internal Revenue Service IRS is responsible for administering the tax laws passed by Congress

2. From 1791 to 1862 the US government relied on tariffs to generate income in 1862 however Congress enacted the first income tax law to pay for the debts of the Civil War

3. Did you know that income taxes were not universally instituted until 1913

4. Following the 1986 tax law only a few major deductions will be allowed mortgage payments state and local taxes medical expenses and charitable contributions

5. Nevada South Dakota Texas Washington and Wyoming these states do not impose a corporate tax based on net income

6. The IRS operates from its various headquarters one national office in Washington seven regional offices sixty-three district offices and ten service centers and processes roughly 200 million returns annually

7. Beginning in 1943 taxes were withheld from wages a plan that increased the number of people who equitably paid taxes

8. According to new tax laws corporate rates will drop from 46 percent to 34 percent however a minimum tax will also be imposed to prevent major companies from paying no taxes

9. The nation's first sales taxes enacted in 1812 affected consumers of only four kinds of commodities gold silver jewelry and watches

10. Did you know that it was Benjamin Franklin who said But in this world nothing can be said to be certain except death and taxes

11. James Otis spoke the sentence that became a catch-phrase of the American Revolution Taxation without representation is tyranny

12. In 1985 the IRS collected a total of $742,871,541,000 in taxes a figure so large it is hard to envision

13. Most Americans do not object to paying taxes many however object to how the tax money is spent

14. Various tables Schedule X Y or Z are used to compute the taxes of people with incomes of more than $50000

15. Taxpayers who wish to appeal a tax charge must follow four steps 1 discuss the charge with a local appeal's office 2 submit a written protest 3 wait for a judgment 4 pay the charge or file yet another appeal with the District Claims Court

Observing the Rules of Mechanics

Mechanical errors in the use of capitalization, italics, quotation marks, apostrophes, hyphenation, number style, abbreviations, and spelling distract readers from the content of your writing. Heeding certain rules as you prepare the final copy of a paper will help ensure that your reader's attention is focused not on preventable mechanical errors but on what you have to say.

29   CAPITALIZATION (CAP)

29a   **Capitalize the first word of every sentence and of every line in conventional poetry.**

> Using a word processor saves time during revision.
>
> Standardized tests present a major problem for minorities: they do not allow for cultural differences.
>
> Whenas in silks my Julia goes
> Then, then, methinks, how sweetly flows
> That liquefaction of her clothes. . . .
>   —Robert Herrick,
>   "Upon Julia's Clothes"

29b   **Distinguish between *proper names,* which require capitalization, and *common names,* which do not.**

> I left the assignment in my professor's mailbox.
>
> *But:* I left the assignment in Professor Sheldon's mailbox.

I worked in summer stock to gain experience.

But: I worked at the Summer Festival Theater to gain experience.

29c   In titles, capitalize the first and last words and all important words.

As a general rule, capitalize all nouns, pronouns, verbs, adjectives, and adverbs. In addition, capitalize all prepositions and conjunctions of four or more letters. In works with two-part titles, the first word of the subtitle is also capitalized, regardless of the word's length.

Zora Neale Hurston's *Their Eyes Were Watching God*

Derrick Ashford's "Eighteenth-Century Comedy on the Modern Stage"

Marya Mannes's "TV Advertising: The Splitting Image"

29d   Capitalize the names of people, races, nationalities, languages, and places, whether used as nouns or as adjectives.

In American usage, the terms *black* and *white* are not capitalized. Native American, Hispanic, and Asian are capitalized.

Thomas Paine	Caucasian
Malaysia	Danish customs
Nairobi	Greek festival

29e   Capitalize the names of historical and cultural periods; historical, political, and cultural events; and documents.

the Age of Reason	the Emancipation Proclamation
the Romantic Movement	Elizabethan drama
the Battle of Hastings	Prohibition

29f   Capitalize the names of days, months, and secular and religious holidays.

Thursday	the Fourth of July
September	Hanukkah

29g   Capitalize the names of businesses and other organizations and government agencies and offices.

General Electric Company	National Rifle Association
Phi Delta Kappa	United States Senate

29h   Capitalize the names of schools, colleges, and universities, academic departments, specific courses, and degrees, but not general references.

Amherst College [But *college classes*]

Thomas Jefferson High School [But *high school teachers*]

Department of Education [But *department meeting*]

Sociology 245 [But *sociology course*]

Bachelor of Arts [But *baccalaureate degree*]

29i **Capitalize the names of religions and their followers and religious terms for sacred persons, books, and events.**

God	Islamic law
Buddha	Christian traditions
the Koran	the Immaculate Conception

29j **Capitalize titles that precede proper names.**

Doctor Erica Weinburg	Prime Minister Winston Churchill
Secretary of State James Baker	President Abraham Lincoln
Professor Leon Edel	

A title used alone or following a proper name is not capitalized.

A college professor is the catalyst in a classroom.

Jimmy Carter, the former president, has contributed even in retirement to the benefit of the country.

29k **Capitalize nouns designating family relationships only when they are used as proper names or when they precede proper names.**

After arthroscopic surgery, Mother's chances of leading a normal life improved.

I arrived at the apartment before Uncle Will got home from work.

Do not capitalize common nouns that name family relationships, even when the noun is preceded by a personal pronoun in the possessive case.

After arthroscopic surgery, my mother's life improved.

I arrived at the apartment before my uncle got home from work.

Never underestimate the influence of brothers and sisters.

29l **Capitalize _A.M._ and _P.M._ and _A.D._ and _B.C._; capitalize the call letters of radio and television stations; capitalize abbreviated forms of business, organization, and document names. (Periods may or may not be required, according to convention; consult a dictionary.)**

705 B.C.	ERA
A.D. 1066	WPFR radio
4:30 A.M.	KTVI television
4:30 P.M.	IBM

29m **Capitalize the first word of a direct quotation if the quotation is a complete sentence or an interjection that can stand alone.**

Mr. Bennett remarked, "Though ornate by present standards, Baroque sculpture remains aesthetically pleasing."

Carla, surprised by the harsh criticism, responded, "Oh."

Supply capitalization in the following sentences, noting the rule that guides each correction.

1. the elizabethan period, a cultural and aesthetic awakening in england, began roughly a century after the italian renaissance.

2. yom kippur, the holiest jewish holiday, was observed on monday, october 13, this year.

3. although my mother and aunt beatrice are both normally critical television viewers, they both love _the young and the restless._

4. an mba from harvard is an excellent passport to a lucrative job on wall street or with a fortune 500 firm.

5. students in french secondary schools are expected to learn english as well as one other foreign language.

6. james baker, the secretary of state, travels extensively in europe and the middle east for the department of state.

7. the reverend thomas r. fitzgerald serves as president of st. louis university, a catholic university enrolling over eleven thousand students.

8. who was it who said, "i cried all the way to the bank"?

9. the abbreviation ira could refer to the irish republican army or the international reading association.

10. dorothy parker once described katharine hepburn's performance in a play with this caustic sentence: "she ran the whole gamut of emotions from a to b."

30 ITALICS (ITAL)

In print, italics, slanted type, is used to give words distinction or emphasis. In handwritten or typed manuscript, the same effects are achieved using underlining.

30a   **Italicize the titles of books, periodicals, newspapers, pamphlets, plays, films, television series (but not individual programs), radio programs, long poems, long musical compositions, record albums, paintings, and sculpture.**

Marcel Proust's *Swann's Way* (book)
the *Washington Post* (newspaper)
NCTE's *Essentials of English* (pamphlet)
Oscar Wilde's *The Importance of Being Earnest* (play)
Sidney Pollack's *Out of Africa* (film)
Norman Lear's *All in the Family* (television program)
Casey Kasem's *Top-Twenty Count Down* (radio program)
Walt Whitman's *Leaves of Grass* (long poem)
Tchaikovsky's *The Nutcracker Suite* (long musical composition)
Paul Simon's *Graceland* (album)
Pablo Picasso's *Three Musicians* (painting)
George Segal's *Girl in Doorway* (sculpture)

30b   **Italicize the names of individual ships, trains, airplanes, and spacecraft.**

Jacques Cousteau's *Calypso* (ship)
the *Orient Express* (train)
Air Force One (airplane)
Voyager 1 (spacecraft)

30c   **Italicize foreign words and phrases.**

Confined to a hospital bed, Rachel had to vote *in absentia*.

Many foreign terms have been assimilated into standard usage and, as a result, do not require italics. Consult a dictionary for guidance.

30d   **Italicize words used as words, letters used as letters, numbers used as numbers, and symbols used as symbols.**

French contains two variations of *you,* one formal and one informal.
The letters *a* and *e* used to be printed *æ.*
Make sure that you distinguish your *1*s from your *7*s.
The ampersand, *&,* is unacceptable in formal prose.

30e   **Italicize words selectively for emphasis.**

In formal prose, this is not considered good usage.

Jason played the song *twenty-three* times in a row!

31   QUOTATION MARKS ("/")

Quotation marks are most commonly used to set off direct quotations, but they have a mechanical use as well.

31a   **Use quotation marks with the titles of brief works or parts of complete works.**

> "Winning Hearts Through Minds" in *Time* (article)
>
> Ernest Hemingway's "Old Man at the Bridge" (short story)
>
> Gerard Manley Hopkins's "God's Grandeur" (poem)
>
> Stephen Jay Gould's "Darwinism Defined: The Difference Between Fact and Theory" (essay)
>
> Manhattan Transfer's "Tuxedo Junction" (song)
>
> "The Spirit of Scholarship" in Richard Altick's *The Art of Literary Research* (chapter in a book)
>
> "Captain Tuttle" from *M*A*S*H* (episode of television program)

—————————————*Exercise*

Insert italics (underlining) and quotation marks in the following sentences. Remember to place them accurately in relation to other punctuation.

1. Paul Conrad won Pulitzer prizes for editorial cartooning when he worked for two different publications: the Denver Post and the Los Angeles Times.

2. Grammies for best song and best album went to Tina Turner for What's Love Got to Do With It? and Private Dancer, respectively.

3. To demonstrate aerodynamic possibilities, engineers developed the Gossamer Albatross, an airplane propelled by peddling.

4. Blattela germanica is an eloquent sounding term to use when you mean cockroach!

5. Stuart called here sixteen times while you were gone this weekend.

6. On your final charts, please write female and male rather than ♀ and ♂.

7. A View to a Death, a pivotal chapter in Golding's novel Lord of the Flies, offers a vision of primitive, ritualistic execution.

8. In an article titled A Man With Titanic Vision, Discover magazine honored Bob Ballard as its 1986 Scientist of the Year.

9. Many American musicals have plays as their source, among them Hello, Dolly (The Matchmaker), My Fair Lady (Pygmalion), and Cabaret (I Am a Camera).

10. Kurtz, a character in Conrad's novel The Heart of Darkness, has re-emerged in T. S. Eliot's Hollow Men, a brief poem, and Apocalypse Now, a long film.

32   APOSTROPHE (')

The apostrophe has three general uses: to indicate the possessive case of nouns and some pronouns, to indicate the omission of letters and numbers, to indicate the plural of letters, numbers, and words used as words.

32a   **Use an apostrophe and an _s_ to form the possessive of a singular noun or indefinite pronoun.**

Oprah Winfrey's guests
somebody's car
the men's dressing room
a month's rental fee
Harry Jones's first flight

32b   **Use only an apostrophe, without an _s_, when a noun is plural.**

scientists' projections
the Joneses' first flight

32c   **To show joint possession, add an apostrophe and an _s_ to the last name in the group. To show individual possession, add an apostrophe and an _s_ to each name in the group.**

Lerner and Lowe's musical reputation [Joint possession]
Shakespeare's and Marlowe's dramatic innovations [Individual possession]

32d   **Use an apostrophe to show the omission of letters and numbers.**

couldn't	could not	there's	there is
I'll	I will (_or_ I shall)	the '84 Olympics	the 1984 Olympics

Use an s to form the plurals of numbers, letters, and words used as words.

Kirsten received four *10*s during the final round of competition.
Her *s*'s look like *8*s.
His writing was cluttered with *very*s, *really*s, and *especially*s.

HYPHENATION (-)

Hyphens are used for two purposes: to divide a multisyllable word at the end of a line and to join two or more words of a compound.

Hyphenate a word that must continue on a new line

Place hyphens between the syllables of words that must be divided (if necessary, consult a dictionary to see where a break may be made). Do not break one-syllable words or leave fewer than three letters at the end or beginning of any line. Do not hyphenate proper names.

The hurricane battered the coastline, damaging property in four cities.

Hyphenate compound words according to convention; consult a dictionary.

Some compound words are hyphenated; others are "closed up," written as one word; still others are written as two words.

Hyphenated	Closed Up	Two Words
sister-in-law	applesauce	wedding ring
razzle-dazzle	blackboard	living room
master-at-arms	landowner	free fall

Hyphenate words that precede a noun and combine to modify it.

heart-to-heart talk
off-the-cuff comments
never-ending problems

When the modifiers follow the noun, no hyphens are necessary.

The comments were off the cuff.
His problems were never ending.

Hyphenate compound numbers ranging from twenty-one to ninety-nine; hyphenate fractions.

a test score of sixty-seven
two-thirds of the voters

33e   **Hyphenate words using the prefixes *all-, ex-,* and *self-;* hyphenate words using the suffix *-elect.***

> all-consuming pride
> ex-wife
> self-motivated student
> secretary-elect of the city council

33f   **Hyphenate a compound consisting of a prefix and a proper noun.**

> anti-Iranian
> un-American
> pre-Enlightenment
> post-Modern

33g   **Hyphenate words formed with a prefix if the unhyphenated form would be a homonym, a word with the same spelling but a different meaning.**

> re-cover (to cover again)   recover (to regain)
> re-lease (to lease again)   release (to let go)

34   NUMBERS (N)

34a   **Spell out numbers that can be expressed in one or two words.**

> thirty-two source cards   twenty-six thousand dollars
> five million voters   fourteen hundred miles

34b   **Use digits for numbers that would require three or more words if spelled out.**

> 319 graduates (*not* three hundred and nineteen)
> 101 pages (*not* one hundred and one)

34c   **Spell out a number that begins a sentence, or revise the sentence so that it does not open with a number.**

> *Not:* 412 art dealers attended the convention.
> *But:* Four hundred and twelve art dealers attended the convention.
> *Or:* There were 412 art dealers at the convention.

34d   **Use digits for addresses, dates, divisions of books and plays, dollars and cents, identification numbers, percentages, scores, and times.**

> 2300 North 12th Street (address)
> 11 January 1912 or January 11, 1912 (dates)
> 700 B.C., A.D. 700 (dates)

Chapter 17, Volume 2, Act 1, Scene 2 (divisions of books and plays)
$7.95, $1,230,000, $4.9 million (dollar amounts)
314-77-2248, UTC 41 69490 (identification numbers)
81 percent, 3 percent (percentages)
117 to 93 (scores)
6:10 A.M., 2:35 P.M. (times)

35 ABBREVIATIONS (AB)

Abbreviations, shortened forms of words, should be used sparingly. Any abbreviations you use should be familiar to your readers, and they must be appropriate to the writing context. To double-check conventional abbreviations, consult a dictionary.

35a Abbreviate titles that precede or follow people's names.

William D. Grenville, Jr.	Judith Haverford, Ph.D.
Ms. Abigail Hample	Rebecca Blair, M.D.
Dr. Terence McDonald	the Rev. Stephen Pierson

35b Use standard abbreviations and acronyms for names of organizations, corporations, and countries. Many of these abbreviations do not require periods.

Organizations: AFL-CIO, YMCA, FBI
Corporations: GTE, NBC, GM
Countries: USA (*or* U.S.A.), USSR (*or* U.S.S.R.), UK (*or* U.K.)

35c Before using an abbreviation that might be unfamiliar to some readers, spell out the complete name or term at its first appearance.

Idaho State University—located in Pocatello, Idaho—is a state-supported university serving over three thousand students. ISU offers especially strong programs in health-related professions.

35d Use standard abbreviations with times, dates, and specific numbers. Use the dollar sign with specific amounts.

Note the placement of the abbreviations *A.M., P.M., B.C.,* and *A.D.*

$1,245.78	500 B.C.
11:20 A.M.	A.D. 496
4:15 P.M.	part no. 339 (*or* No.)

35e Use standard abbreviations in works-cited entries.

(See "Documenting Sources" in Chapter 14.)

Abbreviation	Meaning
ed.	editor, edition
et al.	and others
rev.	revised
rpt.	reprint
trans.	translator, translated by
vol.	volume

35f **Use Latin abbreviations sparingly in prose.**

Latin Abbreviation	English Equivalent
c.f. *(confer)*	compare
e.g. *(exempli gratia)*	for example
et al. *(et alii)*	and others
etc. *(et cetera)*	and others, and so on
i.e. *(id est)*	that is
n.b. *(nota bene)*	note well

35g **In most writing, do not abbreviate business designations (unless the company does), units of measurement, days of the week, months, courses of instruction, divisions of books and plays, geographical names (except in addresses), or personal names.**

Not	But
Co., Inc.	Company, Incorporated
lb, tbs.	pound, tablespoon
Fri., Oct.	Friday, October
psych., Eng.	psychology, English
chap., vol.	chapter, volume
L.A., VA	Los Angeles, Virginia
Wm., Robt.	William, Robert

Exercise

Insert necessary apostrophes and hyphens in the following sentences. In addition, correct the number style and forms of abbreviations.

1. 6 members of the committee returned the questionnaire, refusing to comment on MSUs drug testing program.

2. The suicide that ends Act four of *Hedda Gabler* shocked many narrow minded critics.

3. Doctor Connelly, a graduate of U. of TX at Austin, spoke to our faculty on Oct. 15, 1986.

4. To attract first rate teachers to our public schools, we will have to increase teachers salaries.

5. Stephen Sondheims *Sunday in the Park with George* presents a neo Impressionist view of human relations and art.

6. Karin was delighted to receive 2 8s and 2 9s on her performance until she realized that 15s were possible.

7. The post Civil War period was a time of exploitation and manipulation in the South.

8. The Rams won the game thirty-six to seven, having passed for one hundred and fifty four yards and having made seventy four percent of the games interceptions.

9. My father in laws Social Security check ($24967) covers slightly over two thirds of his monthly expenses.

10. The president elect of the N.C.T.E. felt that her work would require working with a state of the art computer and printer, so she bought the pair.

_Exercise

Revise the following paragraph so that it is mechanically correct and consistent with conventional usage. Errors in capitalization, italics, quotation marks, apostrophes, hyphenation, number style, and abbreviations are present in the paragraph.

1600 Pennsylvania Ave., Washington, District of Columbia, is perhaps the *most famous* address in the U.S. At that site is the "White House," the residence of the President and his family. The design for the Original house was selected by Pres. Washington and Pierre L'Enfant, the french born designer of the city, and the cornerstone was set on Oct. 13, 1792. In 1814, the building was razed during a Battle of the war of 1812, and in subsequent years the interior of the structure had to be rebuilt. But the original design was heavily modified. As Mrs. John N. Pearce notes in The White House: An Historic Guide Ever changing personalities and styles of living and building have inspired the continuing metamorphosis that has marked the history of the White House. Over the years, the "White House" has served as both the official and the private residence of the first family. The 1st floor's rooms are used for public functions like Receptions and State Dinners, and its expansive, public rooms are decorated with such famous artwork as Gilbert Stuarts portrait George Washington. The limited access rooms on the second and third floors are used by the presidents family and friends. In all, the "White House" has one hundred and thirty-two rooms.

36 SPELLING (SP)

Errors in spelling, like other mechanical errors, interfere with communication because readers notice and are distracted by them. To avoid such distractions in your writing, develop good spelling habits. If you are a naturally good speller, then you have only to refresh your memory of common spelling rules. If you are a weak speller, then you need to hone your spelling skills.

Do not worry about spelling while you are planning and working on early drafts of your papers. If you interrupt your writing to check the spelling of a word, you might lose a thought that you cannot recapture. Instead make a mark near the word in question—a checkmark in the margin, the abbreviation *sp.* above the word, or a circle around the word—and continue your writing. Then, when your final draft is complete, look up the spelling of the words you have marked. This approach—checking spelling during revision—will allow you to write with a sense of continuity and attend to potential problems before typing your final copy.

36a Review Spelling Rules

Form plurals according to the pattern of the singular word.

■ When words end in a consonant plus *o,* add *-es.*

fresco	frescoes
motto	mottoes
tomato	tomatoes

Exceptions

auto	autos
dynamo	dynamos
piano	pianos

■ When words end in a vowel plus *o*, add *-s*.

cameo	cameos
radio	radios
studio	studios

■ When words end in a consonant plus *y*, change the *y* to *i* and add *-es*.

daisy	daisies
remedy	remedies
victory	victories

■ When words end in a vowel plus *y*, add *-s*.

attorney	attorneys
key	keys
survey	surveys

■ When words end in *s, ss, sh, ch, x,* or *z,* add *-es*.

bonus	bonuses	match	matches
overpass	overpasses	tax	taxes
wish	wishes	buzz	buzzes

■ When words that are proper names end in *y*, add *-s*.

the Bellamys

the three Marys

two Germanys

Add prefixes, such as *dis-, mis-, non-, pre-, re-, un-,* and others, without altering the spelling of the root word.

similar	dissimilar
spell	misspell
restrictive	nonrestrictive
historic	prehistoric
capture	recapture
natural	unnatural

Add suffixes according to the spelling of both the root word and the suffix.

■ When words end with a silent *e* and the suffix begins with a consonant, retain the *e*.

achieve   achievement
definite   definitely
refine   refinement

Exceptions

argue   argument

awe   awful

true   truly

■ When words end with a silent *e* and the suffix begins with a vowel, drop the *e*.

accommodate   accommodating

grieve   grievance

size   sizable

tolerate   tolerating

■ When words end with a silent *e* that is preceded by a "soft" *c* or *g* and the suffix begins with a vowel, retain the *e*.

notice   noticeable   singe   singeing

trace   traceable   outrage   outrageous

change   changeable

■ When a one-syllable word ends with a single consonant and contains only one vowel and the suffix begins with a vowel, double the final consonant.

blot   blotted

clip   clipping

fit   fitting

skip   skipper

stop   stopping

trip   tripped

Distinguish between words spelled with *ie* and *ei*.

The order of the vowels *ie* and *ei* is explained in this familiar poem:

Write *i* before *e*
Except after *c*
Or when sounded like *ay*
As in *neighbor* and *weigh*.

These are some exceptions to this rule:

counterfeit   leisure

either   neither

foreign   seizure

forfeit   sovereign

height   weird

36b   Improving Your Spelling Skills

Use a full-sized dictionary to check meanings and spellings of words that are often mistaken for each other.

A standard dictionary provides definitions that will help you distinguish between *affect* and *effect, elicit* and *illicit,* and other confusing word pairs.

Use a spelling dictionary for easy reference when you know a word's meaning but are unsure of its spelling.

Spelling dictionaries contain lists of commonly used words with markings to indicate syllable breaks. These special dictionaries are helpful as quick references.

Concentrate on the most troublesome parts of easily misspelled words.

Give particular attention to the parts of words that lead to spelling errors—usually a single syllable or small cluster of letters.

acciden**tal**ly	des**per**ate
sep**ara**te	se**cre**tary
main**ten**ance	

Keep a record of words you have misspelled in your writing.

Most people have individual sets of words that they regularly use and regularly misspell. Use a note card, a sheet of paper, or a small notebook to record your personal list of troublesome words.

Carefully check the spelling of technical terms.

When your writing requires specialized language, verify the spelling of technical terms because their spelling is often tricky.

Use a spelling program if you are using a word-processing program.

If you use a word processor to prepare your papers, take advantage of software that can check spelling. Although spelling programs are not without problems, they can be quite helpful.

Consult the following list of frequently misspelled words.

abbreviate	according	across
absence	accumulate	address
absurd	accustom	aggravate
accelerate	achievement	aggression
accidentally	acoustics	airplane
accommodate	acquaintance	alleviate
accomplish	acquitted	alley

allotted
allowed
ally
although
always
amateur
ambiguous
ammunition
among
amount
analogous
analysis
analyze
annual
antecedent
anxiety
apartment
apparatus
apparent
appearance
appropriate
arctic
argument
arising
arithmetic
arouse
arranging
article
artillery
ascend
association
athlete
athletics
attempt
attractive
audible
audience
authorities

automobile
auxiliary
awkward
bachelor
balance
balloon
barbarous
barring
battalion
bearing
becoming
beggar
beginning
believe
beneficial
benefited
biscuit
boundaries
breathe
brilliant
Britain
Britannica
bulletin
buoyant
bureau
buried
burying
business
busy
cafeteria
calendar
candidate
carburetor
carrying
casualties
causal
ceiling
celebrity

cemetery
certain
changeable
changing
characteristic
chauffeur
chief
choosing
chosen
clause
climbed
clothes
colloquial
colonel
column
coming
commission
commitment
committed
committee
companies
comparatively
compel
compelled
competent
competition
complaint
completely
compulsory
concede
conceivable
conceive
condemn
condescend
connoisseur
conqueror
conscience
conscientious

Continued on the next page.

considered
consistent
contemptible
control
controlled
convenient
copies
corner
coroner
corps
corpse
costume
countries
courteous
courtesy
cries
criticism
criticize
cruelty
cruise
curiosity
curriculum
custom
cylinder
dealt
debater
deceitful
deceive
decide
decision
defendant
deferred
deficient
definite
definition
democracy
dependent
descendant
description

desirable
despair
desperate
destruction
developed
development
diaphragm
diary
dictionary
dietitian
difference
digging
diphtheria
disappearance
disappoint
disastrous
discipline
discussion
disease
dissatisfied
dissipate
distribute
doesn't
dominant
don't
dormitories
dropped
drunkenness
echoes
ecstasy
efficiency
eighth
eligible
eliminate
embarrass
emphasize
employee
encouraging
encyclopedia

enthusiastic
environment
equipment
equipped
equivalent
erroneous
especially
eventually
exaggerate
exceed
excel
excellent
exceptional
excitement
exercise
exhaust
exhilaration
existence
experience
explanation
extensive
extracurricular
extremely
exuberance
fallacious
fallacy
familiar
fascinate
February
fiery
financial
financier
forehead
foreign
foremost
forfeit
forty
frantically
fraternities

friend
fulfill, fulfil
gaiety
generally
genius
genuine
glorious
government
grammar
grandeur
grievous
guarantee
guardian
guidance
handicapped
handkerchief
harass
hearse
height
heinous
heroes
hesitancy
hindrance
hoarse
hoping
horde
humorous
hurries
hygiene
hypocrisy
hysterical
illiterate
illogical
imaginary
imagination
imitative
immediately

implement
impromptu
inadequate
incidentally
incredible
indefinitely
independent
indicted
indispensable
inevitable
influential
innocent
inoculate
intellectual
intelligence
intentionally
intercede
interested
interpret
interrupt
irreligious
irresistible
irresponsible
itself
judicial
khaki
knowledge
laboratory
legitimate
leisure
library
lightning
literature
loneliness
losing
magazine
magnificent

maintain
maintenance
maneuver
manual
manufacture
mathematics
mattress
meant
medicine
medieval
messenger
millionaire
miniature
minute
mischievous
misspelled
modifies
modifying
momentous
mosquitoes
mottoes
mountainous
murmur
muscle
mysterious
necessary
necessity
neither
nervous
nevertheless
nickel
niece
ninety
ninth
noticeable
notorious
nowadays

Continued on the next page.

obedience
obliged
obstacle
occasionally
occur
occurred
occurrence
official
omission
omit
omitted
opinion
opportunity
optimistic
organization
original
orthodox
outrageous
overrun
pamphlet
parallel
parliament
participle
particularly
pastime
peaceable
perceive
perform
permissible
perseverance
persuade
phrase
physical
physician
picnicked
piece
playwright
pleasant
possess
possessive

possible
potatoes
practice
prairie
preceding
predominant
preference
preferred
prejudice
preparation
prevalent
primitive
privilege
probably
professor
prominent
pronounce
pronunciation
propeller
protein
psychology
pursue
pursuing
putting
quantity
quarantine
questionnaire
quizzes
realize
recede
receipt
receive
receiving
recognize
recommend
reference
referred
relevant
religion
religious

remembrance
reminiscence
rendezvous
repetition
replies
representative
reservoir
resistance
restaurant
rhetoric
rheumatism
rhythmical
ridiculous
sacrifice
sacrilegious
safety
salary
sanctuary
sandwich
scarcely
scene
scenic
schedule
secretarial
secretary
seized
sensible
sentence
sentinel
separate
sergeant
severely
shining
shriek
siege
sieve
similar
sincerely
sincerity
skeptical

slight
soliloquy
sophomore
source
specifically
specimen
spontaneous
statement
statue
stomach
stopped
strength
strenuously
stretched
struggle
studying
subordinate
subtle
succeed
success
successful
suffrage
superintendent
supersede
suppress
surprise
swimming
syllable
synonym

synonymous
tangible
tariff
tasting
technical
technique
temperament
tenant
tendency
thorough
thought
tournament
traffic
tragedy
transferred
tremendous
tries
truly
twelfth
typical
tyranny
unanimous
undoubtedly
unnecessary
until
usage
useful
using
usually

vacancy
vacuum
valuable
vengeance
victorious
view
vigilant
vigorous
village
villain
warrant
warring
weird
welfare
whole
wholly
wiry
woman
women
won't
worried
worrying
writing
written
yacht
your
you're (you are)
zoology

_____Exercises_

Use the following activities to help you eliminate any spelling problems that you happen to have. Keep in mind that your work will vary from that of other writers because individuals have individual difficulties with spelling.

1. Scan the list of frequently misspelled words (pages 564–9) and underline the words you know you have trouble spelling. Then, write them on a 4″ × 6″ card for handy reference when you proofread your papers.

2. Review your graded papers from classes this term (or other recent samples of your writing) and make a list of the words you have misspelled. Include in this list any specialized terms that you frequently use.

3. Prepare a 4″ × 6″ card with a list of important names and terms used in your major and minor courses, especially those that present spelling problems. Include the names of writers, theorists, organizations, cities, titles, scientific terms, commonly used foreign phrases, and so on.

Observing the Rules of Mechanics: Review Exercise

Correct the mechanical errors in the following paragraph.

The civil war period in american history has had a tremendous impact on modern Culture, Science, Politics, and Economics—in fact, on almost all aspects of american life. Yet the real influences of the civil war are typically ignored because of the myths which americans prefer to perpetrate. Who has not created a fictionalized view of antebellum culture based on Historical Novels like Margaret Mitchells Gone With The Wind, Harriet Beecher Stowes Uncle Toms Cabin, or Margaret Walkers Jubilee? Who has not been influenced by the mini series The North and the South, The Blue and The Gray, or Roots? Modern Americans have seen president Lincoln portrayed by dozens of actors, have seen reenactments of the battle of Gettysburg, and have witnessed the sea battles of the Iron Ships: The Monitor and others. Who has not seen dramatized versions of soldiers—both from the north and the south—heading to their homes, with The Battle Hymn of the Republic or Dixie as background music. We have stored images of generals Lee and Grant, as often as not based on the idealized statuary of the Franklin Mints Civil War Chess Set. Yet few of us have seen the civil war through the disturbing Psychological perspective of Stephen Cranes The Red Badge of Courage. Few have acknowledged in any real way that the reconstruction depressed the southern economy, gave rise to the ku klux klan, and failed to solve the ideological problems that continued to divide the country long after the deaths of six-hundred and fifty thousand soldiers.

A Glossary of Contemporary Usage

This glossary identifies words and constructions that sometimes require attention in composition classes. Some of the entries are pairs of words that are quite different in meaning yet similar enough in spelling to be confused (see **principal, principle**). Some, such as the use of *without* as a synonym for *unless,* are nonstandard usages that are not acceptable in college writing (see **without = unless**). Some are informal constructions that may be appropriate in some situations but not in others (see **guess**).

The judgments recorded here about usage are based on the Usage Notes contained in the *American Heritage Dictionary,* supplemented by other sources. Because these authorities do not always agree, it has sometimes been necessary for the authors of this textbook to decide which judgments to accept. In coming to decisions, we have attempted to represent a consensus, but readers should be aware that on disputed items the judgments recorded in this glossary are finally those of the authors.

Because dictionaries do not always distinguish between formal, informal, and colloquial usage, it has seemed useful to indicate whether particular usages would be appropriate in college writing. The usefulness of this advice, however, depends on an understanding of its limitations. In any choice of usage, the decision depends less on what dictionaries or textbooks say than on what is consistent with the purpose and style of the writing. The student and instructor, who alone have the context of the paper before them, are in the best position to answer that question. All that the glossary can do is provide a background from which particular decisions can be made. The general assumption in the glossary is that the predominant style in college writing is moderate rather than formal or colloquial. This assumption implies that calling a usage informal in no way suggests that it is less desirable than a formal usage.

ad   *Ad* is the clipped form of *advertisement.* The full form is preferable in a formal style, especially in letters of application. The appropriateness of *ad* in college writing depends on the style of the paper.

adapt, adopt   *Adapt* means "to adjust to meet requirements": "The human body can adapt itself to all sorts of environments"; "It will take a skillful writer to adapt this novel for the movies." *Adopt* means "to take as one's own" ("He immediately adopted the idea") or—in parliamentary procedure—"to accept as law" ("The motion was adopted").

advice, advise   The first form is a noun, the second a verb: "I was advised to ignore his advice."

affect, effect   Both words may be used as nouns, but *effect,* meaning "result," is usually the word wanted: "His speech had an unfortunate effect"; "The treatments had no effect on me." The noun *affect* is a technical term in psychology. Although both words may be used as verbs, *affect* is the more common. As a verb, *affect* means "impress" or "influence": "His advice affected my decision"; "Does music affect you that way?" As a verb, *effect* is rarely required in college writing but may be used to mean "carry out" or "accomplish": "The pilot effected his mission"; "The lawyer effected a settlement."

affective, effective   See **affect, effect.** The common adjective is *effective* ("an effective argument"), meaning "having an effect." The use of *affective* is largely confined to technical discussions of psychology and semantics, in which it is roughly equivalent to "emotional." In this textbook, *affective* is used to describe a tone that is chiefly concerned with creating attitudes in the reader (see pp. 236–37).

aggravate   *Aggravate* may mean either "to make worse" ("His remarks aggravated the dispute") or "to annoy or exasperate" ("Her manners aggravate me"). Both are standard English, but there is still some objection to the second usage. If you mean *annoy, exasperate,* or *provoke,* it would be safer to use whichever of those words best expresses your meaning.

ain't   Except to record nonstandard speech, the use of *ain't* is not acceptable in college writing.

all together, altogether   Distinguish between the phrase ("They were all together at last") and the adverb ("He is altogether to blame"). *All together* means "all in one place"; *altogether* means "entirely" or "wholly."

allow   When used to mean "permit" ("No smoking is allowed on the premises"), *allow* is acceptable. Its use to mean "think" ("He allowed it could be done") is nonstandard and is not acceptable in college writing.

allusion, illusion   An *allusion* is a reference: "The poem contains several allusions to Greek mythology." An *illusion* is an erroneous mental image: "Rouge on pallid skin gives an illusion of health."

alright   A common variant spelling of *all right,* but there is still considerable objection to it. *All right* is the preferred spelling.

among, between See **between, among.**

amount, number *Amount* suggests bulk or weight: "We collected a considerable amount of scrap iron." *Number* is used for items that can be counted: "He has a large number of friends"; "There are a number of letters to be answered."

an Variant of the indefinite article *a.* Used instead of *a* when the word that follows begins with a vowel sound: "an apple," "an easy victory," "an honest opinion," "an hour," "an unknown person." When the word that follows begins with a consonant, or with a *y* sound or a pronounced *h,* the article used should be *a:* "a yell," "a unit," "a history," "a house." Such constructions as "a apple," "a hour" are nonstandard. The use of *an* before *historical* is an older usage that is now dying out.

and/or Many people object to *and/or* in college writing because the expression is associated with legal and commercial writing. Generally avoid it.

angle The use of *angle* to mean "point of view" ("Let's look at it from a new angle") is acceptable. In the sense of personal interest ("What's your angle?"), it is slang.

anxious = eager *Anxious* should not be used in college writing to mean "eager," as in "Gretel is anxious to see her gift." *Eager* is the preferred word in this context.

any = all The use of *any* to mean "all," as in "He is the best qualified of any applicant," is not acceptable. Say "He is the best qualified of all the applicants," or simply "He is the best-qualified applicant."

any = any other The use of *any* to mean "any other" ("The knife she bought cost more than any in the store") should be avoided in college writing. In this context, use *any other.*

anyone = all The singular *anyone* should not be used in writing to mean "all." In "She is the most talented musician of anyone I have met here," drop "of anyone."

anywheres A nonstandard variant of *anywhere.* It is not acceptable in college writing.

apt = likely *Apt* is always appropriate when it means "quick to learn" ("He is an apt student") or "suited to its purpose" ("an apt comment"). It is also appropriate when a predictable characteristic is being spoken of ("When he becomes excited he is apt to tremble"). In other situations the use of *apt* to mean "likely" ("She is apt to leave you"; "He is apt to resent it") may be too colloquial for college writing.

as = because *As* is less effective than *because* in showing causal relation between main and subordinate clauses. Since *as* has other meanings, it may in certain contexts be confusing. For example, in "As I was going home, I decided to telephone," *as* may mean "while" or "because." If there is any possibility of confusion, use either *because* or *while*—whichever is appropriate.

as = that The use of *as* to introduce a noun clause ("I don't know as I would agree to that") is colloquial. In college writing, use *that* or *whether*.

as to, with respect to = about Although *as to* and *with respect to* are standard usage, many writers avoid these phrases because they sound stilted: "I am not concerned as to your cousin's reaction." Here *about* would be more appropriate than either *as to* or *with respect to;* "I am not concerned about your cousin's reaction."

at Avoid the redundant *at* in such sentences as "Where were you at?" and "Where do you live at?"

author *Author* is not fully accepted as a verb. "To write a play" is preferable to "to author a play."

awful, awfully The real objection to *awful* is that it is worked to death. Instead of being reserved for situations in which it means "awe inspiring," it is used excessively as a utility word (see page 263). Use both *awful* and *awfully* sparingly.

bad = badly The ordinary uses of *bad* as an adjective cause no difficulty. As a predicate adjective ("An hour after dinner, I began to feel bad"), it is sometimes confused with the adverb *badly*. After the verbs *look, feel,* and *seem,* the adjective is preferred. Say: "It looks bad for our side," "I feel bad about the quarrel," "Our predicament seemed bad this morning." But do not use *bad* when an adverb is required, as in "He played badly," "a badly torn suit."

bank on = rely on In college writing *rely on* is generally preferred.

being as = because The use of *being as* for "because" or "since" in such sentences as "Being as I am an American, I believe in democracy" is nonstandard. Say "Because I am an American, I believe in democracy."

between, among In general, use *between* in constructions involving two people or objects and *among* in constructions involving more than two: "We had less than a dollar between the two of us"; "We had only a dollar among the three of us." The general distinction, however, should be modified when insistence on it would be unidiomatic. For example, *between* is the accepted form in the following examples:

> He is in the enviable position of having to choose between three equally attractive young women.
>
> A settlement was arranged between the four partners.
>
> Just between us girls . . . (when any number of "girls" is involved)

between you and I Both pronouns are objects of the preposition *between* and so should be in the objective case: "between you and me."

bi-, semi- *Bi-* means "two": "The budget for the biennium was adopted." *Semi-* means "half of": "semicircle." *Bi-* is sometimes used to mean "twice in." A bimonthly paper, for example, may be published twice a month, not once every two months, but this usage is ambiguous; *semimonthly* is preferred.

but that, but what In such a statement as "I don't doubt but that you are correct," *but* is unnecessary. Omit it. "I don't doubt but what . . ." is also unacceptable. Delete *but what* and write *that*.

can = may The distinction that *can* is used to indicate ability and *may* to indicate permission ("If I can do the work, may I have the job?") is not generally observed in informal usage. Either form is acceptable in college writing.

cannot help but In college writing, the form without *but* is preferred: "I cannot help being angry." (Not: "I cannot help but be angry.")

can't hardly A confusion between *cannot* and *can hardly*. The construction is unacceptable in college writing. Use *cannot, can't,* or *can hardly*.

capital, capitol Unless you are referring to a government building, use *capital*. The building in which the U.S. Congress meets is always capitalized ("the Capitol"). For the various meanings of *capital*, consult your dictionary.

censor, censure Both words come from a Latin verb meaning "to set a value on" or "judge." *Censor* is used to mean "appraise" in the sense of evaluating a book or a letter to see if it may be released ("All outgoing mail had to be censored") and is often used as a synonym for *delete* or *cut out* ("That part of the message was censored").

Censure as a verb means "to evaluate adversely" or "to find fault with"; as a noun, it means "disapproval," "rebuke": "The editorial writers censured the speech"; "Such an attitude will invoke public censure."

center around "Center on" is the preferred form.

cite, sight, site *Cite* means "to refer to": "He cited chapter and verse." *Sight* means "spectacle" or "view": "The garden was a beautiful sight." *Site* means "location": "This is the site of the new plant."

compare, contrast *Compare* can imply either differences or similarities; *contrast* always implies differences. *Compare* can be followed by either *to* or *with*. The verb *contrast* is usually followed by *with*.

> Compared to her mother, she's a beauty.
>
> I hope my accomplishments can be compared with those of my predecessor.
>
> His grades this term contrast conspicuously with the ones he received last term.

complement, compliment Both words can be used as nouns and verbs. *Complement* speaks of completion: "the complement of a verb"; "a full complement of soldiers to serve as an honor guard"; "Susan's hat complements the rest of her outfit tastefully." *Compliment* is associated with praise: "The instructor complimented us for writing good papers."

***complement of* to be** The choice between "It is I" and "It's me" is a choice not between standard and nonstandard usage but between formal and colloquial styles. This choice seldom has to be made in college writing, since the expression, in whatever form it is used, is essentially a spoken rather than a written sentence. Its use in writing occurs chiefly in dialogue, and then the form chosen should be appropriate to the speaker.

The use of the objective case with the third person ("That was her") is less common and should be avoided in college writing except when dialogue requires it.

continual, continuous Both words refer to a continued action, but *continual* implies repeated action ("continual interruptions," "continual disagreements"), whereas *continuous* implies that the action never ceases ("continuous pain," "a continuous buzzing in the ears").

could of = could have Although *could of* and *could have* often sound alike in speech, *of* is not acceptable for *have* in college writing. In writing, *could of, should of, would of, might of,* and *must of* are nonstandard.

council, counsel *Council* is a noun meaning "a deliberative body": "a town council," "a student council." *Counsel* can be either a noun meaning "advice" or a verb meaning "to advise": "to seek a lawyer's counsel," "to counsel a person in trouble." A person who offers counsel is a *counselor:* "Because of his low grades Quint made an appointment with his academic counselor."

credible, creditable, credulous All three words come from a Latin verb meaning "to believe," but they are not synonyms. *Credible* means "believable" ("His story is credible"); *creditable* means "commendable" ("John did a creditable job on the committee") or "acceptable for credit" ("The project is creditable toward the course requirements"); *credulous* means "gullible" ("Only a most credulous person could believe such an incredible story").

cute A word used colloquially to indicate the general notion of "attractive" or "pleasing." Its overuse shows lack of discrimination. A more specific term is often preferable.

> His daughter is cute. [lovely? petite? pleasant? charming?]
>
> That is a cute trick. [clever? surprising?]
>
> He has a cute accent. [pleasant? refreshingly unusual?]
>
> She is a little too cute for me. [affected? juvenile? clever?]

data is Because *data* is the Latin plural of *datum,* it logically requires a plural verb and always takes a plural verb in scientific writing: "These data have been double checked." In popular usage and in computer-related contexts, *datum* is almost never used and *data* is treated as a singular noun and given a singular subject: "The data has been double checked." Either *data are* or *data is* may be used in popular writing, but only *data are* is acceptable in scientific writing.

debut *Debut* is a noun meaning "first public appearance." It is not acceptable as a transitive verb ("The Little Theater will debut its new play tonight") or as an intransitive verb ("Cory Martin will debut in the new play").

decent, descent A decent person is one who behaves well, without crude-ness and perhaps with kindness and generosity. *Decent* can mean "satisfactory" ("a decent grade," "a decent living standard"). *Descent* means "a passage downward"; a descent may be either literal ("their descent into the canyon") or figurative ("hereditary descent of children from their parents," "descent of English from a hypothetical language called Indo-European").

desert, dessert   The noun *desert* means "an uncultivated and uninhabited area"; it may be dry and sandy. *Desert* can be an adjective: "a desert island." The verb *desert* means "to abandon." A *dessert* is a sweet food served as the last course at the noon or evening meal.

different from, different than   Although both *different from* and *different than* are common American usages, the preferred idiom is *different from.*

disinterested, uninterested   The distinction between these words is that *disinterested* means "unbiased" and *uninterested* means "apathetic" or "not interested." A disinterested critic is one who comes to a book with no prejudices or prior judgments of its worth; an uninterested critic is one who cannot get interested in the book. Dictionaries disagree about whether this distinction is still valid in contemporary usage and sometimes treat the words as synonyms. But in college writing the distinction is generally observed.

don't   *Don't* is a contraction of "do not," as *doesn't* is a contraction of "does not." It can be used in any college writing in which contractions are appropriate. But it cannot be used with a singular subject. "He don't" and "it don't" are nonstandard usages.

double negative   The use of two negative words within the same construction. In certain forms ("I am not unwilling to go") the double negative is educated usage for an affirmative statement; in other forms ("He hasn't got no money") the double negative is nonstandard usage. The observation that "two negatives make an affirmative" in English usage is a half-truth based on a false analogy with mathematics. "He hasn't got no money" is unacceptable in college writing, not because two negatives make an affirmative, but because it is nonstandard usage.

economic, economical   *Economic* refers to the science of economics or to business in general: "This is an economic law"; "Economic conditions are improving." *Economical* means "inexpensive" or "thrifty": "That is an economical purchase"; "He is economical to the point of miserliness."

effect, affect   See **affect, effect.**

effective, affective   See **affective, effective.**

either   Used to designate one of two things: "Both hats are becoming; I would be perfectly satisfied with either." The use of *either* when more than two things are involved ("There are three ways of working the problem; either way will give the right answer") is a disputed usage. When more than two things are involved, it is better to use *any* or *any one* instead of *either*: "There are three ways of working the problem; any one of them will give the right answer."

elicit, illicit   The first word means "to draw out" ("We could elicit no response from them"); the second means "not permitted" or "unlawful" ("an illicit sale of drugs").

emigrant, immigrant   An emigrant is a person who moves *out* of a country; an immigrant is one who moves *into* a country. Thus, refugees from Central America and elsewhere who settle in the United States are emigrants from their native countries and immigrants here. A similar distinction holds for the verbs *emigrate* and *immigrate.*

eminent, imminent   *Eminent* means "prominent, outstanding": "an eminent scientist." *Imminent* means "ready to happen" or "near in time": "War seems imminent."

enormity, enormous, enormousness   *Enormous* refers to unusual size or measure; synonyms are *huge, vast, immense:* "an enormous fish," "an enormous effort." *Enormousness* is a noun with the same connotations of size and can be applied to either good or bad effects: "The enormousness of their contribution is only beginning to be recognized"; "The enormousness of the lie almost made it believable." But *enormity* is used only for evil acts of great dimension: "The enormity of Hitler's crimes against the Jews shows what can happen when power, passion, and prejudice are all united in one human being."

enthused   *Enthused* is colloquial for *enthusiastic:* "The probability of winning has caused them to be very enthused about the campaign." In college writing use *enthusiastic.*

equally as   In such sentences as "He was equally as good as his brother," the *equally* is unnecessary. Simply write, "He was as good as his brother."

etc.   An abbreviation for the Latin *et cetera,* which means "and others," "and so forth." It should be used only when the style justifies abbreviations and then only after several items in a series have been identified: "The data sheet required the usual personal information: age, height, weight, marital status, etc." An announcement of a painting contest that states, "Entries will be judged on the basis of use of color, etc.," does not tell contestants very much about the standards by which their work is to be judged. Avoid the redundant *and* before *etc.*

expect = suppose or suspect   The use of *expect* for *suppose* or *suspect* is colloquial. In college writing use *suppose* or *suspect:* "I suppose you have written to him"; "I suspect that we have made a mistake."

fact   Distinguish between facts and statements of fact. A fact is something that exists or existed. A fact is neither true nor false; it just *is.* A statement of fact, or a factual statement, may be true or false, depending on whether it does or does not report the facts accurately.

Avoid padding a sentence with "a fact that," as in "It is a fact that all the public opinion polls predicted Truman's defeat in the 1948 election." The first five words of that sentence add no meaning. Similarly, "His guilt is admitted" says all, in fewer words, that is said by "The fact of his guilt is admitted."

famous, notorious *Famous* is a complimentary and *notorious* an uncomplimentary adjective. Well-known people of good repute are famous; those of bad repute are notorious, or infamous.

farther, further The distinction that *farther* indicates distance and *further* degree is not unanimously supported by usage studies. But to mean "in addition," only *further* is used: "Further assistance will be required."

feature = imagine The use of *feature* to mean "give prominence to," as in "This issue of the magazine features an article on juvenile delinquency," is established standard usage and is appropriate in college writing. But this acceptance does not justify the slang use of *feature*, meaning "imagine," in such expressions as "Can you feature that?" "Feature me in a dress suit," "I can't feature him as a nurse."

fewer = less *Fewer* refers to quantities that can be counted individually: "fewer male than female employees." *Less* is used for collective quantities that are not counted individually ("less corn this year than last") and for abstract characteristics ("less determination than enthusiasm").

field *Field,* in the sense of "an area of study or endeavor," is an overused word that often creates redundance: "He is majoring in the field of physics"; "Her new job is in the field of public relations." Delete "the field of" in each of these sentences.

fine = very well The colloquial use of *fine* to mean "very well" ("He is doing fine in his new position") is probably too informal for most college writing.

flaunt = flout Using *flaunt* as a synonym for *flout* confuses two different words. *Flaunt* means "to show off": "She has a habit of flaunting her knowledge to intimidate her friends." *Flout* means "to scorn or show contempt for": "He is better at flouting opposing arguments than at understanding them." In the right context either word can be effective, but the two words are not synonyms and cannot be used interchangeably.

fortuitous, fortunate *Fortuitous* means "by chance," "not planned": "Our meeting was fortuitous; we had never heard of each other before." Do not confuse *fortuitous* with *fortunate,* as the writer of this sentence has done: "My introduction to Professor Kraus was fortuitous for me; today she hired me as her student assistant." *Fortunate* would be the appropriate word here.

funny Often used in conversation as a utility word that has no precise meaning but may be clear enough in its context. It is generally too vague for college writing. Decide in what sense the subject is "funny" and use a more precise term to convey that sense. (See the discussion of vagueness on pages 263–4).

get A utility word. The *American Heritage Dictionary* lists thirty-six meanings for the individual word and more than sixty uses in idiomatic expressions. Most of these uses are acceptable in college writing. But unless the style is deliberately colloquial, avoid slang uses of *get* meaning "to cause harm to" ("She'll get me for that"), "to cause a negative reaction to" ("His bad manners really get me"), "to gain the favor of" ("He tried to get in with his boss"), and "to become up to date" ("Get in the swing of things").

good   The use of *good* as an adverb ("He talks good"; "She played pretty good") is not acceptable. The accepted adverbial form is *well.* The use of *good* as a predicate adjective after verbs of hearing, feeling, seeing, smelling, tasting, and the like is standard. See **bad.**

good and   Used colloquially as an intensive in such expressions as "good and late," "good and ready," "good and tired." The more formal the style, the less appropriate these intensives are. In college writing use them sparingly, if at all.

guess   The use of *guess* to mean "believe," "suppose," or "think" ("I guess I can be there on time") is accepted by all studies on which this glossary is based. There is objection to its use in formal college writing, but it should be acceptable in an informal style.

had (hadn't) ought   Nonstandard for *ought* and *ought not.* Not acceptable in college writing.

hanged, hung   Alternative past participles of *hang.* For referring to an execution, *hanged* is preferred; in other senses, *hung* is preferred.

he or she, she or he   Traditionally the masculine form (*he, his, him*) of the personal pronoun has been used to refer to an individual who could be either male or female: "The writer should revise his draft until he accomplishes his purpose." Substituting pronouns that refer to both males and females in the group, such as *he or she,* or *she or he,* corrects the implicit sexism in the traditional usage but sometimes sounds awkward. An alternative is to use plural forms: "Writers should revise their drafts until they accomplish their purpose."

hopefully   Opinion is divided about the acceptability of attaching this adverb loosely to a sentence and using it to mean "I hope": "Hopefully, the plane will arrive on schedule." This usage is gaining acceptance, but there is still strong objection to it. In college writing the safe decision is to avoid it.

idea   In addition to its formal meaning of "conception," *idea* has acquired so many supplementary meanings that it must be recognized as a utility word. Some of its meanings are illustrated in the following sentences:

> The idea (thesis) of the book is simple.
> The idea (proposal) she suggested is a radical one.
> I got the idea (impression) that he is unhappy.
> It is my idea (belief, opinion) that they are both wrong.
> My idea (intention) is to leave early.

The overuse of *idea,* like the overuse of any utility word, makes for vagueness. Whenever possible, use a more precise synonym.

illicit, elicit See **elicit, illicit.**

illusion, allusion See **allusion, illusion.**

immigrant, emigrant See **emigrant, immigrant.**

imminent, eminent See **eminent, imminent.**

imply, infer The traditional difference between these two words is that *imply* refers to what a statement means, usually to a meaning not specifically stated but suggested in the original statement, whereas *infer* is used for a listener's or reader's judgment or inference based on the statement. For example: "I thought that the weather report implied that the day would be quite pretty and sunny, but Marlene inferred that it meant we'd better take umbrellas." The dictionaries are not unanimous in supporting this distinction, but in your writing it will be better not to use *imply* as a synonym for *infer.*

individual Although the use of *individual* to mean "person" ("He is an energetic individual") is accepted by the dictionaries, college instructors frequently disapprove of this use, probably because it is overdone in college writing. There is no objection to the adjective *individual,* meaning "single," "separate" ("The instructor tries to give us individual attention").

inferior than Possibly a confusion between "inferior to" and "worse than." Use *inferior to:* "Today's workmanship is inferior to that of a few years ago."

ingenious, ingenuous *Ingenious* means "clever" in the sense of "original": "an ingenious solution." *Ingenuous* means "without sophistication," "innocent": "Her ingenuous confession disarmed those who had been suspicious of her motives."

inside of, outside of *Inside of* and *outside of* generally should not be used as compound prepositions. In place of the compound prepositions in "The display is inside of the auditorium" and "The pickets were waiting outside of the gate," write "inside the auditorium" and "outside the gate."

Inside of is acceptable in most college writing when it means "in less than": "I'll be there inside of an hour." The more formal term is *within.*

Both *inside of* and *outside of* are appropriate when *inside* or *outside* is a noun followed by an *of* phrase: "The inside of the house is quite attractive"; "He painted the outside of his boat dark green."

in terms of An imprecise and greatly overused expression. Instead of "In terms of philosophy, we are opposed to his position" and "In terms of our previous experience with the company, we refuse to purchase its products," write "Philosophically, we are opposed to his position" and "Because of our previous experience with the company, we refuse to purchase its products."

irregardless A nonstandard variant of *regardless.* Do not use it.

irrelevant, irreverent *Irrelevant* means "having no relation to" or "lacking pertinence": "That may be true, but it is quite irrelevant." *Irreverent* means "without reverence": "Such conduct in church is irreverent."

it's me This construction is essentially a spoken one. Except in dialogue, it rarely occurs in writing. Its use in educated speech is thoroughly established. The formal expression is "It is I."

-ize The suffix *-ize* is used to change nouns and adjectives into verbs: *civilize, criticize, sterilize.* This practice is often overused, particularly in government and business. Avoid such pretentious and unnecessary jargon as *finalize, prioritize,* and *theorize.*

judicial, judicious Judicial decisions are related to the administering of justice, often by judges or juries. A judicious person is one who demonstrates good judgment: "A judicious person would not have allowed the young boys to shoot the rapids alone."

kind of, sort of Use a singular noun and a singular verb with these phrases: "That kind of person is always troublesome"; "This sort of attitude is deplorable." If the sense of the sentence calls for the plural *kinds* or *sorts,* use a plural noun and a plural verb: "These kinds of services are essential." In questions introduced by *what* or *which,* the singular *kind* or *sort* can be followed by a plural noun and verb: "What kind of shells are these?"

  The use of *a* or *an* after *kind of* ("That kind of a person is always troublesome") is usually not appropriate in college writing.

kind (sort) of = somewhat This usage ("I feel kind of tired"; "He looked sort of foolish") is colloquial. The style of the writing will determine its appropriateness in a paper.

latter *Latter* refers to the second of two. It should not be used to refer to the last of three or more nouns. Instead of *latter* in "Michigan, Alabama, and Notre Dame have had strong football teams for years, and yet the latter has only recently begun to accept invitations to play in bowl games," write *last* or *last-named,* or simply repeat *Notre Dame.*

lay, lie *Lay* is a transitive verb (principal parts: *lay, laid, laid*) that means "put" or "place"; it is nearly always followed by a direct object: "She lay the magazine on the table, hiding the mail I laid there this morning." *Lie* is an intransitive verb (principal parts: *lie, lay, lain*) that means "recline" or "be situated" and does not take an object. "I lay awake all night until I decided I had lain there long enough."

leave = let The use of *leave* for the imperative verb *let* ("Leave us face it") is not acceptable in college writing. Write "Let us face it." But *let* and *leave* are interchangeable when a noun or pronoun and then *alone* follow: "Let me alone"; "Leave me alone."

less See **fewer.**

liable = likely Instructors sometimes object to the use of *liable* to mean "likely," as in "It is liable to rain," "He is liable to hit you." *Liable* is used more precisely to mean "subject to" or "exposed to" or "answerable for": "He is liable to arrest"; "You will be liable for damages."

like = as, as though The use of *like* as a conjunction ("He talks like you do"; "It looks like it will be my turn next") is colloquial. It is not appropriate in a formal style, and many people object to it in an informal style. The safest procedure is to avoid using *like* as a conjunction in college writing.

literally, figuratively *Literally* means "word for word," "following the letter," or "in the strict sense." *Figuratively* is its opposite and means "metaphorically." In informal speech, this distinction is often blurred when *literally* is used to mean *nearly:* "She literally blew her top." Avoid this usage by maintaining the word's true meaning: "To give employees a work vacation means literally to fire them."

loath, loathe *Loath* is an adjective meaning "reluctant," "unwilling" ("I am loath to do that"; "He is loath to risk so great an investment") and is pronounced to rhyme with *both*. *Loathe* is a verb meaning "dislike strongly" ("I loathe teas"; "She loathes an unkempt man") and is pronounced to rhyme with *clothe*.

loose, lose The confusion of these words frequently causes misspelling. *Loose* is most common as an adjective: "a loose button," "The dog is loose." *Lose* is always used as a verb: "You are going to lose your money."

luxuriant, luxurious These words come from the same root but have quite different meanings. *Luxuriant* means "abundant" and is used principally to describe growing things: "luxuriant vegetation," "a luxuriant head of hair." *Luxurious* means "luxury-loving" or "characterized by luxury": "He finds it difficult to maintain so luxurious a life style on so modest an income"; "The furnishings of the clubhouse were luxurious."

mad = angry or annoyed Using *mad* to mean "angry" is colloquial: "My girl is mad at me"; "His insinuations make me mad." More precise terms—*angry, annoyed, irritated, provoked, vexed*—are generally more appropriate in college writing. *Mad* is, of course, appropriately used to mean "insane."

majority, plurality Candidates are elected by a *majority* when they get more than half of the votes cast. A *plurality* is the margin of victory that the winning candidate has over the leading opponent, whether the winner has a majority or not.

mean = unkind, disagreeable, vicious Using *mean* to convey the sense "unkind," "disagreeable," "vicious" ("It was mean of me to do that"; "He was in a mean mood"; "That dog looks mean") is a colloquial use. It is appropriate in most college writing, but since using *mean* loosely sometimes results in vagueness, consider using one of the suggested alternatives to provide a sharper statement.

medium, media, medias *Medium*, not *media*, is the singular form: "The daily newspaper is still an important medium of communication." *Media* is plural: "Figuratively, the electronic media have created a smaller world." *Medias* is not an acceptable form for the plural of *medium*.

might of   See **could of.**

mighty = very   *Mighty* is not appropriate in most college writing as a substitute for *very*. Avoid such constructions as "He gave a mighty good speech."

moral, morale   Roughly, *moral* refers to conduct and *morale* refers to state of mind. A moral man is one who conducts himself according to standards for goodness. People are said to have good morale when they are cheerful, cooperative, and not too much concerned with their own worries.

most = almost   The use of *most* as a synonym for *almost* ("I am most always hungry an hour before mealtime") is colloquial. In college writing *almost* would be preferred in such a sentence.

must (adj. and n.)   The use of *must* as an adjective ("This book is must reading for anyone who wants to understand Russia") and as a noun ("It is reported that the President will classify this proposal as a must") is accepted as established usage by the dictionaries.

must of   See **could of.**

myself = I, me   *Myself* should not be used for *I* or *me*. Avoid such constructions as "John and myself will go." *Myself* is acceptably used as an intensifier ("I saw it myself"; "I myself will go with you") and as a reflexive object ("I hate myself"; "I can't convince myself that he is right.")

nauseous = nauseated   *Nauseous* does not mean "experiencing nausea"; *nauseated* has that meaning: "The thought of making a speech caused her to feel nauseated." *Nauseous* means "causing nausea" or "repulsive": "nauseous odor," "nauseous television program."

nice   A utility word much overused in college writing. Avoid excessive use of *nice* and, whenever possible, choose a more precise synonym.

> That's a nice dress. [*attractive? becoming? fashionable? well-made?*]
>
> She's a nice person. [*agreeable? charming? friendly? well-mannered?*]

not all that   The use of *not all that interested* to mean "not much interested" is generally not acceptable in college writing.

off, off of = from   Neither *off* nor *off of* should be used to mean "from." Write "Jack bought the old car from a stranger," not "off a stranger" or "off of a stranger."

OK, O.K.   Its use in business to mean "endorse" is generally accepted: "The manager OK'd the request." In college writing *OK* is a utility word and is subject to the general precaution concerning all such words: do not overuse it, especially in contexts in which a more specific term would give more efficient communication. For example, contrast the vagueness of *OK* in the first sentence with the discriminated meanings in the second and third sentences:

The mechanic said the tires were OK.

The mechanic said the tread on the tires was still good.

The mechanic said the pressure in the tires was satisfactory.

one   See **you.**

only   The position of *only* in such sentences as "I only need three dollars" and "If only Mother would write!" is sometimes condemned on the grounds of possible ambiguity. In practice, the context usually rules out any but the intended interpretation, but a change in the word order would result in more appropriate emphasis: "I need only three dollars"; "If Mother would only write!"

on the part of   The phrase *on the part of* ("There will be some objection on the part of the students"; "On the part of business people, there will be some concern about taxes") often contributes to wordiness. Simply say: "The students will object," "Business people will be concerned about taxes."

party = person   The use of *party* to mean "person" is appropriate in legal documents and the responses of telephone operators, but these are special uses. Generally avoid this use in college writing.

per, a   "You will be remunerated at the rate of forty dollars per diem" and "The troops advanced three miles per day through the heavy snow" show established use of *per* for *a*. But usually "forty dollars a day" and "three miles a day" would be more natural expressions in college writing.

percent, percentage   *Percent* (alternative form *per cent*) is used when a specific portion is named: "five percent of the expenses." *Percentage* is used when no number is given: "a small percentage of the expenses." When *percent* or *percentage* is part of a subject, the noun or pronoun of the *of* phrase that follows determines the number of the verb: "Forty percent of the wheat is his"; "A large percentage of her customers pay promptly."

personal, personnel   *Personal* means "of a person": "a personal opinion," "a personal matter." *Personnel* refers to the people in an organization, especially employees: "Administrative personnel will not be affected."

phenomenon, phenomena   *Phenomenon* is singular; *phenomena* is plural: "This is a striking phenomenon." "Many new phenomena have been discovered with the radio telescope."

plenty   The use of *plenty* as a noun ("There is plenty of room") is always acceptable. Its use as an adverb ("It was plenty good") is not appropriate in college writing.

practical, practicable   Avoid interchanging the two words. *Practical* means "useful, not theoretical"; *practicable* means "feasible, but not necessarily proved successful"; "The designers are usually practical, but these new blueprints do not seem practicable."

première   *Première* is acceptable as a noun ("The première for the play was held in a small off-Broadway theater"), but do not use it as a verb

("The play premièred in a small off-Broadway theater"). Write "The play opened . . ."

preposition (ending sentence with)   A preposition should not appear at the end of a sentence if its presence there draws undue attention to it or creates an awkward construction, as in "They are the people whom we made the inquiries yesterday about." But there is nothing wrong with writing a preposition at the end of a sentence to achieve an idiomatic construction: "Isn't that the man you are looking for?"

principal, principle   The basic meaning of *principal* is "chief" or "most important." It is used in this sense both as a noun and as an adjective: "the principal of a school," "the principal point." It is also used to refer to a capital sum of money, as contrasted with interest on the money: "He can live on the interest without touching the principal." *Principle* is used only as a noun and means "rule," "law," or "controlling idea": "the principle of 'one man, one vote' "; "Cheating is against my principles."

proceed, precede   To *proceed* is to "go forward"; to *precede* means "to go ahead of": "The blockers preceded the runner as the football team proceeded toward the goal line."

prophecy, prophesy   *Prophecy* is always used as a noun ("The prophecy came true"); *prophesy* is always a verb ("He prophesied another war").

proved, proven   When used as past participles, both forms are standard English, but the preferred form is *proved:* "Having proved the first point, we moved to the second." *Proven* is preferred when the word is used primarily as an adjective: "She is a proven contender for the championship."

quote   The clipped form for *quotation* ("a quote from *Walden*") is not acceptable in most college writing. The verb *quote* ("to quote Thoreau") is acceptable in all styles.

raise, rise   *Raise* is a transitive verb, taking an object, meaning to cause something to move up; *rise* is an intransitive verb meaning to go up (on its own): "I raised the window in the kitchen while I waited for the bread dough to rise."

rarely ever, seldom ever   The *ever* is redundant. Instead of saying, "He is rarely ever late" and "She is seldom ever angry," write, "He is rarely late" and "She is seldom angry."

real = really (very)   The use of *real* to mean "really" or "very" ("It is a real difficult assignment") is a colloquial usage. It is acceptable only in a paper whose style is deliberately colloquial.

reason . . . because   The construction is redundant: "The reason he couldn't complete his essay is because he lost his note cards." Substitute *that* for *because:* "The reason he couldn't complete his essay is that he lost his note cards." Better yet, simply eliminate *the reason* and *is:* "He couldn't complete his essay because he lost his note cards."

refer back   A confusion between *look back* and *refer*. This usage is objected to in college writing on the ground that since the *re-* of *refer* means "back," *refer back* is redundant. *Refer back* is acceptable when it means "refer again" ("The bill was referred back to the committee"); otherwise, use *refer* ("Let me refer you to page 17").

regarding, in regard to, with regard to   These are overused and stuffy substitutes for the following simple terms: *on, about,* or *concerning:* "The attorney spoke to you about the testimony."

respectfully, respectively   *Respectfully* means "with respect": "respectfully submitted." *Respectively* means roughly "each in turn": "These three papers were graded respectively A, C, and B."

right (adv.)   The use of *right* as an adverb is established in such sentences as "He went right home" and "It served her right." Its use to mean *very* ("I was right glad to meet him") is colloquial and should be used in college writing only when the style is colloquial.

right, rite   A *rite* is a ceremony or ritual. This word should not be confused with the various uses of *right*.

said (adj.)   The use of *said* as an adjective ("said documents," "said offense") is restricted to legal phraseology. Do not use it in college writing.

same as = just as   The preferred idiom is "just as": "He acted just as I thought he would."

same, such   Avoid using *same* or *such* as a substitute for *it, this, that, them*. Instead of "I am returning the book because I do not care for same" and "Most people are fond of athletics of all sorts, but I have no use for such," say "I am returning the book because I do not care for it" and "Unlike most people, I am not fond of athletics."

scarcely   In such sentences as "There wasn't scarcely enough" and "We haven't scarcely time," the use of *scarcely* plus a negative creates an unacceptable double negative. Say: "There was scarcely enough" and "We scarcely have time."

scarcely . . . than   The use of *scarcely . . . than* ("I had scarcely met her than she began to denounce her husband") is a confusion between "no sooner . . . than" and "scarcely . . . when." Say "I had no sooner met her than she began to denounce her husband" or "I had scarcely met her when she began to denounce her husband."

seasonable, seasonal   *Seasonable* and its adverb form *seasonably* mean "appropriate(ly) to the season": "She was seasonably dressed for a late-fall football game"; "A seasonable frost convinced us that the persimmons were just right for eating." *Seasonal* means "caused by a season": "increased absenteeism because of seasonal influenza," "flooding caused by seasonal thaws."

-selfs   The plural of *self* is *selves*. Such a usage as "They hurt themselfs" is nonstandard and is not acceptable in college writing.

semi- See **bi-, semi-**.

sensual, sensuous *Sensual* has unfavorable connotations and means "catering to the gratification of physical desires": "Always concerned with satisfying his sexual lust and his craving for drink and rich food, the old baron led a totally sensual existence." *Sensuous* has generally favorable connotations and refers to pleasures experienced through the senses: "the sensuous comfort of a warm bath," "the sensuous imagery of the poem."

set, sit These two verbs are commonly confused. *Set* meaning "to put or place" is a transitive verb and takes an object. *Sit* meaning "to be seated" is an intransitive verb. "You can set your books on the desk and then sit in that chair."

shall, will In American usage the dominant practice is to use *will* in the second and third persons to express either futurity or determination and to use either *will* or *shall* in the first person.

In addition, *shall* is used in statements of law ("Congress shall have the power to . . ."), in military commands ("The regiment shall proceed as directed"), and in formal directives ("All branch offices shall report weekly to the home office").

should, would These words are used as the past forms of *shall* and *will* respectively and follow the same pattern (see **shall, will**): "I would [should] be glad to see him tomorrow"; "He would welcome your ideas on the subject"; "We would [should] never consent to such an arrangement." They are also used to convert *shall* or *will* in direct discourse into indirect discourse:

Direct Discourse	Indirect Discourse
"Shall I try to arrange it?" he asked.	He asked if he should try to arrange it.
I said, "They will need money."	I said that they would need money.

should of See **could of**.

sight, site, cite See **cite, sight, site**.

so (conj.) The use of *so* as a connective ("The salesperson refused to exchange the merchandise; so we went to the manager") is thoroughly respectable, but its overuse in college writing is objectionable. There are other good transitional connectives—*accordingly, for that reason, on that account, therefore*—that could be used to relieve the monotony of a series of *so*'s. Occasional use of subordination ("When the salesperson refused to exchange the merchandise, we went to the manager") also brings variety to the style.

some The use of *some* as an adjective of indeterminate number ("Some friends of yours were here") is acceptable in all levels of writing. Its use as an intensive ("That was some meal!") or as an adverb ("She cried some after you left"; "This draft is some better than the first one") should be avoided in college writing.

sort of See **kind of**.

without = unless *Without* is not accepted as a conjunction meaning "unless." In "There will be no homecoming festivities without student government sponsors them," substitute *unless* for *without*.

with respect to See **as to.**

worst way When *in the worst way* means "very much" ("They wanted to go in the worst way"), it is too informal for college writing.

would, should See **should, would.**

would of See **could of.**

would have = had *Would* is the past-tense form of *will*, but its overuse in student writing often results in awkwardness, especially, but not only, when it is used as a substitute for *had*. Contrast the following sentences:

Awkward	Revised
If they *would have done* that earlier, there *would have been* no trouble.	If they *had done* that earlier, there *would have been* no trouble.
	or:
	Had they *done* that earlier, there *would have been* no trouble.
We *would want* some assurance that they *would accept* before we *would make* such a proposal.	We *would want* some assurance of their acceptance before we *made* such a proposal.

In general, avoid the repetition of *would have* in the same sentence.

you = one The use of *you* as an indefinite pronoun instead of the formal *one* is characteristic of an informal style. If you adopt *you* in an informal paper, be sure that this impersonal use will be recognized by your readers; otherwise, they are likely to interpret a general statement as a personal remark addressed specifically to them. Generally avoid shifting from *one* to *you* within a sentence (see page 485).

yourself *Yourself* is appropriately used as an intensifier ("You yourself told me that") and as a reflexive object ("You are blaming yourself too much"). But usages such as the following are not acceptable: "Marian and yourself must shoulder the responsibility" and "The instructions were intended for Kate and yourself." In these two sentences, replace *yourself* with *you*. The plural form is *yourselves,* not *yourselfs*.

Acknowledgments (continued from p. iv)

From William J. Bennett, "Why the West?" *National Review,* 27 May 1988, pp. 37–39. © 1988 by *National Review,* Inc., 150 East 35th Street, New York, NY 10016. Reprinted by permission.

Drawing by Booth; © 1976 The New Yorker Magazine, Inc.

Source: Suzanne Britt, "The Lean and Hungry Look." First appeared in *Newsweek,* October 9, 1978, pp. 32–33. Reprinted by permission of the author.

Annie Dillard, Excerpt from "Los Angeles Notebook" from *Slouching Toward Bethlehem* by Joan Didion. Copyright © 1967, 1968 by Joan Didion. Reprinted by permission of Farrar, Straus and Giroux, Inc.

Joan Didion, Excerpt from *AN AMERICAN CHILDHOOD* by Annie Dillard. Copyright © 1987 by Annie Dillard. Reprinted by permission of HarperCollins Publishers Inc.

Excerpt from *TEACHING A STONE TO TALK* by Annie Dillard. Copyright 1982 by Annie Dillard. Reprinted by permission of HarperCollins Publishers Inc.

Pages 89–93 from *Teaching a Stone to Talk: Expeditions and Encounters* by Annie Dillard. Copyright © 1982 by Annie Dillard. Reprinted by permission of Harper and Row, Publishers, Inc., and Blanche Gregory, Inc.

From AMERICA REVISED: HISTORY SCHOOLBOOKS IN THE TWENTIETH CENTURY by Frances FitzGerald. Copyright © 1979 by Frances FitzGerald. By permission of Little, Brown and Company.

Source: *THE NINE NATIONS OF NORTH AMERICA* by Joel Garreau. Copyright © 1981 by Joel Garreau. Reprinted by permission of Houghton Mifflin Company. All rights reserved.

Excerpt from "Becoming a Writer" by Gail Godwin. Copyright © 1979 by Gail Godwin. Reprinted by permission of John Hawkins and Associates, Inc.

Ellen Goodman, "Family: The One Social Glue" from CLOSE TO HOME. Copyright © 1979 by The Washington Post Company. Reprinted by permission of Simon & Schuster, Inc.

From "On Safari," *ADAM AND EVE AND THE CITY,* copyright © 1987 by Francine Du Plessix Gray. Reprinted by permission of Simon & Schuster, Inc.

Patricia Hampl, Excerpt "Prague" from *A Sentimental Education,* copyright © 1981, used by permission of Rhoda Weyr Agency.

Excerpt retitled "The Ugly Tourist" from *A SMALL PLACE* by Jamaica Kincaid. Copyright © 1988 by Jamaica Kincaid. Reprinted by permission of Farrar, Straus & Giroux, Inc.

John McPhee, "Under the Snow" from *Table of Contents* by John McPhee. Copyright © 1985 by John McPhee. Originally appeared in *The New Yorker*. Reprinted by permission of Farrar, Straus and Giroux, Inc.

H. L. Mencken, "The Penalty of Death." From A MENCKEN CHRESTOMATHY by H. L. Mencken. Copyright © 1926 by Alfred A. Knopf, Inc. and renewed 1954 by H. L. Mencken. Reprinted by permission of Alfred A. Knopf, Inc.

"Family Feud" by Mark Crispin Miller. In *Boxed In: The Culture of TV.* © 1988 by Northwestern University Press. Reprinted by permission.

"Territorial Behavior" is reprinted from the book *MANWATCHING: A FIELD GUIDE TO HUMAN BEHAVIOR* by Desmond Morris, Published in 1977 by Harry N. Abrams, Inc., New York, Copyright 1977 Desmond Morris. All rights reserved.

Dixie D. Myers, "Two Postcards from Martha's Vineyard." Originally carried title "Between a Rock and a Wall in Washington: Two Postcards from Martha's Vineyard." *The Vineyard Gazette,* 25 May 1990, p. 15. Reprinted with permission of the author.

Source; From the book, *HOLIDAYS IN HELL,* copyright © 1988 by P. J. O'Rourke. Used by permission of the Atlantic Monthly Press.

From *OXFORD ENGLISH DICTIONARY,* Oxford University Press, 1933. Used by permission of Oxford University Press.

Drawing by W.B. Park; © 1988 The New Yorker Magazine, Inc.

"Design as Revision" by Henry Petroski. Copyright © 1982, 1983, 1984, 1985 by Henry Petroski. From the book *TO ENGINEER IS HUMAN* and reprinted with special permission of St. Martin's Press, Inc., New York, N.Y.

Portions of this chapter appeared in "Humanities for the Future: Reflections on the Western Culture Debate at Stanford" by Mary Louise Pratt, *The South Atlantic Quarterly,* Volume 89, # 1, Winter 1990, published by Duke University Press, Durham. Reprinted with permission of the publisher.

Anna Quindlen, "Some Thoughts About Abortion." From LIVING OUT LOUD by Anna Quindlen. Copyright © 1987 by Anna Quindlen. Reprinted by permission of Random House, Inc.

"Living in Sin" is reprinted from THE FACT OF A DOORFRAME. Poems Selected and New, 1950–1984, by Adrienne Rich, by permission of W. W. Norton & Company, Inc. Copyright © 1984 by Adrienne Rich. Copyright © 1975, 1978 by W. w. Norton & Company, Inc. Copyright © 1981 by Adrienne Rich.

"Mr. Flood's Party." Edwin Arlington Robinson. Reprinted with permission of Macmillan Publishing Company from *Collected Poems by Edwin Arlington Robinson.* Copyright 1921 by Edwin Arlington Robinson, renewed 1949 by Ruth Nivison.

"Marita." Mike Rose. Reprinted with permission of The Free Press, a Division of Macmillan, Inc. from *Lives on the Boundary: The Struggle and Achievements of America's Underprepared* by Mike Rose. Copyright © 1989 by Mike Rose.

Copyright © 1986 by Scott Russell Sanders; first appeared in *The North American Review;* reprinted by permission of the author and Virginia Kidd, Literary Agent.

Drawing by Saxon; © 1987 The New Yorker Magazine, Inc.

Richard Selzer, "The Knife," from *MORTAL LESSONS,* copyright © 1974, 1975, 1976 by Richard Selzer. Reprinted by permission of Simon & Schuster, Inc.

Drawing by Sempe; © 1984 The New Yorker Magazine, Inc.

G. B. Shaw, extract from Pygmalion reprinted by permission of The Society of Authors on behalf of the Bernard Shaw Estate.

"The Value of C", from *A FISTFUL OF FIG NEWTONS* by Jean Shepherd. Copyright 1981. Used by permission of Doubleday, a division of Bantam Doubleday Dell Publishing Group, Inc.

Singer, Peter. Excerpt from "Animals in Transit." From ANIMAL LIBERATION, 2nd ed. © 1990 by Random House.

"Powerful Red Dogs: Excerpts from a Painter's Studio Notes" originally appeared in *The Georgia Review,* Vol. 44, Nos. 1 and 2 (Spring/Summer 1990), © 1990 by The University of Georgia, © 1990 by Pam Smith. Reprinted by permission of Pam Smith and *The Georgia Review.*

Source: Brent Staples, "Black Men and Public Space." *Ms.,* September 1986, pp. 54, 86. Reprinted with permission of the author.

Teale, Edwin Way. *Adventures in Nature.* New York: Dodd, 1959. 37–40. Reprinted by permission.

Copyright © 1933, 1961 James Thurber. From "University Days," My Life and Hard Times, published by Harper and Row.

Reprinted by permission; © 1988 Calvin Tomkins. Originally in The New Yorker.

Copyright © 1988 by Calvin Trillin. From *ENOUGH'S ENOUGH* (And Other Rules of Life) by Calvin Trillin, published by Ticknor & Fields

Excerpted from "Hong Kong Dream" by Calvin Trillin, which appears in his book *THIRD HELPINGS,* published by Ticknor & Fields. Copyright © 1983 by Calvin Trillin.

From *LANDSCAPES OF FEAR* by Yi-Fu Tuan. Copyright © 1979 by Yi-Fu Tuan. Reprinted by permission of Pantheon Books, a division of Random House, Inc.

Barbara W. Tuchman, "The Craft." From PRACTICING HISTORY: SELECTED ESSAYS. Copyright 1981 by Barbara W. Tuchman. Reprinted by permission of Alfred A. Knopf, Inc.

"Everyday Use" from *IN LOVE AND TROUBLE* by Alice Walker, copyright © 1973 by Alice Walker, reprinted by permission of Harcourt Brace Jovanovich, Inc.

"In Search of Our Mothers' Gardens" from *IN SEARCH OF OUR MOTHERS' GARDENS* by Alice Walker, copyright © 1974 by Alice Walker, reprinted by permission of Harcourt Brace Jovanovich, Inc.

"Women" from *REVOLUTIONARY PETUNIAS AND OTHER POEMS* by Alice Walker, copyright © 1970 by Alice Walker, reprinted by permission of Harcourt Brace Jovanovich, Inc.

Richard Wilbur, "A Late Aubade" copyright © 1967 by Richard Wilbur. Reprinted by permission of Harcourt Brace Jovanovich, Inc.

Robert S. Winkler, "The Traveling Photographer," *Travel and Leisure* (December 1983): 42–47. Copyright © 1983 Robert S. Winkler. All rights reserved.

From *THE PLUG-IN DRUG* by Marie Winn. Copyright © 1977, 1985 by Marie Winn Miller. Used by permission of Viking Penguin, a division of Penguin Books USA Inc.

Personal interviews, used by permission:
Chapter 1: Calvin Trillin
Chapter 5: John McPhee
Chapter 6: Anna Quindlen
Chapter 7: Bill Barich
Chapter 8: Richard Selzer
Chapter 9: Annie Dillard
Chapter 10: Patricia Hampl

Index of
Authors
and
Titles

This index contains the names of all authors and titles quoted in the text. Names of student writers and titles of student writing are indicated by an asterisk (*).

Index

A BRIEF GUIDE TO THE HANDBOOK

(Continued)

A BRIEF GUIDE TO THE HANDBOOK (Continued)